DEPRESSION

THE TREATMENT AND MANAGEMENT OF DEPRESSION IN ADULTS (UPDATED EDITION)

National Clinical Practice Guideline 90

National Collaborating Centre for Mental Health
commissioned by the
National Institute for Health & Clinical Excellence

published by
The British Psychological Society and The Royal College of Psychiatrists

British Library Cataloguing-in-Publication Data

A catalogue record for this book is available from the British Library.

ISBN: 978-1-904671-85-5

Printed in Great Britain by Stanley Hunt.

Additional material: data CD-Rom created by Pix18 (www.pix18.co.uk)

developed by	National Collaborating Centre for Mental Health The Royal College of Psychiatrists 4th Floor, Standon House 21 Mansell Street London E1 8AA www.nccmh.org.uk
commissioned by	National Institute for Health and Clinical Excellence MidCity Place, 71 High Holborn London WCIV 6NA www.nice.org.uk
published by	The British Psychological Society St Andrews House 48 Princess Road East Leicester LE1 7DR www.bps.org.uk

and

The Royal College of Psychiatrists
17 Belgrave Square
London
SW1X 8PG
www.rcpsych.ac.uk

The British Psychological Society

RC PSYCH
ROYAL COLLEGE OF PSYCHIATRISTS

CONTENTS

GUIDELINE DEVELOPMENT GROUP MEMBERS		**7**
ACKNOWLEDGEMENTS		**10**
1	**PREFACE**	**11**
1.1	National guidelines	11
1.2	The national depression guideline	14
2	**DEPRESSION**	**17**
2.1	The disorder	17
2.2	Aetiology	25
2.3	Economic costs of depression	26
2.4	Treatment and management in the National Health Service	28
3	**METHODS USED TO DEVELOP THIS GUIDELINE**	**34**
3.1	Overview	34
3.2	The scope	34
3.3	The Guideline Development Group	35
3.4	Clinical questions	37
3.5	Systematic clinical literature review	38
3.6	Health economics methods	47
3.7	Methods for reviewing experience of care	49
3.8	Stakeholder contributions	51
3.9	Validation of the guideline	51
4	**EXPERIENCE OF CARE**	**52**
4.1	Introduction	52
4.2	Personal accounts – people with depression	52
4.3	Personal accounts – carers	68
4.4	Qualitative analysis	71
4.5	Review of the qualitative literature	83
4.6	From evidence to recommendations	86
4.7	Recommendations	94
5	**CASE IDENTIFICATION AND SERVICE DELIVERY**	**97**
5.1	Introduction	97
5.2	The identification of depression in primary care and community settings	98
5.3	Service delivery systems in the treatment and management of depression	121
5.4	Stepped care	124
5.5	Collaborative care	129

Contents

5.6	Medication management	141
5.7	Crisis resolution and home treatment teams	146
5.8	Acute day hospital care	149
5.9	Non-acute day hospital care	151
5.10	Non-statutory support	153
5.11	Research recommendation	155

6 INTRODUCTION TO PSYCHOLOGICAL AND PSYCHOSOCIAL INTERVENTIONS — **157**

6.1	Introduction	157
6.2	Recommending psychological and psychosocial treatments	157
6.3	How do psychological and psychosocial interventions become evidence based?	158
6.4	Contextual factors that impact on clinical practice	164
6.5	Databases searched and inclusion/exclusion criteria	168
6.6	Studies considered	168

7 LOW-INTENSITY PSYCHOSOCIAL INTERVENTIONS — **170**

7.1	Computerised cognitive behavioural therapy	170
7.2	Guided self-help	181
7.3	Physical activity programmes	190
7.4	From evidence to recommendations – low-intensity psychosocial interventions	212
7.5	Recommendations	213

8 HIGH-INTENSITY PSYCHOLOGICAL INTERVENTIONS — **215**

8.1	Cognitive behavioural therapies	215
8.2	Behavioural activation	238
8.3	Problem solving	242
8.4	Couples therapy	246
8.5	Interpersonal therapy	249
8.6	Counselling	261
8.7	Short-term psychodynamic psychotherapy	267
8.8	Rational emotive behavioural therapy	272
8.9	Economic modelling	274
8.10	From evidence to recommendations	291
8.11	Recommendations	296
8.12	Research recommendations	300

9 INTRODUCTION TO PHARMACOLOGICAL AND PHYSICAL INTERVENTIONS — **304**

9.1	Introduction	304
9.2	Dose and duration of antidepressant treatment: evidence from clinical practice	306
9.3	Limitations of the literature: problems with randomised controlled trials in pharmacology	308
9.4	Studies considered for review – additional inclusion criteria	309

9.5	Issues and topics covered by this review	311
9.6	Placebo-controlled randomised controlled trials of antidepressants	313
9.7	Selective serotonin reuptake inhibitors versus placebo	315
9.8	Tricyclic antidepressants versus placebo	319
9.9	From evidence to recommendations	326
9.10	Recommendation	327

10 PHARMACOLOGICAL INTERVENTIONS — **328**

10.1	Introduction	328
10.2	Use of individual drugs in the treatment of depression	329
10.3	Tricyclic antidepressants	330
10.4	Selective serotonin reuptake inhibitors	336
10.5	Escitalopram	341
10.6	The thread study	354
10.7	Monoamine oxidase inhibitors	354
10.8	Third-generation antidepressants	360
10.9	St John's wort	387
10.10	Health economics evidence	391
10.11	Network meta-analysis of newer antidepressants	398
10.12	Economic model for the cost-effectiveness of pharmacological interventions for people with depression	399
10.13	From evidence to recommendations	411
10.14	Clinical practice recommendations	412
10.15	When to change antidepressant treatment when symptoms of depression are not improving	413

11 FACTORS INFLUENCING CHOICE OF ANTIDEPRESSANTS — **418**

11.1	Introduction	418
11.2	The pharmacological management of depression in older adults	418
11.3	The effect of sex on antidepressant choice	424
11.4	The pharmacological management of depression with psychotic symptoms	425
11.5	The pharmacological management of atypical depression	427
11.6	The physical and pharmacological management of depression with a seasonal pattern	430
11.7	Dosage issues for tricyclic antidepressants	451
11.8	Antidepressant discontinuation symptoms	453
11.9	The cardiotoxicity of antidepressants	457
11.10	Depression, antidepressants and suicide	462

12 THE PHARMACOLOGICAL AND PHYSICAL MANAGEMENT OF DEPRESSION THAT HAS NOT ADEQUATELY RESPONDED TO TREATMENT, AND RELAPSE PREVENTION — **466**

12.1	Introduction	466
12.2	Approach to the reviews	467
12.3	Pharmacological 'next-step' treatment for depression that has not adequately responded to treatment	469

12.4	Electroconvulsive therapy	508
12.5	Other non-pharmacological physical treatments	528
12.6	The pharmacological management of relapse prevention	530

13 THE MANAGEMENT OF SUBTHRESHOLD DEPRESSIVE SYMPTOMS — **536**

13.1	Introduction	536
13.2	Pharmacological interventions for subthreshold depressive symptoms and persistent subthreshold depressive symptoms (dysthymia)	537
13.3	Psychological and other strategies for the treatment of persistent subthreshold depressive symptoms (dysthymia)	555
13.4	From evidence to recommendations	563
13.5	Recommendations	564
13.6	Research recommendation	564

14 SUMMARY OF RECOMMENDATIONS — **565**

14.1	Care of all people with depression	565
14.2	Stepped care	567
14.3	Step 1: recognition, assessment and initial management	568
14.4	Step 2: recognised depression – persistent subthreshold depressive symptoms or mild to moderate depression	569
14.5	Step 3: persistent subthreshold depressive symptoms or mild to moderate depression with inadequate response to initial interventions, and moderate and severe depression	571
14.6	Treatment choice based on depression subtypes and personal characteristics	576
14.7	Enhanced care for depression	576
14.8	Sequencing treatments after initial inadequate response	577
14.9	Continuation and relapse prevention	579
14.10	Step 4: complex and severe depression	582
14.11	Research recommendations	585

15 APPENDICES — **591**

16 REFERENCES — **647**

17 ABBREVIATIONS — **696**

GUIDELINE DEVELOPMENT GROUP MEMBERS

Professor Ian Anderson (Chair, Guideline Development Group)
Professor of Psychiatry, University of Manchester

Professor Stephen Pilling
Director, National Collaborating Centre for Mental Health
Director, Centre for Outcomes Research and Effectiveness, University College London

Ms Alison Barnes
Service User Member

Ms Linda Bayliss
Research Assistant (May 2008 to August 2008), National Collaborating Centre for Mental Health

Ms Victoria Bird
Research Assistant, National Collaborating Centre for Mental Health

Ms Rachel Burbeck
Lead Systematic Reviewer, National Collaborating Centre for Mental Health

Dr Carolyn Chew-Graham
General Practitioner and Senior Lecturer in Primary Care, University of Manchester

Mr Jeremy Clarke
Psychological Therapist, Lambeth Primary Care Trust

Mr Matthew Dyer
Health Economist, National Collaborating Centre for Mental Health

Ms Esther Flanagan
Project Manager (2009), National Collaborating Centre for Mental Health

Ms Catherine Harris
Carer member and Local Councillor

Ms Sarah Hopkins
Project Manager (until 2008), National Collaborating Centre for Mental Health

Guideline Development Group members

Dr Mark Kenwright
Consultant Cognitive Behavioural Psychotherapist, Ealing Cognitive Behavioural Therapy Service

Professor Willem Kuyken
Professor of Clinical Psychology and Co-Director, Mood Disorders Centre, School of Psychology, University of Exeter

Ms Angela Lewis
Research Assistant, National Collaborating Centre for Mental Health

Professor Glyn Lewis
Professor of Psychiatric Epidemiology, University of Bristol

Mr Ryan Li
Project Manager (2008), National Collaborating Centre for Mental Health

Mr Brendan Masterson
Clinical Nurse Leader, Affective Disorders Unit, Bethlem Royal Hospital

Dr Nick Meader
Systematic Reviewer, National Collaborating Centre for Mental Health

Mr Alan Meudell
Service User Member, Healthy Minds at Work

Dr Alex Mitchell
Consultant Psychiatrist and Honorary Lecturer in Liaison Psychiatry, University of Leicester

Dr Richard Moore
Clinical Psychologist, Cambridge and Peterborough NHS Foundation Trust

Dr Suffiya Omarjee
Health Economist, National Collaborating Centre for Mental Health

Ms Carol Paton
Chief Pharmacist, Oxleas NHS Foundation Trust

Dr Alejandra Perez
Systematic Reviewer, National Collaborating Centre for Mental Health

Ms Peny Retsa
Health Economist (until 2008), National Collaborating Centre for Mental Health

Ms Maria Rizzo
Research Assistant, National Collaborating Centre for Mental Health

Ms Jennie Robertson
Research Assistant (from September 2008), National Collaborating Centre for Mental Health

Mr Rob Saunders
Research Assistant (2008), National Collaborating Centre for Mental Health

Ms Christine Sealey
Centre Manager, National Collaborating Centre for Mental Health

Ms Beth Shackleton
Project Manager (until 2008), National Collaborating Centre for Mental Health

Dr Thomas Shackleton
General Practitioner, Suffolk

Ms Sarah Stockton
Senior Information Scientist, National Collaborating Centre for Mental Health

Dr Clare Taylor
Editor, National Collaborating Centre for Mental Health

Ms Jane Wood
Nurse, Strategic Development Manager, Mental Health, Leeds Primary Care Trust

ACKNOWLEDGEMENTS

Editorial assistance
Ms Nuala Ernest
Ms Marie Halton

1   PREFACE

This guideline was first published in December 2004 (NICE, 2004a; NCCMH, 2004) (referred to as the 'previous guideline'). The present guideline (referred to as the 'update') updates many areas of the previous guideline. There are also new chapters on the experience of depression for people with depression and their carers (Chapter 4), and on the treatment and management of subthreshold depressive symptoms (including dysthymia symptoms) (Chapter 13), which were not part of the scope of the previous guideline. Recommendations categorised as 'good practice points' in the previous guideline were reviewed for their current relevance (including issues around consent and advance directives). Further details of what has been updated and what is left unchanged can be found at the beginning of each evidence chapter. The scope for the update also included updating two National Institute for Health and Clinical Excellence (NICE) technology appraisals (TAs) on the use of electroconvulsive therapy (ECT) (TA59) and on computerised cognitive behaviour therapy (TA51) (NICE, 2003, 2002)[1]. See Appendix 1 for more details on the scope of this update. Sections of the guideline where the evidence has not been updated are marked by asterisks (**_**).

The previous guideline and this update have been developed to advise on the treatment and management of depression. The guideline recommendations in the update have been developed by a multidisciplinary team of healthcare professionals, people with depression, a carer and guideline methodologists after careful consideration of the best available evidence. It is intended that the guideline will be useful to clinicians and service commissioners in providing and planning high-quality care for people with depression while also emphasising the importance of the experience of care for them and their carers.

Although the evidence base is rapidly expanding there are a number of major gaps, and further revisions of this guideline will incorporate new scientific evidence as it develops. The guideline makes a number of research recommendations specifically to address gaps in the evidence base. In the meantime, it is hoped that the guideline will assist clinicians, people with depression and their carers by identifying the merits of particular treatment approaches where the evidence from research and clinical experience exists.

1.1   NATIONAL GUIDELINES

1.1.1   What are clinical practice guidelines?

Clinical practice guidelines are 'systematically developed statements that assist clinicians and patients in making decisions about appropriate treatment for specific condi-

---

[1]Recommendations from TA59 and TA97 were incorporated into the previous depression guideline according to NICE protocol.

tions' (Mann, 1996). They are derived from the best available research evidence, using predetermined and systematic methods to identify and evaluate the evidence relating to the specific condition in question. Where evidence is lacking, the guidelines incorporate statements and recommendations based upon the consensus statements developed by the Guideline Development Group (GDG).

Clinical guidelines are intended to improve the process and outcomes of healthcare in a number of different ways. They can:

- provide up-to-date evidence-based recommendations for the management of conditions and disorders by healthcare professionals
- be used as the basis to set standards to assess the practice of healthcare professionals
- form the basis for education and training of healthcare professionals
- assist people with depression and their carers in making informed decisions about their treatment and care
- improve communication between healthcare professionals, people with depression and their carers
- help identify priority areas for further research.

1.1.2 Uses and limitations of clinical guidelines

Guidelines are not a substitute for professional knowledge and clinical judgement. They can be limited in their usefulness and applicability by a number of different factors: the availability of high-quality research evidence, the quality of the methodology used in the development of the guideline, the generalisability of research findings and the uniqueness of individuals with depression.

Although the quality of research in this field is variable, the methodology used here reflects current international understanding on the appropriate practice for guideline development (AGREE: Appraisal of Guidelines for Research and Evaluation Instrument; www.agreetrust.org; AGREE Collaboration [2003]), ensuring the collection and selection of the best research evidence available and the systematic generation of treatment recommendations applicable to the majority of people with depression. However, there will always be some people and situations for which clinical guideline recommendations are not readily applicable. This guideline does not, therefore, override the individual responsibility of healthcare professionals to make appropriate decisions in the circumstances of the individual, in consultation with the person with depression or their carer.

In addition to the clinical evidence, cost-effectiveness information, where available, is taken into account in the generation of statements and recommendations in clinical guidelines. While national guidelines are concerned with clinical and cost effectiveness, issues of affordability and implementation costs are to be determined by the National Health Service (NHS).

In using guidelines, it is important to remember that the absence of empirical evidence for the effectiveness of a particular intervention is not the same as evidence for ineffectiveness. In addition, of particular relevance in mental health, evidence-based treatments are often delivered within the context of an overall treatment programme including a range of activities, the purpose of which may be to help engage the person and to provide an appropriate context for the delivery of specific interventions. It is important to maintain and enhance the service context in which these interventions are delivered; otherwise the specific benefits of effective interventions will be lost. Indeed, the importance of organising care in order to support and encourage a good therapeutic relationship is at times as important as the specific treatments offered.

1.1.3   Why develop national guidelines?

NICE was established as a Special Health Authority for England and Wales in 1999, with a remit to provide a single source of authoritative and reliable guidance for patients, professionals and the public. NICE guidance aims to improve standards of care, diminish unacceptable variations in the provision and quality of care across the NHS and ensure that the health service is patient centred. All guidance is developed in a transparent and collaborative manner using the best available evidence and involving all relevant stakeholders.

NICE generates guidance in a number of different ways, three of which are relevant here. First, national guidance is produced by the Technology Appraisal Committee to give robust advice about a particular treatment, intervention, procedure or other health technology. Second, NICE commissions public health intervention guidance focused on types of activity (interventions) that help to reduce people's risk of developing a disease or condition or help to promote or maintain a healthy lifestyle. Third, NICE commissions the production of national clinical practice guidelines focused upon the overall treatment and management of a specific condition. To enable this latter development, NICE originally established seven National Collaborating Centres in conjunction with a range of professional organisations involved in healthcare.

1.1.4   The National Collaborating Centre for Mental Health

This guideline has been commissioned by NICE and developed within the National Collaborating Centre for Mental Health (NCCMH). The NCCMH is a collaboration of the professional organisations involved in the field of mental health, national patient and carer organisations, and a number of academic institutions and NICE. The NCCMH is funded by NICE and is led by a partnership between the Royal College of Psychiatrists and the British Psychological Society's Centre for Outcomes Research and Effectiveness.

1.1.5   From national guidelines to local implementation

Once a national guideline has been published and disseminated, local healthcare groups will be expected to produce a plan and identify resources for implementation, along with appropriate timetables. Subsequently, a multidisciplinary group involving commissioners of healthcare, primary care, specialist mental health professionals, and people with depression and their carers should undertake the translation of the implementation plan locally, taking into account both the recommendations set out in this guideline and the priorities set in the National Service Framework for Mental Health (Department of Health, 1999) and related documentation. The nature and pace of the local plan will reflect local healthcare needs and the nature of existing services; full implementation may take considerable time, especially where substantial training needs are identified.

1.1.6   Auditing the implementation of guidelines

This guideline identifies key areas of clinical practice and service delivery for local and national audit. Although the generation of audit standards is an important and necessary step in the implementation of this guidance, a more broadly based implementation strategy will be developed. Nevertheless, it should be noted that the Healthcare Commission will monitor the extent to which Primary Care Trusts, trusts responsible for mental health and social care and Health Authorities have implemented these guidelines.

1.2   THE NATIONAL DEPRESSION GUIDELINE

1.2.1   Who has developed this guideline?

The GDG was convened by the NCCMH and supported by funding from NICE. The GDG included two people with depression and a carer, and professionals from psychiatry, clinical psychology, general practice, nursing and psychiatric pharmacy.

Staff from the NCCMH provided leadership and support throughout the process of guideline development, undertaking systematic searches, information retrieval, appraisal and systematic review of the evidence. Members of the GDG received training in the process of guideline development from NCCMH staff, and the people with depression and the carer received training and support from the NICE Patient and Public Involvement Programme. The NICE Guidelines Technical Adviser provided advice and assistance regarding aspects of the guideline development process.

All GDG members made formal declarations of interest at the outset, which were updated at every GDG meeting. The GDG met a total of 14 times throughout the process of guideline development. It met as a whole, but key topics were led by a national expert in the relevant topic. The GDG was supported by the NCCMH technical team, with additional expert advice from special advisers where needed. The group oversaw the production and synthesis of research evidence before presentation. All statements and recommendations in this guideline have been generated and agreed by the whole GDG.

1.2.2 For whom is this guideline intended?

This guideline is relevant for adults with depression as the primary diagnosis and covers the care provided by primary, community, secondary, tertiary and other health-care professionals who have direct contact with, and make decisions concerning the care of, adults with depression.

The guideline will also be relevant to the work, but will not cover the practice, of those in:

- occupational health services
- social services
- forensic services
- the independent sector.

The experience of depression can affect the whole family and often the community. The guideline recognises the role of both in the treatment and support of people with depression.

1.2.3 Specific aims of this guideline

The guideline makes recommendations for the treatment and management of depression. It aims to:

- improve access and engagement with treatment and services for people with depression
- evaluate the role of specific psychological and psychosocial interventions in the treatment of depression
- evaluate the role of specific pharmacological interventions in the treatment of depression
- evaluate the role of specific service-level interventions for people with depression
- integrate the above to provide best-practice advice on the care of people with depression and their family and carers
- promote the implementation of best clinical practice through the development of recommendations tailored to the requirements of the NHS in England and Wales.

1.2.4 The structure of this guideline

The guideline is divided into chapters, each covering a set of related topics. The first three chapters provide an introduction to guidelines, the topic of depression and the methods used to update this guideline. Chapters 5 to 13 provide the evidence that underpins the recommendations about the treatment and management of depression, with Chapter 4 providing personal accounts from people with depression and carers that offer an insight into their experience of depression.

Each evidence chapter begins with a general introduction to the topic that sets the recommendations in context. Depending on the nature of the evidence, narrative reviews or meta-analyses were conducted, and the structure of the chapters varies accordingly. Where appropriate, details about current practice, the evidence base and any research limitations are provided. Where meta-analyses were conducted, information is given about the review protocol and studies included in the review. Clinical evidence summaries are used to summarise the data presented. Health economic evidence is then presented (where appropriate), followed by a section (from evidence to recommendations) that draws together the clinical and health economic evidence and provides a rationale for the recommendations. On the CD-ROM, further details are provided about included/excluded studies, the evidence, and the previous guideline methodology (see Table 1 for details).

Table 1: Appendices on CD-ROM

Evidence tables for economic studies	Appendix 15
Clinical evidence profiles	Appendix 16
Clinical study characteristics tables	Appendix 17
References to studies from the previous guideline	Appendix 18
Clinical evidence forest plots	Appendix 19
Case identification included and excluded studies	Appendix 20
Previous guideline methodology	Appendix 21

2   DEPRESSION

This guideline is concerned with the treatment and management of adults with a primary diagnosis of depression in primary and secondary care. The terminology and diagnostic criteria used for this heterogeneous group of related disorders have changed over the years, and the previous guideline related only to those identified by *The ICD–10 Classification of Mental and Behavioural Disorders* (ICD–10) (WHO, 1992) as having a depressive episode (F32 in the ICD–10), recurrent depressive episode (F33) or mixed anxiety and depressive disorder (F41.2). In this guideline update the scope was widened to cover the substantial proportion of people who present with less severe forms of depression. Therefore, this updated guideline covers 'subthreshold depressive symptoms', which fall below the criteria for major depression (and which do not have a coding in ICD–10), and subthreshold depressive symptoms persisting for at least 2 years (dysthymia; F34.1).

It should, however, be noted that much of the research forming the evidence base from which this guideline is drawn has used a different classificatory system – the *Diagnostic and Statistical Manual of Mental Disorders* of the American Psychiatric Association, currently in its fourth edition (DSM–IV-TR) (APA, 2000c). The two classificatory systems, while similar, are not identical especially with regard to definitions of severity. After considerable discussion the GDG took the decision to base the guidelines on the DSM–IV-TR (see Section 2.1.5). This covers major depressive disorder single episode (296.2) and recurrent (296.3) together with dysthymic disorder (300.4), and contains research criteria for minor depressive disorder (APA, 2000c). The effect of this change in practice is discussed in Section 2.1.5 (see also Appendix 11). The guideline does not address the management of depression in children and adolescents, depression in bipolar disorder, depression occurring in both antenatal and postnatal periods, or depression associated with chronic physical health problems, all of which are covered by separate guidelines (NICE, 2005, 2006c, 2007e, 2009c). The guideline update does cover psychotic symptoms occurring within the context of an episode of depression (depression with psychotic symptoms), but not depression occurring in a primary psychotic illness, such as schizophrenia or dementia.

2.1   THE DISORDER

2.1.1   Symptoms, presentation and pattern of illness

Depression refers to a wide range of mental health problems characterised by the absence of a positive affect (a loss of interest and enjoyment in ordinary things and experiences), low mood and a range of associated emotional, cognitive, physical and behavioural symptoms. Distinguishing the mood changes between clinically significant

17

degrees of depression (for example, major depression) and those occurring 'normally' remains problematic and it is best to consider the symptoms of depression as occurring on a continuum of severity (Lewinsohn *et al.*, 2000). The identification of major depression is based not only on its severity but also on persistence, the presence of other symptoms, and the degree of functional and social impairment. However, there appears to be no hard-and-fast 'cut-off' between 'clinically significant' and 'normal' degrees of depression; the greater the severity of depression, the greater the morbidity and adverse consequences (Lewinsohn *et al.*, 2000; Kessing, 2007). When taken together with other aspects that need to be considered, such as duration, stage of illness and treatment history, there are considerable problems when attempting to classify depression into categories (see Section 2.1.5).

Commonly, mood and affect in a major depressive illness are unreactive to circumstance, remaining low throughout the course of each day, although for some people mood varies diurnally, with gradual improvement throughout the day only to return to a low mood on waking. For others, a person's mood may be reactive to positive experiences and events, although these elevations in mood are not sustained, with depressive feelings re-emerging, often quickly (Andrews & Jenkins, 1999).

Behavioural and physical symptoms typically include tearfulness, irritability, social withdrawal, an exacerbation of pre-existing pains, pains secondary to increased muscle tension (Gerber *et al.*, 1992), a lack of libido, fatigue and diminished activity, although agitation is common and marked anxiety frequent. Typically there is reduced sleep and lowered appetite (sometimes leading to significant weight loss), but for some people it is recognised that sleep and appetite are increased. A loss of interest and enjoyment in everyday life, and feelings of guilt, worthlessness and that one deserves punishment, are common, as are lowered self-esteem, loss of confidence, feelings of helplessness, suicidal ideation and attempts at self-harm or suicide. Cognitive changes include poor concentration and reduced attention, pessimistic and recurrently negative thoughts about oneself, one's past and the future, mental slowing and rumination (Cassano & Fava, 2002).

Depression is often accompanied by anxiety, and in these circumstances one of three diagnoses can be made: (1) depression; (2) anxiety; or (3) mixed depression and anxiety when both are below the threshold for either disorder, dependent upon which constellation of symptoms dominates the clinical picture. In addition, the presentation of depression can vary with age with the young showing more behavioural symptoms and older adults more somatic symptoms and fewer complaints of low mood (Serby & Yu, 2003).

Major depression is generally diagnosed when a persistent low mood and an absence of positive affect are accompanied by a range of symptoms, the number and combination needed to make a diagnosis being operationally defined (ICD–10, WHO, 1992; DSM–IV, APA, 1994).

Some people are recognised as showing an atypical presentation with reactive mood, increased appetite, weight gain and excessive sleepiness together with the personality feature of sensitivity to rejection (Quitkin *et al.*, 1991) and this is classified as major depression with atypical features in DSM–IV (APA, 1994). The definition of atypical depression has changed over time and it is not specifically recognised in ICD–10.

Some patients have a more severe and typical presentation, including marked physical slowness (or marked agitation), complete lack of reactivity of mood to positive events, and a range of somatic symptoms, including appetite and weight loss, reduced sleep with a particular pattern of waking early in the morning and being unable to get back to sleep. A pattern of the depression being substantially worse in the morning (diurnal variation) is also commonly seen. This presentation is referred to as major depression with melancholic features in DSM–IV and a depressive episode with somatic symptoms in ICD–10.

People with severe depression may also develop psychotic symptoms (hallucinations and/or delusions), most commonly thematically consistent with the negative, self-blaming cognitions and low mood typically encountered in major depression, although others may develop psychotic symptoms unrelated to mood (Andrews & Jenkins, 1999). In the latter case, these mood-incongruent psychotic symptoms can be hard to distinguish from those that occur in other psychoses such as schizophrenia.

2.1.2 Course and prognosis

The average age of the first episode of major depression occurs in the mid-20s and, although the first episode may occur at any time from early childhood through to old age, a substantial proportion of people have their first depression in childhood or adolescence (Fava & Kendler, 2000). Just as the initial presentation and form of a depressive illness varies considerably, so too does the prodromal period. Some individuals experience a range of symptoms in the months prior to the full illness, including anxiety, phobias, milder depressive symptoms and panic attacks; others may develop a severe major depressive illness fairly rapidly, not uncommonly following a major stressful life event. Sometimes somatic symptoms dominate the clinical picture leading the clinician to investigate possible underlying physical illness until mood changes become more obvious.

Although depression has been thought of as a time-limited disorder, lasting on average 4 to 6 months with complete recovery afterwards, it is now clear that incomplete recovery and relapse are common. The WHO study of mental disorders in 14 centres across the world found that 50% of patients still had a diagnosis of depression 1 year later (Simon *et al.*, 2002) and at least 10% had persistent or chronic depression (Kessler *et al.*, 2003). At least 50% of people, following their first episode of major depression, will go on to have at least one more episode (Kupfer, 1991) and, after the second and third episodes, the risk of further relapse rises to 70 and 90%, respectively (Kupfer, 1991). People with early onset depression (at or before 20 years of age) and depression occurring in old age have a significantly increased vulnerability to relapse (Giles *et al.*, 1989; Mitchell & Subramaniam, 2005). Thus, while the outlook for a first episode is good, the outlook for recurrent episodes over the long term can be poor with many patients experiencing symptoms of depression over many years (Akiskal, 1986).

Sometimes, recurrent episodes of depression will follow a seasonal pattern which has been called 'seasonal affective disorder' (SAD; Rosenthal *et al.*, 1984). DSM–IV includes criteria for a seasonal pattern whereas only provisional criteria are given in the research version of ICD–10. Although a seasonal pattern can apply to both recurrent depression and bipolar disorder it appears most common in the former (70 to 80%, Rodin & Thompson, 1997; Westrin & Lam, 2007), with recurrent winter depression far more common than recurrent summer episodes (Rodin & Thompson, 1997; Magnusson & Partonen, 2005).

Depression with a seasonal pattern refers to depression that occurs repeatedly at the same time of year (not accounted for by psychosocial stress) with remission in between and without a lifetime predominance of non-seasonal depression. Decreased activity is reported as nearly always present and atypical depressive symptoms, particularly increased sleep, weight gain and carbohydrate craving are common (Magnusson & Partonen, 2005). The onset is reported as usually in the third decade and is more common in the young (Rodin & Thompson, 1997; Magnusson & Partonen, 2005). Surveys in the UK have found a surprisingly high prevalence in general practitioner (GP) practice attendees ranging from 3.5% in Aberdeen (Eagles *et al.*, 1999) to 5.6% in southern England (Thompson *et al.*, 2004). However, the validity of 'seasonal affective disorder' has been poorly accepted in Europe and may be an extreme form of a dimensional 'seasonality trait' rather than a specific diagnosis (Kasper *et al.*, 1989). Some patients with non-seasonal mood disorders also report seasonal variation (Bauer & Dunner, 1993) and this also occurs in other disorders such as anxiety and eating disorders (Bauer & Dunner, 1993; Magnusson & Partonen, 2005). After 5 to 11 years' follow-up, approximately half of those with continuing depressive episodes no longer display a seasonal pattern (Magnusson & Partonen, 2005).

Up to 10% of people with depression subsequently experience hypomanic/manic episodes (Kovacs, 1996), which emphasises the need to question patients about a history of elevated mood and to be alert to new episodes occurring.

In the WHO study, episodes of depression that were either untreated by the GP or missed entirely had the same outlook as treated episodes of depression; however, they were milder at index consultation (Goldberg *et al.*, 1998). A small longitudinal study (Kessler *et al.*, 2002) found that the majority of undetected people either recovered or were diagnosed during the follow-up period; nevertheless, nearly 20% of the identified cases in this study remained undetected and unwell after 3 years.

The term 'treatment-resistant depression' was used in the previous guideline to describe depression that has failed to respond to two or more antidepressants at an adequate dose for an adequate duration given sequentially. Although the term is commonly used, and it can be seen as a useful 'short-hand' to refer to difficulties in achieving adequate improvement with treatment, it has problems that led the GDG to a move away from its use in this guideline update. The term implies that there is a natural cut-off between people who respond to one or two antidepressants compared with those who do not, which is not supported by the evidence, and the term may be taken by both doctors and patients as a pejorative label. It is also not helpful as it does not take into account different degrees of improvement or stages of illness (whether occurring in an ongoing episode or relapse in spite of ongoing treatment). It takes no account of psychotherapeutic treatment, and non-antidepressant augmenting agents are not easily incorporated. The limited trial evidence base reflects the lack of a natural distinction and different studies incorporate different degrees of treatment failure. Finally, it fails to take into account whether psychosocial factors may be preventing recovery (Andrews & Jenkins, 1999). The GDG preferred to approach the problem of inadequate response by considering sequenced treatment options rather than by a category of patient.

2.1.3   Disability and mortality

Depression is the most common mental disorder in community settings and is a major cause of disability across the world. In 1990 it was the fourth most common cause of loss of disability-adjusted life years (DALYs) in the world, and it is projected to become the second most common cause by 2020 (World Bank, 1993). In 1994, it was estimated that about 1.5 million DALYs were lost each year in the West as a result of depression (Murray *et al.*, 1994). It is even more common in the developing world (for a review, see Institute of Medicine, 2001). There is a clear dose–response relationship between illness severity and the extent of disability (Ormel & Costa e Silva, 1995) and onsets of depression are associated with onsets of disability, with an approximate doubling of both social and occupational disability (Ormel *et al.*, 1999).

Apart from the subjective experiences of people with depression, the impact on social and occupational functioning, physical health and mortality is substantial. Depressive illness causes a greater decrement in health state than the major chronic physical illnesses: angina, arthritis, asthma and diabetes (Moussavi *et al.*, 2007). Emotional, motivational and cognitive effects substantially reduce a person's ability to work effectively, with losses in personal and family income as well as lost contribution to society in tax revenues and employment skills. Wider social effects include: greater dependence upon welfare and benefits, with loss of self-esteem and self-confidence; social impairments, including reduced ability to communicate and sustain relationships during the illness with knock-on effects after an episode; and longer-term impairment in social functioning, especially for those who have chronic or recurrent disorders. The stigma associated with mental health problems generally (Sartorius, 2002), and the public view that others might view a person with depression as unbalanced, neurotic and irritating (Priest *et al.*, 1996), may partly account for the reluctance of people with depression to seek help (Bridges & Goldberg, 1987).

Depression can also exacerbate the pain, distress and disability associated with physical health problems as well as adversely affecting outcomes. Depression combined with chronic physical health problems incrementally worsens health compared with physical disease alone or even combinations of physical diseases (Moussavi *et al.*, 2007). In addition, for a range of physical health problems, findings suggest an increased risk of death when comorbid depression is present (Cassano & Fava, 2002). In coronary heart disease, for example, depressive disorders are associated with an 80% increased risk, both of its development and of subsequent mortality in established disease, at least partly through common contributory factors (Nicholson *et al.*, 2006). Another guideline on depression in adults with a chronic physical health problem accompanies this guideline update (NCCMH, 2010).

Suicide accounts for nearly 1% of all deaths and nearly two-thirds of this figure occur in people with depression (Sartorius, 2001). Looked at another way, having depression leads to over a four-times higher risk of suicide compared with the general population, which rises to nearly 20 times in the most severely ill (Bostwick & Pankratz, 2000). Sometimes depression may also lead to acts of violence against others and may even include homicide. Marital and family relationships are frequently negatively affected, and parental depression may lead to neglect of children and significant disturbances in children (Ramachandani & Stein, 2003).

2.1.4   Incidence and prevalence

Worldwide estimates of the proportion of people who are likely to experience depression in their lifetime vary widely between studies and settings, but the best estimates lie between about 4 and 10% for major depression, and between about 2.5 and 5% for dysthymia (low grade chronic depressive symptoms) (Waraich *et al.*, 2004) with disparities attributable to real differences between countries and the method of assessment. The estimated point prevalence for a depressive episode (F32/33, ICD–10; WHO, 1992) among 16- to 74-year-olds in the UK in 2000 was 2.6% (males 2.3%, females 2.8%), but, if the broader and less specific category of 'mixed depression and anxiety' (F41.2, ICD–10, WHO, 1992) was included, these figures rose dramatically to 11.4% (males 9.1%, females 13.6%) (Singleton *et al.*, 2001).

Prevalence rates have consistently been found to be between 1.5 and 2.5 times higher in women than men and have also been fairly stable in the age range of 18 to 64 years (Waraich *et al.*, 2004), although in the most recent UK survey cited above female preponderance was only marked for a depressive episode in those under 35 years whereas for mixed anxiety and depression it was across the age range. Compared with adults without a neurotic disorder, those with a depressive episode or mixed anxiety and depression were more likely to be aged between 35 and 54 years, separated or divorced and living alone or as a lone parent. This pattern was broadly similar between men and women (Singleton *et al.*, 2001).

A number of socioeconomic factors significantly affected prevalence rates in the UK survey: those with a depressive episode were more likely than those without 'neurotic disorders' (depressive or anxiety disorders) to be unemployed, to belong to social classes 4 and below, to have lower predicted intellectual function, to have no formal educational qualifications and to live in local authority or Housing Association accommodation, to have moved three or more times in the last 2 years and to live in an urban environment (Singleton *et al.*, 2001).

No significant effect of ethnic status on prevalence rates of a depressive episode or mixed anxiety and depression were found, although numerically there was a higher proportion of South Asians in those with depressive or anxiety disorders than in those without (Singleton *et al.*, 2001). Migration has been high in Europe in the last 2 decades, but data on mental health is scarce and results vary between migrant groups (Lindert *et al.*, 2008).

An illustration of the social origins of depression can be found in a general practice survey in which 7.2% (range 2.4 to 13.7%, depending upon the practice) of consecutive attendees had a depressive disorder. Neighbourhood social deprivation accounted for 48.3% of the variance among practices and the variables that accounted for most of that variance were: the proportion of the population having no or only one car; and neighbourhood unemployment (Ostler *et al.*, 2001).

The evidence therefore overwhelmingly supports the view that the prevalence of depression, however it is defined, varies according to gender, and social and economic factors.

2.1.5   Diagnosis

In recent years there has been a greater recognition of the need to consider depression that is 'subthreshold'; that is, where the depression does not meet the full criteria for a depressive/major depressive episode. Subthreshold depressive symptoms cause considerable morbidity and human and economic costs, and are more common in those with a history of major depression as well as being a risk factor for future major depression (Rowe & Rapaport, 2006).

There is no accepted classification for subthreshold depression in the current diagnostic systems, with the closest being minor depression (a research diagnosis in DSM–IV). At least two but less than five symptoms are required and it overlaps with ICD–10 mild depressive episode with four symptoms. Given the practical difficulty and inherent uncertainty in deciding thresholds for significant symptom severity and disability, there is no natural discontinuity between subthreshold depressive symptoms and 'mild major' depression in routine clinical practice.

Diagnostic criteria and methods of classification of depressive disorders have changed substantially over the years. Although the advent of operational diagnostic criteria has improved the reliability of diagnosis, this does not circumvent the fundamental problem of attempting to classify a disorder that is heterogeneous and best considered in a number of dimensions (for a fuller discussion, see Appendix 11). DSM–IV and ICD–10, have virtually the same diagnostic features for a 'clinically important' severity of depression (termed a major depressive episode in DSM–IV or a depressive episode in ICD–10). Nevertheless their thresholds differ, with DSM–IV requiring a minimum of five out of nine symptoms (which must include depressed mood and/or anhedonia) and ICD–10 requiring four out of ten symptoms (including at least two of depressed mood, anhedonia and loss of energy). This may mean that more people may be identified as depressed using ICD–10 criteria compared with DSM–IV (Wittchen *et al.*, 2001a), or at least that somewhat different populations are identified (Andrews *et al.*, 2008), related to the need for only one of two key symptoms for DSM–IV but two out of three for ICD–10. These studies emphasise that, although similar, the two systems are not identical and that this is particularly apparent at the threshold taken to indicate clinical importance. The GDG has widened the range of depressive disorders to be considered in this guideline update and emphasises that the diagnostic 'groupings' it uses should be viewed as pragmatic subdivisions of dimensions in the form of vignettes or exemplars rather than firm categories. The GDG considered it important to acknowledge the uncertainty inherent in our current understanding of depression and its classification, and that assuming a false categorical certainty is likely to be unhelpful and, even worse, damaging.

In contrast with the previous guideline, the GDG for the update used DSM–IV rather than ICD–10 to define the diagnosis of depression because the evidence base for treatments nearly always uses DSM–IV. In addition, the GDG attempted to move away from focusing on one aspect such as severity, which can have the unwanted effect of leading to the categorisation of depression and influencing treatment choice based on a single factor such as a symptom count.

The implication of the change in diagnostic system used in the guideline update, combined with redefining the severity ranges, is that it is likely to raise the thresholds for some specific treatments such as antidepressants. An important motivation has been to provide a strong steer away from only using symptom counting to make the diagnosis of depression and, by extension, to emphasise that symptom severity rating scales should not be used by themselves to make the diagnosis, although they can be an aid in assessing severity and response to treatment. To make a diagnosis of a depression requires assessment of three linked but separate factors: (a) severity, (b) duration and (c) course. Diagnosis requires a minimum of 2 weeks' duration of symptoms that includes at least one key symptom. Individual symptoms should be assessed for severity and impact on function, and be present for most of every day.

It is important to emphasise that making a diagnosis of depression does not automatically imply a specific treatment. A diagnosis is a starting point in considering the most appropriate way of helping that individual in their particular circumstances. The evidence base for treatments considered in this guideline is based primarily on randomised controlled trials (RCTs), in which standardised criteria have been used to determine entry into the trial. Patients seen clinically are rarely assessed using standardised criteria, reinforcing the need to be circumspect about an over-rigid extrapolation from RCTs to clinical practice. The following definitions of depression, adapted from DSM–IV, are used in the guideline update:

- subthreshold depressive symptoms: fewer than five symptoms of depression
- mild depression: few, if any, symptoms in excess of the five required to make the diagnosis, and the symptoms result in only minor functional impairment
- moderate depression: symptoms or functional impairment are between 'mild' and 'severe'
- severe depression: most symptoms, and the symptoms markedly interfere with functioning. Can occur with or without psychotic symptoms.

However, diagnosis using the three factors listed above (severity, duration and course) only provides a partial description of the individual experience of depression. People with depression vary in the pattern of symptoms they experience, their family history, personalities, premorbid difficulties (for example, sexual abuse), psychological mindedness and current relational and social problems – all of which may significantly affect outcomes. It is also common for depressed people to have a comorbid psychiatric diagnosis, such as anxiety, social phobia, panic and various personality disorders (Brown *et al.*, 2001), and physical comorbidity. Gender and socioeconomic factors account for large variations in the population rates of depression and few studies of pharmacological, psychological or indeed other treatments for depression either control for or examine these variations. This serves to emphasise that choice of treatment is a complex process and involves negotiation and discussion with patients, and, given the current limited knowledge about which factors are associated with better antidepressant or psychotherapy response, most decisions will rely upon clinical judgement and patient preference until there is further research evidence. Trials of treatment in unclear cases may be warranted, but the uncertainty needs to be discussed with the patient and benefits from treatment carefully monitored.

The differential diagnosis of depression can be difficult; of particular concern are patients with bipolar disorder presenting with depression. The issue of differential diagnosis in this area is covered in the NICE guideline on bipolar disorder (NICE, 2006c).

2.2 AETIOLOGY

The enormous variation in the presentation, course and outcomes of depressive illnesses is reflected in the breadth of theoretical explanations for their aetiology, including genetic (Kendler & Prescott, 1999), biochemical, endocrine and neurophysiological (Goodwin, 2000; Malhi *et al.*, 2005), psychological (Freud, 1917), and social (Brown & Harris, 1978) processes and/or factors. An emphasis upon physical and especially endocrine theories of causation has been encouraged by the observation that some physical illnesses increase the risk of depression, including diabetes, cardiac disease, hyperthyroidism, hypothyroidism, Cushing's syndrome, Addison's disease and hyperprolactinaemic amenorrhea (Cassano & Fava, 2002). Advances in neuroimaging have reinforced the idea of depression as a disorder of brain structure and function (Drevets *et al.*, 2008) and psychological findings emphasise the importance of cognitive and emotional processes (Beck, 2008).

Most people now believe that all of these factors influence a person's vulnerability to depression, although it is likely that, for different people living in different circumstances, precisely how these factors interact and influence that vulnerability will vary (Harris, 2000). Nevertheless, the factors identified as likely to increase a person's vulnerability to depression include gender, genetic and family factors, adverse childhood experiences, personality factors and social circumstances. In the stress-vulnerability model (Nuechterlein & Dawson, 1984), vulnerability factors interact with social or physical triggers such as stressful life events or physical illness to result in a depressive episode (for example, Harris, 2000).

A family history of depressive illness accounts for around 39% of the variance of depression in both sexes (Kendler *et al.*, 2001), and early life experiences such as a poor parent–child relationship, marital discord and divorce, neglect, and physical and sexual abuse almost certainly increase a person's vulnerability to depression in later life (Fava & Kendler, 2000). Personality traits such as 'neuroticism' also increase the risk of depression when faced with stressful life events (Fava & Kendler, 2000). However, different personalities have different expectancies of stressful life events and some personalities have different rates of dependent life events that are directly related to their personality, such as the end of a relationship (Hammen *et al.*, 2000).

The possession of a specific variation in particular genes has also been reported to make individuals more likely to experience depression when faced with life events (for example, Caspi *et al.*, 2003).

The role of current social circumstances in increasing the risk of depression, such as poverty, homelessness, unemployment and chronic physical or mental illness, cannot be doubted even from a brief examination of the epidemiology of depression (see above). In the UK, an influential study found that social vulnerability factors for depression in women in Camberwell, London, included: having three or more children under the age of 14 years living at home; not having a confiding relationship with another person; and having no paid employment outside the home (Brown & Harris, 1978). Lack of a confiding relationship appears to be a strong risk factor for depression (Patten, 1991).

The 'neatness' of this social model of depression, in which vulnerabilities interact with stressful life events, such as separation or loss of a loved one, triggering a depressive episode, is not always supported by the 'facts': some episodes of depression occur in the absence of a stressful event and, conversely, many such events are not followed by a depressive disorder in those with vulnerabilities. However, it is also the case that some factors, such as having a supportive and confiding relationship with another person (Brown & Harris, 1978) or befriending, do protect against depression following a stressful life event (Harris *et al.*, 1999).

In addition to considering the aetiology of the onset of depressive episodes, it is equally important to consider factors that maintain or perpetuate depression because these are potential targets for intervention. Although many studies have reported on factors that predict outcome (including earlier age of onset, greater severity and chronicity, ongoing social stresses, comorbidity with other psychiatric or physical disorders and certain types of personality disorder), there is a lack of understanding about what determines how long a depressive episode lasts, why it varies so much between individuals and why for some it becomes persistent. It is also clinically apparent that depression, especially when it persists, may lead to secondary disability that compounds, and is difficult to distinguish from, the depression itself. Features include loss of self-esteem and independence, feelings of helplessness and hopelessness (which increase the risk of suicide) and loss of engagement in outside activities with social withdrawal. These are aspects that self-help interventions and organisations often target, but about which there is little systematic evidence. These are likely to relate to, and benefit from, the non-specific effects of interventions and the placebo effect (see Section 2.4.3).

2.3   ECONOMIC COSTS OF DEPRESSION

There is now widespread recognition of the significant burden that depression imposes on people and their carers, health services and communities throughout the world. As mentioned previously, by 2020, depression is projected to become the second leading cause of disability with estimates indicating that unipolar depressive disorders account for 4.4% of the global disease burden or the equivalent of 65 million DALYs (Murray & Lopez, 1997b; WHO, 2002). Within the UK setting, the Psychiatric Morbidity Survey of adults aged 16 to 74 years in 2000 reported a prevalence rate for depression of 26 per 1000 people with slightly higher rates for women compared with men (Singleton *et al.*, 2001). Due to its high prevalence and treatment costs, its role as probably the most important risk factor for suicide (Knapp & Illson, 2002), as well as its large impact on workplace productivity, depression places an enormous burden on both the healthcare system and the wider society.

One UK study estimated the total cost of depression in adults in England in 2000 (Thomas & Morris, 2003). A prevalence-based approach was used by applying rates of depression from Office of National Statistics data to population data for England in 2000. The study measured the direct treatment costs of depression, including primary and secondary care costs as well as indirect costs of lost working days (morbidity) and lost life years (mortality). The direct treatment costs were estimated at £370 million, of which 84% was attributable to antidepressant medication. However, the indirect costs of depression were estimated to be far greater: total morbidity costs were £8 billion and mortality costs were £562 million. In comparison with the findings of earlier UK-based cost-of-illness studies, direct treatment costs shifted from hospital admissions (including specialised psychiatric institutions) towards medication, reflecting changes in patterns of care over time away from expensive inpatient care to relatively less expensive outpatient-based care.

A recent review was conducted by the King's Fund in 2006 to estimate mental health expenditure, including depression, in England for the next 20 years, to 2026 (McCrone *et al.*, 2008). The study combined prevalence rates of depression, taken from Psychiatric Morbidity Survey data, with population estimates for 2007 through to 2026. It was estimated that there were 1.24 million people with depression in England, and this was projected to rise by 17% to 1.45 million by 2026. Based on these figures the authors estimated total costs for depression, including prescribed drugs, inpatient care, other NHS services, supported accommodation, social services and lost employment in terms of workplace absenteeism. Overall, the total cost of services for depression in England in 2007 was estimated to be £1.7 billion, while lost employment increased this total to £7.5 billion. By 2026, these figures were projected to be £3 billion and £12.2 billion, respectively. In contrast to the study by Thomas and Morris (2003), antidepressant medication accounted for only 1% of total service costs while inpatient and outpatient care accounted for over 50%. However, the proportion of lost employment costs (78 to 90%) of the total costs was similar across both studies.

One of the key findings from the cost-of-illness literature is that the indirect costs of depression far outweigh the health service costs. Thomas and Morris (2003) suggest that the effect on lost employment and productivity is 23 times larger than the costs falling to the health service. Other studies have also supported these findings. Based on UK labour market survey data, Almond and Healey (2003) estimated that respondents with self-reported depression/anxiety were three times more likely to be absent from work (equivalent to 15 days per year) than workers without depression/anxiety. Furthermore, a US-based study suggests that depression is a major cause of reduced productivity while at work, in terms of 'work cut-back days' (Kessler *et al.*, 2001). This reduced workplace productivity is unlikely to be adequately measured by absenteeism rates and further emphasises the 'hidden costs' of depression (Knapp, 2003). Other intangible costs of depression include the impact on the quality of life of people with depression and their carers.

Certainly, the cost-of-illness calculations presented here show that depression imposes a significant burden on people and their carers, family members, the healthcare system and on the broader economy through lost productivity and workplace absenteeism. Furthermore, it is anticipated that these costs will continue to rise significantly in future years. It is therefore important that efficient use of available healthcare resources is made, to maximise health benefits for people with depression.

2.4 TREATMENT AND MANAGEMENT IN THE NATIONAL HEALTH SERVICE

Treatment for depressive illnesses in the NHS is hampered by the unwillingness of many people to seek help for depression and the failure to recognise depression, especially in primary care. The improved recognition and treatment of depression in primary care is central to the WHO strategy for mental health (WHO, 2001).

2.4.1 Detection, recognition and referral in primary care

Of the 130 cases of depression (including mild cases) per 1000, only 80 will consult their GP. The most common reasons given for reluctance to contact the family doctor include: not thinking anyone could help (28%); feeling it was a problem one should be able to cope with (28%); not thinking it was necessary to contact a doctor (17%); thinking the problem would get better by itself (15%); feeling too embarrassed to discuss it with anyone (13%); and being afraid of the consequences (for example, treatment, tests, hospitalisation, being sectioned; 10%) (Meltzer *et al.*, 2000). The stigma associated with depression cannot be ignored in this context (Priest *et al.*, 1996).

Of the 80 depressed people per 1000 who do consult their GP, 49 are not recognised as depressed, mainly because most of such patients are consulting for a somatic symptom and do not consider themselves mentally unwell, despite the presence of symptoms of depression (Kisely *et al.*, 1995). This group also has milder illnesses (Goldberg *et al.*, 1998; Thompson *et al.*, 2001). Of those that are recognised as depressed, most are treated in primary care and about one in four or five are referred to secondary mental health services. There is considerable variation among individual GPs in their referral rates to mental health services, but those seen by specialist services are a highly selected group – they are skewed towards those who do not respond to antidepressants, people with more severe illnesses, single women and those below 35 years of age (Goldberg & Huxley, 1980).

GPs are immensely variable in their ability to recognise depressive illnesses, with some recognising virtually all the patients found to be depressed at independent research interview, and others recognising very few (Goldberg & Huxley, 1992; Üstün & Sartorius, 1995). GPs' communication skills make a vital contribution to determining their ability to detect emotional distress and those with superior skills allow their patients to show more evidence of distress during their interviews, thus making detection easy. Those GPs with poor communication skills are more likely to collude with their patients, who may not themselves wish to complain of their distress unless they are asked directly about it (Goldberg & Bridges, 1988; Goldberg *et al.*, 1993).

Attempts to improve the rate of recognition of depression by GPs using guidelines, lectures and discussion groups have not improved recognition or outcomes (Thompson *et al.*, 2000; Kendrick *et al.*, 2001), although similar interventions combined with skills training may improve detection and outcomes in terms of symptoms and level of functioning (Tiemens *et al.*, 1999; Ostler *et al.*, 2001). The inference that these health gains are the result of improved detection and better access to specific treatments, while having face validity, has been contested. For example, Ormel and colleagues (1990) suggested that the benefits of recognition of common mental disorders could not be attributed entirely to specific mental health treatments. Other factors, such as acknowledgement of distress, reinterpretation of symptoms, and providing hope and social support, were suggested to contribute to better patient outcomes.

This view has gained confirmation from a Dutch study in which providing skills training for GPs did not improve detection, but did improve outcomes. Moreover, about half of the observed improvement in patient outcomes was mediated by the combined improvements in process of care. In combination with the strong mediating effect of empathy and psychoeducation they suggest that other, probably also non-specific, aspects of the process of care must be responsible for the training effect on symptoms and disability (Van Os *et al.*, 2004). In addition, the communication skills needed by GPs can be learned and incorporated into routine practice with evident improvement in patient outcomes (Gask *et al.*, 1988; Roter *et al.*, 1995).

In summary, those with more severe disorders, and those presenting with psychological symptoms, are especially likely to be recognised as depressed while those presenting with somatic symptoms for which no obvious cause can be found are less likely to be recognised. The evidence suggests that these very undesirable circumstances, in which large numbers of people each year experience depression, with all of the attendant negative personal and social consequences, could be changed. With 50% of people with depression never consulting a doctor, 95% never entering secondary mental health services, and many more whose depression goes unrecognised and untreated, this is clearly a problem for primary care.

2.4.2 Assessment and co-ordination of care

Given the low detection and recognition rates, it is essential that primary care and mental health practitioners have the required skills to assess people with depression, their social circumstances and relationships, and the risk they may pose to themselves and others. This is especially important in view of the fact that depression is associated with an increased suicide rate, a strong tendency for recurrence, and high personal and social costs. The effective assessment of a patient, including risk assessment and the subsequent co-ordination of their care (through the use of the Care Programme Approach [CPA] in secondary care services), is highly likely to improve outcomes and should, therefore, be comprehensive.

2.4.3   Aim, and non-specific effects, of treatment and the placebo

The aim of intervention is to restore health through the relief of symptoms and restoration of function and, in the longer term, to prevent relapse. Where possible, the key goal of an intervention should be complete relief of symptoms (remission), which is associated with better functioning and a lower likelihood of relapse (Kennedy & Foy, 2005). It may not always be possible to achieve remission, but it is usually possible to improve symptoms and functioning to an important degree. For this reason the GDG examined a range of outcomes (where available), including response, remission, change in symptoms and relapse. The relative importance of these depends on many factors, including the severity of depression, the degree of impairment to everyday functioning experienced and the patient's psychiatric history. Among those seeking treament for depression, those put on waiting lists do improve steadily with time. Posternak and Miller (2001) studied 221 patients assigned to waiting lists in 19 treatment trials of specific interventions and found that 20% improved within 4 to 8 weeks, and 50% improved within 6 months. They estimated that 60% of responders to placebo and 30% of responders to antidepressants may experience spontaneous resolution of symptoms (if untreated). An earlier study by Coryell and colleagues (1994) followed up 114 patients with untreated depression for 6 months: the mean duration of an episode was 6 months, with 50% remission in 25 weeks. It should be noted that there is a high relapse rate associated with depression (see Section 2.1.2, above).

Despite their greater severity and other differences, Furukawa and colleagues (2000) showed that patients treated by psychiatrists with antidepressants showed greater improvements than untreated patients: the median time to recovery was 3 months, with 26% recovering in 1 month, 63% in 6 months; 85% in 1 year, and 88% in 2 years.

Although there is insufficient space here to allow proper discussion, it should be noted that non-specific/placebo effects apply not only to treatment with medication but also to other treatments. Studies comparing any treatment with a waiting list control or treatment as usual (TAU) in which there is minimal intervention are therefore difficult to interpret and improvements could simply be due to the increased support, engagement and monitoring that the intervention involves. The placebo effect in trials of psychiatric drugs is often so large that specific pharmacological effects can be hard to identify, especially when given to people who fall into one of the larger, more heterogeneous diagnostic categories. There can also be suspicion of publication bias, especially with regard to drug company funded trials (Lexchin *et al.*, 2003; Melander *et al.*, 2003). Antidepressants (or other) treatments for depression may offer little or no advantage, on average, over placebo for patients with subthreshold depressive symptoms or mild depression, who often improve spontaneously or who respond well to non-specific measures such as support and monitoring. The evidence does support the efficacy of specific treatments with more severe depression and in those with depression that persists over time. However at present it is not possible to clearly identify people with depression who will respond to the specific aspects of a treatment as opposed to the non-specific effects associated with having a treatment.

2.4.4 Pharmacological treatments

The mainstay of the pharmacological treatment of depression for the last 40 or more years has been antidepressants. Tricyclic antidepressants (TCAs) were introduced in the 1950s, the first being imipramine (Kuhn, 1958). The mode of action of this class of drug, thought to be responsible for their mood-elevating properties, is their ability to block the synaptic reuptake of monoamines, including noradrenaline (NA), 5-hydroxytryptymine (5HT) and dopamine (DA). In fact, the TCAs predominantly affect the reuptake of NA and 5HT rather than DA (Mindham, 1982). The antidepressant properties of monoamine-oxidase inhibitors (MAOIs) were discovered by chance in the 1950s, in parallel with TCAs.

Although the introduction of the TCAs was welcome, given the lack of specific treatments for people with depression, the side effects resulting from their ability to influence anticholinergic, histaminergic and other receptor systems reduced their acceptability. Moreover, overdose with TCAs (with the exception of lofepramine) carries a high mortality and morbidity, which is particularly problematic in the treatment of people with suicidal intentions.

In response to the side-effect profile and the toxicity of TCAs in overdose, new classes of antidepressants have been developed, including: selective serotonin reuptake inhibitors (SSRIs), such as fluoxetine; drugs chemically related to but different from the TCAs, such as trazodone; and a range of other chemically unrelated antidepressants, including mirtazapine (BNF 57, 2009). Their effects and side effects vary considerably, although their mood-elevating effects are again thought to be mediated through increasing intra-synaptic levels of monoamines, some primarily affecting NA, some 5HT and others affecting both to varying degrees and in different ways.

Other drugs used either alone or in combination with antidepressants include lithium salts (BNF 57, 2009) and antipsychotics (BNF 57, 2009), although the use of these drugs is usually reserved for people with severe, psychotic or chronic depressions, or as prophylactics. A full review of the evidence base for the use of the different types of antidepressants is presented in Chapter 10.

In addition, there is preliminary evidence that pharmacogenetic variations may affect the efficacy and tolerability of antidepressant drugs. It is likely that future research on this topic will lead to the development of clinically meaningful pharmacogenetic markers, but at the moment the data is insufficient to make recommendations.

2.4.5 Psychological treatments

In 1917, Freud published 'Mourning and melancholia', which is probably the first modern psychological theory on the causes, meaning and psychological treatment of depression. Since that time, numerous theories and methods for the psychological treatment of psychological disorders have been elaborated and championed, although psychological treatments specifically for depression were developed only over the last 30 to 40 years, and research into their efficacy is more recent still (Roth & Fonagy, 1996). Many, but not all, such therapies are derived from Freudian psychoanalysis, but address the difficulties of treating people with depression using a less rigid psychoanalytic approach (Fonagy, 2003). In any event, the emergence of cognitive and behavioural approaches to the treatment of mental health problems has led to a greater focus upon the evidence base and the development of psychological treatments specifically adapted for people with depression (for example, see Beck *et al.*, 1979).

Psychological treatments for depression currently claiming efficacy in the treatment of people with depressive illnesses and reviewed for this guideline in Chapter 8 include: cognitive behavioural therapies; behavioural activation; interpersonal therapy (IPT); problem-solving therapy; counselling; short-term psychodynamic psychotherapy; and couples therapy. Psychological treatments have expanded rapidly in recent years and generally have more widespread acceptance from patients (Priest *et al.*, 1996). In the last 15 years in the UK there has been a very significant expansion of psychological treatments in primary care for depression, in particular primary care counselling.

2.4.6   Service-level and other interventions

Given the complexity of healthcare organisations, and the variation in the way care is delivered (inpatient, outpatient, day hospital, community teams, and so on), choosing the right service configuration for the delivery of care to specific groups of people has gained increasing interest with regard to both policy (for example, see Department of Health, 1999), and research (for example, evaluating day hospital treatment, Marshall *et al.*, 2001). Research using RCT designs has a number of difficulties; for example, using comparators such as 'standard care' in the US make the results difficult to generalise or apply to countries with very different types of 'standard care'.

Service-level interventions considered for review in this guideline include: organisational developments, crisis teams, day hospital care, non-statutory support and other social supports. Other types of interventions reviewed for this guideline include: physical activity programmes, guided self-help, computerised cognitive behavioural therapy (CCBT) and screening.

2.4.7   Stepped care

In Figure 1, a 'stepped-care' model is developed that draws attention to the different needs that depressed individuals have – depending on the characteristics of their depression and their personal and social circumstances – and the responses that are required from services. Stepped care provides a framework in which to organise the

Figure 1: The stepped-care model

Focus of the intervention	Nature of the intervention
STEP 4: Severe and complex[1] depression; risk to life; severe self-neglect	Medication, high-intensity psychological interventions, ECT, crisis service, combined treatments, multiprofessional and inpatient care
STEP 3: Persistent subthreshold depressive symptoms or mild to moderate depression with inadequate response to initial interventions; moderate and severe depression	Medication, high-intensity psychological interventions, combined treatments, collaborative care[2] and referral for further assessment and interventions
STEP 2: Persistent subthreshold depressive symptoms; mild to moderate depression	Low-intensity psychosocial interventions, psychological interventions, medication and referral for further assessment and interventions
STEP 1: All known and suspected presentations of depression	Assessment, support, psychoeducation, active monitoring and referral for further assessment and interventions

[1] Complex depression includes depression that shows an inadequate response to multiple treatments, is complicated by psychotic symptoms, and/or is associated with significant psychiatric comorbidity or psychosocial factors.
[2] Only for depression where the person also has a chronic physical health problem and associated functional impairment (see NICE, 2009c).

provision of services supporting patients, carers and healthcare professionals in identifying and accessing the most effective interventions.

Of those people whom primary healthcare professionals recognise as having depression, some prefer to avoid medical interventions and others will improve in any case without them. Thus, in depression of only mild severity, many GPs prefer an 'active monitoring' approach, which can be accompanied by general advice on such matters as restoring natural sleep rhythms and getting more structure into the day. However, other people prefer to accept, or indeed require, medical, psychological or social interventions, and these patients are therefore offered more complex interventions. Various interventions are effective, delivered by a range of workers in primary care.

Treatment of depression in primary care, however, often falls short of optimal guideline recommended practice (Donoghue & Tylee, 1996) and outcomes are correspondingly below what is possible (Rost *et al.*, 1995). As we have seen, only about one in five of the patients at this level will need referral to a mental healthcare professional, the main indications being failure of the depression to respond to treatment offered in primary care, incomplete response or frequent recurrences of depression. Those patients who are actively suicidal or whose depression has psychotic features will need specialist referral.

Finally, there are a few patients who will need admission to an inpatient psychiatric bed. Here, they can receive 24-hour care and various special interventions.

3 METHODS USED TO DEVELOP THIS GUIDELINE[2]

3.1 OVERVIEW

The update of this guideline drew upon methods outlined by NICE (The Guidelines Manual, NICE, 2007c). A team of healthcare professionals, lay representatives and technical experts known as the Guideline Development Group (GDG), with support from the NCCMH staff, undertook the update of a patient-centred, evidence-based guideline. There are six basic steps in the process of updating a guideline:

- define the scope, which sets the parameters of the update and provides a focus and steer for the development work
- update the clinical questions developed for the previous guideline
- develop criteria for updating the literature search and conduct the search
- design validated protocols for systematic review and apply to evidence recovered by search
- synthesise and (meta-) analyse data retrieved, guided by the clinical questions, and produce evidence summaries (for both the clinical and health economic evidence)
- decide if there is sufficient new evidence to change existing recommendations and develop new recommendations where necessary.

The update will provide recommendations for good practice that are based on the best available evidence of clinical and cost effectiveness. In addition, to ensure a service user and carer focus, the concerns of people with depression and their carers regarding health and social care have been highlighted and addressed by recommendations agreed by the whole GDG.

3.2 THE SCOPE

NICE commissioned the NCCMH to review recent evidence on the management of depression and to update the existing guideline *Depression: Treatment and Management of Depression in Primary and Secondary Care* (NICE, 2004a; NCCMH, 2004). The NCCMH developed a scope for the guideline update (see Appendix 1). The scope for the update also included updating the NICE technology appraisal on the use of ECT (NICE, 2003), which had been incorporated into the previous guideline.

The purpose of the scope is to:

- provide an overview of what the guideline will include and exclude
- identify the key aspects of care that must be included

---

[2]The methodology for the previous guideline can be found in Appendix 21.

- set the boundaries of the development work and provide a clear framework to enable work to stay within the priorities agreed by NICE and the NCC and the remit from the Department of Health/Welsh Assembly Government
- inform the development of updated clinical questions and search strategy
- inform professionals and the public about the expected content of the guideline
- keep the guideline to a reasonable size to ensure that its development can be carried out within the allocated period.

The draft scope was subject to consultation with registered stakeholders over a 4-week period. During the consultation period, the scope was posted on the NICE website (www.nice.org.uk). Comments were invited from stakeholder organisations and the Guideline Review Panel (GRP). Further information about the GRP can also be found on the NICE website. The NCCMH and NICE reviewed the scope in light of comments received and the revised scope was signed off by the GRP.

3.3   THE GUIDELINE DEVELOPMENT GROUP

The GDG consisted of: professionals in psychiatry, psychiatric pharmacy, clinical psychology, nursing and general practice; academic experts in psychiatry and psychology; and people with depression and a carer. The GDG was recruited according to the specifications set out in the scope and in line with the process set out in the NICE guideline manual (NICE, 2007c). The guideline development process was supported by staff from the NCCMH, who undertook the clinical and health economics literature searches, reviewed and presented the evidence to the GDG, managed the process and contributed to drafting the guideline.

3.3.1   Guideline Development Group meetings

Fourteen GDG meetings were held between November 2007 and January 2009. During each day-long GDG meeting, in a plenary session, clinical questions and clinical and economic evidence were reviewed and assessed, and recommendations formulated. At each meeting, all GDG members declared any potential conflicts of interest, and the concerns of people with depression and carers were routinely discussed as part of a standing agenda item.

3.3.2   Topic groups

The GDG divided its workload along clinically relevant lines to simplify the guideline development process, and GDG members formed smaller topic groups to undertake guideline work in that area of clinical practice. Three topic groups were formed to cover: (1) pharmacological and physical interventions, (2) psychological and psychosocial interventions and (3) services. These groups were designed to efficiently manage the large volume of evidence needing to be appraised prior to presenting it to the GDG as a whole. Each topic group was chaired by a GDG member with expert knowledge of the topic area (one of the healthcare professionals). Topic groups refined the clinical questions and the clinical definitions of treatment interventions, reviewed and prepared the evidence with the systematic reviewer before presenting it to the GDG as a whole and helped the GDG to identify further expertise in the topic. Topic group leaders reported the status of the group's work as part of the standing agenda. They also introduced and led the GDG discussion of the evidence review for that topic and assisted the GDG Chair in drafting the section of the guideline relevant to the work of each topic group. A group was also convened comprising the service user and carer representatives and members of the NCCMH review team to develop the chapter on experience of care (Chapter 4). The service user and carer representatives jointly ran the group and presented their findings at GDG meetings.

3.3.3 People with depression and carers

Individuals with direct experience of services gave an integral service-user focus to the GDG and the guideline. The GDG included three people with depression, one of whom was also a carer. They contributed as full GDG members to writing the clinical questions, helping to ensure that the evidence addressed their views and preferences, highlighting sensitive issues and terminology relevant to the guideline, and bringing service-user research to the attention of the GDG. In drafting the guideline, they contributed to writing the guideline's introduction and Chapter 4 and identified recommendations from the service user and carer perspective.

3.3.4 Special advisers

Special advisers, who had specific expertise in one or more aspects of treatment and management relevant to the guideline, or provided expertise in methodological aspects of evidence synthesis, assisted the GDG, commenting on specific aspects of the developing guideline and, where necessary, making presentations to the GDG. Appendix 3 lists those who agreed to act as special advisers.

3.3.5 National and international experts

National and international experts in the area under review were identified through the literature search and through the experience of the GDG members. These experts were contacted to recommend unpublished or soon-to-be published studies to ensure that up-to-date evidence was included in the development of the guideline. They informed the group about completed trials at the pre-publication stage, systematic reviews in the process of being published, studies relating to the cost effectiveness of treatment, and trial data if the GDG could be provided with full access to the complete trial report. Appendix 6 lists the researchers who were contacted.

3.4   CLINICAL QUESTIONS

Clinical questions were used to guide the identification and interrogation of the evidence base relevant to the topic of the guideline. The draft clinical questions were discussed by the GDG at the first few meetings and amended as necessary. Where appropriate, the questions were refined once the evidence had been searched and, where necessary, subquestions were generated. Questions submitted by stakeholders were also discussed by the GDG and included where appropriate. For the purposes of the systematic review of clinical evidence, the questions were categorised as primary or secondary. The review focused on providing evidence to answer the primary questions. The final list of clinical questions can be found in Appendix 7.

For questions about interventions, the PICO (patient, intervention, comparison and outcome) framework was used. This structured approach divides each question into four components: the patients (the population under study), the interventions (what is being done), the comparisons (other main treatment options) and the outcomes (the measures of how effective the interventions have been) (see Table 2).

In some situations, the prognosis of a particular condition is of fundamental importance, over and above its general significance in relation to specific interventions. Areas where this is particularly likely to occur relate to assessment of risk, for example in terms of early intervention. In addition, questions related to issues of service delivery are occasionally specified in the remit from the Department of Health/Welsh Assembly Government. In these cases, appropriate clinical questions were developed to be clear and concise.

Table 2: Features of a well-formulated question on effectiveness intervention – the PICO guide

Patients/population	Which patients or population of patients are we interested in? How can they be best described? Are there subgroups that need to be considered?
Intervention	Which intervention, treatment or approach should be used?
Comparison	What is/are the main alternative/s to compare with the intervention?
Outcome	What is really important for the patient? Which outcomes should be considered: intermediate or short-term measures; mortality; morbidity and treatment complications; rates of relapse; late morbidity and readmission; return to work; physical and social functioning and other measures, such as quality of life; general health status; costs?

Table 3: Best study design to answer each type of question

Type of question	Best primary study design
Effectiveness or other impact of an intervention	RCT; other studies that may be considered in the absence of an RCT are the following: internally/externally controlled before and after trial, interrupted time-series
Accuracy of information (for example, risk factor, test, prediction rule)	Comparing the information against a valid gold standard in a randomised trial or inception cohort study
Rates (of disease, patient experience, rare side effects)	Cohort, registry, cross-sectional study
Costs	Naturalistic prospective cost study

To help facilitate the literature review, a note was made of the best study design type to answer each question. There are four main types of clinical question of relevance to NICE guidelines. These are listed in Table 3. For each type of question the best primary study design varies, where 'best' is interpreted as 'least likely to give misleading answers to the question'.

However, in all cases a well-conducted systematic review of the appropriate type of study is likely to always yield a better answer than a single study.

Deciding on the best design type to answer a specific clinical question does not mean that studies of different design types addressing the same question were discarded.

3.5   SYSTEMATIC CLINICAL LITERATURE REVIEW

The aim of the clinical literature review was to systematically identify and synthesise relevant evidence from the literature (updating the existing evidence-base where appropriate) to answer the specific clinical questions developed by the GDG. Thus, clinical practice recommendations are evidence-based where possible and, if evidence is not available, informal consensus methods are used (see Section 3.5.11) and the need for future research is specified.

3.5.1   Methodology

A step-wise hierarchical approach was taken to locating and presenting evidence to the GDG. The NCCMH developed this process based on methods set out in *The*

Guidelines Manual (NICE, 2007c) and after considering recommendations from a range of other sources. These included:

- Clinical Policy and Practice Program of the New South Wales Department of Health (Australia)
- Clinical Evidence online
- The Cochrane Collaboration
- New Zealand Guidelines Group
- NHS Centre for Reviews and Dissemination
- Oxford Centre for Evidence-Based Medicine
- Oxford Systematic Review Development Programme
- Scottish Intercollegiate Guidelines Network (SIGN)
- United States Agency for Healthcare Research and Quality.

3.5.2   The review process

During the development of the scope, a more extensive search was undertaken for systematic reviews and guidelines published since the previous depression guideline. These were used to inform the development of review protocols for each topic group. Review protocols included the relevant clinical question(s), the search strategy, the criteria for assessing the eligibility of studies, and any additional assessments.

The initial approach taken to locating primary-level studies depended on the type of clinical question and potential availability of evidence. Based on the previous guideline and GDG knowledge of the literature, a decision was made about which questions were best addressed by good practice based on expert opinion, which questions were likely to have a good evidence base and which questions were likely to have little or no directly relevant evidence. Recommendations based on good practice were developed by informal consensus of the GDG. For questions with a good evidence base, the review process depended on the type of key question (see below). For questions that were unlikely to have a good evidence base, a brief descriptive review was initially undertaken by a member of the GDG.

Searches for evidence were updated between 6 and 8 weeks before the guideline consultation. After this point, studies were included only if they were judged by the GDG to be exceptional (for example, the evidence was likely to change a recommendation).

3.5.3   The search process for questions concerning interventions

For questions related to interventions, the initial evidence base (or updated evidence base) was formed from well-conducted RCTs that addressed at least one of the clinical questions. Although there are a number of difficulties with the use of RCTs in the evaluation of interventions in mental health, the RCT remains the most important method for establishing treatment efficacy. For other clinical questions, searches were for the appropriate study design (see above).

The search was exhaustive, using several databases and other sources. For RCTs the search consisted of terms relating to the clinical condition (that is, depression) and study design only, thereby yielding the largest number of relevant papers that might otherwise be missed by more specific searches, formed around additional elements of the question, including interventions and the outcomes of interest. The GDG did not limit the search to any particular therapeutic modality. Standard mental health related bibliographic databases (that is, CINAHL, Cochrane Library, EMBASE, MEDLINE and PsycINFO) were used for the initial search for all studies potentially relevant to the guideline update. Where the evidence base was large, recent high-quality English-language systematic reviews were used primarily as a source of RCTs (see Appendix 10 for quality criteria used to assess systematic reviews). However, in some circumstances existing datasets were utilised. Where this was the case, data were cross-checked for accuracy before use. New RCTs meeting inclusion criteria set by the GDG were incorporated into the existing reviews and fresh analyses performed.

After the initial search, results were scanned liberally to exclude irrelevant papers, the review team used a purpose-built 'study information' database to manage both the included and the excluded studies (eligibility criteria were developed after consultation with the GDG). Double checking of all excluded studies was not done routinely, but a selection of abstracts was checked to ensure reliability of the sifting. For questions without good-quality evidence (after the initial search), a decision was made by the GDG about whether to (a) repeat the search using subject-specific databases (for example, AMED, ERIC, OpenSIGLE or Sociological Abstracts), (b) conduct a new search for lower levels of evidence or (c) adopt a consensus process (see Section 3.5.11).

In addition, searches were made of the reference lists of all eligible systematic reviews and included studies. Known experts in the field, based both on the references identified in early steps and on advice from GDG members, were sent letters requesting relevant studies that were in the process of being published (see Appendix 6)[3]. In addition, the tables of contents of appropriate journals were periodically checked for relevant studies.

3.5.4   Search filters

Search filters developed by the review team consisted of a combination of subject heading and free-text phrases. Specific filters were developed for the guideline topic and, where necessary, for each clinical question. In addition, the review team used filters developed for systematic reviews, RCTs and other appropriate research designs (Appendix 8).

---

[3]Unpublished full trial reports were also accepted where sufficient information was available to judge eligibility and quality (see Section 3.5.6).

3.5.5 Study selection

All primary-level studies included after the first scan of citations were acquired in full and re-evaluated for eligibility (based on the relevant review protocol) at the time they were being entered into the study database. Eligible systematic reviews and primary-level studies were critically appraised for methodological quality (see Appendix 10 for the quality checklists and Appendix 17 for characteristics of each study including quality assessment). The eligibility of each study was confirmed by consensus during topic group meetings.

For some clinical questions, it was necessary to prioritise the evidence with respect to the UK context (that is, external validity). To make this process explicit, the topic groups took into account the following factors when assessing the evidence:

- participant factors (for example, gender, age and ethnicity)
- provider factors (for example, model fidelity, the conditions under which the intervention was performed and the availability of experienced staff to undertake the procedure)
- cultural factors (for example, differences in standard care and differences in the welfare system).

It was the responsibility of each topic group to decide which prioritisation factors were relevant to each clinical question in light of the UK context and then decide how they should modify their recommendations.

3.5.6 Unpublished evidence

The GDG used a number of criteria when deciding whether or not to accept unpublished data. First, the evidence must have been accompanied by a trial report containing sufficient detail to properly assess the quality of the research; second, where evidence was submitted directly to the GDG, it must have been done so with the understanding that details would be published in the full guideline. However, the GDG recognised that unpublished evidence submitted by investigators might later be retracted by those investigators if the inclusion of such data would jeopardise publication of their research.

3.5.7 Data extraction

Outcome data were extracted from all eligible studies, which met the minimum quality criteria, using Review Manager 4.2.10 (Cochrane Collaboration, 2003) or Review Manager 5 (Cochrane Collaboration, 2008).

For each major area reviewed, the GDG distinguished between outcomes that they considered critical and ones that were important but not critical for the purposes of updating the guideline. Only critical outcomes were initially extracted for data analysis (further details about the critical outcomes can be found in the evidence chapters).

In most circumstances, for a given outcome (continuous and dichotomous) where more than 50% of the number randomised to any group were lost to follow up, the data were excluded from the analysis (except for the outcome 'leaving the study early', in which case the denominator was the number randomised). Where possible, dichotomous efficacy outcomes were calculated on an intention-to-treat basis (that is, a 'once-randomised-always-analyse' basis). Where there was good evidence that those participants who ceased to engage in the study were likely to have an unfavourable outcome, early withdrawals were included in both the numerator and denominator. Adverse events were entered into Review Manager as reported by the study authors because it was usually not possible to determine whether early withdrawals had an unfavourable outcome. Where there was limited data for a particular review, the 50% rule was not applied. In these circumstances, the evidence was downgraded due to the risk of bias.

Where necessary, standard deviations were calculated from standard errors (SEs), confidence intervals (CIs) or p-values according to standard formulae (see the *Cochrane Handbook for Systematic Reviews of Interventions*, Version 5.0.1; Higgins & Green, 2008). Data were summarised using the generic inverse variance method using Review Manager.

Consultation with another reviewer or members of the GDG was used to overcome difficulties with coding. Data from studies included in existing systematic reviews were extracted independently by one reviewer and cross-checked with the existing dataset. Where possible, data extracted by one reviewer was checked by a second reviewer. Disagreements were resolved with discussion. Where consensus could not be reached, a third reviewer or GDG members resolved the disagreement. Masked assessment (that is, blind to the journal from which the article comes, the authors, the institution and the magnitude of the effect) was not used since it is unclear that doing so reduces bias (Jadad *et al.*, 1996; Berlin, 1997).

3.5.8 Synthesising the evidence

Where possible, meta-analysis was used to synthesise the evidence using Review Manager. If necessary, re-analyses of the data or sub-analyses were used to answer clinical questions not addressed in the original studies or reviews. Studies have been given a 'study ID' to make them easier to identify in the text, tables and appendices of this guideline. Study IDs are composed of the first author's surname followed by the year of publication. Studies that were included in the previous guideline (NCCMH, 2004) have a study ID in title case (for example, Smith1999); studies that were found and included in this guideline update only are labelled in capital letters (for example, JONES2005). References to included and excluded studies can be found in Appendix 17.

Dichotomous outcomes were analysed as relative risks (RR) with the associated 95% CI (for an example, see Figure 2). A 'relative risk' (also called a 'risk ratio') is the ratio of the treatment event rate to the control event rate. An RR of 1 indicates no difference between treatment and control. In Figure 2, the overall RR of 0.73

Figure 2: Example of a forest plot displaying dichotomous data

Review: NCCMH clinical guideline review (Example)
Comparison: 01 Intervention A compared to a control group
Outcome: 01 Number of people who did not show remission

Study or sub-category	Intervention A n/N	Control n/N	RR (fixed) 95% CI	Weight %	RR (fixed) 95% CI		
01 Intervention A vs. control							
Griffiths1994	13/23	27/28		38.79	0.59	[0.41,	0.84]
Lee1986	11/15	14/15		22.30	0.79	[0.56,	1.10]
Treasure1994	21/28	24/27		38.92	0.84	[0.66,	1.09]
Subtotal (95% CI)	45/66	65/70		100.00	0.73	[0.61,	0.88]

Test for heterogeneity: Chi² = 2.83, df = 2 (P = 0.24), I² = 29.3%
Test for overall effect: Z = 3.37 (P = 0.0007)

0.2   0.5   1   2   5
Favours intervention   Favours control

indicates that the event rate (that is, non-remission rate) associated with intervention A is about three quarters of that with the control intervention or, in other words, the RR reduction is 27%.

The CI shows with 95% certainty the range within which the true treatment effect should lie and can be used to determine statistical significance. If the CI does not cross the 'line of no effect', the effect is statistically significant.

Continuous outcomes were analysed as weighted mean differences (WMD), or as a standardised mean difference (SMD) when different measures were used in different studies to estimate the same underlying effect (for an example, see Figure 3). If provided, intention-to-treat data, using a method such as 'last observation carried forward', were preferred over data from completers.

To check for consistency between studies, both the I^2 test of heterogeneity and a visual inspection of the forest plots were used. The I^2 statistic describes the proportion of total variation in study estimates that is due to heterogeneity (Higgins & Thompson, 2002). The I^2 statistic was interpreted in the following way:

- >50%: notable heterogeneity (an attempt was made to explain the variation by conducting sub-analyses to examine potential moderators. In addition, studies with effect sizes greater than two standard deviations from the mean of the

Figure 3: Example of a forest plot displaying continuous data

Review: NCCMH clinical guideline review (Example)
Comparison: 01 Intervention A compared to a control group
Outcome: 03 Mean frequency (endpoint)

Study or sub-category	N	Intervention A Mean (SD)	N	Control Mean (SD)	SMD (fixed) 95% CI	Weight %	SMD (fixed) 95% CI		
01 Intervention A vs. control									
Freeman1988	32	1.30(3.40)	20	3.70(3.60)		25.91	-0.68	[-1.25,	-0.10]
Griffiths1994	20	1.25(1.45)	22	4.14(2.21)		17.83	-1.50	[-2.20,	-0.81]
Lee1986	14	3.70(4.00)	14	10.10(17.50)		15.08	-0.49	[-1.24,	0.26]
Treasure1994	28	44.23(27.04)	24	61.40(24.97)		27.28	-0.65	[-1.21,	-0.09]
Wolf1992	15	5.30(5.10)	11	7.10(4.60)		13.90	-0.36	[-1.14,	0.43]
Subtotal (95% CI)	109		91			100.00	-0.74	[-1.04,	-0.45]

Test for heterogeneity: Chi² = 6.13, df = 4 (P = 0.19), I² = 34.8%
Test for overall effect: Z = 4.98 (P < 0.00001)

-4   -2   0   2   4
Favours intervention   Favours control

43

remaining studies were excluded using sensitivity analyses. If studies with hetero-geneous results were found to be comparable with regard to study and participant characteristics, a random-effects model was used to summarise the results [DerSimonian & Laird, 1986]. In the random-effects analysis, heterogeneity is accounted for both in the width of CIs and in the estimate of the treatment effect. With decreasing heterogeneity the random-effects approach moves asymptotically towards a fixed-effects model).

- 30 to 50%: moderate heterogeneity (both the chi-squared test of heterogeneity and a visual inspection of the forest plot were used to decide between a fixed and random-effects model).
- <30%: mild heterogeneity (a fixed-effects model was used to synthesise the results).

3.5.9 Presenting the data to the GDG

Study characteristics tables and, where appropriate, forest plots generated with Review Manager were presented to the GDG to prepare a GRADE evidence profile table for each review and to develop recommendations.

Evidence profile tables

A GRADE evidence profile was used to summarise, with the exception of diagnostic studies (methods for these studies are at present not sufficiently developed), both the quality of the evidence and the results of the evidence synthesis (see Table 4 for an example of an evidence profile). For each outcome, quality may be reduced depend-ing on the following factors:

- study design (randomised trial, observational study, or any other evidence)
- limitations (based on the quality of individual studies; see Appendix 10 for the quality checklists)
- inconsistency (see Section 3.5.8 for how consistency was measured)
- indirectness (that is, how closely the outcome measures, interventions and partic-ipants match those of interest)
- imprecision (based on the CI around the effect size).

For observational studies, the quality may be increased if there is a large effect, if plausible confounding would have changed the effect, or if there is evidence of a dose–response gradient (details would be provided under the other considerations column). Each evidence profile also included a summary of the findings: the number of patients included in each group, an estimate of the magnitude of the effect and the overall quality of the evidence for each outcome.

The quality of the evidence was based on the quality assessment components (study design, limitations to study quality, consistency, directness and any other considerations) and graded using the following definitions:

- High = further research is very unlikely to change our confidence in the estimate of the effect
- Moderate = further research is likely to have an important impact on our confi-dence in the estimate of the effect and may change the estimate

Table 4: Example of GRADE evidence profile

Quality assessment							Summary of findings				Quality
							No. of patients		Effect		
									Relative (95% CI)	Absolute	
No. of studies	Design	Limitations	Inconsistency	Indirectness	Imprecision	Other considerations	Intervention	Control			
Outcome 1											
6	Randomised trial	No serious limitations	No serious inconsistency	No serious indirectness	Serious[1]	None	8/191	7/150	RR 0.94 (0.39 to 2.23)	0 fewer per 100 (from 3 fewer to 6 more)	⊕⊕⊕○ MODERATE
Outcome 2											
6	Randomised trial	No serious limitations	No serious inconsistency	No serious indirectness	Serious[2]	None	55/236	63/196	RR 0.44 (0.21 to 0.94)[3]	18 fewer per 100 (from 2 fewer to 25 fewer)	⊕⊕⊕○ MODERATE
Outcome 3											
3	Randomised trial	No serious limitations	No serious inconsistency	No serious indirectness	Serious[2]	None	83	81	–	MD –1.51 (–3.81 to 0.8)	⊕⊕⊕○ MODERATE
Outcome 4											
3	Randomised trial	No serious limitations	No serious inconsistency	No serious indirectness	Serious[4]	None	88	93	–	SMD –0.26 (–0.56 to 0.03)	⊕⊕⊕○ MODERATE
Outcome 5											
4	Randomised trial	No serious limitations	No serious inconsistency	No serious indirectness	Serious[4]	None	109	114	–	SMD –0.13 (–0.6 to 0.34)	⊕⊕⊕○ MODERATE

[1] The upper confidence limit includes an effect that, if it were real, would represent a benefit that, given the downsides, would still be worth it.
[2] The lower confidence limit crosses a threshold below which, given the downsides of the intervention, one would not recommend the intervention.
[3] Random-effects model.
[4] 95% CI crosses the minimal importance difference threshold.

- Low = further research is very likely to have an important impact on our confidence in the estimate of the effect and is likely to change the estimate
- Very low = any estimate of effect is very uncertain.

For further information about the process and the rationale of producing an evidence profile table, see GRADE (2004).

3.5.10   Forming the clinical summaries and recommendations

Once the GRADE profile tables relating to a particular clinical question were completed, summary tables incorporating important information from the GRADE profiles were developed (these tables are presented in the evidence chapters).

The systematic reviewer in conjunction with the topic group lead produced a clinical evidence summary. Once the GRADE profiles and clinical summaries were finalised and agreed by the GDG and the evidence from depression in the general populations was taken into account, the associated recommendations were drafted, taking into account the trade-off between the benefits and downsides of treatment as well as other important factors. These included economic considerations, the values of the GDG and society, and the GDG's awareness of practical issues (Eccles *et al.*, 1998). The confidence surrounding the evidence in the depression guideline also influenced the GDG's decision to extrapolate.

3.5.11   Method used to answer a clinical question in the absence of appropriately designed, high-quality research

In the absence of appropriately designed, high-quality research, or where the GDG was of the opinion (on the basis of previous searches or their knowledge of the literature) that there were unlikely to be such evidence, either an informal or formal consensus process was adopted. This process focused on those questions that the GDG considered a priority.

Informal consensus
The starting point for the process of informal consensus was that a member of the topic group identified, with help from the systematic reviewer, a narrative review that most directly addressed the clinical question. Where this was not possible, a brief review of the recent literature was initiated.

This existing narrative review or new review was used as a basis for beginning an iterative process to identify lower levels of evidence relevant to the clinical question and to lead to written statements for the guideline. The process involved a number of steps:

- A description of what is known about the issues concerning the clinical question was written by one of the topic group members.
- Evidence from the existing review or new review was then presented in narrative form to the GDG and further comments were sought about the evidence and its perceived relevance to the clinical question.

- Based on the feedback from the GDG, additional information was sought and added to the information collected. This may have included studies that did not directly address the clinical question but were thought to contain relevant data.
- If, during the course of preparing the report, a significant body of primary-level studies (of appropriate design to answer the question) were identified, a full systematic review was done.
- At this time, subject possibly to further reviews of the evidence, a series of statements that directly addressed the clinical question were developed.
- Following this, on occasions and as deemed appropriate by the GDG, the report was then sent to appointed experts outside the GDG for peer review and comment. The information from this process was then fed back to the GDG for further discussion of the statements.
- Recommendations were then developed and could also be sent for further external peer review.
- After this final stage of comment, the statements and recommendations were again reviewed and agreed upon by the GDG.

3.6   HEALTH ECONOMICS METHODS

The aim of health economics was to contribute to the guideline's development by providing evidence on the cost effectiveness of interventions for people with depression covered in the guideline. This was achieved by:

- a systematic literature review of existing economic evidence
- economic modelling, where economic evidence was lacking or was considered inadequate to inform decisions; areas for further economic analysis were prioritised based on anticipated resource implications of the respective recommendations as well as on the quality and availability of respective clinical data.

Systematic search of the economic literature was undertaken on all areas that were updated since the previous guideline. Moreover, literature on health-related quality of life of people with depression was systematically searched to identify studies reporting appropriate utility weights that could be utilised in a cost-utility analysis.

In addition to the systematic review of economic literature, the following economic issues were identified by the GDG in collaboration with the health economist as key priorities for further economic analysis (either costing of interventions or full economic modelling) in the guideline update:

- a cost analysis of low-intensity psychological interventions
- cost-utility of pharmacological interventions
- cost-utility of pharmacological therapy versus combined psychological and pharmacological therapy.

These topics were selected after considering potential resource implications of the respective recommendations.

The rest of this section describes the methods adopted in the systematic literature review of economic studies undertaken for this guideline update. Methods employed in *de novo* economic modelling carried out for this guideline update are described in the respective sections of the guideline.

3.6.1   Search strategy

For the systematic review of economic evidence the standard mental-health-related bibliographic databases (EMBASE, MEDLINE, CINAHL and PsycINFO) were searched. For these databases, a health economics search filter adapted from the Centre for Reviews and Dissemination at the University of York was used in combination with a general search strategy for depression. Additional searches were performed in specific health economics databases (NHS Economic Evaluation Database [EED], Office of Health Economics Health Economic Evaluations Database [OHE HEED]), as well as in the HTA database. For the HTA and NHS EED databases, the general strategy for depression was used. OHE HEED was searched using a shorter, database-specific strategy. Initial searches were performed in November 2007. The searches were updated regularly, with the final search performed in December 2008. Details of the search strategy for economic studies on interventions for people with depression are provided in Appendix 12.

In parallel to searches of electronic databases, reference lists of eligible studies and relevant reviews were searched by hand. Studies included in the clinical evidence review were also screened for economic evidence.

The systematic search of the literature identified approximately 35,000 references (stage 1). Publications that were clearly not relevant were excluded (stage 2). The abstracts of all potentially relevant publications were then assessed against a set of selection criteria by the health economist (stage 3). Full texts of the studies potentially meeting the selection criteria (including those for which eligibility was not clear from the abstract) were obtained (stage 4). Studies that did not meet the inclusion criteria, were duplicates, were secondary publications to a previous study, or had been updated in more recent publications were subsequently excluded (stage 5). Finally, all papers eligible for inclusion were assessed for internal validity and critically appraised (stage 6). The quality assessment was based on the checklists used by the *British Medical Journal* to assist referees in appraising full and partial economic analyses (Drummond & Jefferson, 1996) (see Appendix 13).

3.6.2   Selection criteria

The following inclusion criteria were applied to select studies identified by the economic searches for further analysis:

● Only papers published in English language were considered.
● Studies published from 1998 onwards were included. This date restriction was imposed in order to obtain data relevant to current healthcare settings and costs.

- Only economic evaluations conducted in the UK were selected so as to reflect healthcare resource use and unit costs directly relevant to the UK context. This criterion was in line with selection criteria from the previous guideline. However, this criterion was not applied to studies reporting utility weights that could be potentially used in cost-utility analysis.
- Selection criteria based on types of clinical conditions and patients were identical to the clinical literature review.
- Studies were included provided that sufficient details regarding methods and results were available to enable the methodological quality of the study to be assessed, and provided that the study's data and results were extractable. Poster presentations and abstracts were excluded from the review.
- Full economic evaluations that compared two or more relevant options and considered both costs and consequences (that is, cost–consequence analysis, cost-effectiveness analysis, cost–utility analysis or cost–benefit analysis) were included in the review.
- Studies were included if they used clinical effectiveness data from an RCT, a prospective cohort study, or a systematic review and meta-analysis of clinical studies. Studies were excluded if they had a mirror-image or other retrospective design, or if they utilised efficacy data that were based mainly on assumptions.

3.6.3 Data extraction

Data were extracted by the health economist using a standard economic data extraction form (see Appendix 14).

3.6.4 Presentation of economic evidence

The economic evidence identified by the health economist is summarised in the respective chapters of the guideline, following presentation of the clinical evidence. The references to included studies at stage 5 of the review, as well as the evidence tables with the characteristics and results of economic studies included in the review, are provided in Appendix 15. Methods and results of economic modelling are reported in the economic sections of the respective evidence chapters.

3.7 METHODS FOR REVIEWING EXPERIENCE OF CARE

3.7.1 Introduction

The chapter on experience of care (Chapter 4) presents three different types of evidence: personal accounts that were collected by the service user and carer members of the GDG; interviews from the Healthtalkonline website (www.healthtalkonline.org); and review of the qualitative literature.

3.7.2 Personal accounts

The authors of the personal accounts were contacted primarily through the service user and carer representatives on the GDG, and through various agencies with access to people with depression. In approaching these individuals, the GDG attempted to assemble a range of individual experience that reflected what the GDG considered to be important aspects of the care and treatment of people with depression. All individuals who were approached to write the accounts were asked to consider a number of questions (see Chapter 4) prepared by a service user and carer topic group[4] which oversaw this aspect of the guideline work. Each individual signed a consent form giving permission for their account to be reproduced in this guideline. All personal accounts were read by the members of the service user and carer topic group, and the review team; if necessary, the authors of the accounts were contacted again if parts of their account were unclear or ambiguous, or where it was thought that further information would be helpful. Any changes made for clarity were approved by the authors of the accounts. The full text of the accounts is reproduced in this guideline. The personal accounts were read again by the service user and carer topic group, and the review team, and themes were identified. These themes were developed and reviewed by the topic group and then incorporated in a combined summary with the evidence from the other two sources below.

3.7.3 Interviews from Healthtalkonline

Using the interviews of people with depression available from healthtalkonline.org, the review team analysed the available data and identified emergent themes. Each transcript was read and re-read, and sections of the text were collected under different headings using a qualitative software program (NVivo). Two reviewers independently coded the data and all themes were discussed to generate a list of the main themes. The evidence is presented in the form of these themes, with selected quotations from the interviews. The methods used to synthesise the qualitative data are in line with good practice (Braun & Clarke, 2006).

3.7.4 Review of the qualitative literature

A systematic search for published reviews of relevant qualitative studies of people with depression was undertaken using standard NCCMH procedures as described in the other evidence chapters. Reviews were sought of qualitative studies that used relevant first-hand experiences of people with depression and their families or carers. The GDG did not specify a particular outcome. Instead, the review was concerned with

---

[4]The topic group comprised three service user and carer members of the GDG and two members of the NCCMH review team.

any narrative data that highlighted the experience of care. The evidence is presented in the form of themes, which were again developed and reviewed by the topic group.

3.7.5 From evidence to recommendations

The themes emerging from the personal accounts, the qualitative analysis of the Healthtalkonline transcripts and the literature review were reviewed by the topic group. They are summarised in Chapter 4 and this summary provides the evidence for the recommendations that appear in that chapter.

3.8 STAKEHOLDER CONTRIBUTIONS

Professionals, people with depression and companies have contributed to and commented on the guideline at key stages in its development. Stakeholders for this guideline include:

- people with depression/carer stakeholders: the national organisations for people with depression and carers that represent people whose care is described in this guideline
- professional stakeholders: the national organisations that represent healthcare professionals who are providing services to people with depression
- commercial stakeholders: the companies that manufacture medicines used in the treatment of depression
- Primary Care Trusts
- Department of Health and Welsh Assembly Government.

Stakeholders have been involved in the guideline's development at the following points:

- commenting on the initial scope of the guideline and attending a briefing meeting held by NICE
- contributing possible clinical questions and lists of evidence to the GDG
- commenting on the draft of the guideline (see Appendices 4 and 5).

3.9 VALIDATION OF THE GUIDELINE

Registered stakeholders had an opportunity to comment on the draft guideline, which was posted on the NICE website during the consultation period. Following the consultation, all comments from stakeholders and others were responded to, and the guideline updated as appropriate. The GRP also reviewed the guideline and checked that stakeholders' comments had been addressed.

Following the consultation period, the GDG finalised the recommendations and the NCCMH produced the final documents. These were then submitted to NICE. NICE then formally approved the guideline and issued its guidance to the NHS in England and Wales.

4   EXPERIENCE OF CARE

4.1   INTRODUCTION

This chapter provides an overview of the experience of people with depression and their families/carers. In the first two sections are first-hand personal accounts written by people with depression and carers, which provide some experiences of having the diagnosis, accessing services, having treatment and caring for someone with depression. It should be noted that these accounts are not representative of the experiences of people with depression and therefore can only ever be illustrative. This is followed by a qualitative analysis of transcripts of people with depression from the Healthtalkonline website (www.healthtalkonline.org) and a review of the qualitative literature of the experience of people with depression. There is then a summary of the themes emerging from the personal accounts, the Healthtalkonline transcripts and the literature review, which provides a basis for the recommendations, which appear in the final section.

4.2   PERSONAL ACCOUNTS – PEOPLE WITH DEPRESSION

4.2.1   Introduction

The writers of the personal accounts were contacted primarily through the service user and carer representatives on the GDG and through various agencies that had access to people with depression. The people who were approached to write the accounts were asked to consider a number of questions when composing their narratives. These included:

- When were you diagnosed with depression and how old were you?
- How did you feel about the diagnosis? How has your diagnosis affected you in terms of stigma and within your community?
- Do you think that any life experiences led to the onset of the condition? If so, please describe if you feel able to do so.
- When did you seek help from the NHS and whom did you contact? (Please describe this first contact.) What helped or did not help you gain access to services? If you did not personally seek help, please explain how you gained access to services.
- What possible treatments were discussed with you?
- Do you have any language support needs, including needing help with reading or speaking English? If so, did this have an impact on your receiving or understanding a diagnosis of depression or receiving treatment?
- What treatment(s) did you receive? Please describe both drug treatment and psychological therapy.
- Was the treatment(s) helpful? (Please describe what worked for you and what didn't work for you.)

- How would you describe your relationship with your practitioner(s)? (GP/community psychiatric nurse/psychiatrist, and so on.)
- Did you use any other approaches to help your depression in addition to those provided by NHS services, for example private treatment? If so please describe what was helpful and not helpful.
- Did you attend a support group and was this helpful? Did any people close to you help and support you?
- How has the nature of the condition changed over time?
- How do you feel now?
- If your condition has improved, do you use any strategies to help you to stay well? If so, please describe these strategies.
- In what ways has depression affected your everyday life (such as schooling, employment and making relationships) and the lives of those close to you?

Each author signed a consent form allowing the account to be reproduced in this guideline. Seven personal accounts from people with depression were received in total. Although the questions were aimed at people with any form of depression, all of the personal accounts received were from people who have/have had severe and chronic depression, spanning many years. The themes that are most frequently expressed in the testimonies include trauma or conflict in childhood as a perceived cause of depression; the need for long-term psychotherapy for people with severe and chronic depression; the need to take personal responsibility for and understand the illness to improve outcomes; issues around diversity; paid and unpaid employment as an important part of the recovery process; the negative impact on daily functioning; concerns regarding stigma and discrimination in the workplace; and the relationship between people with depression and professionals.

4.2.2   Personal account A

I was 23 when I was first diagnosed with depression, 35 when diagnosed with major depressive disorder and 43 when diagnosed with dysthymia. However, my first experience of suffering with depression was most probably as a teenager, living in a chaotic household with a parent with alcoholism and a narcissistic personality disorder.

The first treatment I had was when I was 23 with a wonderful GP who told me he had had depression and a breakdown at medical school. He enabled me to go to see him whenever I wanted, to talk to him for 10 to 15 minutes every week. I was also on an antidepressant and tranquilliser for instant tranquillisation whenever I felt miserable. The depression passed within 4 to 5 months. I always think of the GP fondly as a life saver.

For the next few years I used therapy to deal with my depression, low self-esteem and my underlying childhood issues, each year becoming more confident. During my childhood I had had to deal constantly with my mother's tempers, mood swings and cruelty, so I had to learn in therapy how to deal with my own emotions from scratch. Initially I had 3 years of gestalt therapy with a wonderful therapist who came recommended by a friend. I then had psychodynamic psychotherapy for 4 years (while I also ran a self-help group for women). I found this psychotherapist from the UKCP list. During this period I also worked with teenagers and I found hard work to be a great help in having something to focus on and enhance my self-esteem.

In my 30s, however, I had a major depressive episode and I booked myself into hospital which I now see as a big mistake as it was not therapeutic by any means, but my understanding of what hospital offered was not known to me. I had been having some housing problems, family life was difficult and I had been working very long hours at work to solve all of these problems. I knew that I was at danger point. I was given antidepressants, an antipsychotic, a mood stabiliser and benzodiazepines. I was offered no therapeutic help and I found the system of nursing within the ward very damaging – they just observed the patients and didn't talk to us. So I was just left with my depressed thoughts for 11 weeks. I came out and went back to work.

I also didn't realise that there was stigma around these matters, and I had been open with my friends about being depressed and in hospital. Overnight I lost two thirds of my friends and social contacts. This left me feeling very distressed, ashamed and humiliated. Also, within my family, my illness was exploited by my still-crazy mother, to undermine and separate me from any compassion I could expect. This has changed gradually over the years, but it took a long time to heal.

At work, although I was employed in the care environment, some people were not keen about me returning to work. I was marginalised from external meetings for quite some time and my role was circumscribed. This changed over time, but I don't think I should have had to 're-prove' myself as if I had been in prison. But I kept quiet and got on with it. I learnt that it's best to hide having depression, to avoid the stigma. Subsequently, I have discovered through my own experience and working with service users, that it's still best to hide having depression (or indeed any other mental illness) if you want to get a job and keep it.

I have had two recurrences of major depressive disorder. I had to give up work in 1998 to battle with it full time for a couple of years. I begged to have psychotherapy but I now couldn't afford to pay for it myself. I was tried on a series of drugs over a 7-year period: six different antidepressants and various mood stabilisers, tranquillisers, and so on. I got a job in 2000, but I could barely hold a conversation I was so drugged up. It was sheer force of will that got me up and out each day. I was swimming and eventually was able to pay for my own psychotherapy, and gradually the major depression I had been in for 4 to 5 years lifted in 2002. Throughout this time I had battled with pervasive suicidal feelings and only my personal strength got me through. Just getting off the huge amounts of medication was a feat I am proud of in itself, in addition to overcoming the depression caused by childhood issues and living a normal positive life which the medication, not to mention the illness, nearly took from me completely.

I also had a wonderful GP in 2002 to 2003, who took it upon himself to (in his words) 'have a go at' at my consultant psychiatrist for half an hour on the phone about the cocktail of drugs I was taking. Being on a level of medication that was unnecessary and toxic, I had put on seven and a half stone since 2005 and I was threatened with high blood pressure and impaired glucose syndrome. My GP helped me get off this cocktail of unnecessary medication.

Not being drugged up freed me and enabled me to function at work, as I had previously done, and it 'woke' me up. The threatened 'relapse' has never happened. My self-esteem issues over my depression and weight had left me anxious though, and after an 18-month battle involving Mind and my psychiatrist, I got cognitive behavioural therapy (CBT) in 2004. This was even more wonderful in aiding my recovery and I had one session per week for a year working on my anxiety phobias. The psychologist was a wonderful professional who had faith in me and together we worked very hard overcoming the deep beliefs that I had held and which prevented me leading a full, well life.

I have been having psychotherapy again since 2005, working on the final bits of damage done to me by my alcoholic, narcissistic mother. It is hard work but my personal stamina increases all the time. This therapy would not be available in the local mental health trust – there is only one course of psychotherapy available (1 year per patient). Even with lifelong illness you get one 'go' at it. Where I currently live, patients cannot choose whether they would prefer a male or female therapist, nor the style of training they would want their therapist to have had. Choosing a therapist is as important as choosing a GP. Within the NHS there is still a culture that if you don't take any therapist, you are treatment resistant. I have always preferred a woman therapist, and one psychodynamically or psychoanalytically trained.

My psychotherapist is helping me with positive attachment and parenting techniques to get to the point I should have been at, and forming a positive attachment in the psychotherapeutic environment. This enables me to build confidence and be the person I should be, making the most of my abilities and relationships in the present. I am also learning self-analysis and skills building to enable me to keep an eye on stresses and challenges, to self-manage and keep well.

My psychiatrist, who I had from 1995 to 2005, now agrees with me that psychotherapy, building my career and not being on any drugs, have been the best for me in my recovery. She is of the 'old school' and took a lot of convincing, but at some point, she turned her ideas around about me and what I was able to achieve. She still confirms I was very ill, but that with my hard work I have completely changed my life around and, in her terms, I am unlikely to relapse. My psychiatrist put this in writing to my GP in 2006.

Stigma remains a problem however. It is worse if the negative attitudes are expressed by GPs and other medical practitioners. Even now assumptions seem to be made when I have outpatient appointments for physical ailments because computerisation of records has meant even though I have recovered, major depressive disorder is on my records everywhere. I can sometimes see a doctor's face drop when they get to that point – some are not very good at hiding it. In 2006 I was turned away from a gastro clinic and told that my stomach pain and weight loss were because of depression and that the NHS couldn't help me. I complained and the resulting CT scan showed I had cancer which when removed 6 weeks later was at stage 2. I feel quite sick thinking of how many people with depression and mental illness, especially those who are less articulate and bolshie than me, could be being turned away because of the lack of understanding. If I had listened to that doctor in 2006, I would be dead now – and all because I have had depression, not for any other reason.

4.2.3   Personal account B

I first consulted my original GP in the spring of 2006, when I was 55, because of symptoms of what I felt was very severe and prolonged depression. I had experienced a rapid series of distressing life events (a complex bereavement leading to feelings of alienation and isolation) and I had no support. I was working freelance as a trainer but no longer able to seek work and so I was without an income.

I had already tried to help myself for 6 months and had bought many so-called self-help books. I have a Master's degree in social work and at one time taught counselling skills. I am familiar with rational emotive therapy, CBT, person-centred therapy, transactional analysis, and so on. I understand the efficacy of exercise, diet, positive thinking and relaxation. The major problem is that one *cannot* actually do these things when depressed and I believe those who have not been depressed cannot truly comprehend this at all. I am also conscious that any so-called emotional problems affect the way one is perceived and addressed. Because of this, I was very reluctant indeed to seek help and many of my fears were in fact confirmed.

The GP whom I first saw spent more time looking at his computer than me. He asked 'are you depressed?' I told him I was sufficiently distressed to consult a GP. Having said he could refer me to the mental health team, he said that they were 'not very good' and gave me a card for a private counsellor. He told me to complete a 'HADS' test in the waiting room and put it under his door. He offered no medication and no follow-up appointment. I sat in my car in the car park crying for 2 hours before I could drive home.

However, I made an appointment with the private counsellor, although I was anxious about the cost. But I felt I had to try and help myself. The counsellor was a very nice woman but I felt I was not being assessed. She talked a great deal about her upcoming wedding and for half a session explained the essentials of transactional analysis (which I've taught). I also felt that conclusions were drawn rapidly and inaccurately. She told me to keep a diary of angry feelings and never referred to it again. She explained that 'if you haven't had an adolescent rebellion you have one in middle age' and told me to 'get rid of' people who were draining me. This is not entirely bad advice but much too crude. I got the impression she was talking about her own life, not mine. I felt very much more unsettled at the end of each session than when I had arrived.

After three sessions I found another counsellor, who was better than the first but I could not afford to continue the sessions or to travel to see him. Again I found that the counsellor seemed to have a favourite model of human behaviour. I was later even more annoyed when the difficulties with the counsellors were explained away by a mental health team worker as a disturbance of mine in facing the issues. I felt much worse afterwards knowing this and that I could not improve the situation.

Eventually I began a method of self-counselling: occasionally speaking aloud to myself in a deliberate effort to calm myself down since I knew that depression can be a result of over-stimulation.

Fortunately, in the summer of 2006, I was able to change my GP. The new GP provided much more help but unfortunately the initial medication (citalopram), which I took for 4 months, made no difference to me at all.

My new GP referred me again for counselling at the surgery. There was a waiting list: I attended the first session and then there was a gap of some weeks (which was at the end of 2006). I found it disturbing to have to talk to a stranger yet again. The sessions often ended with an emotionally laden question or the advice given was more appropriate for a much older bereaved person. I did very little talking and I could not summon the energy to constantly correct the assumptions being made which, again, seemed based on the counsellor's own life. I attended just a few sessions and then decided that this was a waste of resources.

I felt that if someone would just skilfully listen and question (as I thought good counselling did) I could sort things out myself. My own reasonably sound knowledge of counselling actually seemed to be a disadvantage to me and I had to learn to keep quiet. I still needed help, had very little external support, and my GP was offering what was available so I felt I had to accept it, but it was not even close to what I needed.

In February 2007 I got into a very distressed state but could not get an appointment with any GP although I phoned the surgery four times. The one friend who knows about my condition then took me to the surgery. I now know that I was quite seriously ill at this point. But one can only go to the surgery when one feels capable of doing so. Appointments had to be made on the day at 8.30 a.m. which was one of the worst times for me. So then appointments had to be made a few days ahead. One needs to be able to access help when one needs it during the bad times. In the end it was a registrar GP who saw me in this deeply distressed state. Even then I felt guilty for someone seeing me 'as an emergency' and I felt very bad about that. He was, however, quite good and he referred me again to the mental health team.

The registrar changed my medication to escitalopram. I was deeply grateful as my GP had kept telling me to continue the citalopram and wait for it to take effect. The escitalopram was beneficial and I have continued with it for over a year. I still seem to need this medication. I feel that getting the medication right and promptly at the virulent stage of the depression is vital. I also feel that I was quite poorly and was left to 'wait' to see if I would get better.

Prior to my mental health team assessment interview in May 2007 (the GP registrar I saw in February had written again to the team to ask for an early appointment) I was in a very foggy state and was particularly vulnerable. However, I think that I expressed the issues quite clearly in the limited time. The interviewer described himself as a nurse, said he was trying to clarify why I was there and at one point told me I looked 'alright', which was frustratingly puzzling to me and based on no knowledge of me whatsoever. I quickly lost confidence in my interviewer. He said, 'Yes, I've had bereavements too' and 'I don't know why you have been referred', which was very unhelpful. He also told me I had to 'negotiate' if the counselling is not right. How can someone who is seriously depressed negotiate?

I was also given the Aaron Beck tick box-type diagnostic tool which I found confusing. (For example 'loss of appetite' is difficult to answer; a lot of people who are depressed have 'abnormal appetite'.) I find these tools very simplistic.

I left this appointment and began crying immediately – again I could not drive home for an hour. I took extra medication to try and cope. I called the mental health team and was told that I was bound to get upset 'as I was talking about upsetting things'. Again, the problem is presented as being because of the vulnerability of the patient rather than the competence of the interviewer.

My GP had said that she would be able to refer me to a psychologist but that first I had to be referred to the mental health team. I found this very disappointing and also embarrassing. I was going to have to tell yet another person about my life. When after many weeks I got to see the mental health team counsellor in June 2007 she told me the sessions were for 6 weeks so I knew immediately I could not be helped in this short time: I was taught 'relaxation training' which was inadequate for my needs. It was like offering aspirin for appendicitis. I had to miss one of the six sessions because I was not well enough to attend.

With every other (physical) condition for which I have been referred I have been seen by a consultant at least once. But with a mental health problem, which was the one life-threatening condition which I had, I was referred by a GP and seen by a nurse (who thought I 'looked ok'). This meant that I had problems getting my pension (money problems started to become a major factor when my savings diminished). The occupational health professional said I had to have a consultant diagnosis; but it was almost a year before I could see a psychiatrist for a formal diagnosis, which my former employer paid for.

I at last saw a consultant psychiatrist privately in January 2008. She diagnosed me with post-traumatic stress (I had been severely bullied at work before I left 10 years ago) leading to severe depression. While perhaps dismal, it was a relief to have the diagnosis and it does validate my experience. The psychiatrist saw me for two sessions but explained that she could not see me again (as this was, I expect, very expensive). She did provide details of a freelance psychologist, but told me that I would have to see her privately. I saw this psychologist twice paying £75 each session but just could not afford any further sessions. I have had no further treatment other than the medication. As my GP said very recently, there is no other help available, just 'short fix' stuff.

Over the past 2 years I have had to share my personal details over and over again with about 12 strangers, half of them doctors 'assessing' me. My GP has done her best, but has only so much time, and one wants to be a 'good' patient. At one point I stopped driving as I knew that I was not safe to do so. I told my GP about this but she said I would feel a sense of achievement if I continued to drive! This greatly concerned me. Also, I felt no 'sense of achievement': a lack of achievement is not one of my problems. I felt that my self-report was not being taken seriously and I was very confused about how I could present myself to make myself understood.

I was never clear about the role of the mental health team or what the 'variety of options on offer' actually was (in fact other than counselling there was 'nothing else available'). It was not recognised that I was in a deep fog, akin to being in another universe, and was finding it very hard to concentrate on what was being said. The more contacts I had, the more distressed I felt.

Up until 6 or 7 months ago I was feeling as if in a parallel universe, and at one point as if I was living under water. I could not 'wake up' from dreams, and very unusually for me I could not get up until 10 am on some days. I felt profound grief.

I now have far less faith in getting help so I do not know what I would do if things become worse. I was helped by seeing the consultant psychiatrist and I felt much better having been taken seriously. One problem was being not being able to work.

My own coping strategies are mainly avoiding known triggers, self-monitoring and trying to get proper nutrition. I also swim every day. Distraction helps if I can stop the circularity of thoughts. My everyday life is affected as I am much less outgoing now. I have been 'let down' so many times that I do not want to make the approach now. I am mostly happier on my own though I am also gregarious and socially skilled. I feel a little embarrassed that I do not have the things other people of my acquaintance have (family relationships and so on) and so I cannot talk the currency of that group (children and grandchildren). But I am more accepting of my own isolation/difference from other people. However, I do fear being destabilised by even small life events in the future as I know I am vulnerable and don't manage such challenges well.

4.2.4   Personal account C

Life experiences have definitely led to the onset of depression. I had an accident as a child which affected my eyesight and I have been visually impaired all my teenage and adult life. After I lost my sight I felt I was rejected as a child and teenager by my family, which was exacerbated by being sent away from home to be educated at a school for blind people. As the eldest of four children I bore the brunt of my father's aggression and when I was older had to work in the family business for long hours and was punished at whim.

Because of my impaired sight I have had problems with sensitive hearing that made my life hell. I felt like a prisoner and as if I was being tortured by everybody and everything with so much noise around me.

I was admitted to a psychiatric unit at the age of 30 because I was suicidal. This was due to a variety of reasons which had been building up to that time. The main complication was that my wife was expecting a baby and we were not getting on and constantly arguing. I felt totally lost, I had no friends and there was no support for my depression. Because of my past experience I couldn't go to my parents or brother or sisters who lived near me. I felt totally isolated and not wanted by anybody. Although I received a diagnosis of depression this was not fully explained to me and it didn't do any good because ultimately the staff weren't equipped to help me or my family. They couldn't give proper information in a manner that my family could accept or understand, or communicate with them effectively, and there has been no support since then. I spent 6 days there and was medicated. The treatment was ultimately not helpful because there was no follow-up support.

In 1992 I attended a college for the blind for training in the hope that I would be able to get a job. Unfortunately this didn't happen because I was so unprepared, was having emotional breakdowns, and had too much to cope with at college. I was sent to a local hospital by a doctor from the college and was diagnosed with problematic depression and was given more practical help than previously: I had some psychotherapy, relaxation classes and exercise for my neck. At the end of the college year I was advised to take a break of a few months. This was a very hard time and a struggle for me – both the college and the job centre rejected me by saying they couldn't help me until I was stable.

There is a definite stigma towards mental health problems in my community, which is Muslim. Nobody seemed to want to understand about my diagnosis and I didn't feel I could talk to anybody because people are not equipped to provide support. They believe in leaving it to the power of prayer. When I approached an Imam in a local mosque about a personal problem within the family I was told that religion would resolve it. He stirred up more trouble by visiting the family member with whom I was having difficulties.

I have felt like an outsider and have suffered rejection after rejection. I have been rejected from services, society and family. I feel like my life is messed up physically, mentally, socially and financially, and in terms of work and education.

I had a severe breakdown last year and am concerned about relapse and was referred twice by my GP to the community mental health team. I was not seen by them. I feel like I am wasting my time trying. I feel like I am being pushed back. I am in a situation where I need the support of a therapeutic community or at the very least a safe place where I am able to get away from family pressures.

My relationship with my current GP is better at the moment. I don't have regular check-ups or practical support but I get help with medication and an occasional chat if I bring the subject up. My GP was a bit more helpful when I had my breakdown. The CMHT did not do a good job of giving practical help: instead I was passed on to voluntary groups who were not fully equipped to offer support in a crisis or if I need help for referral from my GP to the CMHT again. It feels like a vicious circle: I have had a total of five breakdowns and have attempted suicide. But this seems to mean nothing to them. The only psychiatrist I have ever met told me that I would have to sort my problems out for myself. He literally let me wander the streets. I felt so bad I could have jumped off the roof. But perhaps God saved me.

I have therefore spent the last 15 years working on complementary therapies and any improvement in my condition is due to the work that I have done. It is more to do with faith and spirituality rather than religion. I feel closer to God now and feel protected. Many times I wanted to die and take the jump and I was saved. So I think I am meant to live and survive – there is a purpose for me otherwise I would have given up long ago or gone to prison or got on drugs and alcohol. So I thank God I have not gone down those roads.

The self-help techniques I have used have included positive affirmation, relaxation and emotional freedom therapy. I have also received qualifications in holistic therapies. I have been instrumental in setting up a local mental health drop-in centre and I am also a director of a local division of Mind and am standing as the BME representative on Mind Link. (I was able to access some CBT through Mind.) I have joined different groups, for example, a bowls club for blind people, and I have friends who have provided me with support.

But despite all this activity I am still disillusioned by the attitude of organisations that are meant to be dealing with mental health problems. I have a lot to offer despite no help being offered to me.

My feelings of alienation and isolation are exacerbated by family members who appear to have little appreciation of how difficult life is for me. I feel very isolated because my sensitive hearing makes me nervous and anxious in public places.

Depression has infected every part of my life. It has slowed me down, led to loss of self-esteem and made it difficult for me to get work.

4.2.5   Personal account D

The depression started when I was young (I am now 57). I came from a poor background – my father was diagnosed with bipolar disorder when he was in the army during the Second World War and after being discharged he spent a year in a psychiatric hospital. He couldn't work most of the time. My father also suffered from agoraphobia, so I ran errands for him – I was his 'skivvy'. My father had bad mood swings, which affected my mother, my siblings and me. He never gave any praise, and he never once said that he loved me or my mother. I missed school in order to care for him or because he had hit me so hard I had a black eye and couldn't go to school. I found it hard to learn at school and later I found out that I had dyslexia.

When I started puberty I felt different from other people. I felt as though I was not as good as the next person, which stemmed from my upbringing. There were a lot of kids at school living in poverty but life with my father made me feel very inadequate. When I was 15 or 16 years old my father tried to kill my mother when he found out she was having a relationship with another man. I felt as if I was always protecting my mother from my father. Both my siblings, who are older than me, married young to get away from my father.

I knew my feelings were different from those of other people so I went to see the doctor by myself when I was 16. The doctor knew immediately that I was suffering from depression. Because of my low self-esteem I couldn't hold a job down because I felt as if I was not good enough to do anything. I was constantly comparing myself to other people. I felt at the time that life wasn't worth living – I thought that practically it would be better to throw myself under a bus. If I hadn't gone to the doctor I would have killed myself. It was a relief to know that my depression could be understood, if not treated, and to speak to someone who knew what I was talking about.

I was first prescribed diazepam, which made me feel good because I was out of it. I was prescribed one tablet a day but I took three or four. I couldn't work but at least it was a lift and that is what I felt I needed. I was on diazepam for about 6 to 9 months and then I came off it. I tried to look for a job but my feelings of inadequacy and paranoia returned: I felt as if people were looking at me and talking about me. I found it difficult to go outside and became agoraphobic.

Nothing else was offered to treat me so I treated myself by using cannabis, speed and barbiturates. Eventually I found a job I liked and when I was 18 years old I started having serious relationships. I was still living at home then and stayed to protect my mother as my father was still beating her, and I didn't want to take anyone home as I was ashamed of my father.

I finally left home at age 21 when I got married; I felt as if life was taking off. I was happily married and away from my father and it felt like depression was behind me. I loved my wife and that was enough in life. Children completed the marriage. By the time I was in my early 30s I was working in the building trade as a site manager and I was earning good money for the first time. I was determined not to be like my father and I appreciated what I had. I felt that there was a crater in my life where my father should have been. I didn't have anyone to look up to – no one to build a personality around. My personality only grew when I got married.

My Dad died in 1983. I stood by his grave and I couldn't cry. I battered myself with questions: what is the matter with me? I was consumed with all the thoughts of what had happened in the past. I felt numb about it all; it seemed like there was a massive void. I felt like I had never had a Dad and I became very good friends with a man in his 60s who I tried to adopt as a father.

In the following year my wife was diagnosed with schizophrenia. She was 28 at the time. My wife's illness made me feel depressed but I couldn't show it. I felt as though I had lost my wife and there was just a shell of a person there who used to be my wife. The illness was like a bereavement. I was offered antidepressants but I didn't take them as I didn't want my wife to see them. I was trying to keep it together but she believed I was having a nervous breakdown. Throughout her illness I was on an adrenaline rush. I was working flat out and didn't have time to think about myself. I was a machine trying to keep my family together: looking after my wife and kids and working. In the end I took time off work. I needed some emotional help and I needed someone to talk to. There was no time for myself and I stopped communicating with people.

After my wife had sufficiently recovered from her first episode of schizophrenia (it took about 9 or 10 months), I realised how badly it had affected me. I thought about what it had taken out of me and I would sink into depression and phone up the Samaritans. I went to see my GP a few times during this time and they were sympathetic to what I was going through. I started taking amitriptyline and I also saw a counsellor for 3 months. The counsellor was better than the antidepressants. It gave me a good lift. This lasted for a few months before I began to feel low again. For a few years I was in a cycle of relapsing and recovering – I was up and down like a yo-yo. I couldn't set a course for a life; everything had been completely obliterated by illness.

But my wife was feeling better and we wanted more children so the doctors took her off her depot antipsychotics and antidepressants. When she became pregnant she was happy and like she used to be before the illness. In 1987 my youngest son was born but 4 months after his birth my wife became very ill; she was hearing voices and it was as if the gates of hell were opened and everything came out. She was hospitalised and I stopped working and looked after the baby – it was like being a one-parent family.

Shortly after this I was diagnosed with asthma, which was considered by my doctors to be my major illness rather than depression. The asthma hit me hard as I was my wife's carer and I looked after the children. I also began to have panic attacks. Although I was convincing my wife that I was coping, this was just a mask. I felt as if I had become invisible, that my purpose was to make someone else become well. I did not see that there was something wrong with me. Then one day I was pushing a trolley around the supermarket and I thought 'I don't want to die in a supermarket; I don't want to die in between the bleach and the biscuits.' This happened several times around this period. I didn't go to doctors as I thought they would think I was nuts.

In 1997 my wife relapsed again and it affected our youngest son very badly as he had not seen his mother this way before. He was badly bullied at school for having a mother who was a 'nutter' and got very depressed. When he was 15 (in 2003) our son was also diagnosed with schizophrenia. I got depressed about what was happening to my son because I didn't want him to go through the same things that his mother and I had been through.

Although people think that I am stable, I recognise that I will never be free of depression but as I get older I understand more about it. I don't want to kill myself. I care for both my son and my wife and I will never turn away from them. I become more depressed when there is a crisis – and there always seems to be a crisis in my family. But I have accepted my depression as I have lived with it for so long; it's like an old nemesis. It's a part of me.

Eighteen months ago I was taking venlafaxine but I am not currently been treated for depression. To be honest, I hate taking tablets. When I was first ill I thought I was a lunatic because I was taking tablets. If I do need help I find that counselling is best for me, although I have not seen a therapist for a few years. I can now recognise when I am becoming depressed. It's a waiting game. I get black days when I wake up in the morning and I am totally unmotivated and I couldn't even care if I won the lottery – it would make no difference because I feel so lousy. If I feel like this for more than one day then I start to worry and I know I am depressed. To try and cope with the symptoms I grin and bear it or I try doing something different – getting away from mundane routine.

I am now able to talk to my wife about being depressed rather than trying to hide it from her and I talk to lots of other depressed people, which, for me, is like a form of counselling. I got involved with voluntary groups when my wife got schizophrenia: I am the chair of one voluntary organisation and I work for another, and I do a lot of media work. The horrid feeling of not being as good as other people is not there now because I feel that I am helping.

I am particularly interested in the political side of how people with mental health problems are treated. I believe that my depression was caused by my childhood experiences, but depression is such an individual illness – it has got many different faces and it can be caused by many different things. Therefore should people with depression be treated in the same way? I am encouraged to see that a lot of resources are being put into providing CBT for people with depression, but CBT is not the right treatment for everyone with depression and this needs to be recognised.

4.2.6   Personal account E

I was 27 years old when I was first diagnosed with depression, 14 years ago. I think I started to get depressed 6 years prior to diagnosis, I just didn't know it at the time.

At first, I was relieved at the diagnosis. I had gone to the doctors knowing something was wrong, but not knowing what it was. I was offered counselling and/or medication. I knew that I had to have medication, as it would make me feel better more quickly. I had already withdrawn from my friends and community (due to the depression) so in terms of stigma, there was none, though I didn't tell family, because they wouldn't have understood.

I knew that this 'breakdown' occurred due to the events that had happened the previous 18 months: the sudden deaths of two close friends and my grandmother, being made redundant from my part-time job, ending a 6-year relationship with my boyfriend, and then being physically assaulted.

Without doubt, my childhood experiences have also contributed to a life of depression. My mother died when I was 5 and after that my two younger brothers and I were not allowed to talk about her. My Dad remarried a woman with three children, but it was not long before my Dad and stepmother hated each other, and were physically and emotionally cruel to each other. My Dad hated her children, and was physically and emotionally cruel to them, and my stepmother hated my brothers and me, and was physically and emotionally cruel to us. One of my stepsisters sexually abused my youngest brother and me.

A month or so after starting medication, I did not feel any better, so was given counselling immediately. I established a good and trusting relationship with the counsellor who helped me to understand what was happening to me. However, I plummeted further, and was seen by a psychiatrist who allocated me a CPN, who I saw for around 18 months, until I was able to slowly start rebuilding my life. When my 'time' was up seeing the counsellor, I saw a psychologist for the following 18 months. I was also prescribed an antipsychotic drug, but I felt like a zombie and could not look after my daughter, so did not take it often.

Of the professionals listed above, without doubt the CPN helped the most; I had a good relationship with her. When I was at my most depressed, I was seeing the psychologist, but I was in no fit state to engage in any meaningful therapy, as I was too ill.

As well as the treatments listed above, while I was having counselling I was told that I should attend a women's group, run by my counsellor through the NHS. I attended and it helped much more than I realised at the time in that I formed friendships that were very supportive. However, in terms of therapeutic input it did nothing – people would talk about their week and how awful life was, but I couldn't do that. How could I tell people that I had spent the week trying not to kill myself, when that was all I wanted to do? It was not that I wanted to die, but I could see no other way of stopping the pain. Depression filled every second of every minute of every day, and it was unbearable. I was fortunate in that I was able to sleep a lot (up to 15 hours a day), though time still went slowly. Reading books about depression and self-help gave me an understanding of what was happening to me.

On one occasion I went to a voluntary agency support group, but I couldn't accept at that time that depression would be part of my life forever: I found it difficult to listen to others about how they were managing their lives living with depression. I thought I was going to get better and it would never come back again – how naïve was I?

Over the years, I have been prescribed most of the SSRIs. They worked to varying degrees, but the most distressing aspect for me is that they all seem to affect my memory and articulation. I have learnt to live with this, but am aware of the limitations this poses for me, especially at work. I did receive further counselling on one occasion, by the NHS, but it was not particularly helpful, as it did not get to the root of the depression.

Over the last 2 years I have paid privately to see a psychotherapist and had psychodynamic therapy. This has been the most helpful in terms of trying to repair and understand the damage I experienced as a child. Financially, though, this has been difficult, and I have had to get another job, in addition to my full time job to pay for this.

Depression for me has changed over time, I believe, due to the psychodynamic therapy I have had. For years when I was depressed I needed to sleep a lot and I also put on weight. Now I struggle to sleep (which has its obvious disadvantages) and I tend to lose weight. I didn't recognise I was depressed for a long while and by the time I went to see my doctor, it was too late to treat successfully, and so took 2 years to recover from. Whereas now it can very quickly become severe, but on a positive note it can ease quickly as well.

Depression is with me all the time, rather like chronic back ache it is always there, but some times are better than others. I have managed to qualify at university in the career I have always wanted, and I love my job, and know that I am pretty good at it. However, there is always the fear that I will get too ill to work. I have had to have the odd day/week off over the last few years, but with the help of my GP (who has been very supportive and allows me to manage my depression my way) I have not had to say it is because of depression. There is a general acceptance at my place of employment about having depression, so long as it doesn't interfere with one's work.

However, I have an excellent manager at work with whom I can be honest. On one occasion I told him that I was going to have to take sick leave as I was very depressed and could not work. He advised me that I could take time off of work, but that if I wanted, he would go through everything I needed to do. He told me that if I felt unable to do something, he would get someone else to do. I went through my work with him, and was able to do everything because he took the pressure off me. He told me to see him at any time I felt unable to do something. Every morning for about a month after that, he would come into my office in the morning to see how I was, and I never took any sick leave.

I have had to build my life around periods of depression, for which I am resentful. I often feel that my life is hanging by a thread – that at any moment, my life, that I have worked so hard to build up, could be taken away from me. It is on this basis that I choose not to engage in a long-term relationship. I am currently seeing someone, but because of his commitments, I do not see him often. This suits me as it means I am under no obligations or pressure from him.

I feel frustrated that there are no services available to me now. On the surface, I function very well; no one would ever believe that I have depression as I am a good actress. But when it is severe, it would be helpful to be able to access services immediately from a team that knows me and can support me without me having to go through a series of assessments and then being told 'well you can go on the waiting list for this service, but you can only have this service for a particular length of time'. I also feel that long-term psychodynamic therapy should be available, on the NHS, which can get to the root of the issues that cause depression. I now know that I will have depression until I can resolve my childhood issues.

4.2.7   Personal account F

I was first diagnosed with depression in 1999 when I was 44 years old and was feeling suicidal. Because of the way I had been feeling I was relieved to have a diagnosis. Only my close friends knew that I had depression – I didn't want people to know because there is very little understanding within my community.

My mother died when I was 15 years old. My father then attempted suicide and was on a life support machine for 2 weeks. He was brain damaged and I looked after him for 25 years until his death. I was married at 18 and my first child was kidnapped by her father after I left him. My daughter was 3 months old at the time and I never got her back. I married for a second time, to a man who became a violent alcoholic. Because of his drinking he lost a lot of jobs because he was too hung over to turn up and we were often in debt and lived in poverty. We had four children but we could not provide them with much at Christmas and for birthdays. We struggled financially to provide food and the basics.

When I became suicidal I went to see my GP. He was very attentive and took me very seriously and referred me to a psychiatrist and a mental health clinic. Antidepressants and counselling were discussed as possible treatment options and I was referred for counselling but had to wait 18 months, which was useless. I tried various medications, such as Prothiaden, which made me worse. In the end I was put on Prozac which did help to improve my symptoms. When I finally saw a counsellor, I was offered hypnotherapy, which I didn't want. I wanted counselling. My relationship with my psychiatrist is non-existent. My doctor doesn't have a clue who I am. I'm just another number in a long queue.

I have attended a Christian counselling organisation in the city where I live which has been brilliant. There were well-trained counsellors available who were very supportive. Two of the counsellors maintained contact in between appointments.

Depression devastated my life. I shut out a lot of people because I could not socialise when I was so ill. I didn't want to make relationships because I lost trust in people. My family suffered as I was not really there for them and I couldn't work because my illness was too severe for me to function normally. The house became a tip.

However, things have improved over the years. At the current time I am still on antidepressants but I am ready to come off them. I am now very seldom depressed. After 9 years of being off work because of illness I am now getting back to work on a job placement. If I have any low moods I go back to my counsellor and exercise regularly and eat healthier food to stay well.

4.2.8　　Personal account G

I was first diagnosed with depression in 2000 at the age of 42. At the time I was diagnosed, I was unemployed having been made redundant several months previously and also my marriage was in difficulties. I think that these things contributed to triggering my depression but neither was responsible in its own right. On reflection there were signs of problems a couple of years previously.

The diagnosis was not a surprise as it had taken a few months for me to decide to go to see my GP as I tried to cope with it as best as I could. At first my GP was reluctant to do anything but after several visits she relented and prescribed me an antidepressant. Unfortunately, this antidepressant did not work and a few months later I returned to see my GP and asked to see someone. Fortunately my wife at the time had accompanied and backed me up otherwise I don't think the GP would have referred me to a psychologist/psychiatrist.

Initially I had three sessions with a psychologist who said that she could not help and referred me to a psychiatrist. He changed my antidepressant and I then saw him on a monthly basis. This second antidepressant did not work and it was changed again. Eventually I was prescribed a mix of a tricyclic antidepressant and lithium carbonate that proved more effective at controlling the symptoms. However this took 18 months, during which time I was unable to work, my marriage broke up, and because of how I was feeling, I isolated myself from my family. Up until that point I had no experience of mental illness or knew anyone who suffered from it. I was given no information about it from my GP, psychologist or psychiatrist. I think that was the reason I isolated myself from my family more and more as time went on.

During the 8 years I have been ill, I have been on medication and although no longer on lithium I feel that it is only over the last year or so that I have been listened to by my GP and psychiatrist. Since being ill I have changed my GP four times due to moving around the area (one GP retired). Their approach has differed, and has often been inconsistent, and it is only my most recent GP who I feel has listened to me and worked with me dealing with any medical issues around my condition, such as side effects. The one real issue I have about my treatment is that over the 8 years I have only had three sessions with a psychologist and the rest of the time it has been purely medication. I feel this has slowed my recovery and has left me to deal with several issues that I feel could have been dealt with by a psychologist or psychiatrist. Once my condition had stabilised the only contact I had with my GP and psychiatrist was to either get my prescription renewed, or seeing my psychiatrist every 3 months for 10 minutes. Other than that the only other contact I had was with the nurse who took blood samples to check my lithium levels. Also it concerns me that I was never offered any help or advice on managing my condition. I have obtained such information from what I have discovered on the internet and from fellow service users and the voluntary sector.

As my condition improved I started to research my illness online and also made online contact with others from across the world suffering from mental illness. I have found the internet very useful for getting information about my condition and when I was very ill and needed to talk, I could usually find someone somewhere in the world to talk to 24 hours a day. The other advantage was that when I didn't feel like talking, I didn't have to. Over the years I have formed an online network of fellow sufferers and we keep each other up to date on anything of interest happening in the various countries regarding mental illness and its treatment.

The biggest effect depression has had on my life is when it comes to employment. Since being diagnosed I have only worked for 8 months in paid employment. I've also done voluntary work for 18 months with a variety of organisations involved with disability and mental health. Although I did not have a problem getting work before being diagnosed, since then I have found it difficult. In October 2002 I went to university as part of my 'recovery' graduating with an MSc in 2003. Although this did not help me find work I found it very beneficial to me in that it kept my mind active and this is something I have continued to try and do since then.

Although I feel well at present, it is noticeable to me that my mood is more variable than when I was on lithium, but the strategies I have in place help me cope with this. Also keeping my mind active helps and doing voluntary work gives me a feeling of having 'value' in society. I still have some issues due to the depression, but know that it will take time to resolve these so I try not to let this affect me.

4.3   PERSONAL ACCOUNTS – CARERS

4.3.1   Introduction

The methods used for obtaining the carers' accounts was the same as outlined in Section 4.2.1, but for carers of people with depression, the questions included:
- How long have you been a carer of someone with depression?
- How involved are/were you in the treatment plans of the person with depression?
- Were you offered support by the person's practitioners?
- Do you yourself have any mental health problems? If so, were you offered an assessment and treatment by a healthcare professional?
- How would you describe your relationship with the person's practitioner(s)? (GP/community psychiatric nurse/psychiatrist, and so on)
- Did you attend a support group and was this helpful? Did any people close to you help and support you in your role as a carer?
- In what ways has being a carer affected your everyday life (such as schooling, employment and making relationships) and the lives of those close to you? Two personal accounts from carers of people with depression were received.

4.3.2   Personal account H

Firstly, I must say that caring for someone is one of the most rewarding things I have done. It can be frustrating, exhausting, challenging to one's own physical and mental health, but ultimately helping someone make the most of their lives by helping them in their most vulnerable moments, is rewarding.

This applies to any caring. I was my mother's carer when I was a child and teenager and I made sure she ate properly and took her tablets. But most of all I provided practical and emotional support. But I think it can be damaging for children to care for an adult without support, because childhood is when we should be able to expect to be nurtured ourselves.

I then became a carer to my partner. My partner has had two long periods of depression; at present he has been ill since 2005. They have tried the newer antidepressants on him but one of the old favourites seems to be doing the trick. I attend his reviews and make sure he is looking after himself as regards to diet and exercise. I also emotionally support him by listening, working through problems with him, and trying to encourage him to be positive. His best male friend and I have decided to only respond to positive subjects that he brings up, as a way of trying to create positive thoughts in his repertoire. I have struggled for 2 years to try and get him CBT without success, as I can see he desperately needs to be helped with changing his thought patterns to positive thoughts, which would help his overwhelming depression.

As his carer, the pressure of his overwhelmingly negative thoughts and depressed ways of thinking can be a burden. He doesn't want to think about bills and money, and runs up huge phone bills when he is depressed. I have to constantly nag him to get him to try and keep an eye on his expenditure as it is a risk to his welfare.

As a result of this illness, we can't live together anymore. I see him two or three times a day at either his home or my home, but the pressure of 24-hour depression wasn't doing me any good and I had to move house to be able to care for him again. It actually has the good effect of getting him out of the house at least once a day, to come and see me. I plan trips out, organise things and occasionally exert pressure to get him out of bed and even out of the house, because sometimes he would rather sleep 18 hours a day every day.

His physical health is suffering as a result of extreme weight gain because of the medication and a lowering of his activity levels both because of medication and depression. I battle with his doctor and social worker over this, trying to get them to take this seriously because his father had two strokes at his age and he himself has been warned about fat around his heart. I am trying to get him a review of his medication plus a referral to an occupational therapist for support around physical exercise.

It's hard for me seeing him suffer, and sometimes I get angry with his social worker, when they can't see that physical health and other risks are associated with his depression, and that these things should be included in his care plan. It's a constant battle to not get services withdrawn. At one point last year he hadn't seen a social worker or a housing support worker for 3 months, so it's an uphill struggle.

I have neuropathy and sometimes this overwhelms me and I have to lie down for a couple of days to let it 'wear off'. My partner is able to get my shopping and visit me and strangely this seems to take his mind off his own suffering for an hour or two, as he still has physical strength. If it goes on too long, though, he gets cross, and wants me there to support him.

In a way, as a carer, I am more like a mother than a partner, and though I wouldn't say this to him, it has changed the dynamic between us forever. Most carers I have met also say this.

When my partner was depressed previously, I was able to support him and get him back to full time work within a year. Now he has been off work since 2006, and his employers have given him until December 2009 to get through this depression, but I know it is a real risk for him and not working in the long run would not help his self-esteem.

I have built my career around being self-employed, and working from home in the mental health and housing fields, mostly regarding carer, resident or service user issues at strategic level. This means I have the time to care, but I am able to keep myself busy and to have time for myself through work. Work is very, very important to most carers: I have heard other carers say that they go to work to get a rest from the overwhelming nature of caring.

The role of being a carer for someone with severe depression has added to my own symptoms of dysthymia over the years because of the sheer pressure of coping with someone who turned down treatment, stopped their antidepressants at one point and crashed into a psychotic depression. This was a huge burden and local services left me to cope with this on my own 24 hours a day, and it nearly broke me.

Carers who become ill with depression or anxiety, or who have a previous history of depression, should be offered support. As I have said, caring is rewarding but it can also be tiring and frustrating.

4.3.3   Personal account I

My Mum has been depressed on and off since I was a 7-year-old boy (I am now 15) and I have been caring for her since then. She's not depressed all of the time, and it's fun when she's well, and normal, like – we do normal things then and she's the normal bossy Mum.

When I was small it was just making her a cuppa now and again, or telling her about school with funny bits to try and make her laugh. Or telling my Nan and Grandad about how she was so they could come and help, but now it's more. I sit down and talk with her, make sure I get in straight away from school because I worry about her when I am out. I get her tablets, make appointments, sort out food shopping, nag her to get dressed when she's depressed, and answer the phone. I am more of a grown-up than when she's well.

Mostly she's well but now and again she gets depression. I know the signs. Then she goes quiet and stops going out and seeing her friends and I try and cheer her up and make things better for her. I wish she was like other Mums sometimes, and, well, all the time. But I wouldn't be without her or want to leave her on her own – she's my Mum!

I try and be positive and jokey, behave myself and be there for her, and make sure she sees her therapist even when she doesn't want to go out and sometimes get her friends around for a surprise to make time pass for her. I hope she gets better soon. I go to my room when I feel cross and sometimes talk to my friends. I go out and do usual things too so that she doesn't worry about me. I do well in school.

My Mum takes tablets and sees her therapist but I think seeing people really helps her. When her friends come round and take her mind off it for a while, she laughs.

Don't forget your friends when they are depressed, I say. And chocolate sometimes helps too!

For a while I had no support but now I go to the Young Carers' Centre in our town, and I meet other people like me caring for their parents. I play pool and we have days out – we went to Alton Towers which was fun. It's good meeting other young people like myself who are carers too, but we don't talk about it all the time. We want to get away from it just for a few hours, fool about, be normal. Sometimes we watch films, have pizza, and there's a support worker if you do want to chat. I had a carer's assessment there too.

People sometimes think or say my life is sad, but I know it's not my Mum's fault, she can't help being depressed. I love her and where else would I want to be? She helps me too.

4.4   QUALITATIVE ANALYSIS

4.4.1   Introduction

The following section consists of a qualitative analysis of personal accounts of people with depression using Healthtalkonline (www.healthtalkonline.org). Healthtalkonline provides interviews with people with both physical illnesses and mental health problems. The review team undertook their own content analysis of the interviews to explore themes that could be used to inform recommendations for the provision of care for people with depression.

The same transcripts were also reviewed by Ridge and Ziebland (2006), which is included in the review of the qualitative literature below. The review team decided to undertake their own analysis to cover a wider range of themes than those focused upon by Ridge and Ziebland.

4.4.2   Methods

Using the interviews available from Healthtalkonline, the review team analysed the experience of 38 patients from across the UK. The methods adopted by Healthtalkonline to collect interviews were two fold. First, the participants were typically asked to describe everything that had happened to them since they first suspected a problem. The researchers tried not to interrupt the interviewees, to obtain a relatively unstructured, narrative dataset. Second, a semi-structured interview was conducted in which the researcher asked about particular issues that were not mentioned in the unstructured narrative but were of interest to the research team.

From the interviews, the review team for this guideline identified emergent themes relevant to the experience of people with depression that could inform the guideline. Each transcript was read and re-read, and sections of the text were collected under different headings using a qualitative software program (NVivo). Two reviewers independently coded the data and all themes were discussed to generate a list of the main themes. The anticipated headings included: 'the experience of depression, 'psychosocial interventions', 'pharmacological interventions' and 'healthcare professionals'. The headings that emerged from the data were: 'coping mechanisms', 'accessing help and getting a diagnosis of depression', 'stigma and telling people about depression' and 'electroconvulsive therapy'.

There are some limitations to the qualitative analysis of people's experience of depression and its management undertaken for this guideline. As the review team relied on transcripts collected by other researchers with their own aims and purposes, information on issues that are particularly pertinent for people with depression that could be used to inform recommendations may not have been collected. Moreover, the review team did not have access to the full interview transcripts and therefore had a selective snapshot of people's experience. However, using Healthtalkonline did highlight issues regarding depression that can be reflected upon for the purpose of this guideline.

4.4.3   Experience of depression

In recounting their experience of depression, some people described life events which they felt had caused the disorder. Some of these events were childhood experiences including both problems in the family and at school. Some people commented that stressful situations at work contributed to the onset of their depression. Many people described the death of a family member or friend as a trigger of their depression. One service user summed up various life events that she believed were associated with her current state of depression:

> *All these experiences from earlier on in life, my Mum dying, being bullied ... being neglected and isolated and being treated different academically. I think they all combined with my lack of social skills, which I'd not had a chance to develop until that point when I got to university ... within a few months ... I was just feeling very low and very lonely, needy ... I think, probably about 4 or 5 months after starting my first year, I did become very depressed.*

Some people used metaphor and allusion to illuminate their experience of having depression. For example, one person described having a 'racing' mind that was 'zooming into miserable places'. Others used analogies such as depression being like a 'brick wall' or 'being inside a balloon' to describe how depression can act as a barrier from experiencing the world:

> *I couldn't feel anything. I couldn't feel anything for [husband's name]. I couldn't feel anything for the children. It [depression] was like being inside a very, very thick balloon and no matter how hard I pushed out, the momentum of the skin of the balloon would just push me back in.*

Other people listed the symptoms they were experiencing: lack of pleasurable experiences, body aches, tearfulness and sleep problems; they also described feelings of loneliness, isolation and feeling withdrawn.

A prevalent theme in the interviews was the presence of negative thoughts. These thoughts were described by people with depression as irrational and often caused them to jump to conclusions. One person explains how she experienced negative thoughts:

I call, what I've got in my head my chatter box. Basically it is my mind, seeing things a particular way. And with depression you see it really negatively. You see everything negatively, you'll always pull out the negative over the positive if you ever see a positive, you'll ... if for one positive you'll give ten negatives.

People also described feelings of suicidal ideation and some disclosed their experiences of attempting suicide. Some of the suicidal thoughts relating to suicide were: the 'world would be a better place without me', 'life wasn't worth going on', and 'life was completely out of my control'. One person described a suicide attempt:

I can remember being almost unconscious, and with a doctor and nurses around the bed. And the doctor said to one of the nurses, 'Go and get so and so ... we've got about 10 minutes or he'll be gone'. And I could hear him, and I just thought, 'I wish you'd leave me alone. I'm warm and comfortable. I don't want this.'

However many people also identified positive aspects of having experienced depression, for example, having become more confident, positive, understanding of others, able to support others and able to do 'something positive and ... creative'. They also said that they had become more aware of themselves and their feelings and more able to cope with stressful events.

Another common theme was that people felt that they appreciated life in a different way after having been depressed. For example, one person said:

I can listen to music and appreciate it in a different way ... it can move me now. Something on the TV can move me now, and I have, I feel things and things affect me.

Many people also felt that experiencing depression had made them re-evaluate their lifestyle and that this had led them to make some important positive life changes. One person described having had a breakdown as a 'breakthrough'. Another person described the positive effects of having had depression:

I think it's [depression has] sort of made me question what I thought was good about my life because I was in a very busy and hard-working career, and whilst the depression wasn't the main, or the only reason, that I left, there was a re-organisation at my work, I do think, oh, thank God I left there when I was 36 rather than 56. You know, I understand that I need sort of time for me now, and

> *that I'm a person in my own right, and I'm important and I have, you know, the right to have some quality time for me.*

4.4.4   Accessing help and getting a diagnosis of depression

Some people detailed how a particular event or problem prompted them to access help, such as sleep deprivation and lack of concentration:

> *I was putting my eldest daughter to bed and trying to read her a child's story, and I actually found . . . I no longer had the concentration to read . . . I couldn't follow the sentences to actually read it out loud. And that was a point where it was clear that . . . I had to seek help. And so I made an appointment with the doctor the next day.*

Once people with depression accessed help, they described their experience of receiving a diagnosis of depression. Some described how there is not enough recognition of depression and how often when they presented with sleep problems or loss of interest in sexual activities to their GP, these symptoms were not initially recognised as symptoms of depression:

> *I went to the doctor and I said . . . 'I sleep but I always feel tired . . . I've tried . . . everything.' And he just said, 'Try getting more sleep.' [laughing] I was like, yes, I could have thought of that, I've tried that, it didn't work . . . my feeling is that really he should have asked a few questions and could possibly have diagnosed that I was depressed.*

4.4.5   Stigma and telling people about depression

Some people described the stigma of having a diagnosis of depression. The majority felt that stigma still existed while a minority thought it was less prevalent than it used to be. There was also stigma around receiving treatment for depression for both psychological and pharmacological interventions:

> *It took a hell of a lot for me to go to therapy. You know A: nutters go to therapy, B: therapy makes you a nutter. These were the kind of things that I grew up with. And it doesn't help. You know, so hostile kind of lower middle class sort of feeling about that sort of thing.*

Conversely one person said it was quite 'fashionable' to be taking medication:

> *Prozac is quite a fashionable antidepressant. And it was OK to say you were on Prozac, it's like a happy pill isn't it. I'm OK I'm taking Prozac and then of course I knew quite a few people who were taking it as well, so it was like ok like join the club.*

Due to the stigma surrounding depression, some people found it difficult to talk to other people about their condition:

> *I can't talk to my family about it. They don't know about the therapy. I think it's the stigma thing ... my perception is that I would be seen as weak and not coping, so it's easier for me not to admit to that weakness.*

However, some people encouraged others to speak openly about their condition:

> *You should tell someone now, it doesn't have to be the doctor or a therapist, it can be a friend you know. The older I've got, the more I've found that it's accept-able to say to people, 'I'm depressed at the moment'.*

Some described their experiences of telling friends and neighbours and stating that it helped them; one person made a joke to ease the situation:

> *I was just really outright, and I just said, 'Ok, I was in a psychiatric hospital for a month and then outpatients for a further month and now I'm at work part-time to try and get back into the swing of things slowly.' And he just looked at me ... I said, 'It's ok though,' I said, 'I'm not loopy' and he just started laughing, because I'd just turned it into a joke.*

4.4.6   Psychosocial interventions

People with depression discussed their positive attitudes towards psychological treat-ments:

> *Sometimes you do need to talk to somebody who you don't know, who under-stands, instead of chatting to the brick wall. And instead of it going round in your head and trying to sort it out. Or you need somebody to talk to you and push the right buttons to help sort yourself out.*

People with depression expressed the need for psychosocial interventions when the cause of depression was deemed to be psychological rather than a 'chemical imbalance'. In addition they explained how they thought psychosocial interventions, rather than medication, were needed to resolve the maladaptive behaviour and distorted thoughts that contributed to their depression:

> *These tablets helped me ... but after a while, I realised it sorted out my brain chemistry, but you have learnt all these negative ways of looking at things, and doing things ... and that is why I believe I need long term therapy as well. I felt better [with medication], but I still didn't have ways of dealing with things.*

Experience of care

The benefit of psychosocial interventions to tackle negative thoughts was a prevalent theme. People described how they learnt to change their thoughts to be more constructive and positive:

> *There are things that keep me in a place of being depressed, and ... that's what the therapy really helps ... me understand how I perpetuate the depression ... I think for me it's about blaming myself ... thinking that I'm a bad person, and I can expend huge amounts of energy on the mental processes that go into making me responsible for everything that goes wrong in the world.*

In the following sections, experiences of different psychosocial interventions are described by people with depression. The psychosocial interventions that were briefly touched upon were counselling, cognitive therapy, self-help material, relaxation therapy and support groups.

Counselling
Overall people who discussed having counselling were positive about their experiences:

> *The main sort of release point was the counselling, which to me was crucial. If I hadn't have had the counselling, I'd probably still be severely ill and wouldn't be, you know, happily now saying that at last I'm enjoying life to a greater extent.*

Some of the outcomes that people achieved from counselling were: an increase in self-esteem, being able to return to work, dealing with bereavement issues, learning more about oneself and helping to deal with thoughts and feelings. Counselling was a positive experience for many because it provided a safe environment in which to talk about their concerns:

> *It was a big relief to have someone who I could tell anything I wanted, anything that was bothering me, and not worry about what they might think about it or how it might affect our relationship. And you know, it also helped to feel that I was doing something about my problems as well.*

Cognitive therapy
People who had cognitive therapy were positive about it, describing it as enabling because it was practical, focused on the real world and allowed them to begin to help themselves:

> *I could change my thinking and I could thereby change my feeling ... A particular example was he [therapist] said, when you go lie down to go to sleep, he said, 'You tend to look back on your day and think of all the failures' ... 'why don't you just think of everything that's been successful?' So ... I started doing that ... So just things like that, a few things like that with cognitive therapy. You know I think they helped quite a bit.*

Self-help

Two people described using self-help books to cope with their depression. One read David Burns' *Feeling Good*, which is based on cognitive and behavioural principles:

> *I sat and read this book, and you know it's quite a hefty one. But it's a really good one ... It's very difficult to sort of ... stop yourself, and realise that just because you have an opinion or you express yourself a certain way, it's not right or wrong, to you know, to act that way ... it's really difficult, 'cos it's everything in the book ties up with other things and you know cognitive therapy for me, is my chatter box and arguing with it.*

Another read Dorothy Rowe's *Depression: The Way out of Your Prison:*

> *Some of it is relevant, some of it is not at all relevant ... It's really good because it's all about ... looking after you and some of the things just make me laugh. You know because it's so like ... 'That's me. I'm in there. That's what I do'.*

Relaxation therapy

Two service users described their experience of relaxation therapy:

> *Relaxation therapy ... when you're depressed is mighty hard to get started. Once you've started and got the grasp of it, then it's quite good, but to actually get relaxed when you're really depressed is damn nigh impossible you know.*

Support groups

People who had attended support groups were positive about their experiences. They described these groups as therapeutic because they were able to meet people with similar problems and share their experiences in an environment where there was no stigma. In addition, people with depression felt relieved to know they were not alone:

> *It was a great source of comfort ... And to find that in fact you weren't the only person to feel like that was actually a great relief. It was also a great relief to find ... people who were non-judgemental.*

> *A self-help group isn't group therapy but it is very therapeutic ... people meeting with a shared interest ... There are people there who, they won't say, 'Pull yourself together, pull your socks up, what have you got to be depressed about?' There is none of that. The mutual support is just unbelievable.*

One described a suicide support group that provided some source of comfort but also had harmful effects:

> *It's a discussion group of people talking ... of essentially extremely depressed people talking about suicide. And talking about suicidal feelings and suicidal*

methods and yeah, from time to time people die on it. But in a weird perverse way it's a source of strength and a source of comfort.

4.4.7   Pharmacological interventions

People with depression had mixed views regarding pharmacological interventions. Some people were concerned about taking tablets; they did not think pills solved the problem or they had a cynical view of drug companies. Others who tried medication who did not have positive experiences said they felt that it 'robbed' them of feelings. One person described why a pharmacological intervention was not the right treatment for him:

I've been prescribed antidepressants in the past but I've always felt reluctant and apprehensive about taking it, largely because a) I feel that the effects are probably short-term, they're not going to actually resolve the depression, b) because they do have side-effects and, c) I didn't feel comfortable, myself, with taking some tablets.

However, the majority had positive experiences regarding medication. For those who benefited from a pharmacological intervention, they described taking medication as a turning point in their lives. People said that they felt more in control and had greater awareness of the world around them (this was in contrast to other people's experience of medication):

It was exactly 7 weeks to the day that I took . . . the first tablet . . . I knew that morning when I woke up that I feel differently, things are different. And that was the turning point. It was this lifting again, this lifting of overall and just . . . contentedness

It [medication] gave me a feeling that I've got some control now of this thing [depression]. And I was having some experiences like increased sensitivity to things like noise and colours and feelings.

One person advised that if someone was not benefiting from their current medication, that they should persevere until they found a drug that works for them:

It isn't a one size fits all . . . I would say to folk if you feel like you're not getting any better . . . on the particular medication . . . go back to your doctor and ask your doctor to change, to consider changing your medication.

Many people with depression reported side effects from taking medication, notably dry mouth, hair loss, increased sweating, weight gain and problems ejaculating. A minority also reported experiencing suicidal thoughts as a consequence of their medication:

For many years I hadn't had any suicide thoughts at all, and I had certainly never thought of cutting myself, but while I was on Seroxat, I did start to get sudden images in my head of you know, cutting long gashes in myself.

Despite this, some people with depression said that the benefits of medication outweighed the potential side effects:

You're given a sheet which tells you what to expect, and I looked it up on the internet as well. I'm very against taking medicine for a long time, but after my experience with the depression I decided I would be prepared to take it ... for the rest of my life if I don't get it again, the depression again, if it stops that.

When some people stopped their medication, they described experiencing discontinuation symptoms, the most prevalent symptom of which was nausea:

Being stupidly pig-headed, just stopped it [Efexor] ... I was just completely off my head with depression ... the symptoms were so acute it was very frightening. You feel sick, nausea, the nausea was awful. And just panic, really.

4.4.8   Electroconvulsive therapy

Four service users recounted their experience of ECT; the majority had negative experiences because of the frightening nature of the intervention and loss of memory post-treatment:

They'd get you to lie down on the bed, and give you an anaesthetic in your hand, which would basically make you go unconscious. But just that 2 minutes when you might have gone into the room and been waiting, I was just so frightened. And then they give you ECT ... that is quite a confusing experience. I did find that it affected my memory a fair bit.

I have massive blanks, short-term and long-term ... I get angry with the professionals that this wasn't explained that this could happen ... I've tried to talk about it with the doctors at the hospital and they say, 'Give me an example' and I give them an example and they say, 'Oh that's normal, that's just normal, that's not the ECT ... that's normal'.

Only one person reported a positive experience regarding ECT:

It all sounds very scary, but you really don't ... you don't see anything because you are anaesthetised, so you are asleep. And you wake up, and I ... you have a slight headache, but apart from that, I had no side-effects ... my mood improved instantly, and I was talking and laughing.

4.4.9   Healthcare professionals

This section covers people's experience of healthcare professionals, including GPs, nurses and psychiatrists.

Experience of care

GPs

As described in Section 4.4.4, people were critical of their GPs because they felt that their depression went undetected. However some people had positive experiences of getting a diagnosis of depression and of how their depression was initially managed:

> *I was very low physically and clearly very low mentally, and the GP ... and I'll be forever thankful for him, actually said, 'I don't think I am helping with the right kind of medication for the right reasons, and if you agree I'd like to refer you on to somebody'. And it was like an immense relief ... somebody's actually going to treat me as somebody who has a problem here.*

People who had positive experiences of their GPs described them as being sympathetic, warm, tender, kind, helpful and supportive. These people felt that they were listened to and responded to:

> *She's [the GP is] good because she is human. She listens and she responds to me as a human being, not as a professional. She gives me time, as much time as I want sometimes. She cares and she's shown me she cares because she has rung me up before at home and said, 'How are you? Will you come and see me tomorrow?' because she knows I'm not going to ring and make an appointment because I ... I mean I'm in isolating mode and things are going wrong.*

Those with negative experiences described how their GP was lacking in the above characteristics:

> *You just didn't get listened to, you didn't get, you know, it was as though what they [GPs] were saying was, 'Well, it's just in your head, you know you don't really understand, I know better.' And I know that they're really busy and I know that they don't have a lot of time, but I really felt that I got no help at all most of the time.*

Nurses

People said that they did not feel that nurses understood the sensitive nature of their depression, that nurses in the NHS were too busy to talk to their patients and that their attitudes may be because of inadequate training:

> *There's an awful lot there who ... you felt as though it was people saying to you, 'Oh, for goodness sake pull yourself out of it', and, 'Get yourself together', which you don't want, it's the last thing at the end of the day. I just don't think that there is enough, in regards to, against private and NHS, there is just not enough funding to be able to ... I don't know, train the nurses in a certain way.*

Psychiatrists

People had mixed experience of psychiatrists. Some did not like how psychiatrists tried to illicit information about their childhood experiences, describing the method as a 'text book' approach that instantly created a barrier. Others did not like to discuss feelings in general:

> *I felt my psychiatrist was a very .... oh ... wet individual. Again, I think because I'd been quite a numerate, factual, organised person, to have someone to talking about feelings and what about this and what about that? And it was ... nothing could ever be pin-pointed or ... I just found it annoying.*

People also had mixed opinions about how their psychiatrist dealt with their medication. The majority had positive experiences: one person described how their psychiatrist was able to change their medication to one with fewer side effects; another described how the psychiatrist prescribed a proper therapeutic dose of anti-depressants. However, one person felt that she was not listened to when she explained to her psychiatrist that her current medication was not working:

> *He'd [psychiatrist] say something like, 'Oh well, continue with the paroxetine.' And if I said, 'Look, this isn't helping me. I've been on this for eight months, it's not making me better.' 'It takes time, you have to have patience.' You know, 'You are better really' I was told by one doctor. 'You're not depressed, you're just a very sad lady.'*

4.4.10   Services

The experiences of mental health services were described by people with depression. Issues regarding referral, waiting lists and getting into NHS services were raised. Some people said that that they waited too long to be referred to a psychiatrist or receive psychotherapy. One person said that while she was on a waiting list she was unable to cope with her depression:

> *I was referred to the psychiatric hospital for assessment. Although I think it probably took about two months I believe between the initial sort of GP's referring letter and getting an appointment. Which again in retrospect was, was way, way too long, way too long. I was really, really ill and barely coping.*

Another person described how she felt that she had to be violent in her GP's surgery in order to be referred to NHS services:

> *It's very difficult to get a hospital bed for quite severe mental illness. You've got to be suicidal ... I was feeling suicidal. I was also quite violent at times. I mean in my own doctor's surgery, I swept all the things off his desk you know ... there was a part of me, kind of watching what I was doing ... saying, 'Right, well make it really dramatic.' I wasn't pretending exactly, but I knew I had to make a song and dance to get heard.*

Once in mental health services, people described a mixture of positive and negative experiences. One person said that a psychiatric intensive care unit was 'a place of safety'. Others described a mental health service as a place where they had no responsibilities, where they could 'hand yourself over' to the care of the service. Accompanying this, however, was the feeling of being institutionalised:

> *In eight weeks, I very quickly became institutionalised myself. I was scared to come out because I was in this enclosed world where I knew what was going to happen. There were routines, mealtimes, getting up times, medication times, OT [occupational therapy] times. There were routines and I had no responsibilities ... I was in a place where I didn't have to think about anything, and nobody could touch me.*

People also had negative experiences of mental health services provided by the NHS, including not feeling cared for. Those who had had private treatment had more favourable accounts, and compared and contrasted the two experiences:

> *The private hospital was, there was a lot of love, a lot of care in there, sincere care. And I won't knock the NHS because they are obviously very limited to money in a way, but there was no care ... In the private hospital you felt like you were being treated as a human being ... You felt that yes, you could get well here because they cared.*

4.4.11   Families and carers

People with depression described the impact that their condition had on families and carers. Some stated that it was harder for the family and carers than it was for the person who had depression. Others described the impact that it had on the partner, often resulting in a change in roles. For example, people described how their partners had to take a more active role in daily chores:

> *I found it difficult to relate on the day-to-day things, which is where she [his wife] was so good. She took over those things.*

Some felt that their depression had an impact on their children:

> *My sons were very good, but they missed a lot because of how I was. And they would have to make allowances, which isn't really what you should have to do when you're growing up.*

Some people said that without their family and carers they would not have been able to cope with their depression:

> *My partner has played a key role in my recovery – he was very supportive during my depression periods – I do not know how I would have coped without him ... Many times he has forced me to do things and helped me out of the house*

in times when I did not feel like doing anything. I believe having a loving and caring partner has helped me get over the most horrible periods of my depression.

4.4.12   Coping strategies

People with depression described coping strategies that they used to overcome their condition. These strategies were those other than pharmacological and psychological interventions employed by people to manage their depression.

Distraction was a common coping strategy. One of the ways in which people distracted themselves from their mental health problem was by having or acquiring a hobby, which ranged from physical activities such as swimming and going to the gym, to those of a more creative nature such as poetry:

Having hobbies, and that ... that gets depressed people through because the thing that you can't think of, you know, two things at once.

I wanted to do something physical ... So I started to garden, I've never been in the garden before. And it was crap at first, but gradually it was alright, you know you start to think, 'Yeah, this is kind of distracting me a bit.'

For other people, voluntary work was a coping strategy because the process of helping others allowed them to help themselves. In addition, people described how voluntary work helped them to increase their confidence and build up their self-esteem:

At the beginning I used to get anxiety attacks and some days I could just phone up and say, 'Look I'm not feeling well.' If you are doing it voluntarily ... I felt I wasn't letting them down ... the same pressure is not there. So ... voluntary work I would definitely advocate because it gives you a sense of ... it helps build your confidence, self-esteem.

Another coping strategy was completing small, manageable tasks:

When I'm depressed ... I wasn't able to do anything about it, really. I just felt overwhelmed by it ... And with my depression, when I was feeling very low, I would, I did decide to just concentrate on small things; going for a walk, baking some bread, you know pottering around in the garden. Just trying to get through day to day, I think, was how I came out of the suicide attempt.

4.5   REVIEW OF THE QUALITATIVE LITERATURE

4.5.1   Introduction

A systematic search for published reviews of relevant qualitative studies of people with depression was undertaken. The aim of the review was to explore the experience

**Table 5: Databases searched and inclusion/exclusion criteria
for clinical evidence**

Electronic databases	CINAHL, EMBASE, MEDLINE, PsycINFO, HMIC, PsycEXTRA, PsycBOOKS
Date searched	Database inception to February 2009
Study design	Systematic reviews of qualitative studies, surveys, observational studies
Population	People with depression and families/carers
Outcomes	None specified

of care for people with depression and their families and carers in terms of the broad topics of receiving the diagnosis, accessing services and having treatment.

4.5.2   Databases searched and inclusion/exclusion criteria

Reviews were sought of qualitative studies that used relevant first-hand experiences of people with depression and families/carers. The GDG did not specify a particular outcome. Instead, the review was concerned with any narrative data that highlighted the experience of care. For more information about the databases searched see Table 5. Details of the search strings used are in Appendix 8.

4.5.3   Studies considered

The search found one systematic review that explored the experience of care for people with depression that met the inclusion/exclusion criteria (Khan *et al.*, 2007). The review team then looked at primary qualitative studies identified by the search and a further two primary studies (Ridge & Ziebland, 2006; Saver *et al.*, 2007) were included in the review that were not already reviewed by Khan and colleagues (2007). A further seven studies were considered for the review but they did not meet the inclusion criteria (Cooper-Patrick *et al.*, 1997; Rogers *et al.*, 2001; Chew-Graham *et al.*, 2002; Van Schaik *et al.*, 2004; MaGPIe, 2005b; Elgie, 2006; Johnston *et al.*, 2007); the most common reasons for exclusion were the studies did not report qualitative data or the population did not meet criteria for depression.

4.5.4   Themes emerging from the studies

Experiencing depression
Khan and colleagues (2007), in their meta-synthesis of qualitative research in guided self-help in primary care mental health services, found that family conflict, problems at work, chronic physical health problems, childhood events, financial

hardship and racism were the most frequent reasons given for causes for depression. People taking part in the studies spoke about their depression in terms of the effect on functioning and ability to cope rather than feelings or symptoms. The most common means of expressing their feelings was through metaphor: being 'on edge', 'boxed in', 'a volcano bursting', 'broken in half', 'prisoner in my own home', and so on.

Accessing help and stigma

Khan and colleagues (2007) found that accessing help from primary care could be difficult, with very little time spent having one-to-one contact with a primary care professional. Because of feelings of shame and 'lack of legitimacy', people may not have presented their problems in an open manner. There was a possibility that seeking help would 'threaten an already weakened sense of self' if treatments were discussed that might be unacceptable to the person, such as medication.

Saver and colleagues (2007) described four barriers to accessing help by people with depression. These were characterised as: (1) a lack of motivation because of their depression; (2) stigma associated with depression and/or denial of their diagnosis; (3) healthcare professionals seeming unresponsive; and (4) a mismatch between how information is offered and how people with depression prefer to seek information, for example:

> *I would never sit down and read something about medicine. It has never interested me. I learned more from watching that commercial on television.*

Getting a diagnosis of depression

For people with depression, Saver and colleagues (2007) found that the majority of people received their initial diagnosis from a mental healthcare professional and a minority reported receiving their diagnosis from a GP. In addition, people said that their GP missed opportunities to diagnose their depression. Some people described their own inability or unwillingness to raise the issue of depression with their GP, while others stated that their GP focused solely on their somatic complaints, seemed uninterested in mental health issues or were purely dismissive of depression when it was suggested.

Experience of treatment

Khan and colleagues (2007) found that taking medication could lead to ambivalent feelings: on the one hand, people felt relief because medication helped them cope with difficulties in their day-to-day life; on the other hand, they felt a lack of control. There was also a moral component regarding personal responsibility and the fear of not being able to function in daily life. When the GP or others (family or friends) offered advice to relieve this ambiguity, people were more willing to accept medication as a possible treatment, but only on the understanding that it would be for short-term use. People were cautious about telling other people that they were taking medication because of perceived stigma. There was a feeling among the people in the studies that they were in some way 'deficient' because they needed to take antidepressants. Feelings of guilt, of letting themselves and others down, and concerns about long-term changes to their personality were also expressed.

Saver and colleagues (2007) found that less than half of the people with depression reported receiving information about psychological interventions. One participant commented that the only 'option' was a pharmacological treatment:

> *They just handed me a drug and said go on it right now ... I felt rushed along, given a prescription, told this will fix it.*

None remembered receiving information about the different treatment options such as CBT, problem-solving therapy or IPT. Only a minority reported that they had some choice in their treatment options.

Ridge and Ziebland (2006) in their analysis of interview transcripts collected by Health talkonline found that people with deep-seated and complex problems needed longer-term psychological therapy.

Self-help and other coping strategies

Khan and colleagues (2007) synthesised qualitative studies of patient experiences of depression management in primary care to develop a framework for a guided self-help intervention with the aim of providing a potential solution to the problem of the gap between demand for CBT and supply of trained therapists. A number of themes were highlighted, including feelings of control and helplessness in engaging with treatment, which might influence the success of a self-help intervention for people with depression in primary care. People said that they used coping strategies such as distraction or thinking of places that were associated with feeling safe and in control. They saw accessing help as an indication that their personal coping strategies had failed.

Recovery

Ridge and Ziebland (2006) analysed the interview transcripts (collected by Healthtalkonline) of 38 men and women who, in the main, had had severe depression, to explore the approaches and meanings attributed to overcoming depression. The focus was on the specific components involved in recovery: authenticity, responsibility and 'rewriting depression into the self'. Recovery involved the need to understand the 'authentic self'. The main findings of the study were that people needed to understand a language and framework of longer-term recovery to tell their own story of improvement; that getting better meant different things to different people; and that people needed to assume responsibility for their own recovery. The majority of the interviewees had used and valued talking therapies as a means of gaining insight into their thoughts and feelings.

4.6   FROM EVIDENCE TO RECOMMENDATIONS

This section is a combined summary of themes from the personal accounts, the qualitative analysis and the literature review. It should be noted that most of the personal accounts received were from people who either have or have had severe and/or chronic depression. Therefore, it is acknowledged that the themes that run through the personal accounts may not be applicable to people who have other forms of depression. Despite these limitations, a number of themes were identified that were present in all three sources of evidence.

4.6.1   Understanding depression

Both the personal accounts and the literature reveal that lack of information from professionals is a barrier to coming to a full understanding of depression, the range of treatments available and the role of the mental health team. There was also a concern that when a person is severely depressed they may find it difficult to concentrate on what is being said. Therefore written information is crucial, although it should be recognised that people with mental health problems may respond to information provided in other forms, such as via video or DVD. One person (B) said that it would be helpful if professionals could be clear about the purpose of any appointments offered. Lack of clarity about how care is organised may increase the person's distress. One person (G), who had been given no information, had empowered himself through the internet and had built up a wide network of fellow sufferers. Lack of accessible information is a particular issue for people from black and Asian minority ethnic groups, as evidenced by personal account C.

4.6.2   Accessing help and getting a diagnosis of depression

Accessing help was also a prevalent theme in the personal accounts, the qualitative analysis and the literature, whether it was during the initial stages of being diagnosed or after years of having treatment. Two people in the personal accounts (B and E) found it difficult to access support when needed, despite having had depression for some years. It was felt that an emergency number to call would be a lifeline for people who live alone and have no carer support. Such means of support would be particularly helpful for people with long-term, severe depression.

The literature also revealed that accessing help may be a problem for some people first experiencing symptoms because of stigma associated with having a mental health problem (see Section 4.6.3), which may leave them unmotivated to raise the issue of depression with their GP.

4.6.3   Stigma

Stigma was frequently discussed in the personal accounts, the qualitative analysis and in the literature. This was experienced both externally and internally. External stigma was felt from employers and colleagues; but many also felt internal stigma and kept their depression concealed from friends, family and work associates. Feelings of shame were expressed and also an anxiety that asking for help would lead to being offered interventions that they did not want, such as medication (the person in account D said that the idea of taking tablets accentuated the feeling of being mentally unwell).

4.6.4   Recognising depression

Recognition of depression and the severity of symptoms was also a prominent theme in the three forms of evidence. In the literature and qualitative analysis, people spoke about how depression is often not recognised and that physical problems may mask the depressive symptoms or may not be seen as part of the depressive symptomatology. In the personal accounts, two people (B and G) commented that they felt that the severity of their depression was not properly recognised within primary care. One person (B) felt that her diagnosis should have been made by a qualified and experienced professional.

4.6.5   Relationships with healthcare professionals

The relationship with the GP was a prevalent theme in the personal accounts, the qualitative analysis and the literature. In the personal accounts, most found their GPs helpful and understanding. The main area of criticism concerned the quality of contact with the GP (see Khan *et al.*, 2007) – a short appointment when a person is distressed is not long enough and people with depression are unlikely to ask for a longer appointment. In the qualitative analysis and the literature, the relationship with the GP was seen negatively if the GP failed to recognise depressive symptoms or focused solely on the person's somatic symptoms. People who had positive experiences highlighted the sympathetic, supportive and helpful qualities of the GP.

The relationship with nurses was not as positive in both the personal accounts (see B) and the qualitative analysis, with lack of understanding about depression being cited as a common complaint.

In the qualitative analysis there were mixed views about psychiatrists, particularly in the way that they prescribed medication. Some people felt that their psychiatrist was able to work with them to find the right medication and the correct dose; another said her psychiatrist did not listen when she said her medication was not working. In the personal accounts, some people had neutral views about their psychiatrist while three people (C, F and G) expressed negative views, such as the psychiatrist being unsupportive and cursory in their attention.

Most of the personal accounts spoke of the importance of a relationship with professionals that was non-judgemental and supportive. But as one person (B) pointed out, sometimes being well-meaning and supportive is not enough. She felt that while her primary care practitioners and counsellors were pleasant and accommodating, her self-report was not listened to closely enough and the severity of her depression was underestimated. A number of people commented that the relationship between patient and therapist is of prime importance, and that ideally there should be some choice in terms of the gender of the therapist and their therapeutic approach. Two people (A and B) commented that it is often seen as the patient's 'fault' if they do not benefit from psychological treatment, when the counsellor or therapist should take some responsibility for a lack of therapeutic effect.

4.6.6   Experience of services

Both the personal accounts and the qualitative analysis described experiences of mental health services. Many people said that they waited too long to be referred to a psychiatrist or receive psychological treatment. Once in mental health services, views were mixed. In both sources of evidence, those who had private treatment had, on the whole, more positive experiences.

4.6.7   Experience of depression and its possible causes

In both the personal accounts and the qualitative analysis, people with depression described some of the negative thoughts that they had experienced and some described suicidal thoughts and behaviour; they also used metaphor and allusion to explain their symptoms. In the qualitative analysis some people said that they were able to experience life differently since being depressed which, for some, was a positive outcome.

It emerged from the qualitative analysis that some people ascribed the onset of their depression to certain life events, including childhood experiences. The majority of the personal accounts also reported childhood events such as trauma, abuse or conflict of one form or another and many of them linked this directly with the onset of their depression. For many people, complex problems in childhood were compounded by multiple difficulties in adulthood. For the person in account D, being a carer of someone with schizophrenia meant that he had to hide his symptoms of depression to fulfil his role as a carer. Khan and colleagues (2007) found that family conflict and childhood events were among the most frequent reasons given for causes for depression. Howe (1995) explains that:

> Internal psychological states and our ability to cope with the external demands of life have roots which reach right back into childhood. The robustness of our early internal representations of self and others lays down the pattern of our future psychological strengths and weaknesses. When children feel that no matter what they think, say or do, they are not able to control what happens to them, physically or emotionally, a feeling of fatalism and helplessness sets in. Attachment relationships in which sexual or physical abuse took place often leave the individual with feelings of passivity and worthlessness. Early attachment relationships that were lost or broken leave people feeling that they cannot control the important things in their lives. Without support they remain

emotionally vulnerable to setbacks and upsets. For those who feel hopeless and helpless, depression is often the psychological result.

4.6.8   Experiences of treatments

Psychological therapy
There was a strong feeling within the service user and carer topic group that the excerpt from Howe (1995) in the section above highlights the reasons why many people opt for private therapy; that is, that psychological treatment offered by the NHS in the form of CBT does not go far enough in addressing the trauma experienced in childhood. The study by Ridge and Ziebland (2006) confirms the opinions of the topic group and the testimony from the personal accounts that people with 'deep and complex problems felt the need for longer term therapy'. Those that have had long-term psychodynamic therapy report that it has been helpful in their understanding of themselves and their depression and that until they have worked through and repaired the damage experienced in childhood, depression will be a major factor in the person's life. The service user and carer topic group do acknowledge, however, that as there has been little research into the efficacy of long-term psychodynamic therapy, it cannot be recommended as a course of treatment in this guideline (see Chapter 8).

The study by Saver and colleagues (2007) points to the fact that few people received information about psychological therapy and the different treatments, such as CBT and IPT.

Psychosocial interventions
This was a theme of both the personal accounts and the qualitative analysis. In the qualitative analysis, people expressed a need for psychosocial interventions when they attributed the cause of their depression to psychological processes rather than a 'chemical imbalance' and to help them cope with negative thoughts.

Overall, people in the qualitative analysis were positive about counselling, as were people in the personal accounts, although concerns were raised by two people (B and E). One found counselling inadequate for her needs because it did not get to the 'root' of her depression and indeed did not stop her depression from becoming more severe. Another felt that the counselling she received was unsatisfactory: she was asked inappropriate questions, incorrect assumptions were made about her life, and she felt that she did not talk enough during the sessions. She felt that for counselling to be effective, the counsellor needed to both listen and question skilfully.

In the qualitative analysis, people were generally positive about cognitive therapy, self-help books and support groups, but less positive about relaxation therapy because people with severe depression find it difficult to relax. The view of relaxation therapy is borne out in personal account B. The personal accounts express mixed views about support groups: one person (D) was very positive about them, but another (E) said that, while it was good to meet other people, she gained no therapeutic value from attending.

Khan and colleagues (2007) synthesised qualitative studies of patient experiences of depression management in primary care to develop a framework for a guided self-help intervention.

Medication

There were mixed reports regarding medication. Some people did not find antidepressants helpful, particularly in the form of a 'drug cocktail'; others were concerned about taking tablets. In the literature, it emerged that taking medication could lead to ambivalent feelings: on the one hand, people felt relief because medication helped them cope with difficulties in their day-to-day life; on the other, they felt a lack of control. In the personal accounts, one person (A) commented on the weight gain associated with the medication leading to self-esteem issues and feeling more depressed. Others benefited from it; one person (B) felt strongly that getting the appropriate medication promptly is vital and that there should be intense support before the antidepressive effects are experienced. The majority of people in the qualitative analysis said that antidepressants were beneficial, despite some experiencing side effects.

Electroconvulsive therapy

This theme was only present in the qualitative analysis. The majority of people who had ECT had negative experiences, including loss of memory after treatment. Only one person had a positive experience with no side effects.

4.6.9   Coping strategies

It is evident from the personal accounts and the literature review that people who have had depression for a long time develop positive coping mechanisms that enable them to manage their illness. These mechanisms range from exercise (A) or personal faith (C), to readjusting one's life to be able to manage depression. The qualitative analysis also identified a number of coping strategies such as distraction, having a hobby, activities and voluntary work.

4.6.10   Employment

The theme of employment was only present in the personal accounts. To contextualise this theme, some of the literature regarding this topic that was not identified in the systematic search is briefly described below.

From the personal accounts there are issues for those with long-standing depression when it comes to accessing and remaining in employment. Several personal accounts spoke of difficulties in getting paid employment: one person (C) stated that both their college and job centre could not help until their condition was stable, and another (B) was self-employed when she became ill, was unable to work and had no income. In personal account G, the person had only worked in paid employment for 8 months in the 8 years he had had depression, but was doing voluntary work with mental health and disability organisations.

Other personal accounts spoke of experiences in work. One person (A) spoke of colleagues not being keen for her to return to work, and instead of returning to her normal activities she was marginalised from external meetings and confined to certain tasks. Another person (E) expressed the fear of getting too ill to work, but with the help of her GP did not have to say that the occasional day or week off with illness was because of depression. However, she also had the support of her manager in whom she confided and who helped with work pressures. In the qualitative analysis, some people commented that stressful situations at work contributed to the onset of their depression.

The issue of employment is also important to carers: in personal account H, the carer has built her career around self-employment so that she has time to care, but is also able to maintain a life outside caring.

Clinical research and government reports suggest that employment plays a part both in exacerbating stress leading to depression, but also, conversely, that it can be crucial component in aiding the recovery process. The Health and Safety Executive (2008) reported that in 2006/07, an estimated 530,000 people in the UK reported they were experiencing stress, depression or anxiety that was caused or exacerbated by their current or past employment. It was estimated that 13.8 million working days (full-day equivalent) were lost in 2006/07 through work-related stress, depression or anxiety. The Sainsbury Centre for Mental Health (2007) also identified the loss in productivity that occurs when employees come to work but function at less than full capacity because of ill health (termed 'presenteeism'). Fearing possible stigma or discrimination, people with mental health problems may turn up for work even if they are feeling unwell rather than be labelled as mentally ill by their employers and co-workers.

Once people with depression become too ill to work, they may remain absent from their place of employment or unemployed for considerable periods of time. The anecdotal evidence from the personal accounts suggests, however, that for people with depression a return to work or continuing with work can aid the recovery process. A report by Waddell and Burton (2006) concluded that work was generally beneficial for both physical and mental health and well-being. It advised that the type of employment should be healthy and safe, and should offer the individual some influence over how the work is done and a sense of self-worth. Overall, the beneficial effects of work were shown to outweigh the risks and to be much greater than the harmful effects of long-term unemployment or prolonged absence because of sickness.

A report by the Royal College of Psychiatrists (2008) found two studies that analysed employment schemes in people with mental health problems. In a systematic review of 11 RCTs comparing prevocational training or supported employment for people with severe mental illness with each other or with standard community care, Crowther and colleagues (2001) found that participants who received supported employment were more likely to be in competitive employment than those who received prevocational training (34% compared with 12% at 12 months). Rinaldi and colleagues (2008) examined a supported employment scheme run by South West London and St George's Mental Health NHS Trust. The results showed that, following the integration of employment specialists into CMHTs, there was a significant increase in the number of clients with various diagnoses (31% with depression – unspecified severity) engaged in mainstream work or educational activity at both 6 and 12 months. The conclusion drawn supports the use of individual placement specialists in clinical practice in CMHTs.

4.6.11   Recovery

In the study by Ridge and Ziebland (2006), the term 'recovery' is used to describe the process by which people learn to understand and then manage their illness. They explain that as the process of recovery develops, the person is able to assume responsibility for their illness through gaining insight into themselves, their thought processes, their concept of themselves and others around them, and their place in the world. Treatments and professionals were seen as the 'tools' needed to aid recovery. The term 'recovery' was the cause of significant debate in the service user and carer topic group and had different meanings for different people. For some it meant an absence of depressive symptoms *and* an ability to function fully to one's potential. But for other long-term sufferers, 'recovery' was a term that they would not use ('self-management' being perhaps a more appropriate term). For others the term 'recovery' was important in demonstrating the positive shift from being severely depressed with an inability to 'function normally', to perhaps currently living with dysthymia, where the user is able to live a full and productive life, with just a few residual symptoms that are manageable.

4.6.12   Families and carers

The literature search did not identify studies of carer experience and the two personal accounts offer very different perspectives, one from an adult caring for her partner (H) and one from a teenage boy caring for his mother (I). But several themes did emerge. The personal accounts both conveyed the experience that caring is rewarding but challenging. Both carers also spoke of the different aspects of caring: undertaking practical tasks for the person, and offering emotional support. Caring can radically change the relationship between partners and between parents and children. The carer in account H felt more like a mother than a partner and the young carer (I) said that he became an adult when he cared for his mother, but that she became a 'normal bossy Mum' again when she was well. Both carers reported that having interests that took them away from caring for a few hours was extremely important.

   The needs of young carers should be recognised and addressed and recent publications from the Social Care Institute for Excellence and the Department of Health (Department of Health *et al.*, 2008; Greene *et al.*, 2008; Roberts *et al.*, 2008; Department of Health *et al.*, 2009) provide guidance on how this can be achieved. It should be recognised that young carers might marginalise themselves from their peer group and experience other social and educational disadvantage. The report by

Roberts and colleagues (2008) suggests that the needs of young carers could be more effectively addressed by respecting their anxieties and acknowledging their input and skills. It is also recommended that young carers should be included in their family member's care planning.

The impact of depression on families and carers was a prolific theme in both the personal accounts and the qualitative analysis, with some people stating that depression was harder for family members and carers than for themselves. Some people remarked on the change of roles that occurred as a result of one person having depression. Many people also commented on the supportive nature of family members and carers, although some people had to cope with their depression alone.

4.7 RECOMMENDATIONS

4.7.1 Providing information and support, and obtaining informed consent

4.7.1.1   When working with people with depression and their families or carers:
- build a trusting relationship and work in an open, engaging and non-judgemental manner
- explore treatment options in an atmosphere of hope and optimism, explaining the different courses of depression and that recovery is possible
- be aware that stigma and discrimination can be associated with a diagnosis of depression
- ensure that discussions take place in settings in which confidentiality, privacy and dignity are respected.

4.7.1.2   When working with people with depression and their families or carers:
- provide information appropriate to their level of understanding about the nature of depression and the range of treatments available
- avoid clinical language without adequate explanation
- ensure that comprehensive written information is available in the appropriate language and in audio format if possible
- provide and work proficiently with independent interpreters (that is, someone who is not known to the person with depression) if needed[5].

4.7.1.3   Inform people with depression about self-help groups, support groups and other local and national resources[6].

4.7.1.4   Make all efforts necessary to ensure that a person with depression can give meaningful and informed consent before treatment starts. This is especially important when a person has severe depression or is subject to the Mental Health Act[7].

---

[5]The evidence for this recommendation has not been updated since the previous guideline. Any wording changes have been made for clarification only.
[6]Ibid.
[7]Ibid.

4.7.1.5   Ensure that consent to treatment is based on the provision of clear information (which should also be available in written form) about the intervention, covering:
● what it comprises
● what is expected of the person while having it
● likely outcomes (including any side effects).

4.7.2   Advance decisions and statements

4.7.2.1   For people with recurrent severe depression or depression with psychotic symptoms and for those who have been treated under the Mental Health Act, consider developing advance decisions and advance statements collaboratively with the person. Record the decisions and statements and include copies in the person's care plan in primary and secondary care. Give copies to the person and to their family or carer, if the person agrees.

4.7.3   Supporting families and carers

4.7.3.1   When families or carers are involved in supporting a person with severe or chronic[8] depression, consider:
● providing written and verbal information on depression and its management, including how families or carers can support the person
● offering a carer's assessment of their caring, physical and mental health needs if necessary
● providing information about local family or carer support groups and voluntary organisations, and helping families or carers to access these
● negotiating between the person and their family or carer about confidentiality and the sharing of information.

4.7.4   Working with people from diverse ethnic and cultural backgrounds

4.7.4.1   Be respectful of, and sensitive to, diverse cultural, ethnic and religious backgrounds when working with people with depression, and be aware of the possible variations in the presentation of depression. Ensure competence in:
● culturally sensitive assessment
● using different explanatory models of depression

---

[8]Depression is described as 'chronic' if symptoms have been present more or less continuously for 2 years or more.

- addressing cultural and ethnic differences when developing and implementing treatment plans
- working with families from diverse ethnic and cultural backgrounds.

4.7.4.2 Consider providing all interventions in the preferred language of the person with depression where possible[9].

---

[9]The evidence for this recommendation has not been updated since the previous guideline. Any wording changes have been made for clarification only.

5   CASE IDENTIFICATION AND SERVICE DELIVERY

5.1   INTRODUCTION[10]

The starting point for providing effective treatment for depression is the recognition of the problem and the first point of access is usually primary care, with the majority of people continuing to be managed in primary care. There is evidence, however, that many cases go unrecognised (Del Piccolo *et al.*, 1998; Raine *et al.*, 2000). Where depression is recognised, care often falls short of optimal recommended practice (Katon *et al.*, 1992; Donoghue & Tylee, 1996) and outcomes are correspondingly below what is possible (Rost *et al.*, 1994). This is a cause of considerable concern. More recent studies, however, suggest that clinically significant depression (moderate to severe depressive illness) is detected by GPs at later consultations by virtue of the longitudinal patient–doctor relationship and it is milder forms, which are more likely to recover spontaneously, that go undetected and untreated (Thompson *et al.*, 2001; Kessler *et al.*, 2003).

In addition to efforts to improve recognition of depression, a number of responses have been developed over the past 20 or so years to address the problem of suboptimal treatment. These responses have included developments in the treatment of depression in primary and secondary care; the organisational and professional structures of primary and secondary care mental health services; and the development and adaptation of models for the management of chronic medical conditions, for example diabetes (Von Korff *et al.*, 1997; Von Korff & Goldberg, 2001). Since the publication of the previous guideline in 2004, in the UK these developments have included the introduction of graduate mental health workers (Department of Health, 2003), which has contributed to increased access to low-intensity psychosocial interventions, including computerised CBT (NICE, 2002; NICE, 2005). The concept of 'stepped care' advocated in the previous guideline has been embraced by many commissioners and providers in the NHS and is now being taken forward by the Improving Access to Psychological Therapies (IAPT) programme (Department of Health, 2007; IAPT, 2009). It is this later development, with £340 million of funding over 6 years along with 3,400 new psychological therapists, that will bring about the single biggest change in the provision of effective treatments for depression in primary and secondary care.

---

[10]For this guideline update, all sections of the 'Service-level and other interventions' chapter in the previous guideline were reviewed. The sections from the previous guideline on screening (now re-named case identification), organisational developments such as collaborative care, stepped care, enhanced care and integrated care (now re-named enhanced care), non-statutory support and crisis resolution and home treatment teams remain in this chapter. The updated reviews for guided self-help, computerised CBT and exercise (now termed physical activity programmes) have been moved to Chapter 7, and the updated review for ECT can be found in Chapter 12.

This chapter focuses on two main issues: the identification of depression in primary and secondary care and the range of different service delivery mechanisms that have emerged in recent years. These approaches to service delivery fall into three main groups, including systematic approaches for organising care and making available appropriate treatment choices, the development of new and existing staff roles in primary care and the introduction of mental health specialists into primary care.

5.2 THE IDENTIFICATION OF DEPRESSION IN PRIMARY CARE AND COMMUNITY SETTINGS

5.2.1 Introduction

As stated above the accurate identification of depression is an essential first step in the management of people with depression. This includes both people who have sought treatment because of depressive symptoms and those being treated for other conditions, including physical health problems. The identification of depression in adults with a chronic physical health problem is covered in a related NICE guideline (NICE, 2009c). This guideline focuses on identifying depression in primary care and community settings.

Studies indicate that up to 50% of people with depression are not recognised when they attend primary care (Williams *et al.*, 1995), a view which is supported by a recent meta-analysis of 37 studies of GPs' unassisted ability to detect depression (Mitchell *et al.*, 2009). Mitchell and colleagues (2009) suggest that GPs are able to rule out depression in most people who are not depressed with reasonable accuracy but may have difficulty diagnosing depression in all true cases. However, as noted below, this under-recognition of depression may be focused more on mild depression than on moderate or severe depression (Kessler *et al.*, 2003).

5.2.2 Identifying depression – a primary care perspective

For over 40 years, it has been suggested that GPs fail to accurately diagnose depression (Goldberg & Huxley, 1992; Kessler *et al.*, 2002). As stated above, some studies suggest that clinically important depression (moderate to severe depressive illness) is detected by GPs at later consultations by virtue of the longitudinal patient–doctor relationship and that its milder forms, which may recover spontaneously, go undetected and untreated (Thompson *et al.*, 2000; Kessler *et al.*, 2002). However, even this suggests that non-clinically important depression may go undetected initially. More recent studies suggest that the probability of prescribing antidepressants in primary care is associated with the severity of the depression, although almost half of the people prescribed antidepressants were not depressed (Kendrick *et al.*, 2005). Other authors draw attention to the dangers of the erroneous diagnosis of depression in patients with a slight psychological malaise and few functional consequences that can lead to the risk of unnecessary and potentially dangerous medicalisation of distress

(Aragones *et al.*, 2006). Given the modest prevalence of depression in most primary care settings the number of false positive errors (people who are incorrectly identified as being at risk of depression) is larger than the number of false negatives (those falsely identified as not being at risk of developing depression). Further work is clearly needed to examine the subsequent outcome of those false positive and false negative diagnoses, and also to clarify the accuracy of GPs in diagnosing anxiety disorders, adjustment disorders and broadly defined distress.

Reasons for lack of recognition fall into four themes: factors related to the person with depression, and practitioner, organisational and societal factors.

5.2.3   Factors related to the person with depression

People may have difficulty in presenting their distress and discussing their concerns with their doctor, especially when they are uncertain that depression is a legitimate reason for seeing the doctor (Gask *et al.*, 2003). The MaGPIe Research Group (2005a, 2005b) suggests that the relationship is important, and that GPs are, in fact, effective at identifying mental health problems in patients they know; however some people believe that the GP is not the right person to talk to, or that such symptoms should not be discussed at all. Negative perceptions about the value of consulting a GP for mental distress may, at least in part, explain low rates of help-seeking among young adults, including those with severe distress (Biddle *et al.*, 2006). The person with depression may feel that they do not deserve to take up the doctor's time, or that it is not possible for doctors to listen to them and understand how they feel (Pollock & Grime, 2002; Gask *et al.*, 2003).

A number of other factors may also influence the identification of depression. Older adults, in particular, may complain less of depressed mood and instead somatise their depressive symptoms (Rabins, 1996). Physical comorbidity can also make the interpretation of depressive symptoms difficult. People may have beliefs that prevent them from seeking help for depression such as a fear of stigmatisation, or that antidepressant medication is addictive or they may misattribute symptoms of depression for 'old age', ill health or grief. Although depression is more frequent in women, differential reporting of symptoms may lead to depression being under-diagnosed in men. From the perspective of the person with depression, it has been suggested that contact with primary care may be of little significance when set against the magnitude of their other problems (Rogers *et al.*, 2001).

5.2.4   Practitioner factors

The construction of 'depression' as a clinical condition is contested amongst GPs (Chew-Graham *et al.*, 2000; May *et al.*, 2004; Pilgrim & Dowrick, 2006). They may be wary of opening a 'Pandora's box' in time-limited consultations and instead collude with the person with depression in what has been called 'therapeutic nihilism' (Burroughs *et al.*, 2006). In deprived areas, primary care physicians have been shown to view depression as a normal response to difficult circumstances, illnesses or life events (May *et al.*, 2004), and depression may be under-diagnosed because of dissatisfaction with the types of treatment that can be offered, especially a lack of availability of psychological interventions. Primary care practitioners may also lack the necessary consultation skills or confidence to correctly diagnose late-life depression.

5.2.5   Organisational factors

The trend in the UK for mental health services to be separate from mainstream medical services may disadvantage people with depression who may have difficulties in attending different sites and/or services for mental and physical disorders.

Organisational factors that inhibit the identification and disclosure of symptoms and problems, together with limited access to mental health services, add to professionals' reluctance to encourage patients to disclose their distress (Popay *et al.*, 2007; Chew-Graham *et al.*, 2008).

5.2.6   Societal factors

The barriers described are likely to be particularly difficult for the economically poor and minority populations who tend to have more health problems and are more disabled. The oft-described barrier of stigma has to be set against the arguments that depression is a social construction within which chronic distress or unhappiness are medicalised (Ellis, 1996; Pilgrim & Bentall, 1999) and the suggestion that chronic unhappiness is not 'treatable' in the normal curative or therapeutic sense. It is therefore important that the healthcare professional recognises and accepts their own reaction to people presenting with depression so that they can acknowledge and go on to diagnose depression, and then discuss a range of possible interventions.

5.2.7   Shifting the emphasis from screening to identification

The identification of people with a disease is often referred to as screening (and was the term used in the previous guideline). Screening has been defined as the systematic application of a test or enquiry to identify individuals at high risk of developing a specific disorder who may benefit from further investigation or preventative action (Peckham & Dezateux, 1998). Screening programmes detect people at risk of having the condition or at risk of developing the condition in the future. They do not establish a diagnosis but give some indication of any action that may be required, such as further diagnostic investigation, closer monitoring or even preventative action. Screening is not necessarily a benign process (Marteau, 1989). Since screening tools are never 100% accurate, people who are incorrectly identified as being at risk of developing a condition (false positives) can be subject to further possibly intrusive, harmful or inappropriate investigations, management or treatment. Those falsely identified as not being at risk of developing a condition (false negatives) will also suffer by not being given the further investigation they need.

Critics of routine screening for depression have advanced a number of arguments against it. These include the low positive predictive value of the instruments (that is, many patients who screen positive do not have depression), the lack of empirical evidence for benefit to patients, the expenditure of resources on patients who may gain little benefit (many patients who are detected by such an approach may be mildly depressed and recover with no formal intervention), and the diversion of resource away from more seriously depressed and known patients who may be inadequately treated as a result. These issues are well covered by Palmer and Coyne (2003) in their review of screening for depression in medical settings. Palmer and Coyne (2003) also go on to make a number of suggestions for improving recognition, including ensuring effective interventions for those identified, focusing on patients with previous histories of depression and people known to have a high risk of developing depression, such as those with a family history of the condition or chronic physical health problems with associated functional impairment. Others (for example, Pignone *et al.*, 2002; Macmillan *et al.*, 2005) have, however, recommended the use of screening of depression for the general adult population, but it should be noted that the systematic review of interventions conducted in support of the recommendations by these groups have included the need for follow-up interventions. The effectiveness of such interventions (for example, feedback to patients or case management) is considered below and the GDG felt it important to first address the value of case identification systems alone, before going on to consider the benefits of integrated systems.

Within the NHS, case identification of depression in people with some chronic conditions (for example, diabetes) is now part of routine clinical work for GPs as stipulated by the GMS Contract (Ellis, 1996). Evidence, however, suggests that such ultra-short screening instruments may fail to detect depression (Mallen & Peat, 2008). It has been suggested that using an additional question ('is this something with which you would like help?' [Arroll *et al.*, 2005]) may improve the specificity of the screening questions. Others, however, caution that the use of such screening instruments may encourage practitioners to take a reductionist, biomedical approach, diverting them from a broader bio-psychosocial approach to both diagnosing and managing depression (Dowrick, 2004).

5.2.8   Case identification

Introduction
The previous NICE guideline on depression, in addition to other NICE mental health guidelines, considered the case for general population screening for a number of mental health disorders and concluded that it should only be undertaken for specific high-risk populations where benefits outweigh the risks (for example, NICE, 2004b). These were people with a history of depression, significant physical illnesses causing disability, or other mental health problems, such as dementia.

Case identification and service delivery

A history of depression has been identified as a significant factor in future episodes. For example, a study of 425 primary care patients found that 85% of those who were depressed had had at least one previous episode (Coyne *et al.*, 1999). In fact, having a history of depression produced a positive predictive value (see below) roughly equal to that produced by using a depression case-finding instrument (Centre of Epidemiology Studies-Depression – CES-D) (0.25 compared with 0.28). This suggests that careful assessment of relevant instruments is required if a number currently in use appears to have no more predictive value than a history of depression. It should be noted that depression can frequently be comorbid with other mental health problems, including borderline personality disorder (for example, Zanarini *et al.*, 1998; Skodol *et al.*, 1999), and dementia (Ballard *et al.*, 1996).

The following sections review available case identification instruments.

Definition

Case identification instruments were defined in the review as validated psychometric measures that were used to identify people with depression. The review was limited to identification tools likely to be used in UK clinical practice, that is, the Beck Depression Inventory (BDI), Patient Health Questionnaire (PHQ), General Health Questionnaire (GHQ), Centre of Epidemiology Studies-Depression (CES-D), Geriatric Depression Scale (GDS), Hospital Anxiety and Depression Scale (HADS), Zung Self Rated Depression Scale and any one- or two-item measures. The identification tools were assessed in consultation (which included primary care and general medical services) and community populations. 'Gold standard' diagnoses were defined as DSM–IV or ICD–10 diagnosis of depression. Studies were sought that compared case identification with one of the above instruments with diagnosis of depression based on DSM–IV or ICD–10 criteria. Studies that did not clearly state the comparator to be DSM–IV or ICD–10, used a scale with greater than 28 items, or did not provide sufficient data to be extracted in the meta-analysis were excluded.

Summary statistics used to evaluate identification instruments

Sensitivity, specificity, positive predictive validity and negative predictive validity

The terms 'sensitivity' and 'specificity' are used in relation to identification methods discussed in this chapter.

The sensitivity of an instrument refers to the proportion of those with the condition who test positive. An instrument that detects a low percentage of cases will not be very helpful in determining the numbers of patients who should receive a known effective treatment, as many individuals who should receive the treatment will not do so. This would lead to an under-estimation of the prevalence of the disorder, contribute to inadequate care and make for poor planning and costing of the need for treatment. As the sensitivity of an instrument increases, the number of false negatives it detects will decrease.

The specificity of an instrument refers to the proportion of those who do not have the condition and test negative. This is important so that healthy people are not offered treatments they do not need. As the specificity of an instrument increases, the number of false positives will decrease.

To illustrate this, from a population in which the point prevalence rate of depression is 10% (that is, 10% of the population has depression at any one time), 1,000 people are given a test which has 90% sensitivity and 85% specificity. It is known that 100 people in this population have depression, but the test detects only 90 (true positives), leaving 10 undetected (false negatives). It is also known that 900 people do not have depression, and the test correctly identifies 765 of these (true negatives), but classifies 135 incorrectly as having depression (false positives). The positive predictive value of the test (the number correctly identified as having depression as a proportion of positive tests) is 40% (90/90+135), and the negative predictive value (the number correctly identified as not having depression as a proportion of negative tests) is 98% (765/765+10). Therefore, in this example, a positive test result is correct in only 40% of cases, while a negative result can be relied upon in 98% of cases.

The example above illustrates some of the main differences between positive predictive values and negative predictive values in comparison with sensitivity and specificity. For both positive and negative predictive values, prevalence explicitly forms part of their calculation (see Altman & Bland, 1994a). When the prevalence of a disorder is low in a population this is generally associated with a higher negative predictive value and a lower positive predictive value. Therefore although these statistics are concerned with issues probably more directly applicable to clinical practice (for example, the probability that a person with a positive test result actually has depression), they are largely dependent on the characteristics of the population sampled and cannot be universally applied (Altman & Bland, 1994a).

On the other hand, sensitivity and specificity do not necessarily depend on prevalence of depression (Altman & Bland, 1994b). For example, sensitivity is concerned with the performance of an identification test conditional on a person having depression. Therefore the higher false positives often associated with samples of low prevalence will not affect such estimates. The advantage of this approach is that sensitivity and specificity can be applied across populations (Altman & Bland, 1994b). However, the main disadvantage is that clinicians tend to find such estimates more difficult to interpret.

When describing the sensitivity and specificity of the different instruments, the GDG defined values above 0.9 as 'excellent', 0.8 to 0.9 as 'good', 0.5 to 0.7 as 'moderate', 0.3 to 0.5 as 'low', and less than 0.3 as 'poor'.

Receiver operator characteristic curves

The qualities of a particular tool are summarised in a receiver operator characteristic (ROC) curve, which plots sensitivity (expressed as a per cent) against (100-specificity) (Figure 4).

A test with perfect discrimination would have an ROC curve that passed through the top left hand corner; that is, it would have 100% specificity and pick up all true positives with no false positives. While this is never achieved in practice, the area under the curve (AUC) measures how close the tool gets to the theoretical ideal. A perfect test would have an AUC of 1, and a test with AUC above 0.5 is better than chance. As discussed above, because these measures are based on sensitivity and 100-specificity, theoretically these estimates are not affected by prevalence.

Figure 4: Receiver operator characteristic curve

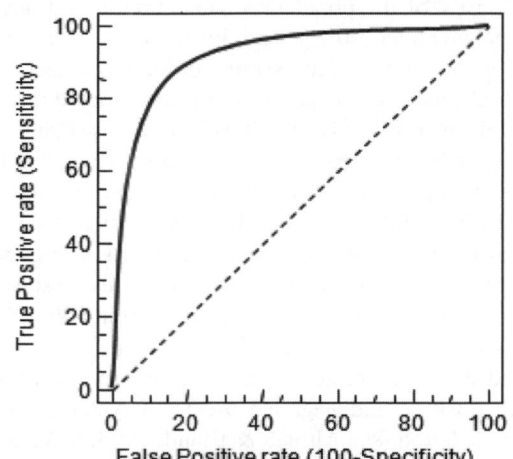

Negative and positive likelihood ratios
Negative (LR−) and positive (LR+) likelihood ratios are thought not to be dependent on prevalence. LR− is calculated by sensitivity/1-specificity and LR+ is 1-sensitivity/specificity. A value of LR+ >5 and LR− <0.3 suggests the test is relatively accurate (Fischer *et al.*, 2003).

Diagnostic odds ratios
The diagnostic odds ratio is LR+/LR−; a value of 20 or greater suggests a good level of accuracy (Fischer *et al.*, 2003).

Databases searched and inclusion/exclusion criteria
The review team conducted a new systematic search for cross-sectional studies to assess tools for identifying depression. This was undertaken as a joint review for this guideline and the guideline for depression in adults with a chronic physical health problem (NICE, 2009c). Information about the databases searched and the inclusion/exclusion criteria used can be found in Table 6. Details of the search strings used are in Appendix 8.

Studies considered
A total of 126 studies met the eligibility criteria of the review; 54 studies were conducted in consultation samples, 45 were on people with chronic physical health problems[11] and 50 were on older people (over 65 years of age). Of these studies, 16

---

[11]Data for the population with chronic physical health problems and information about the included studies is presented in the related guideline, *Depression in Adults with a Chronic Physical Health Problem* (NCCMH, 2010).

Table 6: Databases searched and inclusion/exclusion criteria for the effectiveness of case identification instruments

Electronic databases	MEDLINE, EMBASE, PsycINFO, Cochrane Library
Date searched	Database inception to February 2009
Study design	Cross-sectional studies
Patient population	People in primary care, community, and general hospital settings
Instruments	BDI, PHQ, GHQ, CES-D, GDS, HADS, Zung Self Rated Depression Scale, and any one- or two-item measures of depression
Outcomes	Sensitivity, specificity, AUC, diagnostic odds ratio, positive likelihood, negative likelihood

were on the PHQ-9, five on the PHQ-2, six on the 'Whooley questions', 19 on the BDI, nine on the BDI – short form, two on the GHQ-28, 12 on the GHQ-12, 17 on the CES-D, 20 on the GDS, 11 on the GDS-15, 16 on HADS-D, five on HADS-total and seven on one-item measures (see Appendix 20 for further details).

In addition, 251 studies were excluded from the analysis. The most common reason for exclusion was a lack of a gold standard (DSM/ICD) comparator (see Appendix 20 for further details).

Evaluating identification tools for depression
A bivariate diagnostic accuracy meta-analysis was conducted using Stata 10 with the Module for Meta-analytical Integration of Diagnostic Test Accuracy Studies (MIDAS) (Dwamena, 2007) commands in order to obtain pooled estimates of sensitivity, specificity, likelihood ratios and diagnostic odds ratio (for further details, see Chapter 3). To maximise the available data, the most consistently reported and recommended cut-off points for each of the scales were extracted (see Table 7).

Heterogeneity is usually much greater in meta-analyses of diagnostic accuracy studies compared with RCTs (Gilbody *et al.*, 2007; Cochrane Collaboration, 2008). Therefore, a higher threshold for acceptable heterogeneity in such meta-analyses is required. However when pooling studies resulted in $I^2 > 90\%$, meta-analyses were not conducted.

Table 8 summarises the results of the meta-analysis in terms of pooled sensitivity, specificity, positive likelihood ratios, negative likelihood ratios, and diagnostic odds ratios. Additional subgroup analyses were conducted for older adults.

Patient Health Questionnaire
The PHQ developed out of the more detailed Primary Care Evaluation of Mental Disorders (PRIME-MD) (Spitzer *et al.*, 1994). There are three main instruments that

Table 7: Cut off points used (if available) for each of the identification tools (adapted from Pignone *et al.*, 2002; Gilbody *et al.*, 2007)

Scale	Cut off points
BDI 21 items 13 items Primary care version	 13 4 4
PHQ 9 items 2 items 2 items (Whooley version)	 10 3 1
GHQ 28 items 12 items	 5 3
HADS-D	8–10 mild, 11–14 moderate, 15+ severe
CES-D	16
GDS 30 items 15 items 5 items	 10 5 ?
Zung	50 mild, 60 moderate, 70 severe

have been developed from this scale; the PHQ-9 (Spitzer *et al.*, 1999), PHQ-2 (Kroenke *et al.*, 2003) and the 'Whooley questions' (Whooley *et al.*, 1997).

The PHQ-9 has nine items and has a cut-off of 10. Although the PHQ-2 and the Whooley questions use the same two items, the difference is that while the PHQ-2 follows the scoring format of the PHQ-9 (Likert scales), the Whooley version dichotomises the questions (yes/no) and has a cut-off of 1 compared with 3 for the PHQ-2.

For the PHQ-9 in consultation samples (people in primary care or general medical settings) there was relatively high heterogeneity (although of a similar level to most other scales) ($I^2 = 74.04\%$). The PHQ-9 was found to have good sensitivity (0.82, 95% CI, 0.77, 0.86) and specificity (0.83, 95% CI, 0.76, 0.88).

The PHQ-2 could not be meta-analysed as there was very high heterogeneity. The Whooley questions analysis included studies both on consultation and chronic physically ill samples as there were too few studies to break down by population. This scale was found to have high sensitivity (0.95, 95% CI, 0.91, 0.97) but lower specificity (0.66, 95% CI, 0.55, 0.76). A single study by Arroll and colleagues

Table 8: Evidence summary of depression identification instruments in primary care, people with a chronic physical health problem, and older populations

Population and instrument	Sensitivity	Specificity	Likelihood ratio+	Likelihood ratio−	Diagnostic odds ratio	AUC
PHQ-9 Consultation samples: 11 studies	0.82 (0.77, 0.86)	0.83 (0.76, 0.88)	4.70 (3.29, 6.72)	0.22 (0.17, 0.29)	21.38 (11.87, 38.52)	0.88 (0.85, 0.91)
Whooley*: All populations: 7 studies	0.95 (0.91, 0.97)	0.66 (0.55, 0.76)	2.82 (2.01, 3.96)	0.08 (0.04, 0.15)	36.25 (14.89, 88.24)	0.94 (0.92, 0.96)
BDI Consultation samples: 4 studies	0.85 (0.79, 0.90)	0.83 (0.70, 0.91)	5.14 (2.83, 9.32)	0.18 (0.12, 0.24)	29.29 (15.10, 56.79)	0.90 (0.87, 0.92)
BDI-non somatic items Consultation sample: 5 studies	0.82 (0.57, 0.94)	0.73 (0.61, 0.83)	3.02 (1.87, 4.90)	0.25 (0.09, 0.69)	11.92 (3.02, 47.04)	0.83 (0.79, 0.86)
CES-D Consultation sample: 8 studies	0.84 (0.78, 0.89)	0.74 (0.65, 0.81)	3.19 (2.41, 4.22)	0.21 (0.15, 0.29)	15.02 (9.38, 24.05)	0.87 (0.84, 0.90)
Older adults: 5 studies	0.81 (0.74, 0.87)	0.79 (0.67, 0.88)	3.82 (2.35, 6.22)	0.24 (0.17, 0.33)	15.95 (8.05, 31.60)	0.83 (0.80, 0.86)
GDS-15 Consultation sample: 11 studies	0.87 (0.80, 0.91)	0.75 (0.69, 0.80)	3.40 (2.73, 4.24)	0.18 (0.12, 0.27)	18.98 (10.85, 33.20)	0.86 (0.83, 0.89)
1-item Consultation sample: 6 studies	0.84 (0.78, 0.89)	0.65 (0.55, 0.73)	2.38 (1.81, 3.13)	0.25 (0.17, 0.36)	9.67 (5.35, 17.46)	0.85 (0.82, 0.88)

*It was not possible to conduct separate subgroup analyses for consultation and chronic physical illness samples due to lack of studies for the Zung and Whooley questions.

(2005) added a further question to the two in the PHQ-2, asking the patient if they wanted help with their depression. This increased specificity and the GDG considered the findings of the study and the adoption of the third question, but as there was only a single study showing the effect of this approach the GDG decided not to adopt it.

It was not possible to a conduct meta-analysis on the effects of any of the PHQ scales or the Whooley questions on older adults because of a lack of data (one study each on the PHQ-9, PHQ-2 and Whooley questions).

Beck Depression Inventory

Beck originally developed the BDI in the 1960s (Beck *et al.*, 1961) and subsequently updated the original 21-item version (Beck *et al.*, 1979; Beck *et al.*, 1996). This scale has been used widely as a depression outcome measure and is also used to provide data on the severity of depression; commonly, 13 is used a cut-off in identification studies.

In addition, the cognitive–affective subscale of the BDI has often been used to identify depression. Furthermore, the BDI-fast screen has been specifically developed for use in primary care (Beck *et al.*, 1997).

For the 21-item BDI there was high heterogeneity for consultation samples ($I^2 = 88.61\%$). The BDI appeared to perform relatively well in terms of sensitivity (0.85, 95% CI, 0.79, 0.90) and specificity (0.83, 95% CI, 0.70, 0.91). This was also consistent with the diagnostic odds ratio (29.29, 95% CI, 15.103, 56.79). However, this is based on only four studies so it is difficult to draw firm conclusions. Subgroup analyses on older adults were also not possible as there were only two studies for this population.

Beck Depression Inventory – non-somatic items

Data from BDI fast-screen (Beck *et al.*, 2000) and BDI short-form (Beck *et al.*, 1974, 1996) were combined to assess the impact of removing somatic items as data from both scales were relatively sparse. There was sufficient, although relatively low, consistency between studies to assess these scales (BDI: non-somatic) in consultation ($I^2 = 75.71\%$) populations. There was high sensitivity (0.82, 95% CI, 0.57, 0.94) but lower specificity (0.73, 95% CI, 0.61, 0.83). A meta-analysis was not possible for older adults as there were only two studies.

General Health Questionnaire

The GHQ (Goldberg & Williams, 1991) was developed as a general measure of psychiatric distress and measures a variety of constructs such as depression and anxiety. The main versions used for identification purposes are the GHQ-28 (cut-off of 5) and GHQ-12 (cut-off of 3).

There were only two trials of the GHQ-28, therefore meta-analysis was not conducted. In addition, while there were more studies on the GHQ-12 there was very high heterogeneity ($I^2 > 90\%$) for studies on consultation populations, therefore these studies were also not meta-analysed. Moreover, a meta-analysis specifically for older adults was not possible due to there being only two studies.

Hospital Anxiety and Depression Scale

The HADS (Zigmond & Snaith, 1983) is a measure of depression and anxiety developed for people with physical health problems. The depression subscale has seven items and the cut-off is 8 to 10 points.

A total of 21 studies were included in the review, however meta-analysis could not be conducted due to very high heterogeneity ($I^2 > 90\%$) for all subgroups including consultation populations and older adults.

Center for Epidemiological Studies Depression Scale

The CES-D (Radloff, 1977) has 20 items and the cut-off is 16. This measure is also relatively commonly used as an outcome measure. There are various short forms of the CES-D including an eight-, ten- and 11-item scale.

There was high heterogeneity in the consultation ($I^2 = 84.63\%$) sample. For the older adult population, Haringsma and colleagues (2004) was removed from the analysis resulting in acceptable heterogeneity ($I^2 = 61.09\%$).

For consultation samples sensitivity was high (0.84, 95% CI, 0.78, 0.89) but specificity was lower (0.74, 95% CI, 0.65, 0.81). For older adults, there was relatively low sensitivity (0.81, 95% CI, 0.74, 0.87) and higher specificity (0.79, 95% CI, 0.67, 0.87).

Geriatric Depression Scale

The GDS was developed to assess depression in older people. The original 30-item scale (cut-off of 10 points) was developed by Yesavage and colleagues (1983) and more recently a 15-item (cut-off of 5 points) version has been validated.

Despite the large number of studies (18 studies), there was very high heterogeneity ($I^2 > 90\%$) for the GDS, therefore no meta-analyses could be conducted. However, it was possible to analyse studies on the GDS-15.

In the consultation population there was higher sensitivity (0.87, 95% CI, 0.80, 0.91) but specificity was relatively low (0.75, 95% CI, 0.69, 0.80). The diagnostic odds ratio was just below 20 (18.98, 95% CI, 10.85, 33.20). Heterogeneity was relatively acceptable ($I^2 = 70.96\%$).

No subgroup analyses for older people were conducted as all participants were over 65 years of age.

Zung Self-Rating Depression Scale

The self-rating depression scale was developed by Zung (Zung, 1965) and has been revised (Guy, 1976). This has 20 items where a cut-off of 50 is typically used. It is sometimes used as an outcome measure as well. There were insufficient studies to conduct a meta-analysis.

One-item measures

Five studies were found to assess a one-item measure in consultation samples. There was a relatively good sensitivity (0.84, 95% CI, 0.78, 0.89) but very low specificity (0.65, 95% CI, 0.55, 0.73). The diagnostic odds ratio indicated a lack of accuracy

(9.67, 95% CI, 5.35, 17.46). It was not possible to conduct a subgroup analysis of older adults as there were only two studies.

Comparing validity coefficients for case identification tools in older adults
The impact of old age and residing in a nursing home on the validity coefficients of the case identification tools reviewed above were assessed through meta-regression (see Table 9). Because of a lack of data the PHQ-2, Whooley, Zung, and one-item measures were not included in the analysis.

The GDS and GDS-15 were almost always used for older adults, therefore the validity of these measures in older adults is already accounted for in the previous analysis. However, further analyses were conducted to assess the validity of these measures in nursing home populations.

Table 9: Meta-regressions assessing the impact of differences within populations of studies

Population and instrument	Beta-coefficient	$I^2(\%)$	p-value
PHQ-9 Comparing over 65s with under 65s	Sensitivity = 1.23 Specificity = 1.84	Joint $I^2 = 0$	0.65 0.73 0.83
BDI Comparing over 65s with under 65s	Sensitivity = 1.58 Specificity = 0.74	Joint $I^2 = 0$	0.34 0.79 0.65
BDI-non somatic items Comparing over 65s with under 65s	Sensitivity = 1.58 Specificity = 2.12	Joint $I^2 = 58.64$	0.80 0.02 0.09
CES-D Comparing over 65s with under 65s	Sensitivity = 1.23 Specificity = 1.61	Joint $I^2 = 43.30$	0.09 0.18 0.17
GDS Comparing nursing home with non-nursing home	Sensitivity = 1.54 Specificity = 1.13	Joint $I^2 = 0$	0.85 0.65 0.80
GDS-15 Comparing nursing home with non-nursing home	Sensitivity = 2.14 Specificity = 0.91	Joint $I^2 = 0$	0.36 0.34 0.44
GHQ-12 Comparing over 65s with under 65s	Sensitivity = 0.43 Specificity = 1.45	Joint $I^2 = 11.28$	0.14 0.33 0.32

Older adults

There was some evidence that the BDI versions with no somatic items (p = 0.02) were associated with improved specificity in older adults compared with people under 65 years. There was a trend towards reduction in sensitivity for the CES-D (p = 0.09) in older adults compared with people under 65 years. For all other scales there were no statistically significant differences. However, there was often a lack of power in most studies because only a small number of studies on older adults were found for most scales.

People in nursing homes

Only the GDS and GDS-15 provided sufficient data on people in nursing homes. There appeared to be limited differences in validity when assessing people either in nursing homes or in the community for both scales.

5.2.9   Case identification in black and minority ethnic populations

Introduction

Culture and ethnicity are known to influence both the prevalence and incidence of mental illnesses, including common mental disorders such as depression (Bhui *et al.*, 2001). For example, Shaw and colleagues (1999) indicated that women from black and minority ethnic groups had an increased incidence of common mental disorders including both depression and anxiety. Such findings cannot wholly be explained by differences in factors such as urbanicity, socioeconomic status and perceptions of disadvantage (Bhugra & Cochrane, 2001; Weich *et al.*, 2004). Furthermore, culture is known to exert an influence on the presentation and subjective experience of illness. What a person perceives as an illness and whom they seek for treatment are all affected by their culture and ethnicity. With regard to depression, a number of findings have indicated both ethnic and cultural variations in the subjective experience and initial presentation of the illness. For example, Commander and colleagues (1997) are among researchers who suggest that 'Asians', including Indian, Bangladeshi and Pakistani people, are more likely to present to their GP with physical manifestations, and do so more frequently than their white counterparts. However, both Wilson and MacCarthy (1994) and Williams and Hunt (1997) have indicated that despite this increased GP contact, and even when a psychological problem is present, GPs are less likely to detect depression and more likely to diagnose 'Asians' with a physical disorder.

There is an increasing evidence base to suggest that the reduced identification of depression in different ethnic and cultural groups may be one barrier to receiving appropriate treatment, including both psychological and pharmacological interventions. For example, research has suggested that across mental disorders, particular ethnic groups are often under-represented in primary care services (Bhui *et al.*, 2003; Department of Health, 2008b), whereas a Healthcare Commission survey highlighted how both Asian and black/black British people were less likely to be offered 'talking therapies' (Department of Health, 2008b).

Case identification and service delivery

Despite an increased awareness that different cultural and ethnic factors may influence the presentation of depression, the majority of case identification tools used in routine clinical practice were originally created and validated in white populations (Husain *et al.*, 2007). Owing to the above evidence indicating ethnic and cultural variations in the presentation and subjective experience of illness, one proposed method to improve the identification of depression in black and minority ethnic participants is to assess the validity of ethnic-specific screening tools. Such tools, most of which are still early in their development, aim to incorporate specific cultural idioms and descriptions commonly reported by people from a particular ethnic or cultural group.

Definition and aim of topic of review
The review considered any ethnic-specific case identification instruments aimed at detecting depression in black and minority ethnic populations. This included new identification tools designed for different cultural and ethnic groups, and also existing scales modified and tailored towards the specific needs of particular black and minority ethnic groups. Although the GDG was aware of papers from outside the UK (most notably from the US), the decision was made to only include UK studies. As discussed above, the presentation and subjective experience of depression is known to be influenced by cultural and ethnic factors; therefore, it was felt that findings from non-UK ethnic minority populations would not be generalisable because of the ethnic and cultural differences among the populations studied. The review also assessed the validity of established depression case identification tools for different black and minority ethnic populations within the UK[12].

Databases searched and inclusion/exclusion criteria
The review team conducted a new systematic search for cross-sectional studies aiming to assess tools for identifying depression. This was undertaken as a joint review for this guideline and the guideline for depression in adults with a chronic physical health problem (NCCMH, 2010). Information about the databases searched and the inclusion/exclusion criteria used are presented in Table 10. Details of the search strings used are in Appendix 8.

Studies considered
A total of four studies met the eligibility criteria of the review. All four papers were conducted within the community or primary care. One included study compared the Amritsar Depression Inventory (ADI) with the GHQ-12, and two studies compared the Caribbean Culture-Specific Screen for emotional disorders (CCSS) with the GDS. Only one study assessed the validity of an established scale, the Personal Health Questionnaire, in a UK black and minority ethnic population, namely people of Pakistani family origin.

---

[12]Papers assessing the validity of established scales in UK black and minority ethnic populations were required to have a 'gold standard' diagnosis defined as DSM–IV or ICD–10 diagnosis of depression.

Table 10: Databases searched and inclusion/exclusion criteria for clinical effectiveness of psychological interventions

Electronic databases	MEDLINE, EMBASE, PsycINFO, Cochrane Library
Date searched	Database inception to February 2009
Study design	Cross-sectional studies
Patient population	People in primary care, community, and general hospital settings from black and minority ethnic groups
Instruments	1. Any ethnic-specific depression case identification instrument 2. Any cultural or ethnically adapted version of the following validated case identification instruments: BDI, PHQ, GHQ, CES-D, GDS, HADS, Zung Self Rated Depression Scale, and any one- or two-item measures of depression 3. Any of the above validated identification tools, assessed in a UK black and minority ethnic population
Outcomes	Sensitivity, specificity, AUC, diagnostic odds ratio, positive likelihood, negative likelihood

In addition, ten studies were excluded from the analysis. The most common reason for exclusion was that the paper was a non-UK based study/population or that the paper presented no usable evaluation of a screening tool.

Evaluating identification tools for depression in black and minority ethnic populations
Because of both the paucity of data on ethnic specific scales in the UK and differences in the populations and instruments investigated, it was not possible to conduct a meta-analysis of the included studies. Instead the findings from the included studies are summarised in a narrative review below.

Amritsar Depression Inventory
The ADI is a culturally specific instrument developed in the Punjab in India and is aimed at detecting depression in the Punjabi population of the Indian subcontinent (Singh *et al.*, 1974). The 30-item dichotomous (yes/no) questionnaire was developed on the basis of 50 statements commonly used by Punjabi people with depression. The screen development process also utilised frequently used 'illness statements' and common descriptions of signs and symptoms of depression prevalent in the psychiatric literature.

Using the ADI and the GHQ-12, Bhui and colleagues (2000) screened both Punjabi and white English attendees of five primary care practices in South London. Throughout the study, a cultural screen assessing self-affirmed cultural origin was applied to detect both Punjabi and white English participants. To overcome any additional barriers because of language, the screening tools were administered in English, Punjabi or a combination of the two, depending on the preference of the participant. A two-phase screening protocol was applied in which all 'probable cases', for example, those scoring ≥2 on the GHQ or ≥5 on the ADI, and one third of 'probable non-cases' proceeded to a second interview in which the Clinical Interview Schedule-Revised (CIS-R) was administered by a bilingual psychiatrist.

Results of the validity coefficients and ROC curve analysis using the standard CIS-R thresholds for depression indicated that while the GHQ-12 performed well across both groups, culture had an impact on the validity coefficient of the ADI. In particular, although performing in line with the GHQ-12 for the white English participants, the ADI performed worse in detecting depression in the Punjabi participants. Results indicated that the ADI was no better than chance in identifying cases of depression, particularly for Punjabis who had been resident in the UK for more than 30 years. One additional finding of interest was that the optimal cut-off for the ADI was higher for the Punjabi participants compared with their white English counterparts, although this finding was not sustained for the GHQ-12 in which the same cut-off was optimal for both groups. Analysis of the individual items of both the GHQ-12 and the ADI failed to indicate any specific items that were strongly predictive of depression caseness in either cultural group.

Caribbean Culture-Specific Screen for emotional distress

The CCSS (Abas, 1996) is a 13-item dichotomous (yes/no) culture-specific screen which was developed through a process of generating locally-derived classifications of mental disorders in Caribbean people and gathering commonly used terms for emotional distress. The majority of participants interviewed in the piloting stages of the screen were from Jamaica with a number of participants identifying themselves as from other Caribbean countries including Guyana, Barbados, Trinidad and Grenada.

Two papers assessed the validity of the CCSS screen in older African–Caribbean participants living in two different locations in the UK, namely South London and Manchester. Both papers compared the validity of the CCSS to the GDS and utilised the Geriatric Mental State-Automated Geriatric Examination for Computer Assisted Taxonomy (GMS-AGECAT) as a gold standard for case identification.

The sample in Abas and colleagues (1998) consisted of consecutive African-Caribbean primary care users aged over 60, and included both clinic attendees and those receiving home visits from primary care teams. Participants were firstly administered the CCSS, GDS-15 and the Mini-Mental State Examination (MMSE). Responders were categorised as high scorers if they scored ≥4 on either measure, and low scorers if they attained less than 4 on both screens. A random sample of 80% of the high scorers and 20% of the low scorers was selected to attend a further interview. During this second stage interview, the GMS-AGECAT and a culturally-specific diagnostic interview, which was informed through a process of consultation with African–Caribbean religious healers/ministers, were administered to the selected participants.

Rait and colleagues (1999) included a community sample of African–Caribbean people aged 60 years and over. Registers for general practices with a high-proportion of African–Caribbeans were used to identify members of the community. In stage one, letters were sent to potential participants, with those who consented to take part in the study subsequently interviewed in their homes. All included participants were interviewed by one of two interviewers of a similar cultural background. During this stage, three depression screens were applied, namely the GDS-15, CCSS and the Brief Assessment Schedule Depression Cards (BASDEC). The second stage of the study involved the home administration of the GMS-AGECAT, used as a diagnostic 'gold standard' for the detection of depression.

The ROC curve analyses for the papers indicated that both the GDS and the CCSS performed well in the populations, with a high level of sensitivity and specificity when using the GMS-AGECAT as a gold standard for diagnosis. In both papers, the culturally-specific CCSS did not outperform the GDS. In the Abas and colleagues' (1998) paper it was demonstrated that at a certain cut-off the GDS appeared to perform better than the CCSS, although the authors noted that the small sample size prevented any meaningful test of statistical significance. Because it was noted that considerable variation may exist among people of Caribbean origin from different islands, for example, Jamaica, Trinidad and so on, the results of Rait and colleagues' (1999) paper were presented for the sample as a whole and for a subgroup of Jamaican people who constituted the majority of participants. Although slight variation existed between the two analyses, the results were similar, with the same optimal cut-off occurring in both analyses.

One important feature of the Rait and colleagues' (1999) study was that the authors sought advice from a panel of community resident African–Caribbeans regarding the acceptability of the GDS. The content of the screens was deemed acceptable, and no suggestions for changes were made. Rait and colleagues (1999) argue that the success of case identification measures may be more dependent on the way in which the screen is delivered, for example, the cultural competence of staff and delivering the screen in a culturally sensitive way, rather than the content *per se*. This conclusion was supported by Abas and colleagues (1998) who found that a proportion of participants were more likely to discuss and disclose information during the culturally sensitive diagnostic interview, when compared with the standard GMS-AGECAT. Consequently, both papers have suggested that routine clinical screens may be appropriate for black and minority ethnic participants, particularly when delivered in a culturally sensitive way.

Personal Health Questionnaire
Husain and colleagues (2007) assessed the validity of the Personal Health Questionnaire in Pakistani people who were resident in the UK. The authors noted that, unlike many screening instruments, the Personal Health Questionnaire contains no 'difficult culture specific idioms', thus making translations into other languages possible. In the present study, the Personal Health Questionnaire was translated and back-translated into Urdu, the main language of immigrants from Pakistan, with group discussion utilised to reach a single consensus.

Case identification and service delivery

Consecutive primary care attendees of Pakistani family origin aged 16 to 64 years were included in the sample. Eligible participants were identified through either their name and/or language or via direct questioning. As with the other screening studies, a two stage process was employed. All eligible participants first completed the Personal Health Questionnaire in either English or Urdu, depending on patient preference, with a research psychiatrist administering the screen in the case of illiteracy. In the second stage of the study, all participants were interviewed in either their home or within the primary care practice. A psychiatrist administered the Psychiatric Assessment Schedule, a semi-structured interview resulting in an ICD diagnosis, in either Urdu or English dependent on preference.

Results of the ROC curve analysis indicated that the recommended cut off score of ≥7 produced a sensitivity of 70.4% and a specificity of 89.3%, with a positive predictive value of 82.6 and a negative predictive value of 80.6. The high sensitivity and specificity at the recommended cut-off suggested that the Personal Health Questionnaire is able to detect depression in people of Pakistani family origin when administered in either English or Urdu. Furthermore, the authors noted that participants in this study and in a study conducted in Pakistan (Husain *et al.*, 2000) did not experience any difficulties in understanding and answering the screening questions.

Limitations with the evidence base

It must be noted that a number of potential limitations exist in relation to the above studies. One caveat is the lack of an established gold standard for the diagnosis of depression in people from black and minority ethnic groups. Only one paper used a culturally-sensitive diagnostic tool as a measure of caseness (Abas *et al.*, 1998). The remaining three papers compared the screens with long-standing measures predominantly based on the DSM and ICD–10 classification systems. It is argued that these measures may not be culturally specific and sensitive to cultural differences, but are instead based on ethnocentric ideas of mental illness (Bhui *et al.*, 2000). Consequently, any culturally sensitive measure may not be expected to have a high sensitivity and specificity for caseness when compared with these diagnostic measures. Further research into this area is therefore required to answer such questions.

A further caveat to consider is that three of the four studies that were included assessed consecutive primary care attendees, who may or may not be wholly representative of ethnic minorities, particularly those who experience barriers to accessing and engaging with primary care services. However, the findings of one paper in which a community sample was recruited were consistent with the results of the primary care studies, suggesting the findings may be robust for each particular ethnic group under investigation.

5.2.10 Clinical summary for both reviews

There was very high heterogeneity found for almost all identification tools, which is an important limitation of the reviews. Scales varied a great deal in terms of targeted populations, number of items and scoring systems. When compared with the Whooley questions, other scales such as the PHQ-9 and GDS-15 had better specificity but not as much sensitivity (although they still met the criteria for high sensitivity).

There were also planned subgroup analyses conducted for older adults, which included scales specifically targeted at this population (for example, the GDS and GDS-15) as well as all other measures reviewed. The GDS-15 appeared to be relatively effective in consultation populations. However, the large number of studies on the 30-item GDS could not be meta-analysed as there was very high heterogeneity. There were fewer studies on the CES-D, but the available data suggested a slightly (although not statistically significant) reduced sensitivity compared with consultation populations as a whole. There were studies that targeted older adults for all of the other scales reviewed; however, the number of studies was too small to conduct meta-analyses for any of these measures.

There was a paucity of data concerning ethnic-specific identification tools, with limited data suggesting that the scales, which may be in their developmental infancy, failed to detect depression in different ethnic and cultural groups. In all studies, validated and well researched measures such as the GHQ-12 outperformed the ethnic-specific scales in terms of both sensitivity and specificity. Furthermore, in the case of the Personal Health Questionnaire, this was validated in a particular black and minority ethnic group, namely Pakistani people resident in the UK.

5.2.11   Health economic evidence and considerations

No evidence on the cost effectiveness of case identification tools for depression in primary care and community settings was identified by the systematic search of the economic literature. Details on the methods used for the systematic search of the economic literature are described in Chapter 3, Section 3.6.1.

5.2.12   From evidence to recommendations

The GDG noted the different nature of the scales contained in the review and their psychometric properties, as well as the possible benefit of a two-stage process of identification and diagnosis.

The first stage of case identification would require using a highly sensitive instrument that could be used in routine clinical practice with limited training and implementation difficulties. The data supported the use of the Whooley questions and, given that this measure is already in current use in primary care, the GDG concluded that in the first stage of case identification the Whooley questions remained an appropriate tool for depression. However, given the lack of specificity found with the Whooley questions it was the view of the GDG that people with a positive response would benefit from a more detailed clinical assessment, which may include a more detailed instrument possessing better overall psychometric properties. The data on case-finding instruments in black and minority ethnic groups did not identify any specific measures that in the opinion of the GDG improved upon the results obtained with the Whooley questions, and therefore no specific black and minority ethnic recommendations on case finding tools are made. However, the need for cultural competence of staff in assessments was noted in the review of case-finding instruments in black and minority ethnic groups, and this is reflected in the recommendations. In addition, in performing a more comprehensive mental health assessment, as recommended in the previous guideline, the need to move beyond simple symptom counts was noted, so the recommendation from the previous guideline has been amended. This guideline update also makes recommendations for people with depression and learning disabilities or acquired cognitive impairments because it is likely that depression, which is 'relatively common' (Prasher, 1999) in this population, will be under-diagnosed, particularly if they have autism, a learning disability, established aggressive, self-harming or over-active behaviours or comorbid physical health problems such as epilepsy, diabetes or heart disease (Prasher, 1999; Mind, 2007). Other recommendations from the previous guideline remain essentially the same.

5.2.13 Recommendations

5.2.13.1 Be alert to possible depression (particularly in people with a past history of depression or a chronic physical health problem with associated functional impairment) and consider asking people who may have depression two questions, specifically:
- During the last month, have you often been bothered by feeling down, depressed or hopeless?
- During the last month, have you often been bothered by having little interest or pleasure in doing things?

5.2.13.2 If a person answers 'yes' to either of the depression identification questions (see 5.2.13.1) but the practitioner is not competent to perform a mental health assessment, they should refer the person to an appropriate professional. If this professional is not the person's GP, inform the GP of the referral.

5.2.13.3 If a person answers 'yes' to either of the depression identification questions (see 5.2.13.1), a practitioner who is competent to perform a mental health assessment should review the person's mental state and associated functional, interpersonal and social difficulties.

5.2.13.4 When assessing a person with suspected depression, consider using a validated measure (for example, for symptoms, functions and/or disability) to inform and evaluate treatment.

5.2.13.5 For people with significant language or communication difficulties, for example people with sensory impairments or a learning disability, consider using the Distress Thermometer[13] and/or asking a family member or carer

---

[13]The Distress Thermometer is a single-item question screen that will identify distress coming from any source. The person places a mark on the scale answering: 'How distressed have you been during the past week on a scale of 0 to 10?' Scores of 4 or more indicate a significant level of distress that should be investigated further (Roth *et al.*, 1998).

about the person's symptoms to identify possible depression. If a significant level of distress is identified, investigate further.

5.2.13.6 When assessing a person who may have depression, conduct a comprehensive assessment that does not rely simply on a symptom count. Take into account both the degree of functional impairment and/or disability associated with the possible depression and the duration of the episode.

5.2.13.7 In addition to assessing symptoms and associated functional impairment, consider how the following factors may have affected the development, course and severity of a person's depression:

- any history of depression and comorbid mental health or physical disorders
- any past history of mood elevation (to determine if the depression may be part of bipolar disorder[14])
- any past experience of, and response to, treatments
- the quality of interpersonal relationships
- living conditions and social isolation.

Learning disabilities

5.2.13.8 When assessing a person with suspected depression, be aware of any learning disabilities or acquired cognitive impairments and, if necessary, consider consulting with a relevant specialist when developing treatment plans and strategies.

5.2.13.9 When providing interventions for people with a learning disability or acquired cognitive impairment who have a diagnosis of depression:

- where possible, provide the same interventions as for other people with depression
- if necessary, adjust the method of delivery or duration of the intervention to take account of the disability or impairment.

Depression with anxiety

5.2.13.10 When depression is accompanied by symptoms of anxiety, the first priority should usually be to treat the depression. When the person has an anxiety disorder and comorbid depression or depressive symptoms, consult the NICE guideline for the relevant anxiety disorder and consider treating the anxiety disorder first (since effective treatment of the anxiety disorder will often improve the depression or the depressive symptoms)[15].

---

[14]Refer if necessary to 'Bipolar disorder' (NICE clinical guideline 38; available at www.nice.org. uk/CG38).

[15]The evidence for this recommendation has not been updated since the previous guideline. Any wording changes have been made for clarification only.

Case identification and service delivery

Risk assessment and monitoring

5.2.13.11 Always ask people with depression directly about suicidal ideation and intent. If there is a risk of self-harm or suicide:
- assess whether the person has adequate social support and is aware of sources of help
- arrange help appropriate to the level of risk
- advise the person to seek further help if the situation deteriorates[16].

5.2.13.12 If a person with depression presents considerable immediate risk to themselves or others, refer them urgently to specialist mental health services[17].

5.2.13.13 Advise people with depression of the potential for increased agitation, anxiety and suicidal ideation in the initial stages of treatment; actively seek out these symptoms and:
- ensure that the person knows how to seek help promptly
- review the person's treatment if they develop marked and/or prolonged agitation.

5.2.13.14 Advise a person with depression and their family or carer to be vigilant for mood changes, negativity and hopelessness, and suicidal ideation, and to contact their practitioner if concerned. This is particularly important during high-risk periods, such as starting or changing treatment and at times of increased personal stress[18].

5.2.13.15 If a person with depression is assessed to be at risk of suicide:
- take into account toxicity in overdose if an antidepressant is prescribed or the person is taking other medication; if necessary, limit the amount of drug(s) available
- consider increasing the level of support, such as more frequent direct or telephone contacts
- consider referral to specialist mental health services[19].

Active monitoring

In the previous guideline, a recommendation was made for watchful waiting. In the process of the development of this guideline, in discussion with stakeholders and with the GDG, considerable concern was expressed about the term itself and the fact that it suggested a passive process rather than the more active process of assessment, advice and support that characterises effective interventions for people with mild depression that may spontaneously remit. In light of this, the GDG preferred the term 'active monitoring' and revised the original recommendation accordingly.

5.2.13.16 For people who, in the judgement of the practitioner, may recover with no formal intervention, or people with mild depression who do not want an

---

[16]Ibid.
[17]Ibid.
[18]Ibid.
[19]Ibid.

intervention, or people with subthreshold depressive symptoms who request an intervention:

● discuss the presenting problem(s) and any concerns that the person may have about them
● provide information about the nature and course of depression
● arrange a further assessment, normally within 2 weeks
● make contact if the person does not attend follow-up appointments.

5.3 SERVICE DELIVERY SYSTEMS IN THE TREATMENT AND MANAGEMENT OF DEPRESSION

5.3.1 Introduction

As indicated above, there has been a considerable number of service-focused developments since the publication of the previous guideline. In this guideline update, the over-arching term 'enhanced care' is used to refer to them all. This includes a number of interventions or models that often have some degree of overlap or where individual interventions are contained within large models. For example, collaborative care interventions (Gilbody *et al.*, 2006) may include stepped care (Bower & Gilbody, 2005a) as a component (Katon *et al.*, 1999; Unutzer *et al.*, 2002). Some of the more prominent models are listed below.

Graduated access
One way of changing access is to modify service provision at the point at which people want to access services (Rogers *et al.*, 1999). This may involve 'graduated access' to services, including the use of 'direct health services', which people can access without having face-to-face contact with professionals and which maximise the use of new technologies such as the internet.

The consultation-liaison model
This model (for example, Creed & Marks, 1989; Darling & Tyler, 1990; Gask *et al.*, 1997) is a variant of the training and education model (which is outside of the scope of the guideline), in that it seeks to improve the skills of primary care professionals and improve quality of care through improvements in their skills. However, rather than providing training interventions that teach skills in dealing with patients with depression in general, in this model specialists enter into an ongoing educational relationship with the primary care team, in order to support them in caring for specific patients who are currently undergoing care. Referral to specialist care is only expected to be required in a small proportion of cases. A common implementation of this model involves a psychiatrist visiting practices regularly and discussing patients with primary care professionals.

The attached professional model
In this model (for example, Bower & Sibbald, 2000), a mental health professional has direct responsibility for the care of a person (usually in primary care) focusing on the

121

primary treatment of the problem/disorder, be it pharmacological or psychological. The co-ordination of care remains with the GP/primary care team. Contact is usually limited to treatment and involves little or no follow-up beyond that determined by the specific intervention offered (for example, booster sessions in CBT).

Stepped care

Stepped care (for example, Bower & Gilbody, 2005a) is a system for delivering and monitoring treatment with the explicit aim of providing the most effective yet least burdensome treatment to the patient first, and which has a self-correcting mechanism built in (that is, if a person does not benefit from an initial intervention they are 'stepped up' to a more complex intervention). Typically, stepped care starts by providing low-intensity interventions. In some stepped-care systems, low-intensity care is received by all individuals, although in other systems patients are stepped up to a higher intensity intervention on immediate contact with the service, for example if they are acutely suicidal (this later model is the one adopted in this guideline update and in the previous guideline).

Stratified (or matched care)

This is a hierarchical model of care (for example, Van Straten *et al.*, 2006), moving from low- to high-intensity interventions, where at the patient's point of first contact with services they are matched to the level of need, and the consequent treatment is determined by the assessing professional in consultation with the patient.

Case management

This describes a system where an individual healthcare professional takes responsibility for the co-ordination of the care of an individual patient (for example, Gensichen *et al.*, 2006), but is not necessarily directly involved in the provision of any intervention; it may also involve the co-ordination of follow-up.

Collaborative care

The collaborative care model (for example, Wagner, 1997; Katon *et al.*, 2001) emerged from the chronic disease model and has four essential elements, which are:
- the collaborative definition of problems, in which patient-defined problems are identified alongside medical problems diagnosed by healthcare professionals
- a focus on specific problems where targets, goals and plans are jointly developed by the patient and professional to achieve a reasonable set of objectives, in the context of patient preference and readiness
- the creation of a range of self-management training and support services in which patients have access to services that teach the necessary skill to carry out treatment plans, guided behaviour change and promote emotional support
- the provision of active and sustained follow-up in which patients are contacted at specific intervals to monitor health status, identify possible complications and check and reinforce progress in implementing the care plan.

In mental health services, collaborative care also typically includes a consultation liaison role with a specialist mental health professional and generic primary care staff.

It may also include elements of many of the other interventions described above. In this guideline it is assumed that collaborative care, focused on the treatment and care of depression, is provided as part of a well-developed stepped care programme, and coordinated at either the primary or secondary care level. All sectors of care should be involved in order to ensure a comprehensive and integrated approach to mental and physical healthcare. Typically the programme of care is coordinated by a dedicated case manager supported by a multi-professional team. There will be joint determination with the service user regarding the care plan along with long-term coordination and follow-up. It can be summarised as follows:

● the provision of case management, which is supervised and supported by a senior mental health professional
● the development of a close collaboration between primary and secondary care services
● the provison of a range of interventions consistent with those recommended in this guideline, including patient education, psychological and pharmacological interventions, and medication management
● the provison of long-term coordination of care and follow-up.

5.3.2 Current practice and aims of the review

Over the past 20 years, there has been a growing interest in the development of systems of care for managing depression. This work has been influenced by organisational developments in healthcare in the US, such as managed care and Health Maintenance Organisations (Katon *et al.*, 1999), developments in the treatment of depression, the development of stepped care (Davison, 2000), and influences from physical healthcare (for example, chronic disease management [Wagner & Groves, 2002]). A significant factor in driving these developments has been the recognition that for many people depression is a chronic and disabling disorder.

The implementation in the NHS of the various developments described in the introduction has been variable. Perhaps the model most widely adopted has been the stepped-care model within the IAPT programme (Department of Health, 2007), but outside of demonstration sites and experimental studies (Layard, 2006; Van Straten *et al.*, 2006) there has not been a consistent adoption of any particular model of stepped care. Resource constraints have often been a significant limitation of these developments, but there have also been changes in mental healthcare policies that have influenced implementation, for example the varying developments of the attached professional role over the past 20 years (Bower & Sibbald, 2000).

One consistent factor that links these developments is the limited evidence for most if not all of these interventions. The most notable exception is the evidence base for collaborative care, which has grown considerably in the past 10 years and has led some (for example, Simon, 2006) to call for the widespread implementation of collaborative care. However, it should be noted that the evidence base is largely from the US and, as it is a complex intervention, care must be taken when considering its adoption in different healthcare systems (Campbell *et al.*, 2000).

5.3.3 Interventions included

The GDG considered the range of interventions described above and the extent of current practice and decided to focus the reviews for this update on the following interventions: stepped care (including where possible matched care), collaborative care, the attached professional model and medication management. This was because they were the focus of considerable interest in the NHS and in the case of collaborative care considerable new evidence has emerged since the publication of the previous guideline. No additional studies were found for the attached professional models, so the GDG decided that rather than performing a separate review they would comment on it, particularly in relation to collaborative care. The GDG also decided to review medication management because there was evidence of increased use of this intervention in depression but considerable uncertainty as to whether the evidence supported medication management as a single, stand-alone intervention.

The increased focus on social inclusion and the role of employment in maintaining good mental health led the GDG to also consider an updated review of employment but as no new studies were identified in the searches undertaken for this guideline the GDG decided not to update the review undertaken for the previous guideline. For similar reasons the reviews of social support systems, crisis resolution and home treatment teams and day hospitals were not updated.

Definitions
The definitions adopted are as stated in Section 5.3.1 with the exception of medication management, which is given below.

Medication management
Medication management (for example, Peveler *et al.*, 1999) is an intervention aimed at improving patient adherence to medication. It is usually delivered by a pharmacist or nurse. It involves patient education about the nature and treatment of depression, the delivery of medication adherence strategies, the monitoring of side effects and the promotion of treatment adherence.

5.4 STEPPED CARE

5.4.1 Introduction

Stepped care seeks to identify the least restrictive and least costly intervention that will be effective for a person's presenting problems (Davison, 2000). The low-intensity interventions most often used are those that are less dependent on the availability of professional staff and focus on patient-initiated approaches to treatment. These may include self-help materials such as books (Cuijpers, 1997) and computer programmes (Proudfoot *et al.*, 2004). The use of these materials may be entirely patient managed, which is often referred to as pure self-help, or it may involve some limited input from a professional or paraprofessional, which is often

Table 11: Databases searched and inclusion/exclusion criteria for clinical effectiveness of stepped care

Electronic databases	MEDLINE, EMBASE, PsycINFO, CINAHL
Date searched	Database inception to January 2008
Update searches	July 2008; January 2009
Study design	RCT
Population	People with a diagnosis of depression according to DSM, ICD or similar criteria
Treatments	Stepped care

referred to as guided self-help (Gellatly *et al.*, 2007). Escalating levels of response to the complexity or severity of the disorder are often implicit in the organisation and delivery of many healthcare interventions, but a stepped-care system is an explicit attempt to formalise the delivery and monitoring of patient flows through the system. In establishing a stepped-care approach, consideration should be given to not only the degree of restrictiveness associated with a treatment and its costs and effectiveness, but also the likelihood of its uptake by a patient and the likely impact that an unsuccessful intervention will have on the probability of other interventions being taken up.

5.4.2   Databases searched and the inclusion/exclusion criteria

The review team conducted a new systematic search for studies of stepped care in depression. This was undertaken as a joint review for this guideline and the guideline for depression in adults with a chronic physical health problem (NCCMH, 2010). Information about the databases searched and the inclusion/exclusion criteria used are presented in Table 11. Details of the search strings used are in Appendix 8.

5.4.3   Studies considered[20]

The systematic review identified only one high-quality study (VANSTRATEN2006). However, this study included a sample of mixed depression and anxiety disorders and it was therefore decided to conduct a narrative review, which is set out below.

---

[20]Here and elsewhere in the guideline, each study considered for review is referred to by a 'study ID' made up of first author and publication date (unless a study is in press or only submitted for publication, when first author only is used).

5.4.4 Narrative review

In the field of mental health in the UK, stepped-care models are increasingly common and underpin the organisation and delivery of care in a number of recent NICE mental health guidelines (see for example, the previous guideline on depression [NICE, 2004a] and the guideline on anxiety [NICE, 2004b]). However, despite its widespread adoption, there is a limited evidence-base of studies designed specifically to evaluate stepped care. Bower and Gilbody (2005a) reviewed the evidence for the use of stepped care in the provision of psychological therapies and were unable to identify a significant body of evidence. They set out three assumptions on which they argue a stepped-care framework should be built and which need to be considered in any evaluation of stepped care. These assumptions concern the equivalence of clinical outcomes (between minimal and more intensive interventions, at least for some patients), the efficient use of resources (including healthcare resources outside the immediate provision of stepped care) and the acceptability of low-intensity interventions (to both patients and professionals). They reviewed the existing evidence for stepped care against these three assumptions and found some evidence to suggest that stepped care may be a clinically and cost-effective system for the delivery of psychological therapies, but no evidence that strongly supported the overall effectiveness of the model. Some evidence for the equivalence of low-intensity interventions comes, for example, from work on CCBT (Proudfoot *et al.*, 2004; Kaltenthaler *et al.*, 2008) and the use of written materials (Cuijpers, 1997). For the efficiency assumption, evidence is more difficult to identify, although there is some suggestion that CCBT may be more cost effective than therapist-delivered care (Kaltenthaler *et al.*, 2002). Other evidence suggests that individuals in stepped-care programmes may seek treatment in addition to the low-intensity interventions offered in the study and thereby undermine the efficiency assumption (Treasure *et al.*, 1996; Thiels *et al.*, 1998). Further problems emerge when the acceptability assumption is considered, with some suggestion that stepped-care models may be associated with lower rates of entry into studies (Whitfield *et al.*, 2001; Marks *et al.*, 2003). Bower and Gilbody (2005a) suggest that some of these problems could be addressed by taking into account patient choice (possibly by offering a choice from a range of low-intensity interventions) and also by adjusting the entry level into the stepped-care system to take account of the severity of the disorder. Past experience of treatment or treatment failure may also be a useful indicator of which level a patient should be entered into the stepped-care model.

Since the publication of the Bower and Gilbody (2005a) review, a study of stepped care for over 720 patients by Van Straten and colleagues (2006) has been published; this compared two forms of stepped care with a 'matched care' control. Both forms of stepped care involved assignment to a psychological therapy, brief behaviour therapy with a strong self-help component and therapist-delivered CBT. The matched care control involved patients being allocated to an appropriate psychological treatment as determined by the responsible clinician, unlike the other two arms of the trial where the type and duration of treatment were determined by the trial protocol. Patients in the matched control received more treatment sessions, but outcomes were no better than for those patients in the other two arms. Although the study lacked power to determine whether the difference was statistically significant (despite including over 700 patients), it is possible that the two stepped-care models were more cost effective (Hakkaart-van Roijen *et al.*, 2006). However, both stepped-care arms had higher attrition rates and there was some diversion, especially in the behaviour therapy group, into additional treatments other than those delivered in the study.

Outside the area of stepped care for psychological therapies for depression, considerable use has been made of stepped care programmes most notably in collaborative care (for example, Hunkeler *et al.*, 2006) where stepped care is often integrated into an overall collaborative care programme. (A fuller review of the collaborative care literature is contained in Section 5.5.) Specifically in relation to collaborative care, few of the studies have been built exclusively on a stepped-care model with all individuals receiving a low-intensity intervention at first point of contact. In many collaborative care studies, the prescription of antidepressant drugs has been the first intervention offered (Katon *et al.*, 1999; Swindle *et al.*, 2003). The decision whether to step up to another intervention was then based on no or limited response to treatment. A more limited number of studies have offered psychological interventions as the first point of contact (or the option of a pharmacological or psychological first treatment) in a collaborative care programme (Rost *et al.*, 2001; Unutzer *et al.*, 2002) and where benefit has not been obtained have stepped up either to more intensive pharmacological or psychological treatments or a combination of both.

As may be apparent from this discussion, a number of other factors including the role of case management and other healthcare interventions may have an influence on the outcome. It is also the case that more complex collaborative care interventions (for example, greater duration of intervention and follow-up and a greater range of available interventions, for example, the IMPACT study [Unutzer *et al.*, 2002]) tend to be associated with better outcomes, but whether this reflects the specific contribution of a stepped-care framework is unclear. In addition, meta-regression studies such as those by Bower and colleagues (2006) and Gilbody and colleagues (2006) did not identify the presence of stepped care or specific algorithms of care (which may be taken as a rough equivalent or proxy for stepped care) as being associated with a more positive outcome. Evidence related to stepped care also comes from the Sequenced Treatment Alternatives to Relieve Depression (STAR*D) study (Rush *et al.*, 2003). This was a four-level study designed to assess treatments in patients who had not responded to previous treatment; as such, it can be said to be a form of stepped care. At each level, patients who had not responded to treatment at the previous level were randomised to different treatment options (or 'stepped up'). The study was designed to be as analogous as possible to real clinical practice. In order to achieve this, patients were allowed to opt out of being randomised to drug switching, augmentation treatments and, in level two, to CBT. They were not allowed to opt out of randomisation to a particular agent within the drug switching or drug augmentation arms. The trial did not provide clear evidence on the suitable sequencing of treatment options (in particular, the efficacy of different antidepressants), but it did demonstrate that patients gained some benefit from moving through sequenced or stepped care and that it was possible to investigate this empirically.

The final evidence for the effectiveness of a stepped-care model in mental healthcare comes from the report on the two IAPT demonstration sites (for example, Clark *et al.*, 2008), both of which provide a psychological stepped-care programme. In the demonstration projects there was good evidence for increased patient flows through the system, while at the same time the outcomes obtained were broadly in line with those reported in RCTs for depression and anxiety.

Outside the area of mental health, a number of studies of stepped care have been conducted. These include studies of stepped care in back pain (Von Korff, 1999), obesity (Carels *et al.*, 2005) and acutely injured trauma survivors. In each case there has been a positive benefit associated with stepped care.

In summary, there is limited evidence from direct studies in common mental health problems that provide evidence for the effectiveness of the stepped-care model. Beyond the area of common mental health problems in fields such as addiction (Davison, 2000), there is some evidence for the effectiveness of the model. Bower and Gilbody (2005a) also provide some limited evidence in favour of the model in psychological therapies but, with the exception of the Van Straten and colleagues' (2006) study, no formal trials of the relative efficiency or effectiveness of a pure stepped-care model were identified. The adoption of the stepped-care model within the IAPT pilot sites was associated with the efficient use of healthcare resources and outcomes equivalent to those seen in clinical trials. There is some evidence that the integration of stepped care into a more complex model of collaborative care may be associated with better outcomes but there is no direct evidence that this is the case. Finally, the adoption of stepped-care models in non-mental healthcare has been associated with better physical health outcomes.

5.4.5   Health economic evidence and considerations

No evidence on the cost effectiveness of the stepped care approach was identified by the systematic search of the economic literature. Details on the methods used for the systematic search of the economic literature are described in Chapter 3, Section 3.6.1.

5.4.6   From evidence to recommendations

The previous guideline recommended the adoption of a stepped-care model for the provision of psychological and pharmacological interventions for depression (the model was also used in the NICE guideline on anxiety [NICE, 2004b]). Since that time there has been further but limited evidence providing direct support for the model (Hakkaart-van Roijen *et al.*, 2006; Van Straten *et al.*, 2006; Clark *et al.*, 2008) along with its increasing use in a number of collaborative care interventions. It has also been adopted by the IAPT programme (Department of Health, 2007) as the framework for the delivery of the service. In the view of the GDG, the stepped-care model remains the best developed system for ensuring access to cost-effective interventions for a wide range of people with depression, particularly if supported by systems for routine outcome monitoring, which ensure that there are systems in place that enable prompt stepping up for those who have not benefited from a low-intensity intervention. The

GDG endorsed the model set out in the previous guideline but made some adjustments to the structure and content of the model in light of changes in the recommendations in this guideline update. The model is set out in Figure 1 in Section 2.4.7.

Current models are in development (for example, Richards & Suckling, 2008) that will allow service delivery systems to monitor and review the effectiveness of stepped-care models. Further research however is clearly needed to address the issues of efficacy, efficiency and acceptability of stepped care for depression.

5.5   COLLABORATIVE CARE

5.5.1   Introduction

The origins of collaborative care for depression lie in concerns about the inadequacy of much current treatment for the condition and developments in the field of chronic physical disorders. In many of the earlier studies, mental health professionals provided the enhanced staff input to primary care settings and undertook a care co-ordinator role (Katon *et al.*, 1995; Katon *et al.*, 1996; Unutzer *et al.*, 2002). However, more recently, others, including primary care nurses (Mann *et al.*, 1998; Hunkeler *et al.*, 2000; Rost *et al.*, 2000) or graduates without core mental health professional training (Katzelnick *et al.*, 2000; Simon *et al.*, 2000), have taken on this role. Most studies have been from the US. In the UK, one study used practice nurses in the care co-ordinator role and this did not improve either patient antidepressant uptake or outcomes compared with usual GP care (Mann *et al.*, 1998); more recent studies have used mental health professionals or paraprofessionals (Chew-Graham *et al.*, 2007; Richards & Suckling, 2008; Pilling *et al.*, 2010).

In the UK, there is a concern that there are not sufficient mental health professionals to provide enhanced input and care co-ordination for all primary care patients with depression. Primary care nurses have multiple and increasing demands on their time, and many are also uninterested in working with patients with psychological problems (Nolan *et al.*, 1999). Therefore, it seems unlikely that practice nurses will take on a significant role in the routine care of patients with depression. A major NHS staffing initiative for primary care mental health was the appointment of new graduate primary care mental health workers (Department of Health, 2000; Department of Health, 2003) who may potentially affect this situation. The advent of these posts has recently been superseded by the development of the IAPT programme, where the role of low-intensity staff (in many cases a development of the primary care mental health worker role) has elements that are common to a number of collaborative care interventions.

A number of recent meta-analyses of collaborative care have supported the statistical and clinical effectiveness of the model for depression (Badamgarav *et al.*, 2003; Neumeyer-Gromen *et al.*, 2004; Gilbody *et al.*, 2006; Whittington *et al.*, 2009), but not necessarily the cost effectiveness (Ofman *et al.*, 2004; Gilbody *et al.*, 2006). Other related reviews have focused on the use of case management in depression (Gensichen *et al.*, 2006), which they defined as 'an intervention for continuity of care including at least the systematic monitoring of symptoms. Further elements were possible such as coordination and assessment of treatment and arrangement of referrals'. Given this rather broad definition, the GDG did not consider that a separate analysis of case management from collaborative care was meaningful, particularly in light of the considerable variation in the duration and complexity of the interventions covered in the meta-analyses described above.

The effect sizes on depressive and related symptoms described in the reviews by Badamgarav and colleagues (2003), Neumeyer-Gromen and colleagues (2004), Gilbody and colleagues (2006) and Whittington and colleagues (2009) were generally modest, ranging between 0.25 (95% CI: 0.18, 0.32) (Gilbody *et al.*, 2006) and 0.75 (95% CI: 0.70, 0.81) (Neumeyer-Gromen *et al.*, 2004), with most reviews reporting effect sizes at the lower end of the range indicated. The review by Whittington and colleagues (2009) is the only review that attempts to compare the effectiveness of collaborative care with the effectiveness of the attached professional model (Bower & Sibbald, 2000).

Current practice
The extent of NHS-based provision in the UK has already been reviewed in Section 5.3 and, as can be seen from that section, the formal provision of collaborative care is not very evident in the NHS, although some elements of it are becoming available through the low-intensity arm of the IAPT programme, including medication management (Peveler *et al.*, 1999), care management (Gensichen *et al.*, 2006) and signposting (Grayer & Rudge, 2005).

Definition
This is set out in Section 5.3.

5.5.2   Databases searched and the inclusion/exclusion criteria

The review team conducted a new systematic search for studies of collaborative care of depression. This was undertaken as a joint review for this guideline update and the guideline on depression in adults with a chronic physical health problem (NCCMH, 2010). Information about the databases searched and the inclusion/exclusion criteria used are presented in Table 12. Details of the search strings used are in Appendix 8.

5.5.3   Studies considered[21]

In total, 50 trials were found from searches of electronic databases. Of these, 28 were included and 22 were excluded. Of the included studies, 11 were from the previous

---

[21]Here and elsewhere in the guideline, each study considered for review is referred to by a study ID (primary author and date of study publication, except where a study is in press or only submitted for publication, then a date is not used). Study IDs in title case refer to studies included in the previous guideline and study IDs in capital letters refer to studies found and included in this guideline update. References for studies from the previous guideline are in Appendix 18.

Table 12: Databases searched and inclusion/exclusion criteria for clinical effectiveness of collaborative care

Electronic databases	MEDLINE, EMBASE, PsycINFO, CINAHL
Date searched	Database inception to January 2008
Update searches	July 2008; January 2009
Study design	RCT
Population	People with a diagnosis of depression according to DSM, ICD or similar criteria
Treatments	Collaborative care, case management, monitoring, feedback

guideline (NCCMH, 2004) and of the excluded studies, one had been included in the previous guideline but was removed for the update because only 21% had a diagnosis of depression at baseline. The most common reasons for exclusion were that there was no extractable data or that less than 80% of participants had a diagnosis of depression.

All studies of populations with depression and an identified physical health problem (for example, KATON2004) were excluded at the outset. Of the included studies, Unutzer2002 was removed because of the high percentage of patients with chronic health problems reported in the study sample and this led the GDG to decide that the trial was more appropriately placed in the guideline on depression in adults with a chronic physical health problem (NCCMH, 2010). Araya2003 was also removed in a sensitivity analysis, because it was identified as an outlier producing a great deal of heterogeneity (non-response data pre-sensitivity analysis $I^2 = 82.2\%$; post-sensitivity analysis $I^2 = 69.2\%$). The GDG felt that this was a likely consequence of the study setting; based in Chile, it is possible that the usual care arm, which was utilised as the control, reflected a different healthcare system not relevant to a UK setting. Similarly, the major depression subsample from Katon1996MAJOR was removed from mean endpoint analysis because it too introduced an exceptionally large amount of heterogeneity, which was eradicated after it was taken out of the analysis (mean endpoint pre-sensitivity analysis $I^2 = 43.6\%$; post-sensitivity analysis $I^2 = 0\%$). Wells1999 reported follow-up data at 45 months after the acute phase, which was not extracted because it was felt that the data could not be converted reliably into intention-to-treat analysis given the high attrition rate at that time point.

A range of self-rated and clinician-rated outcomes were reported in the included studies. These included the SCL-20 and SCL-depression subscale which are both depression-specific scales derived from the 90-item Hopkins Symptom Checklist (HSCL; Derogatis, 1974), the BDI (Beck *et al.*, 1961), BDI-II (Beck *et al.*, 1996), PHQ-9 (Spitzer *et al.*, 1999), CES-D (Radloff, 1977) and the Hamilton Rating Scale for Depression (HRSD; Hamilton, 1960). One study reported follow-up relapse prevention data. Data were only extracted where a comparison with usual care was available.

The studies that were identified by the search and included in this review varied considerably in terms of the complexity of the care protocols implemented. In addition to this, the inclusion of both UK and non-UK based trials resulted in inevitable variation in the nature of the usual care used as a comparator. There was also variation in participant diagnoses; studies including patients presenting with an antidepressant prescription were included along with those reporting a more formal diagnosis. Previous meta-regression had identified a number of factors such as mental health background of the care coordinator, antidepressant use, and the provision of supervision as associated with better outcomes. The presence of such elements raises questions about the complexity or comprehensiveness of the intervention in particular when assessed against the criteria originally developed by Wagner (1996). With this in mind a simple checklist (see Appendix 10) to assess the complexity of the intervention provided was used to see if this would help in more reliably characterising the interventions and ascertaining whether or not this would relate to the outcome of the intervention.

In order to reduce the possible confounding crossover effects in which the implementation of collaborative care changes the standard care for all patients in the practice, a number of trials employed a cluster randomised design. In these trials the unit of randomisation was the individual physician, clinic, healthcare firm or geographical area (DATTO2003, DIETRICH2004, DOBSCHA2006, ROST20001a, Rost2001b, SWINDLE2003, and Wells1999). A design effect[22] was applied to the analysis of studies that had not accounted for the clustering in their analysis. Where papers reported the intracluster correlation coefficient (ICC) this was used in the calculations, with the empirically derived value of 0.02 used where the ICC was not reported. A sensitivity analysis was conducted to compare the results of the meta-analysis with and without the application of the design effect. The results indicated that applying the transformation had little to no impact on any of the results reported, thus strengthening the robustness of the original analysis.

Summary study characteristics of the included studies are in Table 13 with full details in Appendix 17a, which also includes details of excluded studies[23].

5.5.4   Clinical evidence

On some key outcome measures of efficacy such as self-rated non-response or mean end point scores, collaborative care was more effective than standard care, although the effect sizes were small. See Table 14 for the summary evidence profile, Appendix 16a for the full profile and Appendix 19a for the forest plots.

---

[22]N (effective) = $(k \times m)/(1 + (m - 1)) * ICC$, where k indicates the number of clusters, m the number of observations per cluster and ICC the intracluster correlation coefficient.

[23]For this review studies from the previous guideline were re-entered into the study database for the guideline update in Appendix 17a.

Table 13: Summary study characteristics of collaborative care

	Collaborative care versus usual care	
No. trials (total participants)	28 RCTs (10,191)	
Study IDs	(1) ADLER2004	(16) MCMAHON2007
	(2) Araya2003	(17) PERAHIA2008
	(3) Blanchard1995	(18) PILLING2010
	(4) CHEWGRAHAM2007	(19) RICHARDS2008
	(5) DATTO2003	(20) RICKLES2005
	(6) DIETRICH2004	(21) ROST2001a[24]
	(7) DOBSCHA2006	(22) Rost2001b
	(8) FINLEY2003	(23) Simon2000*
	(9) Hunkeler2000*	(24) SIMON2004*
	(10) Katon1995	(25) SIMON2006
	(11) Katon1996	(26) SMIT2006[†]
	(12) Katon1999	(27) SWINDLE2003
	(13) Katon2001[‡]	(28) Unutzer2002
	(14) LUDMAN2007[†]	(29) Wells1999*
	(15) Mann1998b	
N/% female	(1) 364/72	(16) Unclear
	(2) 240/100	(17) 617/64
	(3) 82/85	(18) 52/60
	(4) 76/72	(19) 88/77
	(5) 37/61	(20) 53/84
	(6) 325/80	(21) Unclear for 'recently treated' only
	(7) 26/7	
	(8) 106/85	(22) 177/84
	(9) 210/69	(23) 439/72
	(10) 166/78	(24) 446/75
	(11) 113/75	(25) 134/65
	(12) 170/75	(26) 168/63
	(13) 286/74	(27) 9/97
	(14) 74/71	(28) 1168/65
	(15) Unclear for study 2 only	(29) 981/72
Mean age (years)	(1) 42	(16) Unclear
	(2) 43	(17) 46

Continued

[24]Presents acute data of Rost2001b; Rost2001b only used in analysis to avoid double counting.

Table 13: (*Continued*)

	Collaborative care versus usual care	
	(3) 76	(18) 46
	(4) 76	(19) 42
	(5) 37	(20) 38
	(6) 42	(21) Unclear for 'recently treated' only
	(7) 57	(22) 43
	(8) 54	(23) 47
	(9) 55	(24) 45
	(10) 47	(25) 43
	(11) 46	(26) 43
	(12) 47	(27) 56
	(13) 46	(28) 71
	(14) 50	(29) 43
	(15) Unclear for study 2 only	
Diagnosis	(1) MDD, dysthymia or double depression (DSM–IV)	(16) Depressive illness (ICD–10)
	(2) MDD (DSM–IV)	(17) MDD (DSM–IV)
	(3) Probable pervasive depression (Short-CARE)	(18) Clinical diagnosis established by GP (unclear)
	(4) Unclear	(19) MDD (DSM–IV)
	(5) MDD (MINI) or referred with depressive symptoms	(20) Unclear: antidepressant prescription
	(6) MDD, dysthymia or double depression (DSM–IV)	(21) MDD (DSM–III-R)
	(7) Subthreshold depressive symptoms, dysthymia (DSM–IV) or unclear	(22) MDD (DSM–III-R) (23) Unclear: antidepressant prescription
	(8) Unclear: clinical judgment	(24) Unclear: beginning antidepressant treatment
	(9) MDD or dysthymia (DSM–IV)	(25) Depressive disorder (unclear)
	(10) MDD or subthreshold depressive symptoms (DSM–III-R)	(26) MDD (DSM–IV) (27) MDD, dysthymia, partially remitted MDD or double depression (PRIME-MD)
	(11) MDD or subthreshold depressive symptoms (DSM–III-R)	(28) MDD, dysthymia or double depression (DSM–IV)

Continued

Table 13: (*Continued*)

	Collaborative care versus usual care	
	(12) Recurrent depression or dysthymia (DSM–IV) (13) Recovered but high risk of relapse (14) Subthreshold depressive symptoms or dysthymia (treatment resistant; DSM–IV) (15) MDD (DSM–III)	(29) MDD, dysthymic disorder, double depression or subthreshold depression (CIDI)
Setting	(1) US (2) Chile (3)–(4) UK (5)–(14) US (15)–(16) UK	(17) Europe (18)–(19) UK (20)–(25) US (26) Netherlands (27)–(29) US
Length of treatment (days)	(1) 180 (2) 84 (3) 90 (4) 84 (5) 112 (6) 180 (7) 365 (8) 170 (9) 180 (10) 210 (11) 210 (12) 90 (13) 365 (14) 365 (15) 120	(16) 180 (17) 84 (18) 120 (19) 90 (20) 90 (21) 730 (22) 730 (23) 112 (24) 180 (25) 84 (26) 1095 (27) 90 (28) 365 (29) 180
Follow-up	(1) 6 and 12 months (2) 3 months (3)–(10) Not reported (11) 7 months (12) 25 months (13)–(17) Not reported	(18) 4 months (19)–(26) Not reported (27) 9 months (28) 6 and 12 months (29) 6 months

*3-armed trial; †4-armed trial; ‡Relapse prevention study.

Receiving collaborative care appeared to make little difference to the number of people leaving treatment early. However, it improved the number adhering to medication.

One study, Katon2001, looked at relapse prevention in people who had achieved remission. There was no difference between the number relapsing who had received collaborative care and the number relapsing who had received standard care.

5.5.5 Collaborative care: implications of data on the attached professional role

As part of the collaborative care review, the GDG wished to understand the potential impact of collaborative care for depression on the UK healthcare system. This arose from a concern that a significant proportion of the data for the effectiveness of collaborative care was drawn from studies conducted in North America. Given the development of the attached professional role in primary care services in the UK (Bower & Sibbald, 2000), it was decided to explore the potential effect sizes of the attached professional role versus usual GP care or waitlist control and therefore provide a comparator for collaborative care. To estimate the potential effect of the attached professional role, all trials for high-intensity psychological interventions included in the guideline were reviewed. The GDG did consider the inclusion of pharmacological trials based in primary care, but because there were very few and collaborative care often involves antidepressant treatment as a minimum it was not felt to be a useful comparator. The following studies were identified and the study characteristics for these can be found in Chapter 8 and Appendix 17b: Schulberg1996, Scott1992, Scott1997, Simpson2003 and Ward2000[25].

The effect sizes for depressive symptoms obtained in the review for the attached professional role were: BDI, SMD -0.28 (95% CI $-0.66, 0.10$); Hamilton Depression Rating Scale (HAMD), SMD -0.35 (95% CI $-0.58, -0.11$). These effect sizes were similar to that obtained in another review, albeit one with somewhat different inclusion criteria, by Whittington and colleagues (2009). The effect size for depressive symptomatology in that study was -0.35 (SMD, 95% CI $-0.46, -0.25$). The effect size for collaborative care in the review for this guideline was: self-rated outcome, SMD -0.16 (95% CI $-0.25, -0.06$). Given the similarity of effect sizes between the two modes of delivery of care, and the overlapping confidence intervals it seems reasonable to conclude, at least initially in the absence of any direct comparisons, that there may be little difference in effectiveness. When attempting to understand these results, a number of factors need to be considered, including the considerable variation in the nature of the collaborative care provided; in some cases it involved case managers taking on the long-term care of people with depression (for example, Simon

---

[25]<80% of participants met diagnosis of depression. See Chapter 8 for further details.

Table 14: Summary evidence profile for collaborative care versus standard care (acute-phase efficacy data)

	Self-rated	Clinician-rated	DSM criteria	Follow-up
Non-response	RR 0.83 (0.75 to 0.92) (49.7% versus 59.9%)	RR 0.86 (0.69 to 1.06) (44.2% versus 48.7%)	Not reported	Not reported
Quality	High	Moderate	–	–
Number of studies; participants	K = 7; n = 1820	K = 2; n = 1264	–	–
Forest plot number	Service c-care 03.01	Service c-care 03.01	–	–
Non-remission	RR 0.91 (0.86 to 0.97) (70% versus 76%)	RR 0.98 (0.88 to 1.09) (56.4% versus 57.5%)	RR 0.85 (0.70 to 1.04) (29.5% versus 29.3%)	RR 1.05 (0.9 to 1.21) (49.1% versus 47.2%)
Quality	High	High	High	Moderate
Number of studies; participants	K = 3; n = 1480	K = 1; n = 962	K = 6; n = 1173	K = 1; n = 863
Forest plot number	Service c-care 03.02	Service c-care 03.02	Service c-care 03.02	Service c-care 03.03

Continued

137

Table 14: (*Continued*)

	Self-rated	Clinician-rated	DSM criteria	Follow-up
Mean depression scores at endpoint	SMD −0.16 (−0.25 to −0.06)	SMD −0.05 (−0.64 to 0.53)	Not reported	3–4 months SMD −0.36 (−0.63 to −0.09)
Quality	High	High	–	High
Number of studies; participants	K = 11; n = 1876	K = 1; n = 45	–	K = 3; n = 214
Forest plot number	Service c-care 03.05	Service c-care 03.05	–	Service c-care 03.06
Mean depression change scores at endpoint	Not reported	SMD −0.02 (−0.15 to 0.11)	Not reported	Not reported
Quality	–	Moderate	–	–
Number of studies; participants	–	K = 1; n = 958	–	–
Forest plot number	–	Service c-care 03.07	–	–

et al., 2004), in others it involved little more than advice and consultation with a psychiatrist (for example, Katon *et al.*, 1995); there were differences in the nature of the intervention provided – for example, within the attached professional model, the professionals more consistently provided specific psychological interventions (for example, Scott *et al.*, 1997) and this may have had an impact on the effectiveness of the intervention; the populations included in the trials may have been different; and finally the comparators and the nature of the healthcare system in which the interventions were delivered may also have been different. In Whittington and colleagues' (2009) review, for example, the majority of the attached professional studies were based in the UK (26 out of 38) and most of the collaborative care studies were based in the US (13 out of 16).

5.5.6   Clinical summary

The studies of collaborative care reviewed here were limited to people without an accompanying chronic physical health problem. A review of collaborative care for this population, including studies of older people with a high incidence of physical health problems (Unutzer2001) is contained in the related guideline (NCCMH, 2010). The evidence profiles developed for this guideline show that when the review of collaborative care is restricted to the groups with depression and no significant chronic physical health problems, then the effects of the intervention are of limited clinical importance (see, for example, the effect sizes for remission and response) and there is a small effect on endpoint continuous data. It should also be noted that the endpoint continuous data effect sizes were similar to those obtained from an analysis of the attached professional role. The small size of the dataset included here prevented any more detailed analysis, such as a meta-regression. There was considerable variation between studies with some, for example Katon1996MAJOR, reporting a large effect on continuous data: SMD = −1.11 (95% CI −1.64, −0.59), but inclusion of this study in the meta-analysis resulted in considerable heterogeneity, which entirely disappeared when the study was removed in the sensitivity analysis. It is also worth noting that when response data are reviewed, there is a noticeable decline in effect size from the early studies for example, Katon1996MAJOR: RR = 0.49 (95% CI 0.27, 0.92) and Katon1996-MINOR: RR = 0.68 (95% CI 0.41 1.15), to more recent studies such as SIMON2006: RR = 0.97 (95% CI 0.79, 1.18).

5.5.7   Health economic evidence and considerations

The systematic search of the economic literature undertaken for the guideline update identified no eligible studies on service-level interventions for people with depression set in the UK. Details on the methods used for the systematic search of the economic literature are described in Chapter 3, Section 3.6.1.

No UK-based studies evaluating the cost effectiveness of collaborative care were identified in the literature search. The collaborative care meta-analysis conducted for the update points to a small effect size of collaborative care when compared with usual care. A decision was reached by the GDG not to recommend collaborative care interventions in the depressed population in the absence of chronic physical health problems. The effect sizes were considered too small to warrant a formal economic evaluation. Collaborative care studies included in the meta-analysis point to a resource use that is more intensive than usual care, for example, the additional input of a case manager in the co-ordination of care for people with depression and associated liaison time with GPs and specialist psychiatrists. From this one can assume that collaborative care may be more costly than usual care. However this does not exclude the possibility of collaborative care being cost effective when compared with usual care as even small differences in effects and costs could potentially result in a cost-effective intervention.

A significant portion of the effectiveness data was based on studies conducted in the US and collaborative care is a service-level intervention with effects that largely reflect the nature of the healthcare setting in which it is provided. Therefore more studies conducted in the UK healthcare setting may provide more UK-specific effects and resource use estimates.

5.5.8   From evidence to recommendations

The evidence reviewed in this guideline update for collaborative care in depression was not viewed as being sufficiently strong to generate any recommendations. The GDG did recognise that co-ordinated care with long-term follow-up is an important element of effective care for people with severe and complex depression. For example, it is acknowledged in the guideline on depression in adults with a chronic physical health problem (NICE, 2009c; NCCMH, 2010) that collaborative care can play an important role in that population. In addition, co-ordinated multiprofessional interventions are key elements of the care provided in specialist mental health services in Step 4 of the stepped-care model in this guideline (see Figure 1 in Section 2.4.7). In view of this, the GDG thought it appropriate to draw attention in the recommendations to the role of collaborative care for people with depression and a chronic physical health problem and of co-ordinated multi-professional care in specialist mental health services for those with severe and complex depression. The development of an approach to collaborative care for depression built on the provision of low-intensity interventions (such as behavioural activation and medication management) has shown promise in pilot trials in an NHS setting (for example, Richards *et al.*, 2008) and the current multicentre Medical Research Council funded Collaborative Depression Trial ('CADET') may provide more substantial evidence for this type of intervention, which should inform further updates of this guideline.

5.5.9   Recommendations

5.5.9.1   For people with severe depression and those with moderate depression and complex problems, consider:
- referring to specialist mental health services for a programme of co-ordinated multiprofessional care
- providing collaborative care if the depression is in the context of a chronic physical health problem with associated functional impairment[26].

5.5.9.2   Teams working with people with complex and severe depression should develop comprehensive multidisciplinary care plans in collaboration with the person with depression (and their family or carer, if agreed with the person). The care plan should:
- identify clearly the roles and responsibilities of all health and social care professionals involved
- develop a crisis plan that identifies potential triggers that could lead to a crisis and strategies to manage such triggers
- be shared with the GP and the person with depression and other relevant people involved in the person's care.

5.6   MEDICATION MANAGEMENT

5.6.1   Introduction

The effectiveness of antidepressants in the treatment of depression has long been recognised, as has the problem of poor compliance; inevitably this has stimulated interest in developing strategies to promote and support adherence to antidepressant medication.

If the potential benefits of longer-term treatment are to be realised, two conditions need to hold. First, that the drugs are prescribed at an adequate dose and second that the regime of treatment is adhered to. Dunn and colleagues (1999), in a study of over 16,000 primary care patients prescribed either TCAs or SSRIs, reported that while 33% of those prescribed an SSRI were judged to have completed an adequate period of treatment (that is, prescriptions covering at least 120 days' treatment within the first 6 months after diagnosis) only 6% of those prescribed a TCA did. Of course this study does not account for the possibility that some patients may have switched medication and may have done so to their long-term benefit. However, evidence from studies of

---

[26]Refer to 'Depression in adults with a chronic physical health problem: treatment and management' (NICE, 2009c; NCCMH, 2010) for the evidence base for this.

prescribing patterns in primary care suggests that if patients discontinue one form of antidepressant medication they often do not take another medication. For example, Isacsson and colleagues (1999), in a study of nearly 1000 patients, report that only 35% ever received one prescription and only a minority received further prescriptions.

This presents a potentially worrying picture; the effects of antidepressants seem modest and adherence to treatment regimes is also limited. For example, Lingam and Scott (2002) in a systematic review report non-adherence rates between 10 and 60% for antidepressants, with an average around 40%. They were also able to identify only a few well-conducted studies designed to improve antidepressant adherence with, at best, modest effects. Vergouwen and colleagues (2003) in a review of medication adherence compared interventions such as educational interventions not associated with a collaborative care intervention with those adherence programmes nested in collaborative care interventions, such as those developed by Katon and colleagues (2002), and reported improved adherence and better clinical outcomes in the latter. This view of increased adherence to antidepressants in collaborative care was also supported by the meta-regression study of Bower and colleagues (2006), which suggests that collaborative care was associated with increased medication adherence, and by the review conducted for this guideline update of outcomes for collaborative care, which suggests a potentially positive impact on medication adherence (RR 0.58; 95% CI 0.44, 0.75).

Beyond depression and mental health, the problem of poor medication adherence has been the subject of considerable research and debate. Most recently, NICE (2009b) has produced guidance on promoting medication adherence, which has general applicability for promoting adherence across all fields of medical care. However, the GDG was specifically concerned with the effectiveness of medication adherence (medication management programmes) in depression.

5.6.2 Databases searched and the inclusion/exclusion criteria

The review team conducted a new systematic search for studies of medication management. This was undertaken as a joint review for this guideline and the guideline for depression in adults with a chronic physical health problem (NCCMH, 2010). Information about the databases searched and the inclusion/exclusion criteria used are presented in Table 15. Details of the search strings used are in Appendix 8.

5.6.3 Studies considered[27]

In this guideline update four trials with potential relevance to medication management for depression were found from searches of electronic databases. Of these three

---

[27]Each study considered for review is referred to by a study ID in capital letters (primary author and date of study publication, except where a study is in press or only submitted for publication, then a date is not used).

Table 15: Databases searched and inclusion/exclusion criteria for clinical effectiveness of medication management

Electronic databases	MEDLINE, EMBASE, PsycINFO, CINAHL
Date searched	Database inception to January 2008
Update searches	July 2008; January 2009
Study design	RCT
Population	People with a diagnosis of depression according to DSM, ICD or similar criteria
Treatments	Medication management

were included and one was excluded because it did not report any outcomes relevant to the scope. The GDG identified two studies from the collaborative care review that were relevant to medication management so these were also included. None of the studies was included in the previous guideline (NICE, 2004a).

Of the included studies, CROCKETT2006 was a cluster randomised trial but the outcomes could not be adjusted because the number of clusters was not reported in the study. It is therefore reported separately. PEVELER1999 reported both overall outcomes for all participants and an analysis of a subsample of more severely depressed patients. In order to be consistent with the other studies, the overall outcomes were extracted for this review, but it should be noted that the authors reported a significant effect for patients who met criteria for major depression at the outset and received TCAs at doses above 75 mg per day.

Summary study characteristics of the included studies are in Table 16 with full details in Appendix 17a, which also includes details of excluded studies.

5.6.4   Clinical evidence

There was insufficient evidence that medication management helped to reduce symptoms of depression, although it had some effect on medication adherence and appeared acceptable to participants. See Table 17 for the summary evidence profile, Appendix 16a for the full profile and Appendix 19a for the forest plots.

5.6.5   Clinical evidence summary

A total of five studies, focusing specifically on medication management in depression, were reviewed. Overall, the quality of the evidence from these five studies was

**Table 16: Summary study characteristics of medication management
versus usual care**

	Medication management versus usual care
No. trials (Total participants)	5 RCTs (963)
Study IDs	(1) ADLER2004* (2) CROCKETT2006 (3) PEVELER1999[†] (4) RICKLES2005* (5) WILKINSON1993
N/% female	(1) 364/72 (2) 84/71 (3) 157/74 (4) 53/84 (5) 45/74
Mean age	(1) 42 (2) 46 (3) 45 (4) 38 (5) 49
Diagnosis	(1) MDD; dysthymia, double depression (DSM–IV) (2) Antidepressant prescription (unclear) (3) Depressive illness (unclear; clinical diagnosis) (4) Antidepressant prescription (unclear) (5) Depressive disorder (unclear)
Setting	(1) US (2) Australia (3) UK (4) US (5) UK
Length of treatment (days)	(1) 180 (2) 60 (3) 84 (4) 90 (5) 56
Follow-up	(1) 6 and 12 months (2)–(5) Not reported

*From the collaborative care review; [†]4-armed trial.

Table 17: Summary evidence profile for medication management versus usual care

	Self-rated
Non-response	RR 0.94 (0.47 to 1.89) (32.2% versus 34.4%)
Quality	Low
Number of studies; participants	K = 1; n = 63
Forest plot number	Service med-man 01.01
Mean depression scores at endpoint	SMD −0.14 (−0.31 to 0.02)
Quality	High
Number of studies; participants	K = 3; n = 604
Forest plot number	Service med-man 01.02
Adherence	RR 0.7 (0.46 to 1.08) (32.8% versus 40.9%)
Quality	High
Number of studies; participants	K = 2; n = 221
Forest plot number	Service med-man 01.03
Leaving treatment early for any reason (including lost to follow-up)	RR 0.81 (0.63 to 1.05) (25.5% versus 31.4%)
Quality	Moderate
Number of studies; participants	K = 2; n = 594
Forest plot number	Service med-man 02.01

limited, and it was not possible to perform a single meta-analysis of all the studies, focusing on depression outcomes. Where possible data from studies was combined, but even allowing for this, no consistent picture of a clinically important benefit of medication management alone emerged from the data. This is consistent with other reviews in the area (for example, Vergouwen *et al.*, 2003). In light of this, the GDG did not feel able to make any recommendations for medication management alone in the treatment of depression. However, it is recognised that the recommendations set out in the NICE guideline on medicines adherence (NICE, 2009b) are potentially important in improving adherence. Where there are specific concerns about potential problems with adherence (for example increased side effects with TCAs, the delay in onset of antidepressant effects or the possibility of discontinuation symptoms) specific attention is drawn to these within the recommendations on pharmacological interventions (in Chapters 9, 10, 11 and 12).

5.6.6   Health economic evidence and considerations

No evidence on the cost effectiveness of medication management was identified by the systematic search of the economic literature. Details on the methods used for the systematic search of the economic literature are described in Chapter 3, Section 3.6.1.

5.6.7   From evidence to recommendations

The evidence reviewed in this guideline for medication management alone was not viewed as being sufficiently strong to generate any positive recommendations.

5.6.8   Recommendations

5.6.8.1   Medication management as a separate intervention for people with depression should not be provided routinely by services. It is likely to be effective only when provided as part of a more complex intervention.

5.7   CRISIS RESOLUTION AND HOME TREATMENT TEAMS

The following sections marked by asterisks (**_**) are from the previous guideline and have not been updated for this guideline except for style and minor clarification.

5.7.1   Introduction

**Traditionally, a depressive episode marked by serious risk to self (most often suicidal ideation and intent) or very severe deterioration to care for the self is managed by admission to an acute inpatient unit. However, in recent years there has been growing interest in attempting to manage such episodes in the community. If this can be done safely, it may avoid the stigma and costs associated with hospital admission, thus providing benefits to both patients and service providers. Crisis resolution and home treatment teams (CRHTTs) are a form of service that aims to offer intensive home-based support in order to provide the best care for someone with depression where this is the most appropriate setting.

Definition

The GDG adopted the definition of crisis resolution developed by the Cochrane review of crisis intervention for people with serious mental health problems (Joy *et al.*, 2003). Crisis intervention and the comparator treatment were defined as follows:

- Crisis resolution is any type of crisis-oriented treatment of an acute psychiatric episode by staff with a specific remit to deal with such situations, in and beyond 'office hours'.

- 'Standard care' is the normal care given to those experiencing acute psychiatric episodes in the area concerned; this involved hospital-based treatment for all studies included.

5.7.2   Studies considered[28]

The focus of this review is to examine the effects of CRHTT care for people with serious mental illness (where the majority of the sample was diagnosed with non-psychotic disorders) experiencing an acute episode compared with the standard care they would normally receive. Studies were excluded if they were largely restricted to people who were under 18 years or over 65 years old, or to those with a primary diagnosis of substance misuse or organic brain disorder.

The GDG chose to use the Cochrane review of CRHTTs (Joy *et al.*, 2003), which included five RCTs (Fenton1979, Hoult1981, Muijen21992, Pasamanick1964, Stein1975), as the starting point for this section. A further search identified no new RCTs suitable for inclusion. Of the five RCTs included in the Cochrane review, only Stein1975 met the inclusion criteria set by the GDG (all the other studies had a very significant or exclusive focus on schizophrenia), providing data for 130 participants.

Characteristics of the included studies are in Appendix 17a, which also includes details of excluded studies.

5.7.3   Clinical evidence statements[29]

Crisis resolution and home treatment teams versus standard care
Effect of treatment on death (suicide or death in suspicious circumstances)
There is insufficient evidence to determine whether there is a clinically important[30] difference between CRHTTs and 'standard care' on reducing the likelihood of death

---

[28]The study IDs for studies that were in the previous guideline are in title case. References for these studies are in Appendix 18.

[29]The forest plots can be found in Appendix 19a.

[30]Note that the wording in the previous guideline was 'clinically significant'. The GDG for the guideline update preferred the term 'clinically important' to avoid confusion with the term 'statistically significant'.

due to any cause taking place during the study (K = 1; N = 130; RR = 1.00; 95% CI, 0.06 to 15.65).

Effect of treatment on acceptability
There is insufficient evidence to determine whether there is a clinically important difference between CRHTTs and 'standard care' on reducing the likelihood of patients leaving the study early by 6 or 12 months (K = 1; N = 130; RR = 0.60; 95% CI, 0.15 to 2.41) or by 20 months (K = 1; N = 130; RR = 1.17; 95% CI, 0.41 to 3.28).

Effect of treatment on burden to family life
There is insufficient evidence to determine whether there is a clinically important difference between CRHTTs and 'standard care' on reducing the likelihood of a patient's family reporting disruption to their daily routine due to the patient's illness by 3 months (K = 1; N = 130; RR = 0.88; 95% CI, 0.70 to 1.10).

There is insufficient evidence to determine whether there is a clinically important difference between CRHTTs and 'standard care' on reducing the likelihood of a patient's family reporting significant disruption to their social life due to the patient's illness by 3 months (K = 1; N = 130; RR = 0.83; 95% CI, 0.67 to 1.02).

There is evidence suggesting that there is a statistically significant difference favouring CRHTTs over 'standard care' on reducing the likelihood of a patient's family reporting physical illness due to the patient's illness by 3 months but the size of this difference is unlikely to be of clinical importance (K = 1; N = 130; RR = 0.84; 95% CI, 0.73 to 0.96).

There is some evidence suggesting a clinically important difference favouring CRHTTs over 'standard care' on reducing the likelihood of a patient's family reporting physical illness due to the patient's illness by 6 months (K = 1; N = 130; RR = 0.79; 95% CI, 0.66 to 0.95).

Effect of treatment on burden to community
There is insufficient evidence to determine whether there is a clinically important difference between CRHTTs and 'standard care' on reducing the likelihood of patients being arrested (K = 1; N = 130; RR = 0.76; 95% CI, 0.51 to 1.12).

There is insufficient evidence to determine whether there is a clinically important difference between CRHTTs and 'standard care' on reducing the likelihood of patients using emergency services (K = 1; N = 130; RR = 0.86; 95% CI, 0.51 to 1.45).

5.7.4 Clinical summary

The very large majority of patients with depression are never admitted to hospital (in contrast to schizophrenia where 60 to 70% are admitted to hospital at first presentation; McGorry & Jackson, 1999). Therefore, it is unsurprising that much of the evidence base is drawn from the treatment of schizophrenia and this means that there is currently insufficient evidence from RCTs to determine the value of CRHTTs for people with depression. Nevertheless, CRHTTs may have value for that small group of patients with depression who require a higher level of care than can be provided by standard community services.**

5.7.5 Recommendations

5.7.5.1 Use crisis resolution and home treatment teams to manage crises for people with severe depression who present significant risk, and to deliver high-quality acute care. The teams should monitor risk as a high-priority routine activity in a way that allows people to continue their lives without disruption[31].

5.7.5.2 Consider crisis resolution and home treatment teams for people with depression who might benefit from early discharge from hospital after a period of inpatient care[32].

5.7.5.3 Consider inpatient treatment for people with depression who are at significant risk of suicide, self-harm or self-neglect[33].

5.7.5.4 The full range of high-intensity psychological interventions should normally be offered in inpatient settings. However, consider increasing the intensity and duration of the interventions and ensure that they can be provided effectively and efficiently on discharge.

5.8 ACUTE DAY HOSPITAL CARE

The following sections marked by asterisks (**_**) are from the previous guildeline and have not been updated for this guideline except for style and minor clarification.

5.8.1 Introduction

**Given the substantial costs and high level of use of inpatient care, the possibility of day hospital treatment programmes acting as an alternative to acute admission gained credence in the early 1960s, initially in the US (Kris, 1965; Herz *et al.*, 1971) and later in Europe (Wiersma *et al.*, 1989) and the UK (Dick *et al.*, 1985; Creed *et al.*, 1990).

Definition
Acute psychiatric day hospitals were defined for the purposes of the guideline as units that provide diagnostic and treatment services for acutely ill individuals who would

---

[31]The evidence for this recommendation has not been updated since the previous guideline. Any wording changes have been made for clarification only.
[32]Ibid.
[33]Ibid.

otherwise be treated in traditional psychiatric inpatient units. Thus, trials were eligible for inclusion only if they compared admission to an acute day hospital with admission to an inpatient unit. Participants were people with acute psychiatric disorders (where the majority of the sample were diagnosed with non-psychotic disorders) who would have been admitted to inpatient care had the acute day hospital not been available. Studies were excluded if they were largely restricted to people who were under 18 years or over 65 years old, or to those with a primary diagnosis of substance misuse or organic brain disorder.

5.8.2   Studies considered[34]

The GDG selected a Health Technology Assessment (Marshall *et al.*, 2001) as the basis for this section. Marshall and colleagues (2001) focused on adults up to the age of 65 and reviewed nine trials of acute day hospital treatment published between 1966 and 2000. A further search identified no new RCTs suitable for inclusion. Of the nine studies included in the existing review, only two (Dick1985, Sledge1996) met the inclusion criteria set by the GDG, providing data for 288 participants.

Characteristics of the included studies are in Appendix 17a, which also includes details of excluded studies.

5.8.3   Clinical evidence statements[35]

The studies included in this review examined the use of acute day hospitals as an alternative to acute admission to an inpatient unit. The individuals involved in the studies were a diagnostically mixed group, including between 50 and 62% of people with a diagnosis of mood or anxiety disorder. Moreover, acute day hospitals are not suitable for people subject to compulsory treatment, and some studies explicitly excluded people with families unable to provide effective support at home. Clearly, the findings from this review, and the recommendations based upon them, cannot be generalised to all people with depression who present for acute admission.

Effect of treatment on efficacy
There is insufficient evidence to determine whether there is a clinically important difference between acute day hospitals and inpatient care on reducing the likelihood of readmission to hospital after discharge from treatment (K = 2; N = 288; RR = 1.02; 95% CI, 0.74 to 1.43).

---

[34]Study IDs in title case refer to studies included in the previous guideline. References for these studies are in Appendix 18.
[35]The forest plots can be found in Appendix 19a.

Effect of treatment on inpatient days per month

There is some evidence suggesting that there is a clinically important difference favouring acute day hospitals over inpatient care on inpatient days per month (K = 1; N = 197; WMD = –2.11; 95% CI, –3.46 to –0.76).

Effect of treatment on acceptability

There is insufficient evidence to determine whether there is a clinically important difference between acute day hospitals and inpatient care on reducing the likelihood of patients leaving the study early for any reason (K = 2; N = 288; RR = 0.86; 95% CI, 0.29 to 2.59).**

5.9 NON-ACUTE DAY HOSPITAL CARE

The following sections marked by asterisks (**_**) are from the previous guideline and have not been updated for this guideline except for style and minor clarification.

5.9.1 Introduction

**Although the earliest use of day hospitals in mental healthcare was to provide an alternative to inpatient care (Cameron, 1947), non-acute day hospitals have also been used for people with refractory mental health problems unresponsive to treatment in outpatient clinics. Two broad groups of people have been referred for non-acute day hospital care: those with anxiety and depressive disorders who have residual or persistent symptoms, and those with more severe and enduring mental disorders such as schizophrenia.

Given the need for services for people with severe and enduring mental health problems that are refractory to other forms of treatment, the review team undertook a review of the evidence comparing the efficacy of non-acute day hospitals with that of traditional outpatient treatment programmes.

Definition

For this section, the GDG agreed the following definition for non-acute day hospitals, in so far as they apply to people with serious mental health problems:
● psychiatric day hospitals offering continuing care to people with severe mental disorders.

Studies were excluded if the participants were predominantly either over 65 years or under 18 years of age.

5.9.2 Studies considered[36]

The GDG chose to use the Cochrane systematic review (Marshall *et al.*, 2003) that compared day treatment programmes with outpatient care for people with

---

[36]Study IDs in title case refer to studies included in the previous guideline. References for these studies are in Appendix 18.

non-psychotic disorders, as the starting point for this section. Of the four studies included in the Cochrane review (Bateman1999, Dick1991, Piper1993, Tyrer1979), Bateman1999 was excluded from the review for this guideline because the sample were patients diagnosed with borderline personality disorder.

Therefore, three studies (Dick1991, Piper1993, Tyrer1979) were included providing data on 428 participants. Characteristics of the included studies are in Appendix 17a, which also includes details of excluded studies.

5.9.3   Clinical evidence statements[37]

Effect of treatment on death (all causes)
There is insufficient evidence to determine whether there is a clinically important difference between non-acute day hospitals and outpatient care on reducing the likelihood of death during the study (K = 1; N = 106; RR = 2.42; 95% CI, 0.23 to 25.85).

Effect of treatment on efficacy
There is insufficient evidence to determine whether there is a clinically important difference between non-acute day hospitals and outpatient care on reducing the likelihood of admission to hospital during the study at 6 to 8 months (K = 2; N = 202; RR = 1.48; 95% CI, 0.38 to 5.76) and at 24 months (K = 1; N = 106; RR = 1.81; 95% CI, 0.54 to 6.05).

There is insufficient evidence to determine whether there is a clinically important difference between non-acute day hospitals and outpatient care on improving the patient's mental state (change from baseline on the Present State Examination [PSE]) at 4 months (K = 1; N = 89; WMD = –3.72; 95% CI, –8.69 to 1.25) and at 8 months (K = 1; N = 88; WMD = –3.39; 95% CI, –8.96 to 2.18).

Effect of treatment on social functioning
There is insufficient evidence to determine whether there is a clinically important difference between non-acute day hospitals and outpatient care on improving the patient's social functioning (change from baseline on the Social Functioning Schedule [SFS]) at 4 months (K = 1; N = 89; WMD = –3.24; 95% CI, –8.07 to 1.59) and at 8 months (K = 1; N = 89; WMD = –4.38; 95% CI, –9.95 to 1.19).

Effect of treatment on acceptability
There is insufficient evidence to determine whether there is a clinically important difference between non-acute day hospitals and outpatient care on reducing the likelihood of patients reporting that they were not satisfied with care (assuming that people who left early were dissatisfied; K = 2; N = 200; RR = 0.97; 95% CI, 0.68 to 1.39).

---

[37]The forest plots can be found in Appendix 19a.

There is insufficient evidence to determine whether there is a clinically important difference between non-acute day hospitals and outpatient care on reducing the number of people lost to follow-up at 6 to 8 months (K = 2; N = 202; RR = 1.08; 95% CI, 0.49 to 2.38), at about 12 months (K = 1; N = 226; RR = 1.35; 95% CI, 0.94 to 1.94) and at 24 months (K = 1; N = 106; RR = 1.61; 95% CI, 0.85 to 3.07).

5.9.4   Clinical summary

There is currently insufficient evidence to determine whether acute day hospital care differs from inpatient care in terms of readmission to hospital after discharge. With regard to treatment acceptability, the evidence is inconclusive although there is a trend favouring day hospitals.

There is currently insufficient evidence to determine whether non-acute day hospital care differs from outpatient care in terms of admission to hospital, mental state, death, social functioning or acceptability of treatment.**

5.10   NON-STATUTORY SUPPORT

The following sections marked by asterisks (**_**) are from the previous guideline and have not been updated for this guideline except for style and minor clarification.

5.10.1   Introduction

**It is widely accepted that social support can play an important part in a person's propensity to develop depression and their ability to recover from it. Despite this and the considerable amount of work that has described the importance of social support, few formal studies of the potential therapeutic benefits of different forms of social support have been undertaken.

There is evidence from a series of studies that providing social support in the sense of befriending (women with depression) confers benefits (Brown & Harris, 1978). There is also evidence to suggest that supported engagement with a range of non-statutory sector services is beneficial, but this study was not limited to patients with depression and so was excluded from the review (Grant *et al.*, 2000). Given that social isolation is associated with poor outcome and chronicity in depression, this is regrettable. Several descriptive reports suggest that the provision of social support (for example, the Newpin Project; Mills & Pound, 1996) in a variety of non-healthcare settings may confer some benefit and it is hoped that such projects are the subject of more formal evaluation.

There are many organisations offering local group peer support to people with depression, including Depression Alliance and Mind. Although such self-help groups are likely to be beneficial, the review team were unable to find any research evidence for their effectiveness.

Definition

The GDG agreed the following definition for non-statutory support:

● A range of community-based interventions often not provided by healthcare professionals, which provide support, activities and social contact in order to improve the outcome of depression.

5.10.2   Studies considered[38]

The review team found one RCT (Harris1999) of befriending compared with waitlist control in people with depression. Characteristics of the included study are in Appendix 17a, which also includes details of excluded studies.

5.10.3   Clinical evidence statements[39]

Befriending versus wait list control

One RCT of befriending (Harris1999) was identified, so a descriptive review of the data is presented here. In this trial befriending was defined as 'meeting and talking with a depressed woman for a minimum of one hour each week and acting as a friend to her, listening and "being there for her"'. The trained volunteer female befrienders were also encouraged to accompany their 'befriendee' on trips, to broaden their range of activities, to offer practical support with ongoing difficulties and to help create 'fresh start' experiences often found to precede remission in previous work. Befriendees were women with chronic depression in inner London who were interested in being befriended. Women were allowed to be on other treatments such as antidepressants and contact with other healthcare professionals. On an intention-to-treat analysis a clinically important effect upon remission was found at 1 year:

There is some evidence suggesting that there is a clinically important difference favouring befriending over waitlist control on increasing the likelihood of patients achieving remission (defined as patients not meeting 'caseness' for depression[40]) ($K = 1$, $N = 86$, RR = 0.58; 95% CI, 0.36 to 0.93).

Other treatments monitored naturalistically did not relate to remission nor did initial duration of chronic episode or comorbidity. Although remission tended to be higher among those completing the full 12 months of befriending, as opposed to 2 to 6 months, this did not reach statistical significance. This suggests that the benefits of befriending may be obtained by a shorter intervention.

---

[38]Study IDs in title case refer to studies included in the previous guideline. References for these studies are in Appendix 18.

[39]The forest plots can be found in Appendix 19a.

[40]Depressed mood at four out of 10 symptoms on the PSE-10.

Additional trials with less restricted intake conditions and in more naturalistic general practice settings might confirm volunteer befriending as a useful adjunct to current treatments.

5.10.4 Clinical summary

There is some evidence that befriending given to women with chronic depression as an adjunct to drug or psychological treatment may increase the likelihood of remission.**

5.10.5 Recommendation

5.10.5.1 For people with long-standing moderate or severe depression who would benefit from additional social or vocational support, consider:
- befriending as an adjunct to pharmacological or psychological treatments; befriending should be by trained volunteers providing, typically, at least weekly contact for between 2 and 6 months[41]
- a rehabilitation programme if a person's depression has resulted in loss of work or disengagement from other social activities over a longer term.

5.11 RESEARCH RECOMMENDATION

5.11.1.1 The efficacy and cost effectiveness of different systems for the organisation of care for people with depression.

In people with mild, moderate or severe depression, what system of care (stepped care versus matched care) is more clinically effective and cost effective in improving outcomes?

Why this is important
The best structures for the delivery of effective care for depression are poorly understood. Stepped-care models are widely implemented but the efficacy of this model compared with matched care is uncertain. Evidence on the relative benefits of the two approaches and the differential effects by depression severity is needed. The results of this study will have important implications for the structure of depression treatment services in the NHS.

This question should be answered using a randomised controlled design which reports short-term and medium-term outcomes (including cost-effectiveness

---

[41]The evidence for this part of the recommendation has not been updated since the previous guideline. Any wording changes have been made for clarification only.

outcomes) of at least 18 months' duration. In stepped care the majority of patients will first be offered a low-intensity intervention by a paraprofessional unless there are significant risk factors dictating otherwise. In matched care a comprehensive mental health assessment will determine which intervention a patient should receive. The full range of effective interventions (both psychological and pharmacological) should be made available in both arms of the trial. The outcomes chosen should reflect both observer and patient-rated assessments of improvement and an assessment of the acceptability of the treatment options. The study needs to be large enough to determine the presence or absence of clinically important effects, and moderators (including the severity of depression) of response should be investigated.

6 INTRODUCTION TO PSYCHOLOGICAL AND PSYCHOSOCIAL INTERVENTIONS

6.1 INTRODUCTION

A range of psychological and psychosocial interventions for depression have been shown to relieve the symptoms of the condition and there is growing evidence that psychosocial and psychological therapies can help people recover from depression in the longer-term (NICE, 2004a). However, not everyone responds to treatment and of those people who do, not everyone remains free of depression in the long term. Therefore there is a need to offer a range of psychological and psychosocial interventions and for further clinical innovation focused on improving treatment outcomes.

People with depression typically prefer psychological and psychosocial treatments to medication (Prins *et al.*, 2008) and value outcomes beyond symptom reduction that include positive mental health and a return to usual functioning (Zimmerman *et al.*, 2006). Significant national initiatives are beginning to explore how to maximise the accessibility, acceptability and cost effectiveness of psychological and psychosocial interventions. This chapter sets out how these treatments have emerged as evidence-based approaches and some of the contextual issues that are important in translating recommendations based on clinical research to people presenting to the NHS with depression. Research recommendations that, if funded, could inform the recommendations of future clinical guidelines, are made in Chapter 8.

6.2 RECOMMENDING PSYCHOLOGICAL AND PSYCHOSOCIAL TREATMENTS

This guideline is concerned with promoting clinically and cost-effective treatments that should be provided in the NHS. This means that treatments need to have been shown to work against robust criteria that support evidence-based practice (see Chapter 3) and which are likely to be cost effective. Since the previous NICE guideline on depression (NICE, 2004a) there has been significant therapeutic innovation and research effort but in comparison with the research on pharmacological interventions, the extent of the development is limited. However, there are sufficient developments to necessitate a significant review of the literature with consequent refinements to recommendations from the previous guideline. It is important to note the limitations of the available data for making recommendations about psychological and psychosocial treatments (see Pilling [2008] for a fuller discussion of these issues).

Recommendations are made where there is robust evidence to support the effectiveness of an intervention. While a broad array of psychosocial and alternative therapies may be accessed by people seeking help with depression, for many established therapies and promising new developments there will be insufficient evidence to recommend them. However, absence of evidence does not mean evidence of no effect. Just because an approach is not recommended here does not mean that it is not effective or that it should never be provided, rather that the question of efficacy has not yet been adequately addressed to warrant a specific recommendation. In other cases a weak or limited evidence base may lead to a qualified or restricted recommendation. Where established therapies are not recommended, this does not necessarily mean that the withdrawal of provision from the NHS is endorsed but may suggest the need for further research to establish their effectiveness or otherwise.

The majority of available trials of psychological and psychosocial interventions have focused on the acute treatment of depression, usually of mild to moderate severity (although it should be noted that many of the participants in these trials will have had a number of previous episodes of depression). Several of the approaches considered below have shown consistently greater efficacy than control conditions in such trials. However, with even the most effective treatments for depression, a substantial minority of patients do not respond adequately to treatment (both pharmacological and psychological), and of those who do, a substantial proportion relapse. Typically, 50 to 70% of patients in trials will achieve remission but a substantial proportion will go on to relapse (see Chapter 2). The likelihood of relapse will depend on the person's history of depression and is higher in those with a significant past history of depression. For example, in one study of the psychological treatment of people with mostly chronic or recurrent depression (mean duration of episode: 46 months), less than half of treated patients achieved full remission and sustained it over a period of 2 years following treatment (for example, Hollon *et al.*, 2005). However, this should be contrasted with data from the STAR*D trial focusing on pharmacological treatments where remission rates in the initial phase of the study were between 28 and 33% (Trivedi *et al.*, 2006).

In the research recommendations (see Section 8.12), priorities for further research are suggested in order to establish more definitively which therapies work most effectively for people with depression, especially in supporting their longer-term recovery – a pressing concern for those people who experience recurrent depression.

6.3   HOW DO PSYCHOLOGICAL AND PSYCHOSOCIAL INTERVENTIONS BECOME EVIDENCE BASED?

For a therapy to become established as an effective treatment in routine care it typically passes through several phases of treatment development (Rounsaville *et al.*, 2001; Craig *et al.*, 2008). There is ongoing debate among researchers, therapists and policy makers about what constitutes the best evidence for psychological and psychosocial interventions and how this evidence should be used (Kazdin, 2008). The development of the evidence base is nicely illustrated by the 'hourglass model' (Salkovskis, 1995) set out in Figure 5.

In the first phase of treatment development, a theoretical model and therapeutic approach are articulated. As in most clinical sciences, these are normally guided by

Figure 5: The hourglass model

The Hourglass Model of Psychological Therapies Research

Clinical observation; exploratory
research; theory development;
experimental + research +
uncontrolled trials + case series

Randomised controlled trial

Service models research

Real-world research

astute clinical observations and theoretical ideas about processes involved in the disorder, and followed by interventions designed to target these processes. For example, in cognitive therapy negative distortions in thinking were identified as key in maintaining depression, and therapy therefore aims to help clients identify and respond to these distortions. Through a process of careful experimentation and observation, clinical innovators develop novel treatment approaches, often in the form of a treatment manual[42]. For example, a treatment manual for cognitive therapy for depression sets out how to engage people, help people become more active, and test out and change their cognitive distortions and underlying beliefs (Beck *et al.*, 1979).

Often in this initial phase of treatment development, case reports, single case studies and expert opinion provide preliminary evidence that is used to refine the treatment approach. If the treatment appears promising, an uncontrolled open trial enables preliminary research into the potential efficacy of a treatment. This exploratory trial lays the groundwork for a more definitive trial.

The neck of the hourglass represents the stage where a definitive RCT is conducted to establish efficacy. In healthcare research the RCT is considered the gold standard for establishing a treatment's efficacy due to its ability to distinguish, in an unbiased manner, between treatment outcomes and outcomes for the group who did not receive treatment. Thus, the new treatment is compared with a meaningful comparison group; this may include another active treatment, and, if ethically

---

[42]A treatment manual describes how an intervention should be delivered. Typically it contains an account of the disorder and/or problem to be treated and the specific population for which the intervention was developed. It sets out the theoretical rationale for the intervention and specifies the knowledge and skills required to deliver the intervention competently. In many cases manuals also specify the frequency, intensity and duration of the intervention. Manuals usually contain a mix of indicative as well as prescriptive elements, since effective implementation of most interventions involves an element of clinical judgement.

justifiable, with other comparators such as a placebo, an attentional control, usual care or no treatment. This enables the researchers to conclude that the new treatment is better than no active treatment and as good as, or superior to, another established treatment. It is beyond the scope of this chapter to discuss the RCT in detail and its role in evaluating psychosocial treatments. RCTs are explored and critiqued in detail elsewhere (Westen *et al.*, 2004; Stirman *et al.*, 2005; De Los Reyes & Kazdin, 2008; Kazdin, 2008; Rawlins, 2008).

The final phase of treatment development is depicted in the bottom of the hourglass. Having established that the therapy is effective, this phase of treatment development asks: is the treatment exportable to real world settings where therapist competence may be more variable, treatment delivery less adherent and treatment contexts more varied? In short, when the high internal validity expected in an RCT is traded for external validity, do the outcomes hold up? Is the treatment acceptable and accessible? Can therapists be readily trained, is the therapy appropriate for routine care settings, and is it acceptable to clients and therapists? Other research designs, and routinely collected outcomes data, may be suited to answering important questions at this stage. Finally, as the evidence base accumulates, systematic literature reviews and meta-analyses can make sense of larger bodies of data and make inferences about which factors may moderate or mediate treatment effects. These studies also drive the next incremental phases of clinical research.

The phases of treatment development illustrated in the hourglass demand considerable resource and time and this may explain the more limited evidence base for psychological and psychosocial interventions compared with pharmacological interventions. This means that many therapies have not been subjected to a full test of their efficacy. To take the example of CBT, the development work took place in the 1960s and 1970s; the manual was published in 1979 (Beck *et al.*, 1979); the first RCTs were published in the late 1970s and early 1980s (Rush *et al.*, 1977; Kovacs *et al.*, 1981; Rush *et al.*, 1981); the first meta-analysis was conducted in 1990 (Robinson *et al.*, 1990); and the effectiveness and cost-effectiveness studies have only started to emerge in the last decade (Bower *et al.*, 2000; Byford *et al.*, 2003; Scott *et al.*, 2003).

In summary, over the past 50 years there has been a significant expansion of theories and therapies for depression. However, only a relatively small number of these therapies have travelled the full empirical road and demonstrated that they are efficacious and can be cost-effective treatment options for the NHS.

6.3.1   Recent systematic reviews of psychosocial treatments for depression

As part of the development of this guideline update, the GDG and technical team reviewed and evaluated not only relevant RCTs, but also considered recent meta-analyses that had been published since the previous guideline. The intention was to both inform the reviews undertaken for this guideline and provide a better understanding of the context for it. As will be apparent from the summary below, while meta-analysis can be a powerful tool for synthesising the results of several studies, it is not without problems. The most frequent challenges in interpreting meta-analyses are the nature of the studies selected for inclusion, the approach to synthesising the data and the way the results are interpreted.

Of the recent meta-analyses identified during the development of this guideline, seven were considered of particular relevance and they are briefly summarised below. All the meta-analyses were assessed for quality and the references from the included studies were checked to verify that, where appropriate, they had been considered for the reviews in this guideline.

One meta-analysis compared the efficacy of psychological and pharmacological interventions in the treatment of adult depressive disorders (Cuijpers *et al.*, 2008a). Three meta-analyses analysed the efficacy of psychodynamic psychotherapy in several mental health disorders including depression (Leichsenring *et al.*, 2004; Abbass *et al.*, 2008; Leichsenring & Rabung, 2008). A further meta-analysis looked at different types of psychological treatments and analysed their effectiveness in the treatment of depression (Cuijpers *et al.*, 2008b). Ekers and colleagues (2007) reviewed the effectiveness of behavioural activation in the treatment of depression. Finally, a Cochrane review (Mead *et al.*, 2008) evaluated the effectiveness of physical exercise in the treatment of depression.

Cuijpers and colleagues (2008a) concluded that pharmacological and psychological interventions may be equivalent in major depression but that pharmacological interventions may be more effective for dysthymia than psychological interventions (see Chapter 13 for a review of interventions for subthreshold depressive symptoms). This is largely supported by the available data. However, this finding may reflect the fact that the dataset for pharmacological interventions is stronger (it has a more extensive set of high-quality studies and less heterogeneity) than that for psychological interventions, rather than it being due to a large number of high-quality head-to-head studies, which would best inform a study of comparative effectiveness. Cuijpers and colleagues (2008b) concluded that there were no large differences in efficacy between psychological treatments for mild to moderate depression including CBT, problem solving, behavioural activation[43], interpersonal therapy (IPT), short-term psychodynamic psychotherapy, social skills training and non-directive supportive therapy. However, a more accurate conclusion would be that Cuijpers and colleagues (2008a) had failed to find such differences rather than establishing that no differences existed. This failure rests on two main issues: first, the trials they reviewed were designed to test differences in efficacy not establish equivalence (see Piaggio and colleagues [2006] for fuller discussion of this issue); second, the nature of the disorders reviewed (which included physical health problems, dementia and postnatal depression), and the nature of the interventions compared (high- and low-intensity interventions were grouped together), seriously limited the ability of the data to support the conclusions drawn.

Leichsenring and colleagues (2004), Leichsenring and Rabung (2008) and Abbass and colleagues (2008) concluded that psychodynamic psychotherapy is effective in the treatment of a broad range of mental health disorders (and by implication depression). Leichsenring and Rabung (2008) looked at long-term psychodynamic

---

[43]Note that these three interventions may be seen as belonging to a broad school of cognitive and behavioural therapies.

psychotherapy compared with shorter forms of psychotherapy. Leichsenring and colleagues (2004) and Abbass and colleagues (2008) evaluated the effectiveness of short-term psychodynamic psychotherapy versus control groups ranging from medication management to psychotherapeutic support. However, it should be noted that these reviews contained very few studies of depression (three in total across the three reviews from which it was possible to extract data). The fact that so few studies were concerned with depression significantly limits the validity of their conclusions in relation to this guideline. For example in the Knekt and colleagues' (2008) study of short- and long-term psychodynamic versions of solution-focused psychotherapy outpatients with mood or anxiety disorders only 65.8% had recurrent episodes of major depressive disorder. They reported a slow rate of recovery initially in the psychodynamic psychotherapy group and it is difficult to determine whether or not the long-term benefits associated with psychodynamic psychotherapy resulted specifically from the therapy or the prolonged contact with the therapist during that time. In addition, there were a large number of patients in the study who had subsidiary treatments during the same period, which confounds interpretation of the data.

Ekers and colleagues' (2007) review concluded that behavioural activation is an effective treatment for depression, with outcomes superior to those of supportive counselling and brief psychotherapy. However, their conclusion should be treated with some caution for the following reasons: their analysis combined data from trials that included subthreshold symptoms; they combined data on high- and low-intensity behavioural activation; and the studies they included were not all peer-reviewed and did not meet the quality criteria established for this guideline. High- and low-intensity behavioural activation, and other psychological interventions, are considered separately in this guideline. In Ekers and colleagues' (2007) and a number of other reviews, these interventions are combined in the meta-analyses, again leading to caution in the way the results are interpreted.

Mead and colleagues (2008) concluded that physical activity should be recommended for people with depressive symptoms and those who fulfil the diagnostic criteria for depression, but noted that the effects are less convincing for those with an established diagnosis. They did not specify details about particular forms (that is, aerobic, anaerobic, mixed, and so on), whether group or individual, or duration of exercise because of lack of consistent evidence. They state that because discontinuation from exercise can be substantial, it is better to recommend a physical activity that the person will enjoy.

6.3.2 Increasing the availability of psychological and psychosocial therapies in healthcare settings

The previous guideline on depression (NICE, 2004a) has been influential in reshaping the types of psychological and psychosocial treatments available for people with depression. Most notably there has been a recent increase in the accessibility of evidence-based therapies, in particular for people with common mental health disorders (Department of Health, 2007). Alongside the NICE guideline and evidence base, a number of factors determine whether a psychological or psychosocial therapy becomes accessible in the NHS. First, public demand and expectation influence service commissioners. User groups have long advocated the need for psychological and psychosocial approaches and this has influenced commissioning at a national and regional level. The high direct and indirect costs associated with depression, and the suffering experienced by people with depression and their families and carers, have also been drivers. Psychosocial and psychological interventions, particularly high-intensity therapies that involve one-to-one therapy over longer periods of time, are resource intensive. The NHS, like all healthcare systems, has a finite limit on its resources and there is therefore an impetus to find therapies that are as cost effective as possible. This has been one of the drivers for the development of less intensive therapies as well as innovative delivery formats such as group-based work. Finally, there is greater understanding of how depression presents in the NHS and models of care and service delivery have been shaped accordingly (see Chapter 5).

6.3.3   Improving Access to Psychological Therapies initiative as an example of increasing the accessibility of established evidence-based therapies

The IAPT programme (Department of Health, 2007) supports Primary Care Trusts in England in implementing NICE guidelines for people with depression and anxiety disorders (similar programmes are underway in Scotland and Northern Ireland). The goal is to alleviate depression and anxiety using NICE-recommended treatments and help people return to full social and occupational functioning. The development of IAPT was driven by an acknowledgement that the treatments NICE recommended were not as accessible as they should be and sought to redress this imbalance through a large investment of new training and service monies in the NHS.

The IAPT programme began in 2006 with demonstration sites in Doncaster and Newham focused on therapies for adults of working age. In 2007, 11 further IAPT pathfinder sites began to explore the specific benefits of services to vulnerable groups. A national rollout of IAPT delivery sites is now underway and is scheduled to complete in 2013. It is expected that it will lead to large increases in the accessibility of evidence-based psychosocial and psychological interventions. The intention is to provide £340 million of additional funding to train 3,600 therapists and treat a further 45,000 patients per year. The initial focus of the programme is on high- and low-intensity psychological CBT-based interventions focused on new presentations to services and including the opportunity for self-referral. Many of those presenting to services will of course have chronic disorders and will, in the case of depression, require not just the treatment of the acute problems but also help with the prevention of relapse. In 2009 it is expected that other interventions such as IPT will form part of the treatments offered by IAPT.

Another development from the previous guideline that formed part of the IAPT programme is the stepped care framework (see Chapter 5 for further details), which became the organising principle for the provision of IAPT services. A related element of the organisation of psychological therapies in the IAPT programme is the distinction between high-intensity psychological interventions (that is, formal psychological therapies such as CBT, IPT or couples therapy provided by a trained therapists) and low-intensity interventions such as CCBT, physical activity programmes and guided self-help, where a paraprofessional acts to facilitate or support the use of self-help materials and not to provide the therapy *per se*. This distinction between high- and low-intensity is adopted in this guideline and is the basis on which Chapters 7 and 8 are organised.

6.4 CONTEXTUAL FACTORS THAT IMPACT ON CLINICAL PRACTICE

Recommendations in this guideline are largely based on the syntheses of trial data from groups of patients with depression; inevitably they make recommendations about the *average* patient. This approach is consistent with that taken in all clinical guidelines and is set out in Chapter 1 of this guideline; that is, clinical guidelines are a guide for clinicians and not a substitute for clinical judgement, which often involves tailoring the recommendation to the needs of the individual. Unfortunately the relationship of factors that may guide the tailoring of clinical practice recommendations to individual needs, including the impact of such tailoring on outcomes, is poorly understood both for psychological interventions and pharmacological interventions (see Chapters 9 to 12). In the same way that RCTs can be critiqued, so too can some of the assumptions typically made in clinical practice (Kazdin, 2008). There is an increasing research literature addressing factors that can affect treatment choices and outcomes but the research has as yet produced little that directly relates to the outcome of psychosocial and psychological treatments for depression. It is beyond the scope of this chapter to review these in depth, but some of the key factors that may influence treatment decisions are discussed below. Interested readers can refer to several texts for a more detailed review, for example, Lambert and Ogles (2004) and Roth and Pilling (2009).

6.4.1 Patient factors

A broad array of patient factors that could potentially affect treatment choices have been considered, including demographics, marital status, social factors and culture, nature of depression, expectations and preferences and experiences of previous treatment. In the main, few factors consistently predict treatment outcomes except chronicity and severity of depression, which point to reduced treatment effectiveness across treatment modalities (for example, Sotsky *et al.*, 1991).

6.4.2 Therapist factors

Several therapist factors that could potentially affect treatment have been considered, including demographics, professional background, training, use of supervision and competence. Two related aspects are dealt with below, namely the therapeutic alliance and therapist competence.

6.4.3   The therapeutic alliance

There are various definitions of the therapeutic alliance, but in general terms it is viewed as a constructive relationship between therapist and client, characterised by a positive and mutually respectful stance in which both parties work on the joint enterprise of change. Bordin (1979) conceptualised the alliance as having three elements comprising the relationship between therapist and patient: agreement on the relevance of the tasks (or techniques) employed in therapy, agreement about the goals or outcomes the therapy aims to achieve, and the quality of the bond between therapist and patient.

There has been considerable debate about the importance of the alliance as a factor in promoting change, with some commentators arguing that technique is inappropriately privileged over the alliance, a position reflected in many humanistic models where the therapeutic relationship itself is seen as integral to the change process, with technique relegated to a secondary role (for example, Rogers, 1951). The failure of some comparative trials to demonstrate differences in outcome between active psychological therapies (for example, Elkin, 1994) is often cited in support of this argument and is usually referred to as 'the dodo-bird hypothesis' (Luborsky *et al.*, 1975). However, apart from the fact that dodo-bird findings may not be as ubiquitous as is sometimes claimed this does not logically imply that therapy technique is irrelevant to outcome. Identifying and interpreting equivalence of benefit across therapies remains a live debate (for example, Ahn & Wampold, 2001; Stiles *et al.*, 2006) but should also include a consideration of cost effectiveness as well as clinical efficacy (NICE, 2008a).

Meta-analytic reviews report consistent evidence of a positive association of the alliance with better outcomes with a correlation of around 0.25 (for example, Horvath & Symonds, 1991; Martin *et al.*, 2000), a finding that applies across a heterogeneous group of trials (in terms of variables such as type of therapy, patient presentation, type of measures applied and the stage of therapy at which measures are applied). However, it is the consistency, rather than the size of this correlation, which is most striking, since a correlation of 0.25 would suggest it could account for only 6% of the variance in the outcome. It should also be noted that the alliance is itself affected by the process of treatment; for example Feeley and colleagues (1999) reported that alliance quality was related to early symptom change. Therefore it seems reasonable to debate the extent to which a good alliance is necessary for a positive outcome of an intervention, but clearly it is unlikely to be sufficient to account for the majority of the variance in outcome.

6.4.4   Therapist competence

Studies of the relationship between therapist competence and outcome suggest that all therapists have variable outcomes, although some therapists produce consistently better outcomes (for example, Okiishi *et al.*, 2003). There is evidence that more competent therapists produce better outcomes (Barber *et al.*, 1996, 2006; Kuyken & Tsivrikos, 2009). A number of studies have also sought to examine more precisely therapist competence and its relation to outcomes; that is, what is it that therapists do in order to achieve good outcomes? A number of studies are briefly reviewed here.

This section, which focuses mainly on CBT and depression, draws on a more extensive review of the area by Roth and Pilling (2009). In an early study, Shaw and colleagues (1999) examined competence in the treatment of 36 patients treated by eight therapists offering CBT as part of the National Institute of Mental Health in England trial of depression (Elkin *et al.*, 1989). Ratings of competence were made on the Cognitive Therapy Scale (CTS). Although the simple correlation of the CTS with outcome suggested that it contributed little to outcome variance, regression analyses indicated a more specific set of associations; specifically, when controlling for pre-therapy depression scores, adherence and the alliance, the overall CTS score accounted for 15% of the variance in outcome. However, a subset of items on the CTS accounted for most of this association.

Some understanding of what may account for this association emerges from three studies by DeRubeis's research group (DeRubeis & Feeley, 1990; Feeley *et al.*, 1999; Brotman *et al.*, 2009). All of the studies made use of the Collaborative Study Psychotherapy Rating Scale (CSPRS: Hollon *et al.*, 1988), subscales of which contained items specific to CBT. On the basis of factor analysis, the CBT items were separated into two subscales labelled 'cognitive therapy – concrete' and 'cognitive therapy – abstract'. Concrete techniques can be thought of as pragmatic aspects of therapy (such as establishing the session agenda, setting homework tasks or helping clients identify and modify negative automatic thoughts). Both DeRubeis and Feeley (1990) and Feeley and colleagues (1999) found some evidence for a significant association between the use of 'concrete' CBT techniques and better outcomes. The benefits of high levels of competence over and above levels required for basic practice has been studied in most detail in the literature on CBT for depression. In general, high severity and comorbidity, especially with Axis II pathology, have been associated with poorer outcomes in therapies, but the detrimental impact of these factors is lessened for highly competent therapists. DeRubeis and colleagues (2005) found that the most competent therapists had good outcomes even for patients with the most severe levels of depression. Kuyken and Tsivrikos (2009) found that therapists who are more competent have better patient outcomes regardless of the degree of patient comorbidity. In patients with neurotic disorders (Kingdon *et al.*, 1996) and personality disorders (Davidson *et al.*, 2004), higher levels of competence were associated with greater improvements in depressive symptoms. Although competence in psychological therapies is hard to measure in routine practice, degrees of formal training (Brosan *et al.*, 2007) and experience in that modality (James *et al.*, 2001) are associated with competence and are independently associated with better outcomes (Burns & Nolen-Hoeksema, 1992). All therapists should have levels of training and experience adequate to ensure a basic level of competence in the therapy they are practicing, and the highest possible levels of training and experience are desirable for those therapists treating patients with severe, enduring or complex presentations. In routine practice in services providing psychological therapies for depression, therapists should receive regular supervision and monitoring of outcomes.

Trepka and colleagues (2004) examined the impact of competence by analysing outcomes in Cahill and colleagues' (2003) study. Six clinical psychologists (with between 1 and 6 years' post-qualification experience) treated 30 patients with depression using CBT, with ratings of competence made on the CTS. In a completer sample (N = 21) better outcomes were associated with overall competence on the CTS (r = 0.47); in the full sample this association was only found with the 'specific CBT skills' subscale of the CTS. Using a stringent measure of recovery (a BDI score no more than one SD from the non-distressed mean), nine of the 10 completer patients treated by the more competent therapists recovered, compared with four of the 11 clients treated by the less competent therapists. These results remained even when analysis controlled for levels of the therapeutic alliance.

Agreeing and monitoring homework is one of the set of 'concrete' CBT skills identified above. All forms of CBT place an emphasis on the role of homework because it provides a powerful opportunity for patients to test their expectations. A small number of studies have explored whether compliance with homework is related to better outcomes, although rather fewer have examined the therapist behaviours associated with better patient 'compliance' with homework itself. Kazantzis and colleagues (2000) report a meta-analysis of 27 trials of cognitive and/or behavioural interventions that contained data relevant to the link between homework assignment, compliance and outcome. In 19 trials patients were being treated for depression or anxiety; the remainder were seen for a range of other problems. Of these, 11 reported on the effects of assigning homework in therapy and 16 on the impact of compliance. The type of homework varied, as did the way in which compliance was monitored, although this was usually by therapist report. Overall there was a significant, although modest, association between outcome and assigning homework tasks (r = 0.36), and between outcome and homework compliance (r = 0.22). While Kazantzis and colleagues (2000) indicate that homework has greater impact for patients with depression than anxiety disorders, the number of trials on which this comparison is made is small and any conclusions must therefore be tentative.

Bryant and colleagues (1999) examined factors leading to homework compliance in 26 patients with depression receiving CBT from four therapists. As in other studies, greater compliance with homework was associated with better outcome. In terms of therapist behaviours, it was not so much therapists' CBT-specific skills (such as skilfully assigning homework or providing a rationale for homework) that were associated with compliance, but ratings of their general therapeutic skills, and particularly whether they explicitly reviewed the homework assigned in the previous session. There was also some evidence that compliance was increased if therapists checked how the patient felt about the task being set and identified potential difficulties in carrying it out.

The focus of the research on both the alliance and therapist competence has been on high-intensity interventions but it is reasonable to expect that they are potentially of equal importance in the effective delivery of low-intensity interventions.

Table 18: Databases searched and inclusion/exclusion criteria for clinical effectiveness of psychological treatments

Electronic databases	MEDLINE, EMBASE, PsycINFO, CINAHL
Date searched	Database inception to January 2008
Update searches	July 2008
Study design	RCT
Population	People with a diagnosis of depression according to DSM, ICD or similar criteria, or depressive symptoms as indicated by depression scale score for subthreshold and other groups
Treatments	Behavioural activation Cognitive behavioural therapies CCBT Counselling Couples therapy Guided self-help IPT Problem solving Physical activity Rational emotive behaviour therapy Short-term psychodynamic psychotherapy

6.5 DATABASES SEARCHED AND INCLUSION/EXCLUSION CRITERIA

For the guideline update, a new systematic search was conducted looking at both published and unpublished RCTs. The electronic databases searched for published trials are given in Table 18 (further information about the search strategy can be found in Appendix 8).

6.6 STUDIES CONSIDERED[44]

A total of 139 trials relating to clinical evidence met the eligibility criteria set by the GDG, providing data on 12,934 participants. All trials were published in

---

[44]Here and elsewhere in the guideline, each study considered for review is referred to by a 'study ID' made up of first author and publication date (unless a study is in press or only submitted for publication, when first author only is used). Study IDs in title case refer to studies included in the previous guideline and study IDs in capital letters refer to studies found and included in this guideline update. References for studies from the previous guideline are in Appendix 18 and references for studies for the update are in Appendix 17b.

168

peer-reviewed journals between 1979 and 2009. In addition, 95 studies found in the search for this guideline update were excluded from the analysis. Four studies included in the previous guideline were excluded from this guideline update (see Section 7.2.3, Section 8.3.1 and Section 8.6.1). Further information about both included and excluded studies can be found in Appendix 17b[45].

---

[45]Appendix 17b, and also Appendix 16b and 19b, contain a number of studies (such as BROWN2001, CONSTANTINO2008, MANBER2008 and PASSMORE2006) that do not appear in the full guideline. These studies were not excluded because they still met the criteria for the review, but they did not warrant inclusion in the full guideline because they did not show any clear results.

7   LOW-INTENSITY PSYCHOSOCIAL INTERVENTIONS

This chapter reviews the evidence for the effectiveness of a range of low-intensity interventions, including computerised cognitive behavioural therapy (CCBT), guided self-help and physical activity programmes in the treatment of depression.

7.1   COMPUTERISED COGNITIVE BEHAVIOURAL THERAPY

7.1.1   Introduction

The use of information technology to deliver psychological treatments has been explored, for example self-help delivered by telephone (Osgood-Hynes *et al.*, 1998), over the internet (Christensen *et al.*, 2002) and by computer (Proudfoot *et al.*, 2004). Cognitive behavioural therapy (CBT) is currently the main psychological treatment approach that has been computerised. Early studies suggested that patients find computer-based treatment acceptable and they manifest degrees of clinical recovery of similar magnitude to those who have face-to-face therapy (Selmi *et al.*, 1990). The technology more recently available has led to the development of a more sophisticated range of computer-based or internet-based CBT programmes. These have been the subject of a technology appraisal (NICE, 2006a), which covers both depression and anxiety disorders. The review in this guideline supersedes and updates the aspects of the technology appraisal concerned with depression.

Computerised cognitive behavioural therapy (CCBT) programmes engage the patient in a structured programme of care, the content of which is similar to and based on the same principles as treatment provided by a therapist following a standard CBT programme. Direct staff input is usually limited to introducing the programme, brief monitoring and being available for consultation. Most of the programmes have been developed to treat a range of depressive and/or anxiety disorders, often explicitly as part of a stepped-care programme. The programmes vary in style, degree of complexity and content.

Definition
CCBT is defined in this guideline update as a form of CBT, which is delivered using a computer either via a CD-ROM, DVD or the internet. It can be used as the primary treatment intervention with minimal therapist involvement or as augmentation to a therapist-delivered programme where the introduction of CCBT supplements the work of the therapist. In the review for this guideline the focus is on CCBT as a primary intervention and not as a means of augmenting therapist delivered treatment.

7.1.2 Studies considered[46]

Seven RCTs were included, providing data on 1,676 participants. Data were available to compare CCBT with traditional CBT, group CBT, online psychoeducation, an information control, a discussion control, waitlist control and treatment as usual (TAU).

One study, PROUDFOOT2004A, included a population of people with mixed depression and anxiety, depression, subthreshold depression or anxiety. In this study, the review team and GDG calculated that only 39% of the population met criteria for major depressive disorder (MDD). Furthermore, of those people with depression and subthreshold symptoms allocation across the differing severity levels of depression (mild, moderate and severe) was not balanced[47]. The evidence is presented here for the full sample and a sub-analysis was also conducted including only those who met diagnostic criteria for depression. It is important to mention that this sub-analysis gives an indication of the effect in a depressed sample, but results should be interpreted with caution as randomisation to the study was not stratified by diagnosis.

WRIGHT2005 was excluded as the GDG did not consider the intervention provided to be the same as CCBT provided in the NHS (that is, WRIGHT2005 focused on CCBT augmentation of a therapist-delivered intervention).

Summary study characteristics of the included studies are presented in Table 19 with full details in Appendix 17b, which also includes details of excluded studies[48].

Table 19: Summary study characteristics of CCBT studies

	CCBT versus control	**CCBT versus active comparator**
No. trials (Total participants)	7 RCTs (1412)	2 RCTs (548)
Study IDs	(1) ANDERSSON2005A (2) CHRISTENSEN2004A* (3) CLARKE2002 (4) CLARKE2005* (5) PROUDFOOT2004A (6) Selmi1990 (7) SPEK2007*	(1) CHRISTENSEN2004A* (2) SPEK2007*
N/% female/mean age (years)	(1) 117/74/36 (2) 347/71/36	(1) 368/71/36 (2) 191/63/55

Continued

---

[46]Study IDs in capital letters refer to studies found and included in this guideline update.

[47]Severe depression: 39% were assigned to the CCBT group and only 33% were assigned to treatment as usual; moderate depression: 41% CCBT and 56% treatment as usual; mild depression: 20% CCBT and 11% treatment as usual.

[48]For this review studies from the previous guideline were re-entered into the study database for the guideline update in Appendix 17b.

Table 19: (*Continued*)

	CCBT versus control	CCBT versus active comparator
	(3) 223/75/44 (4) 200/77/47 (5) 274/74/44 (6) 36/64/28 (7) 201/63/55	
Diagnosis (average baseline BDI)	(1) Major depression (20.7) (2) No formal diagnosis; $>=$ 12 KPDS (CES-D 21.5) (3) Depression (25% no formal diagnosis) (CES-D 31.0) (4) Depression (22% no formal diagnosis) (CES-D 30.5) (5) Depression and/or anxiety disorders (25.0; depression-only group 30.0) (6) 69% major depression; 11% minor depression; 19% intermittent depressive disorder (22.5) (7) No formal diagnosis; $<$12 EDS (18.4)	(1) No formal diagnosis; $>=$ 12 KPDS (21.5) (2) No formal diagnosis; $<$12 EDS (18.4)
CCBT programme	(1) Not fully described; only mention is that it is based on Beck's cognitive therapy (2) MoodGYM (3)–(4) Overcoming Depression on the Internet (5) Beating the Blues (6) Not reported (7) Coping with Depression	(1) MoodGYM (2) Coping with Depression
CCBT Support	(1) Email feedback from therapist	(1) Phone to direct website use by lay interviewer

Continued

Table 19: (*Continued*)

	CCBT versus control	CCBT versus active comparator
	(2) Phone to direct website use by lay interviewer (3) Email reminders (4) Phone/postcard reminders (5) Nurse facilitating use at clinic (6) Support available at start and end of sessions (7) No support	(2) No support
Comparator	(1) Online discussion group (2) Weekly phone discussion (3)–(4) Health information webpage (5) TAU (6)–(7) Waitlist	(1) BluePages psychoeducation website (2) Group CBT: Coping with Depression course
Length of treatment	(1) 10 weeks (2) 6 weeks (3) Mean = 32 weeks (4) Mean = 16 weeks (5) 8 weeks (6) 6 weeks (7) Not reported	(1) 6 weeks (2) 10 weeks (mean)
Follow-up	(1) 6 months (2) 6 and 12 months (3)–(4) Not reported (5) 2, 3, 5, 8 months (6) 2 months (7) 12 months	(1) 6 and 12 months (2) 12 months

*3-armed trial.

7.1.3　Clinical evidence

Evidence from the important outcomes and overall quality of evidence are presented in Table 20 and Table 21. The full evidence profiles and associated forest plots can be found in Appendix 16b and Appendix 19b, respectively.

Table 20: Summary evidence profile for CCBT versus control

	CCBT versus waitlist control	CCBT versus TAU control	CCBT versus discussion control	CCBT versus information control	CCBT versus any control
Leaving study early for any reason	RR 0.82 (CI 0.57 to 1.16)	RR 1.35 (CI 0.95 to 1.93)	RR 2.23 (CI 1.51 to 3.28)	Not reported	Not reported
Quality	Low	Low	High	–	–
Number of studies; participants	K = 1; n = 202	K = 1; n = 274	K = 2; n = 477	–	–
Forest plot number	CCBT 01.01	CCBT 01.01	CCBT 01.01	–	–
Depression self-report measures at endpoint	SMD –0.27 (CI –0.54 to 0.01)	SMD –0.62 (CI –0.91 to –0.33) At 3 months: SMD –0.40 (CI –0.70 to –0.11)	At endpoint SMD –0.61 (CI –1.22 to 0) At 6 months: SMD –0.20 (CI –0.46 to 0.06)	SMD –0.23 (CI –0.43 to –0.02)	SMD –0.40 (CI –0.58 to –0.22)

	Low	At 5 months: SMD –0.42 (CI –0.73 to –0.11) At 8 months: SMD –0.56 (CI –0.85 to –0.27)	At 12 months: SMD –0.23 (CI –0.43 to –0.04)	High	High
Quality	Low	Low Moderate Moderate Moderate	Low Low High	High	High
Number of studies; participants	K = 1, n = 202	K = 1; n = 195 K = 1; n = 178 K = 1; n = 164 K = 1; n = 186	K = 2; n = 380 K = 1, n = 237 K = 2; n = 420	K = 2; n = 369	K = 7; n = 1146
Forest plot number	CCBT 01.02	CCBT 01.02 CCBT 01.03 CCBT 01.03 CCBT 01.03	CCBT 01.02 CCBT 01.03 CCBT 01.03	CCBT 01.02	CCBT 01.02

Table 21: Summary evidence profile for CCBT versus active comparator

	CCBT versus psychoeducation control	CCBT versus group CBT control
Leaving study early for any reason	RR 1.67 (CI 1.08 to 2.59) (25% versus 15%)	RR 0.79 (CI 0.56 to 1.12) (34% versus 43%)
Quality	Moderate	Low
Number of studies; participants	K = 1; n = 347	K = 1; n = 201
Forest plot number	CCBT 04.02	CCBT 04.02
Depression self-report measures at endpoint	SMD –0.03 (CI –0.27 to 0.2)	SMD 0.06 (CI –0.22 to 0.34)
Quality	Low	Low
Number of studies; participants	K = 1; n = 276	K = 1; n = 201
Forest plot number	CCBT 05.02	CCBT 05.02
	6 months' follow-up	**12 months' follow-up**
Depression self-report measures at follow-up	SMD 0.05 (CI –0.21 to 0.31)	SMD –0.02 (CI –0.22 to 0.17)
Quality	Low	Low
Number of studies; participants	K = 1; n = 221	K = 2; n = 402
Forest plot number	CCBT 06.02	CCBT 06.02

7.1.4 Clinical evidence summary

Seven studies included a comparison of CCBT with control groups. The control groups were varied: waitlist control, treatment as usual, information control and discussion control. Two further studies also compared CCBT with an active comparator: CHRISTENSEN2004A compared CCBT with a psychoeducation website and SPEK2007 compared CCBT with group CBT (delivered by a therapist). The patients in the trials included in this review were drawn predominantly from groups in the mild-to-moderate range of depressive symptoms (mean baseline BDI scores between 18 and 25). Approximately half (53%) met diagnostic criteria while the remainder had no formal diagnosis.

When studies including a non-active control group were analysed together, the results for depression scores at endpoint indicated a significant small-to-medium effect size (SMD –0.40; 95% CI –0.58, –0.22), favouring CCBT in patients with a range of severity of depressive symptoms.

In terms of the effectiveness of CCBT at follow-up, the evidence was more limited. Evidence from two studies (CHRISTENSEN2004A and SPEK2007) that compared CCBT with an active control showed that at 12 months' follow-up, CCBT had a very small effect in reducing depression self-report scores (SMD –0.02; 95% CI –0.22, 0.17); however, this result was not clinically important. One study, PROUD-FOOT2004, reported the results of CCBT in a population with depression and anxiety. The results indicate that CCBT had a significant small/medium-sized effect (SMD –0.40; 95% CI –0.70, –0.11) in reducing self-reported depression scores when compared with treatment as usual at 3 months' follow-up; a significant small/medium-sized effect (SMD –0.42; 95% CI –0.73, –0.11) at 5 months' follow-up; and a significant medium-sized effect (SMD –0.56; 95% CI –0.85, –0.27) at 8 months' follow-up. However, when the mixed depression and anxiety and anxiety only populations were removed, the sub-analysis revealed that there was insufficient evidence to determine a significant effect of CCBT (at endpoint: –0.35; 95% CI –0.90, 0.19; at 3 months: SMD 0.10; 95% CI –0.45, 0.65; and at 5 months: SMD 0.39; 95% CI –0.21, 0.99).

Also, when CCBT was compared with active controls (psychoeducation and group CBT) and results were observed at endpoint, no clinically important difference was identified.

7.1.5   Health economic evidence and considerations

The systematic search of economic literature undertaken for the guideline update identified two studies on CCBT for people with depression set in the UK (McCrone *et al.*, 2003; Kaltenthaler *et al.*, 2008). Details on the methods used for the systematic search of the economic literature are described in Chapter 3, Section 3.6.1.

The paper by McCrone and colleagues (2003) compared the Beating the Blues software package versus standard care in people with a diagnosis of depression, mixed depression and anxiety or anxiety disorders treated in the UK primary care setting.

The study was based on an RCT (PROUDFOOT2004A). It should be pointed out that this study was of a population of mixed depression and anxiety, anxiety only, and depression only. Costing was conducted prospectively on a subsample of the patients included in the RCT. The benefit measures used in the economic analysis were improvements in BDI scores, depression-free days and quality-adjusted life-years (QALYs); these were estimated using the method described by Lave and colleagues (1998). The study adopted a societal perspective. Costs included: contacts with mental healthcare staff (psychiatrists, psychologists, community mental health nurses, counsellors and other therapists); contacts with primary care staff (GPs, practice nurses, district nurses and health visitors); contacts with hospital services (inpatient care for psychiatric and physical health reasons, outpatient care, day surgery and accident and emergency attendance); contacts with home helps; contacts with other services (chiropodists, physiotherapists and dieticians); and medication (antidepressants, anxiolytics and sedatives). The cost of buying the license to use Beating the Blues (plus overheads) was also considered. The price of the computer programme licence was obtained from the manufacturer. The time horizon of the analysis was 8 months.

Results were presented in the form of cost-effectiveness acceptability curves (CEACs), which demonstrate the probability of an intervention being cost effective at different levels of willingness-to-pay per unit of effectiveness (that is, at different cost-effectiveness thresholds the decision-maker may set). The CEAC showed that the probability of Beating the Blues being cost effective over standard care was greater than 80% at a value of £40 per unit reduction in BDI score. In terms of depression-free days, the CEAC suggested that if society placed a value of £5 on a depression-free day, then there would be an 80% chance of the intervention being cost effective. At a cost effectiveness of £15,000 per QALY, the probability of Beating the Blues being cost effective was found to be 99%. At a willingness-to-pay of £5,000 per QALY, the probability of the intervention being cost effective was 85%.

The authors concluded that Beating the Blues had a high probability of being cost effective. The following limitations of the study were noted: sensitivity analysis was conducted only on the cost of the CCBT programme, as this was deemed to be the most uncertain factor. This cost was determined using the throughput levels that were based on assumptions about the number of patients likely to be picked up from a general practice. These throughput levels were highly uncertain because of the novel nature of CCBT in the NHS. The study may benefit from more scrutiny of this uncertainty by the use of sensitivity analysis. In addition, the societal perspective was adopted, which is not recommended by NICE (2009a), and the time horizon spanned just 8 months, which may have led to an underestimation of the potential costs and benefits of the intervention. The indirect method in which QALYs were estimated was also problematic; in particular, the utility value was selected from a study that combined the values from a number of different published studies using a range of sources and methods.

The economic analysis for the health technology appraisal by Kaltenthaler and colleagues (2008) aimed to evaluate a range of CCBT packages for the treatment of depression. The software packages considered included Beating the Blues, Overcoming Depression and Cope. These packages were compared with treatment as usual in primary care over an 18-month time horizon. The study population consisted of patients with mild to moderate, moderate to severe or severe depression. Variation in cost effectiveness by severity of depression was also explored with a subgroup analysis.

The same model structure was used to evaluate all three depression programmes. The decision tree model compared two arms (CCBT and standard care). CCBT was one of the depression products and this was compared with care usually received in primary care. Patients were given either CCBT or standard care over a 2-month period. A proportion of these were assumed to complete the treatment. Patients who complied with treatment were then assumed to be distributed across the four depression severity categories depending on the success of the intervention: minimal, mild to moderate, moderate to severe and severe. Those who did not complete CCBT were assumed to be offered standard care and this resulted in a set of transition probabilities between disease severity categories. Patients were assumed to spend 6 months in their new severity state following treatment. At the end of the 6-month period, which was 8 months after treatment began, patients who improved stayed the same or relapsed. If they relapsed, then at 10 months after initiating treatment they were offered either another course of CCBT or treatment as usual in the CCBT arm. In the second cycle, patients were assumed to move between severity categories as stated previously over the next 2 months and then stabilised for the remaining 6 months of the model. If they did not relapse they stayed in the post-retreatment severity category. If they did not improve in the first place (they were in moderate or severe categories), they also stayed in the same severity category.

Effectiveness estimates in terms of transition probabilities were sourced from published and unpublished trials for each of the products and further assumptions. Beating the Blues was the only product based on an RCT. The authors aimed to find utility values for depression linked to the BDI, the primary outcome in the CCBT studies. Utility values were obtained from a dataset from a recently published UK-based RCT of supervised self-help CBT in primary care by Richards and colleagues (2003). This study incorporated the EQ-5D and CORE (Evans *et al.*, 2000). CORE is a self-report questionnaire of psychological distress that has been mapped onto the BDI. The mapping function was fitted to these data to provide BDI data on each case. Based on the estimated BDI scores, Kaltenthaler and colleagues (2008) categorised patients in this dataset as having minimal (BDI score of ≤9), mild (BDI score 10 to 18), moderate (BDI score 19 to 29) and severe (BDI score 30 to 63) depression and then linked each category with an average EQ-5D score based on people's responses in each category. The ranges of scores were reported to be comparable to those found in other studies.

The study adopted the perspective of the health service. Costs included intervention costs as well as other service costs, depending on the level of severity of depression. The estimated costs of each intervention included licence fees, computer hardware, screening of patients, clinical support, capital overheads and training of support staff. Each product has a licence fee tariff, with all products offering a fixed fee for purchase at the level of general practice. The licence fee is fixed, so the cost per patient depends on the number of patients likely to use each copy. The authors made assumptions about the throughput levels used to estimate the cost per patient using the programme and about the number of patients likely to be picked up from a general practice. For example, for Beating the Blues it was estimated that 100 patients would come forward each year in practices of one to five GPs. This was based on the following assumptions: there are 10,000 patients per practice; 1000 of these have depression; and 10% of these will be treated each year. There is considerable uncertainty surrounding these assumptions and this is one of the main drivers of cost.

Beating the Blues was found to be more effective and more costly than treatment as usual. The incremental cost per QALY of Beating the Blues over treatment as usual was £1,801, for Cope it was £7,139 and for Overcoming Depression it was £5,391. The probability of accepting Beating the Blues over treatment as usual at £30,000 was 86.8%, 62.6% for Cope and 54.4% for Overcoming Depression. The subgroup analysis found no differences across the severity groupings.

All three packages for depression demonstrated an incremental cost-effectiveness ratio (ICER) well below the cost-effectiveness threshold of £20,000/QALY. However,

Beating the Blues was the sole package to be evaluated in the context of an RCT with a control group; it was also the package that demonstrated the highest probability of being cost effective at £30,000/QALY. Subsequently, Beating the Blues was the only package recommended in the technology appraisal.

One of the limitations of the economic model was that a number of parameters such as compliance and relapse rates were based on assumptions because of lack of relevant data. For example, therapist-led CBT relapse rates were used as an estimate for CCBT relapse rates. The authors highlighted this as a strong assumption that needs validation and requires some caution when reviewing the findings of the Kaltenthaler and colleagues' (2008) report. Moreover, although the model assumed more realistic throughput levels, there remains a large amount of uncertainty regarding the costs of the licence per patient. This is due to uncertainty regarding the throughput of people receiving CCBT. There remains scant evidence on the likely uptake in practice.

QALYs were estimated from a population of patients receiving CBT. This study was based in the UK and therefore would be representative of those patients utilising the NHS. However, primary data using generic preference-based measures in the relevant population would have been ideal.

Summary of health economic evidence
Beating the Blues was found to be more cost effective than standard care. Based on the clinical and cost-effectiveness findings of Kaltenthaler and colleagues (2008), Beating the Blues was recommended by NICE (2006a) as suitable treatment for patients with depression.

Since the publication of the technology appraisal on CCBT, no new Beating the Blues RCT data has become available and there have been no new published economic evaluations in the UK related to Beating the Blues or other CCBT packages. The problem of paucity of data mentioned in Kaltenthaler and colleagues (2008) remains and, for Beating the Blues, no data on compliance, relapse rates or costings have been made available since then. Therefore, the economic analysis of Beating the Blues cannot be updated. In addition, an analysis of a depression only sample (some of the participants in the PROUDFOOT2004A trial had a diagnosis of anxiety) undertaken as part of this review suggests further caution in interpreting the outcomes of the trial. Although no further cost-effectiveness analyses were identified, a number of additional trials of CCBT were found and the clinical-effectiveness data reviewed from these trials suggest that other CCBT packages (both CD-ROM and web-based) may be similarly effective to Beating the Blues. The results are based on indirect evidence as no head-to-head trials were identified. Moreover, the clinical trials used different comparators and outcome measures, which suggests caution in making any inferences regarding the relative effectiveness of CCBT packages. Nevertheless, comparison of the effect sizes in each case indicates that the various CCBT packages may offer similar benefits to people with depression compared with a baseline treatment such as waitlist control and treatment as usual.

Regarding costs, other CCBT packages considered in the clinical review are likely to incur lower intervention costs compared with Beating the Blues. A major cost component of Beating the Blues was its licence fee, according to the economic analysis for the technology appraisal; the licence fee for Beating the Blues comprised 73% of the total intervention cost (see Appendix 15 of this guideline update and page 159 of the technology appraisal [NICE, 2006a]). On the other hand, free packages such as MoodGYM do not require a licence fee and therefore intervention costs are greatly reduced. Moreover, where patients can access a CCBT programme over the internet or at locations other than at a GP practice (for example, at home or at a public library), the costs of providing this intervention are going to be further reduced, as they do not include hardware and overhead costs. If a web-based programme were to be offered at a GP practice, providing this service would incur costs for hardware, overheads and supervision. Hardware and overheads are fixed costs and would be the same for both free and licensed programmes. Furthermore, the RCTs of some web-based programmes describe minimal supervision requirements, for example MoodGYM trialled by Christensen and colleagues (2004) described 6- to 10-minute telephonic contacts from lay interviewers to participants to assist in the use of the site.

In addition to intervention costs, other costs associated with the care of people with depression need to be assessed. However, if different packages result in similar improvements for people with depression, as suggested by the findings of the clinical review, it is possible that other service costs associated with provision of CCBT are similar across the packages. The technology appraisal has shown Beating the Blues to be more cost effective than treatment as usual, using conservative estimates of the likely uptake of the intervention. If other CCBT packages are similarly as effective as Beating the Blues (as indicated in the clinical review) and incur lower intervention costs, then they could be also more cost effective than usual care.

Service user preference is important; however, there is little published evidence on this topic regarding CCBT. People may prefer to use CCBT in the privacy of their homes, some may prefer visiting their GP practice to access CCBT, and others with mobility problems may value the flexibility it offers. By offering a range of options for accessing CCBT, this may support a greater range of service user choice.

7.2   GUIDED SELF-HELP

7.2.1   Introduction

Guided self-help is generally accepted as being more than simply giving patients literature to read (this simpler alternative is usually referred to as pure self-help), and often is based on a cognitive or behavioural psychological approach. Contact with professionals is limited and tends to be of a supportive or facilitative nature. It is potentially cost effective for patients with milder disorders, and could support the more effective targeting of resources. Most of the early literature on guided self-help came from the US. In the US there are over 2000 self-help manuals of different sorts published each year, and it is not within the scope of this guideline to make recommendations on specific self-help manuals, but rather the principle and practice of guided self-help in the NHS and related services. See Richardson and colleagues (2008) for a review of publicly available guided self-help materials in the UK.

Guided self-help has some obvious limitations, particularly with written materials, such as a requirement of a certain reading ability and understanding of the language used. For example, 22% of the US population is functionally illiterate, and 44% will not read a book in any year (NCES, 1997). On the other hand, many patients are not keen on using medication, because of antidepressant intolerance, drug interactions, pregnancy, breast-feeding or personal preference, and many patients are understandably worried about having a formal diagnosis of depression recorded in their medical records. For those people, guided self-help can be a more accessible and acceptable form of therapy. Carers and family members can also be involved in understanding the nature and course of depression through the material made available. The majority of guided self-help programmes are in book form and this review is limited to studies of such programmes.

Definition

For the purposes of the guideline, guided self-help is defined as a self-administered intervention designed to treat depression, which makes use of a range of books or other self-help manuals derived from an evidence-based intervention and designed specifi-cally for the purpose. A healthcare professional (or paraprofessional, for example, grad-uate and low-intensity workers in mental health) facilitates the use of this material by introducing, monitoring and reviewing the outcome of such treatment. This intervention would have no other therapeutic goal and would be limited in nature, usually to no less than three contacts and no more than six. Gellatly and colleagues (2007) considered guided self-help to include no more than 3 hours of input from a coach or guide.

7.2.2   Studies considered[49]

Sixteen studies were identified and included in the review of guided self-help; only nine of these had been identified and included in the previous guideline (NICE, 2004a), therefore the review was substantially revised. Two of the studies included in the orig-inal review (Bowman1995, Wollersheim1991) were excluded in the revised review for this guideline because they no longer met inclusion criteria: in the Bowman1995 study, dropouts were replaced, and the Wollersheim1991 study had less than ten participants in each condition. Sixteen of the new studies found were also excluded. The main reasons for exclusion were not being an RCT and participants not meeting diagnostic criteria.

The included studies were grouped based on the nature of support offered to patients. Data were available to examine the following strategies compared with waitlist or treatment as usual:

● individual guided self-help
  – with frequent therapist/coach support (10 to 50 minutes per session)
  – with frequent but minimum duration support (not more than 2 hours overall)

---

[49]Study IDs in title case refer to studies included in the previous guideline and study IDs in capital letters refer to studies found and included in this guideline update. References for studies from the previous guideline are in Appendix 18.

- group guided self-help/psychoeducation
- self-help with support by mail.

Summary study characteristics of the included studies are in Table 22 with full details in Appendix 17b, which also includes details of excluded studies.

7.2.3   Clinical evidence for guided self-help

Evidence from the important outcomes and overall quality of evidence are presented in Table 23. The full evidence profiles and associated forest plots can be found in Appendix 16b and Appendix 19b, respectively.

7.2.4   Clinical evidence summary

Overall, the evidence indicates that guided-self help has a beneficial effect in people with both mild depression and subthreshold depression. Only two studies compared individual guided self-help with frequent and long-duration tutoring with control groups (Brown1984 includes a waitlist control comparison and LOVELL2008 includes a treatment as usual comparison). There is insufficient evidence to indicate a clear effect of either group. While the effect favoured individual guided self-help with support, the results are not significant and the CIs are wide when compared with waitlist control (BDI scores: SMD −0.28; 95% CI −1.08, 0.53) and similarly, when compared with treatment as usual (BDI scores: SMD −0.27; 95% CI −0.88, 0.34).

However, there is clear evidence from five studies to indicate that individual guided self-help with support of frequent but minimum duration has a large effect in reducing depressive self-reported symptoms when compared with waitlist control (SMD −0.98; 95% CI −1.50, −0.47). One study, WILLIAMS2008, reports similar results when comparing individual guided self-help with support of frequent but minimum duration when compared with treatment as usual at endpoint (SMD −0.49; 95% CI −0.77, −0.21) and at 12 months' follow-up (SMD −0.42; 95% CI −0.70, −0.14).

Two studies included group guided self-help, but the data is insufficient and the CIs are too wide to reach any clear conclusions.

Three studies looked at the effectiveness of self-help with support by mail only. One medium-sized study reports BDI scores at endpoint indicating a medium effect (SMD −0.57; 95% CI −1.02, −0.12). Then at 6 months, two studies indicate a small effect (SMD −0.32; 95% CI −0.62, −0.02). The results at shorter follow-up periods (1- and 3-month follow-up) were not significant, with wide CIs. It is important to note that in one of the studies, STICE2007, approximately 50% of the included population was aged 15.

7.2.5   Health economic evidence and considerations

No evidence on the cost effectiveness of individual or group-based guided self-help programmes for people with subthreshold or mild to moderate depression was identified by the systematic search of the health economics literature. Details on the methods used for the systematic search of the economic literature are described in Chapter 3, Section 3.6.1.

Table 22: Summary study characteristics of studies of guided self-help

	Individual guided self-help (with support)	Individual guided self-help (minimal support)	Group guided self-help (psycho-education)	Self-help (with support by mail)
No. trials (no. of participants)	2 RCTs (89)	10 RCTs (904)	3 RCTs (495)	3 RCTs (368)
Study IDs	(1) Brown1984* (2) LOVELL2008	(1) Beutler1991 (2) Brown1984* (3) FLOYD2004 (4) Jamison1995 (5) Landreville1997 (6) Schmidt1983* (7) Scogin1987 (8) Scogin1989 (9) WILLEMSE2004 (10) WILLIAMS2008	(1) BROWN2004 (2) HANSSON2008[‡] (3) Schmidt1983*	(1) GEISNER2006 (2) SALKOVSKIS2006 (3) STICE2007[†]
N/% female/mean age	(1) 30/55/37 (2) 59/73/38	(1) 63/70/47 (2) 30/55/37 (3) 46/76/68 (4) 80/84/40 (5) 23/87/40 (6) 34/86/42 (7) 29/79/70 (8) 67/85/68 (9) 216/66/42 (10) 281/68/41	(1) 120/93/NA (2) 319/73/44 (3) 32/86/42	(1) 177/70/19 (2) 96/80/40 (3) 95/70/18

Inclusion criteria/ diagnosis	(1) MDD (2) GP diagnosis+ BDI >14	(1) MDD (2) MDD/subthreshold depressive symptoms/ intermittent depressive disorder (3)–(4) MDD (5) 74% MDD/26% minor depressive disorder (6) No formal diagnosis; BDI >10 (7)–(8) No formal diagnosis; HAMD >= 10 (9) Subthreshold depression (10) No formal diagnosis; BDI >= 14	(1) No formal diagnosis; BDI >= 10 (70%) (2) Depression (3) BDI >= 10	(1) No formal diagnosis; BDI >= 14 (2) No formal diagnosis; BDI >= 10 (3) No formal diagnosis; ES-D >= 20
Intervention	(1) Coping with Depression (CWD) with individual support (2) Individual guided-self help	(1) Self-directed therapy (2) CWD (3)–(5) Bibliotherapy (Feeling Good) (6) Bibliotherapy (self-help manual) (7)–(8) Bibliotherapy (Feeling Good)	(1) Psychoeducation workshop (2) Psychoeducation Contactus (3) Self-help group (large)	(1) Personalised feedback and brochure with coping strategies by mail (2) Tailored workbook (3) Bibliotherapy (Feeling Good)

Continued

Table 22: (*Continued*)

	Individual guided self-help (with support)	Individual guided self-help (minimal support)	Group guided self-help (psycho-education)	Self-help (with support by mail)
		(9) Minimum contact therapy (based on CWD course) (10) Guided self-help		
Control	(1) Waitlist (2) TAU	(1) Group CBT/focused expressive psychotherapy (2)–(8) Waitlist (9)–(10) TAU	(1) Waitlist (2) TAU (3) Waitlist	(1)–(3) Waitlist
Length of treatment	(1) 8 weeks (2) 12 weeks (mean)	(1) 20 weeks (2) 8 weeks (3) 4–12 weeks	(1) 1 day (mean) (2) 6 weeks (mean) (3) 8 weeks	(1)–(2) Not reported (3) 30 days (mean)

| Follow-up | (1) 1 and 6 months
(2) Not reported | (4)–(5) 4 weeks
(6) 8 weeks
(7) 4 weeks
(8) 1 month
(9) 60 days (mean)
(10) 120 days (mean) | | |
| | | (1) 3 months
(2) 1 and 6 months
(3)–(4) 3 months
(5) 6 months
(6) 10 weeks
(7) 1 month
(8) 6 months
(9)–(10) 12 months | (1) 3 months
(2) Not reported
(3) 10 weeks | (1) 4 weeks
(2) 4 weeks, 12 weeks
and 6 months
(3) 6 months |

*4-armed trial; †3-armed trial; ‡Cluster randomised trial analysed separately.

187

Table 23: Summary evidence profile of guided self-help

	Individual guided self-help (with support)		Individual guided self-help (minimal support)		Group guided self-help (psychoeducation)		Self-help (with support by mail)
	versus waitlist	versus TAU	versus waitlist	versus TAU	versus waitlist	versus TAU	versus waitlist
Leaving study early for any reason	RR 0.50 (0.05 to 4.94)	RR 7.24 (0.95 to 55.26)	RR 1.71 (0.62 to 4.69)	RR 10.77 (0.0 to 31281.62)	Not estimable	RR 2.16 (1.08 to 4.34)	RR 1.75 (0.67 to 4.56)
Quality	Low	Low	Moderate	Moderate	Moderate	Moderate	Moderate
Number of studies; participants	K = 1; n = 30	K = 1; n = 59	K = 6; n = 227	K = 2; n = 497	K = 1; n = 21	K = 1; n = 319	K = 3; n = 368
Forest plot number	GSH 04.01	GSH 02.01	GSH 01.01	GSH 03.01	GSH 05.01	GSH 06.01	GSH 07.01
Depression self-report measures at endpoint	SMD −0.28 (−1.08 to 0.53)	SMD −0.27 (−0.88 to 0.34)	SMD −0.98 (−1.50 to −0.47)	SMD −0.49 (−0.77 to −0.21) At 12 months: SMD −0.42 (−0.70 to −0.14)	SMD −0.67 (−1.56 to 0.21) At 3 months: SMD −0.51 (−1.05 to 0.03)	SMD −0.45 (−0.83 to −0.07)	SMD −0.57 (−1.02 to −0.12) At 1 month: SMD −0.08 (−0.30 to 0.13) At 3 months: SMD 0.02 (−0.38 to 0.42) At 6 months: SMD −0.32 (−0.62 to −0.02)

Quality	Low	Low	Moderate	Moderate Moderate	Low Low	Moderate	Moderate Moderate Low High
Number of studies; participants	K = 1; n = 24	K = 1; n = 42	K = 5; n = 159	K = 1; n = 204 K = 1; n = 204	K = 1; n = 21 K = 1; n = 55	K = 1; n = 122	K = 1; n = 95 K = 3; n = 358 K = 1; n = 96 K = 2; n = 191
Forest plot number	GSH 04.02	GSH 02.02	GSH 01.02	GSH 03.02 GSH 03.03	GSH 05.02 SSH 05.04	GSH 06.02	GSH 07.02 GSH 07.03 GSH 07.04 GSH 07.05
Depression clinician-report measures at endpoint	Not reported	Not reported	SMD −1.54 (−1.90 to −1.18)	Not reported	Not reported	Not reported	Not reported
Quality	–	–	High	–	–	–	–
Number of studies; participants	–	–	K = 4; n = 161	–	–	–	–
Forest plot number	–	–	GSH 01.04	–	–	–	–

189

The clinical evidence review above described interventions consisting of three to ten sessions (typically between four and six sessions) which were of limited duration over a 9- to 12-week period. The intervention could be delivered by a mental health professional or a paraprofessional with each session typically lasting between 15 to 30 minutes.

The total cost of individual or group-based guided self-help consists of the cost of staff plus the written self-help manual. Based on GDG opinion, this intervention is likely to be delivered by a low-intensity therapy worker (essentially a paraprofessional) on the Agenda for Change (AfC) Band 5 salary scale. The unit cost of a low-intensity therapy worker is not currently available but was estimated to be comparable to that of a community mental health nurse at AfC Band 5, and so this was used to estimate total staff costs. The unit cost of an AfC Band 5 community mental health nurse is £51 per hour of patient contact in 2007/08 prices (Curtis, 2009). This cost includes salary, salary on-costs, overheads and capital overheads plus any qualification costs. In addition, as part of their treatment each person receives a copy of the self-help manual; the booklet *A Recovery Programme for Depression* by Lovell and Richards (2008), which currently costs £4.00, was used as an example for costing purposes.

Based on the estimated staff time associated with delivering an individual guided self-help programme as described above and the cost of an AfC Band 5 post (using the community mental health nurse costing), the average cost of the programme would range between £42 and £259 per person in 2007/08 prices. If guided self-help were delivered on a group basis, it is assumed that the resources required to deliver the programme would be identical, except that each patient would receive an individual copy of the self-help manual. Based on the assumption of there being five to six people per group, the average costs of the programme would fall between £28 and £71 per person in 2007/08 prices.

It is difficult to assess whether, based on these health service costs, guided self-help would be a cost-effective intervention for subthreshold or mild to moderate depression. The clinical evidence suggests that individual guided self-help is effective in reducing self-reported depression scores when compared with waitlist control or treatment as usual. However, it is difficult to assess how these clinical improvements can be translated into overall improvements in patient health-related quality of life (HRQoL) that can used in a cost-effectiveness analysis. The cost-effectiveness of individual self-help also depends on the impact on downstream resource use and not just the service costs of delivering the interventions.

7.3   PHYSICAL ACTIVITY PROGRAMMES[50]

7.3.1   Introduction

The effect of physical activity on mental health has been the subject of research for several decades. There is a growing body of literature primarily from the US examining the effects of physical activity in the treatment of depression. The aerobic forms of

---

[50]In the previous guideline the term 'exercise' was used.

physical activity, especially jogging or running, have been most frequently investigated. In the past decade 'exercise on prescription' schemes have become popular in primary care in the UK (Biddle *et al.*, 1994), many of which include depression as a referral criterion.

Guidelines for physical activity referral schemes have been laid down by the Department of Health (2001; Mead *et al.*, 2008). Several plausible mechanisms for how physical activity affects depression have been proposed. In the developed world, regular physical activity is seen as a virtue; the depressed patient who takes regular physical activity may, as a result, get positive feedback from other people and an increased sense of self-worth. Physical activity may act as a diversion from negative thoughts and the mastery of a new skill may be important (Lepore, 1997; Mynors-Wallis *et al.*, 2000). Social contact may be an important benefit, and physical activity may have physiological effects such as changes in endorphin and monoamine concentrations (Thoren *et al.*, 1990; Leith, 1994).

Definition

For the purposes of the guideline, physical activity was defined as a structured physical activity with a recommended frequency, intensity and duration when used as a treatment for depression. It can be undertaken individually or in a group. Physical activity may be divided into aerobic forms (training of cardio-respiratory capacity) and anaerobic forms (training of muscular strength/endurance and flexibility/co-ordination/relaxation) (American College of Sports Medicine, 1980). In addition to the type of physical activity, the frequency, duration and intensity should be described.

7.3.2 Studies considered for all comparisons[51]

In total, 59 RCTs were found, of which 25 were included and 32 were excluded. Principal reasons for exclusion included trials not being RCTs, trials not involving a physical activity intervention, papers not reporting outcome data, or trials not including participants with depression.

Twenty-five studies were included in the review. Of these, nine (Bosscher1993, Fremont1987, Greist1979, Herman2002, Klein1985, McCann1984, McNeil1991, Singh1997, Veale1992) were also included in the previous guideline.

Data were available to compare physical activity with a non-physical activity control, waitlist or pill placebo, psychotherapy, pharmacotherapy, various combination treatments, and different kinds of physical activity. Since there was a wide range of types of physical activity in the included studies, the GDG divided these into aerobic (for example, running) and non-aerobic (for example, resistance training). Combined data are reported here since an initial review of the evidence showed there was little difference between aerobic and non-aerobic physical activity. There were insufficient studies to

---

[51]Throughout the following sections on physical activity programmes, study IDs in title case refer to studies included in the previous guideline and study IDs in capital letters refer to studies found and included in this guideline update. References for studies from the previous guideline are in Appendix 18.

look at specific types of activity separately. The GDG considered supervision to be an important factor in the success of physical activity programmes, and so this factor was also included in the analysis. Since there was a large amount of data to report, dichotomous efficacy outcomes were not extracted since these were reported by a relatively small number of studies, whereas continuous outcomes were more widely reported. The studies described below focus on the comparisons where substantial data were available. The following comparisons are not reported here: physical activity compared with other types of exercise, and some combination strategies (including physical activity plus light therapy) compared with no physical activity control or physical activity alone.

Because of the large number of summary study characteristics and summary evidence profile tables for physical activity, a brief clinical evidence summary follows each of the summary evidence profile tables.

7.3.3 Physical activity versus no physical activity control, pill placebo and waitlist

Studies considered
Seventeen studies compared physical activity with no physical activity control. The review team initially analysed the data combining group and individual physical activity and compared it with relevant control groups. A sub-analysis was then carried out looking at group and individual physical activity separately. Summary study characteristics of the included studies are in Table 24 with full details in Appendix 17b, which also includes details of excluded studies.

Clinical evidence
Evidence from the important outcomes and overall quality of evidence are presented in Table 25 and Table 26. The full evidence profiles and associated forest plots can be found in Appendix 16b and Appendix 19b, respectively.

Clinical evidence summary
Physical activity was more effective in reducing subthreshold symptoms and mild depressive symptoms than no physical activity control, although the effect was reduced at follow-up (see Table 25 and Table 26).

Table 24: Summary of study characteristics of RCTs of physical activity versus no physical activity control, placebo and waitlist

	Group		Individual			
	Supervised aerobic	Supervised non-aerobic	Supervised aerobic	Supervised non-aerobic	Unsupervised aerobic	Unsupervised non-aerobic
No. RCTs (No. of participants)	5 (326)	5 (252)	4 (350)	–	2 (404)	1 (38)
Study IDs	(1) BERLIN 2003* (2) BLUMEN-THAL2007† (3) HABOUSH 2006 (4) McCann1984 (5) TSANG2006 (6) Veale1992	(1) BUTLER 2008* (2) MATHER 2002 (3) Singh1997 (4) SINGH1997A (5) SINGH2005D*	(1) DUNN2005 (2) HOFFMAN 2008† (3) KNUBBEN 2007 (4) McNeil1991		(1) BLUMEN-THAL2007† (2) HOFFMAN 2008†	(1) SIMS2006
N/% female/ mean age	(1) 55/55/40 (2) 202/76/52 (3) 20/65/69 (4) 47/100/Not reported (5) 82/81/82 (6) 124/64/36	(1) 46/74/50 (2) 86/69/65 (3) 32/63/71 (4) 32/53/71 (5) 60/55/69	(1) 80/75/36 (2) 202/76/52 (3) 38/55/50 (4) 30/?/73		(1) 202/76/52 (2) 202/76/52	(1) 38/55/74
Diagnosis (average baseline score)	(1) BDI >= 14 (BDI 25.0) (2) MDD/ subthreshold depressive symptoms/	(1) Dysthymia/ depression/ subthreshold depressive symptoms/mild depressive	(1) Moderate depressive episode (HRSD 19.4) (2) MDD/ subthreshold		(1) MDD/ subthreshold depressive symptoms/ dysthymia (BDI 30.5)	(1) GDS >= 11 (GDS 12.4)

Continued

Table 24: *(Continued)*

| | Group | | Individual | | | |
	Supervised aerobic	Supervised non-aerobic	Supervised aerobic	Supervised non-aerobic	Unsupervised aerobic	Unsupervised non-aerobic
	dysthymia (BDI 30.5) (3) HRSD >= 10 (HRSD 18.13) (4) BDI >= 11 (5) Features of depression/ depression/ dysthymia (GDS 5.8) (6) CIS >= 17 (not reported)	episode (not reported) (2) Mood disorder (HRSD 17.1) (3) MDD/ subthreshold depressive symptoms/ dysthymia (BDI 19.9) (4) Major depression/ subthreshold depressive symptoms/ dysthymia (BDI 19.3) (5) Major depression/MDD/ subthreshold depressive symptoms/dysthymia (HRSD 19.1)	depressive symptoms/ dysthymia (not reported) (3) Moderate depressive episode (CES-D 38.4) (4) BDI >= 12 and <= 24 (not reported)		(2) MDD/ subthreshold depressive symptoms/ dysthymia (not reported)	

Physical activity	(1) Water aerobics (2) Walking/ jogging (3) Ballroom dancing (4) Aerobic exercise (5) Qigong (6) Running	(1) Yoga (2)–(4) Resistance training (5) High- or low-intensity resistance training	(1) Treadmill/biking at different intensities/frequency (2) Aerobics (3) Treadmill (4) Walking	(1) Walking/ jogging (2) Aerobics	(1) Resistance training
Control	(1) No treatment (2) Placebo pill (3) Waitlist (4) No treatment (5) Newspaper reading (6) No treatment	(1)–(4) Health education (5) GP care	(1) Stretching (2) Placebo pill (3) Stretching (4) Waitlist	(1)–(2) Placebo pill	(1) Advice control
Length of treatment	(1) 72 weeks (2) 16 weeks (3) 12 weeks (4) 10 weeks (5) 16 weeks (6) 12 weeks	(1) Not reported (2) 10 weeks (3) 20 weeks (4) 10 weeks (5) 8 weeks	(1) 12 weeks (2) 16 weeks (3) 10 days (4) 6 weeks	(1)–(2) 16 weeks	(1) 10 weeks
Follow-up	(1)–(2) Not reported (3) 3 months (4) Not reported (5) 8 weeks (6) Not reported	(1) Not reported (2) 34 weeks (3) 6 weeks (4)–(5) Not reported	(1)–(4) Not reported	(1)–(2) Not reported	(1) 6 months

*3-arm trial; †4-arm trial.

195

Table 25: Summary evidence profile for physical activity versus no physical activity control

	Supervised	Follow-up	Unsupervised	Follow-up
Clinician-rated mean depression scores at endpoint	SMD −1.26 (CI −2.12 to −0.41)	24 weeks: SMD 0.15 (CI −0.67 to 0.97) 34–36 weeks: SMD −0.38 (CI −0.75 to −0.01)	Not reported	Not reported
Quality	Moderate	24 weeks: Low 34–36 weeks: High	–	–
Number of studies; participants	K = 5; n = 213	24 weeks: K = 1; n = 23 34–36 weeks: K = 2; n = 113	–	–
Forest plot number	PA 01.10	PA 02.01	–	–
Self-rated mean depression change scores at endpoint	SMD −0.74 (CI −1.19 to −0.29)	4 weeks: SMD −1.58 (CI −2.09 to −1.08) 8 weeks: SMD −1.06 (CI −1.53 to −0.59) 34 weeks: SMD −0.24 (CI −0.67 to 0.18)	SMD 0.42 (CI −0.37 to 1.21)	SMD 0.1 (CI −0.6 to 0.8)
Quality	Moderate	4 weeks: Moderate 8 weeks: Moderate 34 weeks: Low	Low	Low
Number of studies; participants	K = 7; n = 368	4 weeks: K = 1; n = 82 8 weeks: K = 1; n = 82 34 weeks: K = 1; n = 86	K = 1; n = 26	K = 1; n = 32
Forest plot number	PA 03.01	PA 04.01	PA 05.01	PA 05.01
Leaving treatment early for any reason	RR 1.47 (CI 0.72 to 3.01) (17.9% versus 12.7%)	Not reported	Not reported	Not reported
Quality	Low	–	–	–
Number of studies; participants	K = 3; n = 195	–	–	–
Forest plot number	PA 06.01	–	–	–

Table 26: Summary evidence profile for physical activity versus control (pill placebo or waitlist)

	Supervised physical activity versus pill placebo	Unsupervised physical activity versus pill placebo	Supervised physical activity versus waitlist	Supervised physical activity versus waitlist at follow-up (12 weeks)
Clinician-rated mean depression scores at endpoint	SMD –0.27 (CI –0.67 to 0.12)	SMD –0.12 (CI –0.50 to 0.27)	SMD –0.49 (CI –1.35 to 0.36)	SMD –0.34 (CI –1.24 to 0.57)
Quality	Low	Low	Low	Low
Number of studies; participants	K = 1; n = 100	K = 1; n = 102	K = 1; n =22	K = 1; n = 19
Forest plot number	PA 07.02	PA 08.02	PA 10.03	PA 11.03
Leaving treatment early for any reason	RR 0.64 (CI 0.33 to 1.23)	RR 0.2 (CI 0.06 to 0.65)	Not reported	Not reported
Quality	Moderate	Moderate	–	–
Number of studies; participants	K = 2; n = 170	K = 1; n = 102	–	–
Forest plot number	PA 09.02	PA 09.02		

7.3.4 Physical activity versus antidepressants

Studies considered
Three studies compared physical activity with sertraline. These studies have been classified based on whether physical activity was supervised or not and whether physical activity was conducted in groups or individually. Summary study characteristics of the included studies are in Table 27, with full details in Appendix 17b, which also includes details of excluded studies.

Clinical evidence
Evidence from the important outcomes and overall quality of evidence are presented in Table 28. The full evidence profiles and associated forest plots can be found in Appendix 16b and Appendix 19b, respectively.

Clinical evidence summary
The data comparing physical activity with sertraline were largely inconclusive being drawn from only three small studies, although there was some evidence suggesting that unsupervised physical activity may be more effective than antidepressants in reducing symptoms in subthreshold and mild depression. People taking antidepressants were more likely to leave treatment early because of side effects (see Table 28).

197

Table 27: Summary study characteristics for physical activity versus antidepressants

	Group		Individual	
	Supervised aerobic	Unsupervised aerobic	Supervised aerobic	Unsupervised aerobic
No. RCTs (No. of participants)	2 (358)	1 (202)	1 (202)	1 (202)
Study IDs	(1) BLUMENTHAL 2007* (2) Herman2002	(1) BLUMENTHAL 2007*	(1) HOFFMAN2008*	(1) HOFFMAN2008*
N/% female/ mean age	(1) 202/76/52 (2) 156/73/57	(1) 202/76/52	(1) 202/76/52	(1) 202/76/52
Diagnosis (average baseline score)	(1) MDD/subthreshold depressive symptoms/ dysthymia (BDI 30.5) (2) MDD/subthreshold depressive symptoms/ dysthymia (BDI 22.5)	(1) MDD/subthreshold depressive symptoms/ dysthymia (BDI 30.5)	(1) MDD/subthreshold depressive symptoms/ dysthymia (not reported)	(1) MDD/subthreshold depressive symptoms/ dysthymia (not reported)
Physical activity	(1)–(2) Walking/jogging	(1) Walking/jogging	(1) Aerobics	(1) Aerobics
Control	(1)–(2) Sertraline	(1) Sertraline	(1) Sertraline	(1) Sertraline
Length of treatment	(1)–(2) 16 weeks	(1) 16 weeks	(1) 16 weeks	(1) 16 weeks
Follow-up	(1) Not reported (2) 24 weeks	(1) Not reported	(1) Not reported	(1) Not reported

*4-armed trial.

Table 28: Summary evidence profile for physical activity compared with antidepressants

	Supervised aerobic	**Unsupervised aerobic**
Clinician-rated mean depression scores at endpoint	SMD –0.75 (CI –1.79 to 0.28)	SMD –1.03 (CI –1.44 to –0.61)
Quality	Low	Moderate
Number of studies; participants	K = 2; n = 201	K = 1; n = 102
Forest plot number	PA 12.04	PA 14.04
Self-rated mean depression scores at endpoint	SMD –0.19 (CI –0.58 to 0.20)	Not reported
Quality	Low	–
Number of studies; participants	K = 1; n = 101	–
Forest plot number	PA 13.04	–
Leaving treatment early for any reason	RR 1.59 (CI 0.87 to 2.9) (23.1% versus 14.4%)	RR 0.4 (CI 0.11 to 1.45) (5.7% versus 14.3%)
Quality	Moderate	Low
Number of studies; participants	K = 2; n = 201	K = 1; n = 102
Forest plot number	PA 15.04	PA 15.04
Leaving treatment early due to side effects	RR 7.41 (CI 1.4 to 39.23) (19.2% versus 6.2%)	RR 2.77 (CI 0.3 to 25.78)
Quality	Moderate	Low
Number of studies; participants	K = 2; n = 149	K = 1; n = 102
Forest plot number	PA 16.04	PA 16.04

7.3.5 Physical activity versus psychosocial and psychological interventions

Studies considered

Four studies compared physical activity with a psychosocial or psychological intervention. Summary study characteristics of the included studies are in Table 29 with full details in Appendix 17b, which also includes details of excluded studies.

Table 29: Summary study characteristics for physical activity versus psychosocial and psychological interventions

	Group		Individual	
	Supervised aerobic	**Supervised non-aerobic**	**Supervised aerobic**	**Supervised non-aerobic**
No. RCTs (No. of participants)	2 (89)	1 (46)	2 (104)	–
Study IDs	(1) Fremont1987 (2) Greist1979	(1) BUTLER2008*	(1) Klein1985 (2) McNeil1991	–
N/% female/mean age	(1) 61/74/unclear (2) 28/54/24	(1) 46/74/50	(1) 74/72/30 (2) 30/?/73	–
Diagnosis (average baseline score)	(1) BDI = 9–30 (not reported) (2) RDC for minor depression and SCL-90 depression cluster score at 50th percentile or above	(1) Dysthymia/depression/ subthreshold depressive symptoms/dysthymia/mild depressive episode (not reported)	(1) Major/subthreshold depressive symptoms (not reported) (2) BDI >= 12 and <= 24 (not reported)	–
Physical activity	(1) Running (2) Running	(1) Yoga	(1) Running (2) Walking	–
Control	(1) Cognitive techniques (2) Time-limited psychotherapy	(1) Hypnosis	(1) Group therapy (2) Social contact	–
Length of treatment	(1) 10 weeks (2) 10 weeks	(1) Not reported	(1) 12 weeks (2) 6 weeks	–
Follow-up	(1) 2 and 4 months (2) Not reported	(1) Not reported	(1) 1, 3 and 9 months (2) Not reported	–

Table 30: Summary evidence profile for physical activity versus psychosocial and psychological interventions

	Supervised aerobic	Follow-up	Supervised non-aerobic	Follow-up
Clinician-rated mean depression scores at endpoint	Not reported	Not reported	SMD 0.80 (CI –0.04 to 1.64)	36 weeks: SMD –0.17 (CI –0.94 to 0.60)
Quality	–	–	Low	Low
Number of studies; participants	–	–	K = 1; n = 24	K = 1; n = 26
Forest plot number	–	–	PA17 05.01	PA17 05.01
Self-rated mean depression scores at endpoint	SMD –0.23 (CI –0.68 to 0.21)	8 weeks: SMD –0.09 (CI –0.79 to 0.62) 16 weeks: SMD –0.41 (CI –1.18 to 0.37) 34 weeks: SMD –0.63 (CI –1.59 to 0.33)	Not reported	Not reported
Quality	Moderate	8 weeks: Low 16 weeks: Low 34 weeks: Low	–	–
Number of studies; participants	K = 3; n = 79	8 weeks: K = 1; n = 31 16 weeks: K = 1; n = 26 34 weeks: K = 1; n = 18	–	–
Forest plot number	PA 18.05	PA 19.05		
Leaving treatment early for any reason	RR 1.2 (CI 0.14 to 10.58) (20% versus 16.7%)	Not reported	Not reported	Not reported
Quality	Low	–	–	–
Number of studies; participants	K = 1; n = 16	–	–	–
Forest plot number	PA 20.05	–	–	–

Clinical evidence

Evidence from the important outcomes and overall quality of evidence are presented in Table 30. The full evidence profiles and associated forest plots can be found in Appendix 16b and Appendix 19b, respectively.

Clinical evidence summary

The data from four studies comparing physical activity with a range of psychosocial and psychological interventions are insufficient to determine a clear picture of the relative effectiveness of physical activity (see Table 30).

7.3.6   Physical activity plus antidepressants versus antidepressants

Studies considered

Two studies compared physical activity and antidepressants versus antidepressants. Summary study characteristics of the included studies are in Table 31 with full details in Appendix 17b, which also includes details of excluded studies.

Table 31: Summary study characteristics for physical activity + antidepressants versus antidepressants

	Group
	Supervised aerobic physical activity + antidepressants versus antidepressants
No. RCTs (No. of participants)	2 (186)
Study IDs	(1) Herman2002 (2) PILU2007
N/% female/mean age	(1) 156/73/57 (2) 30/100/unclear
Diagnosis (average baseline score)	(1) Major depressive disorder (BDI 22.5) (2) MDD/subthreshold depressive symptoms/dysthymia (HAM-D 19.9)
Physical activity	(1) Running + sertraline (2) Running + antidepressant (range of drugs used)
Control	(1) Sertraline (2) Combination antidepressants (range of drugs used)
Length of treatment	(1) 16 weeks (2) 32 weeks
Follow-up	(1) 24 weeks (2) Not reported

Clinical evidence

Evidence from the important outcomes and overall quality of evidence are presented in Table 32. The full evidence profiles and associated forest plots can be found in Appendix 16b and Appendix 19b, respectively.

Table 32: Summary evidence profile for physical activity + antidepressants versus antidepressants

	Supervised aerobic physical activity + antidepressant versus combination antidepressants	Supervised aerobic physical activity + antidepressant versus antidepressant
Clinician-rated mean depression scores at endpoint	SMD −1.04 (CI −1.85 to −0.23)	SMD −0.08 (CI −0.47 to 0.31)
Quality	Moderate	Moderate
Number of studies; participants	K = 1; n = 30	K = 1; n = 103
Forest plot number	PA 21.09	PA 21.09
Self-rated mean depression scores at endpoint	Not reported	SMD 0.08 (CI −0.31 to 0.47)
Quality	–	Moderate
Number of studies; participants	–	K = 1; n = 103
Forest plot number	–	PA22 09.02
Leaving treatment early for any reason	Not reported	RR 1.37 (CI 0.58 to 3.26) (20% versus 14.6%)
Quality	–	Low
Number of studies; participants	–	K = 1; n = 103
Forest plot number	–	PA 23.09
Leaving treatment early because of side effects	RR 0.87 (CI 0.27 to 2.83) (9.1% versus 10.4%)	Not reported
Quality	Low	–
Number of studies; participants	K = 1; n = 103	–
Forest plot number	PA 24.09	–

Low-intensity psychosocial interventions

Clinical evidence summary
Physical activity plus an antidepressant more effectively reduced depression scores than a combination of two antidepressants in one study. There appeared to be no difference between combination treatment versus a single antidepressant. As there was only one study in each comparison, it is difficult to draw any conclusions (see Table 32).

7.3.7 Sub-analysis of group-based versus individual physical activity programmes

Studies considered
A sub-analysis was conducted to examine the indirect effectiveness of group-based physical activity programmes in comparison with individual physical activity. This was performed indirectly, by looking at comparisons between group-based physical activity programmes compared with no physical activity control, and also looking at comparisons between individual physical activity and no physical activity control. The GDG decided to carry out this indirect comparison given that the cost of individual physical activity is considerably greater than group-based. Furthermore, based on the previous results of physical activity, there was no clear benefit of individual over group-based physical activity. Summary study characteristics of the included studies are in Table 33 with full details in Appendix 17b, which also includes details of excluded studies.

Clinical evidence
Evidence from the important outcomes and overall quality of evidence are presented in Table 34 and Table 35. The full evidence profiles and associated forest plots can be found in Appendix 16b and Appendix 19b, respectively.

Clinical evidence summary
The intensity of many of the physical activity programmes (for example, three supervised sessions per week over a 12-week period) raises questions about the cost effectiveness of individual physical activity programmes. To address this, a subgroup analysis of group programmes was undertaken. An indirect comparison can be made by looking at Table 34 and Table 35.

Table 33: Summary study characteristics for group-based and individual physical activity programmes

	Group physical activity versus no physical activity control, placebo and waitlist		Individual physical activity versus no physical activity control	
	Supervised aerobic	Supervised non-aerobic	Supervised aerobic	Unsupervised non-aerobic
No. of RCTs (No. of participants)	5 (326)	5 (252)	2 (118)	1 (38)
Study IDs	(1) BERLIN2003* (2) BLUMENTHAL2007† (3) HABOUSH2006 (4) McCann1984 (5) TSANG2006 Veale1992	(1) BUTLER2008* (2) MATHER2002 (3) Singh1997 (4) SINGH1997A (5) SINGH2005D*	(1) DUNN2005 (2) KNUBBEN2007	(1) SIMS2006
N/% female/Mean age	(1) 55/55/40 (2) 202/76/52 (3) 20/65/69 (4) 47/100/Not reported (5) 82/81/82 (6) 124/64/36	(1) 46/74/50 (2) 86/69/65 (3) 32/63/71 (4) 32/53/71 (5) 60/55/69	(1) 80/75/36 (2) 38/55/50	(1) 38/55/74
Diagnosis (average baseline scores)	(1) BDI >= 14 (BDI 25.0) (2) MDD/subthreshold depressive symptoms/dysthymia (BDI 30.5) (3) HRSD >= 10 (HRSD 18.13)	(1) Dysthymia/depression/subthreshold depressive symptoms/mild depressive episode (not reported) (2) Mood disorder (HRSD 17.1)	(1) Moderate depressive episode (HRSD 19.4) (2) Moderate depressive episode (CES-D 38.4)	(1) GDS >= 11 (GDS 12.4)

Continued

205

Table 33: (*Continued*)

	Group physical activity versus no physical activity control, placebo and waitlist		Individual physical activity versus no physical activity control	
	Supervised aerobic	Supervised non-aerobic	Supervised aerobic	Unsupervised non-aerobic
	(4) BDI $>= 11$ (5) 45% depression, 52% no formal diagnosis, 3% dysthymia (6) CIS $>= 17$ (not reported)	(3) MDD/subthreshold depressive symptoms/dysthymia (BDI 19.9) (4) Major depression/subthreshold depressive symptoms/dysthymia (BDI 19.3) (5) Major depression/MDD/subthreshold depressive symptoms/dysthymia (HRSD 19.1)		
Physical activity	(1) Water aerobics (2) Walking/jogging (3) Ballroom dancing (4) Aerobic exercise (5) Qigong (6) Running	(1) Yoga (2)–(4) Resistance training (5) High- or low-intensity resistance training	(1) Treadmill/biking at different intensities/frequency (2) Treadmill	(1) Resistance training

Comparator	(1) No treatment (2) Placebo pill (3) Waitlist (4) No treatment (5) Newspaper reading (6) No treatment	(1)–(4) Health education (5) GP care	(1)–(2) Stretching	(1) Advice control
Length of treatment	(1) 72 weeks (2) 16 weeks (3) 12 weeks (4) 10 weeks (5) 16 weeks (6) 12 weeks	(1) Not reported (2)–(4) 10 weeks (5) 8 weeks	(1) 12 weeks (2) 10 days	(1) 10 weeks
Follow-up	(1)–(2) Not reported (3) 3 months (4) Not reported (5) 8 weeks (6) Not reported	(1) Not reported (2) 34 weeks (3) 6 weeks (4)–(5) Not reported	(1)–(2) Not reported	(1) 6 months

*3-arm trial; †4-arm trial.

Table 34: Group-based physical activity programmes versus no physical activity control

	Supervised aerobic	Follow-up	Supervised non-aerobic	Follow-up
Clinician-rated mean depression scores at endpoint	Not reported	Not reported	SMD −0.77 (CI −1.08 to −0.45)	24 weeks: SMD 0.15 (CI −0.67 to 0.97) 34–36 weeks: SMD −0.38 (CI −0.75 to −0.01)
Quality	–	–	Moderate	Low High
Number of studies; participants	–	–	K = 4; n = 183	K = 1; n = 23, K = 2; n = 113
Forest plot number	–	–	PA25, 19.01.01	PA26, 19.02.01 PA26, 19.02.02
Self-rated mean depression scores at endpoint	SMD −0.94 (CI −1.29 to −0.59)	4 weeks: SMD −1.58 (CI −2.09 to −1.08) 8 weeks: SMD −1.06 (CI −1.53 to −0.59)	SMD −0.54 (CI −0.84 to −0.24)	34 weeks: SMD −0.24 (CI −0.67 to 0.18)
Quality	High	Moderate Moderate	Moderate	Moderate
Number of studies; participants	K = 2; n = 147	K = 1; n = 82, K = 1; n = 82	K = 4; n = 183	K = 1; n = 86

	PA 27.19	PA 29.19	PA 27.19	PA 29.19
Forest plot number	PA 27.19	PA 29.19	PA 27.19	PA 29.19
Self-rated depression change scores at endpoint	SMD −0.61 (CI −1.26 to 0.03)	Not reported	Not reported	Not reported
Quality	Low	–	Low	–
Number of studies; participants	K = 1; n = 39	–	–	–
Forest plot number	PA 28.19	–	PA 30.19	–
Leaving treatment early for any reason	RR 1.24 (CI 0.56 to 2.79) (20.3% versus 15.7%)	Not reported	RR 2.0 (CI 0.20 to 20.33) (10% versus 5%)	Not reported
Quality	Moderate	–	Low	–
Number of studies; participants	K = 2; n = 115	–	K = 1; n = 40	–
Forest plot number	PA 30.19	–	PA 30.19	–
Leaving treatment early because of side effects	Not reported	Not reported	RR 5.0 (CI 0.26 to 98.00) (10% versus 0%)	Not reported
Quality	–	–	Low	–
Number of studies; participants	–	–	K = 1; n = 40	–
Forest plot number	–	–	PA 31.19	–

Table 35: Individual physical activity versus no physical activity control

	Supervised aerobic	Unsupervised non-aerobic	Follow-up
Clinician-rated mean depression scores at endpoint	SMD –1.16 (CI –1.94 to –0.37)	Not reported	Not reported
Quality	Moderate	–	–
Number of studies; participants	K = 1; n = 30	–	–
Forest plot number	PA 32.20	–	–
Self-rated mean depression scores at endpoint	SMD –0.87 (CI –1.54 to –0.20)	SMD 0.42 (CI –0.37 to 1.21)	24 weeks: SMD 0.10 (CI –0.60 to 0.80)
Quality	Moderate	Low	Low
Number of studies; participants	K = 1; n = 38	K = 1; n = 26	K = 1; n = 32
Forest plot number	PA 33.20	PA 33.20	PA 34. 20

Overall, the evidence indicates that group-based physical activity is effective in the treatment of subthreshold and mild depression. When compared with no physical activity controls, the evidence indicates that supervised non-aerobic group physical activity has a significant effect in patients with largely subthreshold depression in reducing clinician-reported depression scores at endpoint (SMD –0.77, 95% CI –1.08, –0.45) and at 34 to 36 weeks' follow-up (SMD –0.38, 95% CI –0.75, –0.01). Supervised aerobic group physical activity had a beneficial effect in reducing self-rated depression scores at endpoint (SMD –0.94, 95% CI –1.29, –0.59), at 4 weeks' follow-up (SMD –1.58, 95% CI –2.09, –1.08) and at 8 weeks (SMD –1.06, 95% CI –1.53, –0.59). Supervised non-aerobic group physical activity had a positive effect in reducing self-rated depression scores at endpoint (SMD –0.54, 95% CI –0.84, –0.24), and at 34 weeks' follow-up (SMD –0.24, 95% CI –0.67, 0.18). See Table 34 and Table 35.

7.3.8 Clinical evidence summary for physical activity – all comparisons

The evidence is presented for a relatively large dataset of 25 trials and over 2,000 participants, and is a challenging dataset to interpret. This stems from a number of factors including the variation in the populations, which comprised mixed groups of patients with mild major depression, dysthymia and subthreshold depressive symptoms. The participants who were included in the trials in this review who met criteria for major depressive disorder were drawn predominantly from groups in the mild to moderate range of depression (mean baseline BDI scores between 18 and 25). In addition, the nature of the physical activity interventions was also very varied, as indeed were the comparators. Some comparators were also potentially problematic with one study having combined antidepressants as the comparator in a population that included those with a diagnosis of dysthymia and subthreshold depressive symptoms (PILU2007).

Despite these issues, the data suggest that physical activity is more effective in reducing depressive symptoms than a no physical activity control (clinician-rated scores: SMD –1.26; 95% CI –2.12, –0.41; self-reported scores: –0.83; 95% CI –1.31, –0.34), although the effect was reduced at follow-up (clinician-rated scores at 24 weeks: SMD 0.15; 95% CI –0.67, 0.97; and at 34–36 weeks: SMD –0.38; 95% CI –0.75, –0.01; and for self-rated scores at 4 weeks: SMD –1.58; 95% CI –2.09, –1.08; at 8 weeks: SMD –1.06; 95% CI –1.53, –0.59; and at 34 weeks: SMD –0.24; 95% CI –0.67, 0.18). The data comparing physical activity with antidepressants suggests no significant differences; however, the CIs were wide (for clinician-rated scores: SMD –0.75; 95% CI –1.79, 0.28 and for self-rated scores: SMD –0.19; 95% CI –0.58, 0.20); therefore, there is insufficient evidence to identify any differential effect. As expected, people taking antidepressants were more likely to leave treatment early (RR 1.59; 95% CI 0.87, 2.9). The effectiveness for physical activity when compared with pill placebo came from only two studies. The CIs of this dataset were wide and there is insufficient evidence on which to make any clear conclusion. The data for physical activity compared with psychosocial and psychological interventions for depression did not suggest any important differences, but again the results were difficult to interpret given the width of the CIs (for self-rated scores: SMD –0.23; 95% CI –0.68, 0.21).

Taken together, these studies suggest a benefit for physical activity in the treatment of subthreshold depressive symptoms and mild to moderate depression, and, more specifically, a benefit for group-based physical activity. Physical activity also has the advantage of bringing other health gains beyond just improvement in depressive symptoms. In addition to the effectiveness of group-based physical activity, the GDG considered the potentially limited effectiveness of individual physical activity (with a high level of contact: up to three sessions per week over a 10- to 12-week period). In the absence of any clear and direct indication from the data of benefits for a particular kind of physical activity (for example, anaerobic versus aerobic), the GDG took the view that patient preference should be a significant factor in determining the nature of the physical activity.

There were further studies that compared the effectiveness of one type of physical activity with another type of physical activity or a combination of activities. The results did not indicate a clear picture favouring any specific treatment (see Appendix 19b).

7.3.9   Health economic evidence and considerations

No evidence on the cost effectiveness of structured physical activity programmes for people with subthreshold depressive symptoms or mild to moderate depression was identified by the systematic search of the health economics literature. Details on the methods used for the systematic search of the economic literature are described in Chapter 3, Section 3.6.1.

The clinical evidence in the literature review described interventions delivered either individually or in structured groups under the supervision of a competent practitioner or physical activity facilitator. The programme would typically involve two to three sessions per week of 45 minutes' to 1 hour's duration over a 10- to 14-week period.

It is likely that the sessions would be supervised by a physical activity facilitator (an NHS professional or paraprofessional with expertise in the area) who would be a recent graduate from an undergraduate or Masters' level course. The unit cost of a physical activity facilitator is not currently available. Therefore, it is assumed that such workers would be on AfC salary scales 4 or 5, which is likely to be comparable to the salary scales of a community mental health nurse. The unit cost of an AfC Band 5 community mental health nurse is £51 per hour of patient contact in 2007/08 prices (Curtis, 2009). This cost includes salary, salary on-costs, overheads and capital overheads plus any qualification costs.

Based on the estimated staff time associated with delivering and supervising a physical activity programme as described above and the cost of a community mental health nurse, the average cost of a physical activity programme when delivered at an individual level would range between £765 to £2,142 per person in 2007/08 prices. If a physical activity programme were delivered on a structured group basis, it is assumed that the resources required to deliver the programme would be identical. Based on the assumption of five to six people per group, the average costs of the programme would fall between £128 to £428 per person in 2007/08 prices.

It is difficult to assess whether, based on these health service costs, a physical activity programme would be a cost-effective intervention for subthreshold or mild to moderate depression. The clinical evidence suggests that both individual and structured group physical activity interventions are effective in reducing symptoms of depression when compared with a no physical activity control. However, it is difficult to assess how these clinical improvements could be translated into overall improvements in patient HRQoL that could be used in a cost-effectiveness analysis. The relative cost-effectiveness of an individual or group-based physical activity programme also depends on the impact on downstream resource use and not just the service costs of delivering the interventions. Therefore, it is difficult to ascertain whether an individual physical activity programme is more or less clinically effective than a group-based programme. However, given the lower costs of delivering a structured group-based physical activity programme, it is possible that this will be more cost effective than an individual programme for patients with subthreshold or mild to moderate depression.

7.4 FROM EVIDENCE TO RECOMMENDATIONS – LOW-INTENSITY PSYCHOSOCIAL INTERVENTIONS

A range of low-intensity interventions (CCBT, guided self-help and group-based physical activity programmes) have been identified as being effective for subthreshold depressive symptoms and mild to moderate depression. There are few trials that allow for direct clinical or cost-effectiveness comparisons of any of the interventions. As a result the GDG took the view that the decision as to which intervention to offer should, in significant part, be guided by the preference of people with depression and this is reflected in the recommendations. The data also did not support the view that any particular mode of delivery (for example, aerobic versus anaerobic physical activity, internet versus desktop-based CCBT) for any low-intensity intervention had any specific advantage over another, apart from the fact that both guided self-help and CCBT should be based on cognitive behavioural principles and that physical activity should be delivered in a group format. All interventions seem to require some form of support or supervision to be fully effective. The GDG was also concerned that the effective delivery of the interventions may be compromised by differences in the style and content of delivery of the intervention and so has drawn on existing trial data to offer specific recommendations on the content of the interventions.

Based on the health economic evidence a variety of CCBT packages were judged to be cost effective when compared with standard care or treatment as usual in the treatment of subthreshold depressive symptoms or mild to moderate depression (McCrone *et al.*, 2003; Kaltenthaler *et al.*, 2008). No evidence on the cost effectiveness of either guided self-help or physical activity for subthreshold depressive symptoms or mild to moderate depression was identified in the systematic review of the health economic literature. Simple cost analyses combined with the limited clinical evidence suggests that guided self-help interventions may be cost effective compared with control treatments or treatment as usual and that the preferred mode of delivery for physical activity is in groups.

7.5   RECOMMENDATIONS

Low-intensity psychosocial interventions

7.5.1.1   For people with persistent subthreshold depressive symptoms or mild to moderate depression, consider offering one or more of the following interventions, guided by the person's preference:

- individual guided self-help based on the principles of cognitive behavioural therapy (CBT)
- computerised cognitive behavioural therapy (CCBT)[52]
- a structured group physical activity programme.

Delivery of low-intensity psychosocial interventions

7.5.1.2   Individual guided self-help programmes based on the principles of CBT (and including behavioural activation and problem-solving techniques)

---

[52]This recommendation (and recommendation 1.4.2.1 in Clinical Guideline 91 [NICE, 2009c]) updates the recommendations on depression only in 'Computerised cognitive behavioural therapy for depression and anxiety (review)' (NICE technology appraisal 97 [NICE, 2006a]).

for people with persistent subthreshold depressive symptoms or mild to moderate depression should:

- include the provision of written materials of an appropriate reading age (or alternative media to support access)
- be supported by a trained practitioner, who typically facilitates the self-help programme and reviews progress and outcome
- consist of up to six to eight sessions (face-to-face and via telephone) normally taking place over 9 to 12 weeks, including follow-up.

7.5.1.3   CCBT for people with persistent subthreshold depressive symptoms or mild to moderate depression should:

- be provided via a stand-alone computer-based or web-based programme
- include an explanation of the CBT model, encourage tasks between sessions, and use thought-challenging and active monitoring of behaviour, thought patterns and outcomes
- be supported by a trained practitioner, who typically provides limited facilitation of the programme and reviews progress and outcome
- typically take place over 9 to 12 weeks, including follow-up.

7.5.1.4   Physical activity programmes for people with persistent subthreshold depressive symptoms or mild to moderate depression should:

- be delivered in groups with support from a competent practitioner
- consist typically of three sessions per week of moderate duration (45 minutes to 1 hour) over 10 to 14 weeks (average 12 weeks).

Sleep hygiene

7.5.1.5   Offer people with depression advice on sleep hygiene if needed, including:

- establishing regular sleep and wake times
- avoiding excess eating, smoking or drinking alcohol before sleep
- creating a proper environment for sleep
- taking regular physical exercise[53].

---

[53]The evidence for this recommendation has not been updated since the previous guideline. Any wording changes have been made for clarification only.

8 HIGH-INTENSITY PSYCHOLOGICAL INTERVENTIONS

This section covers the high-intensity interventions that were identified in the searches for the guideline update and groups them according to the definitions developed for the previous guideline (NICE, 2004a). Although to some degree cognitive behavioural therapies, behavioural activation, problem solving therapy and couples therapy[54] share a common theoretical base, they are reviewed separately.

8.1 COGNITIVE BEHAVIOURAL THERAPIES

8.1.1 Introduction

Cognitive behavioural therapy (CBT) for depression was developed by Aaron T. Beck during the 1950s and was formalised into a treatment in the late 1970s (Beck *et al.*, 1979). Its original focus was on the styles of conscious thinking and reasoning of depressed people, which Beck posited was the result of the operation of underlying cognitive schemas or beliefs. The cognitive model describes how, when depressed, people focus on negative views of themselves, the world and the future. The therapy takes an educative approach where, through collaboration, the person with depression learns to recognise his or her negative thinking patterns and to re-evaluate his or her thinking. This approach also requires people to practise re-evaluating their thoughts and new behaviours (called homework). The approach does not focus on unconscious conflicts, transference or offer interpretation as in psychodynamic psychotherapy. As with any psychological treatment, cognitive behavioural therapy is not static and has been evolving and changing. There have been important elaborations on the techniques of therapy (Beck, 1997) to address underlying beliefs more directly, which have been applied to particular presentations such as persistent residual depressive symptoms that leave people vulnerable to relapse (Paykel *et al.*, 1999; Scott *et al.*, 2000; Moore & Garland, 2003; Watkins *et al.*, 2007). The guideline refers to 'cognitive behavioural therapies' to indicate the evolution of CBT for depression over several decades.

---

[54]Five out of six of the included studies of couples therapy were based on a behavioural model.

High-intensity psychological interventions

Definition

For the purpose of this review, cognitive behavioural therapies were defined as discrete, time-limited, structured psychological interventions, derived from the cognitive behavioural model of affective disorders and where the patient:

- works collaboratively with the therapist to identify the types and effects of thoughts, beliefs and interpretations on current symptoms, feelings states and/or problem areas
- develops skills to identify, monitor and then counteract problematic thoughts, beliefs and interpretations related to the target symptoms/problems
- learns a repertoire of coping skills appropriate to the target thoughts, beliefs and/or problem areas.

In most individual trials of CBT, the manual used was Beck's *Cognitive Therapy of Depression* (1979) which advocates 16 to 20 sessions for treatment and relapse prevention work.

Group cognitive behavioural therapy

Trials looking at group CBT, which predominantly uses the 'Coping With Depression' approach (Kuehner, 2005; Lewinsohn *et al.*, 1989), were also included. This approach has a strong psychoeducational component focused on teaching people techniques and strategies to cope with the problems that are assumed to be related to their depression. These strategies include improving social skills, addressing negative thinking, increasing pleasant activities, and relaxation training. It consists of 12 sessions of 2 hours' duration over 8 weeks with groups held twice weekly for the first 4 weeks. The groups are highly structured (Lewinsohn *et al.*, 1984; Lewinsohn *et al.*, 1986) and typically consist of six to ten adults, with two group leaders. One- and 6-month follow-up sessions are also held and booster sessions can be used to help prevent relapse.

Mindfulness-based cognitive therapy

Mindfulness-based cognitive therapy (MBCT) was developed with a specific focus on preventing relapse/recurrence of depression (Segal *et al.*, 2002). MBCT is an 8-week group programme with each session lasting 2 hours, and four follow-up sessions in the year after the end of therapy. With 8 to 15 patients per group, MBCT has the potential to help a large number of people.

MBCT is a manualised, group-based skills training programme designed to enable patients to learn skills that prevent the recurrence of depression (Segal *et al.*, 2002). It is derived from mindfulness-based stress reduction, a programme with proven efficacy in ameliorating distress in people with chronic disease (Baer, 2003; Kabat-Zinn, 1990), and CBT for acute depression (Beck *et al.*, 1979), which has demonstrated efficacy in preventing depressive relapse/recurrence (Hollon *et al.*, 2005). MBCT is intended to enable people to learn to become more aware of the bodily sensations, thoughts and feelings associated with depressive relapse, and to relate constructively to these experiences. It is based on theoretical and empirical work demonstrating that depressive relapse is associated with the reinstatement of automatic modes of thinking, feeling and behaving that are counter-productive in contributing to and maintaining depressive relapse and recurrence (for example, self-critical thinking and avoidance) (Lau *et al.*, 2004). Participants learn to recognise these 'automatic pilot' modes, step out of them and respond in healthier ways by intentionally moving into a mode in which they 'de-centre' from negative thoughts and feelings (for example, by learning that 'thoughts are not facts'), accept difficulties using a stance of self-compassion and use bodily awareness to ground and transform experience. In the latter stages of the course, patients develop an 'action plan' that sets out strategies for responding when they become aware of early warning signs of relapse/recurrence (Williams, J.M., *et al.*, 2008).

8.1.2   Studies considered[55]

In total, 68 studies were identified, of which 46 RCTs were included; 24 studies were found in the update search and 22 were also reported in the previous guideline. Furthermore, 22 trials were excluded in this update search. The main reasons for exclusion were: trials included populations that were not diagnosed with depression; authors replaced dropouts; or more than 50% of participants dropped out of the study.

Summary study characteristics of the included studies are presented in Table 36, Table 37 and Table 38, with full details in Appendix 17b, which also includes details of excluded studies.

8.1.3   Clinical evidence for cognitive behavioural therapies

Evidence from the important outcomes and overall quality of evidence are presented in Table 39, Table 40 and Table 41. The full evidence profiles and associated forest plots can be found in Appendix 16b and Appendix 19b, respectively.

---

[55]Here and elsewhere in the guideline, each study considered for review is referred to by a 'study ID' made up of first author and publication date (unless a study is in press or only submitted for publication, when first author only is used). Study IDs in title case refer to studies included in the previous guideline and study IDs in capital letters refer to studies found and included in this guideline update. References for studies from the previous guideline are in Appendix 18 and references for studies for the update are in Appendix 17b.

Table 36: Summary study characteristics of cognitive behavioural therapies

	CBT versus antidepressants	CBT versus comparator	CBT versus rational emotive behavioural therapy	CBT versus behavioural activation	CBT versus interpersonal therapy (IPT)	CBT versus short-term psychodynamic psychotherapy	CBT (primary care) versus GP care
No. trials (total participants)	18 RCTs (1982)	6 RCTs (549)	1 RCT (180)	3 RCTs (216)	4 RCTs (502)	2 RCTs (383)	3 RCTs (202)
Study IDs	(1) BAGBY2008 (2) Blackburn1981 (3) Blackburn1997 (4) DAVID2008 (5) DERUBEIS2005 (6) DIMIDJIAN2006 (7) Elkin1989 (8) Hautzinger (in-pats) (9) Hautzinger1996 (10) Jarrett1999 (11) Keller2000 (12) LAIDLAW2008 (13) MARSHALL2008 (14) Miranda2003 (15) Murphy1984 (16) Murphy1995 (17) Scott1997 (18) Thompson2001	(1) Beach1992 (2) DERUBEIS2005 (3) DIMIDJIAN2006 (4) Elkin1989 (5) Jarrett1999 (6) Selmi1990	(1) DAVID2008	(1) DIMIDJIAN2006 (2) Gallagher1982 (3) JACOBSON1996	(1) Elkin1989 (2) Freeman2002 (3) LUTY2007 (4) MARSHALL2008	(1) Gallagher-Th1994 (2) Shapiro1994	(1) Freeman2002 (2) Scott1992 (3) Scott1997
N/% female	(1) 175/63 (2) Unextractable (3) 31/58	(1) 45/100 (2) 141/59 (3) 159/66	(1) 113/66	(1) 159/66 (2) 23/77 (3) 110/72	(1) 168/70 (2) 96/61 (3)–(4) 70/69	(1) 60/92 (2) 61/52	(1) 96/61 (2) 91/75 (3) 32/67

Continued

	(4) 113/66 (5) 141/59 (6) 159/66 (7) 168/70 (8) 113/63 (9) 113/63 (10) 51/71 (11) 445/65 (12) 29/73 (13) 70/69 (14) 267/100 (15) 52/74 (16) 37/70 (17) 32/67 (18) 67/67	(4) 168/70 (5) 48/67 (6) 23/64				
Mean age	(1) 42 (2) 43 (3) 40 (4) 37 (5)–(6) 40 (7) 35 (8)–(9) 40 (10) 39 (11) 43 (12) 76 (12) No information (13) 33 (14) 29 (15) 41 (16) 39 (17) 67 (18) 67	(1) 39 (2)–(3) 40 (4) 35 (5) 40 (6) 28	(1) 37	(1) 40 (2) 68 (3) 30	(1) 35 (2) 37 (3) 35 (4) No information	(1) 62 (2) 41

(Additional column) (1) 37 (2) 32 (3) 41

Table 36: *(Continued)*

	CBT versus antidepressants	CBT versus comparator	CBT versus rational emotive behavioural therapy	CBT versus behavioural activation	CBT versus IPT	CBT versus short-term psychodynamic psychotherapy	CBT (primary care) versus GP care
Diagnosis	(1) 100% major depressive episode (2) 100% MDD (3) 100% episode of depression (4)–(7) 100% MDD (8)–(9) 80% MDD, 20% dysthymia (10)–(18) 100% MDD	(1) 91% depressive episode, 9% dysthymia (2)–(5) 100% MDD (6) 100% major or intermittent depression, or subthreshold depressive symptoms	(1) 100% MDD	(1)–(3) 100% MDD	(1) 100% MDD (2) 46% mood disorder, 20% anxiety disorder and 34% comorbid diagnosis (3)–(4) 100% MDD	(1) 100% RDC depression (2) Major depressive episode	(1) 46% mood disorder, 20% anxiety disorder and 34 comorbid diagnoses (2)–(3) 100% MDD
Comparator	(1) SSRIs (2) Amitriptyline/ clomipramine (3) Antidepressants of GP's choice (4) Fluoxetine (40–60 mg/day) (5) Paroxetine (38 mg/day) (6) Paroxetine (7) Imipramine (200–300 mg/day) (8)–(9) Amitriptyline (150 mg/day) (10) Phenelzine (0.85 mg/kg)	(1) Waitlist (2)–(3) Placebo (4) Placebo + clinical management (5) Placebo (6) Waitlist	(1) Anti-depressants	(1)–(3) Behavioural activation	(1)–(4) IPT	(1)–(2) Short-term psycho-dynamic psychotherapy	(1)–(2) GP care (3) GP care, usual treatment

	(11) Nefazodone (300–600 mg/day) (12) Desipramine (90 mg/day) (13) Antidepressants (no details) (14) Paroxetine (10–50 mg) (15) Nortiptyline (25 mg) (16) Desipramine (150-300mg) (17) TAU (18) Desipramine (90 mg/day)						
Length of treatment	(1) 16–20 weeks (2) Maximum of 20 weeks (3) 16 weeks (4) 14 weeks (5)–(7) 16 weeks (8)–(9) 8 weeks (10) 10 weeks (11) 12 weeks (12) 18 weeks (13) 16 weeks (14) 8 weeks (15) 12 weeks (16) 16 weeks (17) 6 weeks (18) 8–12 weeks	(1) 15 weeks (2)–(4) 16 weeks (5) 10 weeks (6) 6 weeks	(1) 14 weeks	(1) 16 weeks (2) 12 weeks (3) 20 sessions	(1)–(2) 16 weeks (3) Up to 16 weeks (4) 16 weeks	(1) 16 weeks (2) 8 or 16 weeks	(1) 20 weeks (2) 16 weeks (3) 6 weeks

Continued

Table 36: (*Continued*)

	CBT versus antidepressants	CBT versus comparator	CBT versus rational emotive behavioural therapy	CBT versus behavioural activation	CBT versus IPT	CBT versus short-term psychodynamic psychotherapy	CBT (primary care) versus GP care
Follow-up	(1)–(2) Not reported (3) 24 months (4) 6 months (5)–(6) Not reported (7) 18 months (8)–(9) 12 months (10)–(11) Not reported (12) 6 months (13)–(16) Not reported (17) 12 months (18) No follow-up	(1) 12 months (2)–(3) Not reported (4) 18 months (5) Not reported (6) 2 months	(1) 6 months	(1) Not reported (2) 12 months (3) 6 months	(1) 18 months (2)–(4) Not reported	(1) 12 months (2) Not reported	(1) 5 months (2) Not reported (3) 12 months

Table 37: Summary study characteristics of cognitive behavioural therapy

	CBT + antidepressants versus antidepressants	CBT + antidepressants versus CBT	CBT versus antidepressants	CBT for the elderly	
				CBT + antidepressants versus antidepressants	Group CBT versus waitlist control
No. trials (total partici-pants)	9 RCTs (850)	6 RCTs (731)	2 RCTs (104)	1 RCTs (69)	1 RCT (45)
Study IDs	(1) Blackburn1981 (2) FAVA1998* (3) Hautzinger (in-pats) (4) Hautzinger1996 (5) Keller2000 (6) Miller1989 (7) Murphy1984 (8) Scott1997 (9) Thompson2001	(1) Blackburn1981 (2) Hautzinger (in-pats) (3) Hautzinger1996 (4) Keller2000 (5) Murphy1984 (6) Thompson2001	(1) LAIDLAW2008 (2) Thompson2001	(1) Thompson2001	(1) WILKINSON2009
N/% female	(1) Unextractable (2) 24/60 (3)–(4) 113/63 (5) 445/65 (6) 34/74 (7) 52/74 (8) 32/67 (9) 47/67	(1) Unextractable (2)–(3) 113/63 (4) 445/65 (5) 52/74 (6) 47/69	(1) 29/73 (2) 67/67	(1) 67/67	(1) 28/62

Continued

Table 37: (*Continued*)

	CBT + antidepressants versus antidepressants	CBT + antidepressants versus CBT	CBT versus antidepressants	CBT for the elderly	
				CBT + antidepressants versus antidepressants	Group CBT versus waitlist control
Mean age	(1) 43 (2) 47 (3)–(4) 40 (5) 44 (6) 37 (7) 33 (8) 41 (9) 62	(1) 43 (2)–(3) 40 (4) 43 (5) 33 (6) 67	(1) 76 (2) 67	(1) 67	(1) 74
Diagnosis	(1) 100% MDD (2) Remission after previous treatment (3)–(4) 80% MDD, 20% dysthymia (5)–(9) 100% MDD	(1) 100% MDD (2)–(3) 80% MDD, 20% dysthymia (4)–(6) 100% MDD	(1)–(2) 100% MDD	(1) 100% MDD	(1) Remission from depressive episode
Comparator	(1) Amitriptyline/ clomipramine (2) Range of antidepressants (3)–(4) Amitriptyline (150 mg/day) (5) Nefazodone (300–600 mg/day)	(1) Amitriptyline/ clomipramine (2)–(3) Amitriptyline (150 mg/ day) (4) Nefazodone (300–600 mg/day) (5) Nortriptyline (25 mg) (6) Desipramine	(1) TAU – GP care (2) Desipramine (90 mg/day)	(1) Desipramine (90 mg/day)	(1) TAU

	(6) TCAs (7) Nortriptyline (25 mg) (8) TAU (9) Desipramine (90 mg/day)				
Length of treatment	(1) Maximum 20 weeks (2) 20 weeks (3) 8 weeks (4) 4 weeks (5) 12 weeks (6) 20 weeks (7) 12 weeks (8) 6 weeks (9) 8–12 weeks	(1) Maximum 20 weeks (2)–(3) 8 weeks (4)–(5) 12 weeks (6) 8–12 weeks	(1) 18 weeks (2) 8–12 weeks	(1) 8–12 weeks	(1) 8 weeks
Follow-up	(1) Not reported (2) 24 months (3)–(4) 12 months (5)–(7) Not reported (8) 12 months (9) Not reported	(1) Not reported (2)–(3) 12 months (4)–(6) Not reported	(1) 6 months (2) Not reported	(1) Not reported	(1) 12 months

* Follow-up to Fava1994 (study in the previous guideline).

Table 38: Summary study characteristics of cognitive behavioural therapies

	Group CBT versus other group therapies	Group CBT versus waitlist	Group CBT versus TAU	Relapse prevention studies			
				CBT versus antidepressants	CBT + antidepressants versus antidepressants	MBCT versus antidepressants	MBCT versus comparator
No. trials (total participants)	3 RCTs (144)	5 RCTs (451)	1 RCT (187)	1 RCT (180)	1 RCT (132)	1 RCT (123)	3 RCTs (288)
Study IDs	(1) Beutler1991 (2) Bright1999 (3) Covi1987	(1) ALLARTVANDAM2003 (2) Brown1984 (3) DALGARD2006 (4) HARINGSMA2006A (5) WONG2008	(1) BOCKTING2005	(1) HOLLON2005	(1) PERLIS2002	(1) KUYKEN 2008	(1) CRANE2008 (2) MA2004 (3) Teasdale2000
N/% female	(1) 40/63 (2) 70/71 (3) 42/60	(1) 65/57 (2) 44/55 (3) 118/176 (4) 76/55 (5) 75/78	(1) 137/73	(1) Not reported	(1) 72/55	(1) 94/76	(1) Not reported (2) 57/76 (3) 110/76
Mean age	(1) 47 (2) 46 (3) 44	(1) 48 (2) 37 (3) 47 (4) 64 (5) 37	(1) 44	(1) Not reported	(1) 40	(1) 49	(1) 45 (2) 44 (3) 43

Diagnosis	(1) 100% MDD (2) 100% MDD or dysthymia (3) 100% MDD	(1) 5% dysthymia, 95% no diagnosis but BDI ≥ 10 (2) 44% MDD (RDC), 44% intermittent depressive disorder (RDC), 11% minor depressive disorder (RDC) (3) 100% unipolar depression (4) 60% MDD, 40% MDD + anxiety (5) 100% depression	(1) Remission from depression >10 weeks	(1) Responded to previous treatment	(1) Remission from MDD	(1) Remission from MDD	(1) Remission from depression (2)–(3) Remission from depression (major)
Comparator	(1) Focus expressive psychotherapy (2) Mutual support group therapy (3) Group psycho-therapy	(1) TAU – free to seek (2) Waitlist (3) TAU (4)–(5) Waitlist	(1) TAU	(1) Paroxetine (mean 38 mg/day)	(1) Fluoxetine (40 mg/day) + clinical management	(1) Antide-pressants (no details)	(1) Waitlist (2)–(3) TAU
Length of treatment	(1) 20 weeks (2) 10 weeks (3) 14 weeks	(1) 12 weeks (2)–(3) 8 weeks (4)–(5) 10 weeks	(1) 8 weeks	(1) 12 months	(1) 28 weeks	(1) 8 weeks	(1)–(3) 8 weeks
Follow-up	(1) 3 months (2)–(3) Not reported	(1) 12 months (2)–(3) 6 months (4)–(5) Not reported	(1) 24 months	(1) 24 months	(1) Not reported	(1) 15 months	(1) 2–3 months (2)–(3) 12 months

Table 39: Summary evidence profile for cognitive behavioural therapies

	CBT versus antidepressants	CBT versus comparator		CBT versus rational emotive behavioural therapy	CBT versus behavioural activation	CBT versus IPT	CBT versus short-term psychodynamic psychotherapy	CBT (primary care) versus GP care
		CBT versus waitlist control	CBT versus placebo + clinical management					
Leaving study early for any reason	RR 0.75 (0.63 to 0.91)	Not reported	RR 0.44 (0.12 to 1.61)	RR 1.22 (0.40 to 3.77)	RR 0.56 (0.24 to 1.33)	RR 1.29 (0.91 to 1.85)	RR 0.46 (0.17 to 1.23)	RR 1.54 (0.97 to 2.46)
Quality	High	–	Moderate	Low	Moderate	Moderate	High	High
Number of studies; participants	K = 13, n = 1480	–	K = 2, n = 193	K = 1, n = 113	K = 2, n = 108	K = 3, n = 405	K = 1, n = 66	K = 3, n = 208
Forest plot number	CBT 15.05	–	CBT 03.02	CBT 84.19	CBT 37.17	CBT 81.18	CBT 07.03	CBT 13.04
Depression self-report measures at endpoint	SMD −0.06 (−0.24 to 0.12)	SMD −0.89 (−1.45 to −0.33)	SMD −0.15 (−0.51 to 0.21)	SMD 0 (−0.37 to 0.37)	At 8 weeks: SMD 0.34 (−0.26 to 0.95)	SMD 0.21 (0.01 to 0.41)	SMD − 0.35 (−1.30 to 0.61)	SMD 0.01 (−0.83 to 0.85)
Quality	High	High	Low	Low	Low	High	Moderate	Moderate

Number of studies; participants	K = 8, n = 480	K = 2, n = 54	K = 1, n = 121	K = 1, n = 113	K = 1, n = 43	K = 3, n = 383	K = 1, n = 57	K = 2, n = 120
Forest plot number	CBT 17.05	CBT 01.04	CBT 04.02	CBT 86.19	CBT 74.02	CBT 82.18	CBT 08.03	CBT 14.04
Depression clinician-report measures at endpoint	SMD 0.05 (−0.06 to 0.15)	HRSD >6: RR 0.45 (0.23 to 0.91)	SMD −0.32 (−0.68 to 0.04)	SMD −0.03 (−0.40 to 0.34)	At 8 weeks: SMD −0.03 (−0.62 to 0.57)	SMD 0.13 (−0.06 to 0.32)	Not reported	SMD −0.33 (−0.74 to 0.08)
Quality	High	Low	Low	Low	Low	Low	–	High
Number of studies; participants	K = 13, n = 1403	K = 1, n = 24	K = 1, n = 121	K = 1, n = 113	K = 1, n = 43	K = 4, n = 430	–	K = 2, n = 92
Forest plot number	CBT 17.05	CBT 02.01	CBT 04.02	CBT 86.19	CBT 74.17	CBT 82.18	–	CBT 14.04

Table 40: Summary evidence profile for cognitive behavioural therapies

	CBT + antidepressants versus antidepressants	CBT + antidepressants versus CBT	CBT versus antidepressants	CBT for the elderly	
				CBT + antidepressants versus antidepressants	Group CBT + antidepressants versus antidepressants
Leaving study early for any reason	RR 0.81 (0.65 to 1.01)	RR 1.00 (0.77 to 1.30)	RR 0.57 (0.27 to 1.21)	RR 0.92 (0.48 to 1.75)	RR 0.84 (0.26 to 2.72)
Quality	Moderate	Moderate	Moderate	Low	Low
Number of studies; participants	K = 8, n = 831	K = 5, n = 710	K = 2, n = 108	K = 1, n = 69	K = 1, n = 45
Forest plot number	CBT 31.07	CBT 45.09	CBT 56.12	CBT 60.12	CBT 62.12
Depression self-report measures at endpoint	SMD −0.38 (−0.62 to −0.14)	SMD −0.17 (−0.44 to 0.10)	SMD −0.31 (−0.69 to 0.07)	SMD −0.36 (−0.84 to 0.12)	At 6 months: BDI ≥ 12: RR 1.69 (0.68 to 4.21)
Quality	High	Moderate	Moderate	Low	Low
Number of studies; participants	K = 6, n = 277	K = 4, 219	K = 2, n = 108	K = 1, n = 69	K = 1, n = 37
Forest plot number	CBT 33.07	CBT 47.09	CBT 57.12	CBT 61.12	CBT 62.12
Depression clinician-report measures at endpoint	SMD −0.46 (−0.61 to −0.31)	SMD −0.05 (−0.31 to 0.22)	SMD −0.41 (−0.79 to −0.03)	SMD −0.45 (−0.93 to 0.03)	At 6 months: MADRS ≥ 10: RR 0.26 (0.03 to 2.14)
Quality	High	Moderate	High	Low	Low
Number of studies; participants	K = 7, 724	K = 4, n = 220	K = 2, n = 108	K = 1, n = 69	K = 1, n = 37
Forest plot number	CBT 34.07	CBT 47.09	CBT 57.12	CBT 61.12	CBT 62.12

Table 41: Summary evidence profile for cognitive behavioural therapies

| | Group CBT versus other group therapies | Group CBT versus waitlist | Group CBT versus TAU | Relapse prevention studies | | | |
				CBT versus antidepressants	CBT + antidepressants versus antidepressants	MBCT versus antidepressants	MBCT versus comparator
Leaving study early for any reason	RR 0.94 (0.57 to 1.53)	RR 1.34 (0.44 to 4.11)	RR 2.47 (1.01 to 6.05)	RR 1.20 (0.30 to 4.85)	RR 0.96 (0.61 to 1.52)	RR 0.34 (0.07 to 1.61)	Not reported
Quality	Moderate	Low	Moderate	Low	Low	Low	
Number of studies; participants	K = 3, n = 158	K = 4; n = 369	K = 1, n = 187	K = 1, n = 180	K = 1, n = 132	K = 1, n = 123	–
Forest plot number	CBT 96.22	CBT 89.21	CBT 70.16	CBT 65.14	CBT 68.15	CBT 103.24	–
Depression self-report measures at endpoint	SMD −0.17 (−0.61 to 0.26)	SMD −0.60 (−0.84 to −0.35)	Not reported	Not reported	Not reported	Not reported	At 1 month: SMD −0.36 (−0.98 to 0.25)
Quality	Moderate	High	–	–	–	–	Low
Number of studies; participants	K = 2, n = 83	K = 4; n = 277	–	–	–	–	K = 1; n = 42
Forest plot number	CBT 97.22	CBT 90.21	–	–	–	–	CBT 102.23

Continued

231

Table 41: *(Continued)*

	Group CBT versus other group therapies	Group CBT versus waitlist	Group CBT versus TAU	CBT versus antidepressants	CBT + antidepressants versus antidepressants	MBCT versus antidepressants	MBCT versus comparator
						Relapse prevention studies	
Depression clinician-report measures at endpoint	SMD −0.12 (−0.55 to 0.31)	Not reported	Patients with ≥5 previous episodes: SMD −0.08 (−0.54 to 0.39)	Not reported	SMD −0.18 (−0.52 to 0.16)	Relapse RR 0.80 (0.57 to 1.11)	Relapse: patients with ≥3 episodes: RR 0.46 (0.27 to 0.79)
Quality	Moderate	–	Low	–	Low	Low	Moderate
Number of studies; participants	K = 2, n = 83	–	K = 1, n = 71	–	K = 1, n = 132	K = 1, n = 123	K = 1, n = 55
Forest plot number	CBT 97.22	–	CBT 72.16	–	CBT 69.15	CBT 66.14	CBT 64.13

8.1.4   Clinical evidence summary for cognitive behavioural therapies

Cognitive behavioural therapies versus antidepressants

There were sixteen trials (n = 1793) that reported the effectiveness of CBT compared with antidepressants. Six of those studies were found in the search of the guideline update and ten were reported in the previous guideline. The results for depression scores at post-treatment (BDI: SMD −0.06; 95% CI −0.24 to 0.12; HRSD: SMD 0.05; CI −0.06 to 0.15) and at 1-month follow-up (BDI: SMD −0.02; 95% CI −0.68 to 0.65; HRSD: 0.08; 95% CI −0.59 to 0.74) were not significantly different and this, along with the relatively narrow CIs, suggests broad equivalence between CBT and antidepressants. However, by 12 months' follow-up the evidence from three trials (Hautzinger [in-pats], Hautzinger1996 and Blackburn1997; n = 137) indicates that CBT has a significant medium effect (BDI: −0.41, 95% CI −0.76, −0.07; HRSD: SMD −0.50; 95% CI −0.84, −0.15) over antidepressants. In terms of leaving the study early, there was a significant higher risk of discontinuation (RR 0.75; 95% CI 0.63, 0.91) in the antidepressant group. A 1-year follow-up of the DIMIDJIAN2006 trial indicates that people who had cognitive therapy were less likely to relapse following treatment than those previously treated with antidepressants (RR 0.82; 95% CI 0.60, 1.11).

Cognitive behavioural therapies versus comparator (waitlist control)

Four low quality studies (two reported in the previous guideline: Beach1992 and Selmi1990; and two found in the update search: DERUBEIS2005 and DIMID-JIAN2006) compared the efficacy of cognitive behavioural therapies versus waitlist control. The effectiveness of CBT for the treatment of depression was large (SMD −0.89; 95% CI −1.45; −0.33) in self-reports and showed an effect in clinician-reported depression scores (RR 0.45; 95% CI 0.23, 0.91).

Combination (cognitive behavioural therapy + antidepressants) versus antidepressants

Nine studies included a comparison between combined treatment of CBT plus antidepressants and antidepressants alone. Only one of those studies (FAVA1998[56]) was found in the search for this guideline update. The combination treatment of CBT and antidepressants had a lower risk of discontinuation compared with antidepressants (RR 0.81; 95% CI 0.65, 1.01). There is evidence that the combined treatment has a significant medium effect in the reduction of self-rated (SMD −0.38; 95% CI −0.62, −0.14) and clinician-rated (SMD −0.46; 95% CI −0.61, −0.31) depression scores. At 6 and 12 months' follow-up; however, there was limited data (BDI at 6 months: SMD 0.35; 95% CI −0.69, 1.40; HRSD at 6 months: SMD 0.50; 95% CI −0.53, 1.53; BDI at 12 months: SMD −0.29; 95% CI −0.70, 0.12; HRSD at 12 months: SMD −0.29; 95% CI −0.64, 0.07), which introduced some uncertainty

---

[56]Follow-up to Fava1994 (study in the previous guideline).

about the relative long-term effectiveness of the combination of these two treatments.

Combination (cognitive behavioural therapy + antidepressants) versus cognitive behavioural therapy

Six studies reported in the previous guideline included a comparison of combination treatment and CBT alone. In contrast with the dataset on the combination of CBT and antidepressants versus antidepressants, it was not possible to identify a benefit for adding antidepressants to CBT (BDI at post-treatment: SMD −0.17, 95% CI −0.44, 0.10; BDI at 1-month follow-up: SMD −0.29, 95% CI −0.94, 0.36; HRSD at 1-month follow-up: SMD −0.08, 95% CI −0.72, 0.57). This might suggest that although the CBT and antidepressants dataset supports combined treatment, clinical benefit could still be derived from CBT alone.

Cognitive behavioural therapies versus comparator (placebo plus clinical management)

There was little evidence of the increased effectiveness of CBT when compared with placebo plus clinical management from two studies (also reported in the previous guideline: Elkin1989 and Jarrett1999; n = 193). There was some indication of higher dropout rates in the placebo groups but the effect (RR 0.44, 95% CI 0.12, 1.61) was not significant and therefore inconclusive. There was a small effect on reducing depression scores at endpoint in favour of CBT (self-rated: SMD −0.15, 95% CI −0.51, 0.21 and clinician-rated: SMD −0.32, 95% CI −0.68, 0.04) when compared with placebo plus clinical management. However, the results were not significant and the CIs were fairly wide so the evidence remains inconclusive.

Cognitive behavioural therapies versus other therapies designed for depression (behavioural activation and interpersonal therapy)

There were three studies that compared cognitive behavioural therapies with behavioural activation in the treatment of depression (DIMIDJIAN2006, Gallagher1982, JACOBSON1996). However, the comparison in the Gallagher1982 study included cognitive therapy following the approach of Beck and colleagues (1979) and Emery (1981) and was compared with behavioural therapy that followed Lewinsohn's (1975) approach. In addition, the Gallagher1982 study only reported leaving study early data. There were no clinically important differences identified between CBT and behavioural activation (BDI at endpoint: 0.34; 95% CI −0.26, 0.95; HRSD at endpoint: −0.03; 95% CI −0.62, 0.57). From this evidence it is not possible to draw any clear conclusions about the relative efficacy of the treatments. A 1-year follow-up of the DIMIDJIAN2006 trial indicates that people who had cognitive therapy were less likely to relapse following treatment than those previously treated with antidepressants (RR 0.82; 95% CI, 0.60, 1.11).

Four studies included a comparison of CBT versus IPT (Elkin1989, Freeman2002, LUTY2007, MARSHALL2008). Again, there were no clinically important differences between CBT and IPT (BDI at endpoint: 0.21; 95% CI −0.01, 0.41; HRSD at endpoint: 0.13; 95% CI −0.06, 0.32). This evidence although limited suggests that IPT might be as effective as CBT in the treatment of depression.

Cognitive behavioural therapies versus other psychotherapies not specifically designed for depression

There were three studies that looked at the effectiveness of CBT compared with other therapies not specifically designed for depression. Two studies (Gallagher-Th1994 and Shapiro1994) compared CBT with short-term psychodynamic psychotherapy. One study (Rosner1999) compared CBT with gestalt psychotherapy[57]. The evidence indicates no clinically important differences for the comparison of CBT with short-term psychodynamic psychotherapy in decreasing depression (BDI at endpoint: SMD −0.35; 95% CI −1.30, 0.61) or with Gestalt psychotherapy (BDI at endpoint: SMD 0.17; 95% CI −0.56, 0.91). From this evidence it is not possible to draw any clear conclusions about the relative efficacy of the treatments.

Cognitive behavioural therapies (primary care) versus GP care

Three trials reported in the previous guideline included a comparison between CBT in primary care versus usual GP care. The studies varied in duration: Freeman2002 consisted of 16 sessions over a 5-month period, Scott1992 was 16 weeks' duration and Scott1997 was 6 weeks. In terms of leaving the study early due to any reason, the evidence suggests that there is a higher risk for discontinuation in those in the CBT (primary care) group (RR 1.54; 95% CI 0.97, 2.46). The evidence here is difficult to interpret as many patients in GP care might have been in receipt of antidepressants and the duration of treatment was shorter than that typical of CBT. At the end of treatment self-report depression scores (SMD 0.01; 95% CI −0.83, 0.85) were not significantly different, and neither were clinician-rated depression scores (SMD −0.33; 95% CI −0.74, 0.08).

Group cognitive behavioural therapies

Three studies reported in the previous guideline looked at the effectiveness of group CBT when compared with other psychotherapies (Bright1999, Covi1987, Klein1984) and no new studies were found that looked at this comparison for the guideline update[58]. The results show no significant difference in risk for discontinuation (RR 0.94, 95% CI 0.57, 1.53) or depression scores at post-treatment (BDI: SMD −0.17, 95% CI −0.61, 0.26; HRSD: SMD −0.12, 95% CI −0.55, 0.31). However, when self-rated depression scores were analysed by a cut-off of BDI >9, there was a significant difference favouring group CBT (RR 0.60, 95% CI 0.46, 0.79).

A further analysis was carried out looking at group CBT compared with waitlist control or treatment as usual. Four studies evaluated the Coping with Depression programme (see above) (ALLARTVANDAM2003, BROWN1984, DALGARD2006, HARINGSMA2006). The evidence indicates no clinically important difference in risk for discontinuation (RR 1.34, 95% CI 0.44, 4.11). There was a significant medium effect of group CBT in lowering depression scores at endpoint (SMD −0.60,

---

[57]For reasons of brevity this analysis is not included in the summary evidence table, but can be found in Appendix 16b and 19b. The study characteristics are in Appendix 17b.
[58]Ibid.

95% CI −0.84, −0.35) and at 6 months' follow-up (SMD −0.40, 95% CI −0.83, 0.02). Therefore group CBT (in particular Coping with Depression) appears an effective treatment for people with mild depression.

Cognitive behavioural therapies for the elderly

Three studies looked at the effectiveness of CBT in the treatment of depression in elderly populations. LAIDLAW2008 and Thompson2001 compared CBT with antidepressants. Thompson2001 also included a comparison of the combination of CBT with antidepressants with antidepressants alone. WILKINSON2009 looked at the effectiveness of group CBT in relapse prevention compared with waitlist control.

The evidence was inconclusive regarding leaving the study early. In clinician-rated depression scores, there was a significant medium effect favouring CBT (SMD −0.41; 95% CI −0.79, −0.03). However, the results were not significant for follow-up data (at 3 months: SMD −0.35; 95% CI −0.78, 0.07 and at 6 months: −0.15; 95% CI −0.74, 0.44). The results suggest the effectiveness of CBT seen in adults of working age may be replicated in older adults but some caution is required in interpreting the results.

In the combined treatment of CBT plus antidepressants versus antidepressants alone, there was little to no difference in risk for discontinuation between the two groups (RR 0.92). There were medium effects favouring combined treatments for both self-rated (SMD −0.36; 95% CI −0.84 to 0.12) and clinician-rated depression scores (SMD −0.45; 95% CI −0.93 to 0.03). It should be noted that the CIs for both effects just cross the line of no effect, so these results should be interpreted with caution. The evidence from one trial (WILKINSON2009; n = 43) comparing group CBT plus antidepressants with antidepressants alone in the treatment of depression for the elderly is not significant (BDI ≥12 at 6 months: RR 1.69, 95% CI, 0.68, 4.21; Montgomery–Åsberg Depression Rating Scale [MADRS] ≥10 at 6 months: RR 0.26; 95% CI, 0.03, 2.14) and this prevents any clear conclusion being drawn.

Cognitive behavioural therapies – relapse prevention

This section brings together the impact of relapse prevention studies in different areas (group CBT, individual CBT, combination of CBT and antidepressants, and MBCT). A number of studies have addressed the issue of relapse prevention and have developed a number of different approaches both to the patient population identified and the specific CBT approach taken. The approaches include extending the duration of individual CBT, specific group-based approaches including a programme for those with residual symptoms (BOCKTING2005) and MBCT. In total, seven studies (n = 957) found in the search for the guideline update examined relapse prevention in people who had been administered CBT. Three of these studies compare CBT with antidepressants.

Group cognitive behavioural therapy versus treatment as usual

The evidence from one study (BOCKTING2005) indicates a higher risk for discontinuation in those administered group CBT than treatment as usual (RR 2.47; 95% CI 1.01, 6.05). There is insufficient evidence (one study and wide CIs) to determine the comparative effectiveness between the two groups in terms of relapse or remission rates at 68 weeks. Similarly, the evidence indicates a non-significant difference in self-reports of depression in patients with five or more previous episodes of depression (SMD −0.08; 95% CI −0.54, 0.39). It is important to mention that the study that reports this comparison is based on a series of post-hoc analyses and results should be interpreted with caution.

Cognitive behavioural therapy versus clinical management (not shown in tables)
Two studies (FAVA1998 and PAYKEL2005) compared the effectiveness of individual CBT with clinical management (with antidepressants) as part of a relapse prevention programme. They report a significant difference favouring individual CBT in relapse rates when compared with clinical management (RR 0.54; 95% CI 0.37, 0.79). Furthermore, one of the two studies, PAYKEL2005, reports remission at 68 weeks (RR 1.30; 95% CI 0.94, 1.80). However, data at 68 weeks should be interpreted with caution given that there is only one study and the CIs are wide. The two studies mentioned previously are not shown in the tables of study characteristics or in the summary of evidence profiles in this chapter in the interest of brevity and given that these studies report different outcomes from those listed in the tables. These studies, however, appear in the study characteristics tables in Appendix 17b and the forest plots in Appendix 19b.

Combination cognitive behavioural therapy + antidepressants versus antidepressants
When the combination treatment of CBT plus antidepressants was compared with antidepressants alone there were no significant differences in terms of risk for discontinuation (RR 0.96; 95% CI 0.61, 1.52) or relapse (RR 0.80; 95% CI 0.22, 2.85).

Mindfulness-based cognitive therapy
Four studies (CRANE2008, KUYKEN2008, MA2004, Teasdale2000) evaluated the effectiveness of MBCT group treatment in relapse prevention. Two studies (MA2004, Teasdale2000) compared the combined treatment of group MBCT with GP care versus GP care alone. The evidence indicates a higher risk for discontinuation in the combined treatment (RR 19.11, 95% CI 2.58, 141.35) but a significantly lower risk for relapse (RR 0.74, 95% CI 0.57, 0.96). Regarding the reduction of relapse rates, group MBCT when compared with antidepressants showed a small to medium effect of group MBCT lowering depression scores at 1-month (BDI: SMD −0.37, 95% CI −0.72, −0.01; HRSD: SMD −0.31, 95% CI −0.66, 0.05) and at 15 months' follow-up (BDI: SMD −0.34, 95% CI −0.69, 0.02; HRSD: SMD −0.23, 95% CI −0.59, 0.12).

8.1.5   Health economic evidence and considerations

Two studies were identified in the systematic literature review that evaluated the cost effectiveness of cognitive behavioural therapies for people with depression (Kuyken *et al.*, 2008; Scott *et al.*, 2003). Details on the methods used for the systematic search of the health economics literature are described in Chapter 3, Section 3.6.1. Evidence tables for all health economics studies are presented in Appendix 15.

Kuyken and colleagues (2008) evaluated the cost effectiveness of MBCT compared with maintenance antidepressant medication in 123 patients with a history of depression participating in a primary care-based RCT. The time horizon of the analysis was 15 months and both a health service and societal perspective were taken in separate analyses. Costs included all hospital care, community health and social services and any productivity losses resulting from time off work. The outcome measures used in the cost-effectiveness analysis were the mean total number of relapses/recurrences avoided and the mean total number of depression-free days. Over 15 months' follow-up, there was no significant difference in total mean costs between MBCT and antidepressant treatment (US \$3,370 versus \$2,915; $p = 0.865$). From an NHS and Personal Social Services (PSS) perspective, the ICER was \$429 per relapse/recurrence prevented and \$23 per depression-free day. From a societal perspective, the ICER was \$962 per relapse/recurrence prevented and \$50 per depression-free day. The authors suggested that the additional cost of MBCT may be justified in terms of improvements in the proportion of patients who relapsed.

Scott and colleagues (2003) evaluated the cost effectiveness of cognitive therapy added to antidepressants and clinical management compared with antidepressants and clinical management alone in a UK RCT of 154 patients with partially remitted major depression. The setting was either in local clinics or in participants' homes. The time horizon of the analysis was 68 weeks (including 20 weeks of treatment). The study estimated NHS costs including treatments, clinical management, hospital care, primary care, group and marital therapy and medication for this period. The primary outcomes used in the analysis were relapse rates for the two treatment groups. Overall, the cognitive therapy group was significantly more costly than standard clinical treatment, with a mean difference of £779 per person ($p < 0.01$). The ICER of cognitive therapy versus standard care was £4,328 per relapse averted or £12.50 per additional relapse-free day. The authors concluded that in individuals with depressive symptoms that are resistant to standard treatment, adjunctive cognitive therapy was more costly but more effective than intensive clinical treatment alone.

8.2   BEHAVIOURAL ACTIVATION

8.2.1   Introduction

Behavioural activation for depression evolved from learning theory that posits two types of learning: operant or instrumental learning and classical conditioning. Although classical conditioning theories for depression have been put forward (for example, Wolpe, 1971) with treatment recommendations (Wolpe, 1979) there have been no treatment trials of this approach. Operant or instrumental learning posits that depressive behaviours are learned through the contingencies around those behaviours. In behavioural therapies, depression is seen as the result of a low rate of positive reinforcement and is maintained through negative reinforcement. Most commonly, patients use avoidance to minimise negative emotions and situations they worry will be unpleasant. Behavioural therapies focus on behavioural activation aimed at encouraging the patient to develop more rewarding and task-focused behaviours as well as stepping out of patterns of negative reinforcement. The approach was developed by Lewinsohn (1975). In recent years there has been renewed interest in behavioural activation (for example, Jacobson *et al.*, 2001; Hopko *et al.*, 2003), as it is now known, as a therapy in its own right, although it has always been part of cognitive behavioural treatments of depression (Beck *et al.*, 1997).

Definition
Behavioural activation is defined as a discrete, time-limited, structured psychological intervention, derived from the behavioural model of affective disorders and where the therapist and patient:
● work collaboratively to identify the effects of behaviours on current symptoms, feelings states and/or problem areas
● seek to reduce symptoms and problematic behaviours through behavioural tasks related to: reducing avoidance, graded exposure, activity scheduling, and initiating positively reinforced behaviours.

8.2.2   Studies considered[59]

There were six studies involving a comparison of behavioural activation. Of these, four were found in the searches for the guideline update and two were from the previous guideline. Two further studies were identified, which were excluded: CULLEN2006 because of a lack of extractable data[60] and Thompson 1987 because it was unclear which patient numbers were used in their table reporting outcome measures and the dropout data was not fully reported. Comparisons between behavioural activation and cognitive behavioural therapies can be found in the previous section (see Section 8.1). One study, McLean1979, entailed a comparison with psychotherapy. HOPKO2003 compared behavioural activation with an attentional control (the control had the same duration of contact in a group but no therapy was given) in an inpatient setting. A further study, DIMIDJIAN2006, entailed a comparison between behavioural activation and antidepressants, as well as a comparison between behavioural activation and placebo.

Summary study characteristics of the included studies are presented in Table 42, with full details in Appendix 17b, which also includes details of excluded studies. Studies comparing CBT and behavioural activation are reported in Section 8.1 and therefore have not been included in Table 42.

---

[59]Study IDs in title case refer to studies included in the previous guideline and study IDs in capital letters refer to studies found and included in this guideline update. References for studies from the previous guideline are in Appendix 18.
[60]The review team contacted the authors of the study but did not receive the data.

Table 42: Summary study characteristics of behavioural activation

	Behavioural activation versus placebo	Behavioural activation versus comparator	Behavioural activation versus antidepressants
No. trials (total participants)	1 RCT (96)	2 RCTs (136)	1 RCT (159)
Study IDs	(1) DIMIDJIAN2006	(1) HOPKO2003 (2) McLean1979	(1) DIMIDJIAN2006
N/% female	(1) 159/65	(1) 25/36 (2) 111/72	(1) 159/65
Mean age	(1) 40	(1) 30 (2) 39	(1) 40
Diagnosis	(1) 100% major depression	(1)–(2) 100% major depression	(1) 100% major depression
Comparator	(1) Placebo	(1) Supportive psychotherapy (2) Psychodynamic psychotherapy	(1) 35.17 mg/day paroxetine
Length of treatment	(1) 16 weeks	(1) 2 weeks (2) 10 weeks	(1) 16 weeks
Follow-up	(1) None reported	(1) None reported (2) 3 months	(1) None reported

8.2.3   Clinical evidence

Because there are a relatively small number of studies for behavioural activation a summary of evidence profile table has not been included here. The full evidence profiles and associated forest plots can be found in Appendix 16b and Appendix 19b, respectively.

8.2.4   Clinical evidence summary

Behavioural activation versus cognitive behavioural therapy
Studies comparing behavioural activation and CBT are reported in the CBT summary evidence profile tables – see the section 'Cognitive behavioural therapies versus other therapies designed for depression (behavioural activation and inter-personal therapy)'. In summary, there were three studies included (DIMID-JIAN2006, Gallagher1982[61] and JACOBSON1996). Gallagher1982 only reported

---

[61]Cognitive therapy based on Beck and colleagues (1979) and Emery (1981) and compared with behaviour therapy based on Lewinsohn (1975).

leaving the study early data. There were no clinically important differences identified between CBT and behavioural activation (BDI at endpoint: 0.34; 95% CI −0.26, 0.95; HRSD at endpoint: −0.03; 95% CI −0.62, 0.57). From this evidence it is not possible to draw any clear conclusions about the relative efficacy of the treatments.

Behavioural activation versus placebo
Only one study (DIMIDJIAN2006) included a comparison of behavioural activation versus placebo. The evidence suggests there is no significant difference between treatments in risk for discontinuation (RR 1.23; 95% CI 0.33, 4.64). Similarly, there were no significant differences between treatments in the reduction of depression scores (self-reported, BDI: SMD 0.07; 95% CI, −0.61, 0.75 and clinician reported, HRSD: SMD 0.06; 95% CI, −0.62, 0.73). These results are based on one medium-sized study and given its wide CIs it is difficult to make any firm conclusions from this evidence.

Behavioural activation versus other interventions
One study, McLean1979, compared behavioural activation with an attentional control. The study used a short-term psychotherapy (10 weeks of 1-hour sessions) following Marmor (1973, 1975) and Wolberg (1967), the aim of which is the development of insight of the psychodynamic forces that initiated the patient's current depression. From this study, only leaving the study early data could be extracted, and their results indicate an increased risk for discontinuation in the control group (RR 0.17; 95% CI, 0.04, 0.71). It should be noted that this evidence is based on one study and the CIs are wide.

The second study, HOPKO2003, compared behavioural activation with a supportive treatment (three times weekly, 20 minutes for 14 days), which was a non-directive discussion with the clinician in which the patient was encouraged to share their experiences. The results at post-treatment favoured behavioural activation (BDI: SMD −0.69; 95% CI, −1.52, 0.14). However, this result is not significant and should be interpreted with caution.

Behavioural activation versus antidepressants
There is limited evidence from one study (DIMIDJIAM2006) of the effect of behavioural activation in the treatment of depression when compared with antidepressants. This limited evidence seems to indicate a low risk of discontinuation in the people administered antidepressants when compared with those in the behavioural activation group (RR 0.31; 95% CI 0.12, 0.83). In terms of depression scores, the results were not significant but tended to favour the antidepressant group in those diagnosed with moderate severity (self-reported scores: SMD 0.15; 95% CI −0.47, 0.78 and clinician-reported scores: SMD 0.14; 95% CI −0.49, 0.77) and in those with high severity (self-reported scores: SMD 0.24; 95% CI −0.29, 0.76 and clinician-reported scores: SMD −0.04; 95% CI −0.56, 0.49). There seems to be little to no difference between behavioural activation and antidepressants in terms of relapse rates at 1 year (RR 1.04; 95% CI 0.49, 2.21).

8.2.5 Health economic evidence and considerations

No evidence on the cost effectiveness of behavioural activation for people with depression was identified by the systematic search of the economic literature. Details on the methods used for the systematic search of the economic literature are described in Chapter 3, Section 3.6.1.

8.3 PROBLEM SOLVING

8.3.1 Introduction

It has long been recognised that depression is associated with social problem-solving difficulties (Nezu, 1987). The reasons for this may be various, relating to the effects of depressed state, lack of knowledge, and rumination. As a consequence, helping patients solve problems and develop problem-solving skills has been a focus for therapeutic intervention and development of therapy (Nezu *et al.*, 1989). There has been recent interest in developing problem-solving therapies for depression for use in primary care (Barrett *et al.*, 1999; Dowrick *et al.*, 2000).

Definition
Problem-solving therapy is a discrete, time-limited, structured psychological intervention, which focuses on learning to cope with specific problems areas and where therapist and patient work collaboratively to identify and prioritise key problem areas, to break problems down into specific, manageable tasks, problem solve, and develop appropriate coping behaviours for problems.

8.3.2 Studies considered[62]

No new studies found in the search for the guideline update were included. Two studies were found and excluded on the basis of one study not reporting the outcome data (AREAN2008) and one study having a sample size of less than ten (NEZU1986). Three studies were reported in the previous guideline but only two are included in the update (Mynors-Wallis1995; Mynors-Wallis2000). Dowrick and colleagues (2000) which was included in the previous guideline, was excluded from this update because not all patients met criteria for depression (<80%).

Summary study characteristics of the included studies are presented in Table 43, with full details in Appendix 17b, which also includes details of excluded studies.

---

[62]Study IDs in title case refer to studies included in the previous guideline and study IDs in capital letters refer to studies found and included in this guideline update. References for studies from the previous guideline are in Appendix 18.

Table 43: Summary study characteristics of problem solving

	Problem solving versus placebo	Problem solving versus antidepressants	Problem solving + antidepressants versus antidepressants	Problem solving (GP) versus problem solving (nurse)
No. trials (total participants)	1 RCT (70)	2 RCTs (135)	1 RCT (74)	1 RCT (80)
Study IDs	(1) Mynors-Wallis1995	(1) Mynors-Wallis1995 (2) Mynors-Wallis2000	(1) Mynors-Wallis2000	(1) Mynors-Wallis2000
N/% female	(1) 70/77	(1) 70/77 (2) 116/77	(1) 116/77	(1) 116/77
Mean age	(1) 37	(1) 37 (2) 35	(1) 35	(1) 35
Diagnosis	(1) 100% RDC MDD	(1) 100% RDC MDD (2) 100% depression	(1) 100% depression	(1) 100% depression
Comparator	(1) Placebo	(1) Amitriptyline (150 mg/day) (2) Fluvoxamine/ paroxetine	(1) Fluvoxamine/ paroxetine	(1) Problem solving delivered by a nurse (as opposed to GP)
Length of treatment	(1) 12 weeks	(1)–(2) 12 weeks	(1) 12 weeks	(1) 12 weeks
Follow-up	(1) Not reported	(1) Not reported (2) 12 months	(1) 12 months	(1) 12 months

8.3.3   Clinical evidence

Evidence from the important outcomes and overall quality of evidence are presented in Table 44. The full evidence profiles and associated forest plots can be found in Appendix 16b and Appendix 19b, respectively.

8.3.4   Clinical evidence summary

Only two studies were found that met the inclusion criteria for problem solving and only one study (Mynors-Wallis1995) indicated that this intervention had a significant

Table 44: Summary evidence profile for problem solving

	Problem solving versus placebo	Problem solving versus antidepressants	Problem solving + antidepressants versus antidepressants	Problem solving (GP) versus problem solving (nurse)
Leaving study early for any reason	RR 0.11 (0.03 to 0.44)	RR 0.88 (0.18 to 4.20)	RR 1.03 (0.37 to 2.89)	RR 1.64 (0.80 to 3.34)
Quality	Moderate	Low	Low	Low
Number of studies; participants	K = 1, n = 60	K = 2, n = 177	K = 1, n = 71	K = 1, n = 80
Forest plot number	PS 01.01	PS 08.02	PS 16.03	PS 22.04
Depression self-report measures at endpoint	SMD −0.69 (−1.24, −0.14) BDI >8: RR 0.62 (0.39 to 0.99)	SMD −0.11 (−0.46 to 0.25) BDI >8: RR 0.67 (0.41 to 1.09)	SMD −0.24 (−0.73 to 0.24)	SMD −0.07 (−0.54 to 0.40)
Quality	Moderate Moderate	Moderate Low	Low	Low
Number of studies; participants	K = 1, n = 60	K = 2, n = 124	K = 1, n = 65	K = 1, n = 70
Forest plot number	PS 04.01 & PS 06.01	PS 11.02 & PS 13.02	PS 19.03	PS 26.04
Depression clinician-report measures at endpoint	SMD −0.66 (−1.21, −0.12) HRSD >7: RR 0.55 (0.33 to 0.89)	SMD 0.10 (−0.25 to 0.45) HRSD >7: RR 1.43 (0.85 to 2.39)	SMD 0.18 (−0.30 to 0.67) HRSD >7: RR 1.20 (0.65 to 2.22)	SMD −0.02 (−0.49 to 0.44) HRSD >7: RR 1.05 (0.66 to 1.67)
Quality	Moderate Moderate	Moderate Low	Low Low	Low Low
Number of studies; participants	K = 1, n = 60	K = 2, n = 124	K = 1, n = 71	K = 1, n = 80
Forest plot number	PS 03.01 & PS 05.01	PS 10.02 & PS 12.02	PS 19.03 & PS 18.03	PS 26.04 & PS 24.04

effect in reducing depression scores (clinician-rated: SMD –0.66; 95% CI −1.21, −0.12; self-rated: SMD –0.69; 95% CI −1.24, −0.14) when compared with placebo. This effect was also seen for dichotomous scores: clinician-rated (RR 0.55; 95% CI 0.33, 0.89) and self-rated (RR0.62; 95% CI 0.39, 0.99). A further study (Dowrick2000) indicated a significant decrease in the number of people diagnosed with depressive and subthreshold depressive symptoms after 6 months of treatment (RR 0.83; 95% CI 0.68, 1.02) when compared with placebo. However this trial did not meet the inclusion criteria for the guideline due to 80% or more of the population in the trial not meeting diagnosis for depression and therefore does not appear in the tables above.

There were no significant differences when problem solving was compared with antidepressants or when the combination treatment of problem solving and antidepressants was compared with antidepressants alone, but the uncertainty surrounding these results makes it difficult to draw any conclusions.

8.3.5   Health economic evidence and considerations

One study was identified in the systematic literature review that evaluated the cost effectiveness of problem solving for people with common mental health problems (including depression and anxiety disorders) (Kendrick *et al.*, 2006a). Details on the methods used for the systematic search of the health economics literature are described in Chapter 3, Section 3.6.1. References to included studies and evidence tables for all health economics studies are presented in the form of evidence tables in Appendix 15.

Kendrick and colleagues (2006a) evaluated the cost effectiveness of problem solving delivered by community mental health nurses (CMHNs) compared with usual GP care and generic CMHN care. The setting was primary care and the study population included adult patients with a new episode of anxiety, depression or reaction to life difficulties (33% with a primary diagnosis of depression). The time horizon of the analysis was 26 weeks and two separate analyses were undertaken from a health service and societal perspective. Costs estimated in each treatment group included nurse training and supervision, primary care, social worker and psychiatrist, hospital care plus out-of-pocket patient costs and productivity losses due to time off work. The outcome measures used in the analysis were QALYs, estimated using utility scores derived from the EQ-5D questionnaire. Total direct health service costs and productivity losses were higher over 26 weeks in the problem solving group compared with GP or CMHN care. Overall, the mean cost difference between the problem solving and GP groups was £315 per patient (p < 0.001). No significant differences in utility scores or QALYs were detected between the three treatment groups at 26 weeks' follow-up. The results of the incremental analysis showed that both problem solving and generic CMHN care were dominated by GP care. The mixed population in this study limits its relevance to this guideline.

8.4   COUPLES THERAPY

8.4.1   Introduction

Therapists have noted that a partner's critical behaviour may trigger an episode of depression, and/or maintain or exacerbate relapse in the long term (for example, Hooley & Teasdale, 1989), although other researchers have questioned this (for example, Hayhurst *et al.*, 1997). There has also been some research looking at differences in the vulnerabilities between men and women within an intimate relationship, with physical aggression by a partner predicting depression in women. Difficulties in developing intimacy, and coping with conflict, also predict depression in both men and women (Christian *et al.*, 1994). Like other therapies, couples therapy has evolved in recent years. Systemic couples therapy aims to give the couple new perspectives on the presenting problem (for example, depressing behaviours), and explore new ways of relating (Jones & Asen, 1999). Other developments such as those by Jacobson and colleagues (1993) took a more behavioural approach. In the analysis of couples therapy in this guideline, the focus of the search was not on a specific approach but on couples therapy more generally.

Definition
Couples therapy is defined as a time-limited, psychological intervention derived from a model of the interactional processes in relationships where:
● the intervention aims to help participants understand the effects of their interactions on each other as factors in the development and/or maintenance of symptoms and problems
● the aim is to change the nature of the interactions so that the participants may develop more supportive and less conflictual relationships.

8.4.2   Studies considered[63]

Six RCTs were included in the review of couples therapy. Two studies were found in the search for the guideline update (BODENMANN2008 and JACOBSON1993) and four were also included in the previous guideline. One study (Leff *et al.*, 2000), which was included in the previous guideline, was excluded from the update because more than 50% of the participants dropped out from one arm of the study; this study used a systemic approach based on the Jones and Asen (1999) manual.

Summary study characteristics of the included studies are presented in Table 45, with full details in Appendix 17b, which also includes details of excluded studies.

---

[63]Study IDs in title case refer to studies included in the previous guideline and study IDs in capital letters refer to studies found and included in this guideline update. References for studies from the previous guideline are in Appendix 18.

Table 45: Summary study characteristics of couples therapy

	Couples therapy versus waitlist control	Couples therapy versus CBT	Couples therapy versus IPT	Couples therapy + CBT versus CBT	Couples therapy + CBT versus couples therapy
No. trials (total participants)	2 RCTs (81)	4 RCTs (130)	2 RCTs (109)	1 RCT (41)	1 RCT (40)
Study IDs	(1) Beach1992 (2) O'Leary1990	(1) BODENMANN2008 (2) Emanuels-Zuurveen 1996 (3) JACOBSON1993 (4) O'Leary1990	(1) BODENMANN2008 (2) Foley1989	(1) JACOBSON 1993	(1) JACOBSON 1993
N/% female	(1) 45/100 (2) 36/100	(1) 35/58 (2) 14/52 (3) 60/100 (4) 36/100	(1) 35/58 (2) 13/72	(1) 60/100	(1) 60/100
Mean age	(1)–(2) 39	(1) 45 (2) 38 (3)–(4) 39	(1) 45 (2) 40	(1) 39	(1) 39
Diagnosis	(1) 91% MDD, 9% dysthymia (2) 89% MDD, 11% dysthymia	(1) MDD or dysthymia (2)–(3) 100% MDD (4) 89% MDD, 11% dysthymia	(1) MDD or dysthymia (2) 100% RDC MDD	(1) 100% MDD	(1) 100% MDD
Comparator	(1)–(2) Waitlist control	(1)–(4) CBT	(1)–(2) IPT	(1) CBT	(1) CBT
Length of treatment	(1) 15 weeks (2) 16 weeks	(1) 20 weeks (2) 16 sessions (3) 20 weeks (4) 16 weeks	(1) 20 weeks (2) 16 weeks	(1) 20 sessions	(1) 20 sessions
Follow-up	(1)–(2) 12 months (2) 12 months	(1) 18 months (2) Not reported (3)–(4) 12 months	(1) 18 months (2) Not reported	(1) 12 months	(1) 12 months

8.4.3   Clinical evidence

Evidence from the important outcomes and overall quality of evidence is presented in Table 46. The full evidence profiles and associated forest plots can be found in Appendix 16b and Appendix 19b, respectively.

8.4.4   Clinical evidence summary

In five of the studies included in this review the model used was a behavioural model; two other studies used a model based on IPT. Two studies (Beach1992 and

Table 46: Summary evidence profile for couples therapy

	Couples therapy versus waitlist control	Couples therapy versus CBT	Couples therapy versus IPT
Leaving study early for any reason	Not reported	RR 1.22 (0.55 to 2.71)	RR 0.67 (0.22 to 2.04)
Quality	–	Moderate	Moderate
Number of studies; participants	–	K = 3, n = 101	K = 2, n = 58
Forest plot number	–	CT O2.02	CT 12.05
Depression self-report measures at endpoint	SMD −1.35 (−1.95 to −0.75)	SMD −0.10 (−0.58 to 0.38)	SMD −0.06 (−0.68 to 0.56)
Quality	High	Moderate	Low
Number of studies; participants	K = 2, n = 54	K = 2, n = 67	K = 1, n = 40
Forest plot number	CT O1.01	CT O3.02	CT 13.05
Depression clinician-report measures at endpoint	Not reported	SMD −0.07 (−0.69 to 0.55)	SMD 0.01 (−0.51 to 0.52)
Quality	–	Low	Moderate
Number of studies; participants	–	K = 1, n = 40	K = 2, n = 58
Forest plot number	–	CT O3.02	CT 13.05

O'Leary1990) indicated a significant large effect in reducing depression self-report scores at post-treatment (SMD -1.35; 95% CI -1.95, -0.75) when compared with waitlist control. In a larger dataset where couples therapy is compared with individual CBT, there were no significant differences in risk for discontinuation (RR 1.22; 95% CI 0.55, 2.71) or depression scores at post-treatment (BDI: SMD -0.10; 95% CI -0.58, 0.38; HRSD: -0.07, 95% CI -0.69, 0.55) or at 6 months' follow-up (BDI: SMD -0.05, 95% CI -0.67, 0.57) suggesting couples therapy has broadly similar effects to CBT. There is some indication of an effect in reducing self-reported depression scores at 1 year's follow-up (SMD -0.41; 95% CI -0.90 to 0.09) but this does not persist to 1 and a half years (SMD -0.08, 95% CI -0.70, 0.54). Two studies (BODENMANN2008 and Foley1989) compared couples therapy with IPT. The results from these two small-sized studies had wide CIs and therefore it is difficult to interpret the comparison of the two treatments with any confidence.

8.4.5 Health economic evidence and considerations

No evidence on the cost effectiveness of couples therapy for people with depression was identified by the systematic search of the economic literature. Details on the methods used for the systematic search of the economic literature are described in Chapter 3, Section 3.6.1.

8.5 INTERPERSONAL THERAPY

8.5.1 Introduction

Interpersonal therapy (IPT) was developed by Klerman and Weissman (Klerman *et al.*, 1984) initially for depression although it has now been extended to other disorders (Weissman *et al.*, 2000). IPT focuses on current relationships, not past ones, and on interpersonal processes rather than intra-psychic ones (such as negative core beliefs or automatic thoughts as in CBT, or unconscious conflicts as in psychodynamic psychotherapy). It is time limited and focused on difficulties arising in the daily experience of maintaining relationships and resolving difficulties during an episode of major depression.

The main clinical tasks are to help patients to learn to link their mood with their interpersonal contacts and to recognise that, by appropriately addressing interpersonal situations, they may simultaneously improve both their relationships and their depressive state. Early in the treatment, patient and therapist agree to work on a particular focal area that would include: interpersonal role transitions, interpersonal roles/conflicts, grief and/or interpersonal deficits. IPT is appropriate when a person has a key area of difficulty that is specified by the treatment (for example, grief or interpersonal conflicts). It can be delivered as an individually focused therapy but has also been developed as a group therapy (Wilfley *et al.*, 2000).

The character of the therapy sessions is, largely, facilitating understanding of recent events in interpersonal terms and exploring alternative ways of handling interpersonal situations. Although there is not an explicit emphasis on 'homework', there is an emphasis on effecting changes in interpersonal relationships and tasks towards this end may be undertaken between sessions.

Definition

IPT was defined as a discrete, time-limited, structured psychological intervention, derived from the interpersonal model of affective disorders that focuses on interpersonal issues and where the therapist and patient:

● work collaboratively to identify the effects of key problematic areas related to interpersonal conflicts, role transitions, grief and loss, and social skills, and their effects on current symptoms, feelings states and/or problems
● seek to reduce symptoms by learning to cope with or resolve these interpersonal problem areas.

8.5.2   Studies considered[64]

Twenty-two trials were identified; 14 were included and eight were excluded. The most common reasons for exclusion were: that the trials did not report the outcome data, that they included populations without a diagnosis of depression and that they used an unclear control intervention. Of the 14 studies that were included, six were found in the new search for the guideline update and eight were also included in the previous guideline. Three studies included a comparison of IPT with CBT, and these results are reported in Section 8.1. From the 14 included studies there were three examining IPT as a continuation treatment; two studies looked at IPT as a 3-year maintenance treatment; and four studies looked at IPT in an older population. It is important to mention that one study, Reynolds1999, is a four-arm trial of an elderly population, including IPT as an acute treatment, then as a continuation treatment, and finally, for those who recovered, they were randomised to IPT as a maintenance treatment. The terms 'continuation' and 'maintenance' have been used interchangeably in many trials. In this guideline continuation treatment is defined as a treatment that occurs after the acute symptoms have subsided, when the patient could be considered to be substantially improved and the aim is to achieve remission or significant improvements in symptoms and restore normal function. Maintenance treatment occurs when the episode is considered to have remitted or significantly improved, the patient is stable, but treatment is continued to avoid recurrence.

Summary study characteristics of the included studies are presented in Table 47, Table 48, Table 49 and Table 50 with full details in Appendix 17b, which also includes details of excluded studies.

---

[64]Study IDs in title case refer to studies included in the previous guideline and study IDs in capital letters refer to studies found and included in this guideline update. References for studies from the previous guideline are in Appendix 18.

Table 47: Summary study characteristics of IPT

	IPT versus placebo	IPT versus GP care (including antidepressants)	IPT versus IPT + antidepressants	IPT + antidepressants versus antidepressants	IPT versus antidepressants
No. trials (total participants)	1 RCT (123)	4 RCTs (391)	2 RCTs (78)	4 RCTs (299)	3 RCTs (347)
Study IDs	(1) Elkin1989	(1) Freeman2002 (2) MARSHALL2008 (3) Schulberg1996 (4) SWARTZ2008	(1) Reynolds1999 (2) Weissman1992	(1) BLOM2007 (2) de Mello2001 (3) Reynolds1999 (4) SCHRAMM2007	(1) Elkin1989 (2) Reynolds1999 (3) Schulberg1996
N/% female	(1) 168/70	(1) 96/61 (2) 70/69 (3) 229/83 (4) 47/100	(1) 80/75 (2) 25/71	(1) 96/63 (2) 28/80 (3) 80/75 (4) 81/65	(1) 168/70 (2) 80/75 (3) 229/83
Mean age	(1) 35	(1) 37 (2) Not reported (3) 38 (4) 42	(1) 68 (2) 70	(1)–(2) 35 (3) 70 (4) 41	(1) 35 (2) 70 (3) 38
Diagnosis	(1) 100% RDC MDD	(1)–(4) 100% MDD	(1) 100% MDD (2) 100% moderate/ severe MDD	(1) 100% MDD (2) 100% dysthymia (3)–(4) 100% MDD	(1) 100% RDC MDD (2)–(3) 100% MDD

Continued

Table 47: (*Continued*)

	IPT versus placebo	IPT versus GP care (including antidepressants)	IPT versus IPT + antidepressants	IPT + antidepressants versus antidepressants	IPT versus antidepressants
Comparator	(1) Placebo	(1)–(4) GP care	(1) Nortriptyline (2) Alprazolam (2.2 mg/day) or imipramine (97.5 mg/day)	(1) Nefazodone (2) Moclobemide (150–300 mg/day) (3) Nortriptyline (4) Sertraline (90 mg/day)	(1) Imipramine (150 mg/day) (2) Nortriptyline (3) Nortriptyline (190–270 mg/day)
Length of treatment	(1) 16 weeks	(1) 5 months (2) 16 weeks (3) 4 months (4) Not reported	(1) 16 weeks (2) 6 weeks	(1) 14 weeks (2) 6 months (3) 16 weeks (4) 5 weeks	(1)–(2) 16 weeks (3) 4 months
Follow-up	(1) Not reported	(1) 5 months (2) Not reported (3) 4 months (4) 9 months	(1)–(2) Not reported	(1) Not reported (2) 5 months (3) Not repoerted (4) 12 months	(1)–(2) Not reported (3) 4 months

Table 48: Summary study characteristics of IPT as continuation treatment (up to 6 months)

	IPT versus antidepressants	IPT versus TAU	IPT as continuation treatment			
			IPT + antidepressants versus antidepressants	IPT + antidepressants versus IPT + placebo	IPT + placebo versus medication clinic + placebo
No. trials (total partici-pants)	1 RCT (184)	1 RCT (185)	1 RCT (35)	1 RCT (43)	1 RCT (50)
Study IDs	(1) Schulberg1996	(1) Schulberg1996	(1) de Mello2001	(1) Reynolds1999	(1) Reynolds1999
N/% female	(1) 229/83	(1) 229/83	(1) 28/80	(1) 80/75	(1) 80/75
Mean age	(1) 38	(1) 38	(1) 35	(1) 70	(1) 70
Diagnosis	(1) 100% MDD	(1) 100% MDD	(1) 100% dysthymia	(1) 100% MDD	(1) 100% MDD
Comparator	(1) Nortriptyline (190–270 mg/day)	(1) TAU	(1) Moclobemide (150–300 mg/day)	(1) Nortriptyline	(1) Placebo
Length of treatment	(1) 4 months	(1) 4 months	(1) 6 months	(1) 16 weeks	(1) 16 weeks
Follow-up	(1) 4 months	(1) 4 months	(1) 5 months	(1) Not reported	(1) Not reported

Table 49: Summary study characteristics of IPT as maintenance treatment (3 years)

	IPT as maintenance treatment (3 years)						
	IPT versus IPT + antidepressants	IPT + antidepressants versus IPT + placebo	IPT versus antidepressants	IPT versus placebo	IPT + antidepressants versus antidepressants	IPT + antidepressants versus medication clinic + placebo	IPT versus IPT + placebo
No. trials (total participants)	1 RCT (51)	2 RCTs (94)	1 RCT (54)	1 RCT (49)	2 RCTs (99)	2 RCTs (99)	1 RCT (52)
Study IDs	(1) Frank1990	(1) Frank1990 (2) Reynolds 1999B	(1) Frank1990	(1) Frank1990	(1) Frank1990 (2) Reynolds 1999B	(1) Frank1990 (2) Reynolds 1999B	(1) Frank1990
N/% female	(1) 98/77	(1) 98/77 (2) 80/75	(1) 98/77	(1) 98/77	(1) 98/77 (2) 80/75	(1) 98/77 (2) 80/75	(1) 98/77
Mean age	(1) 40	(1) 40 (2) 68	(1) 40	(1) 40	(1) 40 (2) 68	(1) 40 (2) 68	(1) 40
Diagnosis	(1) 10 week remission from MDD (100%); 14% bipolar	(1) 10 week remission from MDD (100%); 14% bipolar (2) Recovered after continuation treatment	(1) 10 week remission from MDD (100%); 14% bipolar	(1) 10 week remission from MDD (100%); 14% bipolar	(1) 10 week remission from MDD (100%); 14% bipolar (2) Recovered after continuation treatment	(1) 10 week remission from MDD (100%); 14% bipolar (2) Recovered after continuation treatment	(1) 10 week remission from MDD (100%); 14% bipolar
Comparator	(1) Imipramine (150–300 mg/day)	(1) Imipramine (150–300 mg/day) (2) Nortriptyline	(1) Imipramine (150–300 mg/day)	(1) Placebo	(1) Imipramine (150–300 mg/day) (2) Nortriptyline	(1) Imipramine (150–300 mg/day) (2) Nortriptyline	(1) Placebo
Length of treatment	(1) 3 years	(1)–(2) 3 years	(1) 3 years	(1) 3 years	(1)–(2) 3 years	(1)–(2) 3 years	(1) 3 years
Follow-up	(1) Not reported	(1)–(2) Not reported	(1) Not reported	(1) Not reported	(1)–(2) Not reported	(1)–(2) Not reported	(1) Not reported

Table 50: Summary study characteristics of IPT for the elderly

| | IPT for the elderly | | | | |
	IPT versus IPT + antidepressants	IPT + antidepressants versus antidepressants	IPT versus antidepressants	IPT versus standard care (Netherlands)	IPT as maintenance treatment (2/3 years)
No. trials (total participants)	3 RCTs (141)	1 RCT (46)	1 RCT (45)	1 RCT (143)	2 RCTs (223)
Study IDs	(1) Reynolds1999 (2) REYNOLDS2006 (3) Weissman1992	(1) Reynolds1999	(1) Reynolds1999	(1) VAN SCHAIK2006	(1) Reynolds1999 (2) REYNOLDS2006
N/% female	(1) 80/75 (2) 129/66 (3) 25/71	(1) 80/75	(1) 80/75	(1) 99/69	(1) 80/75 (2) 129/66
Mean age	(1) 68 (2) 77 (3) 70	(1) 68	(1) 68	(1) 68	(1) 68 (2) 77
Diagnosis	(1)–(2) 100% MDD (3) 100% moderate/severe MDD	(1) 100% MDD	(1) 100% MDD	(1) 100% depressive disorder	(1)–(2) 100% MDD
Comparator	(1) Nortriptyline (2) Paroxetine (10–40 mg/day) (3) Alprazolam (2.2 mg/day), imipramine (98 mg/day)	(1) Nortriptyline	(1) Nortriptyline	(1) GP care	(1) Nortriptyline, placebo (2) Paroxetine (10–40 mg/day), placebo, clinical management
Length of treatment	(1) 16 weeks (2) 2 years (3) 6 weeks	(1) 16 weeks	(1) 16 weeks	(1) 5 months	(1) 3 years (2) 2 years
Follow-up	(1)–(3) Not reported	(1) Not reported	(1) Not reported	(1) 6 months	(1)–(2) Not reported

8.5.3 Clinical evidence

Evidence from the important outcomes and overall quality of evidence are presented in Table 51, Table 52, Table 53 and Table 54. The full evidence profiles and associated forest plots can be found in Appendix 16b and Appendix 19b, respectively.

8.5.4 Clinical evidence summary

Three studies included a comparison of IPT with CBT, and these results are reported in Section 8.1. Only one study, Elkin1989 (n = 123) looked at IPT when compared with placebo. There was a higher risk for discontinuation in the placebo group when compared with IPT (RR 0.57; 95% CI 0.33, 0.99). Furthermore, there was a significant small to medium effect (SMD –0.43; 95% CI −0.79, 0.07 and RR 0.73; 95% CI 0.56, 0.93) for IPT in reducing clinician-rated depression scores at post-treatment when compared with placebo.

Four studies looked at IPT compared with usual GP care (including medication). The data for the Freeman2002 study is unpublished data the review team for the previous guideline obtained from the authors in anticipation of it being published. However, the study had still not been published when the guideline update was being prepared, and it is important to take this into consideration when interpreting the results. The evidence indicated a significant effect in self-reported depression scores at post-treatment (SMD –0.69; 95% CI −1.22, −0.16). In addition, there was a large effect for IPT in reducing self-report depression scores at 3 months' (SMD –0.88; 95% CI −1.48, −0.28) and 9 months' (SMD –0.73; 95% CI −1.32, −0.13) follow-up. Similarly, in clinician-rated depression reports there was a large effect at 3 months' (SMD –0.81; 95% CI −1.41, −0.21) and 9 months' (SMD –0.98; 95% CI, −1.60, −0.37) follow-up.

Based on the evidence of one study (Reynolds1999) the combination treatment of IPT plus antidepressants when compared with IPT alone had a significant difference in decreasing clinician-rated depression scores (RR 2.26; 95% CI 1.03, 4.97). Furthermore, one study, SCHRAMM2007, showed that when combination treatment was compared with antidepressants alone there was a significant medium effect (SMD −0.40; 95% CI −0.75, −0.05) in the reduction of clinician-rated depression scores post-treatment.

Two studies, Elkin1989 and Schulberg1996, examined the effectiveness of IPT versus antidepressants alone. The evidence showed no significant differences among the two groups (for depression scores: BDI post-treatment SMD 0.04; 95% CI −0.32, 0.40; HRSD post-treatment SMD 0.08; 95% CI, −0.15, 0.30).

Interpersonal therapy as a continuation treatment
The evidence of one study (Schulberg1996) showed a small to medium significant effect (SMD –0.44; 95% CI −0.73, −0.15) for IPT in reducing depression scores after 4 months' continuation treatment when compared with treatment as usual.

Table 51: Summary evidence profile for IPT

	IPT versus placebo	IPT versus usual GP care (including antidepressants)	IPT (with/without placebo) versus IPT + antidepressants	IPT + antidepressants versus antidepressants	IPT versus antidepressants
Leaving study early for any reason	RR 0.57 (0.33 to 0.99)	RR 3.31 (1.94 to 5.63)	RR 1.44 (0.72 to 2.86)	RR 0.77 (0.53 to 1.14)	RR 0.94 (0.72 to 1.22)
Quality	Moderate	Moderate	Moderate	Moderate	Moderate
Number of studies; participants	K = 1, n = 123	K = 2, n = 232	K = 2, n = 58	K = 4, n = 302	K = 3, n = 344
Forest plot number	IPT 01.01	IPT 04.02	IPT 09.03	IPT 11.04	IPT 15.05
Depression self-report measures at endpoint	SMD −0.28 (−0.64 to 0.07)	SMD −0.69 (−1.22 to −0.16)	Not reported	SMD −0.06 (−0.41 to 0.28)	SMD 0.04 (−0.32 to 0.40)
Quality	Low	Moderate	–	Low	Low
Number of studies; participants	K = 1, n = 123	K = 1, n = 72	–	K = 1, n = 130	K = 1, n = 118
Forest plot number	IPT 02.01	IPT 05.02	–	IPT 14.04	IPT 16.05
Depression clinician-report measures at endpoint	SMD −0.43 (−0.79 to −0.07) HRSD >7: RR 0.73 (0.56 to 0.93)	SMD −0.07 (−0.33 to 0.18)	HRSD >7: RR 2.26 (1.03 to 4.97)	HRSD at 5/6 weeks: SMD −0.16 (−0.44 to 0.12) HRSD at 12 weeks: SMD −0.13 (−0.55 to 0.30)	SMD 0.08 (−0.15 to 0.30) HRSD >7: RR 1.12 (0.86 to 1.46)
Quality	Moderate Moderate	Low	Low	Low Moderate	Low Low
Number of studies; participants	K = 1, n = 123; K = 1, n = 123	K = 2, n = 250	K = 1, n = 33	K = 2, n = 200; K = 2, n = 87	K = 2, n = 302; K = 2, n = 160
Forest plot number	IPT 02.01 & IPT 03.01	IPT 05.02	IPT 10.01	IPT 14.04	IPT 16.05 & IPT 17.05

Table 52: Summary evidence profile for IPT as continuation treatment (up to 6 months)

	IPT versus antidepressants	IPT versus TAU	IPT + antidepressants versus antidepressants	IPT + antidepressants versus antidepressants + medication clinic	IPT + antidepressants versus IPT + placebo	IPT + placebo versus medication clinic + placebo
Depression clinician-report measures at endpoint	SMD 0.03 (−0.26 to 0.32) HRSD >7 after 4 months' treatment: RR 1.04 (0.79 to 1.37)	SMD −0.44 (−0.73 to −0.15) HRSD >7 after 4 months' treatment: RR 0.66 (0.53 to 0.82)	After 6 months maintenance: SMD −0.57 (−1.41 to 0.27)	Not reported	Not reported	Not reported
Quality	Low Low	Moderate Moderate	Low	–	–	–
Number of studies; participants	K = 1, n = 184; K = 1, n = 184	K = 1, n = 185; K = 1, n = 185	K = 1, n = 23	–	–	–
Forest plot number	IPT 19.06 & IPT 18.06	IPT 19.06 & IPT 18.06	IPT 19.06	–	–	–
Relapse	Not reported	Not reported	Not reported	RR 0.42 (0.02 to 9.34)	RR 0.17 (0.01 to 3.51)	RR 5.50 (0.26 to 115.22)
Quality	–	–	–	Low	Low	Low
Number of studies; participants	–	–	–	K = 1, n = 25	K = 1, n = 16	K = 1, n = 15
Forest plot number	–	–	–	IPT 20.06	IPT 20.06	IPT 20.06

IPT as continuation treatment (up to 6 months)

Table 53: Summary evidence profile for IPT as maintenance treatment (3 years)

	IPT as maintenance treatment (3 years)								
	IPT versus IPT+antidepressants	IPT + antidepressants versus IPT+placebo	IPT versus antidepressants	IPT versus placebo	IPT+antidepressants versus antidepressants	IPT+antidepressants versus medication clinic + placebo	IPT+placebo versus medication clinic + placebo	IPT versus IPT + placebo	IPT + antidepressants versus medication clinic + antidepressants
Leaving study early for any reason	RR 0.48 (0.10 to 2.40)	RR 0.89 (0.35 to 2.28)	RR 0.24 (0.06 to 1.01)	RR 0.59 (0.11 to 3.22)	RR 0.60 (0.26 to 1.38)	RR 2.11 (0.65 to 6.87)	RR 2.35 (0.74 to 7.44)	RR 0.50 (0.10 to 2.50)	Not reported
Quality	Low	Moderate	Low	Low	Moderate	Moderate	Moderate	Low	–
Number of studies; participants	K = 1, n = 51	K = 2, n = 101	K = 1, n = 54	K = 1, n = 49	K = 2, n = 106	K = 2, n = 102	K = 2, n = 103	K = 1, n = 52	–
Forest plot number	IPT 21.07	IPT 21.07	IPT 21.07	IPT 21.07	IPT 21.07	IPT 21.07	IPT 21.07	IPT 21.07	–
Relapse	RR 1.73 (1.00 to 2.98)	RR 0.42 (0.27 to 0.65)	RR 1.29 (0.84 to 1.99)	RR 0.76 (0.57 to 1.01)	Not reported	RR 0.22 (0.10 to 0.49)	RR 0.80 (0.66 to 0.97)	RR 0.86 (0.62 to 1.18)	RR 0.62 (0.38 to 1.02)
Quality	Moderate	High	Low	Low	–	Moderate	High	Low	Moderate
Number of studies; participants	K = 1, n = 51	K = 2, n = 101	K = 1, n = 54	K = 1, n = 49	–	K = 1, n = 54	K = 2, n = 103	K = 1, n = 52	K = 2, n = 106
Forest plot number	IPT 22.07	IPT 22.07	IPT 22.07	IPT 22.07	–	IPT 22.07	IPT 22.07	IPT 22.07	IPT 22.07

Table 54: Summary evidence profile for IPT for the elderly

	IPT for the elderly			
	IPT versus IPT + antidepressants	IPT + antidepressants versus antidepressants	IPT versus antidepressants	IPT versus standard care (Netherlands)
Leaving study early for any reason	RR 0.87 (0.52 to 1.45)	RR 0.10 (0.01 to 1.67)	RR 0.63 (0.19 to 2.10)	Not reported
Quality	Moderate	Low	Low	–
Number of studies; participants	K = 3, n = 121	K = 1, n = 41	K = 1, n = 42	–
Forest plot number	IPT 23.08	IPT 24.08	IPT 25.08	–
Depression clinician-report measures at endpoint	HRSD >7 RR 2.26 (1.03 to 4.97)	HRSD >7: RR 0.71 (0.30 to 1.66)	HRSD >7: RR 1.60 (0.94 to 2.75)	Not reported
Quality	Moderate	Low	Low	–
Number of studies; participants	K = 1, n = 33	K = 1, n = 41	K = 1, n = 42	–
Forest plot number	IPT 23.08	IPT 24.08	IPT 25.08	–
Depression clinician-report measures at follow-up	Not reported	Not reported	Not reported	MADRS at 2 months: SMD −0.28 (−0.61 to 0.05) MADRS at 6 months: SMD −0.11 (−0.44 to 0.22)
Quality	–	–	–	Low
Number of studies; participants	–	–	–	K = 1, n = 143; K = 1, n = 143
Forest plot number	–	–	–	IPT 26.08

Based on the evidence of two studies with a continuation time of 3 years (Frank1990, Reynolds1990) the evidence indicates that combining interpersonal therapy and antidepressants has a lower risk of relapse when compared with IPT plus placebo (RR 0.17; 95% CI 0.01, 3.51). This significant effect was also seen when combination treatment was compared with antidepressants (RR 0.42; 95% CI 0.02, 9.34) and also when compared with medication clinics (RR 5.50; 95% CI 0.26, 115.22).

Interpersonal therapy as maintenance treatment
Only two studies included a comparison of IPT as a maintenance treatment (Frank1990 and Reynolds1999B). When IPT was studied as a maintenance treatment, combination treatment had a significant effect in lowering the risk of relapse (RR 0.42; 95% CI 0.27, 0.65) when compared with IPT plus placebo and (RR 0.22; 95% CI 0.10, 0.49) when compared with medication clinics.

Interpersonal therapy for the elderly
The evidence for IPT in an elderly population is based on four studies (n = 284). One study (Reynolds1999; n = 33) indicated a significant effect (RR 2.26; 95% CI 1.03, 4.97) for reducing clinician-rated depression scores in an elderly population, favouring combination treatment of IPT plus antidepressants when compared with IPT alone.

Based on the same study (Reynolds1999; n = 42), antidepressants had a significant effect in reducing clinician-rated depression measures (RR 1.60; 95% CI 0.94, 2.75) when compared with IPT.

8.5.5   Health economic evidence and considerations

No evidence on the cost effectiveness of IPT for people with depression was identified by the systematic search of the economic literature. Details on the methods used for the systematic search of the economic literature are described in Chapter 3, Section 3.6.1.

8.6   COUNSELLING

8.6.1   Introduction

Counselling was developed by Carl Rogers (1957) who believed that people had the means for self-healing, problem resolution and growth if the right conditions could be created. These conditions include the provision of positive regard, genuineness and empathy. Rogers's original model was developed into structured counselling approaches by Truax and Carkhuff (1967) and, independently, by Egan (1990) who developed the three stage model: exploration, personalising and action. Voluntary sector counselling training (for example, Relate) tends to draw on these models. However, although many other therapies now use the basic ingredients of client-centred counselling (Roth & Fonagy, 1996), there are differences in how they are used

(Kahn, 1985; Rogers, 1986) and counselling has become a generic term used to describe a broad range of interventions delivered by counsellors usually working in primary care. The content of these various approaches may include psychodynamic, systemic or cognitive behavioural elements (Bower *et al.*, 2003).

Definition
The British Association for Counselling and Psychotherapy (BACP) defines counselling as 'a systematic process which gives individuals an opportunity to explore, discover and clarify ways of living more resourcefully, with a greater sense of well-being'.

8.6.2   Studies considered[65]

Three new studies (GOLDMAN2006, GREENBERG1998, WATSON2003) meeting the inclusion criteria were found in the update search. Three studies (Bedi2000, Simpson2003, Ward2000) were reported in the previous guideline, two of which are included in the guideline update. Ward2000 was excluded because it did not meet inclusion criteria: only 62% met diagnosis for depression and this study was not completely randomised. However, as this study was included in the previous guideline a separate sub-analysis has been conducted to determine whether this would have affected the GDG's conclusions. The results of this sub-analysis do not appear in the tables, but are described in the text below. A further trial (Stiles *et al.*, 2006, a non-RCT) was examined, but it was ultimately excluded because not all patients met criteria for depression and there were concerns about the selection of the study population.

Summary study characteristics of the included studies are in Table 55, with full details in Appendix 17b, which also includes details of excluded studies. Two studies, GOLDMAN2006 and GREENBERG1998, are not listed in Table 55 because these compare two different types of counselling.

8.6.3   Clinical evidence

Evidence from the important outcomes and overall quality of evidence are presented in Table 56. The full evidence profiles and associated forest plots can be found in Appendix 16b and Appendix 19b, respectively.

8.6.4   Clinical evidence summary

One study (Bedi2000) compared the effectiveness of counselling versus antidepressants, although some differences in the baseline scores of the patient preference group

---

[65]Study IDs in title case refer to studies included in the previous guideline and study IDs in capital letters refer to studies found and included in this guideline update. References for studies from the previous guideline are in Appendix 18.

Table 55: Summary study characteristics of counselling

	Counselling versus antidepressants	**Counselling + GP care versus GP care**	**Counselling versus CBT**
No. trials (total participants)	1 RCT (103)	1 RCT (145)	1 RCT (62)
Study IDs	(1) Bedi2000	(1) Simpson2003	(1) WATSON2003
N/% female	(1) 79/77	(1) 116/82	(1) 66/67
Mean age	(1) 39	(1) 43	(1) 41
Diagnosis	(1) 100% MDD	(1) Depressed criteria (14–40 on BDI)	(1) 100% MDD
Comparator	(1) Antidepressants (choice of three antidepressants and continued for 4–6 months)	(1) GP care	(1) CBT
Length of treatment	(1) 8 weeks	(1) 6–12 sessions	(1) 16 weeks
Follow-up	(1) Not reported	(1) 12 months	(1) None

suggest caution in interpreting the data. There were no significant differences and the evidence remains inconclusive (self-reported depression scores at endpoint: SMD 0.04; 95% CI −0.38, 0.47 and at 12-month follow-up: SMD: 0.17; 95% CI −0.32, 0.66; clinician-rated depression scores at endpoint: RR 1.20; 95% CI 0.80, 1.81) and does not support a conclusion that counselling and antidepressants are equivalent. This caution is support by the 12-month follow-up data; clinician-reported depression scores were significantly reduced in the antidepressant group when compared with counselling (RR 1.41; 95% CI 1.08, 1.83). The results of this study should be treated with some caution as the introduction of a patient preference element to the trial led to considerable differences in baseline severity measures between the two arms.

One study (Simpson2003) compared the combination of counselling plus GP care with usual GP care. There was no evidence of any important clinical benefit of counselling plus GP care (BDI at 6 months: SMD 0.06; 95% CI −0.29, 0.40 and at 12 months: SMD 0.03; 95% CI −0.33, 0.40). A sub-analysis was conducted on Ward2000, which did not meet the inclusion criteria but was raised during the consultation process. This study included a comparison of counselling versus GP care. The results indicated a significant medium effect in self-report depression scores at post-treatment (SMD −0.49; 95% CI −0.83, −0.15) but no significant differences between the two treatment groups on discontinuation and self-report depression scores at follow-up.

The comparison of counselling versus CBT was included in one study (WATSON2003). There is insufficient evidence (only one small-sized study with

Table 56: Summary evidence profile for counselling

	Counselling versus antidepressants	Counselling + GP care versus GP care	Counselling versus CBT
Leaving study early for any reason	Not reported	RR 1.13 (0.43 to 2.95)	Not reported
Quality	–	Low	–
Number of studies; participants	–	K = 1, n = 145	–
Forest plot number	–	C 08.05	–
Depression self-report measures at endpoint	SMD 0.04 (−0.39 to 0.47)	Not reported	SMD −0.07 (−0.33 to 0.20)
Quality	Low	–	Low
Number of studies; participants	K = 1, n = 83	–	K = 2, n = 215
Forest plot number	C 02.02	–	C 17.08
Depression clinician-report measures at endpoint	Not reported	Not reported	Not reported
Quality	–	–	–
Number of studies; participants	–	–	–
Forest plot number	–	–	–
Depression self-report measures at follow-up	At 12 months: SMD 0.17 (−0.32 to 0.66)	At 6 months: SMD 0.06 (−0.29 to 0.40) BDI >=14: RR 0.94 (0.73 to 1.22) At 12 months: SMD 0.03 (−0.33 to 0.40) BDI >=14: RR 0.80 (0.62 to 1.02)	Not reported
Quality	Low	Low Low Low Low	–

Table 56: (*Continued*)

	Counselling versus antidepressants	Counselling + GP care versus GP care	Counselling versus CBT
Number of studies; participants	K = 1, n = 65	K = 1, n = 130; K = 1, n = 145; K = 1, n = 115; K = 1, n = 145	–
Forest plot number	C 04.02	C 10.05, C 09.05, C 10.05, C 09.05	–
Depression clinician-report measures at follow-up	RDC >3 at 12 months: RR 1.41 (1.08 to 1.83)	Not reported	Not reported
Quality	Low	–	–
Number of studies; participants	K = 1, n = 103	–	–
Forest plot number	C 05.02	–	–

wide CIs) to reach any definite conclusion about the relative effectiveness of these two treatments (for BDI scores post-treatment: SMD 0.04; 95% CI −0.38, 0.47). This was still the case when a sub-analysis including the Ward2000 study was conducted (SMD −0.07; 95% CI −0.33, 0.20). (Individual outcomes for Ward2000 are: at endpoint BDI: SMD −0.14; 95% CI −0.48, 0.21 and at 12-month follow-up BDI: SMD 0.04; 95% CI −0.31, 0.38.)

Two studies (GOLDMAN2006 and GREENBERG1998), compared two different types of counselling (and therefore are not included in the tables above). GOLD-MAN2006 compared client-centered counselling with emotion-focused counselling. The results favoured emotioned-focused therapy (BDI scores: SMD 0.64; 95% CI −0.02, 1.29). GREENBERG1998 examined the effectiveness of client-centered counselling versus process-experiential counselling. The evidence indicates that there was no significant difference between treatments in reduction of self-reported depression scores (SMD 0.13; 95% CI, −0.57, 0.82). These two studies are small in size and therefore results should be interpreted with caution.

The participants in the trials included in this review were predominantly drawn from groups in the mild-to-moderate range of depression (mean baseline BDI scores between 18 and 26) and two trials included people with minor depression (BDI scores starting from 14) (Bedi2000 and Ward2000).

Overall the evidence for counselling is very limited. Some practice-based evidence was also reviewed (Stiles *et al.*, 2006) but the number of patients with depression in the study fell below the cut-off for inclusion. Furthermore, other diagnoses were included in this study. A smaller practice-based study (Marriott & Kellett, 2009), which included only 34% with a diagnosis of depression, compared counselling, cognitive analytic therapy and CBT but it was small and underpowered and it was not possible to reach any conclusion on the differential effectiveness of the treatments. In addition to the limited data available for counselling, interpretation of the results is complicated by the different therapeutic models adopted in the studies. For example, Bedi2000 and Ward2000 follow a Rogerian client-centred model of counselling, Simpson2003 a psychodynamic model, whereas the studies by WATSON2003, GREENBERG1998 and GOLDMAN2006 adopt a process-experiential/emotion-focused model, which is compared in the latter two trials with the Rogerian client-centred model.

8.6.5 Health economic evidence and considerations

Three studies were identified in the systematic literature review that evaluated the cost effectiveness of counselling for people with depression and other common mental health problems (Friedli *et al.*, 2000; Miller *et al.*, 2003; Simpson *et al.*, 2003). Details on the methods used for the systematic search of the health economics literature are described in Chapter 3, Section 3.6.1. Evidence tables for all health economics studies are presented in Appendix 15.

Friedli and colleagues (2000)[66] compared non-directive counselling with usual GP care in a UK RCT of 136 people with referral symptoms being caused by depression and anxiety disorders (50% were given a GP diagnosis of depression). The time horizon of the analysis was 9 months and direct NHS costs (hospital inpatient stay, outpatient consultations and medications) and non-health service costs (lost productivity, travel and childcare) were estimated over this period. The primary outcome of the clinical analysis was change in BDI scores. However, as no differences in clinical outcomes were detected between the two groups, the study was effectively a cost-minimisation analysis. Over 9 months, total direct NHS costs were £309 and £474 per person while total non-health service costs were £809 and £469 per person, for counselling and GP care, respectively. The authors concluded that counselling in primary care was not cost effective in the short-term if indirect costs were taken into account but that, overall, referral to counselling was no more clinically effective or costly than GP care.

Miller and colleagues (2003)[67] compared counselling with antidepressants in patients with major depression who were recruited from general practice. Sixty five patients were randomised to either treatment modality while a further 183 patients who chose their treatment modality were also analysed. The time horizon of the analysis was 12 months and direct NHS costs (inpatient, outpatient, counselling, GP consultations and medications) were estimated. The primary outcome measure used in the analysis was change in BDI scores. However, no significant differences were

---

[66]Note that this study was excluded from the analysis of clinical effectiveness as only 50% might have met diagnostic criteria for depression.

[67]This is the economic analysis of Bedi2000.

detected between the two treatment groups at 12 months. Overall, no significant differences in total mean costs per person were detected between the two randomised groups while the non-randomised counselling group was significantly more costly than the non-randomised antidepressant treatment group over 12 months. The authors suggested that counselling might be a more cost-effective intervention in patients with mild to moderate depression but, for the larger patient group, antidepressant treatment was likely to be the more cost-effective intervention.

Simpson and colleagues (2003) evaluated the cost effectiveness of short-term psychodynamic counselling compared with routine GP care in a UK RCT of 181 patients with a history of depression. The time horizon of the analysis was 12 months and direct healthcare costs (specialist mental health, hospital, primary care and community health and social care services) were estimated for this period. The primary outcome measure used in the clinical analysis was change in BDI scores. However, since there were no significant clinical differences detected between the two treatment groups, the study was effectively a cost-minimisation analysis. Overall, there was no statistically significant difference between the two treatment groups in total costs per person over 12 months (£1046 versus £1074). The authors suggested that there was no cost-effectiveness advantage of counselling over routine care for general practice attendees with chronic depression.

8.7 SHORT-TERM PSYCHODYNAMIC PSYCHOTHERAPY

8.7.1 Introduction

As with other schools of psychological therapy there are a number of variations on the original model of psychodynamic psychotherapy with some approaches focusing on the dynamic of drives (for example, aggression) while others focus on relationships (Greenberg & Mitchell, 1983). Other forms of this therapy have been influenced by attachment theory (Holmes, 2001). Clinical trials of psychodynamic psychotherapy have focused on short-term psychological therapy (typically 10 to 30 weeks) usually in comparison with antidepressants or CBT. It is this brief version of psychodynamic psychotherapy, often referred to as short-term psychodynamic psychotherapy, which is the focus of this review.

Definition
Psychodynamic psychotherapy is defined as a psychological intervention derived from a psychodynamic/psychoanalytic model, and where:
● Therapist and patient explore and gain insight into conflicts and how these are represented in current situations and relationships including the therapeutic relationship (for example, transference and counter-transference). This leads to patients being given an opportunity to explore feelings and conscious and unconscious conflicts, originating in the past, with a technical focus on interpreting and working through conflicts.

● Therapy is non-directive and recipients are not taught specific skills (for example, thought monitoring, re-evaluating, or problem-solving).

8.7.2   Studies considered[68]

In total, 17 studies were found in the search for trials of short-term psychodynamic psychotherapy. Ten studies were included (six were found in the update search and four were also reported in the previous guideline) and seven were excluded. Reasons for exclusion included: trials not being RCTs, papers not reporting outcome data, trials including participants without a diagnosis of depression and authors replacing dropouts. Two studies (Gallagher-Th1994 and Shapiro1994) included a comparison of short-term psychodynamic psychotherapy with CBT, the results of which are reported in Section 8.1. One study (McLean1979), compared short-term psychodynamic psychotherapy with behavioural activation and this is reported in Section 8.2. One study (Guthrie1999) was not included because in the sample population (which was selected on the basis of high attendance at outpatient clinics) only 73.6% met diagnosis for depression and, therefore, did not meet the inclusion criteria (which is >80% of the total population). However, while it is not included in the main analyses and tables, a sub-analysis including this paper was conducted and is reported below.

It should be noted that all the included studies were of short-term psychodynamic psychotherapy and therefore the analysis and subsequent recommendations are limited to short-term psychodynamic psychotherapy, typically 16 to 20 sessions but with a range of 10 to 30 sessions across the included studies.

Summary study characteristics of the included studies are in Table 57, with full details in Appendix 17b, which also includes details of excluded studies.

8.7.3   Clinical evidence

Evidence from the important outcomes and overall quality of evidence are presented in Table 58. The full evidence profiles and associated forest plots can be found in Appendix 16b and Appendix 19b, respectively.

8.7.4   Clinical evidence summary

Problems with unextractable data and multiple different comparators limited the analyses it was possible to undertake for this review. The evidence from one study (DEKKER2008) showed a significant medium effect (SMD 0.43; 95% CI 0.03, 0.82) favouring antidepressants when compared with short-term psychodynamic

---

[68]Study IDs in title case refer to studies included in the previous guideline and study IDs in capital letters refer to studies found and included in this guideline update. References for studies from the previous guideline are in Appendix 18.

Table 57: Summary study characteristics of short-term psychodynamic psychotherapy

	Short-term psychodynamic psychotherapy (STPP) versus antidepressants	STPP + antidepressants versus supportive therapy + antidepressants	STPP versus STPP + antidepressants	STPP versus waitlist control	STPP versus supportive therapy	Antidepressants versus STPP + antidepressants
No. trials (total participants)	3 RCTs (230)	1 RCT (74)	1 RCT (191)	1 RCT (20)	1 RCT (20)	2 RCTs (220)
Study IDs	(1) DEKKER2008 (2) McLean1979 (3) SALMINEN 2008	(1) Burnand2002	(1) DEJONGHE 2004	(1) MAINA 2005	(1) MAINA 2005	(1) KOOL2003 (2) MAINA2008
N/% female	(1) 76/74 (2) 111/72 (3) 35/68	(1) 45/61	(1) 128/67	(1) 19/63	(1) 19/63	(1) 79/62 (2) 56/61
Mean age	(1) Unextractable (2) 39 (3) 42	(1) 36	(1) Unextractable	(1) 37	(1) 37	(1) 34 (2) 36
Diagnosis	(1) 100% depressive episode (2) 100% MDD (3) Mild/ moderate episode of MDD	(1) 100% MDD	(1) 100% MDD	(1) 100% dysthymia or subthreshold depressive symptoms	(1) 100% dysthymia or subthreshold depressive symptoms	(1) 100% depressive episode (2) Remission from MDD (follow-up of MAINA2005)
Comparator	(1) Venlafaxine (225 mg/day) (2) Amitriptyline (150mg/day) (3) Fluoxetine	(1) Clomipramine (125 mg/day)	(1) GP's choice of antidepressant	(1) Waitlist control	(1) Supportive psychotherapy	(1) Range of antidepressants (2) Citalopram/ paroxetine (20–60 mg/day)
Length of treatment	(1) 24 weeks (2) 10 weeks (3) 16 weeks	(1) 10 weeks	(1) Up to 6 months	(1) 15–30 weeks	(1) 15–30 weeks	(1) 24 weeks (2) 6 months
Follow- up	(1) Not reported (2) 3 months (3) 4 months	(1) Not reported	(1) Not reported	(1) 6 months	(1) 6 months	(1) Not reported (2) 48 months

Table 58: Summary evidence profile for short-term psychodynamic psychotherapy

	STPP versus antidepressants	STPP versus CBT	STPP + antidepressants versus supportive therapy + antidepressants	STPP versus STPP + antidepressants	STPP versus waitlist	STPP versus supportive therapy	STPP + antidepressants versus antidepressants
Leaving study early for any reason	RR 0.90 (0.51 to 1.60)	RR 2.16 (0.81 to 5.76)	RR 1.43 (0.71 to 2.89)	RR 0.06 (0.01 to 0.44)	Not reported	Not reported	Not reported
Quality	Moderate	Low	Low	Moderate	–	–	–
Number of studies; participants	K = 2, n = 193	K = 1, n = 66	K = 1, n = 95	K = 1, n = 208	–	–	–
Forest plot number	PP 01.01	PP 05.03	PP 11.04	PP 15.05	–	–	–
Depression self-report measures at endpoint	Not reported	SMD 0.35 (−0.61 to 1.30)	Not reported	Not reported	Not reported	Not reported	Not reported
Quality	–	Low	–	–	–	–	–
Number of studies; participants	–	K = 1, n = 57	–	–	–	–	–
Forest plot number	–	PP 06.03	–	–	–	–	–
Depression clinician-report measures at endpoint	SMD 0.43 (0.03 to 0.82)	Still meeting RDC criteria post-treatment: RR 1.70 (0.97 to 2.97)	WMD −0.80 (−4.06 to 2.46)	SMD 0.04 (−0.23 to 0.32)	SMD −1.09 (−2.04 to −0.13)	SMD −0.97 (−1.91 to −0.03)	SMD 0.16 (−2.44 to 2.76)
Quality	Moderate	Low	Low	Low	Moderate	Moderate	Very low
Number of studies; participants	K = 1, n = 103	K = 1, 66	K = 1, n = 74	K = 1, n = 208	K = 1, n = 20	K = 1, n = 20	K = 1, n = 128
Forest plot number	PP 02.01	PP 09.03	PP 13.04	PP 14.05	PP 16.06	PP 17.07	PP 18.08

psychotherapy in the reduction of clinician-rated scores at endpoint. However, the results of a further small-sized study (SALMINEN2008) showed no significant differences between short-term psychodynamic psychotherapy and antidepressants when looking at the mean change from baseline to endpoint (SMD 0.03; 95% CI −0.52, 0.58), but given the wide CIs and size of the study it is difficult to establish a clear picture of this comparison. One study (McLean1979) indicated a significantly higher risk of discontinuation in those treated with short-term psychodynamic psychotherapy when compared with behaviour therapy (RR 3.02; 95% CI 1.07, 8.50).

When compared with a waitlist control, one study (MAINA2005) showed a significant and large effect (SMD −1.09; 95% CI −2.04, −0.13) in clinician-rated depression scores at post-treatment, favouring short-term psychodynamic psychotherapy. This study also indicated a large effect (SMD −0.97; 95% CI −1.91, −0.03) for short-term psychodynamic psychotherapy in clinician-rated depression scores at post-treatment when compared with supportive therapy. A follow-up study (MAINA2008) showed that adding short-term psychodynamic psychotherapy to antidepressant treatment had a significant medium to large effect at 24 months (SMD 0.52; 95% CI 0.10, 0.95) and at 48 months (SMD 0.59; 95% CI 0.16, 1.01) in reducing clinician-rated depression scores when compared with antidepressants alone. MAINA2005 and MAINA2008 were conducted in a population diagnosed with minor depression or dysthymia. KOOL2003 compared short-term psychodynamic psychotherapy in two different populations with depression: one with comorbid personality disorder and the second without. The results suggest that short-term psychodynamic psychotherapy is more effective in people diagnosed with depression and personality disorder than those without (SMD −1.15; 95% CI −1.62, −0.69 and SMD 1.50; 95% CI 0.81, 2.18 respectively) but the small sample size in the population without personality disorder suggests caution when interpreting this result.

When a separate analysis was conducted with the Guthrie1999 study, the evidence was inconclusive given the small size of the study and the wide CIs (for SCL-90-R at endpoint: SMD −0.16; 95% CI −0.53, 0.22 and at 6-month follow-up SMD −0.24; 95% CI −0.62, 0.13).

In summary, this is a weak dataset characterised by a number of the findings being contradictory and/or difficult to interpret. Some of the difficulty derives from there being a number of different comparators in a small dataset. There is limited evidence for a benefit of short-term psychodynamic psychotherapy (typically 16 to 20 sessions over 4 to 6 months) in a population with dysthymia and subthreshold depressive symptoms over waitlist or usual care and inconsistent findings when compared with antidepressants. Comparisons against other active psychological interventions are also very limited.

8.7.5 Health economic evidence and considerations

One study (Guthrie *et al.* 1999) was identified in the systematic literature review that evaluated the cost effectiveness of short-term psychodynamic psychotherapy for people who are high utilisers of psychiatric services (with 73.6% having a diagnosis of depression). Details on the methods used for the systematic search of the health economics literature are described in Chapter 3, Section 3.6.1. Evidence tables for all health economics studies are presented in Appendix 15.

The study by Guthrie and colleagues (1999) compared brief psychodynamic interpersonal therapy (equivalent to short-term psychodynamic psychotherapy) with treatment as usual in a UK RCT of 144 patients with non-psychotic disorders (75.5% diagnosed with depression). The time horizon of the analysis was 6 months post-treatment and direct NHS costs (inpatient, outpatient, day cases, A&E visits and medications) and non-health service costs (travel and lost productivity) were estimated during this period. The primary outcome measures used in the economic analysis were quality-adjusted life months (QALMs), which were estimated from utility weights derived from the EQ-5D questionnaire. Overall, total societal costs per person were lower in the brief psychodynamic interpersonal therapy group at 6 months (US $1959 versus $2,465; p = 0.21). The brief psychodynamic interpersonal therapy group also gained more QALMs during this period (4.87 versus 3.48; p = 0.13). While brief psychodynamic interpersonal therapy appeared to dominate treatment as usual, resulting in lower costs but better outcomes, neither the cost nor QALM differences between the two treatment groups were statistically significant.

8.8 RATIONAL EMOTIVE BEHAVIOURAL THERAPY

8.8.1 Introduction

Rational emotive behavioural therapy is a form of CBT developed by Albert Ellis in the 1950s and 1960s (Ellis, 1962). Compared with CBT it has been subject to fewer research trials, and only one study met the criteria of the GDG (DAVID2008). This study compared rational emotive behavioural therapy with antidepressant medication.

Definition
Rational emotive behavioural therapy is a present-focused, relatively short-term therapy usually delivered one-to-one that uncovers and addresses the relationships between thoughts, feelings and behaviours. There is an emphasis on addressing thinking that underpins emotional and behavioural problems. Patients learn how to examine and challenge their unhelpful thinking.

8.8.2 Studies considered[69]

Only one RCT (DAVID2008) was found and was included in the review. This section reports on the comparison of rational emotive behavioural therapy with antidepressants; comparison with CBT can be found in Section 8.1.

---

[69]Each study considered for review is referred to by a study ID in capital letters (primary author and date of study publication, except where a study is in press or only submitted for publication, then a date is not used).

Table 59: Summary study characteristics of rational emotive behaviour therapy

	Rational emotive behavioural therapy versus antidepressants
No. trials (total participants)	1 RCT (180)
Study ID	DAVID2008
N/% female	113/66
Mean age	37
Diagnosis	100% MDD
Comparator	Antidepressants
Length of treatment	14 weeks
Follow-up	6 months

Summary study characteristics of the included studies are in Table 59, with full details in Appendix 17b, which also includes details of excluded studies.

8.8.3   Clinical evidence

Because of the small dataset, a summary of the evidence profile is not included here. The full evidence profiles and associated forest plots can be found in Appendix 16b and Appendix 19b, respectively.

8.8.4   Clinical evidence summary

The evidence of one study (DAVID2008) showed no clinically important different effects of rational emotive behaviour therapy in depressed patients when compared with antidepressants (BDI: SMD −0.07; CI −0.44 to 0.29; HRSD: SMD 0.00; CI −0.37 to 0.37). However, the findings were promising in terms of end-of-treatment depressive symptoms and in terms of acceptability (RR 0.63; 95% CI 0.22 to 1.80) and preventing relapse at 6 months' follow-up (RR 0.20; 95% CI 0.02 to 1.61).

8.8.5   Health economic evidence and considerations

No evidence on the cost effectiveness of rational emotive behavioural therapy for people with depression was identified by the systematic search of the economic literature. Details on the methods used for the systematic search of the economic literature are described in Chapter 3, Section 3.6.1.

8.9 ECONOMIC MODELLING

8.9.1 Background

The aim of this economic analysis is to update the model constructed in the previous guideline (NICE, 2004a), which evaluated the cost effectiveness of antidepressant treatment versus a combination of antidepressant treatment and CBT for the routine treatment of moderate/severe depression. It was anticipated that other high-intensity psychological interventions such as IPT or behavioural activation would be evaluated in an economic model. However, evidence of the clinical effectiveness of IPT or behavioural activation compared with antidepressant treatment for moderate or severe depression was limited. Based on GDG expert opinion, CBT was again chosen as the form of psychological therapy for this analysis as the clinical evidence was superior and CBT remains more widely available in the UK compared with other high-intensity interventions.

Clinical outcome data within the model including rates of discontinuation, remission and relapse remained the same as reported in the previous guideline model. It should be noted that these data were taken from meta-analyses that were undertaken in the previous guideline. Therefore, in this economic analysis, levels of depression severity in relation to the HRSD and BDI were based on those proposed by the APA (2000a) rather than those proposed in this guideline. However, it was necessary to update the economic model in order to better reflect current medical practice within the UK. This included the additional costs of maintenance therapy in both treatment groups while other input parameters, including patient utility scores and unit costs, were also updated.

8.9.2 Methods

A pragmatic decision analytic model was constructed using Microsoft Excel XP. Within the model patients either continue or discontinue their initial treatment, after which they enter remission or no remission health states. Patients in remission can then either relapse or remain in remission health states. A detailed structure of the decision tree is presented in Figure 6. A time horizon of 15 months was chosen to reflect the available comparative clinical evidence. This included 3 months of the initial therapy, followed by 6 months' maintenance therapy and 6 months' follow-up. The following strategies were considered:

Strategy A: Antidepressant treatment given for 12 weeks with 6 months' maintenance therapy and 6 months' follow-up (AD).

Strategy B: Combination of 12 weeks' antidepressant treatment and 16 sessions of CBT with 6 months' maintenance therapy and 6 months' follow-up (COMB).

Figure 6: Structure of the model

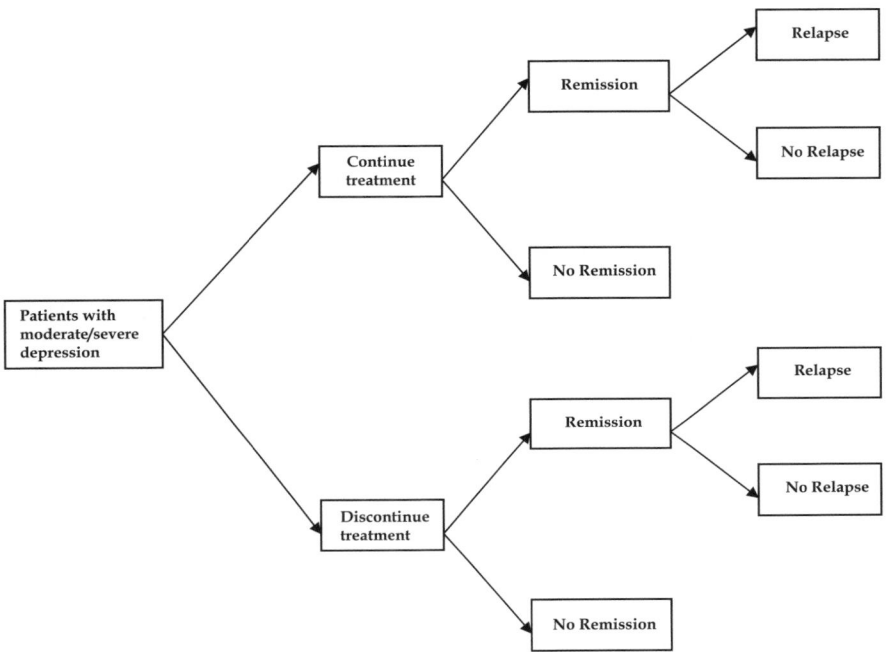

Originally, three specific strategies for the first-line management of depression were considered. However, similar to the previous guideline, the updated clinical evidence review showed no overall superiority for CBT alone on treatment outcomes over antidepressant treatment. The efficacy evidence combined with the significantly higher treatment cost of CBT compared with the cost of antidepressant treatment resulted in the exclusion of CBT alone from the final analysis.

8.9.3 Model assumptions

Population
Two separate models were constructed for a hypothetical cohort of 100 patients in each treatment group with either moderate or severe depression.

Resource use and unit costs
An NHS and PSS perspective was taken for the analysis based on current NICE guidance (NICE, 2008b). Therefore, only direct health and social care costs were considered in the analysis. In order to cost the two therapy pathways, resource utilisation data were collected as part of the literature review or from GDG expert opinion. Unit costs were obtained from a variety of sources including the British National Formulary (BNF 56, 2008) and the Personal Social Services Research Unit (PSSRU)

(Curtis, 2009). Resource utilisation data were then combined with the relevant cost associated with each therapy. All costs were based on 2007/08 prices and were inflated where necessary using Hospital and Community Health Service indices (Curtis, 2009). As in the case of outcomes, no discounting was applied because the time horizon was 15 months.

Antidepressant treatment

The antidepressant treatment protocol consisted of 12 weeks plus 6 months' maintenance period of 40 mg of generic citalopram per day for both moderate and severely depressed patients (GDG expert opinion). Citalopram was used to represent standard pharmacotherapy for patients with moderate or severe depression because it was the most commonly prescribed antidepressant in 2007 in England (Department of Health, 2008a). As part of patient monitoring, it was assumed that all patients with moderate depression and 50% of patients with severe depression would receive standard GP care while the remaining 50% of patients with severe depression would receive specialist mental health outpatient care (GDG expert opinion). It was also assumed that patient monitoring in both primary and secondary care consisted of two fortnightly visits in the first month followed by one visit per month, while the maintenance therapy period consisted of one GP/specialist visit every 2 months (GDG expert opinion).

Combination therapy

For both moderate and severely depressed patients, it was assumed that combination therapy would consist of 16 sessions of CBT over 12 weeks, in addition to the antidepressant treatment protocols described above (GDG expert opinion). One CBT session lasts for 55 minutes and is provided by a specialty doctor, clinical psychologist or mental health nurse (Curtis, 2009). During the 6-month maintenance therapy period, it was assumed that both moderate and severely depressed patients would receive an additional two CBT sessions, in addition to the antidepressant (AD) maintenance therapy protocols described above (GDG expert opinion).

Subsequent healthcare

Patients who discontinued initial treatment did not incur the full costs of treatment. To revise costs downwards, it was assumed that patients who discontinued initial treatment would drop out after 4 weeks of treatment, irrespective of treatment group (Rush *et al.*, 2006; GDG expert opinion). For patients in remission who did not relapse during follow-up, it was assumed that no further additional treatment or mental healthcare resources beyond the 6-month maintenance period were required. However, for patients with unsuccessful treatment outcomes, it was assumed that they would continue to consume additional mental healthcare resources over the 15-month time horizon. Cost data for subsequent mental healthcare were taken from a study published by the King's Fund which estimated annual mental healthcare costs for respondents with mild, moderate and severe depressive disorder based on the UK psychiatric morbidity survey (McCrone *et al.*, 2008). As such, these annual mental healthcare costs may be an under estimate of the actual costs incurred by patients with moderate and severe depression, as one would expect respondents with mild depression to use less mental healthcare on average. These mental healthcare costs included hospital and outpatient care, social services, residential care, GP visits and medication costs. These annual costs were divided into monthly cost estimates and then projected for the periods during which unsuccessfully treated patients would consume subsequent mental healthcare estimated in the model. According to the survey, only 65% of people with depression were in contact or receipt of mental health services. Therefore, these subsequent mental healthcare costs were weighted downwards based on the assumption that 35% of patients would not incur any further healthcare costs. Patients who did not achieve remission following therapy incurred full 3-month treatment costs followed by subsequent mental healthcare thereafter. For patients who relapsed while in remission, it was assumed that the average time to relapse was based on the midpoint of the clinical relapse data elicited in the guideline meta-analysis, which was estimated over a 12-month period (GDG expert opinion). Full details of all resource use and unit cost parameters are presented in Table 60.

Clinical outcomes and event probabilities
The outcome measure used for the economic evaluation was the quality-adjusted life years (QALYs) gained from either treatment. No discounting of outcomes was necessary since the time horizon of the model was 15 months. The key clinical parameter estimates – discontinuation rates, remission rates and relapse rates – were collected as part of the updated clinical systematic review undertaken for the guideline. The dichotomous outcome measure of no remission was defined by scores greater than six on the 17-item HRSD or more than eight on the 24-item HRSD.

For the base case analysis, the baseline absolute rates of remission, discontinuation and relapse for antidepressant treatment as well as the respective relative risks of combination therapy versus antidepressant treatment were taken from the relevant guideline meta-analyses. The guideline meta-analysis of non-remission rates was based on intention-to-treat analysis, with non-completers being considered as an 'unfavourable' outcome (that is, as non-remitters). This means that non-remission rates included people who completed treatment but did not remit plus people who did not complete treatment. For the economic analysis, the proportion of non-remitters in the completer group was estimated from the available data, and was subsequently incorporated in the respective branch of the decision tree.

For patients who did not complete their initial therapy, it was assumed that rather than remaining moderately or severely depressed, a small proportion (20%: 95% CI 10, 30) would spontaneously enter remission (GDG expert opinion). For patients in remission, the rate of relapse was estimated as 67% based on a study of patients who were not receiving maintenance antidepressant treatment (Murphy *et al.*, 1984). Therefore, this is likely to be an over estimate of the relapse rate for patients in this analysis who are receiving maintenance therapy. These two probabilities were applied to patients in both treatment arms. For the sensitivity analyses, 95% CIs around the relevant relative risks of combination (COMB) therapy versus antidepressant (AD) treatment were used. Full details of event probabilities are presented in Table 62.

Table 60: Resource use and cost estimates applied in the economic model

Resource use estimate	Cost	Source of unit costs

Antidepressant treatment (AD)
 - Citalopram (40 mg/day):
   3 months plus 6 months'
   maintenance
	£18	Non-proprietary: £1.87 per
		 28-tab pack (BNF, 2008)

- Patient monitoring (moderate):
   7 GP consultations over
   9 months
	£252	GP consultation: £36 (Curtis,
		 2009)

- Patient monitoring (severe):
   50% mental health outpatient
   consultations (×7) + 50% GP
   consultations (×7) over
   9 months
	£581	Mental health outpatient
		 consultation: £130 (Curtis,
		 2009)

Total cost (moderate) **Total cost (severe)**	**£270** **£599**	

Combination therapy (COMB)
 - 16 sessions over 3 months
   plus 2 sessions during 6-month
   maintenance phase (moderate
   and severe)
	£1044	CBT session (55 minutes):
		 £58 (Curtis, 2009)

- Antidepressant treatment protocol (moderate)	£270	
- Antidepressant treatment protocol (severe)	£599	
Total cost (moderate) **Total cost (severe)**	**£1314** **£1643**	
Patients who discontinue **treatment** - AD: 1 month	£2	
- 2 GP consultations (moderate)	£72	
- 50% GP care (×2) + 50% outpatient care (×2) (severe)	£166	
- CBT sessions: 6 (moderate and severe)	£348	Monthly cost of subsequent mental health care: £165
- Subsequent mental healthcare: 14 months	£1638	Weighted by 65% according to proportion in contact with mental health services (McCrone *et al.*, 2008)
AD total cost (moderate) **AD total cost (severe)** **COMB total cost (moderate)** **COMB total cost (severe)**	**£1712** **£1806** **£2,060** **£2,154**	

Continued

Table 60: (*Continued*)

Resource use estimate	Cost	Source of unit costs
Patients not achieving remission		
- AD: 3 months	£6	
- 4 GP consultations (moderate)	£144	
- 50% GP care (×4) + 50% outpatient care (×4) (severe)	£332	
- CBT sessions: 16 (moderate and severe)	£928	
- Subsequent mental healthcare: 12 months	£1404	
AD total cost (moderate)	**£1554**	
AD total cost (severe)	**£1742**	
COMB total cost (moderate)	**£2,482**	
COMB total cost (severe)	**£2,670**	
Patients who relapse while in remission		
- Antidepressant treatment: (3 + 6 months)	£18	
- 7 GP consultations (moderate)	£252	
- 50% GP care (×7) + 50% outpatient care (×7) (severe)	£581	
- CBT sessions: 17 (moderate and severe)	£1044	
- Subsequent mental healthcare: 8 months	£702	
AD total cost (moderate)	**£972**	
AD total cost (severe)	**£1301**	
COMB total cost (moderate)	**£2,016**	
COMB total cost (severe)	**£2,345**	

Utility data and estimation of quality-adjusted life years

In order to express outcomes in the form of QALYs, the health states of the economic model needed to be linked to appropriate utility scores. Utility scores represent the HRQoL associated with specific health states on a scale from 0 (death) to 1 (perfect health); they are estimated using preference-based measures that capture people's preferences and perceptions on HRQoL characterising the health states under consideration.

8.9.4   Systematic review of published utility scores for adults with depression

Among the studies already assessed for eligibility, eight publications were identified that reported utility scores relating to specific health states and events associated with depression (Revicki & Wood, 1998; Bennett *et al.*, 2000; King *et al.*, 2000; Lenert *et al.*, 2000; Schaffer *et al.*, 2002; Pyne *et al.*, 2003; Sapin *et al.*, 2004; Peveler *et al.*, 2005).

Three studies used the EQ-5D Index instrument, currently recommended by NICE as a measure of patient HRQoL for use in cost-utility analyses (King *et al.*, 2000; Sapin *et al.*, 2004; Peveler *et al.*, 2005). In all three studies, preference values elicited from the UK population sample were used (Dolan & Williams, 1995). King and colleagues (2000) collected patient EQ-5D utility data over 12 months' follow-up in an RCT comparing usual GP care with two types of brief psychological therapy (non-directive counselling and CBT) among patients with depressive or mixed anxiety/depressive symptoms (BDI >14). Patient utility, reported as median scores, improved from baseline in all three treatment groups at 4 and 12 months. However, no differences in median scores were detected between the three patient groups. The study by Peveler and colleagues (2005) was another HTA based on an RCT comparing the cost-utility of TCAs, SSRIs and lofepramine among UK patients with a new episode of depressive illness (based on GP diagnosis). Patients completed the EQ-5D questionnaire on a monthly basis over 12 months. Again, utility scores improved from baseline at 12 months in all three treatment groups but no differences were detected between groups.

The study by Sapin and colleagues (2004) was based on a multicentre, prospective cohort of patients with a new episode of major depressive disorder recruited in the French primary care setting assessed at 8 weeks' follow-up. EQ-5D utility scores were stratified according to depression severity (defined by CGI scores), and by clinical response (defined by MADRS scores) at follow-up. At 8 weeks, patients with MADRS scores lower or equal to 12 were considered as 'remitters' and others considered as 'non-remitters'. Patients with a decrease of at least 50% in relation to baseline score were considered as 'responders' and others as 'non-responders'. These two patient groupings also led to the creation of three mutually exclusive groups: 'responder remitters', 'responder non-remitters' and 'non-responders'.

The other five studies used a variety of instruments to measure patient utility (Revicki & Wood, 1998; Bennett *et al.*, 2000; Lenert *et al.*, 2000; Schaffer *et al.*, 2002; Pyne *et al.*, 2003). Bennett and colleagues (2000) used a disease-specific measure, the McSad instrument, to estimate utility scores for a cross-sectional sample of patients who had experienced at least one episode of major unipolar depression in the previous 2 years. McSad is a direct utility measure in which rating scale (RS) and standard gamble (SG) techniques were used to obtain utilities for specific health states. The health state classification system contains six dimensions (emotion/self-appraisal/cognition/physiology/behaviour/role-function), each with four levels of dysfunction (none/mild/moderate/severe). Utility scores were generated for three temporary clinical marker states of 6 months' duration (mild/moderate/severe depression) and chronic states of lifetime duration (self-reported and severe depression).

Lenert and colleagues (2000) estimated utility scores among depressed US primary care patients based on six health states according to level of depression severity (mild/severe) and physical impairment (mild/moderate/severe). Cluster analysis was applied to the SF-12 HRQoL instrument to generate the six health states. Utilities applied to the six health states were elicited through the use of visual analogue scale (VAS) and SG methods. The resulting six-state health index model was then applied to HRQoL data taken from a longitudinal cohort study of patients with current major depression or dysthymia.

Pyne and colleagues (2003) used the self-administered Quality of Well-Being scale (QWB-SA) in a prospective cohort of US patients treated with antidepressants to measure change in patient HRQoL scores over 4 months' follow-up. The scoring function of the QWB-SA was based on rating scale measurements taken from a random sample of the US population. QWB-SA scores improved during follow-up for treatment responders (defined by a 50% reduction in HRSD-17 scores) but did not improve for non-responders.

Revicki and Wood (1998) used SG techniques in US and Canadian patients with major depressive disorder to generate utility scores for 11 hypothetical depression-related and current health states according to depression severity and antidepressant treatment. The depression-related health states varied depression severity (mild/moderate/severe) and medication (nefazodone/fluoxetine/ imipramine), were framed in terms of 1 month's duration and described symptom severity, functioning and well-being, as well as medication therapy including side effects.

Similarly, the study by Schaffer and colleagues (2002) used SG techniques to elicit utility scores for ten individual symptom profiles of major depression plus three 'clinical marker' depression profiles (mild/moderate/severe) among patients with current or past depression. The individual symptom profiles each consisted of five statements describing a particular aspect of a symptom of depression, incorporating the content of several depression scales and interviews (HRSD, BDI, MADRS, DSM–IV and Structured Clinical Interview for DSM-IV [SCID-IV]).

8.9.5 Summary

Table 61 summarises the methods used to derive health states and estimate utility scores associated with various levels of depression severity and treatments for depression as well as utility scores from each study. Overall, the studies reviewed here reported significant impact of depression on the HRQoL of patients with depression. A number of studies indicated that patients valued the state of severe depression as being close to zero (death) (Revicki & Wood, 1998; Bennett *et al.*, 2000). There was some limited evidence to suggest that generic utility measures such as the EQ-5D may be less sensitive than disease-specific measures such as the McSad health state classification system.

Table 61: Summary of studies reporting utility scores relating to specific health states and events associated with depression

Study	Definition of health states	Valuation method	Population valuing	Results (95% CI/SD)		
Bennett *et al.*, 2000	Utility values were elicited using the McSad health state classification system. The health state descriptions referred to untreated depression.	SG	105 patients with history of major, unipolar depression in the previous 2 years	*Temporary states (6-month):* - Mild depression 0.59 (0.55–0.62) - Moderate depression 0.32 (0.29–0.34) - Severe depression 0.09 (0.05–0.13) *Clinical states (lifetime):* - Self-reported health state 0.79 (0.74–0.83) - Severe depression 0.04 (0.01–0.07)		
King *et al.*, 2000	RCT comparing three treatments: usual GP care and two types of brief psychological therapy (non-directive [ND] counselling and CBT) over 12 months' follow-up.	EQ-5D (TTO)	464 eligible patients with depressive symptoms	*CBT* Baseline 0.73 4 months 0.85 12 months 0.85	*ND counselling* 0.73 0.85 0.85	*GP care* 0.73 0.81 0.85
Lenert *et al.*, 2000	Cluster analysis used to obtain six health states from SF-12. The utility change scores over longitudinal study period were calculated using estimated health state utilities for those in remission, responder – non-remitters, and those with no response.	VAS, SG	104 US depressed primary care patients	Near-normal health (no depression) 0.94 (0.21) Mild mental with mild physical impairment 0.87 (0.18) Severe physical health impairment 0.83 (0.20) Severe mental health impairment 0.81 (0.21) (severe depression) Severe mental and moderate physical impairment 0.78 (0.22) Severe mental and physical impairment 0.66 (0.27)		

Study	Description	Instrument	Sample	Results
Peveler et al., 2005	Pragmatic RCT of three classes of antidepressant: TCAs, SSRIs and lofepramine (LOF) over 12 months' follow-up.	EQ-5D (TTO)	261 UK primary care patients with new episode of depression	

Peveler et al., 2005:

	TCA	SSRI	LOF
Baseline	0.58 (0.27)	0.61 (0.28)	0.57 (0.27)
12 months	0.78 (0.19)	0.78 (0.19)	0.77 (0.21)

Study	Description	Instrument	Sample
Pyne et al., 2003	Prospective observational study conducted over 16 weeks. Treatment with antidepressant and/or mood stabiliser. Depression response data (50% reduction in HRSD-17) collected at baseline, 4 weeks and 4 months.	QWB-SA (Category scaling)	58 US patients treated for MDD

Baseline (HRSD-17: 20.7–21.0; QWB-SA: 0.41–0.43):

	Responders:	Non-responders:
4 weeks	0.54	0.46
4 months	0.63	0.43

Study	Description	Instrument	Sample
Revicki & Wood, 1998	11 hypothetical depression-related states, varying depression severity and antidepressant treatment, and the patient's current health status.	SG	70 patients with MDD from primary care practices in US and Canada

Severe depression, untreated	0.30 (0.22)
Moderate depression	
-Nefazodone	0.63 (0.23)
-Fluoxetine	0.63 (0.19)
-Imipramine	0.55 (0.03)
Mild depression	
-Nefazodone	0.73 (0.21)
-Fluoxetine	0.70 (0.20)
-Imipramine	0.64 (.20)
Depression remission, maintenance treatment	
-Nefazodone	0.83 (0.13)
-Fluoxetine	0.80 (0.15)
-Imipramine	0.72 (0.17)
Remission, no treatment	0.86 (0.16)

Continued

Table 61: (*Continued*)

Study	Definition of health states	Valuation method	Population valuing	Results (95% CI/SD)
Sapin *et al.*, 2004	Multicentre, prospective, non-comparative cohort study, 8 weeks' follow-up. Impact on quality of life measured with EQ-5D instrument. Clinical response, defined by MADRS scores. 'Remitters': MADRS <= 12 'Responder': at least 50% decrease in baseline score	EQ-5D (TTO)	250 patients with new episode of MDD not treated with antidepressant before inclusion; from French primary care	*Baseline* Mild depression 0.45 (0.22) Moderate depression 0.33 (0.24) Severe depression 0.15 (0.21) *8 weeks* No depression 0.86 (0.13) Mild depression 0.74 (0.19) Moderate depression 0.44 (0.27) Severe depression 0.30 (0.27) Responder – remitter 0.85 (0.13) Responder – non-remitter 0.72 (0.20) Non-responders 0.58 (0.28)
Schaffer *et al.*, 2002	Utility scores for ten individual symptoms of depression and three depression severity profiles (mild/moderate/severe).	SG	75 Canadian subjects (19 current depression, 21 past depression, 35 healthy controls)	*Mild* *Moderate* *Severe* Current 0.59 (0.33) 0.51 (0.34) 0.31 (0.31) Past 0.79 (0.28) 0.67 (0.36) 0.47 (0.34) Controls 0.80 (0.21) 0.69 (0.29) 0.46 (0.28) Psychological symptoms (low mood, anhedonia, poor concentration, guilt, suicidal ideation): 0.72 (0.24) Somatic (decreased appetite, energy, sleep, psychomotor agitation, retardation): 0.82 (0.19)

NICE currently recommends the EQ-5D as the preferred measure of HRQoL in adults for use in cost-utility analyses. NICE also suggests that the measurement of changes in HRQoL should be reported directly from people with the condition examined, and the valuation of health states be based on public preferences elicited using a choice-based method such as time trade-off (TTO) or SG, in a representative sample of the UK population (NICE, 2008b). Therefore, based on these recommendations, the EQ-5D utility scores estimated by Sapin and colleagues (2004) were considered to be the most suitable for calculating QALYs in the guideline economic models. Although these utility scores were based on a cohort of French primary care patients, which may limit their applicability to the UK setting, preference values assigned to health states were elicited from the UK population sample. Furthermore, utility scores were stratified according to disease severity and clinical response, which is useful for modelling health states in cost-utility analyses. Full details of utility scores used in the model are presented in Table 62.

Estimation of quality-adjusted life years
By applying the utility scores estimated by Sapin and colleagues (2004), the QALY profiles over 15 months were estimated when patients entered the three end health states in the model (no remission; no relapse; relapse) based on the following assumptions for patients who completed treatment:

● No remission: a linear increase from baseline utility score (0.33 or 0.15) to the 'no response' health state (0.58) over the initial 3-month treatment period; decreasing immediately back to their baseline utility over the remaining 12 months.
● No relapse: a linear increase from baseline utility to the 'response with remission' health state (0.85) over the initial 3-month treatment period; remaining in the 'response with remission' health state for the following 12 months.
● Relapse: a linear increase from baseline utility to the 'response with remission' health state over the initial 3-month treatment period; followed by a linear deterioration back to baseline utility over the remaining 12 months.

For patients who did not complete their initial treatment, the following assumptions were used:

● No response: patient remains at baseline utility (0.33 or 0.15) over 15 months.
● Relapse: a linear increase from baseline utility to the 'response – no remission' health state (0.72) over 3 months; followed by linear decrease back to baseline utility over the remaining 12 months.
● No relapse: a linear increase from baseline utility to the 'response – no remission' health state over 3 months; followed by linear increase to 'response with remission' health state over the remaining 12 months.

Incremental cost effectiveness of COMB versus antidepressant treatment
The incremental cost effectiveness of COMB compared with antidepressant treatment for patients with moderate or severe depression was evaluated by assessing the difference in costs and effectiveness of each therapy. The ICERs were calculated as the difference in the expected healthcare costs divided by the difference in the overall effectiveness of the two strategies.

Table 62: Clinical effectiveness parameters applied in the economic model

Parameter	Base case value (mean)	Range (95% CI)	Source
Clinical outcomes			
Absolute risk of not completing treatment: AD	0.30		
RR of not completing treatment: COMB	0.81	(0.65 to 1.01)	Guideline meta-analysis
Absolute risk of no remission following treatment: AD	0.70		
RR of no remission following treatment: COMB	0.76	(0.55 to 1.03)	Guideline meta-analysis
Absolute risk of relapse during follow-up: AD	0.55		Blackburn *et al.* (1986); Murphy *et al.* (1984)
RR of relapse during follow-up: COMB	0.68	(0.38 to 1.24)	
Probability of spontaneous remission for patients who drop out of initial treatment: BOTH	0.20	(0.10 to 0.30)	GDG expert opinion
Probability of relapse for patients who discontinue initial treatment and in remission: BOTH	0.67	–	Murphy *et al.* (1984)
Quality-of-life weights			
Moderate depression	0.33	(0.29 to 0.37)	Sapin *et al.* (2004)
Severe depression	0.15	(0.08 to 0.22)	
Response with remission	0.85	(0.83 to 0.87)	
Response without remission	0.72	(0.65 to 0.79)	
No response	0.58	(0.50 to 0.66)	

Sensitivity analyses

Deterministic sensitivity analysis

Given the considerable uncertainty around some of the input parameters used in the base case model and ambiguity surrounding any policy implications of point estimates, one-way sensitivity analysis was undertaken. This involved varying a single parameter between its plausible minimum and maximum values while maintaining all remaining parameters in the model at their base case value. Uncertainty around the various transition probabilities and quality-of-life weights, as well as the cost implications of different levels of resource use involved in patient clinical management, were explored.

Probabilistic sensitivity analysis

To demonstrate the joint uncertainty between the different parameters, probabilistic analysis is required. Using the mean point estimates and their 95% CIs, appropriate distributions were assigned for each parameter estimate. For example, lognormal distributions were applied to relative risk estimates, gamma distributions to cost estimates and beta distributions to utility estimates and absolute rates. For cost estimates that did not have 95% CIs, a standard error based on 30% of the mean estimate was applied to reflect any potential uncertainty around these estimates. Effectiveness and cost estimates were then recalculated 10,000 times using Monte Carlo simulation. Whether an intervention is cost effective or not depends on how decision makers value the additional health gain achieved by the therapy. The probability that COMB therapy is cost effective compared with AD treatment as a function of decision makers' maximum willingness-to-pay for an additional successfully treated patient or QALY was illustrated by CEACs (Briggs, 2000).

8.9.6   Results

Clinical outcomes

The systematic review of the clinical evidence showed that the probability of not completing the initial 3-month therapy was higher for AD than for COMB (RR = 0.80, 95% CI 0.65, 1.01) while the probability of not achieving remission following therapy was also lower in the COMB group (RR = 0.76, 95% CI 0.55, 1.03). The two follow-up studies suggested that there is a lower risk of relapse in the COMB therapy arm (RR = 0.68, 95% CI 0.38, 1.24) over a 12-month follow-up period although this was not statistically significant (p = 0.21).

Quality-adjusted life years

The decision model for patients with moderate depression resulted in an average of 0.67 QALYs per patient in the COMB therapy group and 0.58 QALYs per patient in the AD group. The decision model for patients with severe depression resulted in an average of 0.53 QALYs per patient in the COMB therapy group and 0.42 QALYs in the AD group. Therefore, the average gain in QALYs over 15 months for COMB therapy was 0.09 per patient with moderate depression and 0.11 per patient with severe depression.

Costs and cost effectiveness

The full cost of a 3-month course of antidepressant treatment plus 6-month maintenance therapy was £270 for patients with moderate depression and £599 for patients with severe depression. The full cost of 3-month COMB therapy, including a full course of CBT, plus 6 months' maintenance therapy was £1314 for patients with moderate depression and £1643 for patients with severe depression. The expected subsequent health and social care cost over 15 months for patients who did not complete their initial therapy was £1638 for both moderate and severe patients. The expected subsequent health and social care cost over 15 months for patients who did not respond to therapy and achieve remission was £1404 for both patient groups. The expected subsequent health and social care cost of relapse while in remission was £702 for both patient groups.

Incremental cost effectiveness of COMB versus antidepressant treatment
Overall, COMB therapy was estimated to be significantly more effective and more costly than antidepressant treatment for patients with both moderate and severe depression. On average, the strategy of COMB therapy was £624 more costly per patient with moderate depression and £653 more costly per patient with severe depression. The resulting base case ICERs were £7,052 per QALY gained for moderate depression and £5,558 per QALY gained for severe depression.

Sensitivity analyses
Deterministic sensitivity analysis
The parameter values used in the sensitivity analyses and the resultant ICERs are presented in Table 63. The results of the deterministic sensitivity analysis indicated that the results were fairly robust when single parameters were varied over their uncertainty ranges. The cost-effectiveness estimates were most sensitive to: (1) the relative risk of no remission following therapy completion and; (2) the relative risk of relapse while in remission. This is explained by the high uncertainty around the relative risk estimate of no remission and to a lesser extent around the relative risk of relapse for COMB versus AD. Other factors had a much lesser role in the variation of the results.

Probabilistic sensitivity analysis
In order to present the results of the probabilistic sensitivity analysis, CEACs were constructed (see Figure 7). The CEAC indicates the probability of COMB therapy being cost effective for a range of threshold values. The threshold value represents the maximum a decision maker would be willing to pay for a unit of effect, in this case a QALY.

Current NICE guidance sets a threshold range of £20,000 to £30,000 per QALY (NICE, 2008a). Within this threshold range, the probability of COMB therapy being cost effective for patients with moderate depression was 86 to 90% and for patients with severe depression was 88 to 92%.

8.9.7   Discussion

In this economic evaluation, CBT was chosen as the psychological therapy and citalopram as the antidepressant drug being compared. An updated cost-effectiveness model was constructed to investigate the difference in clinical outcomes and direct health and social care costs between the different strategies. The updated clinical evidence review indicated that CBT alone may be more costly yet less clinically effective than antidepressant treatment and so it was excluded from the final model. As combination therapy is both more effective and more costly than antidepressant treatment, these strategies were compared in a formal cost-effectiveness analysis.

Table 63: Deterministic sensitivity analysis

Analysis	Uncertainty range	ICER per QALY (£)	
		Moderate depression	Severe depression
Base case analysis		7,052	5,558
Clinical efficacy (COMB versus AD)			
Relative risk of discontinuation	0.65 to 1.01	6,610 to 7,420	5,187 to 5,866
Relative risk of non-remission	0.55 to 1.03	3,154 to 367,000	2,623 to 227,385
Relative risk of relapse	0.38 to 1.24	5,248 to 14,222	4,143 to 11,254
Relative risk of non-remission following discontinuation	0.7 to 0.9	6,905 to 7,205	5,434 to 5,688
Quality-of-life weights			
Moderate depression	0.29 to 0.37	6,573 to 7,606	N/A
Severe depression	0.08 to 0.22	N/A	5,071 to 6,148
Remission – no relapse	0.83 to 0.87	6,773 to 7,355	5,391 to 5,736
Remission – relapse	0.65 to 0.79	7,012 to 7,092	5,535 to 5,582
No Remission	0.50 to 0.66	6,964 to 7,141	5,506 to 5,611
Resource use and costs			
Severe patients – % receiving specialist care	5 to 50%	N/A	4,984 to 5,558
Moderate patients – number of CBT sessions	8 to 16	2,762 to 7,052	N/A

Figure 7: CEACs of COMB therapy versus AD for patients with moderate and severe depression

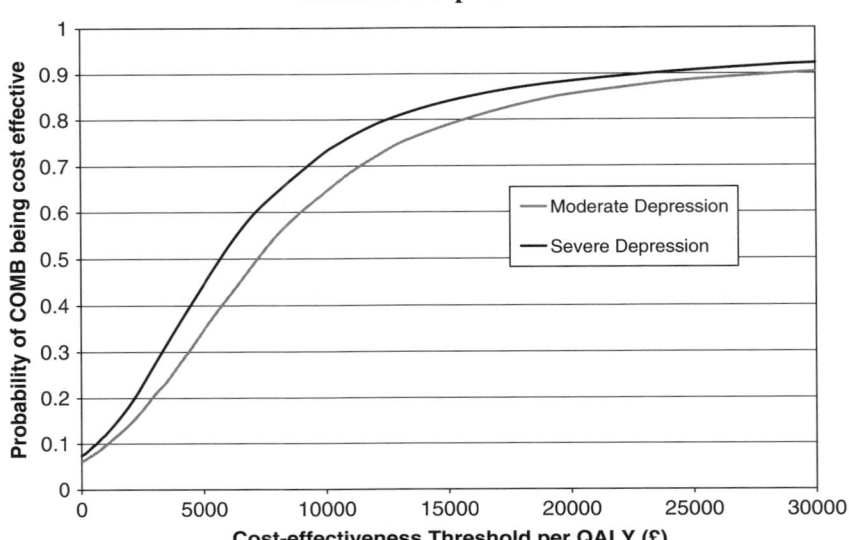

Two separate analyses were conducted for patients with moderate and severe depression. The difference in costs between combination therapy and antidepressant treatment was slightly higher for patients with severe depression, while the difference in QALY gains was also slightly higher. The cost results for patients with both moderate and severe depression suggest that although the initial treatment cost of combination therapy is substantially higher, these costs were partially offset by savings due to lower subsequent treatment costs. Overall, the results of the analysis indicate that combination therapy is likely to be a cost-effective first-line treatment for both moderate and severe depression.

Limitations of the analysis
The clinical effectiveness estimates used in the analyses were based on efficacy data obtained from RCTs, resulting in possible over estimates of successful outcomes for both treatment options provided within the NHS setting. However, this is unlikely to significantly influence the relative effectiveness of the two treatment options.

Another issue concerns the time horizon used for the analysis. A 15-month time horizon was used, with remission rates applied at the end of the initial 3 months of treatment and relapse rates applied during the 12-month follow-up period. One study in the clinical evidence review indicated lower relapse rates with combination therapy versus antidepressant treatment for up to 6 years after treatment (Fava *et al.*, 2004). This suggests that the relative cost effectiveness of combination therapy versus antidepressant treatment may be underestimated when based on a short time horizon.

It would have been preferable to evaluate the two strategies over a longer follow-up period, but the lack of direct clinical evidence beyond 15 months precluded this.

Depression incurs significant non-healthcare costs, such as social service costs, direct costs to patients and their families and lost productivity costs because of morbidity or premature mortality (Thomas & Morris, 2003; McCrone *et al.*, 2008). As this analysis was conducted from the health service and PSS perspective, as per NICE guidance, such non-healthcare costs were not considered. It is likely that the inclusion of these costs would have further increased the probability of combination therapy being cost effective compared with antidepressant treatment.

8.10   FROM EVIDENCE TO RECOMMENDATIONS

This section synthesises the evidence from the clinical summaries of all the psychological interventions reviewed in this chapter and the health economic evidence. This is because some key recommendations about psychological therapies are common to all types of interventions and also because a number of the recommendations draw on evidence from several different reviews. Overall, the evidence indicates that psychological interventions have a beneficial effect in the treatment of people with depression and they do not have an increased risk for discontinuation when compared with antidepressants. However, the evidence suggests that there are differences in the evidence base for the effectiveness among the psychological interventions reviewed in this chapter, and this is the focus of this section.

8.10.1   Cognitive behavioural therapies

With 46 studies, cognitive behavioural therapies have the largest evidence base. Within this group of studies, the largest dataset is that which compares individual CBT with antidepressants and which shows broad equivalence of effect across the range of severity. The clinical effectiveness data also points to a clear advantage of combination treatment over antidepressants alone. This is supported by the outcome of the health economics model, which suggested that combination treatment is cost effective not just for severe depression but also for moderate depression, and as a result the recommendations from the previous guideline were changed. The outcome of the model does not support the simple adoption of combination treatment as the first choice, but as potentially the most cost-effective option because of its greater benefit despite the increased cost. The GDG took the view that for patients with moderate depression a number of options, including antidepressants alone and CBT alone (CBT alone was found to be better than antidepressants alone when both were compared with combined treatment), should be available. This should then allow for a discussion between patient and clinician in which a number of factors are taken into account, including the demands of adhering to the various treatment options and experience of past treatment, when determining treatment choice.

A more limited (because the evidence relates primarily to mild depression) dataset was examined for group CBT. The group CBT approach (based on the Coping with Depression model) showed evidence of benefit at post-treatment and at follow-up over a waitlist control. There was no clear evidence for the effectiveness of other models of group CBT.

Given the relapsing and remitting nature of depression, the GDG looked closely at the evidence for relapse. The most important evidence came from two sources: the studies comparing CBT with antidepressants, which showed a reduced relapse rate for CBT in the follow-up of individual trials; and the data from psychological interventions specifically designed to reduce relapse. The provision of individual CBT is therefore one option when there are concerns over the risk of relapse (an almost ever-present concern with people who have had more than two episodes of depression) and should be considered along with the evidence reviewed for pharmacological interventions and relapse prevention (see Chapter 12). Of the treatments specifically designed to reduce relapse, group-based mindfulness-based cognitive therapy has the strongest evidence base with evidence that it is likely to be effective in people who have experienced three or more depressive episodes.

The GDG also reviewed the relative effectiveness of CBT against a range of other psychological interventions; the detailed outcomes of these reviews are set out in the sections for these interventions below. In brief, the GDG found evidence for some other interventions including IPT and couples therapy that suggested, in some comparisons, broadly similar effects to CBT and, to a lesser extent, for behavioural activation. The GDG did not consider the evidence for counselling, short-term psychodynamic psychotherapy or problem solving therapy to be as strong as that for other interventions (see below).

In making recommendations on CBT, the GDG were conscious of feedback from stakeholders from the previous guideline (NICE, 2004a) and of their experiences of providing or receiving psychological treatments. This led the group to specify in greater detail than previously the ways in which all psychological treatments in this guideline (including CBT) should be provided. It also led the GDG, after considering the evidence, to remove the previous recommendation about the provision of brief CBT because the GDG did not think that the rather limited evidence for brief CBT justified such a specific recommendation. There was concern that this recommendation had led to an unnecessary restriction on the number of sessions of psychological intervention being made available. Instead, the GDG elected to recommend that the duration of treatment should be in line with that found in the majority of trials but also suggested that the target in treatment should be remission and, should that be achieved after fewer than the recommended sessions, then treatment need not be continued beyond that point.

The GDG also took into account the evidence on the delivery of effective psychological interventions reviewed in Chapter 6 and used this to develop a number of recommendations on the need to adhere to, as far as possible, the treatments set out in the trials, as well as the need for routine outcome monitoring and the use of appropriate training and supervision. (Note that this approach has been adopted for all recommendations for psychological therapies in this guideline.)

The GDG felt it was important to locate all psychological interventions in proper relation to each other, having considered the evidence on clinical and cost effectiveness. This meant developing recommendations that locate all psychological interventions at the appropriate place in the stepped-care model. Low-intensity interventions are clinically and cost effective for subthreshold depressive symptoms and mild depression, and therefore are to be preferred over individual and group CBT (and other high-intensity psychological interventions) as the initial treatment for subthreshold depressive symptoms and mild depression. Group CBT is an effective treatment for mild depression but, given the duration of the group and the staffing of such groups, it was viewed on cost-minimisation grounds as less cost effective than low-intensity interventions but more cost effective than individual CBT, and so was placed between them in the stepped-care model.

8.10.2   Behavioural activation

There has been renewed interest in behavioural activation as a treatment for depression and a number of new studies were identified for the review in this guideline. It is also a component part of cognitive behavioural interventions for depression and one of the first important trials of behavioural activation was a deconstruction study (Jacobson1999). No direct evidence on the cost effectiveness of behavioural activation as a high- or low-intensity intervention was identified in the systematic review of the health economics literature, although it should be noted that the duration and frequency of high-intensity behavioural activation is identical to that of high-intensity CBT. It was also not possible to evaluate the cost effectiveness of behavioural activation in an economic model because of the limited clinical evidence available. However, consideration was given to the emergence of new evidence, including data on comparisons with placebo, antidepressants, CBT and usual care, all of which were positive for behavioural activation (that is, there was no evidence of the superiority of these other interventions). Note was also taken of the evidence for the effectiveness of behavioural activation in low-intensity interventions. The GDG decided that although the evidence was not sufficiently robust to recommend behavioural activation as a direct alternative individual treatment option to CBT or IPT, it could be considered as an option. The GDG did, however, decide that healthcare professionals should be made aware of the more limited evidence base for behavioural activation when compared with CBT, IPT and couples therapy (see below).

8.10.3   Problem solving therapy

Problem solving therapy was recommended as a separate intervention in the last guideline. No new studies were identified, leaving a limited dataset based only on two studies with much of the evidence for effectiveness being dependent on one study (Mynors-Wallis1995). In light of the improved evidence for a range of low-intensity interventions that have emerged since the last guideline, the GDG decided not to recommend problem solving therapy as a separate intervention in this guideline. However, the GDG expects that it will continue to be one of the component parts of the low-intensity interventions offered for the treatment of depression (Richards & Whyte, 2008). In the health economics literature, one study was found that suggested that problem solving therapy delivered by community mental health nurses was not cost effective compared with usual GP care in patients with new episodes of anxiety, depression and life difficulties (Kendrick *et al.*, 2006a).

8.10.4   Couples therapy

In the review for this guideline, a number of additional studies were included and one from the previous guideline was excluded. The evidence base for couples therapy is relatively modest with just six studies, but there are indications of a beneficial effect in couples with depression (in particular, those who adopted a behavioural approach to treatment) when compared with waitlist control, and evidence of similar outcomes for couples therapy when compared with individual CBT and IPT (although the evidence in comparison with IPT is more uncertain). As a result of the increased evidence identified in this guideline, couples therapy (based on a behavioural model) is recommended; however, the GDG did not consider it appropriate to offer it as a direct alternative to CBT or IPT, but rather decided that it should be focused on patients in established relationships where the relationship may play a role in the development, maintenance or resolution of depression, because these issues were typical of the patients who entered the trials reviewed in this guideline. Only one study was identified in the health economics literature, which suggested that couples therapy may be a cost-effective treatment compared with antidepressant medication for patients with major depressive disorder (Leff *et al.*, 2000), but this study was excluded from the clinical evidence analyses because of its high attrition rate.

8.10.5   Interpersonal therapy

The evidence for the effectiveness of IPT reviewed in this guideline confirms the picture in the previous guideline of IPT as an effective treatment for depression. However, the dataset is not as large as that for CBT, nor is the evidence for the range of applications for IPT as strong or as wide ranging (for example the evidence on group- or individual-based approaches to relapse prevention). There was also no good economic evidence for the effectiveness of IPT and it was also not possible to evaluate the cost effectiveness of IPT in an economic model because of the limited clinical evidence available. Therefore, the GDG did not develop recommendations for IPT that were as broad in scope as for CBT (for example, the use of combination CBT and antidepressant drugs as the initial treatment for severe depression), but for many patients with mild to moderate depression IPT is an appropriate alternative to CBT.

8.10.6   Counselling

The evidence base for counselling identified in the previous guideline was small (only three studies – one of which, Ward2000, did not meet current inclusion criteria). Of the new studies identified, only one provided relevant data on an important comparison relevant to the effectiveness of counselling (WATSON2003), while one did not meet inclusion criteria and two other studies compared different forms of counselling (GOLDMAN2006, GREENBERG1998). An inconsistent picture of the effectiveness of counselling emerges from the review, with one trial having poorer outcomes against usual care (Simpson2003) and one against antidepressants (Bedi2000), but no difference identifiable in the two comparisons with CBT (Ward2000, WATSON2003). Two studies identified in the health economics literature suggested no advantage, in terms of cost effectiveness, of counselling compared with either usual GP care or antidepressant treatment in adults with depression (Friedli *et al.*, 2000; Miller *et al.*, 2003). Furthermore, a review of the practice-based evidence did not provide clear evidence of a benefit for counselling in depression (for example, Stiles *et al.*, 2008; Marriott & Kellett, 2009). The evidence base for counselling in contrast to that for both CBT and IPT lacked data on both long-term follow-up and relapse prevention. The previous guideline recommended counselling in mild to moderate depression, but in light of the increased evidence for a range of low-intensity interventions and group CBT for mild to moderate depression, the GDG decided not to support the same recommendation for counselling in this guideline update. Nevertheless, the GDG thought that counselling may be considered for people with mild to moderate depression who have declined an antidepressant, CBT, IPT, behavioural activation or behavioural couples therapy, but felt that the limited evidence should be drawn to the attention of the healthcare professional. There was considerable discussion of this recommendation in the GDG, which took into account not only the limited evidence for counselling but also the increased evidence for other interventions, such as CBT, IPT, behavioural activation and behavioural couples therapy.

8.10.7   Short-term psychodynamic psychotherapy

A number of new studies were identified for short-term psychodynamic psychotherapy as a treatment for depression, taking the total number of included studies to ten. The comparators were very varied and so significantly limited the amount of meta-analysis that was possible. Nevertheless, from a review of these studies it was not possible to demonstrate a consistent picture of any clinically important benefit for short-term psychodynamic psychotherapy in depression. For example, the two comparisons with antidepressants revealed directly contradictory results (DEKKER2008, SALMINEN2008) and some of the largest effects were obtained in dysthymic or subthreshold populations (MAINA2005). Two studies identified in the health economics literature suggested no advantage, in terms of cost effectiveness, of short-term psychodynamic psychotherapy compared with usual care for primary care patients with depression (Simpson *et al.*, 2003) or high utilisers of psychiatric services with a significant number of patients with a diagnosis of depression (Guthrie *et al.*, 1999). The previous guideline recommended psychodynamic psychotherapy for complex comorbidities, but the current dataset offered no clear evidence for the effectiveness of short-term psychodynamic psychotherapy for complex comorbidities. As a result of the limited evidence for short-term psychodynamic psychotherapy for depression with or without complex comorbidities, the GDG did not feel able to endorse the recommendation in the previous guideline and developed a more specific recommendation for this update. Results from the KOOL2003 study, which included a subgroup analysis of those with a personality disorder, lacked the power to inform a decision on the use of short-term psychodynamic psychotherapy with comorbidities such as personality disorder. As with the evidence base for counselling, the short-term psychodynamic psychotherapy evidence base lacked data on both long-term follow-up and relapse prevention. Nevertheless, the GDG took the view that short-term psychodynamic psychotherapy may be considered for people with mild to moderate depression who have declined an antidepressant, CBT, IPT, behavioural activation or behavioural couples therapy, but that the limited evidence should be drawn to the attention of the healthcare professional. There was considerable discussion of this recommendation in the GDG which took into account not only the limited evidence for short-term psychodynamic psychotherapy but also the increased evidence for other interventions such as CBT, IPT, behavioural activation and behavioural couples therapy.

8.11 RECOMMENDATIONS

8.11.1 Effective delivery of interventions for depression

8.11.1.1 All interventions for depression should be delivered by competent practitioners. Psychological and psychosocial interventions should be based on the relevant treatment manual(s), which should guide the structure and duration of the intervention. Practitioners should consider using competence frameworks developed from the relevant treatment manual(s) and for all interventions should:
- receive regular high-quality supervision
- use routine outcome measures and ensure that the person with depression is involved in reviewing the efficacy of the treatment
- engage in monitoring and evaluation of treatment adherence and practitioner competence - for example, by using video and audio tapes, and external audit and scrutiny where appropriate.

8.11.2 Group cognitive behavioural therapy

8.11.2.1 Consider group-based CBT for people with persistent subthreshold depressive symptoms or mild to moderate depression who decline low-intensity psychosocial interventions (see 7.5.1.1).

8.11.2.2   Group-based CBT for people with persistent subthreshold depressive symptoms or mild to moderate depression should:

- be based on a structured model such as 'Coping with Depression'
- be delivered by two trained and competent practitioners
- consist of ten to 12 meetings of eight to ten participants
- normally take place over 12 to 16 weeks, including follow-up.

8.11.3   Treatment options

8.11.3.1   For people with persistent subthreshold depressive symptoms or mild to moderate depression who have not benefited from a low-intensity psychosocial intervention, discuss the relative merits of different interventions with the person and provide:

- an antidepressant (normally a selective serotonin reuptake inhibitor [SSRI]) or
- a high-intensity psychological intervention, normally one of the following options:
    - CBT
    - interpersonal therapy (IPT)
    - behavioural activation (but note that the evidence is less robust than for CBT or IPT)
    - behavioural couples therapy for people who have a regular partner and where the relationship may contribute to the development or maintenance of depression, or where involving the partner is considered to be of potential therapeutic benefit[70].

8.11.3.2   For people with moderate or severe depression, provide a combination of antidepressant medication and a high-intensity psychological intervention (CBT or IPT)[71].

8.11.3.3   The choice of intervention should be influenced by the:

- duration of the episode of depression and the trajectory of symptoms
- previous course of depression and response to treatment
- likelihood of adherence to treatment and any potential adverse effects
- person's treatment preference and priorities[72].

8.11.3.4   For people with depression who decline an antidepressant, CBT, IPT, behavioural activation and behavioural couples therapy, consider:

- counselling for people with persistent subthreshold depressive symptoms or mild to moderate depression
- short-term psychodynamic psychotherapy for people with mild to moderate depression.

---

[70]This recommendation also appears in the chapter on pharmacological interventions.
[71]Ibid.
[72]Ibid.

Discuss with the person the uncertainty of the effectiveness of counselling and psychodynamic psychotherapy in treating depression.

8.11.4 Delivering high-intensity psychological interventions

8.11.4.1 For all high-intensity psychological interventions, the duration of treatment should normally be within the limits indicated in this guideline. As the aim of treatment is to obtain significant improvement or remission the duration of treatment may be:
- reduced if remission has been achieved
- increased if progress is being made, and there is agreement between the practitioner and the person with depression that further sessions would be beneficial (for example, if there is a comorbid personality disorder or significant psychosocial factors that impact on the person's ability to benefit from treatment).

8.11.4.2 For all people with depression having individual CBT, the duration of treatment should typically be in the range of 16 to 20 sessions over 3 to 4 months. Also consider providing:
- two sessions per week for the first 2 to 3 weeks of treatment for people with moderate or severe depression
- follow-up sessions typically consisting of three to four sessions over the following 3 to 6 months for all people with depression.

8.11.4.3 For all people with depression having IPT, the duration of treatment should typically be in the range of 16 to 20 sessions over 3 to 4 months. For people with severe depression, consider providing two sessions per week for the first 2 to 3 weeks of treatment.

8.11.4.4 For all people with depression having behavioural activation, the duration of treatment should typically be in the range of 16 to 20 sessions over 3 to 4 months. Also consider providing:
- two sessions per week for the first 3 to 4 weeks of treatment for people with moderate or severe depression
- follow-up sessions typically consisting of three to four sessions over the following 3 to 6 months for all people with depression.

8.11.4.5 Behavioural couples therapy for depression should normally be based on behavioural principles, and an adequate course of therapy should be 15 to 20 sessions over 5 to 6 months.

8.11.5 Delivering counselling

8.11.5.1 For all people with persistent subthreshold depressive symptoms or mild to moderate depression having counselling, the duration of treatment should typically be in the range of six to ten sessions over 8 to 12 weeks.

8.11.6 Delivering short-term psychodynamic psychotherapy

8.11.6.1 For all people with mild to moderate depression having short-term psychodynamic psychotherapy, the duration of treatment should typically be in the range of 16 to 20 sessions over 4 to 6 months.

8.11.7 Combined psychological and drug treatment

8.11.7.1 For a person whose depression has not responded to either pharmacological or psychological interventions, consider combining antidepressant medication with CBT[73].

8.11.8 Psychological interventions for relapse prevention

8.11.8.1 People with depression who are considered to be at significant risk of relapse (including those who have relapsed despite antidepressant treatment or who are unable or choose not to continue antidepressant treatment) or who have residual symptoms, should be offered the following psychological interventions:
- individual CBT for people who have relapsed despite antidepressant medication and for people with a significant history of depression and residual symptoms despite treatment
- mindfulness-based cognitive therapy for people who are currently well but have experienced three or more previous episodes of depression.

8.11.9 Delivering psychological interventions for relapse prevention

8.11.9.1 For all people with depression who are having individual CBT for relapse prevention, the duration of treatment should typically be in the range of 16 to 20 sessions over 3 to 4 months. If the duration of treatment needs to be extended to achieve remission it should:
- consist of two sessions per week for the first 2 to 3 weeks of treatment
- include additional follow-up sessions, typically consisting of four to six sessions over the following 6 months.

8.11.9.2 Mindfulness-based cognitive therapy should normally be delivered in groups of eight to 15 participants and consist of weekly 2-hour meetings over 8 weeks and four follow-up sessions in the 12 months after the end of treatment.

---

[73]This recommendation can also be found in the chapter on pharmacological interventions.

8.12 RESEARCH RECOMMENDATIONS

8.12.1.1 The efficacy of short-term psychodynamic psychotherapy compared with CBT and antidepressants in the treatment of moderate to severe depression.

In well-defined depression of moderate to severe severity, what is the efficacy of short-term psychodynamic psychotherapy compared with CBT and antidepressants?

Why this is important

Psychological treatments are an important therapeutic option for people with depression. CBT has the best evidence base for efficacy but it is not effective for everyone. The availability of alternatives drawing from a different theoretical model is therefore important. Psychotherapy based on psychodynamic principles has historically been provided in the NHS but provision is patchy and a good evidence base is lacking. It is therefore important to establish whether short-term psychodynamic psychotherapy is an effective alternative to CBT and one that should be provided. The results of this study will have important implications for the provision of psychological treatment in the NHS.

This question should be answered using a randomised controlled trial design that reports short- and medium-term outcomes (including cost-effectiveness outcomes) of at least 18 months' duration. Particular attention should be paid to the reproducibility of the treatment model and training and supervision of those providing interventions to ensure that the treatments are both robust and generalisable. The outcomes chosen should reflect both observer- and patient-rated assessments of improvement and an assessment of the acceptability of the treatment options. The study needs to be large enough to determine the presence or absence of clinically important effects using a non-inferiority design, and mediators and moderators of response should be investigated.

8.12.1.2 The cost effectiveness of combined antidepressants and CBT compared with sequenced treatment for moderate to severe depression

What is the cost effectiveness of combined antidepressants and CBT compared with sequenced medication followed by CBT and vice versa for moderate to severe depression?

Why this is important

There is a reasonable evidence base for the superior effectiveness of combined antidepressants and CBT over either treatment alone in moderate to severe depression. However the practicality, acceptability and cost effectiveness of combined treatment over a sequenced approach is less well-established. The answer has important practical implications for service delivery and resource implications for the NHS.

This question should be answered using a randomised controlled trial design in which people with moderate to severe depression receive either combined treatment from the outset, or single modality treatment with the addition of the other modality if there is inadequate response to initial treatment. The outcomes chosen should reflect both observer and patient-rated assessments for acute and medium-term outcomes to at least 6 months, and an assessment of the acceptability and burden of the treatment options. The study needs to be large enough to determine the presence or absence of clinically important effects using a non-inferiority design together with robust health economic measures.

8.12.1.3 The efficacy of CBT compared with antidepressants and placebo for persistent subthreshold depressive symptoms

What is the efficacy of CBT compared with antidepressants and placebo for persistent subthreshold depressive symptoms?

Why this is important

Persistent subthreshold depressive symptoms are increasingly recognised as affecting a considerable number of people and causing significant suffering, but the best way to treat them is not known. There are studies of the efficacy of antidepressants for dysthymia (persistent subthreshold depressive symptoms that have lasted for at least 2 years) but there is a lack of evidence for CBT. Subthreshold depressive symptoms of recent onset tend to improve but how long practitioners should wait before offering medication or psychological treatment is not known. This research recommendation is aimed at informing the treatment options available for this group of people with subthreshold depressive symptoms that persist despite low-intensity interventions.

This question should be answered using a randomised controlled trial design that reports short- and medium-term outcomes (including cost-effectiveness outcomes) of at least 6 months' duration. A careful definition of persistence should be used which needs to include duration of symptoms and consideration of failure of low-intensity interventions and does not necessarily imply a full diagnosis of dysthymia. The outcomes chosen should reflect both observer and patient-rated assessments of improvement, and an assessment of the acceptability of the treatment options. The study needs to be large enough to determine the presence or absence of clinically important effects using a non-inferiority design, and mediators and moderators of response should be investigated.

8.12.1.4 The efficacy of counselling compared with low-intensity cognitive behavioural interventions and treatment as usual in the treatment of persistent subthreshold depressive symptoms and mild depression

In persistent subthreshold depressive symptoms and mild depression, what is the efficacy of counselling compared with low-intensity cognitive behavioural interventions?

Why this is important

Psychological treatments are an important therapeutic option for people with subthreshold symptoms and mild depression. Low-intensity cognitive behavioural interventions have the best evidence base for efficacy but the evidence is limited and longer-term outcomes are uncertain, as are the outcomes for counselling. It is therefore important to establish whether either of these interventions is an effective alternative to treatment as usual and should be provided in the NHS. The results of this study will have important implications for the provision of psychological treatment in the NHS.

This question should be answered using a randomised controlled trial design which reports short-term and medium-term outcomes (including cost-effectiveness outcomes) of at least 18 months' duration. Particular attention should be paid to the reproducibility of the treatment model and training and supervision of those providing interventions in order to ensure that the treatments are both robust and generalisable. The outcomes chosen should reflect both observer and patient-rated assessments of improvement and an assessment of the acceptability of the treatment options. The study needs to be large enough to determine the presence or absence of clinically important effects using a non-inferiority design, and mediators and moderators of response should be investigated.

8.12.1.5 The efficacy of behavioural activation compared with CBT and antidepressants in the treatment of moderate to severe depression

In well-defined depression of moderate to severe severity, what is the efficacy of behavioural activation compared with CBT and antidepressants?

Why this is important
Psychological treatments are an important therapeutic option for people with depression. Behavioural activation is a promising treatment but does not have the substantial evidence base that CBT has. The availability of alternatives drawing from a different theoretical model is important because outcomes are modest even with the best supported treatments. It is therefore important to establish whether behavioural activation is an effective alternative to CBT and one that should be provided. The results of this study will have important implications for the provision of psychological treatment in the NHS.

This question should be answered using a randomised controlled trial design which reports short-term and medium-term outcomes (including cost-effectiveness outcomes) of at least 18 months' duration. Particular attention should be paid to the reproducibility of the treatment model and training and supervision of those providing interventions in order to ensure that the treatments are both robust and generalisable. The outcomes chosen should reflect both observer and patient-rated assessments of improvement, and an assessment of the acceptability of the treatment options. The study needs to be large enough to determine the presence or absence of clinically important effects using a non-inferiority design, and mediators and moderators of response should be investigated.

8.12.1.6 The efficacy and cost effectiveness of cognitive behavioural therapy, interpersonal therapy and antidepressants in prevention of relapse in people with moderate to severe recurrent depression

In people with moderate to severe recurrent depression, what is the relative efficacy of CBT, IPT and antidepressants in preventing relapse?

Why this is important
Psychological and pharmacological treatments are important therapeutic options for people with depression, but evidence on the prevention of relapse (especially for

psychological interventions) is limited. All of these treatments have shown promise in reducing relapse but the relapse rate remains high. New developments in the style and delivery of CBT and IPT show some promise in reducing relapse but need to be tested in a large-scale trial. The results of this study will have important implications for the provision of psychological treatment in the NHS.

This question should be answered using a randomised controlled trial design which reports short-term and medium-term outcomes (including cost-effectiveness outcomes) of at least 24 months' duration. Particular attention should be paid to the development and evaluation of CBT, IPT and medication interventions tailored specifically to prevent relapse, including the nature and duration of the intervention. The outcomes chosen should reflect both observer and patient-rated assessments of improvement and an assessment of the acceptability of the treatment options. The study needs to be large enough to determine the presence or absence of clinically important effects using a non-inferiority design, and mediators (including the focus of the interventions) and moderators (including the severity of the depression) of response should be investigated.

9 INTRODUCTION TO PHARMACOLOGICAL AND PHYSICAL INTERVENTIONS

9.1 INTRODUCTION

For the guideline update the following reviews of pharmacological interventions are updated: escitalopram, relapse prevention and next-step treatments (treatments for treatment-resistant depression in the previous guideline), and the following narrative reviews have been updated with new data: effect of sex on antidepressant choice, dosage, discontinuation, cardiotoxicity, and antidepressants and suicide. There are also new reviews for TCAs, duloxetine and therapies for depression with a seasonal pattern, new narrative reviews of transcranial magnetic stimulation (TMS) and vagus nerve stimulation (VNS), and new sections for chronic depression and residual symptoms. The scope for the update also includes updating the NICE technology appraisal on the use of ECT (for depression) (TA59; NICE, 2003)[74]. Where reviews have not been updated, an explanation has been added to the relevant chapter introduction.

This chapter introduces the pharmacological interventions in the management of depression covered by this guideline update (although other physical interventions are also reviewed). It discusses some of the issues that the GDG addressed in assessing the evidence base in order to form recommendations, including that of placebo response. The reviews of pharmacological interventions themselves are presented in the following chapters.

Since the introduction of the MAOIs and the first TCA, imipramine, in the late 1950s, many new antidepressants have been introduced and approximately 35 different antidepressants in a number of classes are currently available worldwide. There has been intensive research on the effects of drug therapy on depression and how drugs might alter the natural history of the disorder. Excellent reviews of the topic are to be found in the *British Association for Psychopharmacology Evidence-Based Guidelines for Treatment of Depressive Disorder* (Anderson *et al.*, 2008) and in the World Federation of Societies of Biological Psychiatry's (WFSBP) *Guidelines for the Biological Treatment of Unipolar Depressive Disorders Parts 1 and 2* (Bauer *et al.*, 2002a, 2002b).

The severity of depression at which antidepressants show consistent benefits over placebo is poorly defined. In general, the more severe the symptoms, the greater the benefit (Anderson *et al.*, 2008; Kirsch *et al.*, 2008); antidepressants are normally recommended as first-line treatment in patients whose depression is of at least moderate severity. Of this patient group, approximately 20% will respond with no treatment at all, 30% will respond to placebo and 50% will respond to antidepressant drug

---

[74]Recommendations from TA59 were incorporated into the previous depression guideline according to NICE protocol.

treatment (Anderson *et al.*, 2008). This gives a number needed to treat (NNT) of three for antidepressants over waitlist control and five for antidepressants over placebo. It should be noted, however, that response in clinical trials is generally defined as a 50% reduction in depression rating scale scores, a somewhat arbitrary dichotomy, and that change, measured using continuous scales, tends to show a relatively smaller mean difference between active treatment and placebo.

Systematic reviews using meta-analysis suggest that antidepressant drugs, when considered individually or by class, are more effective than placebo in the treatment of major depression, and are generally equally effective (Cochrane Database of Systematic Reviews; Gartlehner *et al.*, 2008; NICE, 2004a). SSRIs are considerably safer in overdose than TCAs, are generally better tolerated than antidepressants from other classes and most are available as generic preparations. An SSRI was recommended as first-line pharmacological treatment of moderate to severe depression in the previous guideline, and SSRIs are now the most commonly prescribed group of antidepressants in the UK (see also Section 9.2).

There are concerns over side effects following short- and long-term treatment, which limit adherence to treatment with antidepressants. Most side effects of antidepressants are dose related. SSRIs as a class are associated with headache and gastrointestinal symptoms, and a relative higher propensity than other antidepressants to cause sexual dysfunction, hyponatraemia and gastrointestinal bleeds. TCAs tend to be associated with a high burden of anticholinergic side effects and a higher propensity than other antidepressants to cause adverse cardiovascular effects including hypotension, tachycardia and corrected QT interval (QTc) prolongation. Overall, venlafaxine is better tolerated than TCAs, but not as well tolerated as SSRIs. Some common antidepressant side effects, such as nausea, tend to resolve within the first week of treatment whereas others, such as anticholinergic effects and, in some patients, sexual dysfunction, tend to persist.

Antidepressant treatment has been associated with an increased risk of suicidal thoughts and acts, particularly in adolescents and young adults, leading to the recommendation that patients should be warned of this potential adverse effect during the early weeks of treatment and know how to seek help if required. All antidepressants have been implicated, as have drugs with a similar pharmacology that are used for an indication other than depression (for example, atomoxetine). Although the relative risk of developing suicidal thoughts and acts may be elevated above placebo rates in some patient groups, the absolute risk remains very small. Overall, the most effective way to prevent suicidal thoughts and acts is to treat depression.

It has been proposed that early non-persistent improvement in depressive symptoms may be due to a placebo response (Quitkin *et al.*, 1987), but recent evidence has emphasised that improvement starts immediately on commencing treatment and early improvement is a strong predictor of eventual response which is unlikely if no improvement is evident after 4 weeks of treatment (Posternak & Zimmerman, 2005; Anderson *et al.*, 2008). At the present time there are a variety of strategies for improving efficacy following initial non-response that are supported by existing evidence-based guidelines or systematic reviews. These include dose escalation, switching to another antidepressant, and combining the antidepressant with another antidepressant, a second drug such as lithium, a second generation antipsychotic or thyroid hormones. Adjunctive use of psychological therapies, particularly CBT, is also supported by an evidence base. Systematic assessment of the evidence for these strategies is a major feature of this guideline update.

An untreated depressive episode typically lasts about 6 months (Angst & Preisig, 1995; Solomon *et al.*, 1997) and, in view of the high recurrence rate if antidepressant medication is stopped immediately after response, it is currently recommended that antidepressant drug treatment is continued for a minimum of 6 months after remission of major depression (12 months in older adults), and longer if there are factors that increase the risk of relapse.

It is recommended that the same dose of antidepressant is used in this continuation phase. It is also recommended that patients with recurrent major depression should go on to receive maintenance antidepressant drug treatment (NICE, 2004a). There is good evidence that patients with residual symptoms are at increasing risk of relapse of major depression and the current practice is to continue treatment for longer in those patients. The recurrence rate is lower when treatment is maintained with the effective acute treatment dose compared with a reduction to half the dose.

All antidepressant drugs can cause discontinuation symptoms with short half-life drugs being most problematic in this respect (see Chapter 11, Section 11.8).

9.2 DOSE AND DURATION OF ANTIDEPRESSANT TREATMENT: EVIDENCE FROM CLINICAL PRACTICE

9.2.1 Prevalence of antidepressant prescribing

In 1992, the Royal College of Psychiatrists launched the 'Defeat Depression' campaign to raise public awareness of depression and improve treatment (Vize & Priest, 1993). During the launch year, 9.9 million prescriptions for antidepressants were dispensed by community pharmacists in England at a total cost of £18.1 million. However, an epidemiological study conducted in 1995 found that treatment remained suboptimal (Lepine *et al.*, 1997). Only a third of people with major depression in the UK received a prescription usually, but not always, for an antidepressant drug.

The number of prescriptions for antidepressants dispensed by community pharmacies in England has risen steadily over the last 15 years. In the 3 months to June 2008, over 4.5 million prescriptions were dispensed for SSRIs (almost half of which were for citalopram), over 2.5 million for tricyclic and related antidepressants (over half of which were for amitriptyline), and over 1 million for other antidepressants (the vast majority of which were for venlafaxine or mirtazapine). Although the number of prescriptions written continues to increase, costs are falling due to the availability of an increasing number of antidepressants as generic preparations. Details of the number of antidepressant prescriptions dispensed in primary care, the costs of individual drugs and prescribing trends can be found on the NHS Business Authority website (www.nhsbsa.nhs.uk).

9.2.2 Dose

Studies of prescribing practice have generally taken 125 mg and above of TCAs (except lofepramine) and licensed doses of SSRIs to be 'an effective dose', and compared prescribing in practice with this ideal. It is generally accepted that response to TCAs is partially dose-related, but no such effect has been demonstrated for SSRIs. SSRIs are consistently found to be prescribed 'at an effective dose' in a much greater proportion of cases than TCAs. For example, a UK prescribing study collecting data from over 750,000 patient records found that if lofepramine was excluded the mean doses prescribed for individual TCAs fell between 58 mg and 80 mg. Only 13.1% of TCA prescriptions were for 'an effective dose' compared with 99.9% of prescriptions for SSRIs (Donoghue *et al.*, 1996). A further UK study that followed prescribing for 20,195 GP patients found that at least 72% of those prescribed TCAs never received 'an effective dose' compared with 8% of those prescribed SSRIs (MacDonald *et al.*, 1996). The prescribing of TCAs in this way is known to be pervasive across different countries and over time (Donoghue, 2000; Donoghue & Hylan, 2001).

In the previous guideline, a systematic review of the efficacy and tolerability of low versus high doses of TCAs was undertaken; no difference was found with respect to remission data, while there was insufficient evidence to determine if there was a difference with respect to response or continuous endpoint data.

9.2.3 Duration

In a UK study of 16,204 patients who were prescribed TCAs or SSRIs by their GP, 33% of those prescribed an SSRI completed 'an adequate period of treatment' compared with 6% of those prescribed a TCA (2.8% if lofepramine was excluded) (Dunn *et al.*, 1999). 'An adequate period of treatment' was defined by the authors as: prescriptions covering at least 120 days' treatment within the first 6 months after diagnosis. A more recent, naturalistic, randomised UK study also found that there was a higher rate of switching to another antidepressant with TCAs (including lofepramine) than SSRIs (Peveler *et al.*, 2005).

There is some evidence that the mean figure quoted for SSRIs may mask important differences between drugs: Donoghue (2000) found that, in a GP population of 6,150 patients who were prescribed SSRIs, 27% of patients taking fluoxetine were still receiving prescriptions after 120 days compared with 23% of patients taking paroxetine and 13.5% of patients taking sertraline. Of course, prescribing patterns cannot be directly linked with outcome in studies of this type.

An RCT conducted in the US randomised 536 adults to receive desipramine, imipramine or fluoxetine (Simon *et al.*, 1996). Sixty percent of the patients taking fluoxetine completed 6 months of treatment compared with less than 40% of the patients taking TCAs. Those who discontinued one antidepressant were offered another. There were no differences in overall completers or response rates at endpoint, suggesting that initial drug choice did not affect outcome. However, outside of clinical trials, patients may not return to their GP to have their treatment changed and outcome may be less positive. For example, a Swedish study of 949 patients found that 35% only ever received one prescription irrespective of whether it was for a TCA or an SSRI (Isacsson *et al.*, 1999); after 6 months, 42% of patients taking an SSRI were still receiving prescriptions compared with 27% of patients taking a TCA. There is some evidence from this study that the relapse rate may have been higher in the TCA group: 28% of TCA-treated patients received a subsequent prescription for an antidepressant after a 9-month treatment-free gap compared with 10% of patients taking an SSRI.

9.3   LIMITATIONS OF THE LITERATURE: PROBLEMS WITH RANDOMISED CONTROLLED TRIALS IN PHARMACOLOGY

In RCTs, patients are assigned randomly to different treatment arms to reduce bias and therefore to reduce systematic differences in the allocation of patients that might affect the results. Primary efficacy is usually based on a placebo-controlled RCT in which one of the treatment arms is a 'placebo' treatment. A placebo is an inert or innocuous substance that began to be used increasingly in control conditions in clinical trials during the 1950s, although at that time it often contained an active ingredient. The response of patients to the inert substances now used should not be equated with the untreated course of the disorder because patients taking placebo have regular meetings with their doctor and receive supportive help. In some trials the participants are allowed to contact the therapist at any time to report problems. In short, they receive everything except the pharmacological help from the tablet in the 'active drug' arm of the trial. This constitutes a treatment in itself and almost 30% of patients assigned to placebo respond within 6 weeks (Walsh *et al.*, 2002). This response can include spontanous improvement, which is a function of the duration and severity of the disorder; with shorter and milder depression, the chance of improvement is greater. The issue of placebo response is discussed further in section 9.6. Unfortunately, there is a tendency for investigators to recruit patients with less severe depression to RCTs and these are more likely to recover spontaneously (Khan *et al.*, 2002). High spontaneous improvement rates are a major cause of 'failed trials' where active treatment is not statistically significantly more effective than placebo.

Conversely, patients with more severe depression are less likely to be thought suitable for RCTs (despite being more likely to show a true drug effect [Angst, 1993; Khan *et al.*, 2002]) because clinicians are reluctant to allow suicidal patients, or patients with severe degrees of depressive phenomena, to run the risk of being randomised to an inactive treatment.

Next, of those enrolled into an RCT, typically 20 to 35% fail to complete the study, either because they drop out of treatment themselves, or they are withdrawn from the RCT by the anxious clinician (for example, Stassen *et al.*, 1993). Worse still, results are often presented only for 'completers' rather than for the full 'intention-to-treat' sample.

Finally, participants may not be representative of patients seen in clinical practice because they are recruited by newspaper advertisement and paid for their participation in the study after completing a screening questionnaire (Greist *et al.*, 2002; Thase, 2002). In the recent naturalistic STAR*D study, only 22% of depressed patients met typical criteria for a phase III clinical trial, and they had higher response and remission rates than the rest (Wisniewski *et al.*, 2009).

The inclusion of individuals likely to improve, whatever they are given, as well as those motivated to receive free medication, taken together with the smaller likelihood of severely depressed patients being included, will all reduce the size of the specific drug effect. A further consideration is that the method of analysis and confining the study to 'completers' may increase apparent drug effects, while intention-to-treat analysis, in which all participants are included using their last recorded value or assuming they have not improved, introduces potential bias the other way.

In addition to the factors related to the type of patient recruited into RCTs, there are measurement-related errors and biases. The pressure to recruit patients may lead to 'rating scale inflation', which not only leads to patients with milder degrees of depression being studied but also may contribute to the drop in scores after the treatment has started when severity may be more realistically assessed. Although raters may be blinded to the treatment arm to which a patient is allocated, they are not blind to the phase of study, so that patient and rater expectations of improvement may confound assessments. The emergence of drug-specific side effects can also 'unblind' a study. In addition, there is the phenomenon of 'regression to the mean', which means that subsequent ratings from an extreme value (such as high depression score) will tend to drop simply by virtue of being remeasured. These all add 'noise' to the assessment leading to increased variability and make it difficult to assess the 'true' size of any treatment effect.

Most studies of the effects of drugs are sponsored by the drug industry and these have been shown to be more than four times as likely to demonstrate positive effects of the sponsor's drug as independent studies (Lexchin *et al.*, 2003). Finally, the tendency of journal editors to publish only studies with positive results (Kirsch & Scoboria, 2001; Melander *et al.*, 2003), and the fact that the same patients may appear in several publications (op. cit.), introduces a severe bias in the other direction.

Despite the limitations of RCTs described above, there are few alternatives to using these data because better ways of assessing efficacy have not been developed. Therefore the bulk of the guideline recommendations are based on RCT evidence. However, the GDG has been careful to consider their application to routine practice.

9.4 STUDIES CONSIDERED FOR REVIEW – ADDITIONAL INCLUSION CRITERIA

In addition to the criteria established for the inclusion of trials for the guideline update as a whole, the following specific criteria relating to RCTs of pharmacological treatments were established by the pharmacology topic group.

9.4.1   Diagnosis

Trials where some participants had a primary diagnosis of bipolar disorder were included provided at least 80% had a primary diagnosis of major depressive disorder and no more than 15% had a primary diagnosis of bipolar disorder. These figures resulted from discussion, expert opinion and involvement with user groups. The GDG considered that these trials would still have adequate validity for determining efficacy in depression. In some situations where trial data were limited a greater proportion of patients with bipolar disorder were permitted but in this case the grade of evidence was reduced and these studies are identified.

Trials where some participants had a primary diagnosis of dysthymia were included provided at least 80% of trial participants had a primary diagnosis of major depressive disorder, and no more than 20% had a primary diagnosis of dysthymia. Trials not meeting these criteria are considered in the chapter on subthreshold depressive symptoms (Chapter 13).

Trials where participants had a diagnosis of atypical depression or depression with a seasonal pattern/seasonal affective disorder (SAD) were included provided all had a primary diagnosis of major depressive disorder.

Studies were included provided data from the HRSD and MADRS could be extracted for the following outcomes:

- the number of participants who remitted[75] (achieved below the equivalent 17-item HRSD score of eight)
- the number of participants who responded[76] (achieved at least a 50% reduction in scores)
- mean endpoint or change scores in the rating scales.

9.4.2   Dose

There is a lack of clear evidence that doses of tricyclics at or below 100 mg are less effective than doses above (Blashki *et al.*, 1971; Thompson & Thompson, 1989; Bollini *et al.*, 1999; Furukawa *et al.*, 2002a), although there might be benefit in more severely ill patients (Ramana *et al.*, 1999). Nevertheless, in order to provide fair comparisons, studies were included provided there was clear evidence that at least 75% of patients received the standard dose or the mean dose used was at least 105% of the standard dose. The standard dose was either that stated by Bollini and colleagues (1999) or by the BNF (2009) for drugs not included in Bollini and colleagues (1999).

---

[75]For statistical reasons, relative risks for this outcome are framed in terms of the number of participants not remitting.

[76]For statistical reasons, relative risks for this outcome are framed in terms of the number of participants not responding.

9.5 ISSUES AND TOPICS COVERED BY THIS REVIEW

In view of the vast numbers of studies performed investigating pharmacological responses in depression and the limited time available, the pharmacology topic group had to decide which aspects of drug treatment were most important to clinicians and patients. Therefore the chapters on pharmacological interventions do not constitute a comprehensive review of all psychopharmacological studies performed in all aspects of the treatment of depression.

9.5.1 Severity

A key issue is whether severity of illness can guide the use of antidepressant medication. Unfortunately there is little data to help with this point. Although most studies report mean baseline HRSD or MADRS, this can be taken only as a guide to baseline severity because of heterogeneous samples with wide standard deviations as well as the fact that results are not presented in a way that allows differential response to be identified.

9.5.2 Setting

Where appropriate, studies were categorised by setting:
- primary care – where this was specifically stated in the study
- outpatients/secondary care – where this was specifically stated in the study
- inpatients – where at least 75% of the patients were initially treated as inpatients.
  This is likely to provide some bearing on the issue of setting and type of depression, although it is not clear how well 'setting' maps onto severity. A further problem is that because of differences among healthcare systems across the world, the nature of the patients in these different groups varies. Thus considerable uncertainty must be associated with conclusions drawn using these categories.

9.5.3 Issues addressed

In broad terms, the GDG tried to address the issue of the comparative efficacy, acceptability and tolerability of the antidepressants most commonly prescribed in the UK, together with specific pharmacological strategies for dealing with depression that has inadequately responded to treatment, with depression with atypical features and with depression with psychotic symptoms. Within each review, where the data allowed, the GDG looked at the effect on outcomes of severity, setting and age. In addition, the GDG looked at some of the issues regarding so-called continuation and maintenance therapy, the cardiac safety of antidepressants, dosage, and issues regarding suicidality and completed suicide with antidepressants. Although the number of trial participants leaving treatment early was used as a measure of the tolerability of drugs reviewed, this guideline cannot be seen as a comprehensive review of the issue of the safety, pharmacology, pharmokinetics and pharmaceutical advice regarding these drugs. Readers are referred to conventional texts, particularly those regarding issues of dosage schedules, acceptability and tolerability for individual patients and drug interactions.

9.5.4   Topics covered

Where there was lack of substantial new evidence, some analyses and conclusions were not updated from the previous guideline (NCCMH, 2004), although their discussion was updated where factual or stylistic adjustments were required. These are indicated with asterisks (**). Agomelatine was not licensed at the time of data analysis and is not included in this guideline. The following topics are covered:

In the rest of this chapter:

- SSRIs versus placebo** (Sections 9.6 and 9.7)
- TCAs versus placebo (Section 9.8).

Chapter 10: Pharmacological interventions

Use of individual drugs in the treatment of depression (Section 10.1):
- TCAs: amitriptyline** and overview of TCA data** (Section 10.3)
- Selective serotonin reuptake inhibitors (except escitalopram): citalopram**, fluoxetine**, fluvoxamine**, paroxetine** and sertraline** (Section 10.4)
- Escitalopram (Section 10.5)
- Monoamine oxidase inhibitors: moclobemide**, phenelzine** (Section 10.7)
- 'Third-generation' drugs: duloxetine, mirtazapine**, reboxetine** and venlafaxine** (Section 10.8)
- St John's wort** (Section 10.9).

Chapter 11: Factors influencing choice of antidepressants

- The pharmacological management of depression in older adults** (Section 11.2)
- The effect of sex on antidepressant choice (Section 11.3)
- The pharmacological management of depression with psychotic symptoms** (Section 11.4)
- The pharmacological management of atypical depression (Section 11.5)**
- The physical and pharmacological management of depression with a seasonal pattern (Section 11.6)
- Dosage issues for tricyclic antidepressants** (Section 11.7)
- Antidepressant discontinuation symptoms** partly updated (Section 11.8)
- The cardiotoxicity of antidepressants (Section 11.9)
- Depression, suicide and antidepressants** (Section 11.10).

Chapter 12: The pharmacological and physical management of depression that has not adequately responded to treatment, and relapse prevention:

- Increasing the dose (Section 12.3.1)
- Switching to another antidepressant (Section 12.3.2)
- Combining an antidepressant with another antidepressant (Section 12.3.3)
- Augmentation an antidepressant with a different drug, including:
  - antipsychotics (Section 12.3.4)
  - lithium (Section 12.3.5)
  - anticonvulsants** (lamotrigine, carbamazepine or valproate) (Section 12.3.6)
  - pindolol** (Section 12.3.7)
  - triiodothyronine (T3)** (Section 12.3.8)
  - benzodiazepines** (Section 12.3.9)
  - buspirone** (Section 12.3.10)
  - atomoxetine (Section 12.3.11)
- ECT (Section 12.4)
- TMS and VNS (Section 12.5)
- Relapse prevention** partly updated (Section 12.6).

In addition, evidence for the pharmacological treatment of symptoms of depression that do not meet threshold for major depressive disorder is considered in Chapter 13.

9.6   PLACEBO-CONTROLLED RANDOMISED CONTROLLED TRIALS OF ANTIDEPRESSANTS

As mentioned above, the response to placebo in an RCT consists of three main components: (1) spontaneous improvement, (2) measurement errors and biases, and (3) the true 'placebo response', which is non-pharmacological benefit due to taking part in a trial. A large part of the placebo response is thought to be due to expectation combined with regular review and monitoring. A recent meta-analysis showed that studies in which patients know they may get a placebo tablet have lower response rates than when they know they will only get active treatments (Sneed *et al.*, 2008). This means that the chance of improvement in response to antidepressants in clinical practice may not be the same as those in clinical trials involving placebo. Another systematic review provides suggestive evidence that the chance of responding to treatment with placebo is higher if monitoring is carried out more frequently in the first few weeks of treatment (Posternak & Zimmerman, 2007). Taking these factors together it is clear that the exact design of any trial will influence the non-specific benefit that participants will obtain and that the placebo response is not a minor distraction but an integral part of treatment not only in RCTs but also in clinical practice.

In recent years there has been an increasing response to placebo, so that the extent of the placebo response has been shown to correlate with the year of publication in studies in depression (r = +0.43) (Walsh *et al.*, 2002). There is a similar but less robust association between the extent of the response to active medication and the year of publication ($r = +0.26$) (op. cit.). This may well indicate an increasing tendency for RCTs to be carried out on people with milder, less chronic disorders that have a greater chance of spontaneously improving or having a placebo response.

An important point is that there is some evidence that the placebo response is greatest with mild depression, and the drug–placebo difference becomes greater with increasing degrees of severity of depression (Angst, 1993; Khan *et al.*, 2002; Kirsch *et al.*, 2008). This effect cannot be demonstrated in the meta-analyses carried out for the guideline update because the published studies do not quote data for individual patients, only for the entire group. Thus, there is considerable overlap between the distributions of HRSD scores between studies with different mean severities of depression at baseline, and between inpatient and outpatient studies, so that any effect of severity is diluted in group analyses.

The placebo response may also be short-lived, with more patients on placebo relapsing compared with those on antidepressants (Ross *et al.*, 2002). Longer trials are required to be able to fully elucidate the contributions of placebo and the treatment to clinical response. Dago and Quitkin (1995) suggest that greater placebo response is more likely when the presenting episode occurs within the context of a psychosocial stressor.

In three meta-analyses (Kirsch & Sapirstein, 1998; Kirsch *et al.*, 2002a; Kirsch *et al.*, 2008), it has been argued that up to 80% of the antidepressant effect may be duplicated by placebo–that is, that 80% of the antidepressant effect is placebo response. Although the earlier meta-analysis was criticised because it included only a limited number of published trials, the later work analysed all data submitted to the US Food and Drug Administration (FDA) for the licensing of new antidepressants, including the SSRIs and venlafaxine, although it is not clear how many of the trials involved have subsequently been published.

Many commentators attribute this finding to placebo effects as discussed above. There is also the problem of 'breaking the blind' as a result of the side effects of antidepressants (Rabkin *et al.*, 1986, in Kirsch *et al.*, 2002b) leading to possible bias in placebo-controlled clinical trials. One way round this problem is to use an active placebo. A meta-analysis of trials using active placebo is more effective than a meta-analysic of trials using only inactive placebos. However, there are few trials of active placebo using modern diagnostic criteria and widely accepted ratings (Moncrieff *et al.*, 2001).

The increasing rate of response to placebo and to a lesser extent to antidepressants (Walsh *et al.*, 2002) means that many trials are underpowered because with placebo response rates above 40%, an active drug effect becomes harder to detect (Thase, 2002). Other methodological problems are highlighted by inter-site differences found in many multi-site trials, probably resulting from subtly different procedures being adopted by different researchers (Schneider & Small, 2002).

The increase in the drug/placebo difference with severity (Elkin *et al.*, 1989; Angst, 1993; Khan *et al.*, 2002) appears due to the decreasing efficacy of placebo with increasing severity of depression, rather than increasing efficacy of the antidepressant drug *per se* (Kirsch *et al.*, 2008). The published data did not allow the GDG to address the question of efficacy related to severity systematically since most RCTs merely give mean depression scores (with standard deviations) of large groups of patients, so that there is very considerable overlap between baseline depression scores of patients in different studies. Therefore, it was only possible to address important questions relating to the effects of severity, age and gender with relatively weak information about patient characteristics. Nonetheless, the GDG's findings were generally in favour of greater drug/placebo differences with increasing severity (see Section 9.7). It should also be borne in mind that there are non-mood-related benefits of prescribing antidepressants, for example in helping patients to sleep better and in dealing with anxiety-related symptoms. Improving these factors may help patients to cope with their daily lives thereby contributing to a reduction in symptoms of depression.

9.7 SELECTIVE SEROTONIN REUPTAKE INHIBITORS VERSUS PLACEBO

The following sections on SSRIs versus placebo marked by asterisks (**_**) are from the previous guideline and have not been updated except for style and minor clarification.

9.7.1 Introduction

The analysis of SSRIs as a class against placebo was not updated for this guideline although evidence for the most recently marketed SSRI, escitalopram, is considered separately in Section 10.5. See Appendix 11 for a discussion of the severity categories used in the analyses in the previous guideline (in brief, the categories shift down so that moderate becomes mild, severe becomes moderate and very severe becomes severe).

9.7.2 Studies considered[77,78]

**One hundred and three studies were found in a search of electronic databases with 48[79] being included and 55 being excluded by the GDG.

---

[77]Details of standard search strings used in all searches are in Appendix 8. Information about each study along with an assessment of methodological quality is in Appendix 17c, which also contains a list of excluded studies with reasons for exclusions.

[78]Here and elsewhere in the guideline, each study considered for review is referred to by a 'study ID' made up of first author and publication date (unless a study is in press or only submitted for publication, when first author only is used). Study IDs in title case refer to studies included in the previous guideline and study IDs in capital letters refer to studies found and included in this guideline update. References for studies from the previous guideline are in Appendix 18 and references for studies for the update are in Appendix 17c.

[79]This figure includes a multicentre trial (Kasper95) as well as two of its constituent trials published independently (Dominguez1985, Lapierre1987) because 'number of participants leaving the study early for any reason' was not extractable from Kasper95. See the SSRIs versus placebo study charactertics table in Appendix 17c.

Six studies were of citalopram (Burke02, Feighner99, Mendels1999, Mont'mery01, Mont'mery92A, Stahl00); 17 of fluoxetine (Andreoli2002, Byerley88, Cohn1985, Coleman01, Dunlop1990, Feighner89a, McGrath00, O'Flynn1991, Rickels1986, Rudolph99, Sil'stne99, Sramek95, Stark85, Thakore1995, Valducci1992, Wernicke-1987, Wernicke1988); 12 of fluvoxamine (Claghorn1996, Conti1988, Dominguez85, Fabre1996, Feighner1989, Itil1983, Kasper95, Lapierre1987, Lydiard1989, Norton1984, Roth90, Walczak1996); eight of paroxetine (Claghorn92a, Edwards93, Feighner92, Hackett96, Miller1989, Rickels1989, Rickels1992, Smith1992) and five of sertraline (Coleman1999, Croft1999, Fabre95, Ravindram1995, Reimherr90). These provided data from up to 7,460 trial participants.

All included studies were published between 1983 and 2003, and were between 4 and 24 weeks' long (mean = 6.75 weeks), with 16 trials of 8 weeks or longer. Three studies were of inpatients, 31 of outpatients, one in primary care and 13 either mixed or unspecified. In no study were more than 80% of study participants aged 65 years or over. It was possible to determine baseline severity in 19 studies, with four being classified as moderate, six as severe and nine as very severe.

Visual inspection of funnel plots of the meta-analyses of the above studies indicated the possibility of publication bias. It was planned to combine these data with the FDA data reported by Kirsch and colleagues (2002a). However, it was not possible to determine which of the FDA data had been subsequently published.

Since it is possible that a placebo response is only short-lived, a sub-analysis of studies which lasted 8 weeks or longer was undertaken.

9.7.3   Clinical evidence statements[80]

Effect of treatment on efficacy outcomes

There is strong evidence suggesting that there is a clinically important difference favouring SSRIs over placebo on increasing the likelihood of patients achieving a 50% reduction in symptoms of depression as measured by the HRSD (K = 17[81]; N = 3143; RR = 0.73; 95% CI, 0.69 to 0.78).

In moderate[82] depression there is some evidence suggesting that there is a clinically important difference favouring SSRIs over placebo on increasing the likelihood of patients achieving a 50% reduction in symptoms of depression as measured by the HRSD (K = 3[83]; N = 729; RR = 0.75; 95% CI, 0.65 to 0.87).

In severe depression there is strong evidence suggesting that there is a clinically important difference favouring SSRIs over placebo on increasing the likelihood of

---

[80]The forest plots can be found in Appendix 19c.

[81]Fifteen studies were excluded from all efficacy outcomes because >50% left treatment early (Claghorn1996, Cohn1985, Conti1988, Dominguez85, Edwards93, Fabre95, Fabre1996, Feighner1989, Feighner92, Itil1983, Lapierre1987, Smith1992, Stahl00, Stark85, Walzak1996).

[82]Severity categories based on APA (2000a) – see previous guideline Appendix 13.

[83]Studies were excluded from sub-analyses of severity if mean baseline scores were not available.

patients achieving a 50% reduction in symptoms of depression as measured by the HRSD (K = 5; N = 619; RR = 0.63; 95% CI, 0.54 to 0.73).

In very severe depression there is strong evidence suggesting that there is a clinically important difference favouring SSRIs over placebo on increasing the likelihood of patients achieving a 50% reduction in symptoms of depression as measured by the HRSD (K = 6; N = 866; RR = 0.72; 95% CI, 0.65 to 0.8).

There is insufficient evidence to determine whether there is a clinically important difference between SSRIs over placebo on increasing the likelihood of achieving remission as measured by the HRSD (K = 3; N = 468; Random effects RR = 0.8; 95% CI, 0.61 to 1.06).

There is evidence suggesting that there is a statistically significant difference favouring SSRIs over placebo on reducing symptoms of depression as measured by the HRSD, but the size of this difference is unlikely to be of clinical importance (K = 16; N = 2223; Random effects SMD = −0.34; 95% CI, −0.47 to –0.22).

In moderate depression there is evidence suggesting that there is a statistically important difference favouring SSRIs over placebo on reducing symptoms of depression as measured by the HRSD, but the size of this difference is unlikely to be of clinical importance (K = 2; N = 386; SMD = −0.28; 95% CI, −0.48 to −0.08).

In severe depression there is some evidence suggesting that there is a clinically important difference favouring SSRIs over placebo on reducing symptoms of depression as measured by the HRSD (K = 4; N = 344; SMD = −0.61; 95% CI, −0.83 to −0.4).

In very severe depression there is evidence suggesting that there is a statistically significant difference favouring SSRIs over placebo on reducing symptoms of depression as measured by the HRSD, but the size of this difference is unlikely to be of clinical importance (K = 5; N = 726; SMD = −0.39; 95% CI, −0.54 to −0.24).

Acceptability and tolerability of treatment

There is evidence suggesting that there is a statistically significant difference favouring placebo over SSRIs on reducing the likelihood of leaving treatment early, but the size of this difference is unlikely to be of clinical importance (K = 39[84]; N = 7274; RR = 0.94; 95% CI, 0.88 to 0.99).

There is strong evidence suggesting that there is a clinically important difference favouring placebo over SSRIs on reducing the likelihood of leaving treatment early due to side effects (K = 39; N = 7460; RR = 2.45; 95% CI, 2.08 to 2.89).

There is some evidence suggesting that there is a clinically important difference favouring placebo over SSRIs on reducing the likelihood of patients reporting side effects (K = 11; N = 2290; RR = 1.19; 95% CI, 1.13 to 1.25).

Sub-analysis of trials lasting 8 weeks or longer

To assess whether the placebo effect was short-lived, trials lasting 8 weeks or longer were analysed separately.

---

[84]One study (Cohn1985) was removed from the meta-analysis to remove heterogeneity from the dataset.

Effect of treatment on efficacy outcomes in trials lasting 8 weeks or longer
In trials lasting 8 weeks or longer, there is strong evidence suggesting that there is a clinically important difference favouring SSRIs over placebo on increasing the likelihood of achieving a 50% reduction in symptoms of depression as measured by the HRSD (K = 8; N = 1764; RR = 0.72; 95% CI, 0.66 to 0.79).

In moderate depression in trials lasting 8 weeks or longer, there is some evidence suggesting that there is a clinically important difference favouring SSRIs over placebo on increasing the likelihood of achieving a 50% reduction in symptoms of depression as measured by the HRSD (K= 3; N = 729; RR = 0.75; 95% CI, 0.65 to 0.87).

In severe depression in trials lasting 8 weeks or longer, there is strong evidence suggesting that there is a clinically important difference favouring SSRIs over placebo on increasing the likelihood of achieving a 50% reduction in symptoms of depression as measured by the HRSD (K = 3; N = 535; RR = 0.63; 95% CI, 0.53 to 0.74).

In very severe depression in trials lasting 8 weeks or longer, there is some evidence suggesting that there is a clinically important difference favouring SSRIs over placebo on increasing the likelihood of achieving a 50% reduction in symptoms of depression as measured by the HRSD (K = 1; N = 299; RR = 0.72; 95% CI, 0.59 to 0.88).

In trials lasting 8 weeks or longer, there is insufficient evidence to determine whether there is a clinically important difference between SSRIs and placebo on increasing the likelihood of achieving remission as measured by the HRSD (K = 2; N = 456; RR = 0.85; 95% CI, 0.67 to 1.07).

In trials lasting 8 weeks or longer, there is evidence suggesting that there is a statistically significant difference favouring SSRIs over placebo on reducing symptoms of depression as measured by the HRSD but the size of this difference is unlikely to be of clinical importance (K = 7; N = 1369; Random effects SMD = −0.28; 95% CI, −0.44 to −0.11).

In moderate depression in trials lasting 8 weeks or longer, there is evidence suggesting that there is a statistically significant difference favouring SSRIs over placebo on reducing symptoms of depression as measured by the HRSD, but the size of this difference is unlikely to be of clinical importance (K = 2; N = 386; SMD = −0.28; 95% CI, −0.48 to −0.08).

In severe depression in trials lasting 8 weeks or longer, there is some evidence suggesting that there is a clinically important difference favouring SSRIs over placebo on reducing symptoms of depression as measured by the HRSD (K = 1; N = 237; SMD = −0.53; 95% CI, −0.79 to −0.27).

In very severe depression in trials lasting 8 weeks or longer, there is evidence suggesting that there is a statistically significant difference favouring SSRIs over placebo on reducing symptoms of depression as measured by the HRSD, but the size of this difference is unlikely to be of clinical importance (K = 1; N = 283; SMD = −0.43; 95% CI, −0.67 to −0.2).

Acceptability and tolerability of treatment in trials lasting 8 weeks or longer
In trials lasting 8 weeks or longer, there is evidence suggesting that there is no clinically important difference between SSRIs and placebo on reducing the likelihood of

leaving treatment early (K = 13; N = 3,069; Random effects RR =0.95; 95% CI, 0.83 to 1.09).

In trials lasting 8 weeks or longer, there is strong evidence suggesting that there is a clinically important difference favouring placebo over SSRIs on reducing the likelihood of leaving treatment early due to side effects (K = 13; N = 3069; Random effects RR = 1.93; 95% CI, 1.23 to 3.03).

In trials lasting 8 weeks or longer, there is evidence suggesting that there is a statistically significant difference favouring placebo over SSRIs on reducing the likelihood of patients reporting side effects, but the size of this difference is unlikely to be of clinical importance (K = 7; N = 1378; RR = 1.09; 95% CI, 1.03 to 1.16).

9.7.4   Clinical summary

There is strong evidence that SSRIs have greater efficacy than placebo on achieving a 50% reduction in depression scores in moderate and severe major depression[85]. There is some evidence for a similar effect in mild depression[86]. The effect was similar in longer trials. These results should be treated with caution because of publication bias (that is, studies with statistically significant findings are more likely to be published than those with non-significant findings).

There is insufficient evidence on the effect on remission because of heterogeneity in the meta-analysis, but the trend is towards a small effect size. There appears to be no difference between SSRIs and placebo on mean endpoint or change scores.

SSRIs produced more side effects than placebo, with more people leaving treatment early because of adverse events. This was also the case in trials lasting 8 weeks or longer.**

9.8   TRICYCLIC ANTIDEPRESSANTS VERSUS PLACEBO

9.8.1   Introduction

In the previous guideline, a review of the efficacy and tolerability of TCAs compared with placebo was not carried out, but for the guideline update these analyses were undertaken. This review informs the assessment of the relative efficacy and tolerability of different classes of antidepressants and, therefore, their utility in everyday clinical practice.

---

[85]The wording has been updated here. The previous guideline used the terms 'severe and very severe depression'.

[86]The wording has been updated here. The previous guideline used the term 'moderate depression'.

Table 64: Databases searched and inclusion/exclusion criteria for clinical effectiveness of pharmacological treatments

Electronic databases	MEDLINE, EMBASE, PsycINFO, CINAHL
Date searched	Database inception to January 2008
Update searches	July 2008, January 2009
Study design	RCT
Population	People with a diagnosis of depression according to DSM, ICD or similar criteria
Treatments	Any TCA with UK marketing authority where a comparison with placebo was available

9.8.2 Databases searched and the inclusion/exclusion criteria

A systematic search for RCTs comparing any TCA with UK marketing authorisation with placebo was undertaken. Information about the databases searched and the inclusion/exclusion criteria used are presented in Table 64. Details of the search strings used are in Appendix 8.

9.8.3 Studies considered[87]

In total, 108 studies were found that met inclusion criteria. Most were for imipramine (66) and amitriptyline (30). The number of studies is summarised in Table 65, with full details in Appendix 17c, which also includes details of excluded studies.

9.8.4 Clinical evidence

Evidence from the important outcomes and overall quality of evidence are presented in (Table 66 and Table 67). The full evidence profiles and associated forest plots can be found in Appendix 16c and Appendix 19c, respectively. There were no extractable data from studies of lofepramine, and little data for some outcomes from studies of clomipramine, dosulepin and nortriptyline (see Table 66).

---

[87]Study IDs in capital letters refer to studies found and included in this guideline update.

Table 65: Summary of studies for TCAs versus placebo

TCA	Number of studies	Study IDs
Amitriptyline	30	AMSTERDAM2003A, BAKISH1992B, BAKISH1992C, BREMNER1995, CLAGHORN1983, CLAGHORN1983B, FEIGHNER1979, GELENBERG1990, GEORGOTAS1982A, GOLDBERG1980, HICKS1988, HOLLYMAN1988, HORMAZ-ABAL1985, HOSCHL1989, KLIESER1988, LAAKMAN1995, LAPIERRE1991, LYDI-ARD1997, MYNORSWALLIS1995, MYNORSWALLIS1997, REIMHERR1990, RICKELS1982D, RICKELS1985, RICK-ELS1991, ROFFMAN1982, ROWAN1982, SMITH1990, SPRING1992, STASSEN1993, WILCOX1994
Clomipramine	3	LARSEN1989, PECKNOLD1976B, RAMPELLO1991
Dosulepin	4	FERGUSON1994B, ITIL1993, MIND-HAM1991, THOMPSON2001B
Imipramine	66	BARGESCHAAPVELD2002, BEASLEY1991B, BOYER1996A, BYER-LEY1988, CASSANO1986, CASSANO1996, CLAGHORN1996A, COHN1984, COHN1985, COHN1990A, COHN1992, COHN1996, DOMINGUEZ1981, DOMINGUEZ1985, DUNBAR1991, ELKIN1989, ENTSUAH1994, ESCO-BAR1980, FABRE1980, FABRE1992, FABRE1996, FEIGER1996A, FEIGH-NER1980, FEIGHNER1982, FEIGH-NER1983A, FEIGHNER1983B, FEIGHNER1989, FEIGHNER1989A, FEIGHNER1989B, FEIGHNER1989C, FEIGHNER1992B, FEIGHNER1993, FONTAINE1994, GELENBERG1990, GERNER1980B, HAYES1983, ITIL1983A, KASPER1995B, KELLAMS1979, LAIRD1993, LAPIERRE1987, LECRU-BIER1997B, LIPMAN1986, LYDIARD1989,

Continued

Table 65: (*Continued*)

TCA	Number of studies	Study IDs
		MARCH1990, MARKOWITZ1985, MENDELS1986, MERIDETH1983, NANDI1976, NORTON1984, PEDERSEN2002, PESELOW1989, PESELOW1989B, PHILIPP1999, QUITKIN1989, RICKELS1981, RICKELS1982A, RICKELS1987, SCHWEIZER1994, SCHWEIZER1998, SHRIVASTAVA1992, SILVERSTONE1994, SMALL1981, UCHA1990, VERSIANI1990, WAKELIN1986
Lofepramine	0	N/A
Nortriptyline	4	GEORGOTAS1986, KATZ1990, NAIR1995, WHITE1984A
Total	108	

On all measures of efficacy TCAs are more effective than placebo. Results were similar for each individual drug where there were sufficient data. There was little difference between TCAs compared with placebo for leaving treatment early, although effect sizes were less certain for individual drugs with few data (for example, dosulepin and clomipramine). However, participants taking TCAs were more likely to leave treatment early because of side effects and to report side effects than those taking placebo. This finding was similar across individual drugs, apart from clomipramine which only showed a similar result for number of participants reporting side effects. However, there was only a single study.

Table 66: Summary evidence profile for TCAs versus placebo (efficacy data)

	Overall (all studies)	Amitriptyline	Clomipramine	Dosulepin	Imipramine	Nortriptyline
Mean depression scores at endpoint	SMD −0.48 (−0.59 to −0.37)	SMD −0.61 (−0.83 to −0.4)	Not reported	SMD −0.49 (−0.7 to −0.29)	SMD −0.41 (−0.54 to −0.27)	SMD −0.8 (−1.37 to −0.24)
Quality	Moderate	High	–	Moderate	Moderate	Moderate
Number of studies; participants	K = 22; n = 2445	K = 6; n = 348	–	K = 1; n = 386	K = 13; n = 1603	K = 2; n = 108
Forest plot number	Pharm TCAs 01.01	Pharm TCAs 01.01	–	Pharm TCAs 01.01	Pharm TCAs 01.01	Pharm TCAs 01.01
Mean depression change scores at endpoint	SMD −0.35 (−0.53 to −0.18)	SMD −0.5 (−0.67 to −0.34)	Not reported	Not reported	SMD −0.21 (−0.41 to −0.01)	Not reported
Quality	Moderate	High	–	–	High	–
Number of studies; participants	K = 7; n = 1173	K = 3; n = 645	–	–	K = 4; n = 528	–
Forest plot number	Pharm TCAs 01.03	Pharm TCAs 01.03	–	–	Pharm TCAs 01.03	–
Non-response	RR 0.70 (0.66 to 0.75) (43 versus 62.7%)	RR 0.71 (0.65 to 0.78) (43.5 versus 67.3%)	Not reported	RR 0.74 (0.62 to 0.88) (48.5 versus 65.6%)	RR 0.68 (0.62 to 0.76) (41.8 versus 63.4%)	Not reported

Continued

323

Table 66: (*Continued*)

	Overall (all studies)	Amitriptyline	Clomipramine	Dosulepin	Imipramine	Nortriptyline
Quality	High	High	–	High	Moderate	–
Number of studies; participants	K = 34; n = 4717	K = 13; n = 2145	–	K = 1; n = 386	K = 20; n = 2186	–
Forest plot number	Pharm TCAs 01.06	Pharm TCAs 01.06	–	Pharm TCAs 01.06	Pharm TCAs 01.06	–
Non-remission	RR 0.74 (0.65 to 0.84) (63 versus 82.6%)	RR 0.66 (0.44 to 1) (51.9 versus 83.1%)	RR 0.58 (0.34 to 1) (45 versus 77.8%)	RR 1.18 (0.18 to 7.48) (11.8 versus 10%)	RR 0.83 (0.75 to 0.91) (70.4 versus 85.4%)	RR 0.68 (0.52 to 0.88) (62.1 versus 92.3%)
Quality	Moderate	Moderate	Moderate	Moderate	Moderate	Moderate
Number of studies; participants	K = 09; n = 954	K = 3; n = 152	K = 1; n = 38	K = 1; n = 37	K = 2; n = 596	K = 2; n = 131
Forest plot number	Pharm TCAs 01.04	Pharm TCAs 01.04	Pharm TCAs 01.04	Pharm TCAs 01.04	Pharm TCAs 01.04	Pharm TCAs 01.04

Table 67: Summary evidence profile for TCAs versus placebo (leaving treatment early and side-effect data)

	Overall (all studies)	Amitriptyline	Clomipramine	Dosulepin	Imipramine	Nortriptyline
Leaving treatment early	RR 0.99 (0.92 to 1.06) (37 versus 37.6%)	RR 0.93 (0.79 to 1.1) (32.6 versus 34.3%)	RR 0.82 (0.3 to 2.19) (20 versus 25%)	RR 1.09 (0.79 to 1.5) (40.7 versus 39.3%)	RR 1.01 (0.93 to 1.09) (38.9 versus 38.8%)	RR 0.73 (0.27 to 2.03) (35.4 versus 46%)
Quality	Moderate	Moderate	Moderate	Moderate	Moderate	Low
Number of studies; participants	K = 84; n = 9901	K = 23; n = 2805	K = 2; n = 58	K = 3; n = 475	K = 53; n = 6288	K = 3; n = 251
Forest plot number	Pharm TCAs 02.01	Pharm TCAs 02.01	Pharm TCAs 02.01	Pharm TCAs 02.01	Pharm TCAs 02.01	Pharm TCAs 02.01
Leaving treatment early due to side effects	RR 4.02 (3.46 to 4.67) (18.7 versus 4.6%)	RR 4.66 (3.38 to 6.44) (16.7 versus 3.5%)	RR 0.9 (0.14 to 5.74) (10 versus 11.1%)	RR 2.92 (1.47 to 5.8) (14.5 versus 5%)	RR 3.91 (3.27 to 4.67) (20 versus 5.1%)	RR 7.98 (1.51 to 42.09) (18.2 versus 1.5%)
Quality	High	High	Low	High	High	High
Number of studies; participants	K = 65; n = 8173	K = 16; n = 2350	K = 1; n = 38	K = 2; n = 409	K = 44; n = 5245	K = 2; n = 113
Forest plot number	Pharm TCAs 02.02	Pharm TCAs 02.02	Pharm TCAs 02.02	Pharm TCAs 02.02	Pharm TCAs 02.02	Pharm TCAs 02.02
Number reporting side effects	RR 1.4 (1.26 to 1.58) (74.9 versus 56.6%)	RR 1.44 (1.15 to 1.79) (75.7 versus 51%)	RR 1.6 (0.8 to 3.2) (80 versus 50%)	RR 3.02 (1.27 to 7.18) (56 versus 18.5%)	RR 1.41 (1.22 to 1.62) (74.2 versus 57.9%)	RR 1.18 (1.03 to 1.34) (95.5 versus 81%)
Quality	Moderate	Moderate	Low	Moderate	Moderate	High
Number of studies; participants	K = 30; n = 4523	K = 7; n = 932	K = 1; n = 20	K = 1; n = 52	K = 19; n = 3390	K = 2; n = 129
Forest plot number	Pharm TCAs 02.03	Pharm TCAs 02.03	Pharm TCAs 02.03	Pharm TCAs 02.03	Pharm TCAs 02.03	Pharm TCAs 02.03

Figure 8: Meta-regression showing relationship between baseline depression scores and effect sizes calculated from mean endpoint or mean change scores

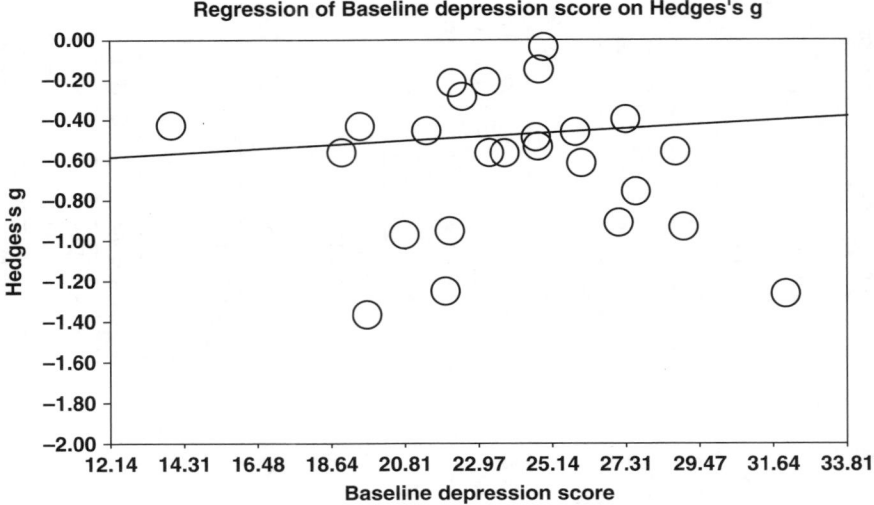

9.8.5   Effect of baseline severity on outcomes

A meta-regression was undertaken using the baseline depression scores as the predictor variable (see Figure 8). This showed no consistent relationship between baseline scores and effect sizes calculated from mean endpoint depression score or change score (regression coefficient 0.01 [p = 0.46]). Sensitivity analyses for mean endpoint scores and mean change scores were performed and a relationship found between mean change scores and baseline scores. However, there were only five studies in the analysis, which is not enough to draw conclusions, and it is not reported here.

9.8.6   Clinical summary

TCAs are more effective than placebo in terms of efficacy, and similar with regard to completing treatment. However, they are more likely to lead to stopping treatment due to side effects and more likely to cause side effects. When compared with the review of SSRIs against placebo, the effect sizes from efficacy outcomes tended to be similar for response outcomes, but larger on mean endpoint data than those seen with SSRIs. This may be explained by the fact that the included studies were mostly older than those in the SSRI review and the differences in effect sizes may be explained by a combination of the timing of the studies and the characteristics of the participants. A review of SSRIs compared with TCAs is in Chapter 10, Section 10.4.2.

The effect sizes for tolerability outcomes were considerably larger than those seen with SSRIs, with those taking TCAs more likely to report side effects or leave treatment early because of side effects.

9.9   FROM EVIDENCE TO RECOMMENDATIONS

There is evidence that antidepressants are more effective than placebo on efficacy outcomes, but that they are less acceptable (based on attrition rates), and produce more side effects. There is some evidence that they are less effective in people with less severe symptoms. The previous guideline recommended that antidepressants should not be prescribed for mild depression based on the poor risk–benefit ratio, but could be considered for persistent symptoms following other interventions or for those with a history of moderate or severe depression. Given the evidence in Chapter 13 reviewed for the guideline update, that antidepressants are not more effective than placebo for recent onset subthreshold depressive symptoms, but may be effective in persistent subthreshold depressive symptoms (dysthymia), this recommendation may be extended to include the TCAs.

9.10   RECOMMENDATION

9.10.1.1   Do not use antidepressants routinely to treat persistent subthreshold depressive symptoms or mild depression because the risk–benefit ratio is poor, but consider them for people with:
- a past history of moderate or severe depression **or**
- initial presentation of subthreshold depressive symptoms that have been present for a long period (typically at least 2 years) **or**
- subthreshold depressive symptoms or mild depression that persist(s) after other interventions[88].

---

[88]This recommendation also appears in Chapter 13.

10 PHARMACOLOGICAL INTERVENTIONS

10.1 INTRODUCTION

This chapter reviews the use of individual drugs in the treatment of depression. The GDG updated its reviews of drugs (including escitalopram and antipsychotic augmentation) where there were substantial new data likely to change the recommendations from the previous guideline, and where studies for newly licensed drugs (duloxetine) were available. It did not update most of the reviews of individual antidepressants undertaken for the previous guideline because most of these were large-scale reviews – a substantial amount of new evidence would have had to have been published to change the overall conclusion that there is little difference in efficacy between individual drugs. This includes SSRIs (apart from escitalopram) and venlafaxine. Although new RCT data on venlafaxine have become available and several meta-analyses (for example, Nemeroff *et al.*, 2008; Weinmann *et al.*, 2008) and systematic reviews (Gartlehner *et al.*, 2008) have been published, these new data do not change the conclusion that if there is an efficacy advantage for venlafaxine over other antidepressants it is small and unlikely to be of clinical importance. Some of the recommendations were revised (NICE, 2007a) in light of the safety review of venlafaxine conducted by the Medicines and Healthcare products Regulatory Agency (MHRA 2006a, 2006b), and further revised in this guideline update.

The relative efficacy and tolerability of SSRIs and serotonin–noradrenaline reuptake inhibitors (SNRIs) have been the subject of several meta-analyses (for example, Cipriani *et al.*, 2008; Gartlehner *et al.*, 2008). A recent network meta-analysis has also been published (Cipriani *et al.*, 2009), which uses direct and indirect methods to rank 12 new antidepressants with regard to relative efficacy and tolerability; this is discussed in more detail in Section 10.11. These analyses do suggest that there may be differences in efficacy and tolerability between individual drugs but, given the modest size of the effect and some methodological uncertainties, the GDG concluded that there was sufficient doubt about the clinical importance of the differences to not justify the development of recommendations for specific drugs. However, differences between drugs relating to tolerability and safety are highlighted where relevant.

The GDG did not update its review of St John's wort. Although further data have become available to suggest that St John's wort may be more effective and better tolerated than standard antidepressants in the acute treatment of mild to moderate depression, there is evidence of publication bias that complicates the interpretation of these data (Linde *et al.*, 2008). In addition, there are few medium-term data (Anghelescu *et al.*, 2006; Kasper *et al.*, 2008) or data that support the use of St John's wort in relapse prevention (Kasper *et al.*, 2008). There is also a lack of efficacy data in people with severe depression and long-term safety data remain scant. The GDG were previously cautious about the use of St John's wort partly because there is uncertainty over the active constituent and the majority of preparations are not standardised to contain fixed quantities of individual constituents. Since the previous guideline was published, Traditional Herbal Registration Certificates have been granted in the UK for standardised preparations of St John's wort; these certificates are not based on RCT evidence of efficacy and tolerability in the same way that a product licence is for a conventional medicine. The recommendations on St John's wort remain, therefore, unchanged.

10.2   USE OF INDIVIDUAL DRUGS IN THE TREATMENT OF DEPRESSION

Where there was lack of substantial new evidence, some analyses and conclusions were not updated from the previous guideline (NCCMH, 2004), although their discussion was updated where factual or stylistic adjustments were required. These are indicated with asterisks (**). The reviews of escitalopram and duloxetine are new for this guideline update.

10.2.1   Introduction

This section reviews the relative efficacy of individual antidepressants in the treatment of depression. Where there were sufficient data, the effect of patient setting (inpatient, outpatient or primary care) on choice of drug was also examined. It covers the following drugs:

- Tricyclic antidepressants (TCAs) (Section 10.3)
  - Amitriptyline**
  - An overview of TCAs used as comparator treatments in trials reviewed elsewhere[89]**
- Selective serotonin reuptake inhibitors (SSRIs) except escitalopram (Section 10.4)
  - Citalopram**
  - Fluoxetine**
  - Fluvoxamine**
  - Paroxetine**
  - Sertraline**
- Escitalopram (Section 10.5)

---

[89]Many studies in the reviews used a TCA as a comparator treatment. These data were combined in a review of TCAs to enable the GDG to gain an overview of this class of drugs. TCAs included clomipramine, doxepin, desipramine, imipramine, dothiepin/dosulepin, nortriptyline, amineptine and lofepramine.

- Monoamine oxidase inhibitors (Section 10.7)
  - Moclobemide**
  - Phenelzine**
- 'Third-generation' drugs (Section 10.8)
  - Duloxetine
  - Mirtazapine**
  - Reboxetine**
  - Venlafaxine**
- Other preparations
  - St John's wort** (Section 10.9)

10.3   TRICYCLIC ANTIDEPRESSANTS

The following sections on TCAs marked by asterisks (**_**) are from the previous guideline and have not been updated except for style and minor clarification.

10.3.1   Introduction

**TCAs have been used to treat depression for over 40 years. Currently, nine TCAs are available in the UK. They are thought to exert their therapeutic effect by inhibiting the re-uptake of monoamine neurotransmitters into the presynaptic neurone, thus enhancing noradrenergic and serotonergic neurotransmission. Although all TCAs block the reuptake of both amines, they vary in their selectivity with, for example, clomipramine being primarily serotonergic and imipramine noradrenergic.

All TCAs cause, to varying degrees, anticholinergic side effects (dry mouth, blurred vision, constipation, urinary retention, and sweating), sedation and postural hypotension. These side effects necessitate starting with a low dose and increasing slowly. In many patients a 'therapeutic dose' is never reached either because the patient cannot tolerate it or because the prescriber does not titrate the dose upwards.

All TCAs except lofepramine are toxic in overdose, with seizures and arrhythmias being a particular concern (see Chapter 11, Section 11.9). This toxicity and the perceived poor tolerability of these drugs in general have led to a decline in their use in the UK over the last decade.

10.3.2   Amitriptyline

Although amitriptyline was not the first TCA and is not the best tolerated or the most widely prescribed, it is the standard drug against which new antidepressants are compared with respect to both efficacy and tolerability. Amitriptyline may be marginally more effective than other antidepressants, a potential benefit that is offset by its poorer tolerability (Barbui & Hotopf, 2001). Efficacy benefits may be more marked in hospitalised patients (Anderson *et al.*, 2000).

Studies considered[90,91]

The GDG used an existing review (Barbui & Hotopf, 2001) as the basis for this section, for which the authors made their data available to the NCCMH team. The original review included 184 studies of which 144 did not meet the inclusion criteria set by the GDG. Eight additional studies were identified from searches undertaken for other sections of this guideline. Thus 48 trials are included in this section providing tolerability data from up to 4,484[92] participants and efficacy data from up to 2,760 participants. A total of 177 trials were excluded. The most common reason for exclusion was an inadequate diagnosis of depression.

All included studies were published between 1977 and 1999 and were between 3 and 10 weeks' long (mean = 5.71 weeks). Sixteen studies were of inpatients, 22 of outpatients and two were undertaken in primary care. In the remaining eight, it was either not clear from where participants were sourced or they were from mixed sources. In three studies all participants were over the age of 65 years (Cohn1990, Geretsegger95, Hutchinson92). Studies reported mean doses equivalent to at least 100 mg of amitriptyline.

Data were available to compare amitriptyline with citalopram, fluoxetine, fluvoxamine, paroxetine, sertraline, amoxapine, desipramine, dothiepin/dosulepin, doxepin, imipramine, lofepramine, minaprine[93], nortriptyline, trimipramine, maprotiline, mianserin, trazodone, phenelzine and mirtazapine.

The original systematic review on which this section is based included two outcome measures, responders and mean endpoint scores. It did not include data on remission and this has not been extracted for the present review.

Clinical evidence statements for amitriptyline[94,95]

Effect of treatment on efficacy[96]

There appears to be no clinically important difference in efficacy between amitriptyline and other antidepressants, either when compared or by class:

There is evidence suggesting that there is no clinically important difference between other antidepressants and amitriptyline on increasing the likelihood of

---

[90]Details of standard search strings used in all searches are in Appendix 8. Information about each study along with an assessment of methodological quality is in Appendix 17c, which also contains a list of excluded studies with reasons for exclusions.

[91]Here and elsewhere in the guideline, each study considered for review is referred to by a 'study ID' made up of first author and publication date (unless a study is in press or only submitted for publication, when first author only is used). Study IDs in title case refer to studies included in the previous guideline and study IDs in capital letters refer to studies found and included in this guideline update. References for studies from the previous guideline are in Appendix 18 and references for studies for the update are in Appendix 17c.

[92]It is not always possible to extract data for all outcomes from each study; therefore, the figures given are for the outcome with the largest number of participants.

[93]Not available in the UK.

[94]The forest plots can be found in Appendix 19c.

[95]The authors of the review on which this review is based entered data into Review Manager so that amitriptyline is on the right-hand side of the forest plot and comparator treatments on the left.

[96]Where it made a difference to results the following studies were removed from efficacy analyses because >50% left treatment early: Cohn1990, Fawcett1989, Guy1983, Preskorn1991, Shaw1986, Stuppaeck1994, Wilcox1994.

achieving a 50% reduction in depression scores as measured by the HRSD (K = 16; N = 1541; RR = 1.06; 95% CI, 0.96 to 1.18).

There is evidence suggesting that there is a statistically significant difference favouring amitriptyline over other antidepressants on reducing symptoms of depression by the end of treatment as measured by the HRSD and MADRS, but the size of this difference is unlikely to be of clinical importance (K = 32; N = 2760; SMD = 0.09; 95% CI, 0.01 to 0.16).

There is evidence suggesting that there is no clinically important difference between:

- other TCAs and amitriptyline on reducing symptoms of depression by the end of treatment as measured by the HRSD or MADRS (K = 5; N = 285; SMD = 0.04; 95% CI, −0.19 to 0.27)
- SSRIs and amitriptyline on increasing the likelihood of achieving a 50% reduction in symptoms of depression as measured by the HRSD (K = 9; N = 837; RR = 1.09; 95% CI, 0.95 to 1.25)
- SSRIs and amitriptyline on reducing symptoms of depression by the end of treatment as measured by the HRSD or MADRS (K = 19; N = 1648; SMD = 0.06; 95% CI, −0.03 to 0.16).

There is insufficient evidence to determine whether there is a clinically important difference between other TCAs and amitriptyline on increasing the likelihood of achieving a 50% reduction in symptoms of depression as measured by the HRSD (K = 2; N = 68; RR = 0.96; 95% CI, 0.60 to 1.53).

Effect of setting on treatment efficacy

There appears to be no clinically important difference between amitriptyline and other antidepressants in different treatment settings:

In inpatients there is evidence suggesting that there is no clinically important difference between other antidepressants and amitriptyline on increasing the likelihood of achieving a 50% reduction in symptoms of depression as measured by the HRSD (K = 6; N = 600; RR = 1.08; 95% CI, 0.9 to 1.29).

In inpatients there is evidence suggesting that there is a statistically significant difference favouring amitriptyline over other antidepressants on reducing symptoms of depression as measured by the HRSD and MADRS, but the size of this difference is unlikely to be of clinical importance (K = 11; N = 752; SMD = 0.16; 95% CI, 0.02 to 0.30).

In outpatients there is evidence suggesting that there is a statistically significant difference favouring amitriptyline over other antidepressants on reducing symptoms of depression as measured by the HRSD and MADRS, but the size of this difference is unlikely to be of clinical importance (K = 9; N = 1002; SMD = 0.13; 95% CI, 0.00 to 0.25).

In outpatients there is evidence suggesting that there is no clinically important difference between other antidepressants and amitriptyline on increasing the likelihood of achieving a 50% reduction in symptoms of depression as measured by the HRSD (K = 7; N = 666; RR = 1.03; 95% CI, 0.89 to 1.2).

In patients in primary care there is evidence suggesting that there is no clinically important difference between other antidepressants and amitriptyline on reducing symptoms of depression by the end of treatment as measured by the HRSD (K = 2; N = 132; SMD = –0.09; 95% CI, –0.44 to 0.27).

Acceptability and tolerability of treatment

When compared with all antidepressants, amitriptyline appears to be equally tolerable in terms of leaving treatment early for any reason. However, patients taking other antidepressants report fewer side effects:

There is evidence suggesting that there is no clinically important difference between amitriptyline and other antidepressants on reducing the likelihood of leaving treatment early for any reason (K = 43; N = 4884; RR = 0.92; 95% CI, 0.84 to 1.003).

There is strong evidence suggesting that there is a clinically important difference favouring other antidepressants over amitriptyline on reducing the likelihood of leaving the study early due to side effects (K = 34; N = 4034; RR = 0.71; 95% CI, 0.61 to 0.83).

There is some evidence suggesting that there is a clinically important difference favouring other antidepressants over amitriptyline on reducing the likelihood of patients reporting side effects (K = 5; N = 773; RR = 0.78; 95% CI, 0.65 to 0.93).

Acceptability and tolerability of treatment by setting

For inpatients, there appears to be little difference between the tolerability of amitriptyline and other antidepressants:

There is evidence suggesting that there is no clinically important difference between other antidepressants and amitriptyline on reducing the likelihood of inpatients leaving the study early for any reason (K = 15; N = 1320; RR = 0.96; 95% CI, 0.82 to 1.13).

There is insufficient evidence to determine whether there is a clinically important difference between other antidepressants and amitriptyline on reducing the likelihood of inpatients leaving treatment early due to side effects (K = 8; N = 855; RR = 0.78; 95% CI, 0.55 to 1.1).

There is evidence suggesting that there is no clinically important difference between paroxetine and amitriptyline on reducing the likelihood of inpatients reporting side effects (K = 2; N = 131; RR = 0.88; 95% CI, 0.68 to 1.12).

Amitriptyline was less well tolerated in outpatients.

There is evidence suggesting that there is no clinically important difference between other antidepressants and amitriptyline on reducing the likelihood of outpatients leaving treatment early for any reason (K = 19; N = 2647; Random effects RR = 0.87; 95% CI, 0.72 to 1.06).

There is some evidence suggesting that there is a clinically important difference favouring other antidepressants over amitriptyline on reducing the likelihood of outpatients leaving treatment early due to side effects (K = 18; N = 2396; RR = 0.75; 95% CI, 0.62 to 0.9).

There is insufficient evidence to determine whether there is a clinically important difference between other antidepressants and amitriptyline on reducing the likelihood of outpatients reporting side effects (K = 2; N = 552; RR = 0.8; 95% CI, 0.61 to 1.04).

Although much of the evidence was too weak to make a valid comparison of tolerability in primary care, more patients reported side effects in amitriptyline than paroxetine, which was the only comparator drug available:

In patients in primary care there is insufficient evidence to determine whether there is a clinically important difference between other antidepressants and amitriptyline on reducing the likelihood of leaving treatment early either for any reason or due to side effects.

There is some evidence suggesting that there is a clinically important difference favouring paroxetine over amitriptyline on reducing the likelihood of primary care patients reporting side effects (K = 1; N = 90; RR = 0.55; 95% CI, 0.35 to 0.86).

Clinical summary
Amitriptyline is as effective as other antidepressants, although patients taking the drug report more adverse events and tend to leave treatment early due to side effects.

10.3.3   Tricyclic antidepressants – an overview of selected data

**This section combines data from other reviews where a TCA was used as a comparator treatment. It is, therefore, not a systematic review since a systematic search for all trials of TCAs was not conducted. It specifically does not include comparisons of TCAs with other TCAs.

Studies considered[97,98]
In all, 94 studies from other reviews included a TCA as a comparator drug. Seventy studies were sourced from the review of SSRIs (Section 10.4), seven from the review of mirtazapine (Section 10.8.3), eight from phenelzine (Section 10.7.3), three from reboxetine (Section 10.8.4) and six from venlafaxine (Section 10.8.5). Data were available from the following TCAs: clomipramine, doxepin, desipramine, imipramine, dothiepin/dosulepin, nortriptyline, amineptine and lofepramine. Efficacy data were available from up to 6,848 patients, and tolerability data from up to 8,967 patients.

All included studies were published between 1981 and 2002. Twenty-four studies were of inpatients, 48 of outpatients and three undertaken in primary care. In the remaining 19, it was either not clear from where participants were sourced or they were from mixed sources. In 11 more than 80% of study participants were aged 65 years and over, and, in two, participants had depression with additional atypical features.

---

[97]Details of standard search strings used in all searches are in Appendix 8. Information about each study along with an assessment of methodological quality is in Appendix 17c, which also contains a list of excluded studies with reasons for exclusions.
[98]Study IDs in title case refer to studies included in the previous guideline. References for these studies guideline are in Appendix 18.

Clinical evidence statements[99]

Effect of treatment on efficacy

There is evidence suggesting that there is no clinically important difference between other antidepressants and TCAs on:

- increasing the likelihood of achieving a 50% reduction in symptoms as measured by the HRSD or the MADRS (K = 15[100]; N = 2364; RR = 0.91; 95% CI, 0.83 to 1.01)
- increasing the likelihood of achieving remission as measured by the HRSD (K = 3[101]; N = 534; RR = 0.98; 95% CI, 0.84 to 1.15)
- reducing symptoms of depression by the end of treatment as measured by the HRSD or MADRS (K = 70; N = 6,848; SMD = 0.02; 95% CI, –0.03 to 0.07).

Effect of setting on treatment efficacy

Inpatients:

There is evidence suggesting that there is no clinically important difference between TCAs and alternative antidepressants on increasing the likelihood of achieving a 50% reduction in symptoms of depression in inpatients as measured by the HRSD (K = 4[102]; N = 765; RR = 0.98; 95% CI, 0.82 to 1.18).

There is evidence suggesting that there is a statistically significant difference favouring TCAs over alternative antidepressants on reducing symptoms of depression, as measured by the HRSD or the MADRS, in inpatients by the end of treatment, but the size of this difference is unlikely to be of clinical importance (K = 20; N = 1681; SMD = 0.12; 95% CI, 0.03 to 0.22).

Outpatients:

There is some evidence suggesting that there is a clinically important difference favouring alternative antidepressants over TCAs on increasing the likelihood of achieving a 50% reduction in symptoms of depression as measured by the HRSD (K = 5; N = 733; RR = 0.74; 95% CI, 0.64 to 0.87).

There is evidence suggesting that there is no clinically important difference between TCAs and alternative antidepressants on reducing symptoms of depression in outpatients by the end of treatment as measured by the HRSD or MADRS (K = 33; N = 3,275; SMD = –0.03; 95% CI, –0.1 to 0.04).

There is insufficient evidence to determine whether there is a clinically important difference between phenelzine and nortriptyline on increasing the likelihood of achieving remission in outpatients by the end of treatment as measured by the HRSD (K= 1[103]; N = 60; RR = 1.28; 95% CI, 0.78 to 2.09).

---

[99]The forest plots can be found in Appendix 19c.
[100]Bruijn1996 and Quitkin1990 were removed from the meta-analysis to remove heterogeneity from the imipramine dataset.
[101]Quitkin1990 was removed from the meta-analysis to remove heterogeneity from the imipramine dataset.
[102]Bruijn1996 was removed from the meta-analysis to remove heterogeneity from the imipramine dataset.
[103]Quitkin1990 was removed from the meta-analysis to remove heterogeneity from the imipramine dataset.

Primary care:
There is insufficient evidence to determine whether there is a clinically important difference between TCAs and alternative antidepressants on reducing symptoms of depression in patients in primary care by the end of treatment as measured by the HRSD or MADRS (K = 2; N = 213; SMD = –0.14; 95% CI, –0.42 to 0.13).

Acceptability and tolerability of treatment
There is evidence suggesting that there are statistically significant differences favouring alternative antidepressants over TCAs on the following outcomes, but the size of these differences is unlikely to be of clinical importance:
- on reducing the likelihood of leaving treatment early for any reason (K = 83; N = 8967; RR = 0.88; 95% CI, 0.83 to 0.94)
- on reducing the likelihood of patients reporting adverse effects (K = 25; N = 3007; random effects RR = 0.91; 95% CI, 0.86 to 0.96).

There is strong evidence suggesting that there is a clinically important difference favouring alternative antidepressants over TCAs on reducing the likelihood of leaving treatment early due to side effects (K = 80; N = 8888; RR = 0.71; 95% CI, 0.65 to 0.78).

When TCAs were examined individually, only dothiepin/dosulepin appears to be more acceptable than alternative antidepressants:
There is some evidence suggesting that there is a clinically important difference favouring dothiepin/dosulepin over alternative antidepressants on reducing the likelihood of leaving treatment early for any reason (K = 5; N = 336; RR = 1.42; 95% CI, 1.02 to 1.98) and on reducing the likelihood of leaving treatment early due to side effects (K = 5; N = 336; RR = 2.02; 95% CI, 1.09 to 3.76).

Clinical summary
TCAs have equal efficacy compared with alternative antidepressants but are less well tolerated particularly in outpatients.**

10.4   SELECTIVE SEROTONIN REUPTAKE INHIBITORS

The following sections on SSRIs marked by asterisks (**_**) are from the previous guideline and have not been updated except for style and minor clarification.

10.4.1   Introduction

**The selective serotonin reuptake inhibitors (SSRIs) inhibit the reuptake of serotonin into the presynaptic neurone thus increasing neurotransmission. Although they 'selectively' inhibit serotonin reuptake, they are not serotonin specific. Some of the drugs in this class also inhibit the reuptake of noradrenaline and/or dopamine to a lesser extent.

As a class, they are associated with less anticholinergic side effects and are less likely to cause postural hypotension or sedation. Dosage titration is not routinely required so subtherapeutic doses are less likely to be prescribed. They are also less cardiotoxic and much safer in overdose than the TCAs or MAOIs. These advantages have led to their widespread use as better-tolerated first-line antidepressants.

The most problematic side effects of this class of drugs are nausea, diarrhoea and headache. Fluvoxamine, fluoxetine and paroxetine are potent inhibitors of various hepatic cytochrome metabolising enzymes (Mitchell, 1997) precipitating many significant drug interactions. Sertraline is less problematic although enzyme inhibition is dose-related, while both citalopram and escitalopram are relatively safe in this regard.

There are other important differences among the SSRIs (Anderson & Edwards, 2001), as outlined below.

Citalopram

Until the introduction of escitalopram, citalopram was the most serotonin selective of the SSRIs. In animals, one of its minor metabolites is cardiotoxic (Van Der Burght, 1994) and it is pro-convulsant at high dose (Boeck *et al.*, 1982). The issue of its safety in overdose is discussed below (see Section 11.9.3). It is available as a generic preparation.

Escitalopram[104]

Citalopram is a racemic mixture of s-citalopram and r-citalopram. With respect to SSRI potency, escitalopram (s-citalopram) is 100 times more potent than r-citalopram. The observation that escitalopram 10 mg is as effective as citalopram 20 mg confirms that escitalopram is responsible for most or perhaps the entire antidepressant efficacy of citalopram (Waugh & Goa, 2003). It has been suggested that r-citalopram contributes to side effects and, by using the active isomer only, efficacy will be maintained and side effects reduced.** Other mechanisms have been attributed to r-citalopram, which may account for some of the differences in efficacy seen between escitalopram and citalopram (Mork *et al.*, 2003), although these are not firmly established.

Fluoxetine

Fluoxetine is associated with a lower incidence of nausea than fluvoxamine but a higher incidence of rash. It has a long half-life, which may cause problems with washout periods when switching to other antidepressant drugs but has the advantage of causing fewer discontinuation symptoms. It is available as a generic preparation.

Fluvoxamine

**Fluvoxamine was the first of the currently available SSRIs to be marketed in the UK. It is associated with a higher incidence of nausea than the other SSRIs and so is not widely prescribed.

Paroxetine

Paroxetine is associated with a higher incidence of sweating, sedation and sexual dysfunction than other SSRIs and more problems on withdrawal (Anderson & Edwards,

---

[104]A new review of escitalopram can be found in Section 10.5.

2001; see also Section 11.8 on antidepressant discontinuation symptoms). It is available as a generic preparation.

Sertraline

Sertraline is a well-tolerated SSRI. It is more likely to be associated with upwards dosage titration during treatment than the other SSRIs (Gregor *et al.*, 1994). It is available as a generic preparation.

10.4.2   Studies considered for review of selective serotonin reuptake inhibitors apart from escitalopram[105,106]

The GDG used an existing review (Geddes *et al.*, 2002) as the basis of this section, for which the authors made their data available to the NCCMH team. Since this review did not cover escitalopram which achieved its UK licence in late 2001, a separate review[107] of this drug was undertaken.

The Geddes and colleagues' (2002) review included 126 studies of which 72 did not meet the inclusion criteria set by the GDG. In addition, one trial (Peselow *et al.*, 1989) included in the original review was considered to be part of a multicentre trial (Feighner92) rather than a separate trial. Another trial (Feighner1989) excluded by Geddes and colleagues (2002) was included in this review because it contained tolerability data (which Geddes and colleagues [2002] did not include). A further two trials excluded by Geddes and colleagues (2002) were also considered part of the Feighner92 multicentre trial (Dunbar *et al.*, 1991; Feighner & Boyer, 1989).

Since the Geddes and colleagues' (2002) review compared SSRIs with TCAs only, 59 additional studies were identified from other reviews undertaken for this guideline, including two identified from hand searching reference lists. Thirty-three of these were included and 26 excluded. Thus 107 trials are included in this review providing data from up to 11,442 participants. A total of 97 trials were excluded.

All included studies were published between 1983 and 2003 and were between 4 and 24 weeks' long (mean = 6.5 weeks). Twenty-four studies were of inpatients, 51 of outpatients and six undertaken in primary care. In the remaining 26, it was either not clear from where participants were sourced, or they were from mixed sources. In 11 studies, more than 80% of participants were aged 65 years and over (although only eight of these reported extractable efficacy outcomes). In two studies participants had depression with additional atypical features.

In addition to the standard diagnostic criteria, most studies required a minimum baseline HRSD score of between 10 and 22 on the 17-item version (61 studies) or

---

[105]Details of standard search strings used in all searches are in Appendix 8. Information about each study along with an assessment of methodological quality is in Appendix 17c, which also contains a list of excluded studies with reasons for exclusions.

[106]Study IDs in title case refer to studies included in the previous guideline. References for these studies are in Appendix 18.

[107]The review on escitalopram was updated for this guideline – see Section 10.5.

between 18 and 22 on the 21-item version (28 studies). The ten studies reporting MADRS scores required minimum baseline scores of between 18 and 30.

Data were available to compare SSRIs (citalopram, fluoxetine, fluvoxamine, paroxetine and sertraline) with amineptine, amitriptyline, clomipramine, desipramine, dothiepin/dosulepin, doxepin, imipramine, lofepramine, nortriptyline, maprotiline, mianserin, trazodone, phenelzine, moclobemide, mirtazapine, venlafaxine and reboxetine.

The Geddes and colleagues' (2002) review, on which this review is based and for which the data were made available to the GDG, included only one outcome measure (mean endpoint scores) and did not include tolerability data. Tolerability data, but not additional efficacy outcomes, have been extracted by the NCCMH team.

10.4.3 Clinical evidence statements for selective serotonin reuptake inhibitors apart from escitalopram[108]

Effect of treatment on efficacy
There is no clinically important difference between SSRIs and other antidepressants, whether combined as a group or divided by drug class:

There is evidence suggesting that there is a statistically significant difference favouring other antidepressants over SSRIs on reducing symptoms of depression as measured by the HRSD or MADRS, but the size of this difference is unlikely to be of clinical importance (K = 82[109]; N = 8,668; SMD = 0.08; 95% CI, 0.03 to 0.12).

There is evidence suggesting that there is no clinically important difference on reducing symptoms of depression as measured by the HRSD or MADRS between:
- SSRIs and TCAs (K = 49; N = 4,073; SMD = 0.05; 95% CI, –0.01 to 0.12)
- SSRIs and MAOIs (K = 7; N = 469; SMD = 0.03; 95% CI, –0.15 to 0.22).

There is evidence suggesting that there is a statistically significant difference favouring third-generation[110] antidepressants over SSRIs on reducing symptoms of depression as measured by the HRSD or MADRS, but the size of this difference is unlikely to be of clinical importance (K = 17; N = 3,665; SMD = 0.13; 95% CI, 0.06 to 0.19).

Effect of setting on treatment efficacy
In inpatients there is no difference between the efficacy of SSRIs and other antidepressants, apart from third-generation antidepressants:

There is evidence suggesting that there is no clinically important difference on reducing symptoms of depression in inpatients as measured by the HRSD or MADRS between:
- SSRIs and other antidepressants (K = 20; N = 1258; SMD = 0.09; 95% CI, –0.02 to 0.2)
- SSRIs and TCAs (K = 15; N = 970; SMD = 0.12; 95% CI, –0.01 to 0.24).

---

[108]The forest plots can be found in Appendix 19c.
[109]Studies where >50% of participants left treatment early were retained in the analysis since removing them made no difference to the results.
[110]Mirtazapine, venlafaxine and reboxetine.

Pharmacological interventions

There is some evidence suggesting that there is a clinically important difference favouring third-generation antidepressants over SSRIs on reducing symptoms of depression as measured by the HRSD or MADRS in inpatients (K = 1; N = 67; SMD = 0.58; 95% CI, 0.09 to 1.07).

There is insufficient evidence to determine whether there is a clinically important difference between SSRIs and MAOIs on reducing symptoms of depression as measured by the HRSD or MADRS in inpatients.

In outpatients there is no difference between the efficacy of SSRIs and other antidepressants:

There is evidence suggesting that there is a statistically significant difference favouring other antidepressants over SSRIs on reducing symptoms of depression as measured by the HRSD or MADRS in outpatients, but the size of this difference is unlikely to be of clinical importance (K = 38; N = 4666; SMD = 0.06; 95% CI, 0 to 0.12).

There is evidence suggesting that there is no clinically important difference on reducing symptoms of depression as measured by the HRSD or MADRS in outpatients between SSRIs and TCAs (K = 24; N = 2304; SMD = 0.02; 95% CI, –0.07 to 0.1).

There is evidence suggesting that there is a statistically significant difference favouring 'third-generation' antidepressants over SSRIs on reducing symptoms of depression as measured by the HRSD or MADRS in outpatients, but the size of this difference is unlikely to be of clinical importance (K = 9; N = 2,096; SMD = 0.13; 95% CI, 0.05 to 0.22).

There is insufficient evidence to determine whether there is a clinically important difference between SSRIs and MAOIs on reducing symptoms of depression as measured by the HRSD or MADRS in outpatients.

There is a similar picture in primary care:

There is evidence suggesting that there is no clinically important difference between SSRIs and other antidepressants on reducing symptoms of depression as measured by the HRSD or MADRS in primary care (K = 4; N = 922; SMD = 0.08; 95% CI, –0.05 to 0.21).

Acceptability and tolerability of treatment
There is evidence suggesting that there is a statistically significant difference favouring SSRIs over alternative antidepressants on reducing the likelihood of patients leaving treatment early for any reason, but the size of this difference is unlikely to be of clinical importance (K = 97; N = 11,442; RR = 0.91; 95% CI, 0.87 to 0.96).

There is strong evidence suggesting that there is a clinically important difference favouring SSRIs over alternative antidepressants on reducing the likelihood of patients leaving treatment early due to side effects (K = 89; N = 10898; RR = 0.78; 95% CI, 0.71 to 0.85).

There is evidence suggesting that there is a statistically significant difference favouring SSRIs over alternative antidepressants on reducing the likelihood of patients reporting adverse effects, but the size of this difference is unlikely to be of clinical importance (K = 42; N = 5658; RR = 0.94; 95% CI, 0.91 to 0.97).

A sub-analysis against TCAs showed similar results:

There is evidence suggesting that there is a statistically significant difference favouring SSRIs over TCAs on reducing the likelihood of patients leaving treatment early for any reason but the size of this difference is unlikely to be of clinical importance (K = 62; N = 6446; RR = 0.88; 95% CI, 0.82 to 0.93).

There is strong evidence suggesting that there is a clinically important difference favouring SSRIs over TCAs on reducing the likelihood of patients leaving treatment early due to side effects (K = 59; N = 6145; RR = 0.69; 95% CI, 0.62 to 0.77).

There is evidence suggesting that there is a statistically significant difference favouring SSRIs over TCAs on the likelihood of patients reporting adverse events, but the size of this difference is unlikely to be of clinical importance (K = 17; N = 1846; RR = 0.86; 95% CI, 0.81 to 0.9).

10.4.4   Clinical summary of selective serotonin reuptake inhibitors apart from escitalopram

SSRIs are relatively well-tolerated drugs with equal efficacy compared with alternative antidepressants. They may have an advantage for those with suicidal intent, due to their safety in overdose (see Section 11.10).**

10.5   ESCITALOPRAM

10.5.1   Introduction

Escitalopram was reviewed in the previous guideline, but a relatively large number of studies (compared with the number previously available) have been published since then and so the review has been updated for this guideline. For the present review, both published and unpublished double-blind RCTs were sought that compared escitalopram either with placebo or with another antidepressant. The marketing authorisation holder, Lundbeck, was also contacted for data.

10.5.2   Databases searched and the inclusion/exclusion criteria

Information about the databases searched for published trials and the inclusion/exclusion criteria used are presented in Table 68. Details of the search strings used are in Appendix 8.

10.5.3   Studies considered[111]

A total of six trials were included in the review in the previous guideline and these were supplemented by another 18 trials. Some of the studies used in the previous

---

[111]Study IDs in title case refer to studies included in the previous guideline and study IDs in capital letters refer to studies found and included in this guideline update. References for studies from the previous guideline are in Appendix 18.

Table 68: Databases searched and inclusion/exclusion criteria for clinical effectiveness of pharmacological treatments

Electronic databases	MEDLINE, EMBASE, PsycINFO, CINAHL
Date searched	Database inception to January 2008
Update searches	July 2008
Study design	RCT
Population	People with a diagnosis of depression according to DSM, ICD or similar criteria
Treatments	Escitalopram, placebo, other antidepressants

review that had been unpublished, have since been published with different first authors; therefore, the study identifier has changed for some studies. Five studies in the current review are unpublished and supplied by the drug's manufacturer.

Data were available to compare escitalopram with placebo, and with a range of other antidepressants. Sub-analyses were undertaken to assess the effect of the severity of depression at baseline and by dose, and to ascertain effectiveness against individual drugs (in particular, citalopram), other SSRIs and non-SSRI antidepressants.

Summary study characteristics of the included studies are presented in Table 69 with full details in Appendix 17c, which also includes details of excluded studies.

10.5.4 Clinical evidence

Escitalopram versus placebo
Eleven studies were found that compared escitalopram with placebo. Those that used a fixed dose of 10 or 20 mg were included in sub-analyses by dose. The summary evidence profile can be found in Table 70. The full evidence profiles and associated forest plots can be found in Appendix 16c and Appendix 19c.

Escitalopram was effective when compared with placebo, although overall effect sizes were small and the quality of evidence graded moderate (largely because of heterogeneity). Sub-analyses by dose indicated that both 10 and 20 mg doses were effective, although effect sizes were greater and graded moderate with the larger dose. However, more people left treatment early for any reason and because of side effects, and more people taking 20 mg reported side effects compared with those taking 10 mg.

Escitalopram versus all other antidepressants
Twenty one studies were found that compared escitalopram with other antidepressants. Table 71 gives the summary evidence table for escitalopram compared with all other antidepressants together. (Separate analyses follow for escitalopram compared with SSRIs, citalopram and other antidepressants are below). The full evidence profiles and associated forest plots can be found in Appendix 16c and Appendix 19c, respectively.

Table 69: Summary study characteristics of escitalopram

	Versus placebo	Versus citalopram	Versus other SSRIs	Versus other antidepressants
No. trials (total participants)	11 RCTs (3409)	6 RCTs (1917)	8 RCTs (2086)	7 RCTs (2191)
Study IDs	(1) BOSE2008 (2) Burke2002* (3) CLAYTON2006C study 1[†] (4) CLAYTON2006C study 2[†] (5) KASPER2005[†] (6) LEPOLA2003[†] (originally Montgomery2001) (7) NIERENBERG 2007B[†] (8) SCT-MD-02[†] (9) SCT-MD-26 (10) SCT-MD-27[†] (11) Wade2002	(1) Burke2002* (2) COLONNA2005 (3) LEPOLA2003[†] (originally Montgomery2001) (4) MOORE2005 (5) SCT-MD-02[†] (6) YEVTUSHENKO 2007[†]	(1) BALDWIN2006D (2) BOULENGER2006 (3) KASPER2005[†] (4) MAO2008 (5) SCT-MD-09 (6) SCT-MD-16 (7) SCT-MD-27[†] (8) VENTURA2007 (originally Alexopoulos2003)	(1) BIELSKI2004 (originally Bielski2003) (2) CLAYTON2006C study 1[†] (3) CLAYTON2006C study 2[†] (4) KHAN2007B (5) Montgomery2002 (6) NIERENBERG 2007B[†] (7) WADE2007
N/% female	(1) 267/58 (2) 366/64 (3) 283/61 (4) 286/54	(1) 369/64 (2) 357/74 (3) 310/72 (4) 294/67	(1) 325/73 (2) 459/68 (3) 338/76 (4) 240/56	(1) 198/58 (2) 284/61 (3) 297/54 (4) 278/60

Continued

343

Table 69: (*Continued*)

	Versus placebo	Versus citalopram	Versus other SSRIs	Versus other antidepressants
	(5) 354/76 (6) 310/72 (7) 411/65 (8) 258/52 (9) 309/59 (10) 271/55 (11) 294/NA	(5) 257/52 (6) 330/57	(5) 30/87 (6) 205/62 (7) 274/55 (8) 215/66	(5) 293/71 (6) 547/65 (7) 294/72
Mean age	(1) 68 (2) 40 (3) 36 (4) 37 (5) 75 (6) 43 (7)–(8) 42 (9) 39 (10) 40 (11) 41	(1) 40 (2) 46 (3) 43 (4) 45 (5) 42 (6) 35	(1) 45 (2) 44 (3) 75 (4) 39 (5) 39 (6) 37 (7) 40 (8) 39	(1) 37 (2) 36 (3) 37 (4) 42 (5) 48 (6) 42 (7) 44
Escitalopram dose (mean, if given)	(1) 20 mg (2) 10 mg and 20 mg (3)–(4) 13 mg (5)–(7) 10 mg (8)–(9) 10–20 mg (10) 16.6 mg (11) 10 mg	(1) 10 mg and 20 mg (2)–(3) 10 mg (4) 20 mg (5) 10–20 mg (6) 10 mg	(1) 13.9 mg (2) 20 mg (3)–(4) 10 mg (5)–(6) 20 mg (7) 16.6 mg (8) 10 mg	(1) 20 mg (2)–(3) 13 mg (4) 10/20 mg (5) 12.1 mg (6) 10 mg (7) 20 mg

Comparator (mean dose, if given)	(1)–(11) Placebo	(1) Citalopram 40 mg (2) 20 mg (3) 20/40 mg (4) 40 mg (5) 20–40 mg (6) 10 mg and 20 mg	(1) Paroxetine 26.3 mg (2) Paroxetine 20–40 mg (3)–(4) Fluoxetine 20 mg (5)–(6) Fluoxetine 40 mg (7) Sertraline 113.1 mg (8) Sertraline 50–200 mg	(1) Venlafaxine extended release (XR) 225 mg (2) Bupropion XL 323 mg (3) Bupropion XL 309 mg (4) Duloxetine 60 mg (5) Venlafaxine-XR 95.2 mg (6)–(7) Duloxetine 60 mg
Setting	(1)–(2) Outpatients (3)–(4) Unclear (5) Primary care and specialist (6) Primary care (7)–(10) Outpatients (11) Primary care	(1)–(2) Outpatients (3) Primary care (4)–(6) Outpatients	(1) Primary care (2) Outpatients (3) Primary care and specialist (4) Outpatients and inpatients (5)–(8) Outpatients	(1)–(3) Unclear (4) Outpatients (5) Primary care (6) Outpatients (7) Outpatients and primary care
Length of treatment (weeks)	(1) 12 days (2)–(6) 8 (7) 8- + 6-month continuation (8) 8 (9) 14 (10)–(11) 8	(1) 8 (2) 6 months (3)–(5) 8 (6) 6	(1) 8 (2) 6 months (3)–(8) 8	(1)–(5) 8 (6) 8- + 6-month continuation (7) 24

*4-armed trial; †3-armed trial.

Table 70: Summary evidence profile for escitalopram versus placebo

	Non-response	Non-remission	Mean depression scores at endpoint/mean change	Leaving treatment early	Leaving treatment early due to side effects	Number reporting side effects
All data: effect size	RR 0.81 (0.75 to 0.88) (49.8 versus 60.2%)	RR 0.88 (0.82 to 0.94) (61.1 versus 68.6%)	SMD −0.24 (−0.35 to −0.13)/ SMD −0.26 (−0.34 to −0.19)	RR 1.11 (0.95 to 1.29) (22 versus 19.3%)	RR 1.8 (1.18 to 2.73) (6.3 versus 3.2%)	RR 1.09 (1.04 to 1.15) (71.7 versus 64.7%)
Quality of evidence	Moderate	Moderate	Moderate High	High	Moderate	High
Number of studies/ participants	K = 11; n = 3495	K = 9; n = 2871	K = 6; n = 1821 K = 10; n = 2930	K = 11; n = 3495	K = 11; n = 3456	K = 8; n = 2490
Forest plot number	Pharm Esc 01.01	Pharm Esc 01.02	Pharm Esc 01.03 Pharm Esc 01.04	Pharm Esc 01.05	Pharm Esc 01.06	Pharm Esc 01.07
10 mg effect size	RR 0.84 (0.72 to 0.98) (53.7 versus 61.8%)	RR 0.92 (0.81 to 1.06) (62.1 versus 65.4%)	SMD −0.23 (−0.46 to −0.01) SMD −0.28 (−0.41 to −0.15)	RR 0.99 (0.75 to 1.3) (19.9 versus 18.9%)	RR 2.02 (0.9 to 4.54) (5.9 versus 2.9%)	RR 1.04 (0.94 to 1.15) (61.1 versus 58.7%)

Quality of evidence	Moderate	Moderate	High / Moderate	Low	Low	High
Number of studies/ participants	K = 4; n = 1386	K = 3; n = 1145	K = 3; n = 964 / K = 3; n = 1025	K = 4; n = 1386	K = 4; n = 1386	K = 3; n = 974
Forest plot number	Pharm Esc 01.01	Pharm Esc 01.02	Pharm Esc 01.03 / Pharm Esc 01.04	Pharm Esc 01.05	Pharm Esc 01.06	Pharm Esc 01.07
20 mg effect size	RR 0.68 (0.55 to 0.84) (49.6 versus 73%)	Not reported	SMD –0.46 (–0.71 to –0.2) / SMD –0.48 (–0.74 to –0.22)	RR 1.17 (0.77 to 1.77) (28.8 versus 24.6%)	RR 4.23 (1.24 to 14.47) (10.4 versus 2.5%)	RR 1.21 (1.06 to 1.39) (85.6 versus 70.5%)
Quality of evidence	Moderate	–	Moderate / Moderate	Low	Moderate	Moderate
Number of studies/ participants	K = 1; n = 247	–	K = 1; n = 242	K = 1; n = 247	K = 1; n = 247	K = 1; n = 247
Forest plot number	Pharm Esc 01.01	–	Pharm Esc 01.03 / Pharm Esc 01.04	Pharm Esc 01.05	Pharm Esc 01.06	Pharm Esc 01.07

347

Table 71: Summary evidence profile for escitalopram versus all other antidepressants

	Non-response	Non-remission	Mean depression scores at endpoint/mean change	Leaving treatment early	Leaving treatment early due to side effects	Number reporting side effects
Effect size	RR 0.9 (0.85 to 0.96) (37.7 versus 41.4%)	RR 0.93 (0.88 to 0.98) (46.3 versus 49.7%)	SMD −0.1 (−0.17 to −0.02) SMD −0.07 (−0.12 to −0.02)	RR 0.85 (0.74 to 0.98) (18.9 versus 21.6%)	RR 0.64 (0.53 to 0.78) (5.6 versus 8.6%)	RR 0.94 (0.91 to 0.98) (63.9 versus 64.4%)
Quality of evidence	High	High	High High	Moderate	High	High
Number of studies/ participants	K = 19; n = 5832	K = 17; n = 5206	K = 11; n = 3009 K = 19; n = 5158	K = 21; n = 6192	K = 20; n = 5807	K = 17; n = 4839
Forest plot number	Pharm Esc 02.01	Pharm Esc 02.02	Pharm Esc 02.03 Pharm Esc 02.04	Pharm Esc 02.05	Pharm Esc 02.06	Pharm Esc 02.07

Compared with all antidepressants for which there are data, escitalopram was more effective although effect sizes were small. Fewer participants taking escitalopram left treatment early for any reason or because of side effects compared with those taking other antidepressants, although the numbers reporting side effects were roughly equal.

Escitalopram versus selective serotonin reuptake inhibitors
Eight studies were found that compared escitalopram with SSRIs. Escitalopram is also compared with citalopram separately. The summary evidence profile can be found in Table 72. The full evidence profiles and associated forest plots can be found in Appendix 16c and Appendix 19c, respectively.

Compared with all SSRIs together, escitalopram is more effective although the effect sizes are small. Compared with individual SSRIs, there were no clinically important differences on efficacy outcomes other than compared with citalopram, where escitalopram was more effective with a small effect size. Escitalopram was also more acceptable and tolerable than SSRIs, apart from sertraline, although differences were again small.

Escitalopram versus non-selective serotonin reuptake inhibitors
Seven studies were found that compared escitalopram with non-SSRI antidepressants. The summary evidence profile can be found in Table 73. The full evidence profiles and associated forest plots can be found in Appendix 16c and Appendix 19c, respectively.

There were no clinically important differences between escitalopram and duloxetine, venlafaxine or bupropion on efficacy measures, although all effect sizes favoured escitalopram. Escitalopram was mostly more acceptable and tolerable, although differences were small.

10.5.5   Clinical summary

Escitalopram is superior to placebo in the treatment of depression. There is some evidence that 20 mg may be more effective than 10 mg, but at the expense of increased side effects. Escitalopram is more effective than citalopram although the effect size is small. It is at least as effective as other SSRIs and marginally better tolerated, except against sertraline.

Escitalopram was more effective than other antidepressants, with statistically significant differences versus SSRIs (although effect sizes are small and unlikely to be clinically important), but not against other antidepressants (duloxetine, venlafaxine and bupropion). Effect sizes compared with citalopram were largest, although these were still relatively small. This was particularly the case for escitalopram at 20 mg. It was also marginally more acceptable and tolerable, apart from compared with sertraline. However, differences were again small and unlikely to be clinically important.

Several more detailed comparisons were considered by the GDG, in addition to those presented above, which helped inform interpretation of the data. These can be found in Appendix 19c (forest plot numbers Pharm Esc 05 to Esc 11).

Table 72: Summary evidence profile for escitalopram versus SSRIs

	Non-response	Non-remission	Mean depression scores at endpoint/mean change	Leaving treatment early	Leaving treatment early due to side effects	Number reporting side effects
All SSRIs effect size	RR 0.89 (0.82 to 0.97) (36.1 versus 39.6%)	RR 0.9 (0.83 to 0.98) (41.6 versus 46.2%)	SMD −0.11 (−0.19 to −0.03) SMD −0.1 (−0.18 to −0.02)	RR 0.86 (0.71 to 1.03) (16.8 versus 18.6%)	RR 0.75 (0.58 to 0.96) (5.8 versus 7.6%)	RR 0.94 (0.9 to 0.98) (64.8 versus 67.7%)
Quality of evidence	High	High	High High	Moderate	High	High
Number of studies/ participants	K = 12; n = 3650	K = 10; n = 3024	K = 9; n = 2434 K = 13; n = 3337	K = 14; n = 4010	K = 13; n = 3639	K = 13; n = 3652
Forest plot number	Pharm Esc 03.02	Pharm Esc 03.04	Pharm Esc 03.05 Pharm Esc 03.06	Pharm Esc 03.07	Pharm Esc 03.08	Pharm Esc 03.10
Citalopram effect size	RR 0.85 (0.76 to 0.95) (40.2 versus 45.6%)	RR 0.82 (0.72 to 0.94) (41 versus 50.1%)	SMD −0.12 (−0.24 to 0) SMD −0.17 (−0.28 to −0.05)	RR 0.82 (0.6 to 1.11) (15.2 versus 15.4%)	RR 0.8 (0.49 to 1.29) (5.6 versus 6.7%)	RR 0.95 (0.89 to 1.02) (64.7 versus 64.2%)
Quality of evidence	High	High	High High	Low	High	High

Number of studies/participants	K = 5; n = 1594	K = 3; n = 968	K = 4; n = 1143 K = 6; n = 1639	K = 6; n = 1924	K = 5; n = 1569	K = 5; n = 1583
Forest plot number	Pharm Esc 03.02	Pharm Esc 03.04	Pharm Esc 03.05 Pharm Esc 03.06	Pharm Esc 03.07	Pharm Esc 03.08	Pharm Esc 03.10
Fluoxetine effect size	RR 0.92 (0.78 to 1.08) (39.8 versus 35.9%)	RR 0.92 (0.8 to 1.06) (44.9 versus 48.7%)	SMD −0.2 (−0.34 to −0.06) SMD −0.06 (−0.24 to 0.13)	RR 0.91 (0.58 to 1.42) (19.98 versus 21.9%)	RR 0.77 (0.47 to 1.26) (6.6 versus 8.6%)	RR 0.92 (0.82 to 1.03) (56.3 versus 61.7%)
Quality of evidence	High	High	High High	Low	High	High
Number of studies/participants	K = 3; n = 783	K = 3; n = 783	K = 3; n = 759 n = 449	K = 4; n = 813	K = 4; n = 805	K = 4; n = 804
Forest plot number	Pharm Esc 03.02	Pharm Esc 03.04	Pharm Esc 03.05 Pharm Esc 03.06	Pharm Esc 03.07	Pharm Esc 03.08	Pharm Esc 03.10
Sertraline effect size	RR 1.01 (0.8 to 1.28) (35.8 versus 35.4%)	RR 1.02 (0.86 to 1.22) (50.6 versus 49.6%)	SMD −0.02 (−0.29 to 0.25) SMD 0.01 (−0.17 to 0.19)	RR 1.19 (0.81 to 1.74) (19.3 versus 16.3%)	RR 1.11 (0.38 to 3.22) (4.2 versus 3.7%)	RR 0.93 (0.87 to 1) (83.2 versus 89%)
Quality of evidence	High	High	Moderate High	Low	High	High
Number of studies/participants	K = 2; n = 489	K = 2; n = 489	K = 1; n = 211 K = 2; n = 477	K = 2; n = 489	K = 2; n = 483	K = 2; n = 483

Continued

Table 72: *(Continued)*

	Non-response	Non-remission	Mean depression scores at endpoint/mean change	Leaving treatment early	Leaving treatment early due to side effects	Number reporting side effects
Forest plot number	Pharm Esc 03.02	Pharm Esc 03.04	Pharm Esc 03.05 Pharm Esc 03.06	Pharm Esc 03.07	Pharm Esc 03.08	Pharm Esc 03.10
Paroxetine effect size	RR 0.92 (0.73 to 1.17) (24.9 versus 26.9%)	RR 0.92 (0.76 to 1.11) (33.7 versus 36.5%)	SMD 0.11 (−0.11 to 0.33) SMD −0.06 (−0.38 to 0.27)	RR 0.65 (0.49 to 0.85) (16.1 versus 24.9%)	RR 0.65 (0.31 to 1.36) (6.3 versus 10.6%)	RR 0.94 (0.85 to 1.04) (62.7 versus 67%)
Quality of evidence	Low	Low	Moderate Very low	High	Low	High
Number of studies/participants	K = 2; n = 784	K = 2; n = 784	K = 1; n = 321 K = 2; n = 772	K = 2; n = 784	K = 2; n = 782	K = 2; n = 782
Forest plot number	Pharm Esc 03.02	Pharm Esc 03.04	Pharm Esc 03.05 Pharm Esc 03.06	Pharm Esc 03.07	Pharm Esc 03.08	Pharm Esc 03.10

Table 73: Summary evidence profile for escitalopram versus non-SSRIs

	Non-response	Non-remission	Mean depression scores at endpoint/ mean change	Leaving treatment early	Leaving treatment early due to side effects	Number reporting side effects
Duloxetine effect size	RR 0.81 (0.57 to 1.15) (43.4 versus 48.8%)	RR 0.97 (0.83 to 1.13) (55.6 versus 56%)	SMD −0.19 (−0.42 to 0.04) SMD 0.03 (−0.11 to 0.17)	RR 0.7 (0.49 to 1) (21.3 versus 29.9%)	RR 0.47 (0.25 to 0.89) (5.4 versus 11.2%)	RR 1.02 (0.94 to 1.11) (78.8 versus 77.2%)
Quality of evidence	Low	Moderate	Moderate High	Moderate	Moderate	High
Number of studies/ participants	K = 3; n = 1120	K = 3; n = 1120	K = 1; n = 287 K = 2; n = 809	K = 3; n = 1120	K = 3; n = 1120	K = 2; n = 572
Forest plot number	Pharm Esc 04.01	Pharm Esc 04.02	Pharm Esc 04.03/04	Pharm Esc 04.05	Pharm Esc 04.06	Pharm Esc 04.07
Venlafaxine effect size	RR 0.86 (0.68 to 1.09) (32.1 versus 36.7%)	RR 0.88 (0.72 to 1.07) (39.8 versus 45.3%)	SMD 0.08 (−0.15 to 0.32) SMD −0.04 (−0.37 to 0.29)	RR 0.88 (0.63 to 1.23) (19.9 versus 22.4%)	RR 0.47 (0.17 to 1.31) (6.5 versus 13.1%)	RR 0.94 (0.81 to 1.1) (66.2 versus 70.3%)
Quality of evidence	Moderate	High	Moderate Low	Moderate	Low	High
Number of studies/ participants	K = 2; n = 491	K = 2; n = 491	K = 1; n = 288 K = 2; n = 483	K = 2; n = 491	K = 2; n = 491	K = 1; n = 293
Forest plot number	Pharm Esc 04.01	Pharm Esc 04.02	Pharm Esc 04.03 Pharm Esc 04.04	Pharm Esc 04.05	Pharm Esc 04.06	Pharm Esc 04.07
Bupropion XL effect size	RR 0.98 (0.78 to 1.22) (40.9 versus 41.8%)	RR 0.98 (0.79 to 1.21) (58.4 versus 59.6%)	Not reported SMD −0.05 (−0.22 to 0.12)	RR 1.08 (0.82 to 1.41) (27.8 versus 25.7%)	RR 0.78 (0.16 to 3.7) (4.3 versus 6.2%)	Not reported
Quality of evidence	Moderate	Moderate	Not reported High	Moderate	Very low	–
Number of studies/ participants	K = 2; n = 571	K = 2; n = 571	Not reported K = 2; n = 529	K = 2; n = 571	K = 2; n = 557	–
Forest plot number	Pharm Esc 04.01	Pharm Esc 04.02	Pharm Esc 04	Pharm Esc 04.05	Pharm Esc 04.06	–

Overall, the quality of the evidence tended to be downgraded because of heterogeneity between trials. Since escitalopram is still in patent its acquisition costs are relatively high compared with antidepressants available in generic form.

10.6   THE THREAD STUDY

The THREAD study (Kendrick *et al.*, 2009) is a pragmatic, open label, multi-centre RCT comparing SSRIs plus supportive care with supportive care alone for mild to moderate depression in primary care. It was designed to address the question of the effectiveness of antidepressants in people with mild to moderate depression because of the uncertainty about the risk–benefit ratio in this group. It did not have a placebo arm and was close to real-life practice. In total, 220 patients were recruited to the trial and outcomes on clinician- and patient-rated measures of depressive symptoms were taken at 12 and 26 weeks. Patients had to meet a minimum criterion score of 12 on the HDRS and symptoms had to have persisted for at least 8 weeks. Supportive care from GPs consisted of follow-up consultations 2, 4, 8 and 12 weeks after the baseline assessment. GPs prescribed and, if thought necessary, switched SSRIs; they were discouraged to do so but GPs could also prescribe antidepressants in the supportive arm of the trial. In total, 87% of patients in the SSRIs plus supportive care arm and 20% in the supportive care alone arm received SSRIs.

The primary outcome reported was the HDRS, which showed a small (2.20 points) difference between the two arms at 12 weeks, which was statistically significant; no significant difference was identified on the BDI. Significant differences were also identified in remission and response rates and a cost-effective analysis suggested that the addition of SSRIs to supportive care might be cost effective, although the cost per QALY was towards the upper end of the accepted NICE range of £20,000/QALY.

The study had a number of limitations including the open label design, the lack of a placebo control, the overall small effect size and the absence of effect on the patient-rated BDI, although it did improve other patient-rated measures. Nevertheless it suggests that SSRIs could be of value in mild to moderate depression for people whose symptoms have persisted for some time. This conclusion is broadly in line with the recommendation developed in the original guideline based on the review of the SSRIs; that is, SSRIs might be considered for patients with mild to moderate depression who have persistent symptoms. However, given the small effect size this study does not suggest changes to the recommendation from the original guideline that SSRIs should not be offered routinely in primary care for people with mild to moderate depression, particularly when other treatments with potentially greater acceptability to patients, such as a range of low-intensity psychosocial interventions, are available.

10.7   MONOAMINE OXIDASE INHIBITORS

The following sections on MAOIs marked by asterisks (**_**) are from the previous guideline and have not been updated except for style and minor clarification.

10.7.1   Introduction

**MAOIs exert their therapeutic effect by binding irreversibly to monoamine oxidase, the enzyme responsible for the degeneration of monoamine neurotransmitters such as NA and serotonin. This results in increased monoamine neurotransmission. The first antidepressant drug synthesised was an irreversible MAOI and drugs in this class have been available in the UK for nearly 50 years.

All MAOIs have the potential to induce hypertensive crisis if foods containing tyramine (which is also metabolised by monoamine oxidase) are eaten (Merriman, 1999) or drugs that increase monoamine neurotransmission are co-prescribed (Livingstone & Livingstone, 1996). These foods and drugs must be avoided for at least 14 days after discontinuing MAOIs. Reversible inhibitors of monoamine oxidase (RIMAs) have a much lower likelihood of causing a hypertensive crisis and dietary restrictions are usually not required. Moclobemide is the only RIMA licensed in the UK.

Dietary restrictions, potentially serious drug interactions and the availability of safer antidepressants have led to the irreversible MAOIs being infrequently prescribed in the UK, even in hospitalised patients. However, MAOIs are still widely cited as being the most effective antidepressants for the treatment of atypical depression (see Section 11.5).

For this class of drugs, the GDG chose to review phenelzine and moclobemide.

10.7.2   Moclobemide

Introduction
Moclobemide is a reversible selective inhibitor of monoamine oxidase A (a RIMA), as opposed to the traditional MAOIs that irreversibly inhibit both monoamine oxidase A and monoamine oxidase B. It has the advantages over the traditional MAOIs that strict dietary restrictions are not required, drug interactions leading to hypertensive crisis are less problematic and shorter washout periods are required when switching to other antidepressants. Moclobemide is generally well-tolerated as it is associated with a low potential for producing anticholinergic side effects, weight gain and symptomatic postural hypotension. It is not widely prescribed in the UK.

Studies considered[112,113]
Forty-four studies were found in a search of electronic databases with 12 meeting the inclusion criteria set by the GDG and 32 being excluded. Twenty-seven additional

---

[112]Details of standard search strings used in all searches are in Appendix 8. Information about each study along with an assessment of methodological quality is in Appendix 17c, which also contains a list of excluded studies with reasons for exclusions.

[113]Study IDs in title case refer to studies included in the previous guideline. References for these studies are in Appendix 18.

studies were identified from other searches undertaken for this guideline, 14 of which met inclusion criteria with 13 being excluded. A total of 26 studies are therefore included in this review (Bakish1992, Barrelet1991, Beaumont1993, Beckers1990, Bougerol1992, Casacchia1984, Duarte1996, Gattaz1995, Geerts1994, Guelfi1992, Hebenstreit90, Hell1994, Jouvent1998, Koczkas1989, KraghSorensen95, Lapierre1997, Larsen1989, Lecrubier1995, Nair1995, Newburn1990, Ose1992, Reynaert1995, Silverstone94, Tanghe1997, Versiani1989, Williams1993) providing efficacy data from up to 1,742 participants and tolerability data from up to 2,149 participants. A total of 45 studies were excluded.

Sixteen studies compared moclobemide with TCAs (Bakish1992, Beaumont1993, Beckers1990, Guelfi1992, Hebenstreit90, Hell1994, Jouvent1998, Koczkas1989, KraghSorensen95, Larsen1989, Lecrubier1995, Nair1995, Newburn1990, Silverstone94, Tanghe1997, Versiani1989), eight with SSRIs (Barrelet1991, Bougerol1992, Duarte1996, Gattaz1995, Geerts1994, Lapierre1997, Reynaert1995, Williams1993) and seven with placebo (Bakish1992, Casacchia1984, Larsen1989, Nair1995, Ose1992, Silverstone1994, Versiani1989).

All included studies were published between 1984 and 1998 and were between 4 and 7 weeks' long (mean = 5.34 weeks). In seven studies, participants were classified as inpatients; in a further seven studies, as outpatients; in two, primary care; and in ten, either a mixture of inpatients and outpatients or the setting was unclear. In one study (Nair1995), the patients were exclusively older adults (aged 60 to 90 years). None of the included studies described participants as having depression with atypical features. Participants received between 150 and 600 mg of moclobemide with most receiving at least 300 mg.

Data were available to compare moclobemide with amitriptyline, clomipramine, dothiepin/dosulepin, imipramine, nortriptyline, fluoxetine, fluvoxamine and placebo.

Clinical evidence statements for moclobemide compared with placebo[114]
Effect of treatment on efficacy outcomes
There is some evidence suggesting that there is a clinically important difference favouring moclobemide over placebo on reducing symptoms of depression by the end of treatment as measured by the HRSD (K = 3; N = 490; Random effects SMD = –0.6; 95% CI, –1.13 to –0.07).

There is some evidence suggesting that there is a clinically important difference favouring moclobemide over placebo on increasing the likelihood of achieving at least a 50% reduction in symptoms of depression as measured by the HRSD (K = 3; N = 606; Random effects RR = 0.7; 95% CI, 0.5 to 0.99).

There is insufficient evidence to determine whether there is a clinically important difference between moclobemide and placebo on increasing the likelihood of achieving remission by the end of treatment as measured by the HRSD (K = 2; N = 111; RR = 0.88; 95% CI, 0.73 to 1.05).

---

[114]The forest plots can be found in Appendix 19c.

Acceptability and tolerability of treatment

There is insufficient evidence to determine if there is a clinically important difference between moclobemide and placebo on:

- reducing the likelihood of leaving treatment early for any reason (K = 7; N = 819; Random effects RR = 0.95; 95% CI, 0.74 to 1.22)
- reducing the likelihood of leaving treatment early due to side effects (K = 6; N = 785; RR = 1.11; 95% CI, 0.6 to 2.04)
- reducing the likelihood of patients reporting side effects (K = 5; N = 615; Random effects RR = 1.12; 95% CI, 0.94 to 1.32).

Clinical evidence statements for moclobemide compared with other antidepressants[115]

Effect of treatment on efficacy outcomes

There is evidence suggesting that there is no clinically important difference between moclobemide and other antidepressants on:

- reducing symptoms of depression by the end of treatment as measured by the HRSD (K = 13[116]; N = 1222; SMD = 0; 95% CI, –0.12 to 0.11)
- increasing the likelihood of achieving remission by the end of treatment as measured by the HRSD (K = 5; N = 402; RR = 1; 95% CI, 0.86 to 1.18)
- increasing the likelihood of achieving at least a 50% reduction in symptoms of depression by the end of treatment as measured by the HRSD or MADRS (K = 13; N= 2070; RR = 1.02; 95% CI, 0.93 to 1.13).

Similar results were found in sub-analyses by antidepressant class and setting.

Acceptability and tolerability of treatment

There is evidence suggesting that there is no clinically important difference between moclobemide and other antidepressants on reducing the likelihood of leaving treatment early for any reason (K = 20; N = 2458; RR = 0.97; 95% CI, 0.85 to 1.11).

Similar results were found in sub-analyses by antidepressant class and setting.

There is strong evidence suggesting that there is a clinically important difference favouring moclobemide over other antidepressants on reducing the likelihood of leaving treatment due to side effects (K = 18; N = 2292; RR = 0.57; 95% CI, 0.44 to 0.75).

There is evidence suggesting that there is a statistically significant difference favouring moclobemide over other antidepressants on reducing the likelihood of patients reporting side effects, but the size of this difference is unlikely to be of clinical importance (K = 12; N = 1472; RR = 0.85; 95% CI, 0.79 to 0.92).

Similar results were found in sub-analyses by setting but not by antidepressant class:

There is evidence suggesting that there is no clinically important difference between moclobemide and SSRIs on reducing the likelihood of patients reporting side effects (K = 6; N = 519; RR = 0.9; 95% CI, 0.79 to 1.03).

---

[115]Ibid.

[116]Two studies (Duarte1996, Tanghe1997) were removed from this analysis to remove heterogeneity from the dataset; this did not affect the results.

Pharmacological interventions

There is insufficient evidence to determine if there is a clinically important difference between moclobemide and SSRIs on reducing the likelihood of leaving treatment early due to side effects (K = 6; N = 660; RR = 0.96; 95% CI, 0.59 to 1.57).

There is strong evidence suggesting that there is a clinically important difference favouring moclobemide over TCAs on reducing the likelihood of leaving treatment due to side effects (K = 12; N = 1632; RR = 0.46; 95% CI, 0.34 to 0.64).

There is evidence suggesting that there is a statistically significant difference favouring moclobemide over TCAs on reducing the likelihood of patients reporting side effects but the size of this difference is unlikely to be of clinical importance (K = 6; N = 953; RR = 0.83; 95% CI, 0.76 to 0.91).

Clinical summary
There is some evidence that moclobemide is more effective than placebo, but insufficient evidence of its tolerability and acceptability. There is evidence that it is equally as effective as other antidepressants (TCAs and SSRIs). While moclobemide is equally as acceptable and tolerable to patients as SSRIs, there is strong evidence that patients receiving moclobemide are less likely to leave treatment early due to side effects than patients receiving TCAs.

10.7.3   Phenelzine

Introduction
Phenelzine is the best tolerated MAOI. Established side effects include hypotension, drowsiness, dizziness, dry mouth and constipation. It has been associated with hepatotoxicity.

Studies considered[117,118]
Twenty-seven studies were found in a search of electronic databases with nine being included and 18 being excluded by the GDG.

Eight studies compared phenelzine with TCAs (Davidson81, Davidson87, Georgotas86, Quitkin1990[119], Raft1981, Robinson1983, Swann1997, Vallejo87) and one with SSRIs (Pande1996). These provided efficacy data from up to 634 trial participants and tolerability data from up to 481 participants.

All included studies were published between 1981 and 1997 and were between 3 and 7 weeks' long (mean = 5.56 weeks). Participants were described as outpatients in eight studies and as inpatients in the other study (Georgotas86). Georgotas86 was also the only study in which all participants were 55 years of age or older (mean

---

[117]Details of standard search strings used in all searches are in Appendix 8. Information about each study along with an assessment of methodological quality is in Appendix 17c, which also contains a list of excluded studies with reasons for exclusions.

[118]Study IDs in title case refer to studies included in the previous guideline. References for these studies are in Appendix 18.

[119]The data from Quitkin1990 was supplied as raw individual patient data by the authors to the NCCMH review team.

age = 65 years). Studies reported mean doses of between 30 and 90 mg of phenelzine. All participants in Pande1996 and 67% of those in Quitkin1990 were diagnosed with depression with additional atypical features.

Data were available to compare phenelzine with amitriptyline, desipramine[120], imipramine, nortriptyline and fluoxetine.

Clinical evidence statements for phenelzine[121]
Effect of treatment on efficacy outcomes
There is some evidence suggesting that there is a clinically important difference favouring phenelzine over other antidepressants on increasing the likelihood of achieving a 50% reduction in symptoms of depression as measured by the HRSD (K = 2; N = 325; RR = 0.66; 95% CI, 0.52 to 0.83).

There is evidence suggesting that there is no clinically important difference between phenelzine and other antidepressants on reducing symptoms of depression by the end of treatment as measured by the HRSD or MADRS (K = 7; N = 634; Random effects SMD = −0.02; 95% CI, −0.33 to 0.28).

There is insufficient evidence to determine whether there is a clinically important difference between phenelzine and other antidepressants on increasing the likelihood of achieving remission by the end of treatment as measured by the HRSD (K = 3; N = 385; Random effects RR = 0.97; 95% CI, 0.55 to 1.70).

There is insufficient evidence to determine whether there is a clinically important difference between phenelzine and SSRIs on any efficacy measure or between phenelzine and TCAs on reducing the likelihood of achieving remission by the end of treatment.

There is some evidence suggesting that there is a clinically important difference favouring phenelzine over TCAs on increasing the likelihood of achieving a 50% reduction in symptoms of depression as measured by the HRSD (K = 1; N = 285; RR = 0.66; 95% CI, 0.52 to 0.83).

There is evidence suggesting that there is no clinically important difference between phenelzine and TCAs on reducing symptoms of depression by the end of treatment as measured by the HRSD or MADRS (K = 6; N = 594; Random effects SMD = −0.07; 95% CI, −0.40 to 0.27).

Acceptability and tolerability of treatment
There is insufficient evidence to determine whether there is a clinically important difference between phenelzine and other antidepressants on reducing the likelihood of leaving treatment early for any reason and on reducing the likelihood of leaving treatment early due to side effects.

There is evidence suggesting that there is no clinically important difference between phenelzine and other antidepressants on reducing the likelihood of patients reporting adverse effects (K = 1; N = 60; RR = 0.97; 95% CI, 0.87 to 1.09).

A sub-analysis by antidepressant class gave similar results.

---

[120]Not licensed for use in the UK.
[121]The forest plots can be found in Appendix 19c.

Clinical summary

There is some evidence suggesting a superior efficacy for response for phenelzine compared with other antidepressants. These findings are probably explained by the high proportion of patients with depression with atypical features in the studies reporting response (71% of patients had depression with atypical features) and remission (56% of patients had depression with atypical features). (A separate review of the pharmacological treatment of atypical depression is provided in Section 11.5.)

There is no difference in mean endpoint scores between the two groups of treatments in patients with depression regardless of additional atypical features. This is also evident in comparisons with TCAs alone. Evidence from studies comparing phenelzine with SSRIs was too weak to draw any conclusions.

There is insufficient evidence to draw any conclusions on the comparative tolerability of phenelzine against alternative antidepressants.

10.8   THIRD-GENERATION ANTIDEPRESSANTS[122]

Sections on third-generation antidepressants marked by asterisks (**_**) are from the previous guideline and have not been updated except for style and minor clarification.

10.8.1   Introduction

This diverse group of antidepressants was marketed after the SSRIs. The aim was to broaden the mechanism of action beyond serotonin in order to improve efficacy without incurring the side effects or toxicity in overdose associated with the TCAs.

The following drugs are reviewed in this section: duloxetine (a new review for this updated guideline), mirtazapine, reboxetine and venlafaxine.

10.8.2   Duloxetine

Introduction

Duloxetine has been licensed since the publication of the previous guideline. It is similar to venlafaxine in that it inhibits the reuptake of both serotonin and NA, and is a weak inhibitor of dopamine reuptake. Duloxetine is associated with nausea and headache, and can also increase blood pressure. It is one of the few antidepressants that has been tested in double-blind, placebo-controlled trials in elderly patients. Duloxetine is available under two brand names from the same manufacturer; one is licensed primarily for depression, and the other for stress urinary incontinence.

---

[122]Although these are classified 'other antidepressants' by the BNF, to avoid confusion with the guideline's use of 'other antidepressants' to mean all other antidepressants, the GDG uses the term 'third-generation antidepressants' to describe this group of drugs.

Table 74: Databases searched and inclusion/exclusion criteria for clinical effectiveness of pharmacological treatments

Electronic databases	MEDLINE, EMBASE, PsycINFO, CINAHL
Date searched	Database inception to January 2008
Update searches	July 2008; January 2009
Study design	RCT
Population	People with a diagnosis of depression according to DSM, ICD or similar criteria
Treatments	Duloxetine, placebo, other antidepressants

Databases searched and the inclusion/exclusion criteria

For the present review, both published and unpublished double-blind RCTs were sought that compared duloxetine either with placebo or with another antidepressant. The marketing authorisation holder, Eli Lilly, was also contacted for data. Information about the databases searched for published trials and the inclusion/exclusion criteria used are presented in Table 74. Details of the search strings used are in Appendix 8.

Studies considered[123]

In total, 27 acute-phase trials were sourced from searches of electronic databases and from the website of the drug's manufacturer, Eli Lilly, which included links to the clinical trials website www.clinicaltrialresults.org from where full trial reports were downloaded. In all, 18 trials (four unpublished) were included with nine excluded (seven unpublished). (One trial is also included in the review of treatment-resistant depression [see Chapter 12, Section 12.3] because it re-randomised patients who did not respond to acute phase treatment.) Only data from patients given at least the licensed dose (60 mg) were included in the analyses, apart from in trials that used a variable dose and in trials where comparisons with the licensed dose were possible.

Data were available to compare duloxetine with placebo, with duloxetine at different doses, and with other antidepressants (SSRIs or venlafaxine). In addition, three trials continued treatment for those with at least a partial response (>30% improvement in baseline depression scores). Summary study characteristics of the included studies are presented in Table 75 with full details in Appendix 17c, which also includes details of excluded studies.

---

[123]Study IDs in title case refer to studies included in the previous guideline and study IDs in capital letters refer to studies found and included in this guideline update. References for studies from the previous guideline are in Appendix 18.

Table 75: Summary study characteristics of studies of duloxetine

	Versus placebo	Versus different doses	Versus other antidepressants
No. trials (total participants)	12 RCTs (3,069)	5 RCTs (1242)	12 RCTs (3,367)
Study IDs	(1) BRANNAN2005A (2) BRECHT2007 (3) DETKE2002 (4) DETKE2002A (5) DETKE2004[†] (6) ELI LILLY HMAQ[‡] (7) ELI LILLY HMAT-A[‡] (8) GOLDSTEIN2002[‡] (9) GOLDSTEIN2004[†] (10) NIERENBERG2007B[‡] (11) PERAHIA2006B[†] (12) RASKIN2007	(1) DETKE2004[†] (2) ELI LILLY HMAT-A[‡] (3) GOLDSTEIN2004[†] (4) PERAHIA2006B[†] (5) WHITMYER2007[‡]	(1) DETKE2004[†] (2) ELI LILLY HMAQ[‡] (3) ELI LILLY HMBU (4) ELI LILLY HMCQ[‡] (5) ELI LILLY HMAT-A[‡] (6) GOLDSTEIN2002[‡] (7) GOLDSTEIN2004[†] (8) KHAN2007B (9) LEE2007 (10) NIERENBERG2007B[‡] (11) PERAHIA2006B[†] (12) WADE2007
N/% female	(1) 282/65 (2) 327/74 (3) 267/69 (4) 245/67 (5) 281/73 (6) 157/67 (7) 174/62 (8) 140/64	(1) 188/73 (2) 175/62 (3) 177/62 (4) 196/70 (5) 506/64	(1) 180/73 (2) 119/67 (3) 323/71 (4) 504/66 (5) 173/62 (6) 103/64 (7) 178/62 (8) 278/60

	(9) 180/62 (10) 410/65 (11) 295/70 (12) 311/60		(9) 478/70 (10) 547/65 (11) 190/70 (12) 294/72
Mean age	(1) 40 (2) 50 (3) 41 (4) 42 (5) 43 (6) 40 (7) 44 (8) 41 (9) 40 (10) 42 (11) 45 (12) 72	(1) 43 (2) 44 (3) 40 (4) 45 (5) 43	(1) 43 (2) 40 (3) 44 (4) 42 (5) 44 (6) 41 (7) 44 (8) 42 (9) 38 (10) 42 (11) 45 (12) 45
Duloxetine dose	(1)–(4) 60 mg (5) 80 mg, 120 mg (6) 40–120 mg (7) 40 mg*, 80 mg (8) 120 mg (9) 40 mg*, 80 mg (10) 60 mg (11) 80 mg, 120 mg (12) 60 mg	(1) 80 mg versus 120 mg (2)–(3) 40 mg versus 80 mg (4) 80 mg versus 120 mg (5) 30 mg versus 60 mg	(1) 80 mg (2) 40–120 mg (3)–(4) 60 mg (5) 80 mg (6) 120 mg (7) 80 mg (8)–(10) 60 mg (11) 80 mg (12) 60 mg

Continued

Table 75: (*Continued*)

	Versus placebo	Versus different doses	Versus other antidepressants
Comparator	Placebo	Duloxetine (doses as above)	(1) Paroxetine 20 mg (2) Fluoxetine 20 mg (3) Venlafaxine 150 mg (4) Venlafaxine 150 mg, 75 mg (5) Paroxetine 20 mg (6) Fluoxetine 20 mg (7) Paroxetine 20 mg (8) Escitalopram 10 mg (9) Paroxetine 20 mg (10) Escitalopram 10 mg (11) Paroxetine 20 mg (12) Escitalopram 10 mg
Setting	Outpatients	Outpatients	Outpatients
Length of treatment	(1) 9 weeks (2) 8 weeks (3)–(4) 9 weeks (5) 8 weeks (6) 10 weeks (7)–(12) 8 weeks	(1)–(4) 8 weeks (5) 6 weeks	(1) 9 weeks (2) 8 weeks (3)–(4) 12 weeks (5) 8 weeks (6) 10 weeks (7)–(12) 8 weeks
Continuation phase (length and inclusion criterion)	(5) 6 months for partial responders (6) 6 months but data not available (11) 6 months for partial responders	(1) 6 months for partial responders (2) 6 months but data not available (4) 6 months for partial responders (5) Non-responders re-randomised (data in Chapter 12, Section 12.3)	(1) 6 months for partial responders (2) 6 months but data not available (11) 6 months for partial responders

*Data not used as dose given less than licensed dose; †4-armed trial; ‡3-armed trial.

Clinical evidence

Duloxetine versus placebo

Although the effect sizes for all three efficacy outcomes for duloxetine (dose at least as large as the licensed dose of 60 mg) versus placebo were statistically significant and favoured duloxetine, with only that for non-response approaching clinical importance, there were similar effect sizes for duloxetine at different doses when these data were looked at separately, although the effect sizes for duloxetine at 120 mg versus placebo was larger than those for lower does (WMD $= -2.57, -3.77$ to -1.37). The data for duloxetine at different doses can be seen in the full evidence profiles and forest plots (Appendix 16c and Appendix 19c, respectively).

Two trials specifically examined depression-related pain using the self-report Brief Pain Inventory (BPI) scale. There was an average reduction of three-quarters of a point (on an 11-point Likert scale) for the 'average pain in last 24 hours' item.

There was little difference between the number of people receiving duloxetine who left treatment early for any reason and those receiving placebo on this measure. However, of those leaving treatment early, twice as many taking duloxetine as those taking placebo left specifically because of side effects while twice as many taking placebo left because of lack of efficacy. The numbers reporting side effects were high in both groups, with more among those taking duloxetine. Those taking duloxetine also experienced a small average weight loss compared with those on placebo, although these data were of low quality largely because of heterogeneity. The quality of the evidence was moderate or low, largely because of the selective population included in the studies.

Evidence from the important outcomes and overall quality of evidence are presented in Table 76. The full evidence profiles and associated forest plots can be found in Appendix 16c and Appendix 19c, respectively.

Three studies continued patients who achieved at least partial response to acute-phase treatment (defined as $>= 30\%$ decrease in baseline HAMD scores) (DETKE-2004, ELI LILLY HMAQ, PERAHIA2006B), although there were no extractable data in ELI LILLY HMAQ. There was no difference in symptoms of depression or on acceptability and tolerability measures between duloxetine at either 80 or 120 mg and placebo.

Evidence from the important outcomes and overall quality of evidence are presented in Table 77. The full evidence profiles and associated forest plots can be found in Appendix 16c and Appendix 19c, respectively.

Duloxetine comparing different doses

Data were available to compare duloxetine at 40 mg (less than the licensed dose) with 80 mg, 30 mg with 60 mg, and 80 mg with 120 mg. There were no statistically or clinically important differences between the doses on either efficacy or acceptability and tolerability outcomes, although there were few trials. Evidence from the important outcomes and overall quality of evidence are presented in Table 78. The full evidence profiles and associated forest plots can be found in Appendix 16c and Appendix 19c, respectively.

One study comparing duloxetine at different doses included a continuation phase for those who achieved at least partial response to acute-phase treatment (defined as

Table 76: Summary evidence profile for duloxetine versus placebo (acute phase)

	Mean depression change scores at endpoint	Non-response	Non-remission	Depression related pain (average pain in last 24 hours)	Leaving treatment early	Leaving treatment early due to side effects	Leaving treatment early due to lack of efficacy	N reporting side effects	Weight change (kg)
Clinician-rated effect size	WMD −1.9 (−2.44 to −1.35)	RR 0.78 (0.74 to 0.83) (51.6 versus 67.3%)	RR 0.83 (0.79 to 0.87) (62 versus 75.2%)	WMD −0.74 (−1.13 to −0.34)	RR 1.02 (0.91 to 1.15) (26.9 versus 28.4%)	RR 2.22 (1.66 to 2.95) (10 versus 5%)	RR 0.34 (0.22 to 0.54) (7.3 versus 11.5%)	RR 1.18 (1.12 to 1.24) (66 versus 51%)	WMD −0.69 (−1 to −0.38)
Quality of evidence	Moderate	Low	Moderate	Moderate	Moderate	Moderate	Moderate	Moderate	Low
Number of studies/ participants	K = 10; n = 2249	K = 12; n = 3078	K = 11; n = 2789	K = 2; n = 583	K = 11; n = 2895	K = 11; n = 2921	K = 6; n = 1763	K = 10; n = 2647	K = 8; n = 1663
Forest plot number	Dul 01.02*	Dul 01.04*	Dul 01.06*	Dul 01.09	Dul 02.02	Dul 02.04	Dul 02.07	Dul 02.09	Dul 02.11

*The full data for these outcomes for different doses are shown in the forest plots Dul 01.01, Dul 01.03 and Dul 01.05 in Appendix 19c.

Table 77: Summary evidence profile for duloxetine versus placebo (continuation phase for partial responders)

	Mean depression change scores at endpoint	Leaving treatment early	Leaving treatment early due to side effects	Leaving treatment early due to lack of efficacy
80 mg Clinician-rated effect size	WMD -1 (-2.5 to 0.5)	RR 0.94 (0.81 to 1.08) (82 versus 87%)	RR 0.96 (0.34 to 2.73) (5 versus 5%)	RR 1 (0.06 to 15.68) (1 versus 1%)
Quality of evidence	Low	Low	Moderate	Low
Number of studies/ participants	K = 1; n = 140	K = 1; n = 142	K = 2; n = 275	K = 1; n = 142
Forest plot number	Dul 07.01	Dul 07.02	Dul 07.03	Dul 07.04
120 mg Clinician-rated effect size	WMD -0.2 (-1.78 to 1.38)	RR 0.88 (0.75 to 1.02) (77 versus 87%)	RR 0.84 (0.28 to 2.54) (4 versus 5%)	RR 3.51 (0.4 to 30.65) (5 versus 1%)
Quality of evidence	Low	Low	Moderate	Low
Number of studies/ participants	K = 1; n = 150	K = 1; n = 152	K = 2; n = 280	K = 1; n = 152
Forest plot number	Dul 07.01	Dul 07.02	Dul 07.03	Dul 07.04

$>=$ 30% decrease in baseline HAMD scores) (PERAHIA2006B). This showed no difference between the doses. The quality of the evidence was low or very low. Evidence from the important outcomes and overall quality of evidence are presented in Table 79. The full evidence profiles and associated forest plots can be found in Appendix 16c and Appendix 19c, respectively.

Duloxetine versus other antidepressants
Data were available to compare duloxetine with paroxetine, fluoxetine, escitalopram and venlafaxine. There was no difference between duloxetine and other antidepressants, except venlafaxine which was more effective on mean change scores at endpoint (although the effect size was small and not quite statistically significant). Duloxetine was less acceptable to patients, as measured by the number leaving treatment early, and more people taking duloxetine left specifically because of adverse reactions. However,

Table 78: Summary evidence profile for duloxetine comparing different doses (acute phase)

	Mean depression change scores at endpoint	Non-response	Non-remission	Leaving treatment early	Leaving treatment early due to side effects	Leaving treatment early due to lack of efficacy	N reporting side effects	Weight change (kg)
40 mg versus 80 mg Clinician-rated effect size	WMD 0.58 (−0.87 to 2.03)	RR 1.05 (0.89 to 1.24) (62 versus 59%)	RR 1.15 (0.92 to 1.43) (72 versus 63%)	RR 0.73 (0.57 to 0.95) (35 versus 47%)	RR 0.77 (0.45 to 1.31) (12 versus 15%)	Not reported	RR 0.99 (0.91 to 1.07) (85 versus 86%)	WMD −0.19 (−0.69 to 0.31)
Quality of evidence	Very low	Low	Moderate	Moderate	Low	–	Moderate	Low
Number of studies/ participants	K = 2; n = 341	K = 2; n = 352	K = 2; n = 353	K = 2; n = 352	K = 2; n = 352	–	K = 2; n = 352	K = 2; n = 325
Forest plot number	Dul 03.01	Dul 03.02	Dul 03.03	Dul 04.01	Dul 04.02	–	Dul 04.04	Dul 04.05
30 mg versus 60 mg Clinician-rated effect size	WMD 0.83 (−0.43 to 2.09)	RR 0.96 (0.84 to 1.08) (62 versus 65%)	RR 0.97 (0.84 to 1.11) (57 versus 59%)	RR 0.82 (0.62 to 1.07) (25 versus 30%)	RR 0.47 (0.24 to 0.91) (5 versus 10%)	RR 0.98 (0.25 to 3.87) 1 versus 1%	RR 0.99 (0.9 to 1.1) (73 versus 74%)	WMD −0.35 (−1 to 0.3)
Quality of evidence	Very low	Moderate	Moderate	Very low	Low	Very low	Low	Low
Number of studies/ participants	K = 1; n = 400	K = 1; n = 647	K = 1; n = 647	K = 1; n = 647	K = 1; n = 647	K = 1; n = 647	K = 1; n = 647	K = 1; n = 323

Forest plot number	Dul 03.01	Dul 03.02	Dul 03.03	Dul 04.01	Dul 04.02	Dul 04.03	Dul 04.04	Dul 04.05
80 mg versus 120 mg Clinician-rated effect size	WMD 0.7 (−0.28 to 1.68)	RR 1.13 (0.85 to 1.5) (35 versus 31%)	RR 1.01 (0.83 to 1.23) (55 versus 55%)	RR 1.15 (0.65 to 2.03) (12 versus 10%)	RR 1.2 (0.44 to 3.24) (4 versus 4%)	RR 1.56 (0.45 to 5.44) (3 versus 2%)	RR 1.12 (0.9 to 1.4) (49 versus 41%)	WMD −0.08 (−0.69 to 0.53)
Quality of evidence	Very low	Low	Low	Low	Very low	Very low	Low	Low
Number of studies/participants	K = 2; n = 381	K = 2; n = 384	K = 2; n = 384	K = 2; n = 384	K = 2; n = 384	K = 2; n = 384	K = 2; n = 384	K = 1; n = 186
Forest plot number	Dul 03.01	Dul 03.02	Dul 03.03	Dul 04.01	Dul 04.02	Dul 04.03	Dul 04.04	Dul 04.05

Table 79: Summary evidence profile for duloxetine comparing different doses (continuation phase for partial responders)

	Mean depression change scores at endpoint*	Leaving treatment early	Leaving treatment early due to side effects	Leaving treatment early due to lack of efficacy
80 mg versus 120 mg Clinician-rated effect size	WMD −0.8 (−2.18 to 0.58)	RR 1.07 (0.91 to 1.26) (82 versus 77%)	RR 0.76 (0.13 to 4.42) (3 versus 4%)	RR 0.29 (0.03 to 2.49) (1 versus 5%)
Quality of evidence	Low	Low	Very low	Very low
Number of studies/ participants	K = 1; n = 150	K = 1; n = 152	K = 1; n = 152	K = 1; n = 152
Forest plot number	Dul 08.01	Dul 08.02	Dul 08.03	Dul 08.04

*Change from end of acute phase.

there was no difference between duloxetine and other antidepressants on numbers leaving treatment early because of lack of efficacy, on the number of people reporting side effects or on weight change. The quality of the evidence was moderate, low or very low, largely because of the selective population included in the studies.

Evidence from the important outcomes and overall quality of evidence are presented in Table 80. The full evidence profiles and associated forest plots can be found in Appendix 16c and Appendix 19c, respectively.

Two studies comparing duloxetine with other antidepressants included a continuation phase for those who achieved at least partial response to acute-phase treatment (defined as >= 30% decrease in baseline HAMD scores) (DETKE2004, PERAHIA2006B). Both studies compared duloxetine with paroxetine. Only one outcome was reported by both studies. This showed no difference between the doses. The quality of the evidence was low. Evidence from the important outcomes and overall quality of evidence are presented in Table 81. The full evidence profiles and associated forest plots can be found in Appendix 16c and Appendix 19c, respectively.

Table 80: Summary evidence profile for duloxetine versus other antidepressants (acute phase)

	All	Paroxetine	Fluoxetine	Escitalopram	Venlafaxine
Mean depression change scores at endpoint	WMD 0.19 (−0.44 to 0.81)	WMD −0.2 (−1.14 to 0.74)	WMD −1.1 (−3.03 to 0.83)	WMD 0.66 (−0.61 to 1.93)	WMD 1.06 (−0.02 to 2.14)
Quality	Low	Low	Very low	Low	Moderate
Number of studies; participants	K = 12; n = 3145	K = 5; n = 1184	K = 2; n = 217	K = 3; n = 1096	K = 2; n = 648
Forest plot number	Dul 05.01	Dul 05.01	Dul 05.01	Dul 05.01	Dul 05.01
Non-response	RR 1.05 (0.95 to 1.17) (49 versus 46%)	RR 1.01 (0.81 to 1.26) (44 versus 43%)	RR 0.99 (0.72 to 1.36) (53 versus 53%)	RR 1.04 (0.94 to 1.16) (59 versus 57%)	RR 1.23 (0.92 to 1.64) (40 versus 32%)
Quality	Low	Low	Low	Moderate	Very low
Number of studies; participants	K = 12; n = 3208	K = 5; n = 1200	K = 2; n = 222	K = 3; n = 1119	K = 2; n = 667
Forest plot number	Dul 05.02	Dul 05.02	Dul 05.02	Dul 05.02	Dul 05.02
Non-remission	RR 1.02 (0.94 to 1.11) (58 versus 56%)	RR 0.99 (0.9 to 1.10) (56 versus 56%)	RR 1.21 (0.56 to 2.61) (61 versus 52%)	RR 1.06 (0.89 to 1.26) (61 versus 60%)	RR 1.06 (0.88 to 1.27) (54 versus 51%)

Continued

371

Table 80: (*Continued*)

	All	Paroxetine	Fluoxetine	Escitalopram	Venlafaxine
Quality	Low	Moderate	Very low	Low	Low
Number of studies; participants	K = 12; n = 3208	K = 5; n = 1200	K = 2; n = 222	K = 3; n = 1119	K = 2; n = 667
Forest plot number	Dul 05.03	Dul 05.03	Dul 05.03	Dul 05.03	Dul 05.03
Leaving treatment early	RR 1.27 (1.01 to 1.45) (32 versus 24%)	RR 1.21 (1.01 to 1.45) (29 versus 24%)	RR 0.87 (0.59 to 1.27) (32 versus 37%)	RR 1.64 (0.97 to 2.78) (32 versus 21%)	RR 1.37 (1.09 to 1.72) (35 versus 26%)
Quality	Low	Moderate	Very low	Low	Moderate
Number of studies; participants	K = 11; n = 2914	K = 5; n = 1200	K = 2; n = 222	K = 2; n = 825	K = 2; n = 667
Forest plot number	Dul 06.01	Dul 06.01	Dul 06.01	Dul 06.01	Dul 06.01
Leaving treatment early due to side effects	RR 1.54 (1.2 to 1.99) (10 versus 7%)	RR 1.32 (0.9 to 1.93) (9 versus 7%)	RR 3.3 (0.42 to 25.74) (10 versus 3%)	RR 2.62 (0.67 to 10.3) (9 versus 4%)	RR 1.58 (1.04 to 2.42) (15 versus 9%)
Quality	Moderate	Low	Very low	Very low	Moderate
Number of studies; participants	K = 10; n = 2795	K = 5; n = 1200	K = 1; n = 103	K = 2; n = 825	K = 2; n = 667

Forest plot number	Dul 06.02	Dul 06.02	Dul 06.02	Dul 06.02	Dul 06.02
Leaving treatment early due to lack of efficacy	RR 1.09 (0.70 to 1.68) (3 versus 3%)	RR 2.29 (0.6 to 8.78) (2 versus 1%)	Not reported	RR 0.88 (0.51 to 1.53) (5 versus 6%)	RR 1.24 (0.52 to 2.95) (3 versus 3%)
Quality	Moderate	Very low		Very low	Very low
Number of studies; participants	K = 7; n = 2341	K = 3; n = 849	–	K = 2; n = 825	K = 2; n = 667
Forest plot number	Dul 06.03	Dul 06.03	–	Dul 06.03	Dul 06.03
N reporting side effects	RR 1.02 (0.98 to 1.07) (79 versus 76%)	RR 1.07 (0.99 to 1.15) (71 versus 65%)	RR 0.97 (0.85 to 1.12) (89 versus 91%)	RR 1.02 (0.96 to 1.09) (88 versus 87%)	RR 0.99 (0.88 to 1.11) (86 versus 87%)
Quality	Moderate	Moderate	Low	Low	Low
Number of studies; participants	K = 9; n = 2517	K = 5; n 1200	K = 1; n = 103	K = 1; n = 547	K = 2; n = 667
Forest plot number	Dul 06.04	Dul 06.04	Dul 06.04	Dul 06.04	Dul 06.04
Weight change (kg)	WMD 0 (−0.03 to 0.03)	WMD 0 (−0.03 to 0.03)	WMD −0.01 (−0.74 to 0.72)	WMD 0.06 (−1.08 to 1.2)	WMD 0.39 (−0.09 to 0.86)
Quality	Moderate	Moderate	Low	Low	Moderate
Number of studies; participants	K = 8; n = 2207	K = 4; n = 834	K = 1; n = 98	K = 1; n = 547	K = 2; n = 579
Forest plot number	Dul 06.05	Dul 06.06	Dul 06.06	Dul 06.06	Dul 06.06

Table 81: Summary evidence profile for duloxetine versus other antidepressants (continuation phase for partial responders)

	Paroxetine
Mean depression change scores at endpoint*	WMD 0.3 (-1.06 to 1.66)
Quality	Low
Number of studies; participants	K = 1; n = 140
Forest plot number	Dul 09.01
Leaving treatment early	RR 0.94 (0.81 to 1.08) (82 versus 87%)
Quality	Low
Number of studies; participants	K = 1; n = 141
Forest plot number	Dul 09.02
Leaving treatment early due to side effects	RR 2.84 (0.7 to 11.6) (5 versus 1%)
Quality	Very low
Number of studies; participants	K = 2; n = 286
Forest plot number	Dul 09.03
Leaving treatment early due to lack of efficacy	RR 0.49 (0.05 to 5.31) (1 versus 3%)
Quality	Very low
Number of studies; participants	K = 1; n = 141
Forest plot number	Dul 09.04

*Change from end of acute phase.

One study comparing duloxetine with other antidepressants included a continuation phase for all those entering the study regardless of response during the acute phase of the study (WADE2007). This compared duloxetine with escitalopram. There was a small difference in favour of escitalopram in efficacy measures, which was not clinically important, and the number of patients leaving treatment early specifically because of side effects favoured escitalopram. Evidence from the important outcomes and overall quality of evidence are presented in Table 82. The full evidence profiles and associated forest plots can be found in Appendix 16c and Appendix 19c, respectively.

Table 82: Summary evidence profile for duloxetine versus other antidepressants (continuation phase for all)

	Escitalopram
Mean depression change scores at endpoint*	WMD 1.34 (-0.25 to 2.93)
Quality	Low
Number of studies; participants	K = 1; n = 287
Forest plot number	Dul 11.01
Non-response	RR 1.16 (0.82 to 1.65) (33 versus 28%)
Quality	Very low
Number of studies; participants	K = 1; n = 294
Forest plot number	Dul 11.02
Non-remission	RR 1.32 (0.86 to 2.02) (26 versus 20%)
Quality	Low
Number of studies; participants	K = 1; n = 294
Forest plot number	Dul 11.03
Leaving treatment early	RR 1.13 (0.74 to 1.72) (25 versus 22%)
Quality	Very low
Number of studies; participants	K = 1; n = 294
Forest plot number	Dul 11.04
Leaving treatment early due to side effects	RR 1.89 (1.01 to 3.54) (17 versus 9%)
Quality	Low
Number of studies; participants	K = 1; n = 294
Forest plot number	Dul 11.05
Leaving treatment early due to lack of efficacy	RR 0.27 (0.06 to 1.28) (1 versus 5%)
Quality	Very low
Number of studies; participants	K = 1; n = 294
Forest plot number	Dul 11.06

*Change from end of acute phase.

Clinical summary

There does not seem to be any advantage for duloxetine over other antidepressants. The difference in endpoint depression scores compared with placebo is small, and there does not seem to be an important reduction in pain associated with depression in those trials that reported this measure (WMD = −0.74 [−1.13 to −0.34] that is, three-quarters of a point difference between the groups). There appears to be no advantage for doses of duloxetine above the licensed dose of 60 mg, although there are few trials comparing higher doses, and no trials comparing 60 mg with higher doses. There was no advantage found for increasing the dose for partial responders.

Overall the quality of the evidence was downgraded because of the highly selective patient populations in the trials, with evidence for some outcome-comparison combinations being downgraded further largely because of low numbers of trials. Since duloxetine is still in patent its acquisition costs are relatively high compared with antidepressants available in generic form (see Section 10.10.2).

10.8.3   Mirtazapine

Introduction

**Mirtazapine is a noradrenaline and specific serotonin antidepressant (NaSSA) that blocks presynaptic alpha 2 receptors on both NA and 5HT neurones and also blocks postsynaptic 5HT2 (less sexual dysfunction but possible worsening of the symptoms of obsessive-compulsive disorder) and 5HT3 (less nausea) receptors. It can cause weight gain and sedation.

Studies considered[124,125]

Twenty-five studies were found in a search of electronic databases and details of a study in press were provided by Organon Laboratories Ltd (Wade2003). Fifteen studies were included (although the efficacy data from one of these, Wade2003, were excluded because more than 50% of participants left treatment early) and 11 were excluded by the GDG.

Nine studies compared mirtazapine with TCAs and related antidepressants (Bremner1995, Bruijn1996, Halikas1995, Marttila1995, Mullin1996, Richou1995, Smith1990, VanMoffaert1995, Zivkov1995), five compared it with SSRIs (Benkert2000, Leinone1999, Schatzberg2002, Wade2003, Wheatley1998), and one with venlafaxine (Guelfi2001). These provided efficacy data from up to 2,491 trial participants and tolerability data from up to 2,637 participants.

All included studies were published between 1990 and 2003 and were between 5 and 24 weeks' long (mode = 6 weeks). In five studies participants were described as inpatients, in six as outpatients, one was from primary care and in the other three

---

[124]Details of standard search strings used in all searches are in Appendix 8. Information about each study along with an assessment of methodological quality is in Appendix 17c, which also contains a list of excluded studies with reasons for exclusions.

[125]Study IDs in title case refer to studies included in the previous guideline. References for these studies are in Appendix 18.

it was either not clear from where participants were sourced or they were from mixed sources. In one study (Schatzberg2002), all participants were 65 years of age or older. Studies reported mean doses of between 22 and 76.2 mg of mirtazapine.

Data were available to compare mirtazapine with amitriptyline, clomipramine, doxepin, imipramine, trazodone, citalopram, fluoxetine, paroxetine and venlafaxine.

Clinical evidence statements[126]
Effect of treatment on efficacy outcomes
There is no difference between the efficacy of mirtazapine and other antidepressants for which comparisons were available:

There is evidence suggesting that there is no clinically important difference between mirtazapine and other antidepressants on:

- increasing the likelihood of achieving a 50% reduction in symptoms of depression by the end of treatment as measured by the HRSD (K = 14[127]; N = 2440; RR = 0.92; 95% CI, 0.84 to 1.01)
- reducing symptoms of depression by the end of treatment as measured by the HRSD or the MADRS (K = 14; N = 2,314; SMD = –0.03; 95% CI, –0.11 to 0.05).

There is evidence suggesting that there is a statistically significant difference favouring mirtazapine over other antidepressants on increasing the likelihood of achieving remission by the end of treatment as measured by the HRSD, but the size of this difference is unlikely to be of clinical importance (K = 4; N = 819; RR = 0.91; 95% CI, 0.83 to 0.99).

Similar results were found in sub-analyses by antidepressant class, other than for SSRIs:

There is evidence suggesting that there is a statistically significant difference favouring mirtazapine over SSRIs on reducing symptoms of depression by the end of treatment, but the size of this difference is unlikely to be of clinical importance (K = 4; N = 888; SMD = –0.13; 95% CI, –0.27 to 0.00).

Effect of setting on efficacy outcomes
There is evidence suggesting that there is no clinically important difference between mirtazapine and other antidepressants on:

- reducing symptoms of depression by the end of treatment in inpatients as measured by the HRSD or MADRS (K = 5; N = 854; Random effects SMD = 0.05; 95% CI, –0.15 to 0.24)
- increasing the likelihood of achieving remission in outpatients by the end of treatment (K = 2; N = 387; RR = 0.93; 95% CI, 0.81 to 1.05)
- reducing symptoms of depression in outpatients by the end of treatment as measured by the HRSD or the MADRS (K = 6; N = 915; SMD = –0.1; 95% CI, –0.23 to 0.03).

In outpatients there is evidence suggesting that there is a statistically significant difference favouring mirtazapine over other antidepressants on increasing the

---

[126]The forest plots can be found in Appendix 19c.
[127]One study (Wade2003) was removed because >50% of participants left the study early.

likelihood of achieving a 50% reduction in symptoms of depression by the end of treatment as measured by the HRSD, but the size of this difference is unlikely to be of clinical importance (K = 6; N = 957; RR = 0.86; 95% CI, 0.73 to 1).

In inpatients there is insufficient evidence to determine whether there is a clinically important difference between mirtazapine and other antidepressants on increasing the likelihood of achieving a 50% reduction in symptoms of depression or on achieving remission.

No data were available to determine efficacy in patients in primary care.

Acceptability and tolerability of treatment
Mirtazapine appears to be as acceptable to patients as other antidepressants, except that fewer patients leave treatment early due to side effects:

There is evidence suggesting that there is no clinically important difference between mirtazapine and other antidepressants on reducing the likelihood of leaving treatment early for any reason (K = 15; N = 2637; RR = 0.88; 95% CI, 0.78 to 1).

There is strong evidence suggesting that there is a clinically important difference favouring mirtazapine over other antidepressants on reducing the likelihood of patients leaving treatment early due to side effects (K = 15; N = 2637; RR = 0.69; 95% CI, 0.55 to 0.87).

There is evidence suggesting that there is no clinically important difference between mirtazapine and other antidepressants on reducing the likelihood of patients reporting side effects (K = 6; N = 1253; RR = 0.99; 95% CI, 0.93 to 1.05).

Findings were similar in sub-analyses by setting and class of antidepressant.

Clinical summary
There is no difference between mirtazapine and other antidepressants on any efficacy measure, although in terms of achieving remission mirtazapine appears to have a statistical though not clinical advantage. In addition, mirtazapine has a statistical advantage over SSRIs in terms of reducing symptoms of depression, but the difference is not clinically important.

However, there is strong evidence that patients taking mirtazapine are less likely to leave treatment early because of side effects, although this is not the case for patients reporting side effects or leaving treatment early for any reason.

Therefore, although mirtazapine is as effective as other antidepressants, it may have an advantage in terms of reducing side effects likely to lead to patients leaving treatment early.**

10.8.4 Reboxetine

Introduction
**Reboxetine is a relatively selective, noradrenergic reuptake inhibitor. Side effects include insomnia, sweating, dizziness, dry mouth and constipation (Holm & Spencer, 1999). It may also lower serum potassium (The Association of the British Pharmaceutical Industry, 2003). It is not licensed for use in older adults.

Studies considered[128,129]

Eight studies were found in a search of electronic databases, with six (Andreoli2002, Ban1998, Berzewski1997, Katona1999, Massana1999, Versiani2000B) being included and two excluded.

Three studies compare reboxetine with placebo (Andreoli2002, Ban1998, Versiani2000B), three with TCAs (Ban1998, Berzewski1997, Katona1999) and two with SSRIs (Andreoli2002, Massana1999). These provided efficacy and tolerability data from up to 1,068 trial participants.

All included studies were published between 1997 and 2002 and were between 4 and 8 weeks' long (mean = 6.66 weeks). In two studies participants were described as inpatients and in the other three it was either not clear from where participants were sourced or they were from mixed sources. In one (Katona1999), all participants were aged 65 years and over. Apart from Katona1999, where participants received a dose of 6 mg, doses were between 8 and 10 mg of reboxetine.

Data were available to compare reboxetine with desipramine, imipramine, fluoxetine and placebo.

Clinical evidence statements for reboxetine compared with placebo[130]

Effect of treatment on efficacy outcomes

There is strong evidence suggesting that there is a clinically important difference favouring reboxetine over placebo on increasing the likelihood of achieving a 50% reduction in symptoms of depression as measured by the HRSD (K = 3; N = 479; RR = 0.61; 95% CI, 0.51 to 0.73).

There is some evidence suggesting that there is a clinically important difference favouring reboxetine over placebo on increasing the likelihood of achieving remission by the end of treatment (K = 1; N = 254; RR = 0.71; 95% CI, 0.59 to 0.87).

Acceptability and tolerability of treatment

There is insufficient evidence to determine whether there is a clinically important difference between reboxetine and placebo on any measure of acceptability or tolerability.

Clinical evidence statements for reboxetine compared with other antidepressants[131]

Effect of treatment on efficacy outcomes

There is evidence suggesting that there is no clinically important difference between reboxetine and other antidepressants on:

● increasing the likelihood of achieving a 50% reduction in symptoms of depression as measured by the HRSD (K = 5; N = 1068; RR = 0.87; 95% CI, 0.76 to 1.01)

---

[128]Details of standard search strings used in all searches are in Appendix 8. Information about each study along with an assessment of methodological quality is in Appendix 17c, which also contains a list of excluded studies with reasons for exclusions.

[129]Study IDs in title case refer to studies included in the previous guideline. References for these studies are in Appendix 18.

[130]The forest plots can be found in Appendix 19c.

[131]The forest plots can be found in Appendix 19c.

- increasing the likelihood of achieving remission by the end of treatment (K = 4; N = 895; RR = 0.96; 95% CI, 0.84 to 1.09)
- reducing symptoms of depression by the end of treatment as measured by the HRSD or MADRS (K = 3; N = 618; SMD = –0.09; 95% CI, –0.24 to 0.07).

Acceptability and tolerability of treatment

There is evidence suggesting that there is no clinically important difference between reboxetine and other antidepressants on increasing the likelihood of patients reporting side effects (K = 4; n = 895; RR = 0.98; 95% CI, 0.9 to 1.06).

There is insufficient evidence to determine whether there is a clinically important difference between reboxetine and other antidepressants on reducing the likelihood of leaving treatment early for any reason or on reducing the likelihood of leaving treatment early due to side effects.

Clinical summary

Reboxetine is superior to placebo and as effective as other antidepressants in the treatment of depression. There is insufficient evidence to comment on reboxetine's tolerability compared with placebo or alternative antidepressants.

10.8.5   Venlafaxine

Introduction

**Venlafaxine was the first of the new generation dual-action antidepressants. It inhibits the reuptake of both serotonin and noradrenaline in the same way as TCAs. At the standard dose of 75 mg it is an SSRI, with dual action emerging at doses of 150 mg and above. At higher doses it also inhibits dopamine reuptake.

Venlafaxine has a broad range of side effects similar to those of TCAs and SSRIs. It can increase blood pressure at higher doses, is associated with a high incidence of discontinuation symptoms (see Section 11.8) and is more toxic than the SSRIs in overdose (see Section 11.9).

Studies considered[132,133]

The GDG used an existing review (Smith *et al.*, 2002) as the basis of this review. The Smith and colleagues' (2002) review included 31 studies of which nine did not meet the inclusion criteria set by the GDG. Fifteen additional studies were identified from new searches and four from another review (Einarson *et al.*, 1999). None of these studies met the inclusion criteria set by the GDG. Two studies were sourced from other reviews in this chapter, both of which met inclusion criteria, and details of ten additional unpublished studies were provided by Wyeth Laboratories, five of which

---

[132]Details of standard search strings used in all searches are in Appendix 8. Information about each study along with an assessment of methodological quality is in Appendix 17c, which also contains a list of excluded studies with reasons for exclusions.
[133]Study IDs in title case refer to studies included in the previous guideline. References for these studies are in Appendix 18.

met inclusion criteria. Thus a total of 33 studies were excluded from this review with 29 trials being included (014Nemeroff, 015Schatzberg, 102Tsai, 332Rickels, 349Wyeth, 428Casabona, 626Kornaat, 671Lenox-Smith, Alves1999, Benkert1996, Bielski2003, Clerc1994, Costa1998, Cunnigham1994, Dierick1996, Guelfi2001, Hackett1996, Lecrubier1997, Mahapatra1997, McPartlin98, Montgomery2002, Poirier1999, Rudolph1999, Samuelian1998, Schweizer1994, Silverstone1999, Smeraldi1998, Tylee1997, Tzanakaki2000). Together, these provide tolerability data from up to 5,063 participants and efficacy data from up to 4,198 participants.

All included studies were published between 1994 and 2003 and were between 4 and 13 weeks' long (mean = 8.03 weeks). Three studies were of inpatients, 16 of outpatients and four were undertaken in primary care. In the remaining six, it was either not clear from where participants were sourced or they were from mixed sources. In three (Mahapatra1997, 015Schatzberg, Smerladi1998) participants were aged 64 years and over. Mean HRSD scores at baseline ranged from 22.4 to 30.6 (various HRSD versions).

Data were available to compare venlafaxine with clomipramine, dothiepin/dosulepin, imipramine, trazodone, citalopram, escitalopram, fluoxetine, paroxetine and mirtazapine.

Studies reported mean doses equivalent to at least 100 mg of amitriptyline. Eight studies (102Tsai, 428Casabona, 671Lenox-Smith, Bielski2003, Hackett1996, Montgomery2002, Rudolph1999, Silverstone1999) used 'extended release' (XR) venlafaxine and the remainder 'immediate release' (IR) venlafaxine. Doses ranged from 75 mg to 375 mg. A sub-analysis was performed by dose of venlafaxine, with studies achieving a maximum dose of no more than 150 mg classified as low dose (102Tsai, 349Wyeth, 428Casabona, Alves1999, Costa1998, Dierick1996, Hackett1996, Lecrubier1997, Mahapatra1997, McPartlin1998, Montgomery2002, Samuelian1998, Smeraldi1998, Tylee1997) and those achieving a minimum dose of no less than 150 mg classified as high dose (332Rickels, Benkert1996, Bielski2003, Clerc1994, Guelfi2001, Poirier99, Tzanakaki2000). In addition, studies with a dose of 75 mg were analysed separately (102Tsai, 428Casabona, McPartlin1998, Tylee1997). Some participants in one study (Guelfi2001) received the comparator treatment (mirtazapine) at a dose higher than BNF limits. Where this gave heterogeneity, sub-analyses were performed removing this study. Results are presented only where clinically important differences were found.

Clinical evidence statements[134]
Effect of treatment on efficacy
Venlafaxine is no more effective in treating depression than other antidepressants:

There is evidence suggesting that there is no clinically important difference between venlafaxine and other antidepressants on:

- increasing the likelihood of achieving a 50% reduction in symptoms of depression as measured by the HRSD (K = 23; N = 4198; Random effects RR = 0.92; 95% CI, 0.83 to 1.02)

---

[134]The forest plots can be found in Appendix 19c.

- increasing the likelihood of achieving remission as measured by the HRSD (K = 20; N= 3849; RR = 0.96; 95% CI, 0.91 to 1.01).

There is evidence suggesting that there is a statistically significant difference favouring venlafaxine over other antidepressants on reducing symptoms of depression, but the size of this difference is unlikely to be of clinical importance (K = 20; N = 3637; SMD = –0.09; 95% CI, –0.15 to –0.02).

Similar results were found in sub-analyses by class of antidepressant:

There is evidence to suggest that there is no clinically important difference between venlafaxine and SSRIs on increasing the likelihood of achieving:

- a 50% reduction in symptoms of depression (K = 16; N = 3268; RR = 0.92; 95% CI, 0.84 to 1.005)
- remission (K = 19; N = 3692; RR = 0.95; 95% CI, 0.9 to 1.002).

There is evidence suggesting that there is a statistically significant difference favouring venlafaxine over SSRIs on reducing symptoms of depression by the end of treatment but the size of this difference is unlikely to be of clinical importance (K = 13; N = 2741; SMD = –0.10; 95% CI, –0.17 to –0.02).

There is insufficient evidence to determine if there is a clinically important difference between venlafaxine and TCAs on increasing the likelihood of patients achieving a 50% reduction in symptoms of depression as measured by the HRSD or MADRS (K = 6; N = 773; Random effects RR = 0.91; 95% CI, 0.71 to 1.17).

There is evidence suggesting that there is no clinically important difference between venlafaxine and TCAs on reducing symptoms of depression by the end of treatment as measured by the HRSD or MADRS (K = 6; N = 744; SMD = –0.12; 95% CI, –0.27 to 0.02).

Effect of setting on treatment efficacy

To assess the efficacy of venlafaxine in inpatients, data were available to compare it with imipramine, fluoxetine and mirtazapine.

Inpatients:

There is evidence suggesting that there is no clinically important difference between venlafaxine and other antidepressants on reducing symptoms of depression in inpatients by the end of treatment as measured by the HRSD or MADRS (K = 3; N = 383; Random effects SMD = –0.04; 95% CI, –0.46 to 0.38).

There is insufficient evidence to determine whether there is a clinically important difference between venlafaxine and other antidepressants on either increasing the likelihood of achieving a 50% reduction in symptoms of depression (K = 3; N = 392; Random effects RR = 1.04; 95% CI, 0.71 to 1.53) or on increasing the likelihood of achieving remission (K = 2; N = 225; Random effects RR = 0.85; 95% CI, 0.45 to 1.62).

However, compared with SSRIs, venlafaxine is more effective in inpatients:

There is some evidence suggesting that there is a clinically important difference favouring venlafaxine over SSRIs on:

- reducing symptoms of depression in inpatients by the end of treatment as measured by the HRSD or MADRS (K = 1; N = 67; SMD = –0.58; 95% CI, –1.07 to –0.09)

● increasing the likelihood of achieving remission in inpatients as measured by the HRSD (K = 1; N = 68; RR = 0.60; 95% CI, 0.39 to 0.92).

Outpatients:
Data from studies of venlafaxine in outpatients were available to make comparisons with imipramine, clomipramine, fluoxetine and paroxetine.

There is some evidence suggesting that there is a clinically important difference favouring venlafaxine over other antidepressants on increasing the likelihood of achieving a 50% reduction in symptoms of depression in outpatients as measured by the HRSD (K = 11; N = 2023; RR = 0.83; 95% CI, 0.74 to 0.93).

There is evidence suggesting that there is a statistically significant difference favouring venlafaxine over other antidepressants on reducing symptoms of depression in outpatients by the end of treatment as measured by the HRSD or MADRS, but the size of this difference is unlikely to be of clinical importance (K = 9; N = 1804; SMD = –0.17; 95% CI, –0.26 to –0.08).

Results were similar against TCAs alone. However, when venlafaxine was compared with SSRIs there is evidence suggesting that there is no clinically important difference between venlafaxine and SSRIs on increasing the likelihood of achieving remission in outpatients (K = 12; N = 2199; RR = 0.95; 95% CI, 0.89 to 1.02).

In outpatients, there is evidence suggesting that there are statistically significant differences favouring venlafaxine over SSRIs on the following outcomes, but the size of these differences is unlikely to be of clinical importance on:
● increasing the likelihood of achieving a 50% reduction in symptoms of depression by the end of treatment (K = 9; N = 1775; RR = 0.85; 95% CI, 0.75 to 0.96)
● reducing symptoms of depression in outpatients by the end of treatment (K = 7; N = 1572; SMD = –0.15; 95% CI, –0.25 to –0.05).

Primary care:
Data were available to compare venlafaxine against imipramine, paroxetine and fluoxetine in primary care.

There is evidence suggesting that there is no clinically important difference between venlafaxine and other antidepressants on reducing symptoms of depression by the end of treatment as measured by the HRSD or MADRS (K = 3; N = 824; SMD = –0.07; 95% CI, –0.21 to 0.06).

There is evidence suggesting that there is no clinically important difference between venlafaxine and SSRIs on increasing the likelihood of achieving remission (K = 3; N = 995; RR = 0.98; 95% CI, 0.88 to 1.11).

Effect of dose on treatment efficacy
Venlafaxine at 75 mg:
Data were available to compare venlafaxine at 75 mg with fluoxetine and paroxetine.

There is insufficient evidence to determine if there is a clinically important difference between venlafaxine (75 mg) and SSRIs on increasing the likelihood of patients achieving a 50% reduction in symptoms of depression as measured by the HRSD or MADRS (K = 4; N = 882; Random effects RR = 0.87; 95% CI, 0.6 to 1.26).

There is evidence to suggest that there is no clinically important difference between venlafaxine (75 mg) and SSRIs on:

- increasing the likelihood of patients achieving remission as measured by the HRSD or MADRS (K = 4; N = 882; RR = 0.98; 95% CI, 0.88 to 1.09)
- reducing symptoms of depression as measured by the HRSD at the end of treatment (K = 3; N = 792; SMD = –0.08; 95% CI, –0.21 to 0.06).

Low-dose venlafaxine (mean ≤150 mg):
There is insufficient evidence to determine if there is a clinically important difference between venlafaxine (≤150 mg) and other antidepressants on increasing the likelihood of patients achieving a 50% reduction in symptoms of depression as measured by the HRSD or MADRS (K = 12; N = 2418; Random effects RR = 0.86; 95% CI, 0.72 to 1.02).

There is evidence suggesting that there is no clinically important difference between venlafaxine (≤150 mg) and other antidepressants on increasing the likelihood of achieving remission (K = 9; N = 2125; RR = 0.98; 95% CI, 0.9 to 1.06).

There is evidence suggesting that there is a statistically significant difference favouring venlafaxine (≤150 mg) over other antidepressants on reducing symptoms of depression as measured by the HRSD or MADRS at the end of treatment but the size of this difference is unlikely to be of clinical importance (K = 11; N = 2256; SMD = –0.11; 95% CI, –0.19 to –0.03).

Results were similar in sub-analyses by antidepressant class.

High-dose venlafaxine (mean ≥150 mg):
There is insufficient evidence to determine if there is a clinically important difference between venlafaxine (≥150 mg) and other antidepressants on increasing the likelihood of patients achieving a 50% reduction in symptoms of depression as measured by the HRSD or MADRS (K = 6; N = 822; Random effects RR = 1; 95% CI, 0.78 to 1.28).

There is evidence suggesting that there is no clinically important difference between venlafaxine (≥150 mg) and other antidepressants on:

- reducing symptoms of depression (K = 6; N = 807; Random effects SMD = 0.03; 95% CI, –0.18 to 0.23)
- increasing the likelihood of achieving remission (K = 6; N = 706; Random effects RR = 0.94; 95% CI, 0.79 to 1.12).

Results were similar in sub-analyses by antidepressant class.

Acceptability and tolerability of treatment
There is evidence suggesting that there is no clinically important difference between venlafaxine and other antidepressants on:

- reducing the likelihood of leaving treatment early for any reason (K = 23; N = 4196; RR = 0.98; 95% CI, 0.88 to 1.08)
- reducing the likelihood of patients reporting adverse events (K = 21; N = 3757; RR = 1.01; 95% CI, 0.97 to 1.05).

There is some evidence suggesting that there is a clinically important difference favouring other antidepressants over venlafaxine on reducing the likelihood of patients leaving treatment early due to side effects (K = 27; N = 5063; RR = 1.21; 95% CI, 1.04 to 1.41).

In sub-analyses by antidepressant class, results were similar for venlafaxine compared with SSRIs, except for fluoxetine:

There is evidence suggesting that there is a statistically significant difference favouring fluoxetine over venlafaxine on reducing the likelihood of patients reporting side effects, but the size of this difference is unlikely to be of clinical importance (K = 10; N = 1871; RR = 1.06; 95% CI, 1 to 1.11).

Acceptability and tolerability of treatment by setting

Inpatients:

To assess the efficacy of venlafaxine in inpatients, data were available to compare it with imipramine, fluoxetine and mirtazapine. Heterogeneity was a problem in the meta-analysis assessing the tolerability of venlafaxine against all antidepressants in inpatients. This was because in the study comparing venlafaxine with mirtazapine, fewer participants taking mirtazapine left the study early compared with those taking venlafaxine, whereas this was not the case in other studies. Therefore, the result against TCAs and SSRIs only were considered:

There is some evidence suggesting that there is a clinically important difference favouring venlafaxine over TCAs and SSRIs on reducing the likelihood of inpatients leaving treatment early (K = 2; N = 235; RR = 0.61; 95% CI, 0.41 to 0.92).

Outpatients:

There is evidence suggesting that there is no clinically important difference between venlafaxine and other antidepressants on:

- reducing the likelihood of outpatients leaving treatment early for any reason (K = 11; N = 2,021; RR = 0.95; 95% CI, 0.82 to 1.1)
- reducing the likelihood of outpatients reporting side effects (K = 10; N = 1736; RR = 1.03; 95% CI, 0.98 to 1.09).

When compared with SSRIs:

There is some evidence suggesting that there is a clinically important difference favouring SSRIs over venlafaxine on reducing the likelihood of outpatients leaving treatment early due to side effects (K = 11; N = 2085; RR = 1.48; 95% CI, 1.16 to 1.90).

Primary care:

There is evidence suggesting that there is no clinically important difference between venlafaxine and other antidepressants on:

- reducing the likelihood of leaving treatment early for any reason (K = 4; N = 1148; RR = 0.94; 95% CI, 0.77 to 1.15)
- reducing the likelihood of patients reporting adverse events (K = 3; N = 787; RR = 1.08; 95% CI, 0.9995 to 1.16).

Acceptability and tolerability of treatment by dose

Venlafaxine at 75 mg:

There is insufficient evidence to determine if there is a clinically important difference between venlafaxine (75 mg) and SSRIs on:

- reducing the likelihood of patients leaving treatment early (K = 3; N = 768; RR = 0.93; 95% CI, 0.75 to 1.16)
- reducing the likelihood of patients leaving treatment early due to side effects (K = 3; N = 768; Random effects RR = 1.07; 95% CI, 0.68 to 1.7)
- reducing the likelihood of patients reporting side effects (K = 3; N = 521; RR = 1.12; 95% CI, 0.996 to 1.25).

Low-dose venlafaxine (≤150 mg):

There is evidence suggesting that there is no clinically important difference between low-dose venlafaxine and other antidepressants on reducing the likelihood of leaving treatment early (K = 12; N = 2471; RR = 1.04; 95% CI, 0.91 to 1.19).

There is evidence suggesting that there is a statistically significant difference favouring other antidepressants over low-dose venlafaxine on reducing the likelihood of patients reporting side effects but the size of this difference is unlikely to be of clinical importance (K = 12; N = 2224; RR = 1.06; 95% CI, 1.001 to 1.12).

There is some evidence suggesting that there is a clinically important difference favouring other antidepressants over venlafaxine (<= 150 mg) on reducing the likelihood of patients leaving treatment early due to side effects (K = 12; N = 2471; RR = 1.25; 95% CI, 1.002 to 1.55).

In sub-analyses by class of antidepressant, results were similar except that:

There is strong evidence that there is a clinically important difference favouring fluoxetine over low-dose venlafaxine on reducing the likelihood of leaving treatment early due to side effects (K = 5; N = 1190; RR = 1.61; 95% CI, 1.15 to 2.24).

There is insufficient evidence to determine whether there is a clinically important difference between low-dose venlafaxine and TCAs on reducing the likelihood of leaving treatment early due to side effects.

High-dose venlafaxine (≥150 mg):

There is insufficient evidence to determine whether there is a clinically important difference between high-dose venlafaxine and other antidepressants on reducing the likelihood of leaving treatment early (K = 6; N = 822; Random effects RR = 1; 95% CI, 0.7 to 1.41) or on reducing the likelihood of leaving treatment early due to side effects (K = 7; N = 873; Random effects RR = 1.48; 95% CI, 0.71 to 3.05).

There is evidence suggesting that there is no clinically important difference between high-dose venlafaxine and other antidepressants on reducing the likelihood of patients reporting side effects (K = 6; N = 674; RR = 0.95; 95% CI, 0.85 to 1.05).

Clinical summary

There are no clinically important differences between venlafaxine (at any dose) and other antidepressants on any efficacy outcome. This was also the case for most acceptability and tolerability outcomes. However, there is some evidence that patients taking venlafaxine are more likely to leave treatment early due to side effects, particularly when low-dose (≤150 mg) venlafaxine is compared with fluoxetine.

Results were similar in sub-analyses by setting, other than for inpatients, with those taking venlafaxine being less likely to stop treatment early compared with TCAs and SSRIs. In addition, one small study of inpatients found that venlafaxine was superior to SSRIs on efficacy. In outpatients, there was some evidence for increased efficacy compared with other antidepressants, but only on response.**

10.9   ST JOHN'S WORT

The following sections on St John's wort marked by asterisks (**_**) are from the previous guideline and have not been updated except for style and minor clarification.

10.9.1   Introduction

**St John's wort, an extract of the plant *Hypericum perforatum*, has been used for centuries for medicinal purposes including the treatment of depression. It is not licensed as a medicine in the UK but can be bought 'over the counter' from health food shops, herbalists and community pharmacies. Many different branded preparations are available. St John's wort is licensed in Germany for the treatment of depression.

St John's wort is known to contain at least ten constituents or groups of components that may contribute to its pharmacological effects (Linde & Mulrow, 2004), but its exact mode of action is unknown. These include naphthodianthrons, flavonoids, xanthons and biflavonoids (Wagner & Bladt, 1994). In common with all herbal preparations, the quantity and proportions of each constituent varies among batches (Wang *et al.*, 2004). Most commercial products are standardised with respect to hypericin content, but it is not known if this is the only active component. Individual brands or batches of the same brand may, therefore, not be therapeutically equivalent. Many clinically important drug interactions have been reported (Committee on Safety of Medicines, 2000). St John's wort may also cause photosensitivity.

10.9.2   Studies considered[135,136]

Forty studies were found in a search of electronic databases, with 19 being included and 21 being excluded by the GDG.

Ten studies were available for a comparison with placebo (Davidson02, Hansgen1996, Kalb2001, Laakmann98, Lecrubier02, Philipp99, Schrader98, Shelton2001, Volz2000, Witte1995); four studies for a comparison with TCAs (Bergmann93, Philipp99, Wheatley97, Woelk2000); one for a comparison with

---

[135]Details of standard search strings used in all searches are in Appendix 8. Information about each study along with an assessment of methodological quality is in Appendix 17c, which also contains a list of excluded studies with reasons for exclusions.

[136]Study IDs in title case refer to studies included in the previous guideline. References for these studies are in Appendix 18.

TCA-related antidepressants (Harrer94); and six studies for a comparison with SSRIs (Behnke2002, Brenner00, Davidson02, Harrer99, Schrader00, VanGurp02)[137]. Data from up to 1520 participants were available from studies comparing St John's wort with placebo, and data from up to 1629 participants were available from comparison with antidepressants.

All included studies were published between 1993 and 2002 and were between 4 and 12 weeks' long (mean = 6.47 weeks). In 16 studies participants were described as outpatients and in the other three it was either not clear from where participants were sourced or they were from mixed sources. In one study (Harrer99), all participants were aged 60 years and over. All participants had either moderate or severe depression.

It is very difficult to assess the exact content of the preparation of St John's wort used in included studies so no study was excluded on grounds of inadequate dose. Included studies described the following range of preparations:

- 2×150 mg (300 mg) at 0.450 to 0.495 mg total hypericin per tablet
- 900 mg LI 160
- 4×200 mg (800 mg) LoHyp-57: drug extract ratio 5–7:1
- 3×300 mg (900 mg) WS5572: drug extract ratio 2.5–5:1, 5% hyperforin
- 3×300 mg (900 mg) WS5573: 0.5% hyperforin
- 3×300 mg (900 mg) WS5570: 0.12 to 0.28% hypericin
- 3×350 mg (1050 mg) STEI 300: 0.2 to 0.3% hypericin, 2 to 3% hyperforin
- 2×200 mg (500 mg) ZE117: 0.5 mg hypericin
- 3 to 6×300 mg (900 mg to 1800 mg) at 0.3% hypericum
- 3×300 mg (900 mg) LI 160 = 720 to 960 mcg hypericin
- 2×250 mg (500 mg) ZE117: 0.2% hypericin
- 900 mg to 1500 mg LI 160: standardised to 0.12 to 0.28% hypericin
- 4×125 mg (500 mg) Neuroplant
- 200–240 mg Psychotonin forte
- 3×30 drops Psychotonin (500 mg)
- 3×30 drops Hyperforat: 0.6 mg hypericin.

In addition, six studies with low doses of standard antidepressants were also included.

10.9.3 Clinical evidence statements for St John's wort compared with placebo[138]

Effect of treatment on efficacy outcomes
There is some evidence suggesting that there is a clinically important difference favouring St John's wort over placebo on increasing the likelihood of achieving a 50% reduction in symptoms of depression as measured by the HRSD in:
- the dataset as a whole (K = 6[139]; N = 995; RR = 0.79; 95% CI, 0.71 to 0.88)

---

[137]Davidson02 and Philipp99 are 3-arm trials.
[138]The forest plots can be found in Appendix 19c.
[139]Three studies (Davidson02, Hangsen1996, Schrader98) were removed from the meta-analysis to remove heterogeneity from the dataset.

- moderate depression (K = 1; N = 162; RR = 0.64; 95% CI, 0.51 to 0.79)
- severe depression (K = 5[140]; N = 898; RR = 0.81; 95% CI, 0.72 to 0.9).

There is insufficient evidence to determine if there is a clinically important difference between St John's wort and placebo on increasing the likelihood of achieving remission by the end of treatment as measured by the HRSD (K = 3; N = 804; Random effects RR = 0.80; 95% CI, 0.53 to 1.22).

There is evidence suggesting that there is a statistically significant difference favouring St John's wort over placebo on reducing symptoms of depression by the end of treatment as measured by the HRSD, but the size of this difference is unlikely to be of clinical importance in:

- the dataset as a whole (K = 6[141]; N = 1031; SMD = –0.35; 95% CI, –0.47 to –0.22)
- severe depression (K = 5[142]; N = 891; SMD = –0.34; 95% CI, –0.47 to –0.2).

However, in moderate depression there is some evidence suggesting that there is a clinically important difference favouring St John's wort over placebo on reducing symptoms of depression by the end of treatment as measured by the HRSD (K = 2; N = 299; Random effects SMD = –0.71; 95% CI, –1.28 to –0.13).

Acceptability and tolerability of treatment
There is evidence suggesting that there is no clinically important difference between St John's wort and placebo on reducing the likelihood of patients leaving treatment early for any reason (K = 8; N = 1472; RR = 0.96; 95% CI, 0.74 to 1.25).

There is insufficient evidence to determine if there is a clinically important difference between St John's wort and placebo on reducing the likelihood of patients leaving treatment early due to adverse effects (K = 5; N = 1127; RR = 0.88; 95% CI, 0.32 to 2.41).

There is evidence suggesting that there is no clinically important difference between St John's wort and placebo on reducing the likelihood of patients reporting adverse effects (K = 7; N = 1106; RR = 0.89; 95% CI, 0.72 to 1.1).

10.9.4   Clinical evidence statements for St John's wort compared with antidepressants[143]

Effect of treatment on efficacy outcomes
There is evidence suggesting that there is no clinically important difference between St John's wort and antidepressants on:

- increasing the likelihood of achieving a 50% reduction in symptoms of depression as measured by the HRSD (K = 10; N = 1612; Random effects RR = 1.03; 95% CI, 0.87 to 1.22)

---

[140]Two studies (Davidson02, Hangsen1996) were removed from the meta-analysis to remove heterogeneity from the dataset.

[141]Three studies (Davidson02, Hangsen1996, Schrader98) were taken out of the meta-analysis to remove heterogeneity from the dataset.

[142]Ibid.

[143]The forest plots can be found in Appendix 19c.

- increasing the likelihood of achieving remission by the end of treatment as measured by the HRSD (K = 1; N = 224; RR = 1.01; 95% CI, 0.87 to 1.17)
- reducing symptoms of depression by the end of treatment as measured by the HRSD (K = 9; N = 1168; SMD = –0.02; 95% CI, –0.13 to 0.1).

A sub-analysis by severity found no difference in these results except for response rates in those with moderate depression:

In moderate depression there is some evidence suggesting that there is a clinically important difference favouring St John's wort over antidepressants on increasing the likelihood of achieving a 50% reduction in symptoms of depression as measured by the HRSD (K = 3; N = 481; RR = 0.77; 95% CI, 0.62 to 0.95).

Sub-analyses by antidepressant class and by antidepressant dose (therapeutic versus low dose) found similar results.

A sub-analysis combining severity and antidepressant dose also found similar results apart from for response rates in severe depression:

In severe depression there is some evidence suggesting that there is a clinically important difference favouring low-dose antidepressants over St John's wort on increasing the likelihood of achieving a 50% reduction in symptoms of depression as measured by the HRSD (K = 4; N = 521; RR = 1.2; 95% CI, 1 to 1.44).

Acceptability and tolerability of treatment

With regard to reducing the likelihood of patients leaving treatment early for any reason, there is insufficient evidence to determine a difference between St John's wort and either all antidepressants or low-dose antidepressants. However, there is some evidence suggesting that there is a clinically important difference favouring St John's wort over antidepressants given at therapeutic doses (K = 5; N = 1011; RR = 0.69; 95% CI, 0.47 to 1).

There is strong evidence suggesting that there is a clinically important difference favouring St John's wort over antidepressants on:

- reducing the likelihood of patients leaving treatment early due to side effects (K = 10; N = 1629; RR = 0.39; 95% CI, 0.26 to 0.6)
- reducing the likelihood of patients reporting adverse effects (K = 8; N = 1358; RR = 0.65; 95% CI, 0.57 to 0.75).

10.9.5   Clinical summary

St John's wort is more effective than placebo on achieving response in both moderate and severe depression, and on reducing symptoms of depression in moderate depression.

There appears to be no difference between St John's wort and other antidepressants, other than in moderate depression where it is better at achieving response and in severe depression where it is less effective than low-dose antidepressants in achieving response.

However, St John's wort appears as acceptable as placebo and more acceptable than antidepressants, particularly TCAs, with fewer people leaving treatment early due to side effects and reporting adverse events.

10.9.6   Recommendation

10.9.6.1   Although there is evidence that St John's wort may be of benefit in mild or moderate depression, practitioners should:

- not prescribe or advise its use by people with depression because of uncertainty about appropriate doses, persistence of effect, variation in the nature of preparations and potential serious interactions with other drugs (including oral contraceptives, anticoagulants and anticonvulsants)
- advise people with depression of the different potencies of the preparations available and of the potential serious interactions of St John's wort with other drugs[144].

10.10   HEALTH ECONOMIC EVIDENCE

10.10.1   Systematic literature review and economic considerations

The systematic search of the economic literature undertaken for this guideline update identified nine studies. Two unpublished evaluations submitted by pharmaceutical companies were also included. Pharmacological companies producing the drugs under review were identified and contacted to provide/recommend unpublished or soon-to-be published studies in order to ensure up-to-date evidence was included in the evidence base for the guideline.

10.10.2   Escitalopram and duloxetine

Five industry-funded studies that assessed the cost effectiveness of escitalopram and duloxetine against various antidepressant comparators in the UK were included in the systematic review of economic literature (Benedicte *et al.*, 2010; Fernandez *et al.*, 2005; Wade *et al.*, 2005a; Wade *et al.*, 2005b; Wade *et al.*, 2008).

Wade and colleagues (2005a) investigated the cost effectiveness of escitalopram at a dose of 20 mg per day compared with citalopram at 40 mg per day in those with severe depression (MADRS => 30) in primary and secondary care in the UK. This cost-effective analysis was reported to be an adaptation of models described in other studies such as Borghi and Guest (2000). A decision tree with a 6-month time horizon was developed. It incorporated effectiveness data derived from a study review and expert opinion. Data for response rates and other relevant inputs such as remission and discontinuation rates were derived from a 506-sample meta-analysis reporting at week 8; these were then extrapolated to 6 months. Costs were calculated from the societal

---

[144]The evidence for this recommendation has not been updated since the previous guideline. Any wording changes have been made for clarification only.

perspective as well as from that of the NHS and reported in 2003 pound sterling. Conventional resource use directly related to treatment as well as treatment-emergent adverse events and attempted suicide were also included. Lost productivity costs due to absenteeism from work were calculated using the human capital approach, based on mean market wages for 2003. Cost estimates for the majority of the resources used were derived from national published studies. The primary outcome measure was patient treated successfully, defined as a patient in remission (MADRS <= 12 at week 24), while the secondary outcome measure was first-line success (that is, remission without switching drug treatment). Univariate sensitivity analysis and Monte Carlo simulations were conducted to evaluate the effect of uncertainty.

From the NHS perspective, the expected total cost per patient was £422 (£404 to £441) for escitalopram and £454 (£436 to £471) for citalopram. Escitalopram also fared better in terms of the effectiveness outcomes. For example, overall success was 53.7% (50.3 to 57.5%) compared with 48.7% (45.8 to 51.7%) for citalopram. Escitalopram was demonstrated to be more effective and less costly, and therefore escitalopram dominated citalopram.

Wade and colleagues (2005a) concluded that escitalopram was a cost saving alternative to citalopram for the treatment of people with severe depression in the UK despite the price of escitalopram being higher than other generic drugs. Cost savings were shown from both perspectives. Multivariate sensitivity analysis further demonstrated that escitalopram was dominant at all ranges of probabilities tested in more than 99% of simulations. This study is deemed to be of good quality; however, depression is a chronic illness and a 6-month time horizon may well be too short to capture all costs and benefits. There are many commonly used drugs for depression and other comparators from other drug classes may have been relevant for analysis and their inclusion would possibly have been more informative.

Another study by Wade and colleagues (2005b) was reviewed, which examined the cost effectiveness of three drug therapies for the treatment of depression in primary care. Escitalopram (10 to 20 mg daily) was compared with venlafaxine-XR (75 to 150 mg daily) and then generic citalopram (20 to 40 mg daily) over a 6-month time horizon from the perspective of the NHS and society. Because of an absence of relevant head-to-head studies, two separate analyses were run. An Austrian cost-effectiveness model (Hemels *et al.*, 2004) was adapted for the UK by Wade and colleagues (2005b). The model encompassed remission, treatment failure, referral to secondary care, dosage titration and switching of antidepressants as required. A decision tree representation was developed. The clinical evidence came from a meta-analysis of four studies (n = 1472) and head-to-head clinical trials. The summary benefit measure was the overall success rate and this was estimated using the decision model. The direct health service costs included in the economic evaluation were drugs, GP visits and psychiatrist visits. The General Practice Research Database (GPRD) was searched for treatment pattern data; expert opinion was also sought and unit costs were taken from published cost data for the UK. The price year was 2003.

When escitalopram was compared with citalopram from the NHS perspective the cost per successfully treated patient was £732 (95% CI 665, 807) for escitalopram and £933 (95% CI 850, 1023) for citalopram. In the comparison between escitalopram and venlafaxine, the cost per successfully treated patient was £546 (95% CI 481, 618) for escitalopram and £607 (95% CI 542, 677) for citalopram. ICERs were not calculated because escitalopram was found to always dominate both citalopram and venlafaxine, which were more expensive and less effective.

Sensitivity analysis showed robust findings for the analysis between escitalopram and citalopram. However, the comparison with venlafaxine was sensitive to changes in parameters such as remission rates and relapse rates used in the model.

Quality of life (QoL) is an important dimension in the depression spectrum and the impact of the interventions under review on QoL may have been informative. An indirect comparison analysis could have been conducted had there been relevant head-to-head trials published. However, the authors argue that an indirect comparison would not have changed the conclusions of the analysis.

Fernandez and colleagues (2005) aimed to assess the cost effectiveness of escitalopram (10 to 20 mg/day) compared with venlafaxine-XR (75 to 150 mg/day) in UK primary care patients with depression. The effectiveness data were derived from a double-blind, multinational[145] RCT with 8-week follow-up (n = 293). Costing was undertaken prospectively on the same patient sample. The perspectives of the NHS and society were adopted. The direct costs for the average patient were reported to be 40% higher for venlafaxine-XR than for escitalopram. The analysis of efficacy data was based on the basis of treatment completers only. The primary health outcome was quality of life measured on the Quality of Life Depression Scale (QLDS). Mean QLDS scores decreased in both groups: from 18.6 to 12.4 for escitalopram-treated patients (p < 0.01) and from 18.8 to 12.1 for venlafaxine-treated patients (p < 0.01). No statistically significant differences were observed between the groups. CEACs were not produced because there were no significant differences in efficacy. The results showed escitalopram to be less costly and equally effective as venlafaxine-XR. The authors concluded that escitalopram is as effective as venlafaxine-XR on the treatment of depression and may be associated with lower costs from both perspectives. Limited details of the effectiveness study were reported making it difficult to assess the study quality or validity. An 8-week follow-up is quite short for a depression-related study and, as a result, long-term costs and benefits may not have been captured. Fernandez and colleagues (2005) acknowledged that larger sample sizes are required to increase the power of performed tests and to enable the detection of differences in costs between escitalopram and venlafaxine-XR.

The study by Benedicte and colleagues (2010)[146] was also reviewed. It described an economic evaluation of duloxetine in comparison with SSRIs, venlafaxine-XR and mirtazapine in primary and secondary care settings in Scotland. Two analyses were conducted; in the first duloxetine was compared with SSRIs, venlafaxine and mirtazapine in patients with moderate to severe depression (HAMD-17 => 19) in primary care. The second analysis set in secondary care compared duloxetine with venlafaxine and mirtazapine in patients with severe depression (HAMD-17 => 25). Efficacy data, drug dosages and resource utilisation differed in both. The perspective adopted

---

[145]Denmark, Finland, France, Germany, Spain and the UK.
[146]This study was unpublished during the development of this guideline update.

was that of the NHS. The clinical effectiveness parameters were from published and unpublished RCT data, other clinical study data and expert interviews. Resource use estimates were sourced from the Scottish Psychiatrists' Panel, literature and UK practicing GPs. Direct medical costs consisted of all outpatient and inpatient visits and drug costs. The main outcome of the model was QALYs.

In the primary care setting, when compared with SSRIs and mirtazapine, duloxetine produced additional benefits at higher costs leading to ICERs of £6,300/QALY and £2,400/QALY gained. It dominated venlafaxine in this setting. Duloxetine also dominated venlafaxine and mirtazapine in the secondary care setting. The cost effectiveness results in the primary care setting were sensitive to changes in efficacy parameters (that is, duloxetine relapse, remission and response rates). The secondary care scenario was less sensitive to changes. The study limitations considered that efficacy data for SSRIs had been collected from other duloxetine trials and for mirtazapine from a single old meta-analysis of limited quality. The authors acknowledged the risk of bias given the problems of comparability of trial populations. Resource use data were collected from a small physician panel that is not considered to be a good source of such evidence.

Wade and colleagues (2008) evaluated the cost effectiveness of escitalopram and duloxetine in the treatment of patients with depression in an outpatient setting. This analysis was carried out alongside a double-blind, multisite randomised study. The study time horizon was 24 weeks. The primary effectiveness outcome of the analysis was the Sheehan Disability Scale (SDS) score. Resource use estimates over this time were sourced from the health economics assessment questionnaires taken alongside the trial. The societal perspective was adopted and results were reported in 2006 UK pound sterling.

The results showed that over the study period escitalopram was associated with significant cost savings compared with duloxetine (£1127 versus £2,001 total/patient cost respectively). Escitalopram also resulted in significantly lower sick leave duration compared with duloxetine (31 versus 62 days). Escitalopram dominated duloxetine in the primary analysis (that is, when assessed with the SDS scale). Indirect costs because of sick leave accounted for two-thirds of the total costs. This study was conducted in several countries in addition to the UK, which limits the generalisability of the results to the UK. Because of the marked differences in healthcare systems there would be differences in healthcare resource use costs and the relative economic burden of sick leave. The perspective adopted in this study is not that of the health services and is therefore less useful for those making decisions on behalf of health services. The short time horizon modelled may not capture all the costs and benefits of the drugs for the treatment of depression.

10.10.3 Selective serotonin reuptake inhibitors, tricyclic antidepressants and lofepramine

One study that assessed the cost effectiveness of SSRIs, TCAs and lofepramine (a newer TCA which is safer in overdose) in the treatment of depression in adult patients in the UK was included in the systematic review of economic literature (Kendrick *et al.*, 2006b). The study was carried out alongside a prospective, randomised, open-label, clinical trial in primary care from the perspective of the health service. This trial provided effectiveness and costing data. The costing was carried out prospectively on the same sample (n = 327) of patients. The length of follow-up was 12 months.

The primary clinical measure was the number of weeks free from depression (HADS-D <8). No statistically significant differences between the groups were observed in this measure. The differences in the total costs did not reach statistical significance either. Cost-effectiveness planes and CEACs were computed to illustrate the uncertainty around the estimates. The cost-effectiveness planes for each comparison included points in all four quadrants reflecting statistically non-significant differences in outcomes and costs. The CEACs suggested that, for values placed on an additional QALY of over £5,000, SSRIs were likely to be most cost effective, although the probability of this did not rise above 0.6. This analysis was based on a trial that was well described and reflected usual practice. It also drew from a population from several centres across the UK, which was representative of the wider UK population. A limitation of the study was the failure to recruit the desired number of patients thereby reducing the study's power to detect differences in effectiveness and costs. Loss to follow-up approaching 50% over 12 months further limited the power.

10.10.4 Mirtazapine and venlafaxine

Two industry funded UK based studies compared mirtazapine to older agents such as TCAs and SSRIs (Borghi & Guest, 2000; Romeo *et al.*, 2004).

Borghi and Guest (2000) aimed to determine the cost effectiveness of mirtazapine compared with amitriptyline and fluoxetine in the treatment of moderate and severe depression in the UK, as well as the costs related to antidepressant discontinuation. Effectiveness data were derived from a literature review and also from a panel of GPs and psychiatrists. Direct costs included costs of hospitalisation, visits to GPs and psychiatrists, antidepressant and concomitant medication, community psychiatric nurse and community mental health team visits, and attendance at day wards. The study adopted the perspective of the health service. The estimation of quantities and costs was based on actual data, a panel of ten GPs and three psychiatrists, and literature. The price year was 1997/1998. The measure of benefit used was the proportion of successfully treated patients, determined by the HAMD-17 score (7 or less). Mirtazapine was observed to be cheaper and more effective than amitriptyline and therefore dominated amitriptyline. Six months' treatment with mirtazapine compared with fluoxetine increased the proportion of successfully treated patients by 22% at a net additional cost to the NHS of £27 per patient. Mirtazapine's cost effectiveness relative to amitriptyline was sensitive to the cost of managing adverse events. Mirtazapine's cost effectiveness relative to fluoxetine was sensitive to the cost of managing patients who discontinue antidepressant treatment, the number of psychiatric consultations with GPs and the percentage of patients who completed 6 weeks' treatment with mirtazapine and achieved a 50% reduction in the HAMD-17 score. A significant limitation of this study was that 6-week data comparing mirtazapine with fluoxetine was extrapolated to 6 months using assumptions derived from published literature due to the lack of available comparison data at the time of the study. The authors recommend an update of the model when longer-term data are available. Another limitation was that resource use data were obtained from interviews with a panel of experts; this is not considered to be ideal.

Romeo and colleagues (2004) compared the cost effectiveness of 30 to 45 mg/day mirtazapine with 20 to 30 mg/day paroxetine for patients with depression treated in primary care. The model data were obtained from an RCT. The effectiveness data and costing, which was conducted prospectively, were obtained from a subgroup of patients participating in the trial (treatment completers only). The study was conducted in general practices in Scotland and had a 24-week follow-up.

Costs were reported from the NHS and societal perspectives. Effectiveness outcomes were reported in the form of number of HAMD responders (that is, patients with a 50% decrease in the HAMD-17 score) and the change in QLDS score (from baseline) at the 24-week end point to capture change in quality of life. Both antidepressants were efficacious for 24 weeks of treatment in depressed primary care patients. Compared with paroxetine, mirtazapine was associated with greater improvements in quality of life. The primary measure of cost effectiveness was the incremental cost per responder. There were no significant differences in costs and effects on the primary outcome measure; therefore, they were not combined in the form of ICERs. In addition, there were no significant differences in the benefits between the two groups when the number of HAMD responders was the outcome considered. However, improvement in quality of life was shown to be significantly higher with mirtazapine than with paroxetine. These results were robust under all scenarios examined in the sensitivity analysis.

Sensitivity analysis revealed that if society were willing to pay nothing for a point improvement in depressive syndromes, there was an 80% probability that mirtazapine would be more cost effective than paroxetine. If the willingness-to-pay increased to £1000, this probability rose to 89%. Romeo and colleagues (2004) concluded that compared with paroxetine, mirtazapine might be a cost-effective treatment choice for depression in a primary care setting. However, when considering improvements in quality of life following the administration of these two agents, it can be inferred that mirtazapine should be considered the treatment of choice. The potential limitations are that the analysis may be subject to potential selection bias. The subgroup used consisted of treatment completers only. Nevertheless, it was reported that patients excluded from the subgroup did not differ from the patients included in terms of baseline characteristics. No further statistical analyses, to account for potential biases and confounding factors, were undertaken.

Doyle and colleagues (2001) described a multinational pharmacoeconomic evaluation which compared the cost effectiveness of venlafaxine, SSRIs and TCAs in acute depression. A decision analytic model with a 6-month time horizon was developed. This model was adapted with country specific estimates from a clinical management analysis, meta-analytic rates and two published meta-analyses and a resource valuation of treatment costs by local health economists in each country. Cost effectiveness was determined using the expected values for both a successful outcome and a composite measure of outcome termed 'symptom-free days'. Venlafaxine dominated the other two options since its expected total health service costs were the lowest and it was more effective in terms of both success rate and symptom free days. These findings were explored with sensitivity analysis. This study was conducted in several countries in addition to the UK, which limits the generalisability of the results to the UK. Because of the marked differences in healthcare systems there would be differences in healthcare resource use patterns and patient variations. The short time horizon modelled may not capture all the costs and benefits of the drugs for the treatment of depression.

10.10.5   Summary of health economic evidence

The pharmacoeconomic evidence (much of it industry funded) presented above suggests that escitalopram is better in terms of costs and benefits compared with some of the antidepressants. There is also a weak trend that reflects that SSRIs may be more cost effective than TCAs. (In the previous guideline, pharmacoeconomic evidence suggested that SSRIs were more cost effective than TCAs for the first-line treatment of depression.)

In the previous guideline, pharmacoeconomic evidence suggested that venlafaxine was more cost effective than SSRIs; however, the clinical evidence review at the time highlighted that the clinical estimates used in the economic studies of the drugs compared were inconsistent with the results of the NCCMH clinical evidence review. Therefore an opportunity cost approach was adopted and primary care costs of the different antidepressants were considered alongside the clinical evidence. It is evident that the nature of the current pharmacoeconomic data is piecemeal – no study compares all the relevant antidepressants drugs in a single evaluation. Such an evaluation could inform future guideline recommendations.

The updated meta-analyses of clinical evidence in this guideline points to similar levels of effectiveness across the antidepressants reviewed; that is, they show no robust clinically important superiority in terms of effectiveness. The guideline update recommends that normally an SSRI should be prescribed because they are as effective as other antidepressants, are better tolerated and are less likely to be discontinued because of side effects. Most SSRIs are off patent and available in generic form. In the case of newer drugs, the lack of any greater effect than older drugs makes the added cost potentially not worthwhile (see Table 83). Additionally, a better tolerated drug may also result in cost savings because of the potential decrease in adverse event related healthcare resource use. Therefore, when making a treatment decision regarding the use of an antidepressant, many factors should be taken into consideration for example, clinical history, side effect profile, cost of drug and patient choice.

The findings from the health economic evidence highlighted the need for *de novo* economic modelling for this guideline (see Section 10.12).

Table 83: Drug acquisition costs

Drug	Average daily quantities unit	Unit cost (BNF 56, September 2008)	Weekly cost
Escitalopram	10 mg	Cipralex® (Lundbeck, 2009) 10 mg (scored), 28-tab pack = £14.91	£3.73
Venlafaxine-XR	100 mg	Efexor® XL (Wyeth Pharmaceuticals, 2008) 75 mg 28-cap pack = £23.41	£7.80
		Non-proprietary 75 mg, 56-tab pack = £31.61*	£5.26
Duloxetine	60 mg	Cymbalta® (Eli Lilly, 2009) 60 mg 28-cap pack = £27.72	£6.93
Agomelatine	Not available	Not available	–
Citalopram	20 mg	20 mg, 28-tab pack = £1.24	£0.31
Sertraline	50 mg	50 mg, net price 28-tab pack = £1.31	£0.33

*Based on the Electronic Drug Tariff as of 23 May 2009 (NHS, Business Services Authority, 2009).

No new pharmacoeconomic evidence on relapse prevention, maintenance therapy or switching and sequencing patterns were identified in the UK setting.

10.11   NETWORK META-ANALYSIS OF NEWER ANTIDEPRESSANTS

A review by Cipriani and colleagues (2009) was published at the end of the guideline development process and was considered by the GDG in view of its method and potential importance. This was a network meta-analysis which looked at the comparative evidence from RCTs for 12 antidepressants using both direct and indirect methods; this provides a valid way of comparing individual drugs taking into account results against other drugs in the 'network' as well as being able to compare drugs in the absence of head-to-head RCT evidence. The authors demonstrated that sertraline, escitalopram, mirtazapine and venlafaxine performed well in terms of efficacy and tolerability compared with the other antidepressants reviewed (bupropion, citalopram, duloxetine, fluoxetine, fluvoxamine, milnaciran, paroxetine and reboxetine). They reported that 'mirtazapine, escitalopram, venlafaxine, and sertraline were significantly more efficacious than duloxetine (odds ratio [OR] 1·39, 1·33, 1·30 and 1·27, respectively), fluoxetine ([OR] 1·37, 1·32, 1·28, and 1·25, respectively), fluvoxamine ([OR] 1·41, 1·35, 1·30, and 1·27, respectively), paroxetine ([OR] 1·35, 1·30, 1·27, and 1·22, respectively), and reboxetine ([OR] 2·03, 1·95, 1·89, and 1·85, respectively). Reboxetine was significantly less efficacious than all of the other antidepressants tested. Escitalopram and sertraline showed the best profile of acceptability, leading to significantly fewer discontinuations than did duloxetine, fluvoxamine, paroxetine, reboxetine, and venlafaxine'. Cipriani and colleagues (2009) concluded that 'clinically important differences exist between commonly prescribed antidepressants for both efficacy and acceptability in favour of escitalopram and sertraline. Sertraline might be the best choice when starting treatment for moderate to severe major depression in adults because it has the most favourable balance between benefits, acceptability, and acquisition cost'. They did not consider other potentially important factors, such as evidence of side effects, toxic effects, discontinuation symptoms and social functioning (Cipriani *et al.*, 2009).

The analysis was based on efficacy data (response rates) and dropout rates using data from 117 trials (about 26,000 participants). There are some methodological aspects of the study that are important to consider. First, the analysis was limited to response rates (some of which were imputed) and this outcome measure may provide a less conservative measure of effect than the other commonly used measures (remission and continuous data). Second, it is not clear to what degree differential dropout rates may have influenced the relative efficacy, for example with drugs like reboxetine and escitalopram, as the method of analysis may favour the drug with fewer dropouts. Third, the size of the efficacy effect when translated from the odds ratio reported in the study to an absolute risk is small. The credibility interval encompassed much higher values. Fourth, total dropouts may not be an accurate way to assess tolerability and usually only half of dropouts are attributed to adverse effects. This adds uncertainty to the analysis. Fifth, this uncertainty aside, the size of the tolerability effect is small when translated from an odds ratio to an absolute risk. For example, it is about 2.7% for sertraline versus fluoxetine, assuming a dropout rate of 28% on fluoxetine from Table 38 in Cipriani and colleagues (2009) (number needed to harm [NNH] 37). The credibility interval again encompassed much higher values. Finally, Cipriani and colleagues' (2009) analysis found that the cumulative probability of being among the four best treatments became slightly smaller for those drugs in trials that were sponsored by the marketing company, with the comparators moving up the ranking slightly. This effect, while likely to be small, highlights the difficulty in excluding potential confounds.

10.12 ECONOMIC MODEL FOR THE COST EFFECTIVENESS OF PHARMACOLOGICAL INTERVENTIONS FOR PEOPLE WITH DEPRESSION

10.12.1 Introduction

As described in Section 10.10, the systematic search of economic literature identified a number of studies on pharmacological treatments for the management of depression in the UK. The studies were characterised by varying quality in the methods employed. The number of antidepressants assessed in this literature was limited and did not include the whole range of drugs available in the UK for the treatment of people with depression. These findings highlighted the need for *de novo* economic modelling for this guideline. The objective of economic modelling was to explore the relative cost effectiveness of antidepressants for people with depression in the current UK clinical setting, incorporating the results of a recently published network meta-analysis (Cipriani *et al.*, 2009), as described in Section 10.11.

10.12.2   Methods

Interventions assessed

The choice of interventions assessed in the model was determined by the antidepressants included in the network meta-analysis by Cipriani and colleagues (2009). The analysis was based on 117 studies including 25,928 participants randomly assigned to 12 different new-generation antidepressants. These included bupropion, citalopram, duloxetine, escitalopram, fluoxetine, fluvoxamine, milnacipran, mirtazapine, paroxetine, reboxetine, sertraline and venlafaxine. For the economic model, bupropion and milnacipran were excluded from the analysis because bupropion is not currently licensed as a treatment for depression and milnacipran does not currently have a licence for treatment in the UK. The remaining ten antidepressants were assessed in the economic model. The exclusion of other categories of antidepressants, such as TCAs and MAOIs, from the network meta-analysis is acknowledged as a potential limitation for the economic analysis.

Model structure

A pragmatic decision analytical model was constructed using Microsoft Excel XP. The model constructed for the economic analysis of combination therapy versus antidepressant treatment in Section 8.9 was adapted for this analysis. Within the antidepressant model, patients were initiated on a specific antidepressant and either continued or discontinued treatment. Patients continuing their initial antidepressant treatment either responded or did not respond. Patients who responded to initial treatment received 6 months of maintenance therapy and then were assumed to either relapse or enter remission. People who discontinued from initial antidepressant treatment were assumed to receive various levels of care for their depression, including no care. Some of these people were assumed to clinically improve, and then either relapse or enter remission. The time horizon of the analysis was 14 months; this consisted of 2 months of treatment, reflecting the time point at which the clinical efficacy and acceptability parameters reported in Cipriani and colleagues (2009) were measured, plus 12-month follow-up, for which relapse data were available. Switching to second-line antidepressants was not considered for those patients who discontinued their first-line antidepressant treatment or who did not respond to treatment. Two separate analyses were conducted for hypothetical cohorts of 100 patients with either moderate or severe depression, each assessing the relative cost effectiveness of the ten antidepressants assessed. A schematic diagram of the economic model is presented in Figure 9.

Costs and outcomes considered in the analysis
The analysis adopted the NHS and PSS perspective. The measure of outcome was the QALY.

Efficacy and discontinuation data
Overview of methods used by Cipriani and colleagues (2009)
In summary, only RCTs that compared the following 12 new-generation antidepressants were considered: bupropion, citalopram, duloxetine, escitalopram, fluoxetine, fluvoxamine, milnacipran, mirtazapine, paroxetine, reboxetine, sertraline and venlafaxine as monotherapy in the acute-phase treatment of adults with depression. Acute treatment was defined as 8 weeks of treatment for both efficacy (response) and discontinuation (drop out) analyses. If 8-week data were not available, data ranging between 6 and 12 weeks were used. Response was defined as the proportion of patients who had a reduction of at least 50% from the baseline score on the HRSD or MADRS or who scored much improved or very much improved on the CGI scale at 8 weeks. Treatment discontinuation was defined as the number of patients who stopped treatment early for any reason during the first 8 weeks.

Figure 9: Schematic diagram of the economic model structure

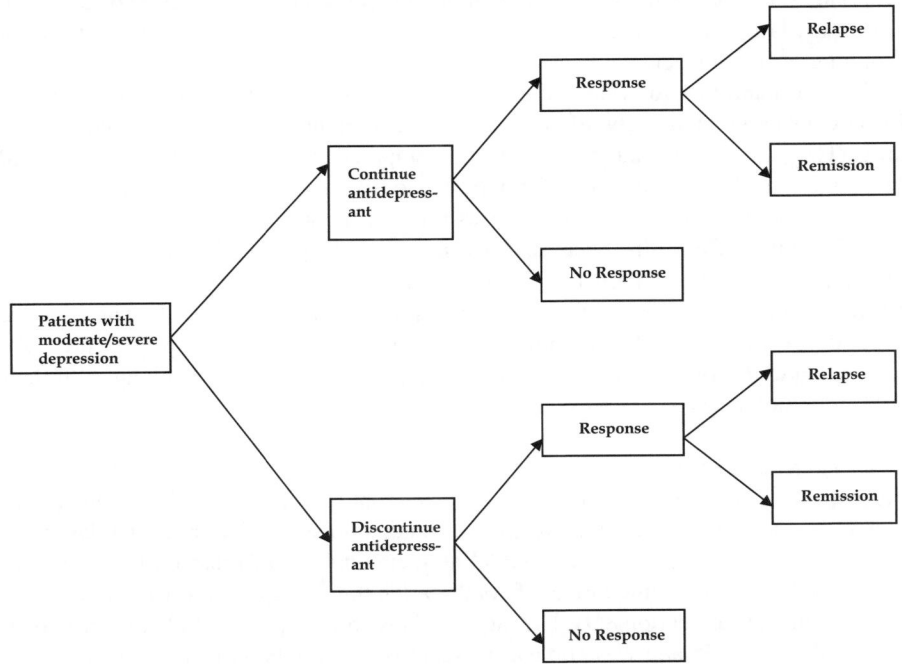

401

Pharmacological interventions

Responders to treatment in each trial were calculated on an intention-to-treat basis. Outcomes were imputed for missing participants assuming that they did not respond to treatment. For the network meta-analysis, a random-effects model within a Bayesian framework using Markov chain Monte Carlo methods was used. Results were reported as odds ratios for all pairs of antidepressants that were considered in the network meta-analysis. The comparative efficacy and acceptability among the 12 antidepressants was shown in terms of odds ratios of each antidepressant versus fluoxetine. Fluoxetine was used as the reference drug, because it was the first among the 12 antidepressants to be marketed in Europe and the US, and it had been consistently used as the reference drug among the different pair-wise comparisons in the RCTs considered in the network meta-analysis.

Estimation of response and discontinuation rates in the economic model
The efficacy and acceptability results from the network meta-analysis by Cipriani and colleagues (2009) are summarised in Table 84. The odds ratios reported for fluoxetine versus each of the other antidepressants were converted into probabilities (response and dropouts) for each antidepressant considered in the economic model using the following formulae:
(1) $Odds_{FL} = P_{FL}/(1 - P_{FL})$
(2) $OR_{(FL,AD)} = Odds_{FL}/Odds_{AD} => Odds_{AD} = Odds_{FL}/OR_{(FL,AD)}$
(3) $P_{AD} = Odds_{AD}/(1 + Odds_{AD})$

$Odds_{FL}$ and P_{FL} are the odds and probability (of relapse or dropping out) for fluoxetine at 8 weeks; $Odds_{AD}$ and P_{AD} are the odds and probability (of relapse or dropping out) for each of the other antidepressants considered at 8 weeks; and $OR_{(FL,AD)}$ is the odds ratio of fluoxetine versus each antidepressant (of relapse or dropping out) at 8 weeks.

The probabilities for fluoxetine were estimated based on data reported for 54 RCTs considered in the network meta-analysis that included fluoxetine in one of their arms. Two of the trials had three arms and compared fluoxetine with paroxetine and sertraline. The data on fluoxetine from these two trials were reported twice, and therefore have been double-counted at the estimation of probabilities on response and dropping out for fluoxetine because it was not possible to identify and isolate respective data coming from these two RCTs. Because both response and dropout rates referred to an 8-week period, the probabilities for discontinuation and response were applied over a period of 2 months in the economic model. The probabilities for response and discontinuation for each antidepressant over 8 weeks, along with their 95% credible intervals, are presented in Table 85.

Other model clinical input parameters
For patients who responded to initial antidepressant treatment after 2 months, it was assumed that they would either relapse or enter remission. The rate of relapse for these patients was taken from the guideline meta-analysis of relapse over 12-month follow-up for the economic model of combination therapy compared with antidepressant treatment (see Section 8.9). The rate of relapse for the pharmacotherapy arm over 12 months was 0.55 and was applied irrespective of initial antidepressant treatment.

Table 84: Efficacy (expressed as response rate) and acceptability (reflected in dropout rates) of antidepressants, expressed as odds ratios (OR) of fluoxetine versus each of the antidepressants assessed (taken from Cipriani *et al.*, 2009)

	Efficacy (response rate) OR (95% credible interval)	Acceptability (dropout rate) OR (95% credible interval)
Bupropion	0.93 (0.77–1.11)	1.12 (0.92–1.36)
Citalopram	0.91 (0.76–1.08)	1.11 (0.91–1.37)
Duloxetine	1.01 (0.81–1.27)	0.84 (0.64–1.10)
Escitalopram	0.76 (0.65–0.89)*	1.19 (0.99–1.44)
Fluvoxamine	1.02 (0.81–1.30)	0.82 (0.62–1.07)
Milnacipran	0.99 (0.74–1.31)	0.97 (0.69–1.32)
Mirtazapine	0.73 (0.60–0.88)*	0.97 (0.77–1.21)
Paroxetine	0.98 (0.86–1.12)	0.91 (0.79–1.05)
Reboxetine	1.48 (1.16–1.90)*	0.70 (0.53–0.92)*
Sertraline	0.80 (0.69–0.93)*	1.14 (0.96–1.36)
Venlafaxine	0.78 (0.68–0.90)*	0.94 (0.81–1.09)

Credible interval; *$p < 0.05$.
For efficacy, OR higher than 1 favours fluoxetine.
For acceptability, OR lower than 1 favours fluoxetine.

All remaining patients in the model of those who responded to initial antidepressant treatment (that is, those who did not relapse) were assumed to enter remission.

For patients who discontinued their initial antidepressant treatment at 8 weeks, it was assumed that rather than remaining moderately or severely depressed, a proportion (20%) would improve from their baseline health state, either spontaneously or following treatment (according to 'response' as defined in Cipriani *et al.*, 2009). Of those patients who improved following discontinuation, again it was assumed that a proportion would relapse and the remaining patients would enter remission. The rate of relapse for these patients was assumed to be 0.67 based on a study of patients who were not receiving maintenance therapy at 12 months (Murphy *et al.*, 1984). Again, these rates were applied to all patient cohorts irrespective of initial antidepressant treatment.

Estimation of quality-adjusted life-years
To calculate QALYs, QoL weights estimated in a study of patients with depression were used (Sapin *et al.*, 2004) (see Section 8.9 for further details). Utility weights used in the economic analysis are presented in Table 86.

Table 85: Probabilities estimated for use in the economic model (adapted from Cipriani *et al.*, 2009)

	Efficacy (response rate) Probability (95% credible interval)	Acceptability (dropout rate) Probability (95% credible interval)
Fluoxetine (reference compound)	0.55 (0.54–0.56)	0.28 (0.27–0.29)
Citalopram	0.57 (0.53–0.62)	0.26 (0.22–0.30)
Duloxetine	0.55 (0.49–0.60)	0.31 (0.26–0.38)
Escitalopram	0.62 (0.58–0.65)	0.24 (0.21–0.28)
Fluvoxamine	0.54 (0.48–0.60)	0.32 (0.26–0.38)
Mirtazapine	0.63 (0.58–0.67)	0.28 (0.24–0.33)
Paroxetine	0.55 (0.52–0.59)	0.30 (0.27–0.33)
Reboxetine	0.45 (0.39–0.51)	0.35 (0.29–0.42)
Sertraline	0.60 (0.57–0.64)	0.25 (0.22–0.29)
Venlafaxine	0.61 (0.58–0.64)	0.29 (0.26–0.32)

Note: Bupropion and milnacipran excluded from economic analysis.

Resource use and unit costs

An NHS and PSS perspective was taken for the analysis based on current NICE guidance (NICE, 2008b). Therefore, only direct health and social care costs were considered in the model. Costs included drug acquisition costs, monitoring costs relating to consultations with psychiatrists and GP visits, as well as other health and social care costs associated with the care of people with depression who discontinued treatment,

Table 86: Quality-of-life weights utilised in the economic model

Health state	Quality-of-life weight (95% CI)
Moderate depression	0.33 (0.29–0.37)
Severe depression	0.15 (0.08–0.22)
Response with remission	0.85 (0.83–0.87)
Response without remission	0.72 (0.65–0.79)
No response (following treatment)	0.58 (0.50–0.66)

or did not respond to treatment, or responded to treatment but relapsed at a later stage. Costs were calculated by combining relevant resource use estimates with national unit costs. Unit costs were obtained from a variety of sources including the BNF (British Medical Association and the Royal Pharmaceutical Society of Great Britain, 2008) and the PSSRU (Curtis, 2009). All costs were based on 2008 prices and were inflated where necessary using the Hospital and Community Health Services Pay and Prices Indices (Curtis, 2009). For both costs and outcomes, no discounting was applied given the short time horizon of the model (14 months).

Drug acquisition costs

Drug acquisition costs were taken from BNF 56 (British Medical Association and the Royal Pharmaceutical Society of Great Britain, 2008), with the exception of the cost of venlafaxine which was obtained from the Electronic Drug Tariff (NHS, Business Services Authority, 2009) because this antidepressant has recently become available in generic form but BNF 56 has not captured this information. The daily dosage of all ten antidepressant drugs was informed by the midpoint of the range of daily dosages presented in Cipriani and colleagues (2009) and by the BNF. It was assumed that patients with moderate or severe depression would both receive the same average daily dosage. For all patients, the total costs of antidepressants were calculated over the 8 weeks of initial therapy. It was assumed that all patients who did not discontinue and responded to their initial treatment after 8 weeks would continue to receive maintenance antidepressant treatment at the same dose over a further 6 months in the model. The average daily dosages and the drug acquisition costs are presented in Table 87.

Monitoring costs

All patients receiving antidepressant treatment were assumed to be actively monitored either in primary or secondary care during both the initial treatment period and the maintenance treatment period. Based on the same assumptions used in the combination therapy versus antidepressant treatment model (see Section 8.9), all patients with moderate depression and 50% of patients with severe depression would receive standard GP care while the remaining 50% of patients with severe depression would receive specialist mental health outpatient care. According to the expert opinion of the GDG, it was estimated that patient monitoring in both primary and secondary care consists of two fortnightly visits in the first month followed by one visit in the second month; the maintenance therapy period consists of one GP/specialist visit every 2 months. The unit costs of a GP consultation (£36) and a mental health outpatient consultation (£130) were both taken from the latest PSSRU estimates (Curtis, 2009). The total antidepressant treatment costs including patient monitoring are presented in Table 88.

Other healthcare costs

It was assumed that patients with moderate or severe depression would require additional subsequent mental health and social care resources if they discontinued their initial therapy, did not respond to their initial antidepressant treatment at 8 weeks, or

Table 87: Average daily dosages and acquisition costs of antidepressant drugs included in the economic model

Antidepressant	Average daily dosage	Unit cost (BNF 56, 2008)
Citalopram	40 mg	Non-proprietary 40 mg, 28-tab = £1.46
Duloxetine	60 mg	Cymbalta 60 mg, 28-tab = £27.72
Escitalopram	10 mg	Cipralex 10 mg, 28-tab = £14.91
Fluoxetine	40 mg	Non-proprietary 20 mg, 30-tab = £1.46
Fluvoxamine	100 mg	Non-proprietary 100 mg, 30-tab = £8.32
Mirtazapine	30 mg	Non-proprietary 30 mg, 28-tab = £3.14
Paroxetine	40 mg	Non-proprietary 20 mg, 30-tab = £2.92
Reboxetine	8 mg	Edronax 4 mg, 60-tab = £18.91
Sertraline	100 mg	Non-proprietary 100 mg, 28-tab = £1.80
Venlafaxine	150 mg	Non-proprietary 75 mg, 56-tab = £31.61*

*Based on the Electronic Drug Tariff as of 23 May 2009 (NHS, Business Services Authority, 2009).

responded to therapy but relapsed at a later stage. Based on the same assumptions used in the combination therapy versus antidepressant treatment model (see Section 8.9), monthly mental health and social care cost estimates (£180 per month) were estimated from a study that calculated annual mental health and social care costs based on responses from the UK psychiatric morbidity survey (McCrone *et al.*, 2008). For both dropouts and non-responders, it was assumed that these costs were incurred over the 12 months following initial antidepressant treatment. People who relapsed over the 12 months following initial therapy were assumed to relapse in the middle of this period, that is, at 6 months. Therefore they were assumed to incur these mental health and social care costs for 6 months at the end of the maintenance therapy period. For patients who responded to initial treatment and did not relapse during follow-up, it was assumed that no further additional treatment or mental health and social care resources beyond the 6-month maintenance period were required. These total subsequent mental health care costs are presented in Table 88.

Sensitivity analysis
Because of time constraints, it was not possible to explore uncertainty around key parameters used in the model, including resource use, cost estimates and health state

Table 88: Total healthcare costs applied in the economic model

Antidepressant	Total antidepressant treatment costs-MODERATE DEPRESSION		Total antidepressant treatment costs-SEVERE DEPRESSION	
	Initial treatment (8 weeks)	Maintenance treatment (6 months)	Initial treatment (8 weeks)	Maintenance treatment (6 months)
Citalopram	£111	£118	£252	£259
Duloxetine	£168	£289	£309	£430
Escitalopram	£140	£205	£281	£346
Fluoxetine	£112	£120	£253	£261
Fluvoxamine	£125	£159	£266	£300
Mirtazapine	£115	£128	£256	£269
Paroxetine	£120	£144	£261	£285
Reboxetine	£146	£223	£287	£364
Sertraline	£112	£120	£253	£261
Venlafaxine	£177	£314	£318	£455
Subsequent health states	**Mental health and social care costs**			
No response/dropout (12 months)	£2,160			
Relapse (6 months)	£1080			

utilities. Deterministic sensitivity analysis was only carried out on the upper and lower 95% credible intervals around the response and dropout probabilities (see Table 85). Furthermore, probabilistic sensitivity analysis was not possible because this required full access to the posterior estimates recorded within every iteration of the network meta-analysis undertaken by Cipriani and colleagues (2009). Full access to this dataset is necessary in order to maintain the correlation between the posterior estimates when running the probabilistic analysis.

10.12.3 Data analysis and presentation of the results

A deterministic analysis was undertaken, where data are analysed as point estimates; results are presented as mean total costs and QALYs associated with each treatment option assessed. Relative cost effectiveness between alternative treatment options is estimated using incremental analysis: all options are first ranked from the most to the least effective; any options that are more expensive than options that are higher in ranking are dominated (because they are also less effective) and excluded from further analysis. Subsequently, ICERs are calculated for all pairs of consecutive options, starting from the most to the least effective. ICERs express the additional cost per additional unit of benefit associated with one treatment option compared with another. Estimation of such a ratio allows consideration of whether the additional benefit is worth the additional cost when choosing one treatment option over another. If the ICER for a given option is higher than the ICER calculated for the previous intervention in ranking, then this strategy is also excluded from further analysis on the basis of extended dominance. After having excluded cases of dominance and extended dominance, ICERs are recalculated. The treatment option with the highest ICER below the cost-effectiveness threshold is the most cost effective option.

10.12.4   Results

Mirtazapine appears to be the most cost-effective option among those assessed for both moderate and severe depression, producing the highest number of QALYs and the lowest costs among all drugs assessed (dominant option). Full results of the deterministic analysis for both moderate and severe depression are presented in Table 89, where the antidepressant drugs have been ranked from the most to the least effective in terms of number of QALYs gained.

If mirtazapine is not a suitable treatment option for patients with moderate or severe depression, the next option would be escitalopram or sertraline because venlafaxine is dominated by escitalopram and the remaining antidepressants are dominated by sertraline. The ICERs of escitalopram versus sertraline are £32,987 per QALY for moderate depression and £27,172 per QALY for severe depression. Both ICERs are above the current cost-effectiveness threshold of £20,000 per QALY recommended by NICE (NICE, 2008b). Therefore, based on the results of the deterministic analysis, for patients with either moderate or severe depression, sertraline is the second most cost-effective option after mirtazapine and escitalopram is the third most cost-effective option. By repeating this process in steps, and excluding from each new incremental analysis all options found to be cost effective in previous analyses, it is possible to rank all antidepressants in terms of cost effectiveness.

The rankings of antidepressants in terms of QALYs in Table 89 were identical for both moderate and severe depression. Reboxetine was ranked last in both cases, resulting in the lowest number of QALYs and the highest costs. Overall, the rankings of antidepressants in terms of cost-effectiveness are very similar to the ranking of antidepressants in terms of efficacy, based on the ORs of fluoxetine versus each antidepressant as reported by Cipriani and colleagues (2009). In their analysis, mirtazapine, followed by escitalopram, venlafaxine, sertraline and citalopram were ranked as the five best antidepressants in terms of efficacy (measured by ORs versus fluoxetine), with results being statistically significant for the first four of them. In the economic analysis, mirtazapine, followed by sertraline, escitalopram, citalopram and venlafaxine were ranked as the five best antidepressants in terms of cost effectiveness for both moderate and severe depression. Escitalopram and venlafaxine both fell slightly in the cost-effective rankings because escitalopram remains under patent and

Table 89: Mean costs and QALYs associated with each antidepressant assessed for patients with depression

Antidepressant	Mean QALYs per person		Mean cost per person	
	MODERATE DEPRESSION	SEVERE DEPRESSION	MODERATE DEPRESSION	SEVERE DEPRESSION
Mirtazapine	**0.620**	**0.468**	**£1459**	**£1781**
Escitalopram	0.616	0.463	£1597	£1918
Venlafaxine	0.615	0.462	£1781	£2,102
Sertraline	0.612	0.458	£1478	£1798
Citalopram	0.602	0.446	£1522	£1840
Paroxetine	0.598	0.441	£1590	£1908
Duloxetine	0.596	0.439	£1831	£2,148
Fluvoxamine	0.596	0.438	£1629	£1946
Fluoxetine	0.595	0.438	£1561	£1878
Reboxetine	0.567	0.403	£1867	£2,177

venlafaxine has only recently become available in generic form and its price remains high (although it may be expected to fall substantially).The other three antidepressants are available in generic form and hence much cheaper. Table 90 presents the rankings of each antidepressant in terms of both their efficacy and cost effectiveness.

Sensitivity analysis was undertaken to explore uncertainty around the ORs for efficacy and acceptability estimated in the network meta-analysis by using the upper and lower limits of the 95% credible intervals. The analysis demonstrated that overall results were robust with mirtazapine remaining the dominant option for both moderate and severe depression.

10.12.5 Discussion – limitations

Given the time constraints involved, a preliminary economic analysis was undertaken based on the results of the network meta-analysis by Cipriani and colleagues (2009). The model used to compare the cost effectiveness of combination therapy and antidepressant treatment was adapted for this analysis. The network meta-analysis examined 12 new-generation antidepressants, of which two (bupropion and milnacipran) were excluded from the economic analysis in this guideline. The study did not analyse older antidepressants including TCAs and MAOIs, which is a limitation in terms of the comprehensiveness of the economic analysis presented here. The study

Table 90: Rankings of each antidepressant in terms of efficacy and cost effectiveness

Efficacy (response)*	Cost effectiveness	
	MODERATE depression	SEVERE depression
(1) Mirtazapine	(1) Mirtazapine	(1) Mirtazapine
(2) Escitalopram	(2) Sertraline	(2) Sertraline
(3) Venlafaxine	(3) Escitalopram	(3) Escitalopram
(4) Sertraline	(4) Citalopram	(4) Citalopram
(5) Citalopram	(5) Venlafaxine	(5) Venlafaxine
(6) Paroxetine	(6) Paroxetine	(6) Paroxetine
(7) Fluoxetine	(7) Fluoxetine	(7) Fluoxetine
(8) Duloxetine	(8) Fluvoxamine	(8) Duloxetine
(9) Fluvoxamine	(9) Duloxetine	(9) Fluvoxamine
(10) Reboxetine	(10) Reboxetine	(10) Reboxetine

*Adapted from Cipriani *et al.* (2009); ranked according to ORs versus fluoxetine as reference compound.

evaluated efficacy regarding response and acceptability in terms of dropouts over the acute phase of depression (8 weeks). As Cipriani and colleagues (2009) acknowledge, other important outcomes such as side effects, toxic effects, discontinuation symptoms and social functioning were not investigated in the meta-analyses. Other possible limitations of the study have been highlighted in the clinical review in Section 10.11. A more comprehensive economic analysis would be able to consider costs and outcomes over a longer time horizon, consider issues of drug sequencing or switching (for patients who discontinue initial antidepressant treatment), and give more explicit consideration (captured in estimation of QALYs) of the side effects of different antidepressants as well as impacts on patient mortality (because of side effects or increased suicide risk).

The economic analysis did not consider the possibility of switching to second-line antidepressants for patients who discontinue their first-line antidepressant, which is another possible limitation. In clinical practice, if a patient discontinues their initial antidepressant because of adverse side affects or other factors, another second-line antidepressant would almost certainly be offered. Another issue relates to the current and future costs of the antidepressants analysed. Venlafaxine has recently been available in generic form and, although the current price listed in the NHS Drug Tariff (NHS, Business Services Authority, 2009) remains high, it is anticipated that this price will fall further to non-proprietary levels. Similarly, it is anticipated that escitalopram will shortly be available in generic form. As the prices of both antidepressants in generic form are likely to be lower in the future, their relative cost effectiveness compared with other antidepressants is likely to be further improved.

Another major limitation of this economic model is the inadequate exploration of uncertainty around the results in terms of the assumptions and the clinical efficacy and acceptability data used. Given the considerable uncertainty around some of the input parameters used in the model, and the underlying assumptions behind them, comprehensive deterministic sensitivity analyses are required. Ideally, probabilistic sensitivity analysis, which demonstrates the joint uncertainty between all of the different parameters used in the model, is also required. However, this would have necessitated full access to the results (posterior estimates of every iteration) of the network meta-analysis by Cipriani and colleagues (2009).

10.12.6   Conclusions

The findings of this preliminary economic analysis suggest that mirtazapine might be more cost effective than other antidepressants in the treatment of people with moderate and severe depression and support the findings of Cipriani and colleagues (2009) regarding the clinical superiority of mirtazapine. However, these economic findings are subject to considerable uncertainty arising from the limitations of the current model and lack of incorporation of data on the relative adverse effects of the drugs in the model. Addressing these issues may alter the outcome of the model.

10.13   FROM EVIDENCE TO RECOMMENDATIONS

Apart from the review of escitalopram, the reviews of individual drugs undertaken for the previous guideline were not updated and, therefore, the recommendations concerning the choice of antidepressants have been updated only to ensure compatibility with the current NICE house style. A review of the clinical evidence for the new antidepressant drug duloxetine was added, but the drug was found to be no more clinically effective than other antidepressant drugs. In addition, the pharmacoeconomic evidence on duloxetine was contradictory and, therefore, it could not be specifically recommended. The updated review of escitalopram showed a small advantage over other antidepressants, but this was not judged to be clinically important over other antidepressants. The economic evidence on escitalopram showed it to be more cost effective in comparison with three other antidepressants. However, the economic evidence had limitations and these comparisons were considered insufficient to make a specific recommendation for this treatment. The overall conclusion that antidepressants have largely equal efficacy and that choice should largely depend on side-effect profile, patient preference and previous experience of treatments, propensity to cause discontinuation symptoms and safety in overdose, is not altered. No advantage for so-called 'dual-action' antidepressants as a class over other drugs was found, including considering duloxetine and venlafaxine separately. An increasing number of newer antidepressants are available as generics, and these drugs are generally preferred on grounds of cost.

The GDG considered the findings from of the review by Cipriani and colleagues (2009) and developed an economic model based on the review. The GDG concluded that the analysis was consistent with the findings from the analyses undertaken for this guideline in suggesting some efficacy and tolerability differences between individual antidepressants. However the size of effect and concerns about potential confounds meant that the findings were not considered sufficiently robust to warrant singling out individual drugs for recommendation.

Clinicians should also consider the potential for drug interactions when prescribing an antidepressant for people taking concomitant medication. More information on this topic is provided in the NICE guideline on treating depression in adults with a chronic physical health problem (NICE, 2009c).

10.14   CLINICAL PRACTICE RECOMMENDATIONS

10.14.1   Choice of antidepressant[147]

10.14.1.1 Discuss antidepressant treatment options with the person with depression, covering:
   ● the choice of antidepressant, including any anticipated adverse events, for example, side effects and discontinuation symptoms (see Section 11.8.7.2) and potential interactions with concomitant medication or physical health problems[148]
   ● their perception of the efficacy and tolerability of any antidepressants they have previously taken.

10.14.1.2 When an antidepressant is to be prescribed, it should normally be an SSRI in a generic form because SSRIs are equally effective as other antidepressants and have a favourable risk–benefit ratio. Also take the following into account:
   ● SSRIs are associated with an increased risk of bleeding, especially in older people or in people taking other drugs that have the potential to damage the gastrointestinal mucosa or interfere with clotting. In particular, consider prescribing a gastroprotective drug in older people who are taking non-steroidal anti-inflammatory drugs (NSAIDs) or aspirin.

---

[147]For additional considerations on the use of antidepressants and other medications (including the assessment of the relative risks and benefits) for women who may become pregnant, please refer to the BNF and individual drug Summary of Product Characteristics. For women in the antenatal and postnatal periods, see also NICE clinical guideline 45 'Antenatal and postnatal mental health'.

[148]Consult Appendix 1 of the BNF for information on drug interactions and 'Depression in adults with a chronic physical health problem' (Clinical Guideline 91; NICE, 2009c).

412

- Fluoxetine, fluvoxamine and paroxetine are associated with a higher propensity for drug interactions than other SSRIs[149].
- Paroxetine is associated with a higher incidence of discontinuation symptoms than other SSRIs[150].

10.14.1.3 When prescribing drugs other than SSRIs, take the following into account:

- The increased likelihood of the person stopping treatment because of side effects (and the consequent need to increase the dose gradually) with venlafaxine, duloxetine and TCAs.
- The specific cautions, contraindications and monitoring requirements for some drugs. For example:
  - the potential for higher doses of venlafaxine to exacerbate cardiac arrhythmias and the need to monitor the person's blood pressure
  - the possible exacerbation of hypertension with venlafaxine and duloxetine
  - the potential for postural hypotension and arrhythmias with TCAs
  - the need for haematological monitoring with mianserin in elderly people[151].
- Non-reversible monoamine oxidase inhibitors (MAOIs), such as phenelzine, should normally be prescribed only by specialist mental health professionals.
- Dosulepin should not be prescribed.

10.15 WHEN TO CHANGE ANTIDEPRESSANT TREATMENT WHEN SYMPTOMS OF DEPRESSION ARE NOT IMPROVING

10.15.1 Introduction

Received wisdom has been that antidepressants have a delayed onset of action and that it takes 2 to 4 weeks for them to begin to work. This is now recognised as incorrect and it has been shown from data from clinical trials that improvement can start immediately, with the greatest degree of improvement occurring in the first week; the curve begins to flatten off thereafter, with a smaller degree of improvement as time goes on. Posternak and Zimmerman (2005), in a meta-analysis of 47 placebo-controlled studies followed up at 6 weeks, found that 35% of the improvement occurred between weeks 0 and 1, and 25% between weeks 1 and 2. However, it is important to recognise that although the curve flattens, some people continue to improve after this and the assessment of the literature is influenced by the duration of follow-up. For example, in the large naturalistic STAR*D study (Trivedi *et al.*, 2006),

---

[149]Ibid.

[150]The evidence for this recommendation has not been updated since the previous guideline. Any wording changes have been made for clarification only.

[151]Consult the BNF for detailed information.

which enrolled nearly 2,876 patients followed up to 12 weeks, the mean time to response with citalopram (defined by at least 50% reduction in the Quick Inventory of Depressive Symptomatology-Self Report [QIDS-SR]) was 5.7 weeks with about 65% of patients responding by 6 weeks, but some patients continuing to respond at 12 weeks and beyond. Malt and colleagues (1999) undertook an RCT of 372 primary care patients randomised to sertraline, mianserin or placebo, and treated for 24 weeks. Response was defined as at least a 50% improvement on the HAMD plus at least much improved and not more than mildly ill on the CGI. Depending on the treatment arm, 58 to 91% of those responding by 24 weeks had done so by 6 weeks and 79 to 98% responded by 12 weeks.

The rate and degree of improvement also appears to be influenced by the frequency of follow up. Posternak and Zimmerman (2007), in a systematic review of 41 RCTs, found that weekly assessment between weeks 2 and 6 led to a greater reduction in HAMD score than less frequent assessment in a dose-related manner. This applied to both placebo and drug treatment arms and they estimated that follow-up frequency accounted for about 40% of the placebo response.

These studies emphasise the importance of the early stages of treatment in response to antidepressants and highlight the role of frequency of monitoring. A key issue related to this is the optimum time to change treatment. Switching treatment too early could lead to rejection of an effective treatment, which in the long run will be unhelpful when future treatment options are considered and could lead to a merry-go-round of treatment changes. Increasing the dose too early could lead to patients unnecessarily being maintained on higher than needed doses of antidepressants over a prolonged period of time with associated increased side effects or treatment discontinuation (Bollini *et al.*, 1999; Furukawa *et al.*, 2002b). Delaying change in treatment too long could prolong the period of depression if symptoms are not going to respond to current drug/dose, lead to a patient's loss of faith in treatment, and increase depression-related morbidity and even mortality.

There is limited but consistent evidence, mostly from studies with SSRIs, that increasing the dose after 3 weeks treatment in those not responding ($<$50% decrease in rating scale) or remitting (HAMD $<$9) at this early stage does not improve outcome at 6 weeks (Adli *et al.*, 2005). However, these are stringent criteria and do not allow clinicians to judge whether altering treatment is beneficial in those not improving at all. Stassen and colleagues (1993) found that the natural variation in assessment makes the minimum reliably detectable improvement in a rating scale in the range of 15 to 25% and most subsequent studies have examined the predictive value of non-improvement using a criterion of 20% or less (these are referred to here as 20% improvers).

10.15.2   Early prediction of eventual response

Most studies have found that early improvement in the first 2 weeks (20% or greater improvement) is a good predictor of response by the end of the study (Nierenberg *et al.*, 1995; Nierenberg *et al.*, 2000; Szegedi *et al.*, 2003; Szegedi *et al.*, 2009). This is consistent with usual clinical practice.

The outcome of concern is the number of non-improvers at each time point who subsequently respond or remit by the end of a certain time frame because this provides some guide as to when changing treatment is likely to improve outcome. This can be assessed using the negative predictive value (NPV), which is the proportion of non-improvers not going on to achieve response/remission at the last evaluation. Where this is low, non-improvement at that time point is not a useful predictor of outcome at endpoint. A matter for debate is: what is a reasonable value for the NPV that should trigger change of treatment? It is suggested that it lies somewhere between 70 and 80%; in other words, if a non-improver still has more than a 20 to 30% chance of responding then it is probably reasonable to persist longer with treatment before adding to the potential side-effect burden by increasing the dose, adding another drug or changing the drug. To put this into context, in the large naturalistic STAR*D study (Rush *et al.*, 2006), changing treatment in non-responders to the first treatment only resulted in an average increase in response of about 30%.

The strongest recent case for changing treatment as early as 2 weeks in non-improvers is Szegedi and colleagues (2009). They pooled data from 41 RCTs in which mirtazapine was compared with active comparators or placebo. Most studies were only 6 weeks in duration. They found that 60 to 76% of patients on antidepressants compared with 52% on placebo were 20% improvers at 2 weeks. Using a definition of stable response (response at both 4 weeks and subsequently, usually 6 weeks), the overall NPV for those not having a 20% improvement at 2 weeks was 89%, in other words only 11% would have a stable response as defined. The limitations are the short time frame of most of the studies and the requirement to have responded by 4 weeks.

It is useful to consider other studies according to the length of follow up. A 5-week study found an NPV for 20% improvement on response at 5 weeks of 48 to 54% at 2 weeks, 74 to 83% at 3 weeks and 96 to 99% at 4 weeks (Stassen *et al.*, 1993). A 6-week study found an NPV defined in the same way as 65 to 72% at 2 weeks, 77 to 94% at 3 weeks and 82 to 94% at 4 weeks (Szegedi *et al.*, 2003). Two 8-week studies of fluoxetine (defining improvement as 20% reduction in one and 30% in another) (Nierenberg *et al.*, 1995; Nierenberg *et al.*, 2000) and a pooled analysis of 14 escitalopram studies (20% improvement) (Baldwin *et al.*, 2009) found NPVs of 55 to 64% at 2 weeks, 80 to 82% at 4 weeks and 90 to 93% at 6 weeks. In contrast, an open 12-week study of fluoxetine (Quitkin *et al.*, 2003) using 25% improvement to predict remission (HAMD <8) found an NPV of only 49% at 4 weeks, 59 to 69% at 6 weeks and 77% at 8 weeks. Finally, a naturalistic study of 795 inpatients (Henkel *et al.*, 2009) with a variable follow-up (discharge, mean = 60 days), using 20% improvement found only a 37% NPV at 2 weeks for response and 43% at 4 weeks. NPVs for remission (HAMD <8) were higher at 69% and 72% respectively.

It is possible to draw only tentative conclusions from these studies. Higher early NPVs are associated with shorter studies and RCTs and lower NPVs with longer, open studies and possibly more severe patients. Taking the middle ground with an assessment period of 8 weeks and an NPV based on less than 20% improvement predicting lack of response at 8 weeks, a reasonable time to consider a change of treatment in these patients would be at 3 to 4 weeks. In patients who have failed

415

previous trials of treatment, and in more severely ill patients, longer trials of treatment may be warranted before making changes.

10.15.3   From evidence to recommendations

Antidepressant studies examining the onset of improvement in relation to response or remission at the end of the study vary in their findings according to the exact methodology used. Taking studies evaluating response over an 8-week time frame, which was thought by the GDG to present a realistic clinical situation, and using less than a 20% improvement on the HAMD score to indicate patients with a lack of, or barely detectable, response, when evaluated at 2 weeks these patients had about a 40% chance of achieving a response at 8 weeks falling to a 20% chance if they had failed to improve by 4 weeks. The rate of improvement after 6 to 8 weeks of treatment is slower and only a minority of non-responders at this stage will go on to have an adequate response over the next 6 to 18 weeks.

In addition, the GDG noted that there is some evidence that a higher frequency of assessment between weeks 2 and 6 is associated with a better outcome. Taken together these led to the recommendation that if there is no, or barely any detectable improvement at 2 to 4 weeks, patients should be followed weekly and consideration given to changing treatment at 3 to 4 weeks. Patients who are improving should have their improvement monitored and if there has been insufficient response at 6 weeks in the absence of a continuing trajectory of improvement, consideration should be given to changing treatment at that stage.

10.15.4   Clinical practice recommendations

10.15.4.1 For people started on antidepressants who are not considered to be at increased risk of suicide, normally see them after 2 weeks. See them regularly thereafter; for example, at intervals of 2 to 4 weeks in the first 3 months, and then at longer intervals if response is good.[152]

10.15.4.2 If a person with depression develops side effects early in antidepressant treatment, provide appropriate information and consider one of the following strategies:
- monitor symptoms closely where side effects are mild and acceptable to the person **or**
- stop the antidepressant or change to a different antidepressant if the person prefers **or**
- in discussion with the person, consider short-term concomitant treatment with a benzodiazepine if anxiety, agitation and/or insomnia are problematic (except in people with chronic symptoms of anxiety); this

---

[152]The evidence for this recommendation has not been updated since the previous NICE guideline. Any wording changes have been made for clarification only.

should usually be for no longer than 2 weeks in order to prevent the development of dependence.

10.15.4.3 If the person's depression shows no improvement after 2 to 4 weeks with the first antidepressant, check that the drug has been taken regularly and in the prescribed dose.

10.15.4.4 If response is absent or minimal after 3 to 4 weeks of treatment with a therapeutic dose of an antidepressant, increase the level of support (for example, by weekly face-to-face or telephone contact) and consider:

- increasing the dose in line with the Summary of Product Characteristics if there are no significant side effects **or**
- switching to another antidepressant as described in Section 12.3.16 if there are side effects or if the person prefers.

10.15.4.5 If the person's depression shows some improvement by 4 weeks, continue treatment for another 2 to 4 weeks. Consider switching to another antidepressant as described in 12.3.16 if:

- response is still not adequate **or**
- there are side effects **or**
- the person prefers to change treatment.

11 FACTORS INFLUENCING CHOICE OF ANTIDEPRESSANTS

11.1 INTRODUCTION

While the previous chapter reviewed the relative efficacy of different antidepressants, this chapter looks at factors that may affect the choice of antidepressant, including:
● the pharmacological management of depression in older adults (Section 11.2)
● the effect of sex on antidepressant choice (Section 11.3)
● the pharmacological management of depression with psychotic symptoms (Section 11.4)
● the pharmacological management of atypical depression (Section 11.5)
● the physical and pharmacological management of depression with a seasonal pattern (Section 11.6)
● dosage issues for tricyclic antidepressants (Section 11.7)
● antidepressant discontinuation symptoms (Section 11.8)
● the cardiotoxicity of antidepressants (Section 11.9)
● depression, antidepressants and suicide (Section 11.10).

This chapter updates the reviews on the effect of sex on antidepressant choice, antidepressant discontinuation symptoms, cardiotoxicity of antidepressants, and antidepressants and suicide. It includes a new review of treatments for depression with a seasonal pattern because this diagnosis was added to the scope of the updated guideline.

The review of the pharmacological management of depression in older adults was not updated because there were little new data in older adults to indicate that the existing recommendations should be amended. In addition, since the previous guideline, a separate guideline has been developed specifically for depression in adults with a chronic physical health problem, which covers many issues relevant to older people with depression (NICE, 2009c; NCCMH, 2010).

The section on depression with psychotic sypmtoms was not updated and the recommendations were left unchanged. The review of atypical depression was also not updated. However, the GDG felt that the previous recommendations should be removed since there was no reason why treatment for people whose depression had atypical features should not follow that for those with major depression. The review of low-dose versus high-dose TCAs was not updated.

11.2 THE PHARMACOLOGICAL MANAGEMENT OF DEPRESSION IN OLDER ADULTS

The following sections on the pharmacological management of depression in older adults marked by asterisks (**_**) are from the previous guideline and have not been updated except for style and minor clarification.

418

11.2.1   Introduction

**Depression is the most common mental health problem of later life affecting approximately 15% of older people (Beekman *et al.*, 1999). Untreated it shortens life and increases healthcare costs, as well as adding to disability from medical illnesses, and is the leading cause of suicide among older people (Lebowitz *et al.*, 1997). Most depression in older adults is treated in primary care (Plummer *et al.*, 1997) but there is evidence of poor detection (Plummer *et al.*, 1997) and sub-optimal treatment (Iliffe *et al.*, 1991). In this population the monitoring of self-harm is particularly important. It is also very important to educate the patient and caregivers about depression and involve them in treatment decisions. Older adults are at risk of co-existing physical disorders, sensory deficits and other disabilities and, therefore, medication needs to be carefully monitored in these groups.

The efficacy of antidepressants in older adults has been summarised in a Cochrane systematic review (Wilson *et al.*, 2001). There is some evidence that older people take longer to recover than younger adults and adverse events need to be carefully monitored for, since they might substantially affect function in a vulnerable individual.

There are a variety of potential differences in older adults in terms of absorption and metabolism of drugs and increased potential for interaction with other drugs. The maxim is, therefore, to start low and increase slowly but it is clear that much more research involving older patients with depression is required on this and other points.

It was possible to review the following pharmacological strategies for the treatment of depression in older adults:

- use of individual antidepressants (amitriptyline, TCAs as a group, SSRIs, phenelzine, mirtazapine, venlafaxine) and St John's wort; studies were also available for reboxetine but, since this drug is not licensed for the treatment of depression in older adults, it is not reviewed
- augmentation of an antidepressant with lithium
- strategies for relapse prevention.

11.2.2   Use of individual antidepressants in the treatment of depression in older adults

Studies considered[153,154]

This review brings together studies from other reviews undertaken for this guideline where more than 80% of study participants were aged 65 years and over. A separate

---

[153]Details of standard search strings used in all searches are in Appendix 8. Information about each study along with an assessment of methodological quality is in Appendix 17c, which also contains a list of excluded studies with reasons for exclusions.

[154]Here and elsewhere in the guideline, each study considered for review is referred to by a 'study ID' made up of first author and publication date (unless a study is in press or only submitted for publication, when first author only is used). Study IDs in title case refer to studies included in the previous guideline and study IDs in capital letters refer to studies found and included in this guideline update. References for studies from the previous guideline are in Appendix 18 and references for studies for the update are in Appendix 17c.

systematic search of the literature was not undertaken and, therefore, studies undertaken with elderly populations using drugs not reviewed for this guideline are not included.

In all, 15 studies from other reviews of individual antidepressants enrolled participants who were at least 60 years of age (Cohn1990, Dorman1992, Feighner1985a, GeorgotaS86, Geretsegger95, Guillibert89, Harrer99, Hutchinson92, LaPia1992, Mahapatra1997, Pelicier1993, Phanjoo1991, Rahman1991, Schatzberg02, Smeraldi1998). Ten studies were sourced from the review of SSRIs, two from venlafaxine and one each from mirtazapine, phenelzine and St John's wort. Studies were included provided the mean dose achieved was at least half the 'standard' adult dose. Efficacy data were available from up to 1,083 patients, and tolerability data from up to 1,620 patients.

All included studies were published between 1985 and 2002. Two were classified as inpatient, eight as outpatient and one as primary care. In four, participants were either from mixed sources or it was not possible determine the source. Studies ranged from 5 to 8 weeks long.

Clinical evidence statements[155]
Effect of treatment on efficacy
There is evidence suggesting that there is no clinically important difference on reducing symptoms of depression in older adults:
- between amitriptyline and paroxetine (K = 2; N = 126; SMD = –0.1; 95% CI, –0.46 to 0.27)
- between SSRIs and alternative antidepressants (K = 8; N = 602; SMD = –0.01; 95% CI, –0.17 to 0.15)
- between venlafaxine and TCAs (K = 2; N = 202; SMD = 0.02; 95% CI, –0.26 to 0.29)
- between alternative antidepressants and TCAs (K = 6, N = 443; SMD = 0.00; 95% CI, –0.19 to 0.19)
- between St John's wort and fluoxetine (K = 1; N = 149; SMD = –0.04; 95% CI, –0.36 to 0.28)
- between mirtazapine and paroxetine (K = 1, N = 254; SMD = –0.12; 95% CI, –0.37 to 0.13).

There is insufficient evidence to determine if there is a clinically important difference in older adults on increasing the likelihood of achieving a 50% reduction in symptoms of depression between:
- amitriptyline and paroxetine
- venlafaxine and TCAs
- alternative antidepressants and TCAs
- St John's wort and fluoxetine
- mirtazapine and paroxetine.

---

[155]The forest plots can be found in Appendix 19c.

There is evidence suggesting that there is no clinically important difference between mirtazapine and paroxetine on increasing the likelihood of achieving remission in older adults (K = 1, N = 254; RR = 0.87; 95% CI, 0.73 to 1.03).

There is insufficient evidence to determine if there is a clinically important difference in older adults on increasing the likelihood of achieving remission:
- between phenelzine and nortriptyline
- alternative antidepressants and TCAs.

Acceptability and tolerability of treatment

There is some evidence suggesting that there is a clinically important difference favouring mirtazapine over paroxetine on reducing the likelihood of older adults leaving treatment early due to side effects (K = 1, N = 254; RR = 0.57; 95% CI, 0.34 to 0.94).

There is evidence suggesting that there is no clinically important difference between alternative antidepressants and TCAs on reducing the likelihood of older adults reporting adverse effects (K = 7, N = 581; RR = 0.89; 95% CI, 0.79 to 1.02).

There is evidence suggesting that there is no clinically important difference on reducing the likelihood of older adults leaving treatment early between:
- amitriptyline and SSRIs (K = 3; N = 422; RR = 0.89; 95% CI, 0.7 to 1.12)
- SSRIs and alternative antidepressants (K = 10; N = 1115; RR = 0.96; 95% CI, 0.82 to 1.13)
- alternative antidepressants and TCAs (K = 10; N = 1058; RR = 0.97; 95% CI, 0.83 to 1.13).

There is evidence suggesting that there is no clinically important difference between SSRIs and alternative antidepressants on reducing the likelihood of older adults leaving treatment early due to side effects (K = 10; N = 1154; RR = 1; 95% CI, 0.81 to 1.23).

There is evidence suggesting that there is no clinically important difference on reducing the likelihood of older adults reporting adverse events between:
- SSRIs and alternative antidepressants (K = 8; N = 717; RR = 0.95; 95% CI, 0.85 to 1.05)
- phenelzine and nortriptyline (K = 1; N = 60; RR = 0.97; 95% CI, 0.87 to 1.09)
- mirtazapine and paroxetine (K = 1, N = 254; RR = 0.97; 95% CI, 0.86 to 1.09).

There is insufficient evidence to determine if there is a clinically important difference between other drug comparisons on other tolerability measures.

Effect of setting on treatment efficacy and tolerability

There is evidence suggesting that there is no clinically important difference between SSRIs and TCAs on reducing symptoms of depression in older inpatients (K = 2; N = 95; SMD = –0.07; 95% CI, –0.48 to 0.33).

There is insufficient evidence to determine any difference on any efficacy measure in older outpatients or patients in primary care.

There is some evidence suggesting that there is a clinically important difference favouring paroxetine over amitriptyline on reducing the likelihood of older adults in primary care reporting adverse effects (K = 1; N = 90; RR = 0.55; 95% CI, 0.35 to 0.86).

Factors influencing choice of antidepressants

There is insufficient evidence to determine any difference on tolerability measures for any other patient setting.

11.2.3   Augmentation of an antidepressant with lithium in older adults

Studies considered[156,157]
In the review of lithium augmentation[158] all participants in one study (Jensen1992) were aged 65 years or over. This was of inpatients, and compared nortriptyline (25 to 100 mg, median = 75 mg) plus lithium with nortriptyline (50 to 100 mg, median = 75 mg) plus placebo.

Clinical evidence statements[159]
Effect of treatment on efficacy outcomes
There is some evidence suggesting that there is a clinically important difference favouring nortriptyline alone over nortriptyline plus lithium on increasing the likelihood of achieving remission in older adults (K = 1; N = 44; RR = 2.28; 95% CI, 1.09 to 4.78).

Acceptability and tolerability of treatment
There is some evidence suggesting that there is a clinically important difference favouring nortriptyline alone over nortriptyline plus lithium on reducing the likelihood of older adults leaving treatment early (K = 1; N = 44; RR = 5.02; 95% CI, 1.26 to 20.07).

There is insufficient evidence to determine if there is a clinically important difference between nortriptyline plus lithium and nortriptyline alone on reducing the likelihood of older adults leaving treatment early due to side effects (K = 1; N = 44; RR = 5.48; 95% CI, 0.72 to 41.82).

11.2.4   Relapse prevention in older adults

Studies considered[160,161]
Five studies looked at relapse prevention in older adults (all at least 65 years of age or with a mean age of 65 years) (Alexopoulos2000, Cook1986, Georgotas1989,

---

[156]Details of standard search strings used in all searches are in Appendix 8. Information about each study along with an assessment of methodological quality is in Appendix 17c, which also contains a list of excluded studies with reasons for exclusions.

[157]Study IDs in title case refer to studies included in the previous guideline. References for these studies guideline are in Appendix 18.

[158]See Chapter 12, Section 12.3.5.

[159]The forest plots can be found in Appendix 19c.

[160]Details of standard search strings used in all searches are in Appendix 8. Information about each study along with an assessment of methodological quality is in Appendix 17c, which also contains a list of excluded studies with reasons for exclusions.

[161]Study IDs in title case refer to studies included in the previous guideline. References for these studies are in Appendix 18.

Klysner2002, Wilson2003), one in patients in primary care (Wilson2003) and four in outpatients (Alexopoulos00, Cook1986, Georgotas1989, Klysner2002).

Clinical evidence statements[162]

In an analysis of all available data comparing maintenance treatment with an anti-depressant with placebo there is strong evidence suggesting that there is a clinically important difference favouring continuing treatment with antidepressants over discontinuing antidepressants on reducing the likelihood of relapse in elderly patients (K = 5; N = 345; RR = 0.55; 95% CI, 0.43 to 0.71).

Where there was sufficient evidence, there was little difference in the results of sub-analyses by length of pre-randomisation treatment or by post-randomisation treatment, by a combination of these factors, or between results for SSRIs and TCAs analysed separately. Nor was any difference found for patients in their first episode or for those with previous episodes.

11.2.5   Clinical summary

There is no difference in the efficacy of the various antidepressants for which studies have been undertaken in older adults. There is also no evidence of differences in acceptability. There is no evidence that there is a difference by setting, apart from in primary care, where fewer patients taking paroxetine report adverse events compared with those taking amitriptyline.

With regard to augmenting an antidepressant with lithium, elderly patients appear to be more likely to achieve remission without the addition of lithium. These patients are also less likely to leave treatment early.

It appears to be worthwhile continuing pharmacological treatment in elderly patients with multiple depressive episodes in order to avoid relapse.

These results are similar to those found in the reviews of studies for all adult patients elsewhere in this guideline.**

11.2.6   From evidence to recommendations

The review of pharmacological treatments for older adults was not updated because there were little new data, and the overall conclusions in the previous guideline were that management of older adults should follow general principles. These were based on the fact that older people tend to metabolise drugs more slowly and are more likely to be taking concomitant medication and to be in poorer physical health than younger people. These recommendations are unchanged. However, they have been amended to bring them up to date with current NICE style. Since the publication of the previous guideline, a guideline on the management of dementia has been published

---

[162]The forest plots can be found in Appendix 19c.

(NICE, 2006b). This covers the management of depression comorbid with dementia and, therefore, recommendations relating to this topic have been removed.

11.2.7   Recommendation

11.2.7.1   When prescribing antidepressants for older people:
- prescribe at an age-appropriate dose taking into account the effect of general physical health and concomitant medication on pharmaco-kinetics and pharmacodynamics
- carefully monitor for side effects.

11.3   THE EFFECT OF SEX ON ANTIDEPRESSANT CHOICE

11.3.1   Review of the evidence

Although the female preponderance in the prevalence of unipolar depression has been well established (Weissman *et al.*, 1993), relatively little attention has been paid to gender differences in treatment response to antidepressant medication. A meta-analysis of 35 studies published between 1957 and 1991 that reported imipramine response rates separately by sex reported that men responded more favourably to imipramine than women (Hamilton *et al.*, 1996). Some studies since then have suggested that younger women may respond preferentially to SSRIs over noradrenaline reuptake inhibitors (TCAs, maprotiline, reboxetine) with predominantly no difference found for men (Kornstein *et al.*, 2000; Martenyi *et al.*, 2001; Joyce *et al.*, 2002; Baca *et al.*, 2004; Berlanga & Flores-Ramos, 2006). This may be accounted for by a poorer tolerability of TCAs in younger women (Kornstein *et al.*, 2000; Joyce *et al.*, 2002; Baca *et al.*, 2004). Results are inconsistent as to whether men respond better than women to TCAs (Quitkin *et al.*, 2001). A study comparing TCAs and MAOIs found that in patients with atypical depression and associated panic attacks, women showed a more favourable response to MAOIs and men to TCAs (Davidson & Pelton, 1986).

However, the data are not consistent, and several studies have failed to show any significant effect of sex on antidepressant response, for example, when SSRIs were compared with clomipramine in inpatients (Hildebrandt *et al.*, 2003), and no effect of sex has been found with venlafaxine (Hildebrandt *et al.*, 2003), duloxetine (Kornstein *et al.*, 2006), and amfebutamone (bupropion) (Papakostas *et al.*, 2007). A large obser-vational study of sertraline treatment in over 5,000 patients failed to find a clinically relevant effect of sex on response to treatment (Thiels *et al.*, 2005).

Taken as a whole, no convincing data showing differential benefits for antidepres-sants based on sex have accrued since the previous guideline; the GDG considered that the previous recommendations should be removed from the guideline update. However, recommendations from the guideline *Antenatal and Postnatal Mental Health: Clinical Management and Service Guidance* (NICE, 2007e) should be considered when treating women of childbearing age who have depression.

11.3.2   Recommendation

11.3.2.1   Do not routinely vary the treatment strategies for depression described in this guideline either by depression subtype (for example, atypical depression or seasonal depression) or by personal characteristics (for example, sex or ethnicity) as there is no convincing evidence to support such action.

11.4   THE PHARMACOLOGICAL MANAGEMENT OF DEPRESSION WITH PSYCHOTIC SYMPTOMS

The following sections on the pharmacological management of depression with psychotic symptoms marked by asterisks (**_**) are from the previous guideline and have not been updated except for style and minor clarification.

11.4.1   Introduction

**Major depression with psychotic features is a disorder with considerable morbidity and mortality. In an epidemiologic catchment area study (Johnson *et al.*, 1991), 14.7% of patients who met the criteria for major depression had a history of psychotic features. The prevalence is higher in samples of elderly patients. The disorder is often not diagnosed accurately because the psychosis may be subtle, intermittent or concealed. There has been a long-standing debate as to whether major depression with psychotic features is a distinct syndrome or represents a more severe depressive subtype. The weight of evidence suggests that severity alone does not account for the differences in symptoms, biological features and treatment response (Rothschild, 2003). The systematic study of major depression with psychotic features has been limited by the fact that the disorder does not exist as a distinct diagnostic subtype in DSM–IV and because of the difficulties in enrolling such patients in research studies. As a result there are few controlled studies on the acute treatment of psychotic depression and no long-term maintenance studies. There is some evidence that patients with major depression with psychotic features exhibit more frequent relapses or recurrences than patients with non-psychotic depression; however, not all studies are in agreement (see Rothschild, 2003). Patients with major depression with psychotic features demonstrate more severe psychomotor disturbance more frequently than patients without psychosis.

11.4.2   Studies considered for review[163,164]

Twenty studies were found in a search of electronic databases, six of which met the inclusion criteria set by the GDG (Anton1990, Bellini1994, Mulsant2001,

---

[163]Details of standard search strings used in all searches are in Appendix 8. Information about each study along with an assessment of methodological quality is in Appendix 17c, which also contains a list of excluded studies with reasons for exclusions.

[164]Study IDs in title case refer to studies included in the previous guideline. References for these studies are in Appendix 18.

Spiker1985, Zanardi1996, Zanardi2000) and 14 of which did not, mainly because too many participants had been diagnosed with bipolar depression and, therefore, fell outside the inclusion criteria set by the GDG.

Four studies (Anton1990, Bellini1994, Mulsant2001, Spiker1985) looked at augmenting an antidepressant with an antipsychotic and two (Zanardi1996, Zanardi2000) compared a single antidepressant with another. The following comparisons were possible:

- amitriptyline plus perphenazine versus amoxapine
- nortriptyline plus perphenazine versus nortriptyline plus placebo
- amitriptyline plus perphenazine versus amitriptyline
- desipramine plus haloperidol versus desipramine plus placebo[165]
- fluvoxamine plus haloperidol versus fluvoxamine plus placebo[166]
- paroxetine versus sertraline
- fluvoxamine versus venlafaxine.

In comparisons involving antipsychotic augmentation, efficacy data were available from up to 103 participants and tolerability data from up to 87 participants. In comparisons comparing single antidepressants, both efficacy and tolerability data were available from up to 60 participants. All included studies were published between 1985 and 2001 and were between 4 days and 16 weeks (mean = 7.17 weeks).

All studies were of inpatients, and in one all patients were at least 50 years of age (mean = 71 years) (Mulsant2001). Participants had a diagnosis of major depressive disorder with psychotic features. In two studies (Anton1990, Zanardi2000) up to 25% (the limit allowed in the inclusion criteria set by the GDG is 15%) of participants were diagnosed with bipolar disorder. Two sets of analyses were performed including and excluding these two studies. There was no difference in results, so statements from the analysis excluding these studies are presented below.

11.4.3   Clinical evidence statements[167]

Effect of treatment on efficacy
There is some evidence suggesting that there is a clinically important difference favouring sertraline over paroxetine on increasing the likelihood of achieving remission as measured by the HRSD in patients with psychotic depression (K = 1; N = 32; RR = 2.83; 95% CI, 1.28 to 6.25).

There is insufficient evidence on any efficacy measure to determine if there is a clinically important difference between a TCA plus an antipsychotic and either amoxapine or a TCA in patients with psychotic depression.

---

[165]Four-armed trial (Bellini1994).
[166]Ibid.
[167]The forest plots can be found in Appendix 19c.

Acceptability and tolerability of treatment

There is insufficient evidence to determine if there is a clinically important difference on the acceptability of treatment between:

- perphenazine augmentation of a TCA and tricyclic monotherapy
- paroxetine and sertraline.

11.4.4   Clinical summary

There is no good quality evidence for pharmacological treatments of psychotic depression. However, there are practical problems in recruiting sufficient numbers of patients with psychotic depression and, therefore, practitioners may wish to consider lower levels of evidence.**

11.4.5   Recommendation

11.4.5.1   For people who have depression with psychotic symptoms, consider augmenting the current treatment plan with antipsychotic medication (although the optimum dose and duration of treatment are unknown)[168].

11.5   THE PHARMACOLOGICAL MANAGEMENT OF ATYPICAL DEPRESSION

The following sections on the pharmacological management of atypical depression marked by asterisks (**_**) are from the previous guideline and have not been updated except for style and minor clarification.

11.5.1   Introduction

**Depression with atypical features is described in DSM–IV (APA, 1994). The introduction of a formally defined type of depression with atypical features was in response to research and clinical data indicating that patients with atypical depression have specific characteristics. The classical atypical features are over-eating and over-sleeping (sometimes referred to as reverse vegetative symptoms). The syndrome is also associated with mood reactivity, leaden paralysis and a long-standing pattern of interpersonal rejection sensitivity. In comparison with major depressive disorder without atypical features, patients with atypical depression are more often female,

---

[168]The evidence for this recommendation has not been updated since the previous NICE guideline. Any wording changes have been made for clarification only.

have a younger age of onset and a more severe degree of psychomotor slowing. Co-existing diagnoses of panic disorder, substance misuse and somatisation disorder are common. The high incidence and severity of anxiety symptoms in these patients increases the likelihood of their being misclassified as having an anxiety disorder. The major treatment implication of atypical depression is that patients are said to be more likely to respond to MAOIs than TCAs. However, the significance of atypical features remains controversial as does the preferential treatment response to MAOIs. The absence of specific diagnostic criteria has limited the ability to assess the aetiology, prevalence and validity of the condition.

11.5.2   Studies considered[169,170]

This section brings together studies from other reviews undertaken for this guideline where participants were diagnosed with atypical depression. A separate systematic search of the literature was not undertaken and, therefore, studies of atypical depression using drugs not reviewed for this guideline are not included.**

No new studies were found in the update search for the guideline update.

**In all, three studies from other reviews were of atypical depression (Mcgrath00, Pande1996, Quitkin1990). Two came from the review of phenelzine and one from the review of SSRIs. Data were available to look at the efficacy of phenelzine compared with imipramine/desipramine or with fluoxetine, and fluoxetine compared with imipramine. But there was only tolerability data available for phenelzine compared with fluoxetine. Efficacy data were available from up to 334 patients, and tolerability data from up to 40 patients. All included studies were published between 1990 and 2000. Two were classified outpatient studies and in the other it was not possible to determine the source.

11.5.3   Clinical evidence statements[171]

Effect of treatment on efficacy
In people with atypical depression there is some evidence suggesting that there is a clinically important difference favouring phenelzine over other antidepressants (imipramine/ desipramine and fluoxetine) on increasing the likelihood of achieving a 50% decrease in symptoms of depression by the end of treatment as measured by the HRSD (K = 2; N = 232; RR= 0.69; 95% CI, 0.52 to 0.9).

---

[169]Details of standard search strings used in all searches are in Appendix 8. Information about each study along with an assessment of methodological quality is in Appendix 17c, which also contains a list of excluded studies with reasons for exclusions.

[170]Study IDs in title case refer to studies included in the previous guideline. References for these studies are in Appendix 18.

[171]The forest plots can be found in Appendix 19c.

In people with atypical depression there is insufficient evidence to determine if there is a clinically important difference between phenelzine and other antidepressants on:

- increasing the likelihood of patients achieving remission by the end of treatment as measured by the HRSD (K = 2; N = 232; Random effects RR = 0.83; 95% CI, 0.39 to 1.75)
- reducing symptoms of depression as measured by the HRSD (K = 2; N = 232; Random effects SMD = −0.31; 95% CI, −0.88 to 0.26).

In a sub-analysis by antidepressant class, there is some evidence suggesting that there is a clinically important difference favouring phenelzine over TCAs (imipramine/desipramine) on:

- increasing the likelihood of patients achieving a 50% decrease in symptoms of depression by the end of treatment as measured by the HRSD (K = 1; N = 192; RR = 0.68; 95% CI, 0.52 to 0.9)
- increasing the likelihood of patients achieving remission by the end of treatment as measured by the HRSD (K = 1; N = 192; RR = 0.65; 95% CI, 0.49 to 0.87)
- reducing symptoms of depression as measured by the HRSD (K = 1; N = 192; WMD = −3.15; 95% CI, −4.83 to −1.47).

Compared with SSRIs (fluoxetine), there is evidence suggesting that there is no clinically important difference between phenelzine and fluoxetine on reducing symptoms of depression by the end of treatment as measured by the HRSD (K = 1; N = 40; WMD = 0.20; 95% CI, −2.11 to 2.51).

There is insufficient evidence to determine if there is a clinically important difference between phenelzine and fluoxetine, or between fluoxetine and TCAs on any other efficacy measure.

Acceptability and tolerability of treatment
In people with atypical depression there is insufficient evidence to determine if there is a clinically important difference between phenelzine and fluoxetine on reducing the likelihood of leaving treatment early for any reason or on reducing the likelihood of leaving treatment early due to side effects.

11.5.4 Clinical summary

In patients with atypical depression there is some evidence suggesting a clinical advantage for phenelzine over TCAs (imipramine/desipramine) in terms of achieving remission and response. However, compared with SSRIs (fluoxetine), there is evidence of no difference on mean endpoint scores, and insufficient evidence on other outcome measures. There is insufficient evidence for the acceptability and tolerability of any antidepressant.**

11.5.5 From evidence to recommendations

The previous guideline recommended treatment with an SSRI for people with atypical depression. Since this is the treatment of choice for all people with depression, the guideline group decided to remove the recommendation from the updated guideline. They also considered that the other recommendations for treating atypical depression were adequately covered elsewhere in the guideline (cautions about the use of phenelzine, and referring to a mental health specialist), and that no special management of people with atypical depression could be recommended.

11.5.6 Recommendation

11.5.6.1 See recommendation 11.3.2.1.

11.6 THE PHYSICAL AND PHARMACOLOGICAL MANAGEMENT OF DEPRESSION WITH A SEASONAL PATTERN

11.6.1 Introduction

The term seasonal affective disorder (SAD), introduced by Rosenthal and colleagues (1984) to describe recurrent depressions that have a seasonal pattern and occur annually at the same time each year, includes bipolar depression but most people affected have recurrent unipolar depression (70 to 80%). Winter depression with a seasonal pattern is far more common than summer depression with a seasonal pattern. DSM–IV includes criteria for a seasonal pattern for depressive episodes whereas only provisional criteria are given in the research version of ICD–10. The characteristic quality of major depression with a seasonal pattern is that symptoms usually present during the winter and remit in the spring. The symptoms of depression with a seasonal pattern do not clearly delineate it from other types of depression but in reported samples decreased activity was nearly always present and atypical depressive symptoms were common, particularly increased sleep, weight gain and carbohydrate craving.

Depression with a seasonal pattern as a separate diagnosis has been less accepted in Europe than North America, and an alternative view is that major depression with a seasonal pattern is an extreme form of a dimensional 'seasonality trait' rather than a specific diagnosis with so-called 'subsyndromal major depression with a seasonal pattern' appearing to be common. Nevertheless there are some patients with recurrent major depression who experience a seasonal pattern to their illness, at least for a time. There also appear to be people who experience seasonal fluctuations in mood that do not reach criteria for major depression.

The hypothesis that light therapy (that is, increasing the amount or duration of light exposure) might be an effective treatment is based on the presumption that depression with a seasonal pattern is caused by a lack of light in the winter months. There have subsequently been a number of controlled studies and meta-analyses (for example, Golden *et al.*, 2005) that have concluded that light therapy may be effective. There has been little research into other treatments in patients with depression with a seasonal pattern.

11.6.2   Databases searched and the inclusion/exclusion criteria

Information about the databases searched for published trials and the inclusion/exclusion criteria used are presented in Table 91. Details of the search strings used are in Appendix 8.

11.6.3   Light therapy for depression with a seasonal pattern

Depression with a seasonal pattern was not included in the scope of the previous guideline. Light therapy, which has been developed as a treatment specifically for major depression with a seasonal pattern, was therefore not reviewed, but has been included here as an additional review for the guideline update. For this review both published and unpublished RCTs investigating light therapy in patients diagnosed with major or subsyndromal major depression with a seasonal pattern were sought. There are a range of methods for administering light therapy; this review included a range of light treatments such as a light box, light room or visor and dawn simulation. Trials comparing a light treatment with a control condition, another light treatment or light administered at different times of day were included in this review.

A special adviser was consulted regarding a number of issues for this review (see Appendix 3). He advised the GDG that 5,000 lux hours[172] per day is a reasonable

Table 91: Databases searched and inclusion/exclusion criteria for clinical effectiveness of psychological treatments

Electronic databases	MEDLINE, EMBASE, PsycINFO, CINAHL
Date searched	Database inception to January 2008
Update searches	July 2008; January 2009
Study design	RCT
Population	People with a diagnosis of depression with a seasonal pattern according to DSM, ICD or similar criteria, or seasonal affective disorder according to Rosenthal's (1984) criteria or subsyndromal major depression with a seasonal pattern as indicated by score on seasonal depression scale
Treatments	Light therapy, dawn simulation, antidepressants, psychological therapies, other physical treatments

---

[172]Lux is a standard measure of illuminance; 1 lux is equal to 1 lumen per square metre [lumen is the unit of luminous flux].

minimum dose for light box treatment, but that a minimum effective dose of light administered by a light visor has not yet been established. For the control light condition a placebo light of not more than 300 lux is appropriate. He suggested that a minimum trial duration of a week would be reasonable for evaluating the efficacy of light treatment. His advice was also sought regarding dawn simulation; he suggested that it would be informative to include this type of light treatment in the review and that a simulation of around an hour and a half peaking at 250 lux is an appropriate minimum, with a control condition of a light of less than 2 lux.

Studies considered[173]

In total, 61 trials were found from searches of electronic databases. Of these, 19 were included and 42 were excluded. The most common reasons for exclusion were that papers were not RCTs or participants did not have a diagnosis of depression or subsyndromal depressive symptoms with a seasonal pattern. In addition, studies that used a cross-over design (where participants serve as their own controls by receiving both treatments) were not used unless pre-crossover data were available.

The studies that were found by the search and included in this review varied considerably in methodology. The intensity and duration of light, time of day, mode of administration of light, and the comparison conditions were different across studies. A range of outcomes were reported by the included studies, including the HRSD (termed 'typical' depression rating scale to distinguish it from scales measuring depression with seasonal pattern symptoms), and scales adapted for measuring symptoms in depression with a seasonal pattern. These included the Structured Interview Guide for the Hamilton Depression Rating Scale (SIGH) for major depression with a seasonal pattern (Williams *et al.*, 1988), which combines the HRSD with an additional eight items relevant to depression with a seasonal pattern. Some studies report the eight additional items separately. Both typical and atypical symptoms were measured using clinician- and self-rated scales. All data were extracted and can be seen in the full evidence profiles and forest plots (Appendix 16c and Appendix 19c, respectively). Only data for the SIGH for major depression with a seasonal pattern (clinician- and self-rated) are presented here.

Data were available to compare light therapy with a range of control conditions including waitlist, attentional controls and active treatment controls. In addition administration of light in the morning versus evening was compared and dawn simulation was compared with attentional control and with bright light. One study included a combination treatment of light and CBT and one trial reported on light therapy for relapse prevention.

Summary study characteristics of the included studies are presented in Table 92 and Table 93 with full details in Appendix 17c, which also includes details of excluded studies.

---

[173]Study IDs in capital letters refer to studies found and included in this guideline update.

Table 92: Summary study characteristics of light therapy studies versus control and morning light versus afternoon/evening light

	Light versus waitlist control	Light versus attentional control	Light versus active treatment control	Morning versus afternoon/evening light
No. trials (total participants)	2 RCTs (82)	8 RCTs (401)	4 RCTs (243)	4 RCTs (144)
Study IDs	(1) RASTAD2008 (2) ROHAN2007	(1) DESAN2007 (2) EASTMAN1998 (3) JOFFE1993 (4) LEVITT1996 (5) ROSENTHAL1993 (6) STRONG2008 (7) TERMAN1998[†] (8) WILEMAN2001	(1) LAM2006F (2) MARTINEZ1994 (3) ROHAN2004 (4) ROHAN2007	(1) AVERY2001A (2) EASTMAN1998 (3) LAFER1994[‡] (4) TERMAN1998[†]
N/% female	(1) 51/80 (2) 31/84	(1) 26/77 (2) 81/88 (3) 67/87 (4) 44/72 (5) 55/84 (6) 30/78 (7) 39/80 (8) 59/88	(1) 96/67 (2) 20/65 (3) 26/92 (4) 61/94	(1) 31/90 (2) 81/85 (3) 32/65 (4) 39/80

Continued

Table 92: *(Continued)*

	Light versus waitlist control	Light versus attentional control	Light versus active treatment control	Morning versus afternoon/evening light
Mean age	(1) 46 (2) 45	(1) 46 (2) 37 (3) 40 (4) 35 (5) 42 (6) 44 (7) 39 (8) 41	(1) 43 (2) 46 (3) 51 (4) 45	(1) 40 (2) 37 (3) 35 (4) 39
Diagnosis	(1)–(2) MDD with seasonal pattern (DSM–IV)	(1) MDD with seasonal pattern (DSM–IV) (2) Major depression with a seasonal pattern (Rosenthal) (3) MDD or bipolar with seasonal pattern (DSM–III–R) or major depression with a seasonal pattern (Rosenthal) (4) MDD with seasonal pattern (DSM–III–R) (5) Major depression with a seasonal pattern (Rosenthal)	(1) MDD or bipolar with seasonal pattern (DSM–IV) (2) MDD with seasonal pattern (DSM–III–R) (3)–(4) MDD with seasonal pattern (DSM–IV)	(1) Subsyndromal major depression with a seasonal pattern (2) Major depression with a seasonal pattern (Rosenthal) (3) Major depressive episode with a seasonal pattern (DSM–III–R) (4) Mood disorder with major depression with a seasonal pattern (DSM–III–R)

	(6) MDD with seasonal pattern (DSM–IV) (7) Mood disorder with major depression with a seasonal pattern (DSM–III–R) (8) MDD with seasonal pattern (DSM–IV)				
Light therapy	(1) Fluorescent light room (2) Fluorescent light box	(1) LED Litebook device (2) Fluorescent light box (3) Light visor (4a) Fluorescent light box (4b) LED visor (5) Light visor (6) Narrow-band blue light panel (7)–(8) Light box	(1) Fluorescent light box + placebo pill (2) Light box + hypericum (3) Light box (4) Fluorescent light box	(1) Light box used between 7 am–12 pm (2) Fluorescent light box used as soon as possible after waking (3) Bright light for 2 hours (4) Light box 10 minutes after waking	
Lux hours/day	(1) Varies 1650–8600 (2) 15000 in 1st week, varies after week 1	(1) 675 (2) 9000 (3) Mean 1762 (4a) Mean 3800 (4b) Mean 323 (5) 3000 or 6000 (6) 470 nm 176 lux × 45 minutes (7) 10000	(1) 5000 (2) 3000 (3) 15000 (4) 15000 in 1st week, varies after week 1	(1) 5000 (2) 9000 (3) 2,500 (4) 10000	

Continued

435

Table 92: (*Continued*)

	Light versus waitlist control	Light versus attentional control	Light versus active treatment control	Morning versus afternoon/evening light
Comparator(s)	(1)–(2) Waitlist	(8) 5000 in 1st week, 7500 in 2nd week, 10000 in last 2 weeks (1)–(2) Deactivated negative ion generator (3) Dim 67 lux light visor (4a) Light box producing no light (4b) Visor producing no light (5) Dim 400 lux light visor (6) Red light (7) Low-density negative ions (8) Dim 500 lux red light box	(1) Dim 100 lux light + 20 mg/day fluoxetine (2) Dim light + hypericum (3) Group CBT/light + group CBT (4) Group CBT	(1) Light box used between 12–5 p.m. (2) Fluorescent light box used within 1 hour of bedtime (3) Bright light for 2 hours (4) Light box 2–3 hours before bedtime
Length of treatment (days)	(1) 21 (2) 42	(1)–(2) 28 (3)–(4) 14 (5) 7 (6) 21 (7) 14 (8) 28	(1) 56 (2) 28 (3)–(4) 42	(1) 14 (2) 28 (3) 7 (4) 14

*3-armed trial, †5-armed trial and ‡3-armed trial but 1 arm not used (bright light alternating morning and evening).

Table 93: Summary study characteristics of dawn simulation and relapse prevention studies

	Dawn simulation versus attentional control	Light versus dawn simulation	Relapse prevention
No. trials (total participants)	3 RCTs (139)	2 RCTs (112)	1 RCT (46)
Study IDs	(1) AVERY1993 (2) AVERY2001 (3) TERMAN2006	(1) AVERY2001 (2) TERMAN2006	(1) MEESTERS 1999
N/% female	(1) 27/70 (2) 62/87 (3) 50/79	(1) 64/88 (2) 48	(1) 46/71
Mean age	(1) 35 (2) 41 (3) 40	(1) 41 (2) 40	(1) 40
Diagnosis	(1) Major depression with a seasonal pattern (Rosenthal) (2) MDD or bipolar with seasonal pattern (DSM–IV) (3) MDD with seasonal pattern (DSM–III-R)	(1) MDD or bipolar with seasonal pattern (DSM–IV) (2) MDD with seasonal pattern (DSM–III-R)	(1) MDD with seasonal pattern (DSM–IV)
Light therapy	(1) Gradual dawn simulation over 2 hours (2) Gradual dawn simulation over 1.5 hours (3) Gradual dawn simulation over 3.5 hours	(1)–(2) Light box	(1) Light visor
Lux hours/day	(1)–(3) 250 lux peak intensity	(1) 5000 (2) 10000	(1) 1250
Comparator	(1) Rapid dim 0.2 lux dawn (2) Dim 0.5 lux red dawn (3) Pulse dawn 250 lux 30 minutes	(1) Gradual dawn simulation over 1.5 hours peaking at 250 lux (2) Gradual dawn simulation over 3.5 hours	(1a) No treatment (1b) Dim 0.18 lux infrared light
Length of treatment (days)	(1) 7 (2) 42 (3) 21	(1) 42 (2) 21	(1) 182

Clinical evidence
Bright light versus waitlist or attentional control
Compared with waitlist control, bright light (either light room or light box) shows a strong effect on symptoms in depression with a seasonal pattern although there are few studies. Compared with attentional controls, such as deactivated negative ion generator, dim red light, and sham light boxes, bright light (either via light box or light visor) shows a small effect on symptoms in depression with a seasonal pattern that was not clinically important. Evidence from the important outcomes and overall quality of evidence are presented in Table 94. The full evidence profiles and associated forest plots can be found in Appendix 16c and Appendix 19c, respectively.

Bright light versus active treatment control
There were data to compare light therapy with group CBT, light therapy plus CBT, and dim light plus fluoxetine. There was also a study comparing light therapy plus St John's wort with dim light plus St John's wort.

Compared with group CBT (tailored to depression with a seasonal pattern) bright light therapy was no better in terms of reducing depressive symptoms in depression with a seasonal pattern, although the effect size is not statistically significant and was graded low quality. However, more participants achieved remission with bright light therapy than with group CBT (52% compared with 37.5%), although the result is not clinically important. Similarly, light therapy appeared to be more acceptable than group CBT with fewer people leaving treatment early (8% compared with 16.7%) although the effect size is not statistically significant. Treatment lasted for 6 weeks.

Combination treatment (bright light plus CBT) was more effective than light therapy alone on both the SIGH for major depression with a seasonal pattern and the BDI, although the effect sizes were not statistically significant. Roughly equal numbers of participants left treatment early.

There appeared to be little difference between bright light therapy and fluoxetine (20 mg) on efficacy outcomes (both treatments given with a sham treatment mimicking the other). Treatment lasted for 8 weeks.

There was no evidence for the efficacy of light therapy combined with St John's wort compared with a sham light condition plus St John's wort. There was only a single small 4-week study (n = 20).

Evidence from the important outcomes and overall quality of evidence are presented in Table 95. The full evidence profiles and associated forest plots can be found in Appendix 16c and Appendix 19c, respectively.

Morning light versus afternoon/evening light
Three studies compared light therapy administered in the morning compared with light therapy in the afternoon or evening, one of which was in participants with subsyndromal major depression with a seasonal pattern. There were no significant differences in outcome measures for those given light therapy in the morning compared with those given light therapy in the afternoon or evening. Evidence from the important outcomes and overall quality of evidence are presented in Table 96. The full evidence profiles and associated forest plots can be found in Appendix 16c and Appendix 19c, respectively.

Table 94: Summary evidence profile for bright light versus waitlist or attentional controls

	Bright light versus waitlist control	Bright light versus attentional control
Leaving treatment early	RR 0.95 (0.21 to 4.32) (7.1 versus 7.5%)	RR 0.88 (0.50 to 1.54) (13.4 versus 14.5%)
Quality	Low	Low
Number of studies; participants	K = 2; n = 82	K = 6; n = 266
Forest plot number	Pharm SAD 01.01	Pharm SAD 02.01
Reported side effects	Not reported	RR 0.98 (0.73 to 1.32) (55.6 versus 58.3%)
Quality	–	Low
Number of studies; participants	–	K = 2; n = 81
Forest plot number	–	Pharm SAD 02.03
Clinician-rated endpoint (SIGH-SAD)	WMD −10.4 (−15.99 to −4.81)	WMD −3.07 (−6.71 to 0.58)
Quality	Moderate	Low
Number of studies; participants	K = 1; n = 31	K = 8; n = 300
Forest plot number	Pharm SAD 01.04	Pharm SAD 02.04
Self-rated endpoint (SIGH-SAD-SR)	WMD −12.8 (−18.52 to −7.08)	Not reported
Quality	Moderate	–
Number of studies; participants	K = 1; n = 44	–
Forest plot number	Pharm SAD 01.03	–
Non-remission (based on SIGH-SAD-SR)	RR 0.53 (0.38 to 0.74) (47.6 versus 90%)	RR 0.89 (0.66 to 1.2) (56.3 versus 61.3%)
Quality	High	Low
Number of studies; participants	K = 2; n = 82	K = 6; n = 336
Forest plot number	Pharm SAD 01.10	Pharm SAD 02.08
Non-response (based on SIGH-SAD	RR 0.50 (0.34 to 0.73) (50 versus 100%)	RR 0.86 (0.64 to 1.15) (45.4 versus 53.8%)
Quality	Moderate	Low
Number of studies; participants	K = 1; n = 51	K = 7; n = 354
Forest plot number	Pharm SAD 01.11	Pharm SAD 02.09

Table 95: Summary evidence profile for bright light versus active treatment control

	Light box versus group CBT	Light box versus light box + group CBT	Light box + placebo pill versus dim light box + fluoxetine	Light box + St John's wort versus dim light + St John's wort
Leaving treatment early	RR 0.53 (0.12 to 2.31) (8 versus 16.7%)	RR 0.92 (0.17 to 4.91) (8 versus 8.7%)	RR 1.14 (0.45 to 2.90) (16.7 versus 14.6%)	Not reported
Quality	Moderate	Moderate	Moderate	–
Number of studies; participants	K = 2; n = 49	K = 2; n = 48	K = 1; n = 96	–
Forest plot number	Pharm SAD 03.01	Pharm SAD 04.01	Pharm SAD 03.01	–
Reported side effects	Not reported	Not reported	RR 1.03 (0.82 to 1.29) (77.1 versus 75%)	Not reported
Quality	–	–	Moderate	–
Number of studies; participants	–	–	K = 1; n = 96	–
Forest plot number	–	–	Pharm SAD 03.04	–
Clinician-rated mean endpoint	WMD –0.2 (–6.5 to 6.1) (SIGH-SAD)	WMD 4.2 (–0.52 to 8.92) (SIGH-SAD)	WMD –0.00 (–3.88 to 3.88) (SIGH-SAD)	SMD –0.32 (–1.2 to 0.57) (HRSD)
Quality	Low	Moderate	High	Low
Number of studies; participants	K = 1; n = 31	K = 1; n = 31	K = 1; n = 96	K = 1; n = 20
Forest plot number	Pharm SAD 03.05	Pharm SAD 04.03	Pharm SAD 03.05	Pharm SAD 03.06

Self-rated mean endpoint	WMD –0.7 (–7.16 to 5.76) (BDI)	SMD 2.3 (–2.47 to 7.07) (BDI)	WMD –1.6 (–5.68 to 2.48) (BDI)	Not reported
Quality	Low	Low	Low	–
Number of studies; participants	K = 1; n = 31	K = 1; n = 31	K = 1; n = 96	–
Forest plot number	Pharm SAD 03.08	Pharm SAD 04.06	Pharm SAD 03.08	–
Non-remission (based on SIGH-SAD-SR)	RR 0.77 (0.46 to 1.28) (48 versus 62.5%)	RR 2.22 (0.92 to 5.32) (48 versus 21.7%)	RR 1.09 (0.57 to 1.76) (50 versus 45.8%)	Not reported
Quality	High	High	Low	–
Number of studies; participants	K = 2; n = 49	K = 2; n = 48	K = 1; n = 96	–
Forest plot number	Pharm SAD 03.09	Pharm SAD 04.07	Pharm SAD 03.09	–
Non-response (based on SIGH-SAD-SR)	Not reported	Not reported	RR 1 (0.57 to 1.76) (33.3 versus 33.3%)	Not reported
Quality	–	–	Low	–
Number of studies; participants	–	–	K = 1; n = 96	–
Forest plot	–	–	03.10	–

Table 96: Summary evidence profile for morning light versus evening light

	Overall results	Subsyndromal major depression with a seasonal pattern only
Leaving treatment early	RR 0.98 (0.41 to 2.35) (12.1 versus 12.5%)	Not reported
Quality	Moderate	–
Number of studies; participants	K = 3; n = 130	–
Forest plot number	Pharm SAD 05.01	–
Reported side effects	RR 0.47 (0.05 to 4.65) (6.3 versus 13.3%)	RR 0.47 (0.05 to 4.65) (6.3 versus 13.3%)
Quality	Low	Low
Number of studies; participants	K = 1; n = 31	K = 1; n = 31
Forest plot number	Pharm SAD 05.03	Pharm SAD 05.03
Clinician-rated mean endpoint	WMD −1.38 (−5.49 to 2.73) (SIGH-SAD)	WMD 0.6 (−3.89 to 5.09) (SIGH-SAD)
Quality	Low	Low
Number of studies; participants	K = 2; n = 68	K = 1; n = 30
Forest plot number	Pharm SAD 05.04	Pharm SAD 05.04
Self-rated mean endpoint	WMD −0.9 (−4.66 to 2.86) (BDI)	Not reported
Quality	Low	–
Number of studies; participants	K = 1; n = 65	–
Forest plot number	Pharm SAD 05.07	–
Non-remission (based on SIGH-SAD-SR)	RR 1.0 (0.69 to 1.45) (54 versus 54.2%)	Not reported
Quality	Low	–
Number of studies; participants	K = 2; n = 98	–
Forest plot number	Pharm SAD 05.08	–
Non-response (based on SIGH-SAD-SR)	RR 1.0 (0.51 to 1.98) (44 versus 42.9%)	RR 0.52 (0.23 to 1.20) (31.3 versus 60%)
Quality	Low	Moderate
Number of studies; participants	K = 3; n = 129	K = 1; n = 31
Forest plot number	Pharm SAD 05.09	Pharm SAD 05.09

Dawn simulation versus attentional control or light therapy
Three studies compared dawn simulation with an attentional control. There was some evidence that dawn simulation improved symptoms of depression but it was not clinically important and was not supported by other outcomes including the major depression with a seasonal pattern subscale. Similarly, there was no evidence of superiority of dawn simulation over regular light therapy. Evidence from the important outcomes and overall quality of evidence are presented in Table 97. The full evidence profiles and associated forest plots can be found in Appendix 16c and Appendix 19c, respectively.

Table 97: Summary evidence profile for dawn simulation studies

	Dawn simulation versus attentional control	Light therapy versus dawn simulation
Leaving treatment early	RR 0.27 (0.08 to 0.92) (2.9 versus 14.1%)	RR 3.72 (0.62 to 22.22) (8.9 versus 1.8%)
Quality	Low	Moderate
Number of studies; participants	K = 3; n = 141	K = 2; n = 112
Forest plot number	Pharm SAD 06.01	Pharm SAD 07.01
Reported side effects	RR 5.57 (0.77 to 40.26) (42.9 versus 7.7%)	Not reported
Quality	Low	–
Number of studies; participants	K = 1; n = 27	–
Forest plot number	Pharm SAD 06.04	–
Clinician-rated mean endpoint	SMD −0.53 (−1.62 to 0.15) (HRSD) WMD −2.20 (−7.52 to 3.11) (SAD subscale)	WMD −0.9 (−4 to 2.2) (HRSD) WMD −1.8 (−6.98 to 3.38) (SAD subscale)
Quality	Moderate (HRSD) Very low (SAD subscale)	Very low (HRSD) Low (SAD subscale)
Number of studies; participants	K = 2; n = 73	K = 1; n = 45
Forest plot number	Pharm SAD 06.05/06	Pharm SAD 07.06/07
Self-rated mean endpoint	Not reported	Not reported
Quality	–	–

Continued

Table 97: (*Continued*)

	Dawn simulation versus attentional control	Light therapy versus dawn simulation
Number of studies; participants	–	–
Forest plot number	–	–
Non-remission (based on SIGH-SAD)	RR 0.9 (0.46 to 1.78) (44.6 versus 50%)	RR 1.19 (0.70 to 2.00) (53.6 versus 44.6%)
Quality	Low	Very low
Number of studies; participants	K = 2; n = 114	K = 2; n = 112
Forest plot number	Pharm SAD 06.07	Pharm SAD 07.04
Non-response (based on SIGH-SAD)	RR 0.71 (0.34 to 1.48) (25 versus 38%)	RR 1.45 (0.82 to 2.58) (35.7 versus 25%)
Quality	Moderate	Moderate
Number of studies; participants	K = 2; n = 114	K = 2; n = 112
Forest plot number	Pharm SAD 06.08	Pharm SAD 07.05

Prevention of future episodes using light therapy

One study compared bight light therapy with a control treatment and with no treatment as relapse prevention in people who had a history of depression with a seasonal pattern but had not yet developed symptoms. This showed that those receiving light therapy were less likely to develop symptoms of depression compared with those receiving no treatment. However, those using the infrared light visor were less likely to develop symptoms of depression than those using the bright white light visor. Neither finding was clinically important. Evidence from the important outcomes and overall quality of evidence are presented in Table 98. The full evidence profiles and associated forest plots can be found in Appendix 16c and Appendix 19c, respectively.

Clinical summary

Although there are a large number of studies that address the efficacy of light treatment in people with depression that follows a seasonal pattern, these studies are difficult to interpret due to methodological differences. The doses and colours of light, methods of delivery, comparator treatments, and clinical populations included in studies are diverse. While bright light is clearly more effective than waitlist control, it is unclear if this is more than a placebo effect (see discussion on the placebo effect in Chapter 2, Section 2.4.3). Studies that compare bright light with other treatments that are not known to be effective give equivocal results. There are too few data

Table 98: Summary evidence profile for relapse prevention using bright light

	Bright white light visor versus no treatment control	Bright white light visor versus infrared light visor
Leaving treatment early	RR 2.22 (0.29 to 17.27) (22.2 versus 10%)	RR 1.33 (0.35 to 5.13) (22.2 versus 16.7%)
Quality	Low	Low
Number of studies; participants	K = 1; n = 28	K = 1; n = 36
Forest plot number	Pharm SAD 08.01	Pharm SAD 08.01
Relapse (BDI >13 for 2 consecutive weeks)	RR 0.63 (0.36 to 1.09) (50 versus 80%)	RR 2.25 (0.84 to 5.99) (50 versus 22.2%)
Quality	Moderate	Moderate
Number of studies; participants	K = 1; n = 28	K = 1; n = 36
Forest plot number	Pharm SAD 08.02	Pharm SAD 08.02

relating to active controls to determine non-inferiority, and few systematic data relating to side effects. In clinical practice, where bright light is used, a minimum daily dose of 5,000 lux administered in the morning during the winter months is the most common treatment strategy. The most common side effect seen is mild agitation.

11.6.4   Other therapies for depression with a seasonal pattern

Studies considered[174]

In total, 14 trials of interventions other than bright light were found, mostly of anti-depressants, of which five met inclusion criteria for a review of acute-phase treatment, one for a review of continuation treatment in people who had responded to open-label treatment, and three (published in the same paper) for a review of prevention in people with a history of depression with a seasonal pattern. Summary study characteristics of the included studies are presented in Table 99, with full details in Appendix 17c, which also includes details of excluded studies.

---

[174]Study IDs in title case refer to studies included in the previous guideline and study IDs in capital letters refer to studies found and included in this guideline update. References for studies from the previous guideline are in Appendix 18.

Table 99: Summary study characteristics for interventions other than bright light for major depression with a seasonal pattern

	Acute phase treatments	Continuation treatment	Prevention treatment
No. trials (total participants)	5 RCTs (346)	1 RCTs (23)	3 RCTs (1061)
Study IDs	(1) LAM1995 (2) LINGJAERDE1993 (3) MOSCOVITCH2004 (4) PARTONEN1996 (5) TERMAN1995	(1) SCHLAGER1994*	(1) MODELL2005 study 1 (2) MODELL2005 study 2 (3) MODELL2005 study 3
N/% female	(1) 68/66 (2) 34/74 (3) 187/78 (4) 32/66 (5) 25/88	(1) 23 (not available)	(1) 277/72 (2) 311/67 (3) 473/68
Mean age	(1) 36 (2) 43 (3) 40 (4) 44 (5) 38	(1) Not given	(1) 42 (2) 42 (3) 41
Diagnosis	(1) Recurrent major depressive episodes with seasonal pattern (2) Mood disorder with seasonal pattern (3) 79% major depression with seasonal pattern; 13%	(1) Responders to initial treatment for recurrent major depressive episodes with seasonal pattern	(1)–(3) History of MDD with seasonal pattern (DSM-IV)

Treatment	depression NOS with seasonal pattern; 7% bipolar disorder with seasonal pattern; 2% bipolar disorder NOS with seasonal pattern (4) 100% MDD; 18% mood disorder with seasonal pattern (5) Major depression with a seasonal pattern, MDD with seasonal pattern, or bipolar disorder NOS with seasonal pattern - % not clear (1) Fluoxetine 20 mg (2) Moclobemide 400 mg (3) Sertraline 50–200 mg (4) Moclobemide 300–450 mg (5) High density negative ions	(1) Propanolol 33 mg	(1) Buspirone 150–300 mg (2)–(3) Bupropion XL 150–300 mg
Comparator	(1)–(3) Placebo (4) Fluoxetine 20–40 mg (5) Low density negative ions	(1) Placebo	(1)–(3) Placebo
Length of treatment (days)	(1) 5 weeks (2) 3 weeks (3) 8 weeks (4) 6 weeks (5) 3 weeks	(1) 2 weeks	(1) 6 months (2)–(3) Unclear

*Continuation trial.

447

Clinical evidence

Acute-phase treatments

The data for acute-phase treatment comparing antidepressants with placebo were largely inconclusive, although on one outcome (response) there appeared to be little difference. Acceptability and tolerability data were inconclusive. There was no evidence to suggest a difference between moclobemide and fluoxetine, which was the only head-to-head evidence available. There was some evidence to suggest that high ion density was more effective than low ion density, although there was only one study. Evidence from the important outcomes and overall quality of evidence are presented in Table 100. The full evidence profiles and associated forest plots can be found in Appendix 16c and Appendix 19c, respectively.

Table 100: Summary evidence profile for acute-phase treatments (not light therapy) for major depression with a seasonal pattern

	Antidepressants versus placebo	Antidepressants versus antidepressants	High ion density versus low ion density
Non-response (based on SIGH-SAD)	RR 0.82 (0.63 to 1.05) (44.2 versus 54%)	Not reported	RR 0.49 (0.24 to 1) (41.7 versus 84.6%)
Quality	High	–	Moderate
Number of studies; participants	K = 2; n = 255	–	K = 1; n = 25
Forest plot number	Pharm SAD 09.01	–	Pharm SAD 12.01
Clinician-rated mean endpoint SIGH-SAD	SMD −0.11 (−0.65 to 0.42)	Moclobemide versus fluoxetine: WMD −1.6 (−7.01 to 3.81)	Not reported
Quality	Low	Low	–
Number of studies; participants	K = 2; n = 99	K = 1; n = 29	–
Forest plot number	Pharm SAD 09.02	Pharm SAD 11.01	–
Self-rated mean endpoint BDI	WMD −1.7 (−6.53 to 3.13)	Not reported	Not reported
Quality	Low	–	–
Number of studies; participants	K = 1; n = 68	–	–
Forest plot number	Pharm SAD 09.02	–	–

Continued

Table 100: (*Continued*)

	Antidepressants versus placebo	Antidepressants versus antidepressants	High ion density versus low ion density
Leaving treatment early	RR 0.7 (0.16 to 3.05) (18.3 versus 20.5%)	Not reported	Not reported
Quality	Very low	–	–
Number of studies; participants	K = 2; n = 221	–	–
Forest plot number	Pharm SAD 10.01	–	
Leaving treatment early due to side effects	RR 1.48 (0.63 to 3.47) (8.3 versus 5.6%)	Not reported	Not reported
Quality	Low	–	–
Number of studies; participants	K = 3; n = 289	–	–
Forest plot number	Pharm SAD 10.02	–	–

Continuation treatment and prevention of future episodes

One small study compared the β-blocker, propanolol, with placebo for people who had responded to previous open treatment. This showed that symptoms of depression in those continuing treatment remained lower compared with those switched to placebo. Another three trials compared bupropion with placebo to prevent episodes in people with a history of depression. Treatment started before the onset of winter and continued until early spring. There was a clinically important reduction in the number of recurrences among those taking bupropion compared with the rate in those taking placebo. Evidence from the important outcomes and overall quality of evidence are presented in Table 101. The full evidence profiles and associated forest plots can be found in Appendix 16c and Appendix 19c, respectively.

Clinical summary

There was a lack of evidence for the effectiveness of antidepressants in the treatment of major depression with a seasonal pattern once symptoms have begun but evidence for a prophylactic effect of starting treatment before symptoms start and continuing until early spring.

11.6.5   From evidence to recommendations

The evidence for light therapy for major depression with a seasonal pattern is poorly developed, with many trials comparing different elements of treatment, including

449

Table 101: Summary evidence profile of continuation treatment and prevention of future episodes for people with major depression with a seasonal pattern

	Continuation treatment: propanolol versus placebo	**Prevention: bupropion versus placebo**
Efficacy outcome	HAMD-21: WMD −7 (−11.24 to −2.76)	Recurrence: RR 0.58 (0.46 to 0.72) (17% versu 29.5%)
Quality	Moderate	High
Number of studies; participants	K = 1; n = 23	K = 3; n = 1061
Forest plot number	Pharm SAD 13.01	Pharm SAD 14.01
Leaving treatment early	RR 2.57 (0.12 to 57.44) (7.7 versus 0%)	Not reported
Quality	Low	–
Number of studies; participants	K = 1; n = 24	–
Forest plot number	Pharm SAD 13.02	–

time of day, level of light and length of treatment. There is little evidence for the efficacy of bright light in the treatment of major depression with a seasonal pattern compared with placebo treatment.

The evidence for other treatments is sparse. Evidence is lacking that antidepressants are effective once symptoms have begun, but they may be worthwhile as prophylactics. For depression with a seasonal pattern practitioners should follow the guidance for depression elsewhere in this guideline.

11.6.6   Recommendations

11.6.6.1   See recommendation 11.3.2.1

11.6.6.2   Advise people with winter depression that follows a seasonal pattern and who wish to try light therapy in preference to antidepressant or psychological treatment that the evidence for the efficacy of light therapy is uncertain.

11.6.7   Research recommendations

11.6.7.1   The efficacy of light therapy compared with antidepressants for mild to moderate depression with a seasonal pattern

How effective is light therapy compared with antidepressants for mild to moderate depression with a seasonal pattern?

Why this is important

Although the status of seasonal depression as a separate entity is not entirely clear, surveys have consistently reported a high prevalence of seasonal (predominantly winter) depression in the UK. This reflects a considerable degree of morbidity, predominantly in the winter months, for people with this condition. Light therapy has been proposed as a specific treatment for winter depression but only small, inconclusive trials have been carried out, from which it is not possible to tell whether either light therapy or antidepressants are effective in its treatment. Clarification of whether, and to what degree, treatments are effective would help to inform the decisions that people with seasonal depression and practitioners have to make about the treatment of winter depression.

This question should be answered using a randomised controlled trial design in which people with mild to moderate depression with a seasonal pattern (seasonal affective disorder) receive light therapy or an SSRI antidepressant in a partially placebo-controlled design. The doses of both light and SSRI should be at accepted or proposed therapeutic levels and there should be an initial phase over a few weeks in which a plausible placebo treatment is administered followed by randomisation to one of the active treatments. The outcomes chosen should reflect both observer and patient-rated assessments of improvement and an assessment of the acceptability of the treatment options. The study needs to be large enough to determine the presence or absence of clinically important effects, and mediators and moderators of response should be investigated.

11.7   DOSAGE ISSUES FOR TRICYCLIC ANTIDEPRESSANTS

The following sections on dosage issues for tricyclic antidepressants marked by asterisks (**_**) are from the previous guideline and have not been updated except for style and minor clarification.

11.7.1   Low-dose versus high-dose TCAs

**There is controversy over whether the existing recommended dosages for TCAs (100 mg/day, Bollini *et al.*, 1999) are too high. Some GPs are criticised for prescribing at doses that are too low, and evidence for dosing levels has not been established (Furukawa *et al.*, 2002a). This review compares the efficacy and tolerability of low and high doses of TCAs. Low doses were those where the mean dose achieved was less than the equivalent of 100 mg of amitriptyline.

11.7.2   Studies considered for review[175,176]

The GDG used an existing review (Furukawa *et al.*, 2002a) as the basis for this review. The Furukawa and colleagues' (2002a) review included 38 studies of which 33 did not meet the inclusion criteria set by the GDG, mainly because of inadequate diagnosis of depression. Therefore, five trials (Burch1988, Danish1999, Rouillon1994, Simpson1988, WHO1986) are included in this review providing data from up to 222 participants.

All included studies were published between 1988 and 1999 and were between 4 and 8 weeks' long (mean = 6 weeks). One study was of inpatients and two of outpatients, with none in primary care. Patients in one study were from mixed sources (Danish1999). It was not possible to discern the setting in WHO1986. No study included all elderly participants or those whose depression has atypical features. Study inclusion criteria ensured a minimum HRSD score at baseline of between 16 and 22 or a MADRS score of 15.

Data were available to compare low doses with high doses of clomipramine, amitriptyline, trimipramine and imipramine. Data were also available to compare low-dose clomipramine with placebo.

Mean low dose was 60.8 mg (total range 25 mg to 75 mg) and mean high dose was 161.9 mg (total range 75 mg to 200 mg) (low-dose versus high-dose studies).

11.7.3   Clinical evidence statements[177]

Effect of treatment on efficacy
There is evidence suggesting that there is no clinically important difference between low-dose TCAs and high-dose TCAs on increasing the likelihood of achieving remission by the end of treatment (K = 3; N = 222; RR = 0.99; 95% CI, 0.84 to 1.16).

There is insufficient evidence to determine whether there is a clinically important difference between low-dose TCAs and high-dose TCAs on increasing the likelihood of achieving a 50% reduction in symptoms of depression or on reducing symptoms of depression as measured by the HRSD.

There is insufficient evidence to determine whether there is a clinically important difference between low-dose TCAs and placebo on reducing depressions symptoms by the end of treatment as measured by the MADRS or on increasing the likelihood of achieving a 50% reduction in symptoms of depression by the end of treatment as measured by the HRSD.

---

[175]Details of standard search strings used in all searches are in Appendix 8. Information about each study along with an assessment of methodological quality is in Appendix 17c, which also contains a list of excluded studies with reasons for exclusions.

[176]Study IDs in title case refer to studies included in the previous guideline. References for these studies are in Appendix 18.

[177]The forest plots can be found in Appendix 19c.

Acceptability and tolerability of treatment

There is some evidence suggesting that there is a clinically important difference favouring low-dose TCAs over high-dose TCAs on leaving the study early due to side effects (K = 1; N = 151; RR = 0.35; 95% CI, 0.16 to 0.78).

There is insufficient evidence to determine whether there is a clinically important difference between low-dose TCAs and high-dose TCAs on reducing the likelihood of patients leaving treatment early.

11.7.4   Clinical summary

There is no clinically important difference on achieving response between low-dose TCAs (mean dose = 60.8 mg) and therapeutic dose TCAs (mean dose = 161.9 mg). Of the four studies that compared low-dose TCAs with high-dose TCAs, two reported completer data only. Patients receiving a low-dose TCA were less likely to leave treatment early due to side effects.**

11.7.5   From evidence to recommendations

This review was not updated by the GDG and the recommendation to maintain a low-dose TCA in people whose depression had responded was retained. However, the recommendation to monitor outcomes and increase dose depending on efficacy and side effects was removed since the points made are adequately covered by other recommendations in the guideline.

11.7.6   Recommendation

11.7.6.1   People who start on low-dose tricyclic antidepressants and who have a clear clinical response can be maintained on that dose with careful monitoring[178].

11.8   ANTIDEPRESSANT DISCONTINUATION SYMPTOMS

The following sections on antidepressant discontinuation symptoms marked by asterisks (**_**) are from the previous guideline and have not been updated except for style and minor clarification.

---

[178]The evidence for this recommendation has not been updated since the previous guideline. Any wording changes have been made for clarification only.

11.8.1   Introduction

There can be confusion over the use of the terms 'addiction', 'psychological dependence' and 'physical dependence' when referring to drugs. This has been associated with concern in the mind of the public about whether antidepressants (and indeed other psychotropic drugs) may be addictive. The DSM–IV (APA, 1994) definition of 'substance dependence' consists of a combination of psychological, physiological and behavioural effects that together comprise what is commonly called addiction. The diagnosis of substance dependence/addiction requires at least three of the following:

(1)   tolerance (marked increase in amount; marked decrease in effect)
(2)   characteristic 'withdrawal' symptoms or substance taken to relieve withdrawal
(3)   substance taken in larger amount and for longer period than intended
(4)   persistent desire or repeated unsuccessful attempt to quit
(5)   much time/activity taken to obtain, use and recover from the substance
(6)   important social, occupational, or recreational activities given up or reduced
(7)   use continues despite knowledge of adverse consequences (for example, failure to fulfill role obligation, using when physically hazardous).

Physical dependence refers to the first two features (tolerance to the effect and 'withdrawal' symptoms) and substance dependence/addiction can be with or without physical dependence. There is no evidence that antidepressants cause psychological dependence or adverse behavioural and functional effects in the sense defined by criteria 3 to 7 above, and therefore antidepressants are not 'addictive' in the accepted sense of the word used to describe dependence on drugs like alcohol or opioids. There is also no good evidence to support tolerance to the therapeutic effect of antidepressants (Zimmerman & Thongy, 2007) and therefore the debate about whether or not antidepressants cause physical dependence centres on the symptoms some people experience when stopping antidepressants. It is important to understand the nature of the phenomenon and its implications for people with depression who have antidepressant treatment. In this guideline these are described as 'discontinuation symptoms', which is a term that makes no assumption about their status.

Discontinuation symptoms can be broadly divided into six groups; affective (for example, irritability), gastrointestinal (for example, nausea), neuromotor (for example, ataxia), vasomotor (for example, sweating), neurosensory (for example, paraesthesia), and other neurological (for example, dreaming; Delgrado, 2006). They may be new or hard to distinguish from some of the original symptoms of the underlying illness. By definition they must not be attributable to other causes. They are experienced by at least a third of patients (Lejoyeux *et al.*, 1996; MHRA, 2004) and are seen to some extent with all antidepressants (Taylor *et al.*, 2006). Of the commonly used antidepressants, the risk of discontinuation symptoms seems to be greatest with paroxetine, venlafaxine and amitriptyline (Taylor *et al.*, 2006). There have been prospective studies, including some RCTs and quasi-randomised trials, which have examined the effect of discontinuation in people taking paroxetine and other antidepressants. These studies suggest an increase in discontinuation symptoms in those taking paroxetine compared with escitalopram (Baldwin *et al.*, 2006), fluoxetine (Rosenbaum *et al.*, 1998; Bogetto *et al.*, 2002; Hindmarch *et al.*, 2000; Judge *et al.*, 2002; Michelson *et al.*, 2000), sertraline (Hindmarch *et al.*, 2000; Michelson *et al.*, 2000), and citalopram (Hindmarch *et al.*, 2000). In addition two RCTs measuring discontinuation symptoms when stopping antidepressants after 8 weeks of treatment found that these were more common with venlafaxine than escitalopram (Montgomery *et al.*, 2004) and moderate and severe symptoms were more common with venlafaxine compared with sertraline (Sir *et al.*, 2005).

The onset is usually within 5 days of stopping treatment, or occasionally during taper or after missed doses (Rosenbaum *et al.*, 1998; Michelson *et al.*, 2000). This is influenced by a number of factors, which may include a drug's half-life. Symptoms can vary in form and intensity and occur in any combination. They are usually mild and self-limiting, but can be severe and prolonged, particularly if withdrawal is abrupt. Some symptoms are more likely with individual drugs, for example dizziness and electric shock-like sensations with SSRIs, and sweating and headache with TCAs (Lejoyeux *et al.*, 1996; Haddad, 2001).

11.8.2   Factors affecting the development of discontinuation symptoms

**Although anyone can experience discontinuation symptoms, the risk is increased in those prescribed short half-life drugs (Rosenbaum *et al.*, 1998), such as paroxetine and venlafaxine (Fava *et al.*, 1997; Hindmarch *et al.*, 2000; MHRA, 2004). They can also occur in patients who do not take their medication regularly. Two-thirds of patients prescribed antidepressants skip a few doses from time to time (Meijer *et al.*, 2001). The risk is also increased in those who have been taking antidepressants for 8 weeks or longer (Haddad, 2001); those who developed anxiety symptoms at the start of antidepressant treatment (particularly with SSRIs); those receiving other centrally acting medications (for example, antihypertensives, antihistamines, antipsychotics); children and adolescents; and those who have experienced discontinuation symptoms before (Lejoyeux & Ades, 1997; Haddad, 2001).

Discontinuation symptoms may also be more common in those who relapse on stopping antidepressants (Zajecka *et al.*, 1998; Markowitz *et al.*, 2000).

11.8.3   Clinical relevance

The symptoms of a discontinuation reaction may be mistaken for a relapse of illness or the emergence of a new physical illness (Haddad, 2001) leading to unnecessary investigations or reintroduction of the antidepressant. Symptoms may be severe enough to interfere with daily functioning. Another point of clinical relevance is that patients who experience discontinuation symptoms may assume that this means that antidepressants are addictive and not wish to accept further treatment. It is very important to counsel patients before, during and after antidepressant treatment about the nature of this syndrome.**

11.8.4 How to avoid discontinuation symptoms

Although it is generally advised that antidepressants (except fluoxetine) should be discontinued over a period of at least 4 weeks, preliminary data suggest that it may be the half-life of the antidepressant rather than the rate of taper that ultimately influences the risk of discontinuation symptoms (Tint *et al.*, 2008).

When switching from one antidepressant to another with a similar pharmacological profile, the risk of discontinuation symptoms may be reduced by completing the switch as quickly as possible (a few days at most). A different approach may be required at the end of treatment where a slower taper is likely to be beneficial.

The half-life of the drug should be taken into account. The end of the taper may need to be slower as symptoms may not appear until the reduction in the total daily dosage of the antidepressant is substantial. Patients receiving MAOIs may need dosage to be tapered over a longer period. Tranylcypromine may be particularly difficult to stop. It is not clear if the need for slow discontinuation of MAOIs, and particularly tranylcypromine, is due to the discontinuation syndrome or the loss of other neurochemical effects of these drugs. Since it is not possible to disentangle these phenomena, the clinical advice is that patients on MAOIs and those at-risk patients need a slower taper (Haddad, 2001).

Many patients experience discontinuation symptoms despite a slow taper. For these patients, the option of abrupt withdrawal should be discussed. Some may prefer a short period of intense symptoms over a prolonged period of milder symptoms.

11.8.5 How to treat

There are no systematic randomised studies in this area. Treatment is pragmatic. If symptoms are mild, reassure the patient that these symptoms are not uncommon after discontinuing an antidepressant and that they will pass in a few days. If symptoms are severe, reintroduce the original antidepressant (or another with a longer half-life from the same class) and taper gradually while monitoring for symptoms (Haddad, 2001; Lejoyeux & Ades, 1997).

11.8.6 From evidence to recommendations

Since the previous guideline, the evidence base for discontinuation symptoms with antidepressants is largely unchanged. Practitioners should ensure that they discuss the issue fully with all patients, and consider prescribing antidepressants that are associated with fewer discontinuation symptoms (for example, fluoxetine), particularly for patients who have had previous experience of these. The previous recommendations are therefore retained, but rewritten to fit the updated NICE style.

11.8.7 Clinical practice recommendations

11.8.7.1 When prescribing antidepressants, explore any concerns the person with depression has about taking medication, explain fully the reasons for prescribing, and provide information about taking antidepressants, including:
- the gradual development of the full antidepressant effect
- the importance of taking medication as prescribed and the need to continue treatment after remission
- potential side effects
- the potential for interactions with other medications
- the risk and nature of discontinuation symptoms with all antidepressants, particularly with drugs with a shorter half-life (such as paroxetine and venlafaxine), and how these symptoms can be minimised
- the fact that addiction does not occur with antidepressants.

Offer written information appropriate to the person's needs.

11.8.7.2 Advise people with depression who are taking antidepressants that discontinuation symptoms[179] may occur on stopping, missing doses or, occasionally, on reducing the dose of the drug. Explain that symptoms are usually mild and self-limiting over about 1 week, but can be severe, particularly if the drug is stopped abruptly.

11.8.7.3 When stopping an antidepressant, gradually reduce the dose, normally over a 4-week period, although some people may require longer periods, particularly with drugs with a shorter half-life (such as paroxetine and venlafaxine). This is not required with fluoxetine because of its long half-life:

11.8.7.4 Inform the person that they should seek advice from their practitioner if they experience significant discontinuation symptoms. If discontinuation symptoms occur:
- monitor symptoms and reassure the person if symptoms are mild
- consider reintroducing the original antidepressant at the dose that was effective (or another antidepressant with a longer half-life from the same class) if symptoms are severe, and reduce the dose gradually while monitoring symptoms.

11.9 THE CARDIOTOXICITY OF ANTIDEPRESSANTS

The following sections on the cardiotoxicity of antidepressants marked by asterisks (**_**) are from the previous guideline and have not been updated except for style and minor clarification.

---

[179]Discontinuation symptoms include increased mood change, restlessness, difficulty sleeping, unsteadiness, sweating, abdominal symptoms and altered sensations.

11.9.1 Introduction

**Consistent associations between depression and cardiovascular morbidity and mortality have been identified (Glassman & Shapiro, 1998). Depression is a significant independent risk factor for both first myocardial infarction and cardiovascular mortality with an adjusted relative risk in the range of 1.5 to 2 (Ford *et al.*, 1998). In patients with ischaemic heart disease, depression has been found to be associated with a three- to four-fold increase in cardiovascular morbidity and mortality (Carney *et al.*, 1997). The prevalence of depression in patients with coronary heart disease is approximately 20% (Glassman *et al.*, 2002).

In view of the above associations and factors it is important to use antidepressant drugs that either reduce or do not increase the cardiovascular risk of the condition itself and to establish a safe and effective treatment strategy for depressed patients with heart disease. There is evidence that adequate treatment of depression appears either to lower (Avery & Winokur, 1976) or not to change (Pratt *et al.*, 1996) the risk of heart disease. However, two large-scale follow-up studies have shown an increase in myocardial infarction in users of antidepressants with an average odds ratio of 5.8 (Penttinen & Valonen, 1996; Thorogood *et al.*, 1992). The antidepressants used in these studies were predominately TCAs. A similar association has been identified in the UK for dothiepin/dosulepin (Hippisley-Cox *et al.*, 2001).

However, these studies do not distinguish between the effects of drugs and the condition itself. Thus it is necessary to look at the effects of antidepressants on cardiovascular function and what trials are available (Roose, 2003).

11.9.2 Tricyclic antidepressants

Sinus tachycardia, postural hypotension and episodic hypertension are side effects frequently observed. Electrocardiogram (ECG) changes are frequent, such as lengthening of the QT, PR and QRS intervals relating to alterations in atrioventricular conduction and repolarisation (Roose & Glassman, 1989). These effects are due to the wide-ranging pharmacological actions of TCAs that are not correlated with recognised mechanisms of antidepressant action. In healthy patients such changes may be asymptomatic or clinically unimportant, but in those with heart disease they may lead to significant morbidity and mortality (Glassman *et al.*, 1993). For example, prolonged increased heart rate (mean 11%, Roose & Glassman, 1989) could have a major impact in terms of cardiac work (Roose, 2003).

In patients with left ventricular impairment on TCAs, orthostatic hypotension is three to seven times more common and potentially clinically harmful (Glassman *et al.*, 1993). The TCA induced prolongation of conduction may be clinically unimportant in healthy patients, but can lead to complications in those with conduction disease, in particular bundle branch block, and these can be severe in 20% of subjects (Roose *et al.*, 1987). TCAs may be regarded as Class I arrhythmic drugs. Evidence suggests that this class of drug is associated with an increase in mortality in post-infarction patients and in patients with a broader range of ischaemic disease, probably because they turn out to be arrhythmogenic when cardiac tissue becomes anoxic. Overdose of TCAs or elevated plasma levels as a result of interactions with other drugs, liver disease and age is associated with serious hypotension and atrial and ventricular arrhythmias may arise even to the extent of complete atrioventricular block, which in a number of cases may be fatal (deaths from TCAs represent 20% of overdose deaths; Shah *et al.*, 2001).

Individual tricyclics
The tertiary amine tricyclics (amitriptyline, imipramine and clomipramine) have more cardiovascular effects than the secondary amine tricyclics (for example, nortriptyline). These drugs, such as nortriptyline, have been shown to have less postural hypotension and, therefore, may be considered in those with cardiovascular disease and in the elderly in whom postural hypotension can be very hazardous. There is evidence (although not from an RCT) that lofepramine is safer in overdose than other tricyclics (Lancaster & Gonzalez, 1989). It is thought that lofepramine blocks the cardiotoxic effects of the main metabolite desipramine. Dothiepin/dosulepin has marked toxicity in overdose in uncontrolled studies (Henry & Antao, 1992; Buckley *et al.*, 1994).

11.9.3   Selective serotonin reuptake inhibitors

Depression in untreated populations has been demonstrated to increase cardiovascular morbidity and mortality. SSRIs appear to reduce that risk, since two studies have reported no difference in cardiovascular risk between SSRI-treated depressed patients and non-treated non-depressed controls (Cohen *et al.*, 2000; Meier *et al.*, 2001). Sauer and colleagues (2001) compared the rate of myocardial infarction (MI) in patients on an SSRI with those on no antidepressants. The SSRI-treated patients had a significantly lower rate of MI than did the non SSRI-treated patients. Multiple studies (Roose, 2001) reveal no clinically significant effects of SSRIs on heart rate, cardiac conduction or blood pressure (see further details below). Studies of depressed patients with and without ischaemic heart disease (IHD) have documented increased platelet activation and aggregation, which potentially contributes to thrombus formation (Musselman *et al.*, 1998). Treatment with SSRIs normalises elevated indices of platelet activation and aggregation seen in non-treated patients with depression and IHD. There is evidence that this effect occurs at relatively low doses and before the antidepressant effect (Pollock *et al.*, 2000). However, the effects on platelet serotonin are not always advantageous: SSRIs increase the probability of having a serious gastrointestinal bleed, particularly in the very old (Walraven *et al.*, 2001).

Citalopram
The cardiac safety of citalopram has been studied in prospective studies in volunteers and patients and in retrospective evaluations of all ECG data from 40 clinical trials (1,789 citalopram-treated patients) (Rasmussen *et al.*, 1999). The only effect of citalopram was the reduction in heart rate (of eight beats per minute) but no other

ECG change. There have been case reports of bradycardia with citalopram (Isbister *et al.*, 2001) and a low frequency of hypotension and arrhythmias including left bundle branch block (Mucci, 1997).

Fluoxetine

In a 7-week open trial of older adults with cardiac disease, Roose and colleagues (1998b) showed that fluoxetine caused no major cardiovascular change. Strik and colleagues (2000) showed that fluoxetine was safe in 27 patients with recent MI (more than 3 months since the MI) and there was no change in cardiovascular indices in these patients compared with placebo. However, fluoxetine did not demonstrate clinical efficacy in this group compared with placebo (N = 54; WMD = –2.50, 95% CI, –5.64 to 0.64). It is noteworthy that fluoxetine has significant potential to interact with drugs commonly used in the management of heart disease (Mitchell, 1997).

Fluvoxamine

Fluvoxamine has not been found to be associated with cardiovascular or ECG changes (Hewer *et al.*, 1995). Fluvoxamine appears to be safe in overdose (Garnier *et al.*, 1993). Cardiotoxicity was not a serious problem; sinus bradycardia requiring no treatment was noted in a few cases.

Paroxetine

A daily dose of 20 to 30 mg of paroxetine was compared with nortriptyline (dose adjusted to give plasma concentrations of 80 to 120 mg/ml) in a double-blind study of 41 patients with major depressive disorder and IHD (Roose *et al.*, 1998a). Paroxetine was not associated with clinically importantly sustained changes in heart rate, blood pressure or conduction intervals whereas nortriptyline caused 'clinically significant' changes in these measures and 'more serious cardiac events'.

Sertraline

Three hundred and sixty nine patients with either unstable angina (26%) or recent (within 30 days) MI (74%) were randomised to receive either placebo or sertraline (flexible dose, 50 to 200 mg per day in a randomised double-blind trial) (Glassman *et al.*, 2002). Sertraline had no significant effect on left ventricular function compared with placebo or on a range of clinical or laboratory investigations. The incidence of severe cardiovascular events was 14.5% with sertraline, numerically, but not significantly, less than placebo at 22.4%.

There was no overall difference between sertraline and placebo in terms of antidepressant response in all patients studied. However, in more severely depressed patients (HRSD >= 18 and at least two previous depressive episodes), there was some evidence of a greater decrease in symptoms of depression in those taking SSRIs compared with those taking placebo (N = 90; WMD= –3.4, 95% CI, –6.47 to –0.33[180]). However, this study and others in the field are not adequately powered

---

[180]These data were calculated from data in the paper.

or of sufficient length to determine cardiovascular morbidity or mortality in the longer term.

Overdose

In contrast to the TCAs, the SSRIs, if taken alone, are only rarely lethal in overdose (Barbey & Roose, 1998; Goeringer *et al.*, 2000). Deaths have occurred when citalopram has been ingested in very high doses (Ostrom *et al.*, 1996). However, other studies, while reporting complications with high-dose citalopram overdoses, have not reported deaths (Grundemar *et al.*, 1997; Personne *et al.*, 1997b). The mechanisms of the deaths reported by Ostrom and colleagues (1996) are not clear. There is some evidence that high-dose citalopram overdoses have been associated with ECG abnormalities (Personne *et al.*, 1997a) and QTc prolongation (Catalano *et al.*, 2001). However, Boeck and colleagues (1982) did not report cardiotoxicity with high-dose citalopram in the dog, and in the deaths reported by Ostrom and colleagues (1996) levels of the potentially cardiotoxic metabolite were low. Another potential mechanism of toxicity is that high-dose citalopram overdoses induce seizures and this has been shown in animals (Boeck *et al.*, 1982) and man (Grundemar *et al.*, 1997; Personne *et al.*, 1997a). Glassman (1997) suggested that all high dose SSRI overdoses were a cause for concern and advised prudence over the prescription of large amounts of tablets.

11.9.4   Other drugs

Lithium

Lithium has a number of cardiac effects and they can be of clinical importance in patients with heart disease, the elderly, those with higher lithium levels, hypokalaemia and when lithium is used with other drugs such as diuretics, hydroxyzine and TCAs (Chong *et al.*, 2001). Common, often subclinical, effects of lithium include the 'sick sinus' syndrome, first degree heart block, ventricular ectopics, flattened T-waves and increased QT dispersion (Reilly *et al.*, 2000), but adverse clinical outcomes are rare. Caution and periodic ECG monitoring is advised in those at risk or with cardiac symptoms.

Mianserin

Cardiac effects with mianserin are rare (Peet *et al.*, 1977; Edwards & Goldie, 1983; Jackson *et al.*, 1987) although there have been some reports of bradycardia and complete heart block in overdose (Hla & Boyd, 1987; Haefeli *et al.*, 1991) and, rarely, bradycardia at therapeutic doses (Carcone *et al.*, 1991). Bucknall and colleagues (1988) showed that mianserin was well tolerated in most, but not all, cardiac patients.

Mirtazapine

No significant cardiovascular effects from mirtazapine have been noted (Nutt, 2002). It appears to have a benign safety profile in overdose (Velazquez *et al.*, 2001).

Moclobemide

Moclobemide is not associated with any significant cardiovascular effects (Fulton & Benfield, 1996) and there are no reports of death in overdose with moclobemide as the sole agent.

Phenelzine

Phenelzine causes marked postural hypotension particularly in the early weeks of treatment and it is associated with a significant bradycardia. It does not cause conduction defects (McGrath *et al.*, 1987a). Its fatal toxicity index in overdose appears to be less than most tricyclics (Henry & Antao, 1992). There is no data on the safety or clinical efficacy of phenelzine in patients with IHD.

Reboxetine

No specific clinical or ECG abnormalities have been noted with reboxetine (Fleishaker *et al.*, 2001) and it has relative safety in overdose.

Trazodone

Trazodone is generally believed to have low cardiotoxicity, although there have been some reports of postural hypotension and, rarely, arrhythmias (Janowsky *et al.*, 1983).

Venlafaxine

No obvious laboratory or clinical cardiac changes have been found with venlafaxine in routine use (Feighner, 1995). There is evidence that in higher doses (greater than 200 mg), hypertension occurs in a small but significant minority, and others have recommended regular blood pressure monitoring at and above this dose (for example, Feighner, 1995). There is also evidence that in overdose (greater than 900 mg) venlafaxine is pro-convulsant compared with TCAs and SSRIs (Whyte *et al.*, 2003) and has a higher fatal toxicity index in overdose than SSRIs (Buckley & McManus, 2002). The MHRA also raised concerns about the increased incidence of adverse cardiovascular events and the use of venlafaxine in individuals with pre-existing cardiovascular disease (MHRA, 2004).**

11.9.5   Recommendation

11.9.5.1   See recommendation 10.14.1.3.

11.10   DEPRESSION, ANTIDEPRESSANTS AND SUICIDE

The following sections on depression, antidepressants and suicide marked by asterisks (**_**) are from the previous guideline and have not been updated except for style and minor clarification.

11.10.1   Introduction

**The majority of patients with depression have at least episodic suicidal ideation often linked to general negativity and hopelessness. Two-thirds of people who attempt suicide are experiencing depression, and suicide is the main cause of the increased mortality of depression and is commonest in those with comorbid physical and mental illness. Suicidal behaviour also occurs with milder forms of depression. In a meta-analysis of 36 studies the lifetime prevalence of suicide has been reported to be 4% in hospitalised depressed patients, rising to 8.6% if hospitalised for suicidality. In mixed inpatient/outpatient populations the lifetime prevalence is 2.2% compared with less than 0.5% in the non-affectively ill population (Bostwick & Pankratz, 2000). Harris and Barraclough (1997) found a suicide risk of 12 times that expected in a cohort of patients with dysthymia (DSM–III) (APA, 1980). Therefore, the effective recognition and treatment of depression should lead to a fall in the overall suicide rate.

11.10.2   Suicidality and antidepressants

There is evidence for a small but significant increase in the presence of suicidal thoughts in the early stages of antidepressant treatment (Jick *et al.*, 2004). However this must be put against recent data showing that the risk of clinically important suicidal behaviour is highest in the month before starting antidepressants and declines thereafter (Simon *et al.*, 2006). The highest rates of suicidal behaviour were seen in patients treated by psychiatrists but the same pattern was also seen with psychological treatments and in primary care (Simon & Savarino, 2007). No temporal pattern of completed suicide was found in the 6 months after starting an antidepressant (Simon *et al.*, 2006). No increase in suicide/suicidal thoughts or attempts was seen with SSRIs compared with other antidepressants (Jick *et al.*, 2004; Simon *et al.*, 2006).

It is therefore not clear from these naturalistic data to what extent suicidal thoughts or behaviour can be attributable to a direct result of taking an antidepressant (the effect was seen with all classes of antidepressant) as opposed to the timing of when help was sought. Two meta-analyses of RCTs (Fergusson *et al.*, 2005; Gunnell *et al.*, 2005) with 702 and 477 studies respectively and a large nested case-control study comparing new prescriptions of SSRIs and TCAs (Martinez *et al.*, 2005) found no evidence of an increase in completed suicide with SSRIs but possible evidence of increased suicidal/self-harming behaviour with SSRIs compared with placebo (NNH 684 and 754 in the two meta-analyses). There was no overall difference between SSRIs and TCAs (Fergusson *et al.*, 2005; Martinez *et al.*, 2005) but Martinez and colleagues (2005) found some evidence for increased self-harming behaviour with SSRIs compared with TCAs in those under 19 years. A review by Möller and colleagues (2008) concluded that all antidepressants carry a small risk of inducing suicidal thoughts and suicide attempts in age groups below 25 years, the risk reducing further at the age of about 30 to 40 years.

There may be a delay in noticeable improvement after starting antidepressants, and, just after initiation of treatment, mood remains low with prominent feelings of guilt and hopelessness, but energy and motivation can increase and may be related to the increased suicidal thoughts. A similar situation can arise with patients who develop akathisia or increased anxiety due to a direct effect of some SSRIs and related drugs and it has been hypothesised that this may increase the propensity to suicidal ideation and suicidal behaviour (Healey, 2003). Careful monitoring is therefore indicated when treatment is initiated with an antidepressant. Patients should be monitored regardless of the apparent severity of their depression.

A meta-analysis of observational studies (Barbui *et al.*, 2009) found that compared with depressed people who did not take antidepressants, adolescents receiving SSRIs had a significantly higher risk of suicide attempts and completed suicide. In contrast adults, especially older adults, had a significantly lower risk of suicide attempts and completed suicide. Ecological data has failed to find any link between SSRI use and higher completed suicide rates (Gibbons *et al.*, 2005; Hall & Lucke, 2006), in fact it has been suggested that the overall reduction in suicide rate may be partly due to more effective treatment of depression with newer antidepressants. In particular, it has been argued that the significant reductions in suicide rates in Sweden, Hungary, the US and Australia have been due to treatment with these drugs (Isacsson *et al.*, 1997; Hall *et al.*, 2003). However, a number of other factors may account for this trend including changing socioeconomic circumstances, and demonstrating a causal link between increased antidepressant prescription and falling suicide rates is not straightforward and has not been conclusively established (Gunnell & Ashby, 2004).

The use of antidepressants in the treatment of depression is also not without risk not least because of their toxicity in overdose. Antidepressants were involved in 18% of deaths from drug poisoning between 1993 and 2002 (Morgan *et al.*, 2004), with TCAs, which are cardiotoxic in overdose (see Section 8.2.9), accounting for 89% of these. This is equivalent to 30.1 deaths per million prescriptions. Dothiepin/dosulepin alone accounted for 48.5 deaths per million prescriptions (Morgan *et al.*, 2004). By contrast, over the same period, SSRIs accounted for around 6% of deaths by suicide, and other antidepressants, including venlafaxine, around 3%. This is equivalent to 1 and 5.2 deaths per million prescriptions respectively (Morgan *et al.*, 2004). Venlafaxine alone accounted for 8.5 deaths per million prescriptions. Morgan and colleagues (2004) showed an overall reduction in mortality rates over the time period studied, with a fall in rates related to TCAs, little change for SSRIs, but an increase for other antidepressants largely due to venlafaxine. These data are based on analyses of coroners' records for England and Wales, and prescription data for drugs dispensed in England (regardless of the prescription's country of origin). They may be subject to bias because indication is not recorded on prescriptions. Some antidepressants are licensed for conditions such as obsessive-compulsive disorder and post-traumatic stress disorder in addition to depression. Also, coroners record antidepressant information voluntarily and only if they consider the antidepressant contributed to the cause of death (Morgan *et al.*, 2004). Interpretation of these data is complicated by the possibility of differential prescribing, that is patients at high risk of suicide may have been prescribed different drugs from those at low risk.** The MHRA (2006a and b) concluded that the increased rate seen with venlafaxine was partly, but not wholly, attributable to patient characteristics.

11.10.3   From evidence to recommendations

There is a small risk of inducing suicidal ideation in younger people starting antidepressants. Although the most recent data suggests the cut-off for this is around 25 years old, previous advice from the MHRA suggests the cut-off should be around 30. Practitioners should seek strategies to reduce risk as far as possible for people who are at increased risk of suicide, including prescribing drugs with relatively low toxicity and prescribing small amounts of drugs. They should refer people at high risk to specialist mental health services. The recommendations in this section are unchanged from the previous guideline, but have been reworded to fit current NICE house style and to fit with new recommendations developed for the updated guideline.

11.10.4   Recommendations

11.10.4.1 A person with depression started on antidepressants who is considered to present an increased suicide risk or is younger than 30 years (because of the potential increased prevalence of suicidal thoughts in the early stages of antidepressant treatment for this group) should normally be seen after 1 week and frequently thereafter as appropriate until the risk is no longer considered clinically important[181].

11.10.4.2 See recommendation 5.2.24.15.

11.10.4.3 See recommendation 5.2.24.13.

11.10.4.4 Take into account toxicity in overdose when choosing an antidepressant for people at significant risk of suicide. Be aware that:
- compared with other equally effective antidepressants recommended for routine use in primary care, venlafaxine is associated with a greater risk of death from overdose
- tricyclic antidepressants (TCAs), except for lofepramine, are associated with the greatest risk in overdose.

---

[181]The evidence for this recommendation has not been updated since the previous guideline. Any wording changes have been made for clarification only.

12 THE PHARMACOLOGICAL AND PHYSICAL MANAGEMENT OF DEPRESSION THAT HAS NOT ADEQUATELY RESPONDED TO TREATMENT, AND RELAPSE PREVENTION

In this chapter, sections marked by asterisks (**__**) are from the previous guideline and have not been updated except for style and minor clarification.

12.1 INTRODUCTION

**Despite major developments in the management of mood disorders, in clinical practice the problem of incomplete, or lack of, response to treatment continues to be problematic. Numerous outcome studies have demonstrated that approximately one-third of patients treated for depression do not respond satisfactorily to first-line anti-depressant pharmacotherapy. Follow-up observations reveal that a considerable number of patients have a poor prognosis with as many as 20% remaining unwell 2 years after the onset of illness (Keller *et al.*, 1986). Even after multiple treatments, up to 10% of patients remain depressed (Nierenberg & Amsterdam, 1990). A range of studies suggests that between 10 and 20% of patients with depression have a long-term poor outcome (Lee & Murray, 1988; Winokur *et al.*, 1993).

It is difficult, however, to evaluate the true degree of poor response to treatment for depression from these figures. Although poor response is relatively common in clinical practice, a major problem has been the inconsistent way in which it has been characterised and defined, limiting systematic research. In recent years there have been attempts to agree definitions of 'treatment resistance' in order to improve the characterisation of the phenomenon, although there is still disagreement on some of the items. The key parameters that have been used to characterise and define treatment resistance include the basic criteria used to specify the diagnosis, response to treatment, previous treatment trials and the adequacy of treatment (Nierenberg & Amsterdam, 1990).**

While it is important to be able to describe these parameters, this guideline update, as discussed in Chapter 2, does not use the term 'treatment-resistant depression', which was defined in the previous guideline as depression that had not responded adequately to two courses of antidepressants (of adequate dose and length). The term implies that following two antidepressant-treatment failures, depression enters a new 'difficult-to-treat' category. Furthermore, the term may be taken by both clinicians and patients as a pejorative label. It is also not supported by the evidence. For example, it does not take into account the fact that there are different degrees of improvement and stage of illness, or the possible impact of other treatments including psychosocial treatments and non-antidepressant augmenting agents. The GDG for this guideline update preferred to approach the problem of inadequate response from the direction of 'next-step' treatment options rather than categorising by patient response.

12.2   APPROACH TO THE REVIEWS

The major reviews undertaken for the previous guideline are represented here and updated with new studies where these were available. Previously, studies had been categorised 'treatment-resistant' where participants had been recruited because their depression had not responded to two sequential antidepressant drugs prescribed in an adequate dose for an adequate duration of time, and 'acute-phase non-responder' where participants' depression had not adequately responded to one antidepressant. These distinctions were not made in the present review, although the studies were coded for the number of antidepressant courses 'failed' both historically and prospectively (for example, H2P1 denoted that participants had inadequately responded to two antidepressants historically and one prospectively). In addition, studies of augmentation strategies that had not recruited people specifically because their depression had not responded to at least one previous treatment were removed from the analyses. A few studies used an open-label design. Since there are relatively few data on this topic, these were analysed separately and described narratively.

The electronic databases searched for published trials are given in Table 102. Details of the search strings used are in Appendix 8. In total, 11 new trials were found to supplement the previous reviews. Data were available to examine the following next-step strategies:
- Increasing the dose (Section 12.3.1)
- Switching to another antidepressant (Section 12.3.2).

Table 102: Databases searched and inclusion/exclusion criteria for clinical effectiveness of pharmacological treatments

Electronic databases	MEDLINE, EMBASE, PsycINFO, CINAHL
Date searched	Database inception to January 2008
Update searches	July 2008, January 2009
Study design	RCT
Population	People with a diagnosis of depression according to DSM, ICD or similar criteria whose depression has failed to respond to treatment
Treatments	Any pharmacological or physical treatment

- Combining an antidepressant with another antidepressant (Section 12.3.3)
- Augmenting an antidepressant with a different drug, including:
  - antipsychotics (Section 12.3.4)
  - lithium (Section 12.3.5)
  - anticonvulsants (Section 12.3.6)
  - pindolol (Section 12.3.7)
  - triiodothyronine (T3) (Section 12.3.8)
  - benzodiazepines (Section 12.3.9)
  - buspirone (Section 12.3.10)
  - atomoxetine (Section 12.3.11)
  - ECT[182] (Section 12.4).

In addition, narrative reviews of evidence for transcranial magnetic stimulation (TMS) and vagal nerve stimulation (VNS) were included (Section 12.5).

There were no new data for augmentation with lithium, anticonvulsants, pindolol or benzodiazepines, but augmentation was part of a topic that was restructured for the guideline update. Sections on acute-phase non-responders and treatment-resistant depression in the previous guideline became 'next-step treatments' in this guideline update and some of the sections have been redrafted.

**The above strategies were reviewed because there is sufficient evidence to come to a conclusion about efficacy and/or there is significant clinical usage of such strategies in the UK. There is, however, a wide range of other strategies used where first-line treatment has not been effective, for which either the evidence base is so weak or the clinical usage so low that the GDG did not include them in this review. Examples of these latter strategies include the use of stimulants or glucocorticoid antagonists either alone or to augment antidepressants.

Details of the available information about these strategies (for example, case reports, open studies, expert opinion) can be found elsewhere (Thase & Rush, 1997; Price *et al.*, 2001; Bauer *et al.*, 2002b). These papers also include details of the pharmacological issues associated with these strategies. Wide varieties of new treatments to augment antidepressants are being developed or are in pilot trial phase. These are beyond the scope of this review and details can be found elsewhere (Tamminga *et al.*, 2002).

MAOIs have been used extensively in the management of 'treatment-resistant' depression for 4 decades but there is no randomised data on which to base recommendations. Most information and experience is with phenelzine. McGrath and colleagues (1987b) treated patients in a cross-over design with high doses of phenelzine (maximum 90 mg), imipramine (maximum 300 mg) or placebo and found that of the non-responders only four of the 14 patients responded to a tricyclic cross-over with 17 of the 26 patients responding to an MAOI cross-over. There was some evidence of a preferential response in treatment-resistant patients with atypical symptoms of depression, but Nolen and colleagues (1988) subsequently showed that not only patients with atypical depressive symptoms but also patients with depression and

---

[182]This section updates the NICE Technology Appraisal on ECT (for depression only).

melancholia responded to MAOIs, in particular tranylcypramine. It does not appear that moclobemide has the same spectrum of efficacy in treatment resistance as the classical MAOIs. Nolen and colleagues (1994) switched patients with resistant depression stabilised on tranylcypromine to moclobemide. About 60% of the patients showed deterioration and one-third relapsed.**

12.3 PHARMACOLOGICAL 'NEXT-STEP' TREATMENT FOR DEPRESSION THAT HAS NOT ADEQUATELY RESPONDED TO TREATMENT

12.3.1 Increasing the dose

Introduction

When depression does not respond adequately, a common treatment strategy is to increase the dose of the antidepressant within the licensed dosage range. There is little objective evidence to support higher response rates with increasing dose (within the licensed dosage range) for the majority of antidepressants, but this does not preclude the possibility of a beneficial effect being seen in individual patients. Any beneficial effect is likely to be at least partially determined by individual differences in hepatic metabolising enzymes.

Studies considered[183]

Nine studies were found that compared drugs at different doses following lack of response to the initial dose (see Table 103), of which one was found in the update search (WHITMYER2007), but only two included a treatment group that remained on the previous dose after an adequate trial of the initial treatment (summary study characteristics of these two studies are in Table 104, with full details of the studies in Appendix 17c). Only one study (Licht2002) used a licensed dose for all patients in the initial phase, allowed adequate time to respond to this dose, and then randomised patients to remain on this dose or receive a higher dose.

Clinical evidence

There was evidence that increasing the dose led to small improvements in outcomes compared with continuing with the current dose, although these are not clinically important. However, there are few randomised trials (see Table 105) for the summary evidence profile. The full evidence profile and associated forest plots can be found in Appendix 16c and Appendix 19c, respectively.

---

[183]Here and elsewhere in the guideline, each study considered for review is referred to by a 'study ID' made up of first author and publication date (unless a study is in press or only submitted for publication, when first author only is used). Study IDs in title case refer to studies included in the previous guideline and study IDs in capital letters refer to studies found and included in this guideline update. References for studies from the previous guideline are in Appendix 18 and references for studies for the update are in Appendix 17c.

Table 103: Studies (RCTs) comparing antidepressants at different doses in people whose depression is resistant to treatment

Study ID	Initial treatment	Randomised treatment group 1	Randomised treatment group 2	Randomised treatment group 3	Comment
Fava1994	Fluoxetine 20 mg 8 weeks	Fluoxetine hi-dose 40–60 mg	Fluoxetine + mianserin	Fluoxetine + lithium	No same dose group
Fava2002	Fluoxetine 20 mg 8 weeks	Fluoxetine hi-dose 40–60 mg	Fluoxetine + desipramine	Fluoxetine + lithium	No same dose group
Licht2002	Sertraline 50 mg 4 weeks then 100 mg 2 weeks	Sertraline same-dose 100 mg	Sertraline hi-dose 200 mg	Sertraline + mianserin	Allows comparison
Benkert et al., 1997	Maprotiline 100 mg 3 weeks	Maprotiline same-dose 100 mg	Maprotiline hi-dose 150 mg	N/A	Open-label phase too short
Benkert et al., 1997 (2nd cf)	Paroxetine 20 mg 3 weeks	Paroxetine same-dose 20 mg	Paroxetine hi-dose 40 mg	N/A	Open-label phase too short
Schweizer et al., 2001	Sertraline 50 mg 3 weeks	Sertraline same-dose 50 mg	Sertraline hi-dose 150 mg	N/A	Open-label phase too short
Dornseif et al., 1989	Fluoxetine 20 mg 3 weeks	Fluoxetine same-dose 20 mg	Fluoxetine hi-dose 60 mg	N/A	Open-label phase too short and hi-dose fluoxetine dose too high
Schweizer 1990	Fluoxetine 20 mg 3 weeks	Fluoxetine same-dose 20 mg	Fluoxetine hi-dose 60 mg	N/A	Open-label phase too short and hi-dose fluoxetine dose too high
WHITMYER 2007	Duloxetine 30 mg or 60 mg 6 weeks	Duloxetine 60 mg	Duloxetine 120 mg	N/A	Allows comparison, although some participants were on a sub-therapeutic dose during the open-label phase

**Table 104: Summary study characteristics of included studies of
dose escalation in people whose depression had failed to respond
adequately to treatment**

No. trials (Total participants)	2 RCTs (540)
Study IDs	(1) Licht2002 (2) WHITMYER2007
N/% female	(1) 34/? (2) 506/64
Mean age	(1) Not given (2) 43
Initial treatment	(1) Sertraline 50 mg 4 weeks then 100 mg 2 weeks (2) Duloxetine 30 mg or 60 mg 6 weeks
Antidepressant	(1) Sertraline 100 mg (2) Duloxetine 60 mg
High-dose antidepressant	(1) Sertraline 200 mg (2) Duloxetine 120 mg
Setting	(1)–(2) Outpatients
Length of initial treatment	(1)–(2) 6 weeks
Length of randomised treatment	(1) 5 weeks (2) 6 weeks

Clinical summary

There is little objective evidence that increasing the dose improves outcomes,
although there are very few randomised studies. It is known that there are geneti-
cally determined differences in the activity of several hepatic enzymes that are
involved in the metabolism of antidepressant drugs. Fast or extensive metabolisers
may therefore need higher doses. Until further data are available, it is reasonable to
consider increasing the dose of an antidepressant within the SPC recommended
range, particularly where there has been a partial response and side effects are not
problematic.

Table 105: Summary evidence profile for dose escalation following inadequate treatment response

	Dose escalation
Mean depression scores at endpoint (clinician-rated)	SMD −0.11 (−0.29 to 0.08)
Quality	High
Number of studies; participants	K = 1; n = 443
Forest plot number	Pharm next-step 01.01
Non-response	RR 0.8 (0.59 to 1.1) (44.8% versus 54.5%)
Quality	Low
Number of studies; participants	K = 2; n = 452
Forest plot number	Pharm next-step 01.03
Non-remission	RR 0.94 (0.83 to 1.06) (67% versus 71.2%)
Quality	High
Number of studies; participants	K = 2; n = 452
Forest plot number	Pharm next-step 01.02
Leaving treatment early	RR 0.7 (0.48 to 1.04) (15.7% versus 22.1%)
Quality	Moderate
Number of studies; participants	K = 2; n = 452
Forest plot number	Pharm next-step 01.04
Leaving treatment early due to side effects	RR 0.97 (0.45 to 2.11) (5.2% versus 5.4%)
Quality	Low
Number of studies; participants	K = 2; n = 453
Forest plot number	Pharm next-step 01.05

12.3.2 Switching to another antidepressant

Introduction

Approximately 20 to 30% of patients with depression do not respond to the first antidepressant prescribed (assuming an adequate dose, duration of treatment and compliance with medication; Cowen, 1998). It is normal clinical practice at this point to increase the dose to the maximum tolerated (within licensed limits; see section 12.3.1) and, if there is still no or minimal response, to switch to an alternative antidepressant (Anderson *et al.*, 2008). Most prescribers select an antidepressant from a different class to the 'failed' drug (Fredman *et al.*, 2000). Randomised studies of switching are difficult to interpret as they either include patients who may be expected to fare poorly on one of the treatments (for example, patients with atypical depression in a study with an MAOI and TCA arm; McGrath *et al.*, 1993) or employ a cross-over design (Thase *et al.*, 1992; McGrath *et al.*, 1993). Open studies, however, show that approximately 50% of patients who do not respond to their first treatment are likely to respond to the second antidepressant irrespective of whether it comes from the same class or a different one (Thase & Rush, 1997).

Studies considered[184]
Altogether, six studies met inclusion criteria for the update, three of which were included in the previous guideline (two in other reviews) (Ferreri2001; Poirier1999; Thase2002a). Data were available to compare various switching strategies, including continuing with antidepressant treatment versus switching, comparison of switches to other single antidepressants, and comparison of switches to a single antidepressant versus switching to combinations of drugs. Data were available to compare continuing antidepressant treatment versus switching to olanzapine, but the GDG did not consider this relevant to clinical practice so the data are not reported (but are included in the forest plots for completeness). Summary study characteristics of the included studies are presented in Table 106, with full details in Appendix 17c, which also includes details of excluded studies.

Clinical evidence
Continuing with antidepressant treatment versus switching
Data were available to compare continuing nortriptyline with switching to fluoxetine, continuing fluoxetine with switching to mianserin, and continuing venlafaxine with switching to fluoxetine. There was no evidence that either strategy was more effective, or more acceptable and tolerable. Evidence from the important outcomes and overall quality of evidence are presented in Table 107. The full profile and associated forest plots can be found in Appendix 16c and Appendix 19c, respectively.

Switching antidepressant treatment (comparison of strategies)
Data available to compare the following switching strategies: switching to venlafaxine versus switching to an SSRI (citalopram or paroxetine) and switching to fluoxetine plus olanzapine versus switching to fluoxetine. This part of the review updates the review of venlafaxine for treatment-resistant depression included in the previous guideline.

---

[184]Study IDs in title case refer to studies included in the previous guideline and study IDs in capital letters refer to studies found and included in this guideline update. References for studies from the previous guideline are in Appendix 18.

Table 106: Summary study characteristics of included studies for continuing antidepressant treatment versus switching or switching treatment(s)

	Continuing antidepressant treatment versus switching	Switching treatment(s) (comparison of drugs)
No. trials (Total participants)	3 RCTs (433)	5 RCTs (1285)
Study IDs	(1) CORYA2006 (2) Ferreri2001 (3) SHELTON2005	(1) CORYA2006 (2) LENOXSMITH2008 (3) Poirier1999 (4) SHELTON2005 (5) Thase2002a*
N/% female	(1) 119/73 (2) 104/unclear (3) 210/68	(1) 303/73 (2) 406/42 (3) 122/72 (4) 288/68 (5) 166/68
Mean age (range if not available)	(1) 46 (2) Not given (3) 42	(1) 46 (2) 42 (3) 21–62 (4) 42 (5) 21–65
Treatment group 1	(1) Continuing venlafaxine (2) Continuing fluoxetine (3) Continuing nortriptyline	(1) Switching to fluoxetine + olanzapine (2) Switching to venlafaxine (3) Switching to venlafaxine (4) Switching to fluoxetine + olanzapine (5) Switching to imipramine
Treatment group 2	(1) Switching to fluoxetine (2) Switching to mianserin (3) Switching to fluoxetine	(1) Switching to fluoxetine (2) Switching to citalopram (3) Switching to paroxetine (4) Switching to fluoxetine (5) Switching to sertraline
Setting	(1) Unclear (2) In/outpatients (3) Unclear	(1) Unclear (2)–(3) In/outpatients (4) Unclear (5) Outpatients
Length of treatment	(1) 12 weeks (2) 6 weeks (3) 8 weeks	(1)–(2) 12 weeks (3) 4 weeks (4) 8 weeks (5) 12 weeks

*Participants in this study were randomised to both initial treatment and switching strategy and it is therefore analysed separately.

Table 107: Summary evidence profile for continuing antidepressant treatment versus switching following inadequate response to treatment

	Nortriptyline versus fluoxetine	Fluoxetine versus mianserin	Venlafaxine versus fluoxetine
Mean depression scores at endpoint (self-rated)	WMD 1.05 (−1.31 to 3.41)	WMD 1.8 (−1.63 to 5.23)	WMD −2.03 (−5.22 to 1.16)
Quality	Moderate	Low	Low
Number of studies; participants	K = 1; n = 210	K = 1; n = 72	K = 1; n = 119
Forest plot number	Pharm next-step 02.03	Pharm next-step 02.03	Pharm next-step 02.03
Non-response	RR 1.07 (0.69 to 1.66) (30.9% versus 28.9%)	RR 1.19 (0.8 to 1.78) (63.2% versus 52.9%)	RR 0.94 (0.78 to 1.12) (78% versus 83.3%)
Quality	Low	Low	Moderate
Number of studies; participants	K = 1; n = 210	K = 1; n = 72	K = 1; n = 119
Forest plot number	Pharm next-step 02.01	Pharm next-step 02.01	Pharm next-step 02.01
Non-remission	RR 1.32 (0.68 to 2.56) (17.6% versus 13.4%)	RR 1.26 (0.94 to 1.69) (81.6% versus 64.7%)	RR 0.74 (0.55 to 1.01) (50.8% versus 68.3%)
Quality	Low	Low	Moderate
Number of studies; participants	K = 1; n = 210	K = 1; n = 72	K = 1; n = 119
Forest plot number	Pharm next-step 02.02	Pharm next-step 02.02	Pharm next-step 02.02

Continued

Table 107: *(Continued)*

	Nortriptyline versus fluoxetine	Fluoxetine versus mianserin	Venlafaxine versus fluoxetine
Leaving treatment early	RR 0.6 (0.29 to 1.24) (11.8% versus 19.7%)	RR 1.27 (0.65 to 2.48) (25.4% versus 20%)	Not reported
Quality	Low	Low	–
Number of studies; participants	K = 1; n = 210	K = 1; n = 119	–
Forest plot number	Pharm next-step 02.04	Pharm next-step 02.04	
Leaving treatment early due to side effects	RR 1.04 (0.20 to 5.56) (2.9% versus 2.8%)	RR 0.52 (0.23 to 1.17) (18.4% versus 35.3%)	RR 0.34 (0.04 to 3.17) (1.7% versus 5%)
Quality	Low	Low	Low
Number of studies; participants	K = 1; n = 210	K = 1; n = 72	K = 1; n = 119
Forest plot number	Pharm next-step 02.05	Pharm next-step 02.05	Pharm next-step 02.05

There was no difference between the switching strategies for which data were available on any measure, other than on the number of people leaving treatment early because of side effects, which favoured fluoxetine over fluoxetine plus olanzapine. Combining the two RCTs in which non-responders were randomised to venlafaxine or an SSRI did not show a significant advantage to venlafaxine (LENOX-SMITH2008; Poirier1999). The earlier study (in severely ill patients) did suggest an advantage to venlafaxine in some outcomes as reported in the previous guideline but the later study did not. A secondary analysis of the later study did however report an advantage to venlafaxine in a secondary analysis of severely ill patients. Whether venlafaxine has an advantage in severely depressed patients is therefore undetermined. Evidence from the important outcomes and overall quality of evidence are presented in Table 108. The full profile and associated forest plots can be found in Appendix 16c and Appendix 19c, respectively.

Table 108: Summary evidence profile for switching antidepressant treatment (comparison of strategies) following inadequate antidepressant response

	Venlafaxine versus SSRI	**Fluoxetine + olanzapine versus fluoxetine**
Mean depression scores at endpoint (self-rated)	WMD -0.5 (-2.09 to 1.09)	WMD -1.13 (-3.22 to 0.97)
Quality	Moderate	Low
Number of studies; participants	K = 2; n = 526	K = 2; n = 591
Forest plot number	Pharm next-step 03.02	Pharm next-step 03.04
Non-response	RR 0.91 (0.73 to 1.14) (61.6% versus 65.5%)	RR 0.88 (0.74 to 1.05) (47% versus 40.6%)
Quality	Low	Moderate
Number of studies; participants	K = 2; n = 519	K = 2; n = 591
Forest plot number	Pharm next-step 03.01	Pharm next-step 03.04
Non-remission	RR 0.91 (0.67 to 1.24) (52.2% versus 54.5%)	RR 1 (0.69 to 1.47) (5.37% versus 34.2%)
Quality	Low	Very low
Number of studies; participants	K = 2; n = 519	K = 2; n = 591
Forest plot number	Pharm next-step 03.01	Pharm next-step 03.04

Continued

Table 108: (*Continued*)

	Venlafaxine versus SSRI	Fluoxetine + olanzapine versus fluoxetine
Leaving treatment early for any reason	RR 1.19 (0.85 to 1.67) (22.2% versus 18.7%)	RR 1.12 (0.79 to 1.59) (23.1% versus 19.8%)
Quality	Low	Low
Number of studies; participants	K = 2; n = 529	K = 2; n = 591
Forest plot number	Pharm next-step 03.03	Pharm next-step 03.04
Leaving treatment early due to side effects	RR 1.17 (0.58 to 2.36) (6.1% versus 5.2%)	RR 2.41 (1.07 to 5.43) (10% versus 3.5%)
Quality	Low	High
Number of studies; participants	K = 2; n = 529	K = 2; n = 591
Forest plot number	Pharm next-step 03.03	Pharm next-step 03.04

One study randomised to both initial treatment and switching strategy, and this was analysed separately (Thase2002a). It showed no statistically significant advantage for either strategy (sertraline to imipramine or imipramine to sertraline), although there was an advantage for those starting on imipramine and switching to sertraline following inadequate response (see Appendix 16c).

In addition to the blinded RCTs that were included in the meta-analyses, the search yielded two large open randomised studies. In the first (Baldomero *et al.*, 2005), non-responders to a single antidepressant were randomised to receive venlafaxine or another antidepressant; in the second (STAR*D, Rush *et al.*, 2003)[185], non-responders to citalopram were randomised to switch to another antidepressant or receive an augmenting drug; those who did not remit were further randomised. Both these studies were excluded from the main analyses because they were open-label, but are described narraitavely here because of their importance in the field.

The first large 24-week open-label study (Baldomero *et al.*, 2005) comprised 3502 outpatients with major depressive disorder, subthreshold depressive symptoms (8.7%) and dysthymia (16%) whose depressive symptoms (HRSD scores above 17) had not responded to treatment with an antidepressant (most commonly an SSRI) for at least 4 weeks; 1830 of the participants were randomised to venlafaxine-XR (mean dose 164 mg) and 1672 to other antidepressants different from those used in earlier treatment

---

[185]Many papers have been published from the STAR*D study. Those containing data used in this guideline are listed in Appendix 17, and the study is referred to with the Rush and colleagues (2003) reference which gives an overview of the study design.

and including fluoxetine (17%), paroxetine (21.3%), citalopram (20.1%), sertraline (19.1%) and mirtazapine (7.9%). There was little difference in mean endpoint depression scores between the venlafaxine group and the other antidepressant group: venlafaxine 7.89 (SD 6.5) and other antidepressants 8.84 (6.7). However, 967 people (52% of the number randomised) taking venlafaxine achieved remission (HRSD $<=$ 7) as did 755 (45% of the number randomised) taking other antidepressants. The response rate (50% reduction in baseline HRSD scores) was 1262 (69%) in the venlafaxine group and 1034 (62%) in the other antidepressants group. Figures are calculated from the number randomised rather than the 'intention to treat' population used by the study authors.

As the STAR*D (Rush *et al.*, 2003) study contained both switching and augmentation arms, the data from these studies are summarised in the augmentation section below.

Clinical summary

Given the paucity of evidence from switching studies, evidence from primary efficacy studies in which antidepressants were directly compared were also considered. Caution is required in extrapolating from these studies to those whose illness has not responded to sequential trials of antidepressant drugs.

Data from switching studies and head-to-head studies suggest that there may be a very small efficacy advantage for venlafaxine and escitalopram over other antidepressants. This advantage is too small to be clinically meaningful when all people with depression are considered together, but may be large enough to be clinically worthwhile in those who have not benefited from treatment with a first or second antidepressant. However, the current evidence is not sufficiently robust to form the basis of a recommendation.

12.3.3   Combining an antidepressant with another antidepressant

Introduction

**Combining antidepressant drugs with different modes of action is increasingly used in clinical practice. Combinations of serotonergic and noradrenergic drugs may result in a 'dual action' combination, while combinations of serotonergic drugs with different modes of action may be expected to increase serotonergic neurotransmission more than either drug alone.

While the efficacy of these combinations may be additive (this is not proven for the majority of combinations), so too may the toxicity. Both pharmacokinetic and pharmacodynamic interactions must be considered. Fluoxetine, fluvoxamine and paroxetine may increase TCA serum levels substantially and unpredictably, thereby increasing the risk of adverse effects (Taylor, 1995). Combinations of serotonergic antidepressants increase the risk of developing serotonin syndrome, which can be fatal. Features include confusion, delirium, shivering, sweating, changes in blood pressure and myoclonus.**

Studies considered[186]

No new studies of combination with a second antidepressant were found after inadequate response to the first, but so that the data could be analysed together the studies

---

[186]Study IDs in title case refer to studies included in the previous guideline and study IDs in capital letters refer to studies found and included in this guideline update. References for studies from the previous guideline are in Appendix 18.

are presented in the style of the update in this section. There were data for a range of strategies, including adding mianserin, desipramine (not available in the UK), mirtazapine, moclobemide and atomoxetine to an antidepressant. Summary study characteristics of the included studies are presented in Table 109, with full details in Appendix 17c, which also includes details of excluded studies.

Table 109: Summary study characteristics of included studies of combining antidepressants in people whose depression had not responded adequately to treatment

	Combining with a second antidepressant
No. trials (Total participants)	7 RCTs (518)
Study IDs	(1) Carpenter2002 (2) Fava1994 (3) Fava2002 (4) Ferreri2001 (5) Licht2002 (6) Maes1999 (7) Tanghe1997
N/% female	(1) 26/62 (2) 41/unclear (3) 101/unclear (4) 104 (unclear) (5) 295 (unclear) (6) 34/? (7) 59/?
Mean age	(1) 46 (2) 39 (3)–(6) Not given (7) 43
Combining agent	(1) Mirtazapine 15 mg (30 mg in three patients) (2) Desipramine (dose unclear) (3) Desipramine (dose unclear) (4) Mianserin 60 mg (5)–(6) Mianserin 30 mg (7) Moclobemide 200–600 mg
Antidepressant	(1) SSRIs, venlafaxine or bupropion (2)–(4) Fluoxetine 20 mg

Continued

Table 109: (*Continued*)

	Combining with a second antidepressant
	(5) Sertraline 100 mg (6) Fluoxetine 20 mg (7) Amitriptyline up to 280 mg
Setting	(1)–(3) Outpatients (4) In/outpatients (5) Outpatients (6)–(7) Inpatients
Length of treatment	(1)–(3) 4 weeks (4) 6 weeks (5)–(6) 5 weeks (7) 4 weeks

Clinical evidence

Evidence from the important outcomes and overall quality of evidence are presented in Table 110. The full profile and associated forest plots can be found in Appendix 16c and Appendix 19c, respectively.

Results showed that combination treatment tended to reduce symptoms of depression more than continuing with the existing single antidepressant at 'standard' dose. However, the data are not strong, and participants taking combination treatment reported more side effects than those taking a single antidepressant.

In a mixed population of patients there is some evidence that combining one antidepressant with another leads to better outcomes on response, remission and mean endpoint scores compared with a single antidepressant at 'standard' dose. There is insufficient evidence to determine whether this is the case when compared with a single antidepressant at high dose.

Since the majority of studies used mianserin as the second antidepressant, the analyses are weighted towards this drug. Importantly, there are no RCTs of combinations of a TCA and irreversible MAOI or any two from a choice of venlafaxine, mirtazapine and reboxetine.

Clinical summary

There is some evidence that combinations of antidepressants are associated with a higher burden of side effects than a single antidepressant at either standard or high dose, but there is insufficient evidence to comment on the number of patients leaving treatment early.

Table 110: Summary evidence profile for combining an antidepressant versus antidepressant with/without placebo

	SSRI + mianserin	Fluoxetine + desipramine versus hi-dose fluoxetine	Antidepressant + mirtazapine	Amitriptyline + moclobemide
Mean depression change scores at endpoint	SMD −0.46 (−1.07 to 0.15)	SMD 0.67 (0.05 to 1.28)	SMD −0.83 (−1.64 to −0.01)	SMD −0.63 (−1.28 to 0.01)
Quality	Low	Low	Moderate	Moderate
Number of studies; participants	K = 3; n = 288	K = 2; n = 96	K = 1; n = 26	K = 1; n = 39
Forest plot number	Pharm next-step 07.03	Pharm next-step 07.03	Pharm next-step 07.03	Pharm next-step 07.03
Non-response	RR 0.71 (0.44 to 1.17) (34.8% versus 43.6%)	Not reported	RR 0.45 (0.2 to 1.03) (36.4% versus 80%)	Not reported
Quality	Low	–	Moderate	–
Number of studies; participants	K = 3; n = 290	–	K = 1; n = 26	–
Forest plot number	Pharm next-step 07.01	–	Pharm next-step 07.01	–
Non-remission	RR 0.81 (0.62 to 1.04) (56.2% versus 67.9%)	RR 1.32 (0.96 to 1.81) (71.7% versus 54.2%)	RR 0.63 (0.35 to 1.12) (54.5% versus 86.7%)	Not reported

Quality	Low	Moderate	Moderate	–
Number of studies; participants	K = 2; n = 267	K = 2; n = 96	K = 1; n = 26	–
Forest plot number	Pharm next-step 07.02	Pharm next-step 07.02	Pharm next-step 07.02	–
Leaving treatment early	RR 1.44 (0.81 to 2.58) (17.7% versus 12.4%)	RR 1.71 (0.61 to 4.83) (17.4% versus 10.4%)	RR 0.68 (0.07 to 6.61) (9.1% versus 13.3%)	Not reported
Quality	Low	Low	Low	–
Number of studies; participants	K = 2; n = 267	K = 2; n = 96	K = 1; n = 26	–
Forest plot number	Pharm next-step 07.05	Pharm next-step 07.05	Pharm next-step 07.05	–
Leaving treatment early due to side effects	RR 1.52 (0.58 to 3.96) (6.9% versus 4.4%)	Not reported	Not reported	Not reported
Quality	Low	–	–	–
Number of studies; participants	K = 2; n = 167	–	–	–
Forest plot number	Pharm next-step 07.06	–	–	–

12.3.4   Augmenting an antidepressant with an antipsychotic

Studies considered[187]
A total of five nine studies found in the update search met inclusion criteria for the review of antipsychotic augmentation (BERMAN2007, CORYA2006, KEIT-NER2009, MAHMOUD2007, MARCUS2008, MCINTRYRE2007B, SONG2007, THASE2007 [two studies reported in the same paper]). The previous guideline included only one study (Shelton2001). Summary study characteristics of the included studies are presented in Table 111, with full details in Appendix 17c, which also includes details of excluded studies.

Clinical evidence
There were data for augmentation with aripiprazole, olanzapine, risperidone and quetiapine. Evidence from the important outcomes and overall quality of evidence are presented in Table 112. The full profile and associated forest plots can be found in Appendix 16c and Appendix 19c, respectively.

Overall, there was a moderate, clinical important effect on symptoms of depression favouring antipsychotic augmentation, which was mirrored in small effects on remission and response. Results for individual antipsychotics were similar, but tended not to be statistically significant because of the small number of studies for each drug. There were no head-to-head trials. Participants taking antipsychotics were more likely to leave treatment early for any reason and specifically because of side effects. There were also more likely to report side effects.

Clinical summary
The previous guideline found little evidence on which to make an evidence-based recommendation regarding antipsychotic augmentation of antidepressants for people whose depression had not responded to treatment with an antidepressant alone. A number of studies have been published since, which when considered together, show a statistically significant, but clinically modest advantage for antipsychotic augmentation of an antidepressant over an antidepressant alone. Patients whose antidepressant is augmented by an antipsychotic are much more likely to leave treatment early because of side effects. This was most marked for quetiapine.

---

[187]Study IDs in title case refer to studies included in the previous guideline and study IDs in capital letters refer to studies found and included in this guideline update. References for studies from the previous guideline are in Appendix 18.

Table 111: Summary study characteristics for antipsychotic augmentation

	Augmentation with an antipsychotic
No. trials (Total participants)	10 RCTs (2554)
Study IDs	(1) BERMAN2007 (2) CORYA2006 (3) KEITNER2009 (4) MAHMOUD2007 (5) MARCUS2008 (6) MCINTRYRE2007B (7) Shelton2001 (8) SONG2007 (9) THASE2007 study 1 (10) THASE2007 study 2
N/% female	(1) 362/70 (2) 483/73 (3) 55/57 (4) 274/72 (5) 381/67 (6) 58/64 (7) 28/unclear (8) 50/50 (9) 404/63 (10) 459/68
Mean age	(1) 45 (2) 46 (3) 45 (4) 46 (5)–(6) 44 (7) 42 (8)–(10) 44
Augmenting agent	(1) Aripiprazole (2) Olanzapine (3)–(4) Risperidone (5) Aripiprazole (6) Quetiapine (7) Olanzapine (8) Risperidone (9)–(10) Olanzapine

Continued

Table 111: (*Continued*)

	Augmentation with an antipsychotic
Antidepressant	(1) SSRIs or venlafaxine (2) Fluoxetine (3) Range (4) Range of ADs (5)–(6) SSRI or venlafaxine (7) Fluoxetine (8) Venlafaxine (9)–(10) Fluoxetine
Setting	(1) Outpatients (2) Unclear (3) Outpatients (4) Mixed including primary care (5) Unclear (6) Primary care and outpatients (7) Outpatients (8) Mixed (9)–(10) Unclear
Length of treatment	(1) 6 weeks (2) 12 weeks (3) 4 weeks (4)–(5) 6 weeks (6)–(7) 8 weeks (8) 6 weeks (9)–(10) 8 weeks

Table 112: Summary evidence profile for augmentation with an antipsychotic versus antidepressant with/without placebo

	Overall	Aripiprazole	Olanzapine	Risperidone	Quetiapine
Mean depression change scores at endpoint*	SMD −0.45 (−0.62 to −0.28)	SMD −0.32 (−0.53 to −0.12)	SMD −0.35 (−0.77 to 0.07)	SMD −0.56 (−0.78 to −0.33)	SMD −0.77 (−1.3 to −0.23)
Quality	Moderate	Moderate	Low	High	Moderate
Number of studies; participants	K = 6; n = 1146	K = 1; n = 369	K = 2; n = 401	K = 2; n = 318	K = 1; n = 58
Forest plot number	Pharm next-step 08.03	Pharm next-step 08.03	Pharm next-step 08.03	Pharm next-step 08.03	Pharm next-step 08.03
Non-response	RR 0.88 (0.82 to 0.95) (64.3% versus 73%)	RR 0.94 (0.81 to 1.1) (67% versus 72%)	RR 0.81 (0.67 to 1) (59% versus 71.8%)	RR 0.86 (0.77 to 0.97) (65.5% versus 96.9%)	RR 0.71 (0.47 to 1.08) (51.7% versus 72.4%)
Quality	High	Moderate	Low	High	Low
Number of studies; participants	K = 9; n = 1689	K = 2; n = 734	K = 3; n = 436	K = 3; n = 471	K = 1; n = 58
Forest plot number	Pharm next-step 08.01	Pharm next-step 08.01	Pharm next-step 08.01	Pharm next-step 08.01	Pharm next-step 08.01
Non-remission	RR 0.88 (0.84 to 0.92) (74.7% versus 85.2%)	RR 0.88 (0.82 to 0.95) (74.7% versus 84.8%)	RR 0.87 (0.79 to 0.97) (73% versus 83.5%)	RR 0.88 (0.81 to 0.96) (76.6% versus 88%)	RR 0.83 (0.62 to 1.12) (69% versus 82.8%)
Quality	High	High	High	High	Moderate
Number of studies; participants	K = 8; n = 1670	K = 2; n = 734	K = 2; n = 406	K = 3; n = 472	K = 1; n = 58
Forest plot number	Pharm next-step 08.02	Pharm next-step 08.02	Pharm next-step 08.02	Pharm next-step 08.02	Pharm next-step 08.02

Continued

487

Table 112: *(Continued)*

	Overall	Aripiprazole	Olanzapine	Risperidone	Quetiapine
Leaving treatment early	RR 1.19 (0.93 to 1.51) (19.3% versus 16.3%)	RR 1.3 (0.71 to 2.39) (12.1% versus 9.3%)	RR 1.29 (0.9 to 1.84) (25.2% versus 19.9%)	RR 1.21 (0.64 to 2.29) (17.1% versus 13.3%)	RR 0.79 (0.43 to 1.43) (37.9% versus 48.3%)
Quality	Moderate	Low	Moderate	Very low	Low
Number of studies; participants	K = 7; n = 1209	K = 1; n = 354	K = 3; n = 436	K = 2; n = 371	K = 1; n = 58
Forest plot number	Pharm next-step 08.04	Pharm next-step 08.04	Pharm next-step 08.04	Pharm next-step 08.04	Pharm next-step 08.04
Leaving treatment early due to side effects	RR 2.43 (1.18 to 5.03) (7.9% versus 3%)	RR 2.01 (0.76 to 5.33) (3.5% versus 1.7%)	RR 5.53 (2.17 to 14.08) (13.5% versus 2.4%)	RR 1.13 (0.27 to 4.74) (7.8% versus 6%)	RR 4 (0.93 to 17.25) (27.6% versus 6.9%)
Quality	Moderate	Moderate	High	Low	Low
Number of studies; participants	K = 7; n = 1566	K = 2; n = 735	K = 2; n = 406	K = 2; n = 371	K = 1; n = 58
Forest plot number	Pharm next-step 08.05	Pharm next-step 08.05	Pharm next-step 08.05	Pharm next-step 08.05	Pharm next-step 08.05

12.3.5   Augmenting an antidepressant with lithium

Introduction

Lithium is an established mood stabilising drug that is used in the treatment of mania and the prophylaxis of bipolar affective disorder. It is also widely used to augment antidepressant response in depression that has not responded adequately to initial treatment with an antidepressant.

Lithium is primarily excreted renally and can cause hypothyroidism, renal damage and a number of other adverse effects. Baseline biochemical tests and ongoing monitoring are essential. For example, serum lithium levels must be monitored to achieve a stable therapeutic level (see below). This should include monitoring 1 week after initiation (and 1 week after any dose change) until stable and then every 3 months; more details can be found in the NICE guideline on bipolar disorder (NICE, 2006c).

Lithium is a potentially toxic drug. Plasma levels of 0.5 to 1.0 mmol/L are usually considered to be therapeutic. Above 1.5 mmol/L toxicity invariably develops and death may occur at levels as low as 2.0 mmol/L. Many commonly prescribed drugs can interact with lithium to precipitate lithium toxicity (British Medical Association and the Royal Pharmaceutical Society of Great Britain, 2009; Taylor *et al.*, 2007).

Studies considered[188]

No new studies were found that met inclusion criteria, but so that the data could be analysed together the studies are presented in the style of the update in this section. The data from the ten remaining studies were reanalysed without dividing the dataset by antidepressant-response history. Summary study characteristics of the included studies are presented in Table 113, with full details in Appendix 17c, which also includes details of excluded studies.

Clinical evidence

There was some evidence that lithium augmentation was effective in reducing symptoms of depression. Evidence from the important outcomes and overall quality of evidence are presented in Table 114. The full profile and associated forest plots can be found in Appendix 16c and Appendix 19c, respectively.

Clinical summary

There is some evidence of a clinically important advantage of adding lithium to an antidepressant over adding placebo, although this effect was not found for mean endpoint scores on all outcome measures. Adding lithium to an antidepressant appears to be less acceptable to patients, with just over 30% leaving treatment early compared with 17.4% taking placebo. There is insufficient evidence to determine whether this is due to side effects.

---

[188]Study IDs in title case refer to studies included in the previous guideline. References for studies from the previous guideline are in Appendix 18.

Table 113: Summary study characteristics for lithium augmentation

	Augmentation with lithium
No. trials (Total participants)	10 RCTs (408)
Study IDs	(1) Baumann1996 (2) Bloch1997 (3) Cappiello1998 (4) Januel2002 (5) Jensen1992 (6) Joffe1993a (7) Nierenberg2003 (8) Shahal1996 (9) Stein1993 (10) Zusky1988
N/% female	(1) 24/(unclear) (2) 31/(unclear) (3) 149/(unclear) (4) 44/(unclear) (6) 51/(unclear) (7) 35/45 (8) 22/(unclear) (9) 34/79 (10) 18/(unclear)
Mean age (range if mean not given)	(1)–(2) Not given (3) 40 (4) 18–65 (5) 65+ (6) 37 (7) Not given (8) 53 (10) 47
Lithium dose	(1) Lithium 800 mg (2)–(3) Lithium 900 mg (4) Lithium 750 mg (5)–(6) Lithium 450 mg (7) Lithium (unclear) (8) Lithium 630 mg (10) Lithium 250 mg
Antidepressant	(1) Citalopram 40–60 mg (2)–(3) Desipramine 200 mg

Continued

Table 113: (*Continued*)

	Augmentation with lithium
	(4) Clomipramine 150 mg (5) Nortriptyline 75 mg (6) TCA (7) Nortriptyline 100 mg (8) Imipramine (105–175 mg) (9) Amitriptyline $>= 150$ mg (10) Any
Setting	(1) Inpatients (2) Outpatients (3) In/outpatients (4)–(5) Inpatients (6)–(7) Outpatients (8) Inpatients (9)–(10) Unclear
Length of treatment	(1) 1 week (2)–(3) 5 weeks (4)–(5) 6 weeks (6)–(7) 2 weeks (8) 5 weeks (9)–(10) 3 weeks

12.3.6 Augmenting an antidepressant with anticonvulsants

The following sections on augmenting an antidepressant with anticonvulsants marked by asterisks (**_**) are from the previous guideline and have not been updated except for style and minor clarification.

Introduction
Anticonvulsants are increasingly being prescribed for people with bipolar disorder; there is growing data related to their efficacy in the treatment of depression and mania and in the prophylaxis of bipolar disorder. No new data were found for augmentation of an antidepressant with carbamazepine or valproate.

Carbamazepine
**Carbamazepine has attracted the most interest because it was the first anticonvulsant to be shown to have efficacy in bipolar disorder and because it shares some neurochemical properties with tricyclic antidepressants. However, no RCTs met the inclusion criteria set by the GDG. There are some open studies (Dietrich & Emrich, 1998), and one RCT in major depression (Zhang *et al.*, 2008), and some open studies

Table 114: Summary evidence profile for augmentation with lithium versus antidepressant with/without placebo

	Lithium
Mean depression change scores at endpoint	SMD -0.32 (-0.56 to -0.08)
Quality	High
Number of studies; participants	K = 7; n = 273
Forest plot number	Pharm next-step 09.03
Non-response	RR 0.83 (0.66 to 1.03) (64.4% versus 79.1%)
Quality	Moderate
Number of studies; participants	K = 6; n = 172
Forest plot number	Pharm next-step 09.01
Non-remission	RR 1.26 (0.72 to 2.17) (53.3% versus 48.6%)
Quality	Low
Number of studies; participants	K = 3; n = 216
Forest plot number	Pharm next-step 09.02
Leaving treatment early	RR 1.79 (1.23 to 2.6) (30.9% versus 17.4%)
Quality	High
Number of studies; participants	K = 8; n = 356
Forest plot number	Pharm next-step 09.04
Leaving treatment early due to side effects	Not reported
Quality	–
Number of studies; participants	–
Forest plot number	–

in treatment-resistant depression (Cullen *et al.*, 1991; Ketter *et al.*, 1995) that show some benefit. It is noteworthy that in Cullen's study a high percentage of the older patients who responded had to discontinue carbamazepine because of adverse effects.

Carbamazepine has a wide range of side effects, contraindications and interactions with other drugs. In the context of depression, it is noteworthy that co-administration of carbamazepine reduces TCA levels by up to 50% (Dietrich & Emrich, 1998) and SSRIs may interfere with carbamazepine metabolism leading to intoxication.

There is a lack of controlled data and a high likelihood of adverse effects or clinically important interactions and, therefore, carbamazepine cannot be recommended as a routine next-step treatment for poorly responsive depression.**

Valproate

There are no RCTs of valproate in unipolar major depression. Evidence to date suggests that valproate is more effective in preventing hypomania rather than depression in people with bipolar disorder.

One open study enrolled 33 patients with major depressive disorder in an 8-week study of valproate as monotherapy (Davis *et al.*, 1996). Approximately 50% of the patients achieved remission. Valproate is associated with a number of side effects including significant weight gain. It can also increase plasma levels of other commonly prescribed drugs such as TCAs, quetiapine and warfarin. Fluoxetine may elevate valproate levels by interfering with its metabolism. Valproate is also a major human teratogen.

There are a lack of controlled data and a high likelihood of adverse effects or clinically important interactions and, therefore, valproate cannot be recommended in the routine management of depression that has not responded adequately to other treatments.

Lamotrigine

Lamotrigine is used in the treatment of partial and generalised seizures. In clinical trials in epilepsy it was noted that those who received lamotrigine reported improvements in mood, alertness and social interaction.

Studies have shown evidence of efficacy for lamotrigine in bipolar depression (Geddes *et al.*, 2009). However, in a study of 437 patients with major depressive disorder randomised to lamotrigine, desipramine or placebo, 'last observation carried forward', ratings demonstrated no difference between groups (Hurley, 2002). In a further RCT (Normann *et al.*, 2002), 40 patients with depression (30 unipolar, 10 bipolar) were given lamotrigine (200 mg) or placebo added to paroxetine (40 mg) for 9 weeks. There was no benefit for lamotrigine over placebo in HRSD scores at endpoint. There was a high frequency of adverse effects and dropouts in both groups. Barbosa and colleagues (2003) reported on 23 patients with depression (65% major depressive disorder) who had failed at least one trial of an antidepressant, and were randomised to receive either placebo or 25 mg to 100 mg of lamotrigine in addition to fluoxetine 20 mg/day. There was no statistical difference in HRSD or MADRS ratings between the two groups at 6 weeks, although there was a benefit in a secondary outcome measure of responders based on the CGI. A further small study (Santos *et al.*, 2008; N = 34) of outpatients whose depression had not responded to at least two antidepressants of different classes for at least 6 weeks at the highest tolerated dose, compared augmentation with lamotrigine in doses up to 200 mg with augmentation with placebo for 8 weeks. Participants continued with their existing antidepressant. There was no advantage for lamotrigine augmentation when endpoint depression scores were compared.

Finally, in an 8-week randomised open-label study of antidepressant augmentation with either lamotrigine (150 mg) or lithium (serum level 0.6 to 0.8 mmol/L) in 34 inpatients with a diagnosis of major depressive disorder whose depression had not responded to two trials of different antidepressants, Schindler and Anghelescu (2007) reported no significant difference between the treatment groups at endpoint based on HRSD scores, remission or response.

**In view of the lack of positive data, lamotrigine cannot be recommended for use in unipolar disorder. Although it is generally well tolerated and free of major interactions, it can cause a severe rash that can be life-threatening in a small minority of cases. Its profile in epilepsy and bipolar disorder suggests that further trials of lamotrigine in treatment-resistant depression are worthwhile.

There are no data that indicate that other anticonvulsants – for example, gabapentin or topiramate – can be recommended in the treatment of depression.**

12.3.7 Augmenting an antidepressant with pindolol

The following sections on augmenting an antidepressant with pindolol marked by asterisks (**_**) are from the previous guideline and have not been updated except for style and minor clarification.

Introduction
**Serotonergic antidepressants inhibit the reuptake of serotonin into the presynaptic neurone thus increasing serotonergic neurotransmission. The immediate effect of this increase is to stimulate serotonin 1a autoreceptors, which results in a decrease in serotonin release. In time, these autoreceptors become desensitised and serotonin release returns to normal. This, in combination with the inhibition of serotonin reuptake, is thought to lead to the onset of the antidepressant effect.

Pindolol is primarily an adrenergic b-blocking drug, which also blocks serotonin 1a autoreceptors. The co-administration of pindolol with a serotonergic antidepressant could be expected to result in an immediate increase in serotonin neurotransmission, thus eliminating the delay in onset of antidepressant response.

As well as being used to speed the onset of antidepressant response, pindolol has also been used to augment the efficacy of antidepressant drugs in acute-phase non-responders and treatment-resistant depression.**

Studies considered[189,190]
Twenty-four studies were found in a search of electronic databases, six of which met the inclusion criteria set by the GDG (Bordet1998, Maes1999, Perez1997, Perez1999, Tome1997, Zanardi1997) and 18 of which did not. No new studies were found in the update search.

---

[189]Details of standard search strings used in all searches are in Appendix 8. Information about each study along with an assessment of methodological quality is in Appendix 17c, which also contains a list of excluded studies with reasons for exclusions.

[190]Study IDs in title case refer to studies included in the previous guideline. References for these studies are in Appendix 18.

**Only studies comparing pindolol plus an antidepressant with pindolol plus placebo were included in the analyses. Apart from one study (Perez1999), which included clomipramine as well as a range of SSRIs, all studies used a single SSRI as the antidepressant. Efficacy data were available from up to 282 participants and tolerability data from up to 333 participants.

All included studies were published between 1997 and 1999 with participants being randomised to an experimental treatment phase of between 10 days and 6 weeks (mean = 4.25 weeks).

In two studies participants were described as inpatients (Maes1999, Zanardi1997), in a further two as outpatients (Perez1999, Tome1997), in one as primary care (Perez1997) and in the remaining trial participants were from mixed sources (Bordet1998). In no trial were participants exclusively older or experiencing atypical depression. The mean dose of pindolol was 9.23 mg, ranging from 7.5 mg to 15 mg.

No trial was classified acute-phase non-responder, and only one study included patients who had not responded to previous antidepressant treatment (Perez1999). Here patients were randomised to receive augmentation for 10 days with either pindolol (7.5 mg) or placebo after receiving fluoxetine (40 mg), fluvoxamine (200 mg), paroxetine (40 mg) or clomipramine (150 mg) for at least 6 weeks beforehand. In addition the participants' depression had already failed to respond to between one and four courses of antidepressants (median two). Most patients were outpatients aged 18 to 65. Results from a separate analysis of this trial are presented below.

Outcomes are classified according to when assessment measures were taken. Up to 14 days after treatment was begun was categorised 'early assessment point' and more than 20 days was categorised 'late assessment point'. Three studies (Bordet1998, Tome1997, Zanardi1997) gave outcomes at both assessment points.

Clinical evidence statements: effect of treatment on efficacy[191]
Early assessment point
There is evidence suggesting that there is no clinically important difference between SSRIs plus pindolol and SSRIs plus placebo on increasing the likelihood of achieving a 50% reduction in symptoms of depression by the tenth day of treatment (N = 2; n = 160; RR = 0.95; 95% CI, 0.82 to 1.11).

There is insufficient evidence to determine whether there is a clinically important difference between SSRIs plus pindolol and SSRIs plus placebo on:
● increasing the likelihood of achieving remission by the 10th or 14th day of treatment (K = 3; N = 222; Random effects RR = 0.73; 95% CI, 0.44 to 1.20)
● reducing symptoms of depression by the 10th or 14th day of treatment (K = 3; N = 237; Random effects SMD = –0.30; 95% CI, –0.88 to 0.28).

Late assessment point
There is insufficient evidence to determine whether there is a clinically important difference between SSRIs plus pindolol and SSRIs plus placebo on increasing the

---

[191]The forest plots can be found in Appendix 19c.

likelihood of achieving a 50% reduction in symptoms of depression by the 35th or 42nd day of treatment (K = 3; N = 214; RR = 0.75; 95% CI, 0.54 to 1.03).

There is some evidence suggesting that there is a clinically important difference favouring SSRIs plus pindolol over SSRIs plus placebo on increasing the likelihood of achieving remission by the 21st, 28th or 42nd day of treatment (K = 3; N = 253; RR = 0.73; 95% CI, 0.55 to 0.98).

There is evidence suggesting that there is a clinically important difference favouring SSRIs plus pindolol over SSRIs plus placebo on reducing symptoms of depression by the 21st, 35th or 42nd day of treatment, but the size of this difference is unlikely to be of clinical importance (K = 4; N = 282; SMD = −0.26; 95% CI, −0.49 to −0.02).

Acceptability of treatment
There is insufficient evidence to determine whether there is a clinically important difference between SSRIs plus pindolol and SSRIs plus placebo on any measure of tolerability.

Clinical evidence statements: effect of treatment on efficacy for people whose depression is treatment resistant[192]
Early assessment point
For people whose depression is treatment resistant there is evidence suggesting that there is no clinically important difference when assessment is made between days 10 and 14 between pindolol augmentation and antidepressant monotherapy on:
- increasing the likelihood of achieving a 50% reduction in symptoms of depression (K = 1; N = 80; RR = 1; 95% CI, 0.85 to 1.18)
- increasing the likelihood of achieving remission (K = 1; N = 80; RR = 1.03; 95% CI, 0.88 to 1.2).

There is insufficient evidence to determine if there is a clinically important difference between pindolol augmentation and antidepressant monotherapy on reducing symptoms of depression in people whose depression is treatment resistant (K = 1; N = 80; WMD = 1.6; 95% CI, −0.96 to 4.16).

Acceptability of treatment
There are no data on the acceptability of treatment for people whose depression is treatment resistant.

Clinical summary
While there is some evidence of a modest advantage at 21 to 42 days favouring the addition of pindolol to antidepressants over adding placebo on achieving remission, this effect is not evident for response or mean endpoint scores. There is no evidence of any effect on outcomes in people whose depression is treatment resistant at early assessment point. No data were available for late assessment points.

---

[192]The forest plots can be found in Appendix 19c.

There is insufficient evidence to comment on the tolerability of adding pindolol to antidepressants.

It should be noted that there is uncertainty regarding optimum dose and duration of treatment.**

12.3.8 Augmenting an antidepressant with triiodothyronine

The following sections on augmenting an antidepressant with triiodothyronine (T3) marked by asterisks (**_**) are from the previous guideline and have not been updated except for style and minor clarification.

Introduction
**Consistent with the observations that the prevalence of depression is increased in hypothyroidism (Loosen, 1987), and subclinical hypothyroidism is more prevalent in people who are clinically depressed (Maes *et al.*, 1993), T3 has been used as an anti-depressant augmenting agent both to increase the speed of onset of antidepressant response and to increase the magnitude of response.

Increase the speed of onset of antidepressant response
T3, at a dose of 25 mcg per day, may hasten response to TCAs and this effect may be more robust in women (Altshuler *et al.*, 2001). The optimal duration of treatment is unknown although there is a suggestion in the literature that T3 may be safely with-drawn once response has been achieved (Altshuler *et al.*, 2001). There are no studies with SSRIs or any of the newer antidepressants.**

Increase the magnitude of antidepressant response
Although the RCT that satisfied the inclusion criteria set by the GDG found T3 and lithium to be equally effective and superior to placebo (see below), several 'negative' non-RCTs also exist (Steiner *et al.*, 1978; Gitlin *et al.*, 1987; Thase *et al.*, 1989). The response rate has been variable across studies (Aronson *et al.*, 1996). All studies used TCAs. There are no studies with SSRIs or any of the newer antidepressants apart from STAR*D (Rush *et al.*, 2003), which used an open-label design. T4 has been shown to be inferior to T3 in one study (Joffe & Singer, 1990). Most studies used a dose of 37.5 mcg T3 per day. The optimum duration of treatment is unknown.

Studies considered[193,194]
One study was found in a search of electronic databases (Joffe1993a), and this met the inclusion criteria set by the GDG. It compared a range of antidepressants

---

[193]Details of standard search strings used in all searches are in Appendix 8. Information about each study along with an assessment of methodological quality is in Appendix 17c, which also contains a list of excluded studies with reasons for exclusions.

[194]Study IDs in title case refer to studies included in the previous guideline. References for these studies are in Appendix 18.

augmented with T3 (37.5 mcg) with antidepressants augmented with placebo. Participants were outpatients who had not achieved remission after 5 weeks' treatment with either desipramine or imipramine. No new double-blind studies were found in the update search, although the STAR*D (Rush *et al.*, 2003) trial includes a T3 augmentation arm (described elsewhere in this chapter).

Clinical evidence statements[195]

Effect of treatment on efficacy outcomes

**There is some evidence suggesting that there is a clinically important difference favouring T3 augmentation over antidepressant plus placebo on increasing the likelihood of achieving a 50% reduction in symptoms of depression (K = 1; N = 33; RR = 0.51; 95% CI, 0.27 to 0.94).

There is insufficient evidence to determine if there is a clinically important difference between T3 augmentation and antidepressant plus placebo on reducing symptoms of depression (K = 1; N = 33; WMD = -3.9; 95% CI, -8.86 to 1.06).

Acceptability of treatment

There was no evidence on which to assess the acceptability of treatment.

Clinical summary

There is little evidence on which to make an evidence-based recommendation of augmentation of antidepressants with T3 for the treatment of treatment-resistant depression. The prevalence of cardiovascular disease is increased in people with depression (Glassman & Shapiro, 1998) and T3 should be used with caution in cardiovascular disease. Potential adverse effects include tachycardia, anginal pain and arrhythmias. TCAs also have cardiac side effects including arrhythmias, tachycardia and postural hypotension. Caution is advised in combining TCAs and T3.**

12.3.9   Augmenting an antidepressant with a benzodiazepine

The following sections on augmenting an antidepressant with a benzodiazepine marked by asterisks (**_**) are from the previous guideline and have not been updated except for style and minor clarification.

Introduction

**Depression and anxiety commonly co-exist and insomnia is a common symptom of depression. Antidepressants usually take 2 to 4 weeks to have a clinically important effect.

Benzodiazepines are effective anxiolytic and hypnotic drugs with an immediate onset of action and therefore could be expected to produce early improvement in some symptoms of depression. They do not have a specific antidepressant effect.

Benzodiazepines are associated with tolerance and dependence and withdrawal symptoms can occur after 4 to 6 weeks of continuous use. To avoid these problems,

---

[195]The forest plots can be found in Appendix 19c.

it is recommended that they should not routinely be prescribed for their hypnotic or anxiolytic effects for longer than 4 weeks (Royal College of Psychiatrists, 1997; British Medical Association and the Royal Pharmaceutical Society of Great Britain, 2009).

The National Service Framework for Mental Health (Department of Health, 1999) discourages the use of benzodiazepines and many primary care prescribing incentive schemes include low prescribing rates for benzodiazepines as a marker of good practice. A Cochrane review, however, concludes that early time-limited use of benzodiazepines in combination with an antidepressant drug may accelerate treatment response (Furukawa *et al.*, 2002b).

Studies considered[196,197]

The GDG used an existing review (Furukawa *et al.*, 2002b) as the basis for this section. The original review included nine studies of which four met the inclusion criteria set by the GDG (Feet1985, Nolen1993, Scharf1986, Smith1998). New searches of electronic databases found an additional study (Smith2002), which was included in the review. Together these studies provided tolerability data from up to 196 participants and efficacy data from up to 186 participants.**

No new studies were found in the update search.

**All included studies were published between 1985 and 2002 and were between 3 and 12 weeks' long (mean = 7 weeks). One study was of inpatients (Nolen1993), three of outpatients (Feet1985, Smith1998, Smith2002) and in the remaining study (Scharf1986) participants were from mixed sources. No study was undertaken in primary care and none was exclusively of older participants or people with atypical depression. Other than in Feet1985, where participants had been 'treated in general practice without success', study participants were not described as having failed previous courses of antidepressants.

All studies compared an antidepressant plus benzodiazepine with an antidepressant plus placebo. The included trials used the following antidepressant/benzodiazepine combinations:

- maprotiline or nortriptyline plus flunitrazepam (2 mg) or lormetazepam (2 mg) (Nolen1993)
- fluoxetine plus clonazepam (0.5 mg up to 1 mg) (Smith1998, Smith2002)
- imipramine plus diazepam (10 mg) (Feet1985)
- amitriptyline plus chlordiazepoxide (mean 44 mg) (Scharf1986).

The mean dose of TCAs was between 122.5 mg and 200 mg, and fluoxetine was given at between 20 mg and 40 mg.

---

[196]Details of standard search strings used in all searches are in Appendix 8. Information about each study along with an assessment of methodological quality is in Appendix 17c, which also contains a list of excluded studies with reasons for exclusions.

[197]Study IDs in title case refer to studies included in the previous guideline. References for these studies are in Appendix 18.

Clinical evidence statements[198]

Effect of treatment on efficacy

There is insufficient evidence to determine whether there is a clinically important difference between antidepressants plus a benzodiazepine and antidepressants plus placebo on any efficacy measure.

Acceptability of treatment

There is insufficient evidence to determine whether there is a clinically important difference between antidepressants plus a benzodiazepine and antidepressants plus placebo on any tolerability measure.

Clinical summary

There is insufficient evidence to determine whether there is any effect of adding a benzodiazepine to antidepressant treatment in terms of both efficacy and tolerability.**

12.3.10 Augmenting an antidepressant with buspirone

The sections on augmenting an antidepressant with buspirone marked by asterisks (**_**) are from the previous guideline and have not been updated except for style and minor clarification.

Introduction

There are no extractable efficacy data from double-blind RCTS of buspirone augmentation. Buspirone was used in the STAR*D study (Rush *et al.*, 2003), which had an open-label randomised design in which buspirone augmentation of citalopram did not differ significantly in efficacy from bupropion addition in terms of response to treatment, but there was a greater reduction in self-rated depression scores in people taking bupropion.

Clinical evidence statements[199]

Acceptability of treatment

There is insufficient evidence to determine if there is a clinically important difference between buspirone augmentation and SSRI monotherapy on any tolerability measure. In the STAR*D study (Rush *et al.*, 2003), dropout because of side effects was greater with buspirone augmentation than bupropion addition to citalopram.

Clinical summary

There is no double-blind placebo-controlled evidence on which to make an evidence-based recommendation of augmentation of antidepressants with buspirone for the treatment of treatment-resistant depression.

---

[198]The forest plots can be found in Appendix 19c.
[199]Ibid.

12.3.11   Augmenting an antidepressant with atomoxetine

The following section on augmenting an antidepressant with atomoxetine is new for this guideline update.

Studies considered[200]
One study was found in the update search of augmentation with atomoxetine. Summary study characteristics of the included studies are presented in Table 115, with full details in Appendix 17c, which also includes details of excluded studies.

Clinical evidence
Evidence from the important outcomes and overall quality of evidence are presented in Table 116. The full evidence profiles and associated forest plots can be found in Appendix 16c and Appendix 19c, respectively.

Clinical summary
Augmenting an antidepressant with atomoxetine showed no significant effect on symptoms of depression, and increased the number of people leaving treatment early for any reason because of side effects compared with those taking an antidepressant alone.

Table 115: Summary study characteristics for augmentation with atomoxetine

No. trials (Total participants)	1 (146)
Study ID	MICHELSON2007
N/% female	146/71
Mean age (range if mean not given)	45
Study drug	Atomoxetine 66 mg
Antidepressant	Sertraline 146 mg
Setting	Unclear
Length of treatment	8 weeks

---

[200]Study IDs in capital letters refer to studies found and included in this guideline update.

Table 116: Summary evidence profile for atomoxetine augmentation

	Atomoxetine
Mean depression change scores at endpoint	SMD -0.23 (-0.56 to 0.1)
Quality	Moderate
Number of studies; participants	K = 1; n = 141
Forest plot number	Pharm next-step 09.03
Non-response	Not reported
Quality	–
Number of studies; participants	–
Forest plot number	–
Non-remission	RR 1.23 (0.91 to 1.66) (59.7% versus 48.6%)
Quality	Low
Number of studies; participants	K = 1; n = 146
Forest plot number	Pharm next-step 09.02
Leaving treatment early	RR 1.03 (0.51 to 2.06) (18.1% versus 17.6%)
Quality	Low
Number of studies; participants	K = 1; n = 146
Forest plot number	Pharm next-step 09.04
Leaving treatment early due to side effects	RR 1.8 (0.55 to 5.88) (9.7% versus 5.4%)
Quality	Low
Number of studies; participants	K = 1; n = 146
Forest plot number	Pharm next-step 09.05

12.3.12 Sequenced Treatment Alternatives to Relieve Depression (Rush *et al.*, 2003)

Sequenced Treatment Alternatives to Relieve Depression (STAR*D) (Rush *et al.*, 2003) is a four-level study designed to assess treatments in patients who had not responded to previous treatment. At each level patients who had not responded to treatment at the previous level were randomised to different treatment options. At the first level, all patients received citalopram. Those not responding (QIDS-SR >5) moved to level 2 where they were randomised to switch to another antidepressant (bupropion, sertraline or venlafaxine-ER) or to receive an augmentation treatment (bupropion, buspirone or CBT). Those not responding to treatment in level 2 moved to level 3 where they were randomised again to switch to mirtazapine or nortriptyline or to receive an augmentation agent (lithium or T3 for those on bupropion, sertraline or venlafaxine-ER). In addition, those who had not responded to CBT at level 2 were randomised to bupropion or venlafaxine-ER to ensure that all those in level 3 had failed two courses of antidepressants. Those not responding moved to level 3. Those not responding to level 3 treatment moved to level 4 and were re-randomised to tranylcypromine or mirtazapine plus venlafaxine-ER.

The study was designed to be as analogous as possible to real clinical practice. In order to achieve this, patients were allowed to opt out of being randomised to drug switching, augmentation treatments and, in level 2, to CBT. They were not allowed to opt out of randomisation to a particular agent within the drug switching or drug augmentation arms. Also all treatments were given open label. Medication was free to trial participants but they had to pay for CBT treatment (Weissman, 2007). The patient preference aspect of the trial meant that there were 12 permutations of randomisation preferences at level 2, which greatly adds to the complexity of the trial. For example, only data from patients accepting randomisation to an augmenting or switching option including CBT can be used in comparisons with CBT (either as a switching option or as an augmenting treatment).

It is difficult to draw conclusions about suitable sequencing options since there are so many permutations of treatments possible within the trial. Patients who reach level 4 (that is, have failed three drug trials or three drugs plus a course of CBT) will have taken a variety of routes through the study. They may have taken citalopram continuously (augmented with two separate agents), or may have tried three different single antidepressants, or switched from single to combination drugs and back again. The percentage remission achieved by each treatment strategy is shown in Table 117.

Data from RCTs (see Table 118) suggest that switching from one antidepressant to another may be clinically worthwhile, with increased remission rates of around 20% but with some drugs reporting higher remission rates; within-class switches are associated with remission rates of approximately 20%. Open switching studies report higher remission rates when SSRI non-responders are switched to venlafaxine (BALDOMERO2005 [Baldermero *et al.*, 2005]; Rush *et al.*, 2003). This advantage holds in blinded studies, but the magnitude of the benefit is considerably more modest (Rush *et al.*, 2003).

Table 117: Percentage remission by treatment strategy in STAR*D
(Rush *et al.*, 2003)

STAR*D level 1	% remission
Citalopram	28%
STAR*D level 2	**% remission**
Venlafaxine	25%
Sertraline	18%
Bupropion	21%
CBT	25%
Citalopram + bupropion	30%
Citalopram + buspirone	30%
Citalopram + CBT	23%
STAR*D level 3	
Mirtazapine	12%
Nortriptyline	20%
Lithium augmentation	16%
T3 augmentation	21%
STAR*D level 4	
Tranylcypromine	7%
Venlafaxine + mirtazapine	14%

12.3.13 Clinical summary for 'next-step' treatments

The evidence for effective strategies in people whose depression has not responded adequately to treatment is not strong. A common first-line strategy, increasing the dose, is also not supported by convincing evidence of effectiveness, although this strategy may well be effective in some people, particularly if they have been able to tolerate the drug at the initial dose.

The evidence for switching to another antidepressant is stronger, but data for switching between classes of antidepressant is not. Overall, however, switching is likely to be a worthwhile strategy, and data from primary efficacy head-to-head studies suggest that venlafaxine and escitalopram may offer marginal benefits over other antidepressants in this regard. Augmenting with lithium, a second antidepressant or an antipsychotic is also worthwhile, but the effect size is modest clinically and the side effect burden increased. The main message from the STAR*D study (Rush

Table 118: Raw remission rates following switch to another antidepressant (data from RCTs)

	Previous drug	Class	Drug (mean dose [SD])	% remission
STAR*D (Rush *et al.*, 2003) – level 2	Citalopram	SSRI	Sertraline (135 [57.4] mg)	18%
Poirier1999	SSRIs	SSRI	Paroxetine (36.3 mg [4.9])	18%
Ferreri2001[†]	Fluoxetine	TCA-related	Mianserin (60 mg)	18%
STAR*D (Rush *et al.*, 2003) – level 3	Range of ADs	TCA	Nortriptyline (96.8 mg [41.1])	20%
STAR*D (Rush *et al.*, 2003) – level 2	Citalopram	SNRI	Venlafaxine-XR (193.6 mg [106.2])	25%
Poirier1999	SSRIs	SNRI	Venlafaxine (269 mg [46.7])	36%
BALDOMERO2005	SSRIs	SNRI	Venlafaxine-XR (164 mg [64])	52% [Calculated from number randomised rather than ITT population used by study authors]
STAR*D (Rush *et al.*, 2003) – level 2	Citalopram	Other	Bupropion[‡]	21%

[†]Comparators in this trial were continuing with fluoxetine and mianserin augmentation; [‡]Not licensed for depression in the UK.

et al., 2003) is that some patients will achieve remission with each successive treatment strategy although the proportion doing so falls each time. The lack of good objective data to clearly demonstrate the superior efficacy of one strategy over another probably reflects the fact that the overall difference in effect size between strategies is likely to be small. As was seen in the STAR*D study (Rush *et al.*, 2003), some patients have clear preferences for one treatment over another based, at least in part, on perceived acceptability of the treatment and on degree of response to the current treatment.

12.3.14   Health economic evidence and considerations

No evidence on the cost effectiveness of 'next-step' treatments was identified by the systematic search of the economic literature. Details on the methods used for the systematic search of the economic literature are described in Chapter 3, Section 3.6.1.

12.3.15   From evidence to recommendations

Since the evidence for sequencing pharmacological strategies for people whose depression has not responded adequately to initial treatment is weak, the recommendations in the previous guideline are largely unchanged, although they have been updated to reflect new NICE style. Choice of new medication should be guided by similar principles to those guiding choice of initial medication, for example, a drug's potential for side effects. Since it is possible that poor response to initial treatment may be because the treatment was not properly initiated or adhered to, these factors should be reviewed first and increased frequency of follow-up considered.

12.3.16   Clinical practice recommendations

12.3.16.1   When reviewing drug treatment for a person with depression whose symptoms have not adequately responded to initial pharmacological interventions:
- check adherence to, and side effects from, initial treatment
- increase the frequency of appointments using outcome monitoring with a validated outcome measure
- be aware that using a single antidepressant rather than combination medication or augmentation (see 12.3.16.9 to 12.3.16.13) is usually associated with a lower side-effect burden
- consider reintroducing previous treatments that have been inadequately delivered or adhered to, including increasing the dose
- consider switching to an alternative antidepressant.

The evidence for an advantage of switching to another antidepressant over continuing treatment with the existing antidepressant is not strong. In addition, there is insufficient

506

robust evidence about which antidepressant to switch to. Choice should therefore be guided by side effects and possible interactions during the period of the switch.

12.3.16.2 When switching to another antidepressant, be aware that the evidence for the relative advantage of switching either within or between classes is weak. Consider switching to:
- initially a different SSRI or a better tolerated newer-generation antidepressant
- subsequently an antidepressant of a different pharmacological class that may be less well tolerated, for example venlafaxine, a TCA or an MAOI.

12.3.16.3 Do not switch to, or start, dosulepin because evidence supporting its tolerability relative to other antidepressants is outweighed by the increased cardiac risk and toxicity in overdose.

12.3.16.4 When switching to another antidepressant, which can normally be achieved within 1 week when switching from drugs with a short half-life, consider the potential for interactions in determining the choice of new drug and the nature and duration of the transition. Exercise particular caution when switching:
- from fluoxetine to other antidepressants, because fluoxetine has a long half-life (approximately 1 week)
- from fluoxetine or paroxetine to a TCA, because both of these drugs inhibit the metabolism of TCAs; a lower starting dose of the TCA will be required, particularly if switching from fluoxetine because of its long half-life
- to a new serotonergic antidepressant or MAOI, because of the risk of serotonin syndrome[201]
- from a non-reversible MAOI: a 2-week washout period is required (other antidepressants should not be prescribed routinely during this period).

Following several courses of treatment it may be appropriate to refer someone with depression to a specialist (for example, someone with a special interest in treating depression or a specialist service). Before deciding the next course of action, there should be a thorough assessment of factors affecting treatment choice, including suicide risk and associated comorbidities. It may be appropriate to re-introduce previous treatments, if these were not adequately delivered or adhered to.

12.3.16.5 For a person whose depression has failed to respond to various strategies for augmentation and combination treatments, consider referral to a practitioner with a specialist interest in treating depression, or to a specialist service[202].

---

[201]Features of serotonin syndrome include confusion, delirium, shivering, sweating, changes in blood pressure and myoclonus.
[202]The evidence for this recommendation has not been updated since the previous guideline. Any wording changes have been made for clarification only.

12.3.16.6 The assessment of a person with depression referred to specialist mental health services should include:

- their symptom profile, suicide risk and, where appropriate, previous treatment history
- associated psychosocial stressors, personality factors and significant relationship difficulties, particularly where the depression is chronic or recurrent
- associated comorbidities including alcohol and substance misuse, and personality disorders[203].

12.3.16.7 In specialist mental health services, after thoroughly reviewing previous treatments for depression, consider reintroducing previous treatments that have been inadequately delivered or adhered to[204].

12.3.16.8 Medication in secondary care mental health services should be started under the supervision of a consultant psychiatrist.

Given the higher side-effect burden of taking two drugs rather than one, combining medication would not normally be an initial next-step option. However, there is some evidence of efficacy. Most of the data published since the previous guideline are for augmentation of an antidepressant with an antipsychotic, and this shows some benefit. However, antipsychotics do not have UK marketing authorisation for use in depression. There is still limited evidence for combinations of antidepressants. The recommendations are largely unchanged, but the one for augmentation with a benzodiazepine has been amended since this strategy is recommended elsewhere in the guideline for the short-term management of agitation.

12.3.16.9 When using combinations of medications (which should only normally be started in primary care in consultation with a consultant psychiatrist):

- select medications that are known to be safe when used together
- be aware of the increased side-effect burden this usually causes
- discuss the rationale for any combination with the person with depression, follow GMC guidance if off-label medication is prescribed, and monitor carefully for adverse effects
- be familiar with primary evidence and consider obtaining a second opinion when using unusual combinations, the evidence for the efficacy of a chosen strategy is limited or the risk–benefit ratio is unclear
- document the rationale for the chosen combination.

12.3.16.10 If a person with depression is informed about, and prepared to tolerate, the increased side-effect burden, consider combining or augmenting an antidepressant with:

- lithium **or**

---

[203]Ibid.
[204]Ibid.

- an antipsychotic such as aripiprazole, olanzapine, quetiapine or risperidone[205] **or**
- another antidepressant such as mirtazapine or mianserin.

12.3.16.11 When prescribing lithium:
- monitor renal and thyroid function before treatment and every 6 months during treatment (more often if there is evidence of renal impairment).
- consider ECG monitoring in people with depression who are at high risk of cardiovascular disease
- monitor serum lithium levels 1 week after initiation and each dose change until stable, and every 3 months thereafter.

12.3.16.12 When prescribing an antipsychotic, monitor weight, lipid and glucose levels, and side effects (for example, extrapyramidal side effects and prolactin-related side effects with risperidone).

12.3.16.13 The following strategies should not be used routinely:
- augmentation of an antidepressant with a benzodiazepine for more than 2 weeks as there is a risk of dependence
- augmentation of an antidepressant with buspirone, carbamazepine, lamotrigine or valproate as there is insufficient evidence for their use
- augmentation of an antidepressant with pindolol or thyroid hormones as there is inconsistent evidence of effectiveness[206].

12.4   ELECTROCONVULSIVE THERAPY

12.4.1   Introduction

Electroconvulsive therapy (ECT) has been used as a treatment for depression since the 1930s. In its modern form ECT is perceived by many healthcare professionals to be a safe and effective treatment for severe depression that has not responded to other standard treatments (Geddes *et al.*, 2003b). But many others, including many patient groups, consider it to be an outdated and potentially damaging treatment (Rose *et al.*, 2003). During ECT, an electric current is passed briefly through the brain, via electrodes applied to the scalp, to induce generalised seizure activity. The individual receiving treatment is placed under general anaesthetic and muscle relaxants are given to prevent body spasms. The ECT electrodes can be placed on both sides of the head (bilateral placement) or on one side of the head (unilateral placement). Unilateral placement is usually to the non-dominant side of the brain, with the aim of reducing cognitive side effects. The standard bilateral placement is bitemporal/temporofrontal but some studies have used bifrontal placement in the hope of reducing cognitive side effects associated with the standard placement. The number

---

[205]Aripiprazole, olanzapine, quetiapine and risperidone do not have UK marketing authorisation for the indication in question at the time of publication. Informed consent should be obtained and documented.

[206]Buspirone, carbamazepine, lamotrigine, valproate, pindolol and thyroid hormones do not have UK marketing authorisation for the indication in question at the time of publication. Informed consent should be obtained and documented.

of sessions undertaken during a course of ECT usually ranges from six to twelve, although a substantial minority of patients responds to fewer than six sessions. ECT is usually given twice a week in the UK; less commonly it is given once a fortnight or once a month as continuation or maintenance therapy to prevent the relapse of symptoms. It can be given on either an inpatient or day patient basis.

ECT causes short-term disorientation immediately after treatment and may cause short- or long-term memory impairment for past events (retrograde amnesia) and current events (anterograde amnesia). These effects appear to be dose related and depend on electrode placement, possibly the type of electrical stimulus and patient characteristics (Ingram *et al.*, 2008). However the persistence, severity and precise characterisation of such impairments are still a subject of debate. There is preliminary evidence that prolonged short-term disorientation immediately after treatment predicts retrograde amnesia after the end of a course of treatment (Sobin *et al.*, 1995) but not 2 months after the course. Cognitive impairments have been highlighted as a particular concern by many patients, especially retrograde amnesia for autobiographical events (Rose *et al.*, 2003). There is no simple relationship between subjective cognitive impairment and cognitive test measures, which has contributed to polarising views about the relative risks and benefits of ECT.

At present there is a lack of consensus as to the best method of assessing cognitive function during a course of ECT. The benefit of using only a global measure such as the MMSE in its original or modified form (3MSE) is uncertain given the inconsistent effects of ECT on these measures in trials. And given the evidence that the ability to learn new material (anterograde memory) recovers after the end of ECT treatment, a main concern is in the early detection and minimisation of persistent retrograde memory loss, particularly for important autobiographical memories. Detecting cognitive impairments only at the end of treatment does not give the practitioner the opportunity to alter treatment to attempt to minimise this, although it may lead the practitioner to consider cognitive remediation; there is no evidence, however, to show that this is effective. A battery consisting of a formal mood rating scale (MADRS), the 3MSE, an autobiographical memory task, a word learning task, and tests of digit span forward and backward has been suggested (Porter *et al.*, 2008), but it takes an hour to administer.

In line with NICE policy regarding the relationship of technology appraisals to clinical practice guidelines, this guideline updates the NICE technology appraisal on ECT (TA59) only for depression in adults (the TA covered the use of ECT in the treatment of mania and schizophrenia as well as depression in children and adolescents; NICE, 2003).

Key points to emerge from the reviews underpinning the NICE TA on ECT (NICE, 2003), which concluded that ECT is an effective treatment, include:

- real ECT had greater short-term benefit than sham ECT
- ECT had greater benefit than the use of certain antidepressants
- bilateral ECT was reported to be more effective than unilateral ECT
- the combination of ECT with pharmacotherapy was not shown to have greater short-term benefit than ECT alone
- cognitive impairment does occur but may only be short term

- compared with placebo, continuation pharmacotherapy with tricyclic antidepressants and/or lithium reduced the rate of relapses in people who had responded to ECT
- preliminary studies indicate that ECT is more effective than repetitive transcranial magnetic stimulation.

12.4.2   Databases searched and the inclusion/exclusion criteria

For the updated review double-blind RCTs were sought that compared ECT either with sham ECT or another active treatment in the treatment of people experiencing an acute depressive episode or in relapse prevention following successful treatment (either with ECT or another treatment). Information about the databases searched and the inclusion/exclusion criteria used are presented in Table 119. Details of the search strings used are in Appendix 8.

12.4.3   Studies considered[207]

In total, 21 new trials were found from searches of electronic databases. These included: ten trials comparing ECT with transcranial magnetic stimulation (TMS), which the GDG did not review since NICE has produced guidance on TMS (NICE, 2007d); four trials of continuation treatment following successful treatment with ECT (two of which included continuation ECT), which are considered in the section on relapse prevention, and eight comparing bilateral with unilateral ECT, which are considered in the section on next-step treatments. Several studies included populations with a relatively high proportion of participants with bipolar disorder (up to 30%). These were included since ECT is not known to cause switching to mania (and, indeed, is used as a treatment for mania).

Summary study characteristics of the included studies are presented in Table 120, with full details in Appendix 17c, which also includes details of excluded studies.

Table 119: Databases searched and inclusion/exclusion criteria for clinical effectiveness of ECT

Electronic databases	MEDLINE, EMBASE, PsycINFO, CINAHL
Date searched	January 2002 to January 2008
Update searches	July 2008; January 2009
Study design	RCT
Population	People with a diagnosis of depression according to DSM, ICD or similar criteria
Treatments	ECT

---

[207]Study IDs in capital letters refer to studies found and included in this guideline update.

Table 120: Summary study characteristics of studies of ECT or of treatment following successful ECT published since the systematic reviews underpinning the NICE TA were undertaken

	Relapse prevention studies following remission with ECT	Next-step treatment studies (bilateral ECT versus unilateral ECT)
No. trials (Total participants)	4 RCTs (305)	8 RCTs (472)
Study IDs	(1) GRUNHAUS2001 (2) KELLNER2006 (3) NAVARRO2008 (4) VAN den BROEK2006	(1) ESCHWEILER2007 (2) HEIKMAN2002B (3) McCALL2002 (4) RANJKESH2005 (5) SACKEIM2008 (6) SIENAERT2009 (7) STOPPE2006 (8) TEW2002
N/% female	(1) 39/56 (2) 201/68 (3) 38/55 (4) 27/74	(1) 92/58 (2) 24/54 (3) 77/64 (4) 45/60 (5) 90/57 (6) 81/60 (7) 39/56 (8) 24/not reported
Mean age	(1) 60 (2) 57 (3) 70 (4) 51	(1) 54 (2)–(3) 57 (4) 35 (5) 50 (6) 55 (7) 75 (8) 67
Diagnosis	(1) MDD, 17% psychotic features (2) MDD, 39% psychotic features (3) MDD, 100% psychotic features (4) MDD, 33% psychotic features	(1) MDD and failed $>= 2$ antidepressants courses (2) MDD, 21% psychotic features (3)–(4) MDD (5) MDD, 30% with bipolar disorder

Continued

Table 120: (*Continued*)

	Relapse prevention studies following remission with ECT	**Next-step treatment studies (bilateral ECT versus unilateral ECT)**
		(6) MDD, 20% with bipolar disorder, 27% with psychotic features (7) MDD, 33% psychotic features (8) MDD, some psychotic features (% not reported), insufficient response to 5–8 unilateral ECT (150% above seizure threshold)
Treatments (% above seizure threshold)	(1) Fluoxetine 20 mg – 40 mg + melatonin 5 mg or 10 mg versus fluoxetine 20 mg–40 mg (2) ECT versus nortriptyline + lithium (3) Nortriptyline versus nortriptyline + ECT (4) Imipramine versus placebo	(1) Bilateral 50% versus unilateral 150% (2) Bilateral 0% versus unilateral 400% versus unilateral 150% (3) Bilateral 50% versus unilateral 700% (4) Bilateral 50% versus bilateral 0% versus unilateral 400% (5) Bilateral 150% (separate groups for ultra brief and brief ECT) versus unilateral ECT 500% (separate groups for ultra brief and brief ECT) (6) Bilateral 50% versus unilateral 500% (7) Bilateral 'high' dose versus unilateral 'high' dose (8) Bilateral 150% versus unilateral 450%
Placement	Not examined	(1)–(2) Bifrontal (3) Bitemporal (4)–(6) Bifrontal (7)–(8) Bitemporal

Continued

513

Table 120: (*Continued*)

	Relapse prevention studies following remission with ECT	Next-step treatment studies (bilateral ECT versus unilateral ECT)
Setting	(1) Israel; unclear (2) US; unclear (3) Spain; inpatients + outpatients (4) Holland; inpatients	(1) Germany and Austria; inpatients (2) Finland; inpatients (3) US; unclear (4) Iran; unclear (people referred for ECT) (5) US; inpatients (6) US; unclear (7) Brazil; inpatients (8) US; unclear
Length of treatment	(1) 12 weeks (2) 6 months (3) 24 months (outcomes at 6 months and 24 months) (4) 6 months	(1) 6 treatments (2) Unclear (3) Mean 5.8 sessions (4) >= 8 treatments (5) >= 5 treatments (6) Mean 8 sessions (7) 4–16 treatments (8) >= 3 treatments

0% = just above seizure threshold.

Two older trials on relapse prevention following response to ECT were also discussed narratively (Lauritzen1996, Sackheim2001); see Section 12.4.5.

12.4.4 Clinical evidence for ECT as a next-step treatment

The TA reviews of ECT compared with sham ECT and with pharmacological interventions were not updated because no new studies were found. However, the review comparing bilateral ECT with unilateral ECT, including a sub-analysis by dose, was updated. In addition a narrative review of cognitive impairment related to electrode placement and dose was undertaken.

Bilateral ECT versus unilateral ECT
A review by Geddes and colleagues (2003b) was used as the basis of this review. The effect sizes reported in the published paper were input into CMA (Comprehensive Meta-Analysis) and combined with effect sizes from the eight new studies found (see Table 120 for a summary of these studies). The overall SMD calculated by Geddes

and colleagues (2003b) from 22 studies and 1,137 particpiants was -0.322 (Random effects) (-0.458 to -0.186). With the addition of the relevant new data the SMD effect size was reduced slightly to -0.23 (Random effects) (-0.37, -0.09) (31[208] studies, 1,693 participants; $I^2 = 39\%$), thus confirming an overall small to medium effect favouring bilateral ECT (see Figure 10).

Bilateral ECT versus unilateral ECT – the effect of dose and electrode placement on efficacy

For this guideline update, a sub-analysis by dose was also undertaken on efficacy related to electrode placement. This topic was also included in the review by Geddes and colleagues (2003b), which included seven studies comparing different doses of unilateral ECT and different doses of bilateral ECT, as well as five that specifically compared bilateral ECT with unilateral ECT at doses related to seizure threshold. These five studies were included in the sub-analysis (SACKHEIM1993, SACK-HEIM2000; Malitz *et al.*, 1986; Sackeim *et al.*, 1987; Letemendia *et al.*, 1993).

Dose was classified based on percentage above seizure threshold (one new study described doses as 'high' [STOPPE2006]). Doses described as 'just above seizure threshold' were classified 0%. The doses given in the studies available for the sub-analysis are in Table 121.

Low-dose unilateral ECT was defined as doses up to 150% above seizure threshold (that is, including low and standard doses used clinically) and high-dose unilateral ECT was defined as doses over 150% above seizure threshold. There was insufficient evidence to show a difference between low-dose bilateral ECT and low-dose unilateral ECT from the available studies in this subset, although the direction of effect was similar to that in the full set (see Table 122). On one outcome measure (non-remission) high-dose unilateral ECT tended to be more effective than low-dose bilateral ECT but this was not clinically important and no differential benefit was suggested with the other outcome measures. Evidence from the important outcomes and overall quality of evidence are presented in Table 122. The full evidence profiles and associated forest plots can be found in Appendix 16c and Appendix 19c, respectively.

A visual inspection of the forest plots indicated that there appears to be neither no consistent effect for different bilateral electrode placement (bifrontal or bitemporal) nor a consistent relationship between electrode placement and dose, although there are insufficient studies to allow these factors to be explored systematically.

Cognitive side effects related to electrode placement and dose

Geddes and colleagues (2003b) reported that patients who received bilateral ECT seemed to take longer to recover orientation than those treated with unilateral ECT (based on six trials that reported this), and that they showed greater impairment in retrograde memory (based on four trials that reported this) and anterograde memory (seven trials reported this). Geddes and colleagues (2003b) also report that they found only two trials reporting long-term data, which were both small and underpowered,

---

[208]There are 30 studies, but SACKHEIM2008 includes four treatment groups that were used as two separate comparisons.

Figure 10: Bilateral ECT versus unilateral ECT: updated forest plot

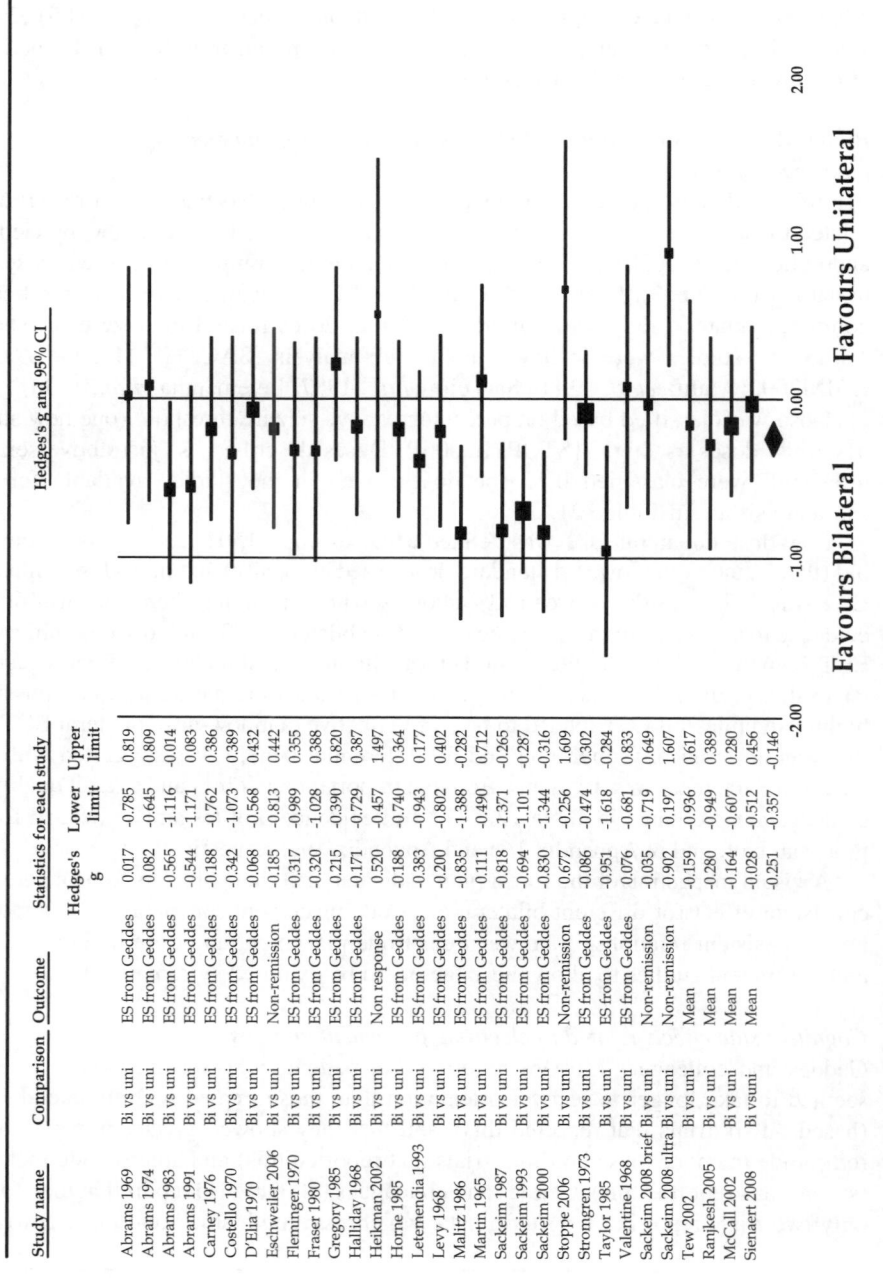

Table 121: Doses (% above seizure threshold) of bilateral ECT and unilateral ECT given in the available studies

	Bilateral group 1	Bilateral group 2	Unilateral group 1	Unilateral group 2	Unilateral group 3
ESCHWEILER2007	50%	–	150%	–	–
HEIKMAN2002	0%	–	400%	150%	–
Letemendia *et al.*, 1993*	0%	–	0%	–	–
Malitz *et al.*, 1986*	0%	–	0%	–	–
MCCALL2002	150	–	800%	–	–
RANJKESH2005	0%	50%	400%	–	–
SACKEIM1993*	0%[†]	250%[†]	0%[†]	250%[†]	–
SACKEIM2000*	150%	–	50%[†]	150%	500%[†]
SACKEIM 2008	150%	–	50%[†]	150%	500%[†]
SIENAERT2009	–	–	–	–	–
STOPPE2006	'High'	–	'High'	–	–
TEW2002	150%	–	450%	–	–

0% indicates just above seizure threshold; *From Geddes *et al.* (2003) review; [†]Groups used in Geddes *et al.* (2003) analysis of dose effects.

and which found no long-term differences between bilateral and unilateral ECT on cognitive functioning.

In the studies considered the GDG has taken bifronto-temporal placement as bitemporal. Combining the new studies with relevant studies from Geddes and colleagues (2003b) there was comparison between different doses of bitemporal ECT and unilateral ECT in six studies, between bifrontal ECT and unilateral ECT in four studies and between bifrontal ECT and bitemporal ECT in one study (see Table 123). In SACKHEIM1993 and SACKEIM2008 approximately 30% of patients had bipolar disorder and in SIENAERT2008 20% of patients had bipolar disorder; both were included in this review of cognitive effects.

The new studies had differences in bilateral electrode placement (bifrontal compared with the standard bitemporal placement) and in stimulus pulse width (ultra brief pulse compared with standard brief pulse). There was variation in the lower/'standard' dose of bitemporal ECT with 150% above seizure threshold often used in key US studies compared with lower UK recommendations from the Royal College of Psychiatrists (50 to 100% above seizure threshold) (Royal College of Psychiatrists, 2005). As explored quantitatively below (see Table 123), high dose (≥400% above seizure threshold) unilateral ECT generally appeared as effective as low/standard dose (0 to 150% above seizure threshold) bilateral ECT, whether bitemporal or bifrontal.

Table 122: Summary evidence profile for acute-phase ECT: bilateral ECT versus unilateral ECT

	Low-dose bilateral ECT versus low-dose unilateral ECT	Low-dose bilateral ECT versus high-dose unilateral ECT
Mean depression scores at endpoint (clinician-rated)	SMD −0.46 (−1.69 to 0.76)	SMD 0.01 (−0.27 to 0.29)
Quality	Very low	Moderate
Number of studies; participants	K = 2; n = 91	K = 4; n = 204
Forest plot number	Pharm next-step 12.05	Pharm next-step 12.08
Non-response	RR 0.65 (0.35 to 1.21) (52% versus 69.7%)	RR 0.98 (0.74 to 1.29) (35.2% versus 36.1%)
Quality	Very low	High
Number of studies; participants	K = 4; n = 217	K = 7; n =362
Forest plot number	Pharm next-step 12.04	Pharm next-step 12.06
Non-remission	RR 0.93 (0.77 to 1.14) (64.2% versus 68.7%)	RR 1.24 (0.97 to 1.6) (52.5% versus 42.9%)
Quality	High	Moderate
Number of studies; participants	K = 2; n = 134	K = 5; n = 237
Forest plot number	Pharm next-step 12.05	Pharm next-step 12.07

One study including low dose unilateral ECT arms found them to be less effective than standard dose bilateral and high dose unilateral ECT. Another study found that threshold dose unilateral ECT was less effective than low/standard dose bilateral ECT.

The range of cognitive side-effects assessments varied between studies and were not consistent with regard to global scores (MMSE/3MS), but more consistent memory effects (including autobiographical memory impairment) were seen.

Previous studies have suggested that bifrontal ECT may cause fewer cognitive effects than bitemporal ECT but with similar efficacy (Lawson *et al.*, 1990; Letemendia *et al.*, 1993; Bailine *et al.*, 2000) so the two types of bilateral ECT were considered separately.

In the five studies in which bitemporal low/standard dose ECT was compared with unilateral high dose ECT, two found no difference in cognitive effects, two found that

Table 123: Studies comparing bilateral and unilateral ECT: reported differences in cognitive functioning and efficacy

Study	Comparison	Dose above threshold	MMSE/3MS	Other cognition	Efficacy
ESCHWEILER2007	BF versus UL	50% versus 150%	No change with treatment (BF = UL)	Reorientation time BF = UL. Non-verbal anterograde amnesia (BF < UL) and decreased verbal fluency with treatment (BF = UL)	Equal (low response rate)
HEIKMAN2002	BF versus high dose UL versus lower dose UL	0% versus 400% versus 150%	No change with treatment (BF = UL)	–	High dose UL faster onset, tendency to greater response
MCCALL2002	BT versus UL	50% versus 700%	–	AMI, anterograde amnesia with treatment but improved at 4 weeks; still below baseline for AMI (BT = UL)	Equal
RANJKESH2005	BT versus BF versus UL	0% versus 50% versus 400%	Decreased with treatment (BF < BT = UL)	–	Equal
SACKEIM1993	BT versus BT versus UL versus UL	0% versus 150% versus 0% versus 150%	Decreased BT versus UL after treatment; improved versus baseline after 2 months (BT = UL)	Prolonged disorientation BT > UL. Retrograde and anterograde amnesia: BT > UL/ higher dose > lower dose/ interaction site x dose depending on test used after treatment. Improved or no change versus baseline at 2 months	Both BT ≥ higher dose UL > lower dose UL

Continued

Table 123: *(Continued)*

Study	Comparison	Dose above threshold	MMSE/3MS	Other cognition	Efficacy
SACKEIM2000/LISANBY2000	BT versus 3 doses UL	150% versus 50% versus 150% versus 500%	Decreased with treatment (BT > UL-dose related)	Anterograde and retrograde amnesia, AMI, persisting to 2 months (BT > UL-mostly dose related)	BT = high dose UL, both > lower dose UL
SACKEIM2008	BT versus $\dagger BT_{ub}$ versus UL versus $\dagger UL_{ub}$	150% versus 150% versus 450% versus 450%	Decrease with treatment standard versus ub (BT = UL)	Reorientation time, anterograde and retrograde amnesia, AMI less in ub groups (AMI difference persisting to 6 months). AMI less in UL groups. $\dagger UL_{ub}$ group had no significant cognitive effects	$\dagger BT_{ub} <$ other groups
SIENAERT2008	$\dagger BF_{ub}$ versus $\dagger UL_{ub}$	50% versus 500%	Increased with treatment (BF = UL)	–	UL faster onset, equal response
STOPPE2006	BT versus UL	Both fixed high dose	Decrease with treatment in BT versus UL	Trend to more delirium with BT versus UL. No significant change in anterograde and retrograde amnesia, AMI 1 month after treatment, some improvement with UL not BL. Overall BT = UL	Equal
TEW2002	*BT versus UL	150% versus 450%	Decrease with treatment in BT versus UL	–	Equal

*Bilateral mode not explicitly stated but taken as bitemporal; †Ultra brief pulse (0.3 msec).
Abbreviations: AMI, autobiographical memory impairment; BF, bifrontal; BT, bitemporal; UL, right unilateral; ub, ultra brief pulse.

bitemporal ECT caused a greater global decrease and one found that bitemporal ECT caused greater impairment of autobiographical memory but not other measures of retrograde and anterograde memory. In one study a global decrease in cognitive function with high dose bitemporal ECT compared with high dose unilateral ECT was seen. The studies in which bitemporal ECT worsened cognitive function compared with unilateral ECT mostly used high standard doses (150% above seizure threshold).

In the three studies where bifrontal low/standard dose ECT was compared with high dose unilateral ECT, two studies found no difference in global cognitive effects and one found less impairment. A study where both doses were low found no difference in most cognitive effects except less non-verbal anterograde amnesia with bifrontal ECT. A study of low and standard doses of bitemporal and unilateral ECT found effects of both dose, electrode placement and their interaction depending on the test used, which had recovered to above baseline 2 months after ECT. In two studies there was faster onset of improvement with high dose unilateral ECT.

Ultra-brief pulse (0.3 msec) high dose ECT caused no cognitive impairment in two studies and cognitive impairment was significantly less than standard brief pulse (1.5 msec) treatment in one study.

A soon-to-be reported large study comparing bitemporal (50% above seizure threshold), bifrontal (50% above seizure threshold) and right unilateral (400% above seizure threshold) with a 1msec pulse width, similar to treatment practice in the UK, has found few differences in cognitive effects and efficacy between placements (Charles Kellner, personal communication, 2009).

The NICE TA on ECT (NICE, 2003) concluded that cognitive impairment is greater in individuals who have had electrodes applied bilaterally than in those who have had them placed unilaterally, and that unilateral placement to the dominant hemisphere causes more impairment than placement to the non-dominant hemisphere. They also found that raising the stimulus threshold above the individual's seizure threshold increased the efficacy of unilateral ECT at the expense of increased cognitive impairment. Overall the conclusion was that reduction in the risk of cognitive impairment is mirrored by a reduction in efficacy.

The new studies provide insufficient evidence to determine whether efficacy and cognitive side effects can be dissociated by manipulating electrode placement and stimulus dose or parameters. Results with high dose ultra-brief unilateral ECT need to be replicated.

Effect of ethnicity

The data from the acute phase of the KELLNER2006 trial included in the analyses above were also analysed by race, looking at data for black and white participants separately (Williams, M. D., *et al.*, 2008). Of 515 participants, 483 were white and 32 black. Of these, 63.4% of white participants and 71.9% of black participants achieved remission. The difference was not statistically significant, although may indicate a trend towards ECT being more effective in black participants. It should be noted that the study was undertaken in the US where the ethnic populations are different from those in England and Wales so the results of this study are unlikely to be generalisable.

12.4.5 Relapse prevention following successful treatment with ECT in relapse prevention

Four studies were found of continuation treatment after successful treatment with ECT, two of which included maintenance ECT (see Table 124; the full evidence profiles and associated forest plots can be found in Appendix 16c and Appendix 19c, respectively). In these studies, there was little difference after 6 months between adding ECT to an antidepressant and maintaining the antidepressant alone, or between ECT alone compared with a combination of nortriptyline and lithium. However, at 12 months, fewer participants experienced relapse if they had received ECT plus nortriptyline compared with those continuing treatment with nortriptyline alone. Similar data were not available for the other study.

In studies of pharmacological maintenance strategies (see Table 125), only nortriptyline plus lithium was effective (compared with placebo), although there was a trend towards nortriptyline plus lithium compared with nortriptyline alone being more effective. The data are weak since there is only one study comparing each strategy, with relatively low numbers. However, the data suggest that combination treatment with nortriptyline and lithium may be effective in reducing the likelihood of relapse following successful treatment with ECT.

A further small study randomised 74 patients following response to ECT to paroxetine or placebo in those with cardiovascular disease and paroxetine or

Table 124: Summary evidence profile for relapse prevention with ECT

	ECT + nortriptyline versus nortriptyline	ECT versus nortriptyline + lithium
Relapse – 1st follow-up	6 months RR 0.5 (0.05 to 4.98) (6.3% versus 12.5%)	6 months RR 1.16 (0.77 to 1.74) (33.7% versus 29.1%)
Quality	Low	Low
Number of studies; participants	K = 1; n = 32	K = 1; n = 201
Forest plot number	Pharm Relapse prevention 10.01	Pharm Relapse prevention 10.01
Relapse – 2nd follow-up	12 months RR 0.12 (0.02 to 0.89)	Not reported
Quality	Moderate	–
Number of studies; participants	K = 1; n = 32	–
Forest plot number	Pharm relapse-prevention 10.01	–

Table 125: Summary evidence profile for studies of pharmacological strategies for relapse prevention following successful ECT

	Fluoxetine + placebo versus fluoxetine + melatonin	Nortriptyline + lithium versus placebo	Nortriptyline versus placebo	Nortriptyline + lithium versus nortriptyline
Relapse – 1st follow-up	12 weeks RR 1.17 (0.4 to 3.39) (27.8% versus 23.8%)	6 months RR 0.44 (0.25 to 0.8) (32.1% versus 72.4%)	6 months RR 0.77 (0.51 to 1.15) (56.6% versus 72.4%)	6 months RR 0.6 (0.32 to 1.14) (32.1% versus 53.6%)
Quality	Low	Moderate	Low	Low
Number of studies; participants	K = 1; n = 39	K = 1; n = 57	K = 1; n = 56	K = 1; n = 56
Forest plot number	Pharm Relapse prevention 10.01	Pharm Relapse prevention 10.01	Pharm Relapse prevention 10.01	Pharm Relapse prevention 10.01

imipramine in those without (Lauritzen *et al.*, 1996). Using survival analysis there was a significant benefit for paroxetine over placebo although this was only at trend level at the end of 6 months, and for paroxetine over imipramine.

12.4.6 Continuation/maintenance ECT and cognitive function

A particular concern in the NICE TA on ECT (NICE, 2003) about continuation or maintenance ECT was the lack of evidence about potential long-term cognitive effects. Since then there have been further data published although the numbers of patients studied remains relatively small.

In the only prospective RCT of continuation ECT compared with continuation antidepressants after acute ECT treatment (Kellner *et al.*, 2007), the MMSE improved in both groups over the 6 months after the end of acute-phase treatment with no difference between those who had not relapsed or dropped out. At 3 months, however, the continuation ECT group had improved less than the antidepressant group and one of the 15 who stopped treatment early in the ECT group did so because of memory loss. Russell and colleagues (2003) reported a retrospective evaluation of 43 patients who had received maintenance ECT for at least a year. They had an improved clinical status and slight improvement in their MMSE scores compared with before starting ECT. Adverse effects included falls, delirium and cardiac dysrhythmia, each in about 10% of patients but none causing significant morbidity. Rami-Gonzalez and colleagues (2003) undertook a cross sectional study of 11 patients on maintenance ECT compared with a matched group not receiving ECT. The patients receiving ECT had impaired encoding of new information and frontal lobe test results compared with the control group but no difference in delayed recall. Vothknecht and colleagues (2003) undertook a prospective study (mean 61 weeks) of 11 patients receiving maintenance ECT compared with 13 patients receiving only antidepressants. There was no difference between groups on a test battery including attention and concentration, anterograde memory and frontal lobe function. An equal number in each group had subjective memory complaints. Rami and colleagues (2004) reported results on a prospective assessment of 26 patients of whom 20 carried on with maintenance ECT over 1 year in comparison with 10 controls. There were no differences found between groups or significant changes over 1 year in attention and concentration, anterograde memory and frontal lobe function. There have also been a few case reports showing no effects on cognitive function with maintenance ECT (Wijkstra & Nolen, 2005; Zisselman *et al.*, 2007).

12.4.7   Health economic evidence and considerations

The systematic literature search identified only one economic evaluation on ECT by Greenhalgh and colleagues (2005) as part of the HTA on ECT. The economic evaluation was undertaken to determine the cost effectiveness of ECT for depressive illness as well as schizophrenia, catatonia and mania. The authors developed an economic model based on how ECT is used in the UK for people with major depressive disorder who require hospitalisation. The analysis compared inpatient administered ECT with other pharmacological treatments (TCAs, SSRIs, SNRIs and lithium augmentation). These therapies were sequenced in several ways so as to form eight scenarios in which ECT featured as a first-, second- and third-line therapy. Expert opinion and data from the clinical effectiveness evidence review and other relevant studies were used to develop the model. Resource use patterns and costs were sourced from published literature. Health utility scores were adapted from a study by Bennett and colleagues (2000) and incorporated in the model. The evaluation failed to demonstrate, however, that any of the scenarios had a clear economic benefit over any of the others. This was due to high levels of uncertainty around the effectiveness data and the utility estimates.

The Greenhalgh and colleagues' (2005) study was one of the first attempts to evaluate the cost effectiveness of ECT and although many of the model inputs were based on published literature many assumptions underlay the results due to the lack of available data. The authors pointed out that one of the main drawbacks in terms of cost effectiveness of prescribing ECT was the associated high resource use. They also mention a higher rate of relapse with ECT than pharmacological therapies. This statement points to one of the limitations of this evaluation. Studies with very dissimilar populations were combined to compute model inputs such as relapse and response rates, while medication trials with patient populations that were less depressed or not treatment resistant were combined with populations who were treatment resistant or referred specifically for ECT. Underlying patient characteristics do play a vital role in determining the outcomes of studies and using data in this way makes the accuracy of the effectiveness estimates used in the model questionable. However, the authors did acknowledge the lack of data and conducted many sensitivity analyses, which further emphasised the uncertainty of the results. The authors of the HTA pointed to the clear need for RCTs that directly compare the efficacy of treating severely depressed patients with ECT versus pharmacological treatments.

For the effectiveness update, reviews of ECT with pharmacological interventions were not updated since no new studies were found. As a result, the cost effective analysis was not updated. However, the review comparing bilateral ECT with unilateral ECT, including a sub-analysis by dose, was updated. The HTA explored these differences by varying the efficacy, outcomes and cost in the sensitivity analysis to incorporate the different approaches used in providing ECT with no effect on results. There should be no resource use differences between bilateral versus unilateral treatment. The clinical evidence review shows little difference in effect between bilateral and unilateral ECT with a slight advantage for bilateral ECT. These results are in keeping with previous effectiveness evidence.

The authors also mentioned uncertainty around the utility estimates used from the study by Bennett and colleagues (2000). In this study the depression-specific McSad health state classification system was utilised; NICE recommends using a generic tool (NICE, 2004a). The health state descriptions used referred to untreated depression. The population of the study consisted of patients who had experienced at least one episode of major unipolar depression in the previous 2 years but who were currently in remission. This is not typical of the patients who are usually prescribed ECT. This study therefore, may underestimate quality of life gains from the treatment and also potentially overestimate benefit if cognitive impairment following ECT is taken into account. However, utility data for mental health related conditions are very sparse and at the time this study was one of a very small number of studies available for patients with depression. The utility values were also subject to sensitivity analysis, with no effect on the results. To date no studies have been found describing health-related quality of life in which the health states have been determined in a group of patients with chronic or severe depression requiring or having received ECT.

ECT is resource intensive, however, patients who require such treatment usually have a chronic form of the illness or undergo several treatment options before being referred on for ECT. This group of people usually makes up a small proportion of the entire depressive population in a health system and the costs they incur to health systems can be quite significant. The clinical evidence points to ECT having a higher success rate for certain groups of people with severe depression, and providing this high cost intervention may prove to be cost effective as it may reduce subsequent resource use and potentially improve quality of life if prescribed as recommended.

12.4.8   From evidence to recommendations

The review of ECT for the updated guideline found relatively little additional data to update the reviews undertaken for the original NICE TA (NICE, 2003). There were no new data comparing ECT with sham ECT, antidepressants, or combination treatment in the acute phase and limited new data in the continuation phase after acute treatment.

Integrating the evidence for ECT with that for other treatments for depression it is evident that many people with depression have a poor response to treatment. In addition the definition of the severity of depression has altered between the previous guideline and this guideline update so that many patients previously defined as severely depressed would now be included in the moderate severity category. For this reason, while ECT is still not recommended as a routine treatment for moderately severe depression, it is presented as an option in those with moderate depression who have repeatedly not responded to both drug and psychological treatment.

The new data comparing bilateral ECT with unilateral ECT did not change the conclusion that bilateral ECT is more effective than unilateral for people with depression, although the effect size is small and complicated by variations in dosing and electrode placement. A sub-analysis by dose suggests that high dose unilateral ECT (doses over 150% above seizure threshold) may be at least as effective as low/standard dose bilateral ECT but there are relatively few data and it was not possible to explore this quantitatively.

For cognitive impairment, it is still not clear to what degree the trade-off between efficacy and cognitive side effects can be avoided by manipulating dose and electrode placement. There is, however, evidence that bilateral ECT causes more cognitive impairment than unilateral ECT and that the cognitive impairment and efficacy from unilateral ECT are dose related. This has now been included in the guidance together with more detailed advice on how and when to measure cognitive side effects and on the principles of choice of electrode placement and dose in relation to efficacy and cognitive side effects.

There are some data on continuation/maintenance ECT that support at least equal efficacy in preventing relapse compared with pharmacotherapy but the evidence is limited. Systematic, prospective assessment of longer-term cognitive effects of continuation/maintenance ECT are also limited although those available do not suggest cumulative cognitive adverse effects. Given the relative lack of data, no treatment recommendation is made with regard to continuation/maintenance ECT.

However, in recognition that continuation/maintenance ECT will continue to be used in exceptional circumstances, and that conclusive RCT data are unlikely to be available in the short-to- medium term, a research recommendation on collecting data for national audit when continuation/maintenance ECT is used has been added (see Section 12.4.10).

Relapse prevention using pharmacological strategies has also been examined, and the data suggest that continuation antidepressants particularly with lithium augmentation of antidepressants is effective.

12.4.9   Recommendations

12.4.9.1   Consider ECT for acute treatment of severe depression that is life-threatening and when a rapid response is required, or when other treatments have failed.

12.4.9.2   Do not use ECT routinely for people with moderate depression but consider it if their depression has not responded to multiple drug treatments and psychological treatment.

12.4.9.3   For people whose depression has not responded well to a previous course of ECT, consider a repeat trial of ECT only after:

● reviewing the adequacy of the previous treatment course **and**

- considering all other options **and**
- discussing the risks and benefits with the person and/or, where appropriate, their advocate or carer.

12.4.9.4 When considering ECT as a treatment choice, ensure that the person with depression is fully informed of the risks associated with ECT, and with the risks and benefits specific to them. Document the assessment and consider:
- the risks associated with a general anaesthetic
- current medical comorbidities
- potential adverse events, notably cognitive impairment
- the risks associated with not receiving ECT.

The risks associated with ECT may be greater in older people; exercise particular caution when considering ECT treatment in this group.

12.4.9.5 A decision to use ECT should be made jointly with the person with depression as far as possible, taking into account, where applicable, the requirements of the Mental Health Act 2007. Also be aware that:
- valid informed consent should be obtained (if the person has the capacity to grant or refuse consent) without the pressure or coercion that might occur as a result of the circumstances and clinical setting
- the person should be reminded of their right to withdraw consent at any time
- there should be strict adherence to recognised guidelines about consent, and advocates or carers should be involved to facilitate informed discussions
- if informed consent is not possible, ECT should only be given if it does not conflict with a valid advance decision and the person's advocate or carer should be consulted.

12.4.9.6 The choice of electrode placement and stimulus dose related to seizure threshold should balance efficacy against the risk of cognitive impairment. Take into account that:
- bilateral ECT is more effective than unilateral ECT but may cause more cognitive impairment
- with unilateral ECT, a higher stimulus dose is associated with greater efficacy, but also increased cognitive impairment compared with a lower stimulus dose.

12.4.9.7 Assess clinical status after each ECT treatment using a formal valid outcome measure, and stop treatment when remission has been achieved, or sooner if side effects outweigh the potential benefits.

12.4.9.8 Assess cognitive function before the first ECT treatment and monitor at least every three to four treatments, and at the end of a course of treatment.

12.4.9.9 Assessment of cognitive function should include:
- orientation and time to reorientation after each treatment
- measures of new learning, retrograde amnesia and subjective memory impairment carried out at least 24 hours after a treatment.

If there is evidence of significant cognitive impairment at any stage consider, in discussion with the person with depression, changing from bilateral to unilateral electrode placement, reducing the stimulus dose or stopping treatment depending on the balance of risks and benefits.

12.4.9.10 If a person's depression has responded to a course of ECT, antidepressant medication should be started or continued to prevent relapse. Consider lithium augmentation of antidepressants.

12.4.10   Research recommendations

12.4.10.1 The effectiveness of maintenance ECT for relapse prevention in people with severe and recurring depression that does not respond to pharmacological or psychological interventions

Is maintenance ECT effective for relapse prevention in people with severe and recurring depression that does not respond to pharmacological or psychological interventions?

Why this is important

A small number of people do not benefit in any significant way from pharmacological or psychological interventions but do respond to ECT. However, many of these people relapse and need repeated treatment with ECT. This results in considerable suffering to them and it is also costly, because ECT often necessitates inpatient care. A small number of studies suggest possible benefits from maintenance ECT but it is used little in the NHS. The outcome of the audit and clinical trial should supply information on patient characteristics, outcomes, feasibility and acceptability in relation to the use of maintenance ECT and potentially inform its wider use in the NHS. The results therefore may have important implications for the provision of ECT in the NHS.

This question should be addressed through first establishing a national audit for the collection of data on all people receiving maintenance ECT. The characteristics of the people who are likely to be considered for maintenance ECT make a randomised controlled trial unfeasible, but a clinical trial using alternative methods (for example, mirror image or a carefully characterised non-randomised study) should be undertaken depending on the outcome of the audit.

The number of people receiving maintenance ECT is small, and considerable uncertainty surrounds its use, such as its long-term efficacy and acceptability and possible side effects, which include cognitive impairment. The outcomes chosen for the audit and clinical trial should reflect both observer and patient-rated assessments of improvement, the impact on cognitive function and an assessment of the acceptability of ECT as a maintenance treatment.

12.5   OTHER NON-PHARMACOLOGICAL PHYSICAL TREATMENTS

12.5.1   Transcranial magnetic stimulation

Transcranial magnetic stimulation (TMS) involves focal stimulation of the superficial layers of the cerebral cortex using a rapidly changing magnetic field applied using an external coil. It does not require anaesthesia and can be performed on an outpatient basis. Treatment with TMS usually involves daily sessions lasting about 30 minutes for 2 to 4 weeks and possibly longer. Its use in the treatment of depression has recently been the subject of NICE Interventional Procedures Guidance (IPG 242; NICE, 2007d).

The main points highlighted in the review and guidance were:

● Uncertainty about the procedure's clinical efficacy, which may depend on higher intensity, greater frequency, bilateral application and/or longer treatment durations than have appeared in the evidence to date.

● No major safety concerns associated with TMS.

Included in the review was consideration of a meta-analysis of 33 short-term RCTs in depression (Herrmann & Ebmeier, 2006), which found a large significant effect size of 0.71 against sham treatment. However, the studies were small, heterogeneous in methodology and effect size and it was not possible to identify any significant predictors of outcome. A more recent meta-analysis for patients with treatment-resistant depression, which included 24 studies (1,092 patients) meeting their inclusion criteria (Lam *et al.*, 2008), found that active repetitive transcranial magnetic stimulation (rTMS) was significantly superior to sham conditions in producing clinical response, with a risk difference of 17%. However the pooled response and remission rates were only 25% and 17%, and 9% and 6% for active rTMS and sham conditions respectively. They concluded that further studies are required before adopting rTMS as a first-line treatment for treatment-resistant depression.

12.5.2 From evidence to recommendations

The guideline uses the recommendation from the current NICE Interventional Procedure Guidance on TMS (IPG 242, NICE, 2007d).

12.5.3 Recommendation

12.5.3.1 Current evidence suggests that there are no major safety concerns associated with transcranial magnetic stimulation (TMS) for severe depression. There is uncertainty about the procedure's clinical efficacy, which may depend on higher intensity, greater frequency, bilateral application and/or longer treatment durations than have appeared in the evidence to date. TMS should therefore be performed only in research studies designed to investigate these factors.

12.5.4 Vagus nerve stimulation

Vagus nerve stimulation (VNS) therapy is a type of treatment where a small electrical pulse is administered through an implanted neurostimulator to a bipolar lead attached to the left vagus nerve. A battery-powered pulse-generating device is implanted under the skin of the upper left chest. A wire is tunnelled under the skin and connected to the left vagus nerve in the neck.

The stimulation parameters (pulse width and frequency, current intensity, and on/off cycles) are programmed into the pulse generator via a programming wand. The battery lasts 8 to 10 years and can be replaced under local anaesthesia. A typical treatment regimen might comprise intermittent stimulation for 30 seconds every 5 minutes throughout the day and night. This procedure has been studied in patients with treatment-resistant epilepsy and it is indicated for use as an adjunctive therapy in reducing the frequency of seizures in patients who are refractory to anti-epileptic medication. NICE guidance on VNS for refractory epilepsy in children concluded that current evidence appears adequate to support the use of this procedure 'provided that the normal arrangements are in place for consent, audit and clinical governance' (IPG 50, NICE, 2004c). In addition antidepressant effects of VNS in epilepsy patients have been described, independent of reduction of seizure frequency (for example, Harden *et al.*, 2000).

The efficacy and safety of VNS for treatment-resistant depression is currently under consideration by the NICE Interventional Procedures Advisory Programme. Readers concerned with the efficacy and safety of VNS, and recommendations about its use to treat depression, should refer to this document which is expected to be published in 2010.

12.6 THE PHARMACOLOGICAL MANAGEMENT OF RELAPSE PREVENTION

The following sections on the pharmacological management of relapse prevention marked by asterisks (**_**) are from the previous guideline and have not been updated except for style and minor clarification.

12.6.1 Introduction

Major depressive disorder is among the most important causes of death and disability worldwide in both developing and developed countries (Murray & Lopez, 1997a). Because of the long-term nature of depression, with many patients at substantial risk of later recurrence, there is a considerable need to establish how long such patients should stay on antidepressants. Existing clinical guidelines recommend that treatment should be continued for 4 to 6 months after the acute episode (Anderson *et al.*, 2000; APA, 2000b; Bauer *et al.*, 2002a). There is considerable variation in practice, suggesting that many patients do not receive optimum treatment. Geddes and colleagues (2003a) reviewed all published and unpublished trials available for review by August 2000 in which continued antidepressant drug therapy was compared with placebo in patients who had responded to acute treatment with antidepressants. It was found that antidepressants reduced the risk of relapse in depression and continued treatment with antidepressants appeared to benefit many patients with recurrent depression. The treatment benefit for an individual patient depended on their absolute risk of relapse with greater absolute benefits in those at higher risk. It was estimated that for patients who were still at appreciable risk of recurrence after 4 to 6 months of treatment with antidepressants, another year of continuation treatment would approximately halve their risk. The authors found no evidence to support the contention that the risk of relapse after withdrawal from active treatment in the placebo group was due to a direct pharmacological effect (for example, 'withdrawal' or 'rebound') since there was not an excess of cases within a month of drug discontinuation.

12.6.2   Studies considered[209],[210]

The GDG used the review by Geddes and colleagues (2003a) as the basis for the review in the previous guideline. This included 37 studies of which 20 met the inclusion criteria set by the GDG. An additional five studies were identified in searches for the previous guideline, one of which was excluded. Another study was identified through searching journal tables of contents and a further study was identified from searches undertaken for the review of lithium augmentation elsewhere in this guideline. Both of these were included. Therefore, 26 studies formed the basis of this review in the previous guideline (Alexopoulous2000, Bauer2000, Cook1986, Doogan1992, Feiger1999, Frank1990, Georgotas1989, Gilaberte2001, Hochstrasser-2001, Keller1998, Kishimoto1994, Klysner2002, Kupfer1992, Montgomery1988, Montgomery1992, Montgomery1993, Prien1984, Reimherr1998, Robert1995, Robinson1991, Sackheim2001, Schmidt2000, Terra1998, Thase2001, Versiani1999, Wilson2003) and 18 were excluded.

A further nine studies were identified in update searches and added to the review (GORWOOD2007 [escitalopram versus placebo]; KORNSTEIN2006A [escitalopram versus placebo]; MCGRATH2006 [fluoxetine versus placebo]; PERAHIA2006 [duloxetine versus placebo]; PREVENT STUDY [studyA and study B: venlafaxine-ER versus placebo]; RAPAPORT2004 [escitalopram versus placebo]; RAPA-PORT2006A [risperidone + citalopram versus placebo + citalopram]; VAN den BROEK2006 [imipramine versus placebo]).

**Studies included a pre-maintenance phase during which participants continued to receive medication after they had achieved remission. This was followed by a maintenance phase in which participants who had achieved remission were randomised either to pharmacological treatment or to placebo. Studies were included provided participants were classified as remitted, only if they no longer met diagnosis for major depression or had achieved an HRSD or MADRS score below the cut-off for mild depression. Similarly, studies were included only if participants had been assessed as having relapsed using some kind of formal criteria such as exceeding a specific HRSD or MADRS score or meeting formal diagnostic criteria for depression rather than clinical judgement alone.

---

[209]Details of standard search strings used in all searches are in Appendix 8. Information about each study along with an assessment of methodological quality is in Appendix 17c, which also contains a list of excluded studies with reasons for exclusions.

[210]Study IDs in title case refer to studies included in the previous guideline and study IDs in capital letters refer to studies found and included in this guideline update. References for studies from the previous guideline are in Appendix 18.

A single outcome (number of study participants experiencing relapse) was extracted. Since the length of both the pre-maintenance and the maintenance phase varied between studies, sub-analyses were undertaken splitting the dataset as follows:

● by length of continuation treatment (that is, length of time continued with medication after remission but before randomisation) – less than or more than 6 months

● by length of maintenance treatment – less than or more than 12 months.

The longest maintenance phase was 2 years. Further sub-analyses were undertaken combining these factors – for example, studies with pre-maintenance treatment of less than 6 months and maintenance treatment of less than 12 months.**

Fifteen studies used an SSRI as the maintenance treatment, eight studies used a TCA, and seven studies used other antidepressants. Three studies compared lithium (with and without an antidepressant) with an antidepressant or placebo[211]. One study compared SSRIs augmented with other agents with the SSRI alone. Twenty-seven studies used the same treatment in both acute and maintenance phases and four did not.

All included studies were published between 1984 and 2008. In 21 studies participants were described as outpatients, one was from primary care and in the others it was either not clear from where participants were sourced or they were from mixed sources. There were no studies of inpatients. Five studies were classified elderly, and none was of atypical depression.

Of the 25 trials of antidepressant medication, 13 (Bauer2000, Cook1986, Frank1990, Gilaberte2001, Hochstrasser2001, Kishimoto1994, Kupfer1992, Montgomery1988, Montgomery1993, PERAHIA2006, Robinson1991, Terra1998, Versiani1999) included only participants who had had at least one previous depressive episode. Five studies (Alexopoulos2000, Feiger1999, Klysner2002, Thase2001, Wilson2003) were of participants with a mix of first episode and previous episode depression. For the purpose of a sub-analysis by number of episodes, two of these (Klysner2002, Wilson2003) were classified first episode since more than 70% of participants were in their first episode. In the remaining seven studies (Doogan 1992, Georgotas1989, Keller1998, Montgomery1992, Robert1995, Schmidt2000, Sackheim2001) it was not possible to assess the proportion of participants with first or subsequent episode depression. Additional sub-analyses were undertaken by number of previous episodes.

12.6.3   Clinical evidence statements[212]

Effect of treatment on relapse
In an analysis of all available data comparing maintenance treatment with an antidepressant with placebo, there is strong evidence suggesting that there is a clinically important difference favouring continuing antidepressant treatment over discontinuing antidepressant treatment on reducing the likelihood of relapse (K = 32; N = 4982; RR = 0.46; 95% CI, 0.4 to 0.52; RD = −0.25 [−0.29 to −0.22]).

---

[211]One four-arm trial (Prien1984) has both antidepressant and lithium treatment groups.
[212]The forest plots can be found in Appendix 19c.

**There was little difference in the results of sub-analyses by length of pre-randomisation treatment or by post-randomisation treatment, by a combination of these factors, or between results for SSRIs and TCAs analysed separately. Nor was any difference found for patients in their first episode or for those with previous episodes.

With regard to lithium augmentation:

There is some evidence suggesting that there is a clinically important difference on reducing the likelihood of relapse favouring continuing lithium augmentation of an antidepressant over:

- discontinuing lithium (that is, continuing on antidepressant monotherapy) (K = 3; N = 160; RR = 0.58; 95% CI, 0.37 to 0.92).
- discontinuing lithium and antidepressant treatment (that is, taking a placebo) (K = 2; N = 129; RR = 0.42; 95% CI, 0.28 to 0.64).

In patients who have achieved remission while taking an antidepressant plus lithium, there is some evidence suggesting that there is a clinically important difference favouring discontinuing lithium treatment (that is, continuing with the antidepressant alone) over discontinuing antidepressant treatment (that is, continuing lithium alone) on reducing the likelihood of patients experiencing a relapse in symptoms of depression (K = 1; N = 77; RR = 1.75; 95% CI, 1.03 to 2.96).

In patients who have achieved remission while taking an antidepressant plus lithium, there is insufficient evidence to determine if there is a clinically important difference between discontinuing antidepressant treatment (that is, continuing with lithium alone) and discontinuing antidepressant and lithium treatment (that is, taking a placebo) on reducing the likelihood of patients experiencing a relapse in symptoms of depression (K =1; N = 71; RR = 0.88; 95% CI, 0.60 to 1.28).

12.6.4   Clinical summary

The majority of study participants in this review had experienced multiple depressive episodes. There is strong evidence that responders to medication, who have had multiple relapses, should stay on medication to avoid relapse, irrespective of the length of treatment pre-response (between 6 weeks and 12 months). This effect holds true beyond 12 months. From the available data, it is not possible to determine effects beyond 2 years. These effects were evident with both TCAs and SSRIs. Whether this effect is evident in those recovering from a first episode or with placebo is unknown. Since most studies randomised participants either to continue with medication or to a placebo, there is little data comparing lengths of maintenance treatment with active medication.

12.6.5   Health economic evidence and considerations

No evidence on the cost effectiveness of the pharmacological management of relapse prevention was identified by the systematic search of the economic literature. Details on the methods used for the systematic search of the economic literature are described in Chapter 3, Section 3.6.1.

12.6.6 From evidence into recommendations

The previous guideline recommended initially continuing treatment for at least 6 months after remission, and up to 2 years for patients who are high risk of relapse. There is no new evidence that suggests that these recommendations should be changed. For patients who have achieved remission while taking lithium in addition to an antidepressant it appears to be worthwhile continuing both treatments. If one or other drug is stopped, the evidence, while suggestive that lithium should be stopped in preference to the antidepressant, is based on a single small study and this was not considered sufficient to support a strong recommendation. The recommendations have been updated to match the new NICE style.

12.6.7 Recommendations

12.6.7.1 Support and encourage a person who has benefited from taking an antidepressant to continue medication for at least 6 months after remission of an episode of depression. Discuss with the person that:
- this greatly reduces the risk of relapse
- antidepressants are not associated with addiction.

12.6.7.2 Review with the person with depression the need for continued antidepressant treatment beyond 6 months after remission, taking into account:
- the number of previous episodes of depression
- the presence of residual symptoms
- concurrent physical health problems and psychosocial difficulties.

12.6.7.3 For people with depression who are at significant risk of relapse or have a history of recurrent depression, discuss with the person treatments to reduce the risk of recurrence, including continuing medication, augmentation of medication or psychological treatment (CBT). Treatment choice should be influenced by:
- previous treatment history, including the consequences of a relapse, residual symptoms, response to previous treatment and any discontinuation symptoms
- the person's preference.

12.6.7.4 Advise people with depression to continue antidepressants for at least 2 years if they are at risk of relapse. Maintain the level of medication at which acute treatment was effective (unless there is good reason to reduce the dose, such as unacceptable adverse effects) if:
- they have had two or more episodes of depression in the recent past, during which they experienced significant functional impairment
- they have other risk factors for relapse such as residual symptoms, multiple previous episodes, or a history of severe or prolonged episodes or of inadequate response

- the consequences of relapse are likely to be severe (for example, suicide attempts, loss of functioning, severe life disruption, and inability to work).

12.6.7.5 When deciding whether to continue maintenance treatment beyond 2 years, re-evaluate with the person with depression, taking into account age, comorbid conditions and other risk factors.

12.6.7.6 People with depression on long-term maintenance treatment should be regularly re-evaluated, with frequency of contact determined by:
- comorbid conditions
- risk factors for relapse
- severity and frequency of episodes of depression.

12.6.7.7 People who have had multiple episodes of depression, and who have had a good response to treatment with an antidepressant and an augmenting agent, should remain on this combination after remission if they find the side effects tolerable and acceptable. If one medication is stopped, it should usually be the augmenting agent. Lithium should not be used as a sole agent to prevent recurrence.

12.6.8   Research recommendations

12.6.8.1   Sequencing antidepressant treatment after inadequate initial response
What is the best medication strategy for people with depression who have not had sufficient response to a first SSRI antidepressant after 6 to 8 weeks of adequate treatment?

Why this is important
Inadequate response to a first antidepressant is a frequent problem but the best way of sequencing treatments is not clear from the available evidence. There is good evidence that the likelihood of eventual response decreases with the duration of depression and number of failed treatment attempts so that maximising the response at an early stage may be an important factor in final outcome. The results of this study will be generalisable to a large number of people with depression and will inform choice of treatment.

This question should be addressed using a randomised controlled trial design and compare the effects of continuing on the same antidepressant (with dose increase if appropriate) and switching to another SSRI or to an antidepressant of another class. Built into the design should be an assessment of the effect of increased frequency of follow-up and monitoring alone on improvement. The outcomes chosen should reflect both observer and patient-rated assessments of improvement and an assessment of the acceptability of the treatment options. The study needs to be large enough to determine the presence or absence of clinically important effects using a non-inferiority design, and mediators and moderators of response should be investigated.

13 THE MANAGEMENT OF SUBTHRESHOLD DEPRESSIVE SYMPTOMS

13.1 INTRODUCTION

The previous guideline made recommendations only for major depressive disorder. However, the scope for the update included the management of milder depressive disorders, including subthreshold depressive symptoms and persistent subthreshold depressive symptoms (including dysthymia). This chapter brings together the evidence for pharmacological and psychological interventions for this group.

Depression that is 'subthreshold', that is, does not meet the full criteria for a depressive/major depressive episode is increasingly recognised as causing considerable morbidity and human and economic costs. It is more common in those with a history of major depression and is a risk factor for future major depression (Rowe & Rapaport, 2006).

There is no accepted classification for this in the current diagnostic systems with the closest being minor depression, a research diagnosis in DSM–IV. At least two but less than five symptoms are required of which one must be depressed mood or diminished interest. It is important to realise that this overlaps with ICD–10 depressive episode with four symptoms (see also Appendix 11). Given the practical difficulty and inherent uncertainty in deciding thresholds for significant symptom severity and disability, there is no natural discontinuity between subthreshold depressive symptoms and mild major depression in routine clinical practice.

Both DSM–IV and ICD–10 have the category of dysthymia, which consists of depressive symptoms which are subthreshold for major depression but which persist (by definition for more than 2 years). There appears to be no empirical evidence that dysthymia is distinct from subthreshold depressive symptoms apart from duration of symptoms, and the term persistent subthreshold depressive symptoms is preferred in this guideline. The term dysthymia is still used in this chapter when describing the evidence from studies using this term.

ICD–10 has a category of mixed anxiety and depression, which is less clearly defined than minor depression in DSM–IV, and is largely a diagnosis of exclusion in those with anxiety and depressive symptoms subthreshold for specific disorders. It is a heterogeneous category with a lack of diagnostic stability over time and for this reason it has not been specifically included in this guideline.

This chapter is in two major sections: the first considers pharmacological strategies and the second psychological interventions (including studies comparing pharmacological treatments with psychological interventions) for subthreshold depressive symptoms and persistent subthreshold depressive symptoms (dysthymia).

13.2 PHARMACOLOGICAL INTERVENTIONS FOR SUBTHRESHOLD DEPRESSIVE SYMPTOMS AND PERSISTENT SUBTHRESHOLD DEPRESSIVE SYMPTOMS (DYSTHYMIA)

13.2.1 Introduction

Although milder depressive disorders are common there has been much less research carried out into their treatment and their definitions have been more varied. Best recognised in classification systems has been dysthymia (subthreshold depressive symptoms that have persisted for at least 2 years), an acknowledgment that chronic disorders tend to persist and therefore may warrant treatment even if relatively mild. The assumption has been that acute subthreshold depressive symptoms have a high natural remission rate and therefore do not benefit from active treatment. This is supported by post-hoc analyses of two studies (Stewart *et al.*, 1983; Paykel *et al.*, 1988), which found that patients with depression below the threshold for major depression generally responded well and showed no advantage for a TCA over placebo, unlike those with major depression. Similarly two RCTs in primary care of enhanced treatment resulting in improved medication adherence showed benefits for the intervention over treatment as usual in those with major depression but not in those with subthreshold depressive symptoms, where, again, improvement was the rule (Katon *et al.*, 1996; Peveler *et al.*, 1999).

A problem in the evidence base is that many studies involving people with persistent subthreshold depressive symptoms often have a mixed population including those with major depression. There is also the difficulty that because dysthymia requires 2 years of symptoms, there is little evidence on outcomes in patients with intermediate durations of illness (for example, from about 3 months to 2 years) on which to determine the point at which subthreshold depressive symptoms become sufficiently persistent to warrant specific treatment; it is unlikely that this occurs only after 2 years. In UK clinical practice the term dysthymia has not been embraced, probably because of confusion about what it includes, the duration required, difficulty in ruling out prior major depression (which would technically make it partially remitted major depression), and lack of guidelines on its treatment.

13.2.2 Databases searched and the inclusion/exclusion criteria

Information about the databases searched for published trials and the inclusion/exclusion criteria used are presented in Table 126. Details of the search strings used are in Appendix 8.

Table 126: Databases searched and inclusion/exclusion criteria for clinical effectiveness of pharmacological treatments

Electronic databases	MEDLINE, EMBASE, PsycINFO, CINAHL
Date searched	Database inception to January 2008
Update searches	July 2008; January 2009
Study design	RCT
Population	People with a diagnosis of dysthymia, minor depression or subthreshold according to DSM, ICD or similar criteria
Treatments	Any pharmacological treatment

13.2.3 Study characteristics[213]

In total, 52 trials were sourced from searches of electronic databases, with 20 being included and 32 excluded. A number of trials included populations with a mixture of diagnoses, including dysthymia, subthreshold depressive symptoms and major depressive disorder. Trials in which more than 50% of participants had a diagnosis of major depressive disorder were excluded from this review (but included in other reviews where appropriate). The majority of trials were of acute-phase treatments, with one being of relapse prevention. Summary study characteristics of the included studies are presented in the following sections, with full details in Appendix 17d, which also includes details of excluded studies.

Data were available to compare antidepressants and one antipsychotic with placebo, and to compare a range of antidepressants, and antidepressants with antipsychotics.

13.2.4 Acute-phase pharmacological interventions for persistent subthreshold depressive symptoms (dysthymia)

Studies considered for placebo-controlled trials
A total of nine placebo-controlled trials met inclusion criteria. Summary study characteristics of the included studies are presented in Table 127, with full details in Appendix 17d, which also includes details of excluded studies.

---

[213]Here and elsewhere in the guideline, each study considered for review is referred to by a 'study ID' made up of first author and publication date (unless a study is in press or only submitted for publication, when first author only is used). Study IDs in capital letters refer to studies found and included in this guideline update. References for studies from the update are in Appendix 17d.

Table 127: Summary study characteristics of placebo-controlled RCTs of pharmacological treatments for dysthymia

	SSRIs	TCAs	MAOIs	Antipsychotics
No. trials (Total participants)	6 RCTs (1226)	4 RCTs (654)	1 RCT (212)	1 RCT (219)
Study IDs	(1) BARRETT1999* (2) HELLERSTEIN1993 (3) RAVINDRAN1999 (4) RAVINDRAN2000 (5) THASE1996A (6) VANELLE1997	(1) BAKISH1993 (2) BOYER1999 (3) THASE1996A (4) VERSIANI1997	(1) VERSIANI1997	(1) BOYER1999
N/% female	(1) 232†/50 (2) 35/46 (3) 97/58 (4) 310/67 (5) 274†/65 (6) 140/76	(1) 50/50 (2) 121†/75 (3) 276†/65 (4) 207†/71	(1) 212†/71	(1) 219†/75
Mean age (range if not given)	(1) 61 (2) 36 (3) 21–54 (4) 45 (5) 42 (6) 43	(1) 38 (2) 48 (3) 42 (4) 41	(1) 41	(1) 48

Continued

Table 127: *(Continued)*

	SSRIs	TCAs	MAOIs	Antipsychotics
Drug	(1) Paroxetine (2) Fluoxetine (3)–(5) Sertraline (6) Fluoxetine	(1) Imipramine (2) Amineptine (3)–(4) Imipramine	(1) Moclobemide	(1) Amisulpride
Setting	(1) Primary care (2) Community/referral (3) Community (4)–(5) Outpatients (6) Mixed	(1)–(4) Outpatients	(1) Outpatients	(1) Outpatients
Length of treatment	(1) 11 weeks (2) 8 weeks (3)–(5) 12 weeks (6) 13 weeks	(1) 7 weeks (2)–(3) 12 weeks (4) 8 weeks	(1) 8 weeks	(1) 12 weeks

*Sample divided into dysthymia or minor depression and included in relevant analysis accordingly; †N with dysthymia in relevant antidepressant and placebo groups.

Clinical evidence for placebo-controlled trials

All treatments were effective compared with placebo (quality of evidence: low, moderate and high). Compared with placebo, fewer participants taking an SSRI or an MAOI left treatment early for any reason, but more participants left treatment early if they took a TCA or an antipsychotic. More left treatment early specifically because of side effects if they had taken a psychotropic drug than if they had taken placebo, while the number reporting side effects (not reported for MAOIs) was also greater in the active treatment groups. Evidence from the important outcomes and overall quality of evidence are presented in Table 128 and Table 129. The full evidence profiles and associated forest plots can be found in Appendix 16d and Appendix 19d, respectively.

Studies considered for head-to-head studies

There were 11 studies making head-to-head comparisons of active treatments, including antidepressants and antipsychotics. Four studies had fewer than 100% of participants with dysthymia (although all had at least 50% with dysthymia). These studies were analysed separately. Two studies used a mixed sample but it was possible to extract dysthymia data separately. Summary study characteristics of the included studies are presented in Table 130, with full details in Appendix 17d, which also includes details of excluded studies.

Clinical evidence for head-to-head studies

For those with dysthymia there was no difference in efficacy either between different antidepressants (quality of evidence: low) or between antidepressants and antipsychotics (quality of evidence: moderate or high). However, in studies with participants with other subthreshold depressive symptoms (see Table 132) an antipsychotic was more effective than an SSRI (amisulpride compared with sertraline), although this was not the case when an antipsychotic was compared with a TCA where there was no difference (quality of evidence: low or moderate). See Table 131 and Table 132 for the summary evidence profiles of efficacy data.

In studies where all participants had dysthymia, SSRIs were more acceptable to participants than other antidepressants, with fewer leaving treatment early for any reason (quality of evidence: moderate), and fewer leaving early specifically because of side effects (quality of evidence: moderate). Amisulpride appeared more acceptable and tolerable than amitriptyline, but the effect sizes were small and not clinically important (quality of evidence: moderate or low). In studies where not all participants had dysthymia, there was inconclusive evidence on the acceptability of an SSRI compared with another antidepressant (quality of evidence: low), some evidence that an SSRI was more acceptable than an antipsychotic (quality of evidence: moderate), but other evidence was inconclusive and graded low in quality.

Evidence from the important outcomes and overall quality of evidence are presented in Table 131, Table 132, Table 133 and Table 134. The full evidence profiles and associated forest plots can be found in Appendix 16d and Appendix 19d, respectively.

Table 128: Summary evidence profile for pharmacological treatments versus placebo for dysthymia (efficacy data)

	SSRIs	TCAs	MAOIs	Antipsychotics
Non-response	RR 0.72 (0.63 to 0.82) (41.6% versus 64.6%)	RR 0.52 (0.37 to 0.73) (36.8% versus 71.1%)	RR 0.5 (0.36 to 0.71) (35.7% versus 71.1%)	Not reported
Quality of evidence	High	Moderate	Moderate	–
Number of studies/ participants	K = 5; n = 727	K = 1; n = 144	K = 1; n = 146	–
Forest plot number	Pharm subthreshold 01.01	Pharm subthreshold 01.01	Pharm subthreshold 01.01	–
Non-remission	RR 0.78 (0.68 to 0.89) (52.7% versus 66.7%)	RR 0.81 (0.63 to 1.03) (58.8% versus 71.3%)	Not reported	Not reported
Quality of evidence	High	Low	–	–
Number of studies/ participants	K = 3; n = 608	K = 2; n = 420	–	–

Forest plot number	Pharm subthreshold 01.02	Pharm subthreshold 01.02	–	–
Mean endpoint/ mean change	SMD −0.56 (−0.83 to −0.29) SMD −0.31 (−0.51 to −0.11)	SMD −0.62 (−0.9 to −0.35) SMD −0.61 (−0.9 to −0.31)	Not reported SMD −0.97 (−1.32 to −0.62)	SMD −0.66 (−0.94 to −0.38) SMD −0.67 (−0.95 to −0.39)
Quality of evidence	High High	Moderate Moderate	Not reported Moderate	Moderate Moderate
Number of studies/ participants	K = 2; n = 219 K = 2; n = 385	K = 1; n = 212 K = 3; n = 623	Not reported K = 1; n = 139	K = 1; n = 206 K = 1; n = 206
Forest plot number	Pharm subthreshold 01.03 Pharm subthreshold 01.05	Pharm subthreshold 01.03 Pharm subthreshold 01.05	Not reported Pharm subthreshold 01.05	Pharm subthreshold 01.03 Pharm subthreshold 01.05

Table 129: Summary evidence profile for treatments versus placebo for dysthymia (acceptability/tolerability data)

	SSRIs	TCAs	MAOI	Antipsychotics
Leaving treatment early for any reason	RR 0.84 (0.57 to 1.24) (18.9% versus 21.8%)	RR 1.1 (0.84 to 1.44) (23.2% versus 21.2%)	RR 0.83 (0.42 to 1.67) (12% versus 14.4%)	RR 0.66 (0.36 to 1.22) (14.5% versus 20.4%)
Quality of evidence	Low	Moderate	Low	Moderate
Number of studies/participants	K = 6; n = 1030	K = 4; n = 734	K = 1; n = 212	K = 1; n = 212
Forest plot number	Pharm subthreshold 02.01	Pharm subthreshold 02.01	Pharm subthreshold 02.01	Pharm subthreshold 02.01
Leaving treatment early due to side effects	RR 1.77 (0.71 to 4.41) (4.9% versus 2.8%)	RR 5.44 (2.66 to 11.11) (12.3% versus 2.2%)	RR 3.37 (0.72 to 15.85) (6.5% versus 1.9%)	RR 3.12 (0.33 to 29.47) (2.9% versus 0.9%)
Quality of evidence	Moderate	High	Moderate	Low
Number of studies/participants	K = 2; n = 497	K = 4; n = 735	K = 1; n = 212	K = 1; n = 212
Forest plot number	Pharm subthreshold 02.02	Pharm subthreshold 02.02	Pharm subthreshold 02.02	Pharm subthreshold 02.02
Number reporting side effects	RR 1.09 (0.95 to 1.25) (52.2% versus 48.9%)	RR 1.4 (1.08 to 1.81) (62.2% versus 44.4%)	Not reported	RR 1.23 (0.94 to 1.62) (54.8% versus 44.4%)
Quality of evidence	High	Moderate	–	Moderate
Number of studies/participants	K = 3; n = 673	K = 1; n = 219	–	K = 1; n = 212
Forest plot number	Pharm subthreshold 02.02	Pharm subthreshold 02.02	–	Pharm subthreshold 02.02

Table 130: Summary study characteristics of studies comparing active treatments for dysthymia

	Antidepressants versus antidepressants	Antidepressants versus antipsychotics
No. trials (Total participants)	6 RCTs (383)	5 RCTs (1237)
Study IDs	(1) BAKISH1993 (2) DEJONGHE1991* (3) SALZMANN1995 (4) THASE1996A (5) VALLEJO1987‡ (6) VERSIANI1997‡	(1) AMORE2001* (2) BOYER1999 (3) GEISLER1992 (4) RAVIZZA1999* (5) SMERALDI1996*
N/% female	(1) 50/48 (2) 48/60 (3) 67/81 (4) 274†/65 (5) 73/71 (6) 211/71	(1) 313/68 (2) 323/75 (3) 67/78 (4) 253/64 (5) 281/65
Mean age (range if not given)	(1) 38 (2) 40 (3) 55 (4)–(5) 42 (6) 41	(1) 47 (2)–(3) 48 (4) 47 (5) 55
Drugs	(1) Imipramine versus ritanserin (2) Fluvoxamine versus maprotiline (3) Imipramine versus minaprine (4)–(5) Sertraline versus imipramine (6) Imipramine versus moclobemide	(1) Amisulpride versus sertraline (2) Amisulpride versus amineptine (3) Flupentixol versus ritanserin (4) Amisulpride versus amitriptyline (5) Amisulpride versus fluoxetine
Setting	(1)–(6) Outpatients	(1)–(2) Outpatients (3) Primary care (4)–(5) Outpatients
Length of treatment	(1) 7 weeks (2)–(3) 6 weeks (4) 12 weeks (5) 7 weeks (6) 8 weeks	(1)–(2) 12 weeks (3) 6 weeks (4) 6 months (5) 12 weeks

*Studies have fewer than 100% of participants with dysthymia (AMORE2001 11% double depression; DEJONGHE1991 46% major depression; RAVIZZA1999 2% major depression in partial remission; SMERALDI1996 6% MDD in partial remission); †N with dysthymia in relevant antidepressant and placebo groups; ‡Mixed sample but dysthymia group only extracted here (VALLEJO1987 dysthymia group extracted for efficacy data; mixed sample extracted for attrition data).

Table 131: Summary evidence profile for active treatment comparisons for dysthymia (efficacy)

	SSRI versus other antidepressant	TCA versus other antidepressant	TCA versus antipsychotic	Antipsychotic versus other drug
Non-response	Not reported	RR 1.07 (0.79 to 1.46) (45.1% versus 41.7%)	Not reported	Not reported
Quality of evidence	–	Low	–	–
Number of studies/ participants (comparison)	–	K = 2; n = 205 (imipramine versus minaprine or moclobemide)	–	–
Forest plot number	–	Pharm subthreshold 03.02	–	–
Non-remission	RR 0.87 (0.7 to 1.07) (53% versus 61%)	RR 1.12 (0.81 to 1.55) (54.4% versus 48.6%)	Not reported	Not reported
Quality of evidence	Moderate	Moderate	–	–
Number of studies/ participants (comparison)	K = 1; n = 270 (sertraline versus imipramine)	K = 1; n = 138 (imipramine versus moclobemide)	–	–
Forest plot number	Pharm subthreshold 03.03	Pharm subthreshold 03.04	–	–

Mean endpoint	Not reported	SMD 0.34 (−0.10 to 0.77)	SMD 0.04 (−0.23 to 0.31)	SMD −0.26 (−0.74 to 0.22)
Quality of evidence	–	Low	Moderate	Low
Number of studies/ participants (comparison)	–	K = 2; n = 83 (imipramine versus minaprine; phenelzine)	K = 1; n = 208 (amitriptyline versus amisulpride)	K = 1; n = 67 (flupentixol versus ritanserin)
Forest plot number	–	Pharm subthreshold 03.06	Pharm subthreshold 03.06	Pharm subthreshold 03.07
Mean change	SMD 0.05 (−0.19 to 0.29)	SMD 0.12 (−0.23 to 0.46)	SMD 0.06 (−0.22 to 0.33)	Not reported
Quality of evidence	Moderate	Moderate	Moderate	–
Number of studies/ participants (comparison)	K = 1; n = 270 (sertraline versus imipramine)	K = 1; n = 130 (imipramine versus moclobemide)	K = 1; n = 208 (amitriptyline versus amisulpride)	–
Forest plot number	Pharm subthreshold 03.08	Pharm subthreshold 03.09	Pharm subthreshold 03.09	–

Table 132: Summary evidence profile for active treatment comparisons for studies where fewer than 100% (but at least 50%) participants have dysthymia (efficacy)

	SSRI versus other antidepressant	SSRI versus antipsychotic	TCA versus antipsychotic
Non-response	RR 1 (0.72 to 1.39) (75% versus 75%)	RR 1.39 (1.06 to 1.83) (30.2% versus 21.7%)	RR 0.97 (0.7 to 1.33) (39.1% versus 40.4%)
Quality of evidence	Low	High	Low
Number of studies/participants (comparison)	K = 1; n = 48 (fluvoxamine versus maprotiline)	K = 2; n = 594 (SSRI versus amisulpride)	K = 1; n = 253 (amitriptyline versus amisulpride)
Forest plot number	Pharm subthreshold 03.01	Pharm subthreshold 03.01	Pharm subthreshold 03.02
Non-remission	Not reported	RR 1.29 (0.92 to 1.81) (34.6% versus 26.8%)	Not reported
Quality of evidence	–	Moderate	–
Number of studies/participants (comparison)	–	K = 1; n = 313 (SSRI versus amisulpride)	–
Forest plot number	–	Pharm subthreshold 03.03	–
Mean endpoint	SMD −0.01 (−0.62 to 0.59)	SMD 0.16 (0 to 0.32)	SMD −0.01 (−0.27 to 0.25)
Quality of evidence	Low	High	Moderate
Number of studies/participants (comparison)	K = 1; n = 42 (fluvoxamine versus maprotiline)	K = 2; n = 574 (SSRI versus amisulpride)	K = 1; n = 250 (amitriptyline versus amisulpride)
Forest plot number	Pharm subthreshold 03.05	Pharm subthreshold 03.05	Pharm subthreshold 03.06

Table 133: Summary evidence profile for active treatment comparisons for dysthymia (acceptability/tolerability)

	SSRI versus other antidepressant	TCA versus other antidepressant	TCA versus antipsychotic	Antipsychotic versus antipsychotic or other drug
Leaving treatment early for any reason	RR 0.47 (0.3 to 0.75) (15.7% versus 33.1%)	RR 1.21 (0.61 to 2.42) (14.6% versus 12%)	RR 1.34 (0.71 to 2.51) (18% versus 13.5%)	RR 1.29 (0.23 to 7.24) (8.3% versus 6.5%)
Quality of evidence	Moderate	Low	Low	Low
Number of studies/ participants (comparison)	K = 1; n = 270 (sertraline versus imipramine)	K = 1; n = 211 (imipramine versus moclobemide)	K = 1; n = 215 (amitriptyline versus amisulpride)	K = 1; n = 67 (flupentixol versus ritanserin)
Forest plot number	Pharm subthreshold 04.01	Pharm subthreshold 04.02	Pharm subthreshold 04.02	Pharm subthreshold 04.03
Leaving treatment early due to side effects	RR 0.32 (0.15 to 0.69) (6% versus 18.4%)	RR 1.54 (0.72 to 3.3) (10.9% versus 7.1%)	RR 1.87 (0.48 to 7.3) (5.4% versus 2.9%)	RR 0.92 (0.14 to 6.14) (5.6% versus 6.1%)
Quality of evidence	Moderate	Low	Low	Low
Number of studies/ participants (comparison)	K = 1; n = 270 (sertraline versus imipramine)	K = 2; n = 278 (imipramine versus minaprine/moclobemide)	K = 1; n = 115 (amitriptyline versus amisulpride)	K = 1; n = 69 (flupentixol versus ritanserin)
Forest plot number	Pharm subthreshold 04.04	Pharm subthreshold 04.05	Pharm subthreshold 04.05	Pharm subthreshold 04.06
Number reporting side effects	Not reported	RR 1.39 (0.85 to 2.26) (58.8% versus 42.4%)	RR 1.13 (0.9 to 1.42) (62.2% versus 54.8%)	RR 0.98 (0.58 to 1.65) (44.4% versus 45.5%)
Quality of evidence	–	Moderate	Moderate	Low
Number of studies/ participants (comparison)	–	K = 1; n = 67 (imipramine versus minaprine)	K = 1; n = 115 (amitriptyline versus amisulpride)	K = 1; n = 69 (flupentixol versus ritanserin)
Forest plot number	–	Pharm subthreshold 04.08	Pharm subthreshold 04.08	Pharm subthreshold 04.09

Table 134: Summary evidence profile for active treatment comparisons for studies where fewer than 100% (but at least 50%) participants have dysthymia (acceptability/tolerability)

	SSRI versus other antidepressant	SSRI versus antipsychotic	TCA versus other antidepressant	TCA versus antipsychotic
Leaving treatment early for any reason	RR 0.67 (0.22 to 2.07) (16.7% versus 25%)	RR 1.36 (0.98 to 1.89) (22.7% versus 16.7%)	RR 1.22 (0.35 to 4.17) (13.5% versus 11.1%)	RR 1.07 (0.81 to 1.42) (47.1% versus 44%)
Quality of evidence	Low	Moderate	Low	Low
Number of studies/ participants (comparison)	K = 1; n = 48 (fluvoxamine versus maprotiline)	K = 2; n = 594 (SSRI versus amisulpride)	K = 1; n = 73 (imipramine versus phenelzine)	K = 1; n = 253 (amitriptyline versus amisulpride)
Forest plot number	Pharm subthreshold 04.01	Pharm subthreshold 04.01	Pharm subthreshold 04.02	Pharm subthreshold 04.02
Leaving treatment early due to side effects	Not reported	RR 0.97 (0.55 to 1.7) (7.5% versus 7.7%)	Not reported	RR 0.91 (0.47 to 1.78) (12.6% versus 13.9%)
Quality of evidence	–	Low	–	Low
Number of studies/ participants (comparison)	–	K = 2; n = 594 (sertraline/fluoxetine versus amisulpride)	–	K = 1; n = 253 (amitriptyline versus amisulpride)
Forest plot number	–	Pharm subthreshold 04.04	–	Pharm subthreshold 04.05

Relapse prevention

A single trial (MILLER2001A) was found that considered treatment to prevent relapse in patients who had achieved remission from dysthymia (study characteristics can be found in Appendix 17d). Patients were randomised following remission or partial remission to open-label acute-phase treatment and 16 weeks' continuation treatment. The acute and continuation phases included patients with major depressive disorder.

Far more participants taking placebo experienced relapse compared with those taking desipramine, although because there is only a single small study, the effect size is not clinically important. The full evidence profiles and associated forest plots can be found in Appendix 16d and Appendix 19d, respectively.

13.2.5   Acute-phase pharmacological interventions for subthreshold depressive symptoms

Study characteristics

Four studies included participants with a diagnosis of subthreshold depressive symptoms, with two including mixed populations. In this group baseline entry rates were very low (for example, HAMD-17 10.85; JUDD2004), and in contrast to the previous analysis, participants were characterised by a more recent onset than that which is typical of dysthymia. Summary study characteristics of the included studies are presented in Table 135, with full details in Appendix 17d, which also includes details of excluded studies.

Clinical evidence

Evidence from the important outcomes and overall quality of evidence are presented in Table 136 and Table 137. The full evidence profiles and associated forest plots can be found in Appendix 16d and Appendix 19d, respectively.

In people with subthreshold depressive symptoms, antidepressants (paroxetine) appeared to be no better than placebo (quality of evidence: moderate or high), although in head-to-head trials paroxetine was more effective than maprotiline, and citalopram was more effective than sertraline.

13.2.6   Clinical summary of pharmacological interventions for subthreshold depressive symptoms and persistent subthreshold depressive symptoms (dysthymia)

There was some evidence the drugs may be effective in treating people with persistent subthreshold depressive symptoms (including dysthymia), this included a range of antidepressants and antipsychotics. SSRIs and MAOIs were more acceptable to participants compared with TCAs or antipsychotics. There was no clear advantage for one drug over another, although in studies with participants

Table 135: Summary study characteristics for treatments for subthreshold depressive symptoms

	SSRIs versus placebo	Antidepressants versus other antidepressants
No. trials (Total participants)	2 RCTs	2 RCTs
Study IDs	(1) BARRETT1999* (2) JUDD2004	(1) ROCCA2005[†] (2) SZEGEDI1997[‡]
N/% female	(1) 656/50 (2) 162/59	(1) 138/28 (2) 543/72
Mean age (range if not given)	(1) 61 (2) 44	(1) 72 (2) Not reported
Drug	(1) Paroxetine (2) Fluoxetine	(1) Citalopram versus sertraline (2) Paroxetine versus maprotiline
Setting	(1) Primary care (2) Unclear	(1)–(2) Outpatients
Length of treatment	(1) 11 weeks (2) 12 weeks	(1) 1 year (2) 7 weeks

*Sample divided into dysthymia or minor depression and included in relevant analysis accordingly; [†]49% subthreshold depressive symptoms; [‡]45% subthreshold depressive symptoms.

with a broader range of subthreshold depressive symptoms (including dysthymia) an antipsychotic was more effective than an SSRI (amisulpride compared with sertraline), but not a TCA.

In people with subthreshold depressive symptoms, antidepressants (paroxetine) appeared to be no better than placebo (quality of evidence: moderate or high), although in head-to-head trials paroxetine was more effective than maprotiline, and citalopram was more effective than sertraline.

Antidepressants are not clearly better than placebo in people with recent onset subthreshold depressive symptoms, but are effective in people with persistent subthreshold depressive symptoms. People with recent onset subthreshold depressive symptoms should be offered the same treatment options as those with mild major depression. Antidepressant treatment may be beneficial in those whose symptoms persist. SSRIs are tolerated better than TCAs.

Table 136: Summary evidence profile for treatments for subthreshold depressive symptoms (efficacy data)

	SSRI versus placebo	Antidepressant versus antidepressant
Non-response	RR 0.99 (0.77 to 1.28) (51.9% versus 52.3%)	RR 0.73 (0.48 to 1.09) (23.8% versus 32.8%)
Quality of evidence	Moderate	Moderate
Number of studies/participants (comparison)	K = 1; n = 215 (paroxetine)	K = 1; n = 245 (paroxetine versus maprotiline)
Forest plot number	Pharm subthreshold 01.01	Pharm subthreshold 03.01
Non-remission	RR 1.06 (0.84 to 1.34) (58.5% versus 55%)	RR 1.24 (0.9 to 1.71) (58.3% versus 47%)
Quality of evidence	Moderate	Moderate
Number of studies/participants (comparison)	K = 1; n = 215 (paroxetine)	K = 1; n = 138 (sertraline versus citalopram)
Forest plot number	Pharm subthreshold 01.02	Pharm subthreshold 03.03
Mean endpoint	SMD -0.19 (-0.41 to 0.03)	Not reported
Quality of evidence	High	–
Number of studies/ participants (comparison)	K = 2; n = 322 (paroxetine or fluoxetine)	–
Forest plot number	Pharm subthreshold 01.03	–

Table 137: Summary evidence profile for treatments for subthreshold depressive symptoms (acceptability/tolerability data)

	SSRIs versus placebo	Antidepressant versus antidepressant
Leaving treatment early for any reason	RR 1.2 (0.87 to 1.65) (31.6% versus 26.3%)	RR 1.02 (0.59 to 1.75) (27.8% versus 27.3%)
Quality of evidence	Low	Low
Number of studies/ participants (comparison)	K = 2; n = 377 (paroxetine or fluoxetine)	K = 1; n = 138 (sertraline versus citalopram)
Forest plot number	Pharm subthreshold 02.01	Pharm subthreshold 04.01
Leaving treatment early due to side effects	RR 1.55 (0.51 to 4.68) (9.1% versus 5.3%)	RR 0.73 (0.31 to 1.75) (11.1% versus 15.2%)
Quality of evidence	Very low	Low
Number of studies/ participants (comparison)	K = 2; n = 377 (paroxetine or fluoxetine)	K = 1; n = 138 (sertraline versus citalopram)
Forest plot number	Pharm subthreshold 02.02	Pharm subthreshold 04.04
Number reporting side effects	RR 0.76 (0.49 to 1.18) (23.6% versus 31.2%)	Not reported
Quality of evidence	Moderate	–
Number of studies/ participants (comparison)	K = 1; n = 215 (paroxetine)	–
Forest plot number	Pharm subthreshold 02.03	–

13.2.7   Health economic evidence and considerations

No evidence on the cost effectiveness of pharmacological strategies in these populations were identified by the systematic search of the economic literature. Details on the methods used for the systematic search of the economic literature are described in Chapter 3, Section 3.6.1.

13.3   PSYCHOLOGICAL AND OTHER STRATEGIES FOR THE TREATMENT OF PERSISTENT SUBTHRESHOLD DEPRESSIVE SYMPTOMS (DYSTHYMIA)

13.3.1   Introduction

There have been few psychological treatment studies in people with well-defined subthreshold depressive symptoms and the range of therapies and definitions of subthreshold depression have varied (Cuijpers *et al.*, 2007).

This section covers psychological treatments and psychological treatments combined with antidepressants. The definitions for psychological interventions are given in Chapter 8, with the exception of short-term psychodynamic art therapy, which is defined below.

Definition
Short-term psychodynamic art therapy has a focus on the transference relationship and uses:
- the creative process to facilitate self-expression
- the aesthetic form to 'contain' and give meaning to the patient's experience
- the artistic medium as a bridge to verbal dialogue and insight-based psychological development if appropriate

The aim is to enable the patient to experience him/herself differently and develop new ways of relating to others.

13.3.2   Databases searched and the inclusion/exclusion criteria

Information about the databases searched and the inclusion/exclusion criteria used are presented in Table 138. Details of the search strings used are in Appendix 8.

Table 138: Databases searched and inclusion/exclusion criteria for clinical effectiveness of non-pharmacological treatments

Electronic databases	MEDLINE, EMBASE, PsycINFO, CINAHL
Date searched	Database inception to January 2008
Update searches	July 2008; January 2009
Study design	RCT
Population	People with a diagnosis of dysthymia, minor depression or subthreshold according to DSM, ICD or similar criteria
Treatments	Any psychological, psychosocial or other non-pharmacological intervention

13.3.3   Study characteristics[214]

In total, eight trials met inclusion criteria and 24 were excluded. A number of trials included populations with a mixture of diagnoses, including dysthymia, subthreshold depressive symptoms and major depressive disorder; where this is the case these trials have been included in the reviews of psychological interventions (see Chapters 7 and 8). As studies with mixed diagnoses are covered elsewhere, the following reviews include trials of dysthymia only. Trials in which more than 50% of participants had a diagnosis of major depressive disorder were excluded from this review (but included in other reviews where appropriate). Summary study characteristics of the included studies are presented in Table 139, with full details in Appendix 17d, which also includes details of excluded studies.

13.3.4   Clinical evidence

Evidence from the important outcomes and overall quality of evidence are presented in Table 140, Table 141 and Table 142. The full evidence profiles and associated forest plots can be found in Appendix 16d and Appendix 19d, respectively.

Psychological interventions versus placebo
There was some evidence of a small but non-significant effect for psychological interventions for people with persistent subthreshold depressive symptoms (dysthymia) compared with placebo.

Psychological interventions versus antidepressants
On some outcomes there was evidence that psychological interventions for people whose symptoms of depression do not meet threshold for major depressive disorder are as effective as antidepressants (non-response and non-remission), while on mean depressions scores at endpoint, antidepressants seem more effective, although the effect size is small. The evidence for combination therapy was inconclusive compared with antidepressants, but compared with psychological therapy there was some evidence that combination treatment was more effective.

The evidence from the study of combination treatment compared with antidepressants alone was inconclusive.

Short-term psychodynamic verbal psychotherapy versus short-term psychodynamic art therapy
There was no evidence of a significant difference in treatment effect for short-term psychodynamic verbal psychotherapy compared with short-term psychodynamic art therapy.

---

[214]Study IDs in capital letters refer to studies found and included in this guideline update.

Table 139: Summary of study characteristics of RCTs of psychological and other non-pharmacological treatments

	Psychological intervention versus no-treatment control	Psychological intervention (with and without antidepressants) versus antidepressants	Short-term psychodynamic verbal psychotherapy versus short-term psychodynamic art therapy
No. trials (Total participants)	2 RCTs (753)	6 RCTs (1625)	1 RCT (43)
Study IDs	(1) BARRETT1999* (2) RAVINDRAN1999*	(1) BARRETT1999* (2) BROWNE2002* (3) DUNNER1996 (4) HELLERSTEIN2001A[†] (5) MARKOWITZ2005* (6) RAVINDRAN1999*	(1) THYME2007
N/% female	(1) 656/50 (2) 97/58	(1) 656/50 (2) 707/56 (3) 31/36 (4) 40/50 (5) 94/60 (6) 97/58	(1) 43/100
Mean age (range if not given)	(1) 61 (2) 21–54	(1) 61 (2) 42 (3) 36 (4) 45 (5) 42 (6) 21–54	(1) 34
Treatment/ second treatment group	(1) Problem solving (2) CBT + placebo	(1) Problem solving (2) IPT/IPT + sertraline (3) CBT (4) Group CBT + fluoxetine 37 mg (5) IPT/IPT + sertraline/ supportive therapy (6) CBT + placebo/ CBT + sertraline	(1) Short-term psychodynamic verbal psycho-therapy
Comparison	(1)–(2) Placebo	(1) Paroxetine 20 mg (2) Sertraline 200 mg (3) Fluoxetine 20 mg (4) Fluoxetine 39 mg	(1) Short-term psychodynamic art therapy

Continued

557

Table 139: *(Continued)*

	Psychological intervention versus no-treatment control	Psychological intervention (with and without antidepressants) versus antidepressants	Short-term psychodynamic verbal psychotherapy versus short-term psychodynamic art therapy
		(5) Sertraline 112 mg (6) Sertraline 178 mg	
Diagnosis	(1) 52% dysthymia; 48% subthreshold depressive symptoms (2) Dysthymia	(1) 52% dysthymia; 48% subthreshold depressive symptoms (2)–(3) Dysthymia (4) Dysthymia (partial responders to previous 8-week fluoxetine trial) (5)–(6) Dysthymia	(1) 64% dysthymic disorder DSM-IV, 36% depressive symptoms and difficulties
Setting	(1) Primary care (2) Community	(1)–(2) Primary care (3) Outpatients (4) Tertiary care (5) Community/primary care (6) Community	(1) Outpatients
Length of treatment	(1) 10 weeks (2) 12 weeks	(1) 10 weeks (2) 6 months (3) 16 weeks (4) 6 months (5) 16 weeks (6) 12 weeks	(1) 10 weeks

*Trial with >2 arms; †analysed separately because participants are partial responders to previous treatment.

13.3.5   Clinical summary

The evidence for psychological interventions in the treatment of persistent subthreshold depressive symptoms (dysthymia) is limited and covers a range of different types of treatments (including IPT, CBT and problem solving therapy) making it difficult to assess the efficacy of the different treatments. There is limited evidence suggesting some benefit for psychological treatments when compared with placebo. In populations with persistent subthreshold depressive symptoms (dysthymia) there is

**Table 140: Summary evidence profile for psychological
interventions versus placebo**

	Psychological intervention versus placebo
Non-response	RR 0.86 (0.70 to 1.06) (51.8% versus 60.9%)
Quality of evidence	High
Number of studies/participants	K = 2; n = 277
Forest plot number	Psych sub-thresh 01.01
Non-remission	RR 0.86 (0.69 to 1.08) (54% versus 62.5%)
Quality of evidence	Low
Number of studies/participants	K = 1; n = 227
Forest plot number	Psych sub-thresh 01.01
Mean endpoint (clinician-rated)	SMD −0.27 (−0.55 to 0.01)
Quality of evidence	Moderate
Number of studies/participants	K = 1; n = 196
Forest plot number	Psych sub-thresh 01.02
Leaving treatment early for any reason	RR 0.86 (0.50, 1.47) (14.4% versus 16.7%)
Quality of evidence	High
Number of studies/participants	K = 2; n = 277
Forest plot number	Psych sub-thresh 01.03

inconclusive evidence about the relative efficacy of antidepressants and psychological interventions.

Combined antidepressants and psychological interventions are more effective than psychological interventions alone, but not more effective than antidepressants alone. The evidence for combination treatment in people who have partially responded to initial treatment was inconclusive. However, the datasets for these interventions are small, and further studies would help to clarify whether these interventions are helpful.

In one small trial that compared two psychological interventions (short term psychodynamic verbal psychotherapy and short-term psychodynamic art therapy) there were no clinically important differences between the treatments.

Table 141: Summary evidence profile for psychological interventions (with and without antidepressants) versus antidepressants or psychological treatment alone

	Psychological intervention versus antidepressants	Follow-up	Psychological intervention + antidepressants versus antidepressants	Follow-up	Psychological intervention + antidepressants versus psychological intervention	Follow-up
Non-response	RR 1.09 (0.92 to 1.29) (56.8% versus 51.6%)	Not reported	RR 0.96 (0.52 to 1.79) (60.9% versus 65.2%)	Not reported	RR 0.48 (0.25 to 0.91) (32% versus 66.7%)	Not reported
Quality of evidence	High	–	Low	–	Moderate	–
Number of studies/participants	K = 3; n = 319	–	K = 2; n = 92	–	K = 1; n = 49	–
Forest plot number	Psych sub-thresh 02.01	–	Psych sub-thresh 03.01	–	Psych sub-thresh 04.01	–
Non-remission	RR 1.14 (0.92 to 1.41) (58% versus 51.9%)	Not reported	RR 0.82 (0.47 to 1.43) (47.6% versus 58.3%)	Not reported	Not reported	Not reported
Quality of evidence	Moderate	–	Low	–	–	–
Number of studies/participants	K = 2; n = 273	–	K = 1; n = 45	–	–	–

Forest plot number	Psych sub-thresh 02.01	–	Psych sub-thresh 03.01	–	–	–
Mean endpoint (clinician-rated)	SMD 0.29 (0.13 to 0.45)	6-month: SMD 0.19 (−0.02 to 0.4) 18-month: SMD 0.26 (0.05 to 0.48)	SMD 0.09 (−0.1 to 0.27)	6-month: SMD 0.01 (−0.19 to 0.21) 18-month: SMD 0.06 (−0.14 to 0.27)	SMD −0.17 (−0.37 to 0.03)	6-month: SMD −0.18 (−0.38 to 0.03) 18-month: SMD −0.2 (−0.41 to 0.01)
Quality of evidence	High	Moderate Moderate	Moderate	Moderate Moderate	Moderate	Moderate Moderate
Number of studies/participants	K = 4; n = 628	K = 1; n = 353 K = 1; n = 335	K = 2; n = 453	K = 1; n = 382 K = 1; n = 369	K = 1; n = 390	K = 1; n = 363 K = 1; n = 346
Forest plot number	Psych sub-thresh 02.02	Psych sub-thresh 02.02	Psych sub-thresh 03.02	Psych sub-thresh 03.02	Psych sub-thresh 04.02	Psych sub-thresh 04.02
Mean endpoint (self-rated)	SMD 0.37 (0.11 to 0.86)	Not reported	Not reported	Not reported	Not reported	Not reported
Quality of evidence	High	–	–	–	–	–
Number of studies/participants	K = 2; n = 67	–	–	–	–	–
Forest plot number	Psych sub-thresh 02.02	–	–	–	–	–
Leaving treatment early for any reason	RR 0.67 (0.42 to 1.06) (14.3% versus 22.3%)	Not reported	RR 1.09 (0.37 to 3.25) (10.9% versus 10.9%)	Not reported	Not reported	Not reported

Continued

561

Table 141: (*Continued*)

	Psychological intervention versus antidepressants	Follow-up	Psychological intervention + antidepressants versus antidepressants	Follow-up	Psychological intervention + antidepressants versus psychological intervention	Follow-up
Quality of evidence	Moderate	–	Moderate	–	–	–
Number of studies/ participants	K = 4; n = 350	–	K = 2; n = 92	–	–	–
Forest plot number	Psych sub-thresh 02.03	–	Psych sub-thresh 03.03	–	–	–
Leaving treatment early due to side effects	RR 0.45 (0.02 to 10.3) (0% versus 5.6%)	Not reported	Not reported	Not reported	Not reported	Not reported
Quality of evidence	Low	–	–	–	–	–
Number of studies/ participants	K = 1; n = 31	–	–	–	–	–
Forest plot number	Psych sub-thresh 02.03	–	–	–	–	–

Table 142: Summary evidence profile for short-term psychodynamic verbal psychotherapy versus short-term psychodynamic art therapy

	Short-term psycho-dynamic verbal psychotherapy versus short-term psychodynamic art therapy	Follow-up
Mean endpoint (self-rated)	SMD −0.11 (−0.74 to 0.52)	3-month: SMD −0.26 (−0.9 to 0.37)
Quality of evidence	Low	Low
Number of studies/participants	K = 1; n = 43	K = 1; n = 43
Forest plot number	Pharm sub-thresh 05.01	Pharm sub-thresh 05.01
Leaving treatment early for any reason	RR 0.32 (0.04 to 2.82) (4.5% versus 14.3%)	Not reported
Quality of evidence	Low	–
Number of studies/participants	K = 1; n = 43	–
Forest plot number	Pharm sub-thresh 07.02	–

13.3.6   Health economic evidence and considerations

No evidence on the cost effectiveness of psychological and non-pharmacological strategies in these populations was identified by the systematic search of the economic literature. Details on the methods used for the systematic search of the economic literature are described in Chapter 3, Section 3.6.1.

13.4   FROM EVIDENCE TO RECOMMENDATIONS

The datasets for both pharmacological and psychological treatments are relatively small, particularly compared with those in major depressive disorder. However, there appears to be some benefit for antidepressants in people with persistent subthreshold depressive symptoms (dysthymia) but not in people with a diagnosis of recent onset subthreshold depressive symptoms. With regard to psychological interventions, the evidence is limited because there are few relevant studies and therefore no evidence base on which a recommendation could be based. For psychosocial interventions of potential benefit for this group see Chapter 7 on low-intensity interventions because a number of the trials in the reviews undertaken in that chapter included patients entered into the trials on the basis of scores on depression rating scales and which potentially included a significant number of patients with subthreshold symptoms.

13.5   RECOMMENDATIONS

13.5.1.1   See recommendation 9.10.1.1.

13.6   RESEARCH RECOMMENDATION

13.6.1.1   See recommendation 8.12.1.3.
13.6.1.2   See recommendation 8.12.1.4.

14 SUMMARY OF RECOMMENDATIONS

14.1 CARE OF ALL PEOPLE WITH DEPRESSION

14.1.1 Providing information and support, and obtaining informed consent

14.1.1.1 When working with people with depression and their families or carers:
- build a trusting relationship and work in an open, engaging and non-judgemental manner
- explore treatment options in an atmosphere of hope and optimism, explaining the different courses of depression and that recovery is possible
- be aware that stigma and discrimination can be associated with a diagnosis of depression
- ensure that discussions take place in settings in which confidentiality, privacy and dignity are respected.

14.1.1.2 When working with people with depression and their families or carers:
- provide information appropriate to their level of understanding about the nature of depression and the range of treatments available
- avoid clinical language without adequate explanation
- ensure that comprehensive written information is available in the appropriate language and in audio format if possible
- provide and work proficiently with independent interpreters (that is, someone who is not known to the person with depression) if needed.

14.1.1.3 Inform people with depression about self-help groups, support groups and other local and national resources.

14.1.1.4 Make all efforts necessary to ensure that a person with depression can give meaningful and informed consent before treatment starts. This is especially important when a person has severe depression or is subject to the Mental Health Act.

14.1.1.5 Ensure that consent to treatment is based on the provision of clear information (which should also be available in written form) about the intervention, covering:
- what it comprises
- what is expected of the person while having it
- likely outcomes (including any side effects).

14.1.2 Advance decisions and statements

14.1.2.1 For people with recurrent severe depression or depression with psychotic symptoms and for those who have been treated under the Mental Health

Act, consider developing advance decisions and advance statements collaboratively with the person. Record the decisions and statements and include copies in the person's care plan in primary and secondary care. Give copies to the person and to their family or carer, if the person agrees.

14.1.3　Supporting families and carers

14.1.3.1　When families or carers are involved in supporting a person with severe or chronic[215] depression, consider:
- providing written and verbal information on depression and its management, including how families or carers can support the person
- offering a carer's assessment of their caring, physical and mental health needs if necessary
- providing information about local family or carer support groups and voluntary organisations, and helping families or carers to access these
- negotiating between the person and their family or carer about confidentiality and the sharing of information.

14.1.4　Principles for assessment, coordination of care and choosing treatments

14.1.4.1　When assessing a person who may have depression, conduct a comprehensive assessment that does not rely simply on a symptom count. Take into account both the degree of functional impairment and/or disability associated with the possible depression and the duration of the episode.

14.1.4.2　In addition to assessing symptoms and associated functional impairment, consider how the following factors may have affected the development, course and severity of a person's depression:
- any history of depression and comorbid mental health or physical disorders
- any past history of mood elevation (to determine if the depression may be part of bipolar disorder[216])
- any past experience of, and response to, treatments
- the quality of interpersonal relationships
- living conditions and social isolation.

14.1.4.3　Be respectful of, and sensitive to, diverse cultural, ethnic and religious backgrounds when working with people with depression, and be aware of

---

[215]Depression is described as 'chronic' if symptoms have been present more or less continuously for 2 years or more.

[216]Refer if necessary to 'Bipolar disorder' (NICE clinical guideline 38; available at www.nice.org. uk/CG38).

the possible variations in the presentation of depression. Ensure competence in:

- culturally sensitive assessment
- using different explanatory models of depression
- addressing cultural and ethnic differences when developing and implementing treatment plans
- working with families from diverse ethnic and cultural backgrounds.

14.1.4.4 When assessing a person with suspected depression, be aware of any learning disabilities or acquired cognitive impairments, and if necessary consider consulting with a relevant specialist when developing treatment plans and strategies.

14.1.4.5 When providing interventions for people with a learning disability or acquired cognitive impairment who have a diagnosis of depression:

- where possible, provide the same interventions as for other people with depression
- if necessary, adjust the method of delivery or duration of the intervention to take account of the disability or impairment.

14.1.4.6 Always ask people with depression directly about suicidal ideation and intent. If there is a risk of self-harm or suicide:

- assess whether the person has adequate social support and is aware of sources of help
- arrange help appropriate to the level of risk (see section 14.3.2)
- advise the person to seek further help if the situation deteriorates.

14.1.5 Effective delivery of interventions for depression

14.1.5.1 All interventions for depression should be delivered by competent practitioners. Psychological and psychosocial interventions should be based on the relevant treatment manual(s), which should guide the structure and duration of the intervention. Practitioners should consider using competence frameworks developed from the relevant treatment manual(s) and for all interventions should:

- receive regular high-quality supervision
- use routine outcome measures and ensure that the person with depression is involved in reviewing the efficacy of the treatment
- engage in monitoring and evaluation of treatment adherence and practitioner competence – for example, by using video and audio tapes, and external audit and scrutiny where appropriate.

14.1.5.2 Consider providing all interventions in the preferred language of the person with depression where possible.

14.2 STEPPED CARE

The stepped-care model provides a framework in which to organise the provision of services, and supports patients, carers and practitioners in identifying and accessing the most effective interventions (see the figure below). In stepped care the least intrusive, most effective intervention is provided first; if a person does not benefit from the intervention initially offered, or declines an intervention, they should be offered an appropriate intervention from the next step.

Figure 11: The stepped-care model

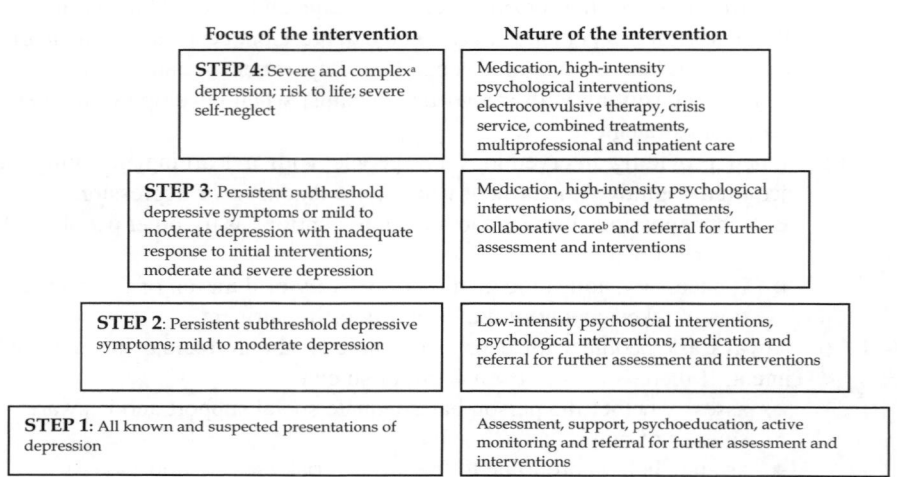

aComplex depression includes depression that shows an inadequate response to multiple treatments, is complicated by psychotic symptoms, and/or is associated with significant psychiatric comorbidity or psychosocial factors.
bOnly for depression where the person also has a chronic physical health problem and associated functional impairment (see 'Depression in adults with a chronic physical health problem: treatment and management' [NICE clinical guideline 91]).

14.3   STEP 1: RECOGNITION, ASSESSMENT AND INITIAL MANAGEMENT

14.3.1   Case identification and recognition

14.3.1.1   Be alert to possible depression (particularly in people with a past history of depression or a chronic physical health problem with associated functional impairment) and consider asking people who may have depression two questions, specifically:
   ● During the last month, have you often been bothered by feeling down, depressed or hopeless?
   ● During the last month, have you often been bothered by having little interest or pleasure in doing things?

14.3.1.2   If a person answers 'yes' to either of the depression identification questions (see 14.3.1.1) but the practitioner is not competent to perform a mental health assessment, they should refer the person to an appropriate professional. If this professional is not the person's GP, inform the GP of the referral.

14.3.1.3   If a person answers 'yes' to either of the depression identification questions (see 14.3.1.1), a practitioner who is competent to perform a mental health assessment should review the person's mental state and associated functional, interpersonal and social difficulties.

14.3.1.4   When assessing a person with suspected depression, consider using a validated measure (for example, for symptoms, functions and/or disability) to inform and evaluate treatment.

14.3.1.5   For people with significant language or communication difficulties, for example people with sensory impairments or a learning disability, consider using the Distress Thermometer[217] and/or asking a family member or carer about the person's symptoms to identify possible depression. If a significant level of distress is identified, investigate further.

14.3.2   Risk assessment and monitoring

14.3.2.1   If a person with depression presents considerable immediate risk to themselves or others, refer them urgently to specialist mental health services.

14.3.2.2   Advise people with depression of the potential for increased agitation, anxiety and suicidal ideation in the initial stages of treatment; actively seek out these symptoms and:
- ensure that the person knows how to seek help promptly
- review the person's treatment if they develop marked and/or prolonged agitation.

14.3.2.3   Advise a person with depression and their family or carer to be vigilant for mood changes, negativity and hopelessness, and suicidal ideation, and to contact their practitioner if concerned. This is particularly important during high-risk periods, such as starting or changing treatment and at times of increased personal stress.

14.3.2.4   If a person with depression is assessed to be at risk of suicide:
- take into account toxicity in overdose if an antidepressant is prescribed or the person is taking other medication; if necessary, limit the amount of drug(s) available
- consider increasing the level of support, such as more frequent direct or telephone contacts
- consider referral to specialist mental health services.

---

[217]The Distress Thermometer is a single-item question screen that will identify distress coming from any source. The person places a mark on the scale answering: 'How distressed have you been during the past week on a scale of 0 to 10?' Scores of 4 or more indicate a significant level of distress that should be investigated further (Roth *et al.*, 1998).

14.4 STEP 2: RECOGNISED DEPRESSION – PERSISTENT SUBTHRESHOLD DEPRESSIVE SYMPTOMS OR MILD TO MODERATE DEPRESSION

14.4.1 General measures

Depression with anxiety

14.4.1.1 When depression is accompanied by symptoms of anxiety, the first priority should usually be to treat the depression. When the person has an anxiety disorder and comorbid depression or depressive symptoms, consult the NICE guideline for the relevant anxiety disorder and consider treating the anxiety disorder first (since effective treatment of the anxiety disorder will often improve the depression or the depressive symptoms).

Sleep hygiene

14.4.1.2 Offer people with depression advice on sleep hygiene if needed, including:
- establishing regular sleep and wake times
- avoiding excess eating, smoking or drinking alcohol before sleep
- creating a proper environment for sleep
- taking regular physical exercise.

Active monitoring

14.4.1.3 For people who, in the judgement of the practitioner, may recover with no formal intervention, or people with mild depression who do not want an intervention, or people with subthreshold depressive symptoms who request an intervention:
- discuss the presenting problem(s) and any concerns that the person may have about them
- provide information about the nature and course of depression
- arrange a further assessment, normally within 2 weeks
- make contact if the person does not attend follow-up appointments.

14.4.2 Low-intensity psychosocial interventions

14.4.2.1 For people with persistent subthreshold depressive symptoms or mild to moderate depression, consider offering one or more of the following interventions, guided by the person's preference:
- individual guided self-help based on the principles of cognitive behavioural therapy (CBT)
- computerised cognitive behavioural therapy (CCBT)[218]
- a structured group physical activity programme.

---

[218]This recommendation (and recommendation 1.4.2.1 in CG91) updates the recommendations on depression only in 'Computerised cognitive behaviour therapy for depression and anxiety (review)' (NICE technology appraisal guidance 97).

Delivery of low-intensity psychosocial interventions

14.4.2.2 Individual guided self-help programmes based on the principles of CBT (and including behavioural activation and problem-solving techniques) for people with persistent subthreshold depressive symptoms or mild to moderate depression should:

- include the provision of written materials of an appropriate reading age (or alternative media to support access)
- be supported by a trained practitioner, who typically facilitates the self help programme and reviews progress and outcome
- consist of up to six to eight sessions (face-to-face and via telephone) normally taking place over 9 to 12 weeks, including follow-up.

14.4.2.3 CCBT for people with persistent subthreshold depressive symptoms or mild to moderate depression should:

- be provided via a stand-alone computer-based or web-based programme
- include an explanation of the CBT model, encourage tasks between sessions, and use thought-challenging and active monitoring of behaviour, thought patterns and outcomes
- be supported by a trained practitioner, who typically provides limited facilitation of the programme and reviews progress and outcome
- typically take place over 9 to 12 weeks, including follow up.

14.4.2.4 Physical activity programmes for people with persistent subthreshold depressive symptoms or mild to moderate depression should:

- be delivered in groups with support from a competent practitioner
- consist typically of three sessions per week of moderate duration (45 minutes to 1 hour) over 10 to 14 weeks (average 12 weeks).

14.4.3 Group cognitive behavioural therapy

14.4.3.1 Consider group-based CBT for people with persistent subthreshold depressive symptoms or mild to moderate depression who decline low intensity psychosocial interventions (see 14.4.2.1).

14.4.3.2 Group-based CBT for people with persistent subthreshold depressive symptoms or mild to moderate depression should:

- be based on a structured model such as 'Coping with Depression'
- be delivered by two trained and competent practitioners
- consist of 10 to 12 meetings of eight to ten participants
- normally take place over 12 to 16 weeks, including follow-up.

14.4.4 Drug treatment

14.4.4.1 Do not use antidepressants routinely to treat persistent subthreshold depressive symptoms or mild depression because the risk–benefit ratio is poor, but consider them for people with:

- a past history of moderate or severe depression or

- initial presentation of subthreshold depressive symptoms that have been present for a long period (typically at least 2 years) or
- subthreshold depressive symptoms or mild depression that persist(s) after other interventions.

14.4.4.2 Although there is evidence that St John's wort may be of benefit in mild or moderate depression, practitioners should:

- not prescribe or advise its use by people with depression because of uncertainty about appropriate doses, persistence of effect, variation in the nature of preparations and potential serious interactions with other drugs (including oral contraceptives, anticoagulants and anticonvulsants)
- advise people with depression of the different potencies of the preparations available and of the potential serious interactions of St John's wort with other drugs.

14.5 STEP 3: PERSISTENT SUBTHRESHOLD DEPRESSIVE SYMPTOMS OR MILD TO MODERATE DEPRESSION WITH INADEQUATE RESPONSE TO INITIAL INTERVENTIONS, AND MODERATE AND SEVERE DEPRESSION

14.5.1 Treatment options

14.5.1.1 For people with persistent subthreshold depressive symptoms or mild to moderate depression who have not benefited from a low-intensity psychosocial intervention, discuss the relative merits of different interventions with the person and provide:

- an antidepressant (normally a selective serotonin reuptake inhibitor [SSRI]) or
- a high-intensity psychological intervention, normally one of the following options:
  - CBT
  - interpersonal therapy (IPT)
  - behavioural activation (but note that the evidence is less robust than for CBT or IPT)
  - behavioural couples therapy for people who have a regular partner and where the relationship may contribute to the development or maintenance of depression, or where involving the partner is considered to be of potential therapeutic benefit.

14.5.1.2 For people with moderate or severe depression, provide a combination of antidepressant medication and a high-intensity psychological intervention (CBT or IPT).

14.5.1.3 The choice of intervention should be influenced by the:

- duration of the episode of depression and the trajectory of symptoms
- previous course of depression and response to treatment

- likelihood of adherence to treatment and any potential adverse effects
- person's treatment preference and priorities.

14.5.1.4 For people with depression who decline an antidepressant, CBT, IPT, behavioural activation and behavioural couples therapy, consider:

- counselling for people with persistent subthreshold depressive symptoms or mild to moderate depression
- short-term psychodynamic psychotherapy for people with mild to moderate depression.

Discuss with the person the uncertainty of the effectiveness of counselling and psychodynamic psychotherapy in treating depression.

14.5.2   Antidepressant drugs

Choice of antidepressant[219]

14.5.2.1 Discuss antidepressant treatment options with the person with depression, covering:

- the choice of antidepressant, including any anticipated adverse events, for example side effects and discontinuation symptoms (see 14.9.2.1), and potential interactions with concomitant medication or physical health problems[220]
- their perception of the efficacy and tolerability of any antidepressants they have previously taken.

14.5.2.2 When an antidepressant is to be prescribed, it should normally be an SSRI in a generic form because SSRIs are equally effective as other antidepressants and have a favourable risk–benefit ratio. Also take the following into account:

- SSRIs are associated with an increased risk of bleeding, especially in older people or in people taking other drugs that have the potential to damage the gastrointestinal mucosa or interfere with clotting. In particular, consider prescribing a gastroprotective drug in older people who are taking non-steroidal anti-inflammatory drugs (NSAIDs) or aspirin.
- Fluoxetine, fluvoxamine and paroxetine are associated with a higher propensity for drug interactions than other SSRIs[221].
- Paroxetine is associated with a higher incidence of discontinuation symptoms than other SSRIs.

---

[219]For additional considerations on the use of antidepressants and other medications (including the assessment of the relative risks and benefits) for women who may become pregnant, please refer to the BNF and individual drug SPCs. For women in the antenatal and postnatal periods, see also NICE clinical guideline 45 'Antenatal and postnatal mental health'.

[220]Consult appendix 1 of the BNF for information on drug interactions and 'Depression in adults with a chronic physical health problem: treatment and management' (NICE clinical guideline 91).

[221]Ibid.

14.5.2.3 Take into account toxicity in overdose when choosing an antidepressant for people at significant risk of suicide. Be aware that:
- compared with other equally effective antidepressants recommended for routine use in primary care, venlafaxine is associated with a greater risk of death from overdose
- tricyclic antidepressants (TCAs), except for lofepramine, are associated with the greatest risk in overdose.

14.5.2.4 When prescribing drugs other than SSRIs, take the following into account:
- The increased likelihood of the person stopping treatment because of side effects (and the consequent need to increase the dose gradually) with venlafaxine, duloxetine and TCAs.
- The specific cautions, contraindications and monitoring requirements for some drugs. For example:
  - the potential for higher doses of venlafaxine to exacerbate cardiac arrhythmias and the need to monitor the person's blood pressure
  - the possible exacerbation of hypertension with venlafaxine and duloxetine
  - the potential for postural hypotension and arrhythmias with TCAs
  - the need for haematological monitoring with mianserin in elderly people[222].
- Non-reversible monoamine oxidase inhibitors (MAOIs), such as phenelzine, should normally be prescribed only by specialist mental health professionals.
- Dosulepin should not be prescribed.

Starting and initial phase of treatment

14.5.2.5 When prescribing antidepressants, explore any concerns the person with depression has about taking medication, explain fully the reasons for prescribing, and provide information about taking antidepressants, including:
- the gradual development of the full antidepressant effect
- the importance of taking medication as prescribed and the need to continue treatment after remission
- potential side effects
- the potential for interactions with other medications
- the risk and nature of discontinuation symptoms with all antidepressants, particularly with drugs with a shorter half-life (such as paroxetine and venlafaxine), and how these symptoms can be minimised
- the fact that addiction does not occur with antidepressants.

Offer written information appropriate to the person's needs.

---

[222]Consult the BNF for detailed information.

14.5.2.6 For people started on antidepressants who are not considered to be at increased risk of suicide, normally see them after 2 weeks. See them regularly thereafter, for example at intervals of 2 to 4 weeks in the first 3 months, and then at longer intervals if response is good.

14.5.2.7 A person with depression started on antidepressants who is considered to present an increased suicide risk or is younger than 30 years (because of the potential increased prevalence of suicidal thoughts in the early stages of antidepressant treatment for this group) should normally be seen after 1 week and frequently thereafter as appropriate until the risk is no longer considered clinically important.

14.5.2.8 If a person with depression develops side effects early in antidepressant treatment, provide appropriate information and consider one of the following strategies:
- monitor symptoms closely where side effects are mild and acceptable to the person or
- stop the antidepressant or change to a different antidepressant if the person prefers or
- in discussion with the person, consider short-term concomitant treatment with a benzodiazepine if anxiety, agitation and/or insomnia are problematic (except in people with chronic symptoms of anxiety); this should usually be for no longer than 2 weeks in order to prevent the development of dependence.

14.5.2.9 People who start on low-dose TCAs and who have a clear clinical response can be maintained on that dose with careful monitoring.

14.5.2.10 If the person's depression shows no improvement after 2 to 4 weeks with the first antidepressant, check that the drug has been taken regularly and in the prescribed dose.

14.5.2.11 If response is absent or minimal after 3 to 4 weeks of treatment with a therapeutic dose of an antidepressant, increase the level of support (for example, by weekly face-to-face or telephone contact) and consider:
- increasing the dose in line with the SPC if there are no significant side effects or
- switching to another antidepressant as described in Section 14.8 if there are side effects or if the person prefers.

14.5.2.12 If the person's depression shows some improvement by 4 weeks, continue treatment for another 2 to 4 weeks. Consider switching to another antidepressant as described in Section 14.8 if:
- response is still not adequate or
- there are side effects or
- the person prefers to change treatment.

14.5.3 Psychological interventions

Delivering high-intensity psychological interventions

14.5.3.1 For all high-intensity psychological interventions, the duration of treatment should normally be within the limits indicated in this guideline. As the aim of treatment is to obtain significant improvement or remission the duration of treatment may be:

- reduced if remission has been achieved
- increased if progress is being made, and there is agreement between the practitioner and the person with depression that further sessions would be beneficial (for example, if there is a comorbid personality disorder or significant psychosocial factors that impact on the person's ability to benefit from treatment).

14.5.3.2 For all people with depression having individual CBT, the duration of treatment should typically be in the range of 16 to 20 sessions over 3 to 4 months. Also consider providing:

- two sessions per week for the first 2 to 3 weeks of treatment for people with moderate or severe depression
- follow-up sessions typically consisting of three to four sessions over the following 3 to 6 months for all people with depression.

14.5.3.3 For all people with depression having IPT, the duration of treatment should typically be in the range of 16 to 20 sessions over 3 to 4 months. For people with severe depression, consider providing two sessions per week for the first 2 to 3 weeks of treatment.

14.5.3.4 For all people with depression having behavioural activation, the duration of treatment should typically be in the range of 16 to 20 sessions over 3 to 4 months. Also consider providing:

- two sessions per week for the first 3 to 4 weeks of treatment for people with moderate or severe depression
- follow-up sessions typically consisting of three to four sessions over the following 3 to 6 months for all people with depression.

14.5.3.5 Behavioural couples therapy for depression should normally be based on behavioural principles, and an adequate course of therapy should be 15 to 20 sessions over 5 to 6 months.

Delivering counselling

14.5.3.6 For all people with persistent subthreshold depressive symptoms or mild to moderate depression having counselling, the duration of treatment should typically be in the range of six to ten sessions over 8 to 12 weeks.

Delivering short-term psychodynamic psychotherapy

14.5.3.7 For all people with mild to moderate depression having short-term psycho-dynamic psychotherapy, the duration of treatment should typically be in the range of 16 to 20 sessions over 4 to 6 months.

14.6 TREATMENT CHOICE BASED ON DEPRESSION SUBTYPES AND PERSONAL CHARACTERISTICS

14.6.1.1 Do not routinely vary the treatment strategies for depression described in this guideline either by depression subtype (for example, atypical depression or seasonal depression) or by personal characteristics (for example, sex or ethnicity) as there is no convincing evidence to support such action.

14.6.1.2 Advise people with winter depression that follows a seasonal pattern and who wish to try light therapy in preference to antidepressant or psychological treatment that the evidence for the efficacy of light therapy is uncertain.

14.6.1.3 When prescribing antidepressants for older people:

- prescribe at an age-appropriate dose taking into account the effect of general physical health and concomitant medication on pharmacokinetics and pharmacodynamics
- carefully monitor for side effects.

14.6.1.4 For people with long-standing moderate or severe depression who would benefit from additional social or vocational support, consider:

- befriending as an adjunct to pharmacological or psychological treatments; befriending should be by trained volunteers providing, typically, at least weekly contact for between 2 and 6 months
- a rehabilitation programme if a person's depression has resulted in loss of work or disengagement from other social activities over a longer term.

14.7   ENHANCED CARE FOR DEPRESSION

14.7.1.1 Medication management as a separate intervention for people with depression should not be provided routinely by services. It is likely to be effective only when provided as part of a more complex intervention.

14.7.1.2 For people with severe depression and those with moderate depression and complex problems, consider:

- referring to specialist mental health services for a programme of coordinated multiprofessional care
- providing collaborative care if the depression is in the context of a chronic physical health problem with associated functional impairment[223].

14.8   SEQUENCING TREATMENTS AFTER INITIAL INADEQUATE RESPONSE

14.8.1   Drug treatments

14.8.1.1 When reviewing drug treatment for a person with depression whose symptoms have not adequately responded to initial pharmacological interventions:

- check adherence to, and side effects from, initial treatment
- increase the frequency of appointments using outcome monitoring with a validated outcome measure

---

[223]Refer to 'Depression in adults with a chronic physical health problem: treatment and management' (NICE clinical guideline 91) for the evidence base for this.

- be aware that using a single antidepressant rather than combination medication or augmentation (see 14.8.1.5 to 14.8.1.9) is usually associated with a lower side effect burden
- consider reintroducing previous treatments that have been inadequately delivered or adhered to, including increasing the dose
- consider switching to an alternative antidepressant.

Switching antidepressants

14.8.1.2 When switching to another antidepressant, be aware that the evidence for the relative advantage of switching either within or between classes is weak. Consider switching to:
- initially a different SSRI or a better tolerated newer-generation antidepressant
- subsequently an antidepressant of a different pharmacological class that may be less well tolerated, for example venlafaxine, a TCA or an MAOI.

14.8.1.3 Do not switch to, or start, dosulepin because evidence supporting its tolerability relative to other antidepressants is outweighed by the increased cardiac risk and toxicity in overdose.

14.8.1.4 When switching to another antidepressant, which can normally be achieved within 1 week when switching from drugs with a short half life, consider the potential for interactions in determining the choice of new drug and the nature and duration of the transition. Exercise particular caution when switching:
- from fluoxetine to other antidepressants, because fluoxetine has a long half-life (approximately 1 week)
- from fluoxetine or paroxetine to a TCA, because both of these drugs inhibit the metabolism of TCAs; a lower starting dose of the TCA will be required, particularly if switching from fluoxetine because of its long half-life
- to a new serotonergic antidepressant or MAOI, because of the risk of serotonin syndrome[224]
- from a non-reversible MAOI: a 2-week washout period is required (other antidepressants should not be prescribed routinely during this period).

Combining and augmenting medications

14.8.1.5 When using combinations of medications (which should only normally be started in primary care in consultation with a consultant psychiatrist):
- select medications that are known to be safe when used together
- be aware of the increased side-effect burden this usually causes

---

[224]Features of serotonin syndrome include confusion, delirium, shivering, sweating, changes in blood pressure and myoclonus.

578

- discuss the rationale for any combination with the person with depression, follow GMC guidance if off-label medication is prescribed, and monitor carefully for adverse effects
- be familiar with primary evidence and consider obtaining a second opinion when using unusual combinations, the evidence for the efficacy of a chosen strategy is limited or the risk–benefit ratio is unclear
- document the rationale for the chosen combination.

14.8.1.6 If a person with depression is informed about, and prepared to tolerate, the increased side-effect burden, consider combining or augmenting an antidepressant with:

- lithium or
- an antipsychotic such as aripiprazole*, olanzapine*, quetiapine* or risperidone* or[225]
- another antidepressant such as mirtazapine or mianserin.

14.8.1.7 When prescribing lithium:

- monitor renal and thyroid function before treatment and every 6 months during treatment (more often if there is evidence of renal impairment)
- consider ECG monitoring in people with depression who are at high risk of cardiovascular disease
- monitor serum lithium levels 1 week after initiation and each dose change until stable, and every 3 months thereafter.

14.8.1.8 When prescribing an antipsychotic, monitor weight, lipid and glucose levels, and side effects (for example, extrapyramidal side effects and prolactin-related side effects with risperidone).

14.8.1.9 The following strategies should not be used routinely:

- augmentation of an antidepressant with a benzodiazepine for more than 2 weeks as there is a risk of dependence
- augmentation of an antidepressant with buspirone*, carbamazepine*, lamotrigine* or valproate* as there is insufficient evidence for their use
- augmentation of an antidepressant with pindolol* or thyroid hormones* as there is inconsistent evidence of effectiveness[226].

Combined psychological and drug treatment

14.8.1.10 For a person whose depression has not responded to either pharmacological or psychological interventions, consider combining antidepressant medication with CBT.

Referral

14.8.1.11 For a person whose depression has failed to respond to various strategies for augmentation and combination treatments, consider referral to a

---

[225]Drug names are marked with an asterisk if they do not have UK marketing authorisation for the indication in question at the time of publication. Informed consent should be obtained and documented.
[226]Ibid.

practitioner with a specialist interest in treating depression, or to a specialist service.

14.9   CONTINUATION AND RELAPSE PREVENTION

14.9.1.1   Support and encourage a person who has benefited from taking an antidepressant to continue medication for at least 6 months after remission of an episode of depression. Discuss with the person that:
- this greatly reduces the risk of relapse
- antidepressants are not associated with addiction.

14.9.1.2   Review with the person with depression the need for continued antidepressant treatment beyond 6 months after remission, taking into account:
- the number of previous episodes of depression
- the presence of residual symptoms
- concurrent physical health problems and psychosocial difficulties.

14.9.1.3   For people with depression who are at significant risk of relapse or have a history of recurrent depression, discuss with the person treatments to reduce the risk of recurrence, including continuing medication, augmentation of medication or psychological treatment (CBT). Treatment choice should be influenced by:
- previous treatment history, including the consequences of a relapse, residual symptoms, response to previous treatment and any discontinuation symptoms
- the person's preference.

Using medication for relapse prevention

14.9.1.4   Advise people with depression to continue antidepressants for at least 2 years if they are at risk of relapse. Maintain the level of medication at which acute treatment was effective (unless there is good reason to reduce the dose, such as unacceptable adverse effects) if:
- they have had two or more episodes of depression in the recent past, during which they experienced significant functional impairment
- they have other risk factors for relapse such as residual symptoms, multiple previous episodes, or a history of severe or prolonged episodes or of inadequate response
- the consequences of relapse are likely to be severe (for example, suicide attempts, loss of functioning, severe life disruption, and inability to work).

14.9.1.5   When deciding whether to continue maintenance treatment beyond 2 years, re-evaluate with the person with depression, taking into account age, comorbid conditions and other risk factors.

14.9.1.6   People with depression on long-term maintenance treatment should be regularly re-evaluated, with frequency of contact determined by:
- comorbid conditions

- risk factors for relapse
- severity and frequency of episodes of depression.

14.9.1.7 People who have had multiple episodes of depression, and who have had a good response to treatment with an antidepressant and an augmenting agent, should remain on this combination after remission if they find the side effects tolerable and acceptable. If one medication is stopped, it should usually be the augmenting agent. Lithium should not be used as a sole agent to prevent recurrence.

Psychological interventions for relapse prevention

14.9.1.8 People with depression who are considered to be at significant risk of relapse (including those who have relapsed despite antidepressant treatment or who are unable or choose not to continue antidepressant treatment) or who have residual symptoms, should be offered one of the following psychological interventions:
- individual CBT for people who have relapsed despite antidepressant medication and for people with a significant history of depression and residual symptoms despite treatment
- mindfulness-based cognitive therapy for people who are currently well but have experienced three or more previous episodes of depression.

Delivering psychological interventions for relapse prevention

14.9.1.9 For all people with depression who are having individual CBT for relapse prevention, the duration of treatment should typically be in the range of 16 to 20 sessions over 3 to 4 months. If the duration of treatment needs to be extended to achieve remission it should:
- consist of two sessions per week for the first 2 to 3 weeks of treatment
- include additional follow-up sessions, typically consisting of four to six sessions over the following 6 months.

14.9.1.10 Mindfulness-based cognitive therapy should normally be delivered in groups of 8 to 15 participants and consist of weekly 2-hour meetings over 8 weeks and four follow-up sessions in the 12 months after the end of treatment.

14.9.2 Stopping or reducing antidepressants

14.9.2.1 Advise people with depression who are taking antidepressants that discontinuation symptoms[227] may occur on stopping, missing doses or, occasionally, on reducing the dose of the drug. Explain that symptoms are usually

---

[227]Discontinuation symptoms include increased mood change, restlessness, difficulty sleeping, unsteadiness, sweating, abdominal symptoms and altered sensations.

mild and self-limiting over about 1 week, but can be severe, particularly if the drug is stopped abruptly.

14.9.2.2 When stopping an antidepressant, gradually reduce the dose, normally over a 4-week period, although some people may require longer periods, particularly with drugs with a shorter half-life (such as paroxetine and venlafaxine). This is not required with fluoxetine because of its long half-life.

14.9.2.3 Inform the person that they should seek advice from their practitioner if they experience significant discontinuation symptoms. If discontinuation symptoms occur:

- monitor symptoms and reassure the person if symptoms are mild
- consider reintroducing the original antidepressant at the dose that was effective (or another antidepressant with a longer half-life from the same class) if symptoms are severe, and reduce the dose gradually while monitoring symptoms.

14.10   STEP 4: COMPLEX AND SEVERE DEPRESSION

14.10.1.1 The assessment of a person with depression referred to specialist mental health services should include:

- their symptom profile, suicide risk and, where appropriate, previous treatment history
- associated psychosocial stressors, personality factors and significant relationship difficulties, particularly where the depression is chronic or recurrent
- associated comorbidities including alcohol and substance misuse, and personality disorders.

14.10.1.2 In specialist mental health services, after thoroughly reviewing previous treatments for depression, consider reintroducing previous treatments that have been inadequately delivered or adhered to.

14.10.1.3 Use crisis resolution and home treatment teams to manage crises for people with severe depression who present significant risk, and to deliver high-quality acute care. The teams should monitor risk as a high-priority routine activity in a way that allows people to continue their lives without disruption.

14.10.1.4 Medication in secondary care mental health services should be started under the supervision of a consultant psychiatrist.

14.10.1.5 Teams working with people with complex and severe depression should develop comprehensive multidisciplinary care plans in collaboration with the person with depression (and their family or carer, if agreed with the person). The care plan should:

- identify clearly the roles and responsibilities of all health and social care professionals involved
- develop a crisis plan that identifies potential triggers that could lead to a crisis and strategies to manage such triggers

● be shared with the GP and the person with depression and other relevant people involved in the person's care.

14.10.2   Inpatient care, and crisis resolution and home treatment teams

14.10.2.1 Consider inpatient treatment for people with depression who are at significant risk of suicide, self-harm or self-neglect.

14.10.2.2 The full range of high-intensity psychological interventions should normally be offered in inpatient settings. However, consider increasing the intensity and duration of the interventions and ensure that they can be provided effectively and efficiently on discharge.

14.10.2.3 Consider crisis resolution and home treatment teams for people with depression who might benefit from early discharge from hospital after a period of inpatient care.

14.10.3   Pharmacological management of depression with psychotic symptoms

14.10.3.1 For people who have depression with psychotic symptoms, consider augmenting the current treatment plan with antipsychotic medication (although the optimum dose and duration of treatment are unknown).

14.10.4   Electroconvulsive therapy (ECT)[228]

14.10.4.1 Consider ECT for acute treatment of severe depression that is life threatening and when a rapid response is required, or when other treatments have failed.

14.10.4.2 Do not use ECT routinely for people with moderate depression but consider it if their depression has not responded to multiple drug treatments and psychological treatment.

14.10.4.3 For people whose depression has not responded well to a previous course of ECT, consider a repeat trial of ECT only after:
● reviewing the adequacy of the previous treatment course and
● considering all other options and
● discussing the risks and benefits with the person and/or, where appropriate, their advocate or carer.

14.10.4.4 When considering ECT as a treatment choice, ensure that the person with depression is fully informed of the risks associated with ECT, and with the risks and benefits specific to them. Document the assessment and consider:
● the risks associated with a general anaesthetic

---

[228]The recommendations in this section update the depression aspects only of 'Guidance on the use of electroconvulsive therapy' (NICE technology appraisal guidance 59).

- current medical comorbidities
- potential adverse events, notably cognitive impairment
- the risks associated with not receiving ECT.

The risks associated with ECT may be greater in older people; exercise particular caution when considering ECT treatment in this group.

14.10.4.5 A decision to use ECT should be made jointly with the person with depression as far as possible, taking into account, where applicable, the requirements of the Mental Health Act 2007. Also be aware that:

- valid informed consent should be obtained (if the person has the capacity to grant or refuse consent) without the pressure or coercion that might occur as a result of the circumstances and clinical setting
- the person should be reminded of their right to withdraw consent at any time
- there should be strict adherence to recognised guidelines about consent, and advocates or carers should be involved to facilitate informed discussions
- if informed consent is not possible, ECT should only be given if it does not conflict with a valid advance decision, and the person's advocate or carer should be consulted.

14.10.4.6 The choice of electrode placement and stimulus dose related to seizure threshold should balance efficacy against the risk of cognitive impairment. Take into account that:

- bilateral ECT is more effective than unilateral ECT but may cause more cognitive impairment
- with unilateral ECT, a higher stimulus dose is associated with greater efficacy, but also increased cognitive impairment compared with a lower stimulus dose.

14.10.4.7 Assess clinical status after each ECT treatment using a formal valid outcome measure, and stop treatment when remission has been achieved, or sooner if side effects outweigh the potential benefits.

14.10.4.8 Assess cognitive function before the first ECT treatment and monitor at least every three to four treatments, and at the end of a course of treatment.

14.10.4.9 Assessment of cognitive function should include:

- orientation and time to reorientation after each treatment
- measures of new learning, retrograde amnesia and subjective memory impairment carried out at least 24 hours after a treatment.

If there is evidence of significant cognitive impairment at any stage consider, in discussion with the person with depression, changing from bilateral to unilateral electrode placement, reducing the stimulus dose or stopping treatment depending on the balance of risks and benefits.

14.10.4.10 If a person's depression has responded to a course of ECT, antidepressant medication should be started or continued to prevent relapse. Consider lithium augmentation of antidepressants.

14.10.5   Transcranial magnetic stimulation

14.10.5.1 Current evidence suggests that there are no major safety concerns associated with transcranial magnetic stimulation (TMS) for severe depression. There is uncertainty about the procedure's clinical efficacy, which may depend on higher intensity, greater frequency, bilateral application and/or longer treatment durations than have appeared in the evidence to date. TMS should therefore be performed only in research studies designed to investigate these factors[229].

14.11   RESEARCH RECOMMENDATIONS

14.11.1.1 Sequencing antidepressant treatment after inadequate initial response
What is the best medication strategy for people with depression who have not had sufficient response to a first SSRI antidepressant after 6 to 8 weeks of adequate treatment?

Why this is important
Inadequate response to a first antidepressant is a frequent problem but the best way of sequencing treatments is not clear from the available evidence. There is good evidence that the likelihood of eventual response decreases with the duration of depression and number of failed treatment attempts, so maximising the response at an early stage may be an important factor in the final outcome. The results of this study will be generalisable to a large number of people with depression and will inform choice of treatment.

This question should be addressed using a randomised controlled trial design to compare the effects of continuing on the same antidepressant (with dose increase if appropriate) and switching to another SSRI or to an antidepressant of another class. Built into the design should be an assessment of the effect of increased frequency of follow-up and monitoring alone on improvement. The outcomes chosen should reflect both observer and patient-rated assessments of improvement and an assessment of the acceptability of the treatment options. The study needs to be large enough to determine the presence or absence of clinically important effects using a non-inferiority design, and mediators and moderators of response should be investigated.

14.11.1.2 The efficacy of short-term psychodynamic psychotherapy compared with CBT and antidepressants in the treatment of moderate to severe depression
In well-defined depression of moderate to severe severity, what is the efficacy of short-term psychodynamic psychotherapy compared with CBT and antidepressants?

---

[229]This recommendation is taken from 'Transcranial magnetic stimulation for severe depression' (NICE interventional procedure guidance 242).

Why this is important

Psychological treatments are an important therapeutic option for people with depression. CBT has the best evidence base for efficacy but it is not effective for everyone. The availability of alternatives drawing from a different theoretical model is therefore important. Psychotherapy based on psychodynamic principles has historically been provided in the NHS but provision is patchy and a good evidence base is lacking. It is therefore important to establish whether short-term psychodynamic psychotherapy is an effective alternative to CBT and one that should be provided. The results of this study will have important implications for the provision of psychological treatment in the NHS.

This question should be answered using a randomised controlled trial design that reports short-term and medium-term outcomes (including cost-effectiveness outcomes) of at least 18 months' duration. Particular attention should be paid to the reproducibility of the treatment model and training and supervision of those providing interventions in order to ensure that the treatments are both robust and generalisable. The outcomes chosen should reflect both observer and patient-rated assessments of improvement and an assessment of the acceptability of the treatment options. The study needs to be large enough to determine the presence or absence of clinically important effects using a non-inferiority design, and mediators and moderators of response should be investigated.

14.11.1.3 The cost effectiveness of combined antidepressants and CBT compared with sequenced treatment for moderate to severe depression

What is the cost effectiveness of combined antidepressants and CBT compared with sequenced medication followed by CBT and vice versa for moderate to severe depression?

Why this is important

There is a reasonable evidence base for the superior effectiveness of combined antidepressants and CBT over either treatment alone in moderate to severe depression. However the practicality, acceptability and cost effectiveness of combined treatment over a sequenced approach is less well-established. The answer has important practical implications for service delivery and resource implications for the NHS.

This question should be answered using a randomised controlled trial design in which people with moderate to severe depression receive either combined treatment from the outset, or single modality treatment with the addition of the other modality if there is inadequate response to initial treatment. The outcomes chosen should reflect both observer and patient-rated assessments for acute and medium-term outcomes to at least 6 months, and an assessment of the acceptability and burden of the treatment options. The study needs to be large enough to determine the presence or absence of clinically important effects using a non-inferiority design together with robust health economic measures.

14.11.1.4 The efficacy of light therapy compared with antidepressants for mild to moderate depression with a seasonal pattern

How effective is light therapy compared with antidepressants for mild to moderate depression with a seasonal pattern?

Why this is important

Although the status of seasonal depression as a separate entity is not entirely clear, surveys have consistently reported a high prevalence of seasonal (predominantly winter) depression in the UK. This reflects a considerable degree of morbidity, predominantly in the winter months, for people with this condition. Light therapy has been proposed as a specific treatment for winter depression but only small, inconclusive trials have been carried out, from which it is not possible to tell whether either light therapy or antidepressants are effective in its treatment. Clarification of whether, and to what degree, treatments are effective would help to inform the decisions that people with seasonal depression and practitioners have to make about the treatment of winter depression.

This question should be answered using a randomised controlled trial design in which people with mild to moderate depression with a seasonal pattern (seasonal affective disorder) receive light therapy or an SSRI antidepressant in a partially placebo-controlled design. The doses of both light and SSRI should be at accepted or proposed therapeutic levels and there should be an initial phase over a few weeks in which a plausible placebo treatment is administered followed by randomisation to one of the active treatments. The outcomes chosen should reflect both observer and patient-rated assessments of improvement and an assessment of the acceptability of the treatment options. The study needs to be large enough to determine the presence or absence of clinically important effects, and mediators and moderators of response should be investigated.

14.11.1.5 The efficacy of CBT compared with antidepressants and placebo for persistent subthreshold depressive symptoms

What is the efficacy of CBT compared with antidepressants and placebo for persistent subthreshold depressive symptoms?

Why this is important

Persistent subthreshold depressive symptoms are increasingly recognised as affecting a considerable number of people and causing significant suffering, but the best way to treat it is not known. There are studies of the efficacy of antidepressants for dysthymia (persistent subthreshold depressive symptoms that have lasted for at least 2 years) but there is a lack of evidence for CBT. Subthreshold depressive symptoms of recent onset tend to improve but how long practitioners should wait before offering medication or psychological treatment is not known. This research recommendation is aimed at informing the treatment options available for this group of people with subthreshold depressive symptoms that persist despite low-intensity interventions.

This question should be answered using a randomised controlled trial design that reports short-term and medium-term outcomes (including cost-effectiveness outcomes) of at least 6 months' duration. A careful definition of persistence should be used which needs to include duration of symptoms and consideration of failure of low-intensity interventions and does not necessarily imply a full diagnosis of dysthymia. The outcomes chosen should reflect both observer and patient-rated assessments of improvement and an assessment of the acceptability of the treatment options. The study needs to be large enough to determine the presence or absence of clinically important effects using a non-inferiority design, and mediators and moderators of response should be investigated.

14.11.1.6 The efficacy of counselling compared with low-intensity cognitive behavioural interventions and treatment as usual in the treatment of persistent subthreshold depressive symptoms and mild depression

In persistent subthreshold depressive symptoms and mild depression, what is the efficacy of counselling compared with low-intensity cognitive behavioural interventions?

Why this is important

Psychological treatments are an important therapeutic option for people with subthreshold symptoms and mild depression. Low-intensity cognitive and behavioural interventions have the best evidence base for efficacy but the evidence is limited and longer-term outcomes are uncertain, as are the outcomes for counselling. It is therefore important to establish whether either of these interventions is an effective alternative to treatment as usual and should be provided in the NHS. The results of this study will have important implications for the provision of psychological treatment in the NHS.

This question should be answered using a randomised controlled trial design which reports short-term and medium-term outcomes (including cost-effectiveness outcomes) of at least 18 months' duration. Particular attention should be paid to the reproducibility of the treatment model and training and supervision of those providing interventions in order to ensure that the treatments are both robust and generalisable. The outcomes chosen should reflect both observer and patient-rated assessments of improvement and an assessment of the acceptability of the treatment options. The study needs to be large enough to determine the presence or absence of clinically important effects using a non-inferiority design, and mediators and moderators of response should be investigated.

14.11.1.7 The efficacy of behavioural activation compared with CBT and antidepressants in the treatment of moderate to severe depression

In well-defined depression of moderate to severe severity, what is the efficacy of behavioural activation compared with CBT and antidepressants?

Why this is important

Psychological treatments are an important therapeutic option for people with depression. Behavioural activation is a promising treatment but does not have the substantial evidence base that CBT has. The availability of alternatives drawing from a different theoretical model is important because outcomes are modest even with the best supported treatments. It is therefore important to establish whether behavioural activation is an effective alternative to CBT and one that should be provided. The results of this study will have important implications for the provision of psychological treatment in the NHS.

This question should be answered using a randomised controlled trial design which reports short-term and medium-term outcomes (including cost-effectiveness outcomes) of at least 18 months' duration. Particular attention should be paid to the reproducibility of the treatment model and training and supervision of those providing interventions in order to ensure that the treatments are both robust and generalisable. The outcomes chosen should reflect both observer and patient-rated assessments of improvement and an assessment of the acceptability of the treatment options. The study needs to be large enough to determine the presence or absence of clinically important effects using a non-inferiority design, and mediators and moderators of response should be investigated.

14.11.1.8 The efficacy and cost effectiveness of different systems for the organisation of care for people with depression
In people with mild, moderate or severe depression, what system of care (stepped care versus matched care) is more clinically effective and cost effective in improving outcomes?

Why this is important
The best structures for the delivery of effective care for depression are poorly understood. Stepped-care models are widely implemented but the efficacy of this model compared with matched care is uncertain. Evidence on the relative benefits of the two approaches and the differential effects by depression severity is needed. The results of this study will have important implications for the structure of depression treatment services in the NHS.

This question should be answered using a randomised controlled trial design which reports short-term and medium-term outcomes (including cost-effectiveness outcomes) of at least 18 months' duration. In stepped care the majority of patients will first be offered a low-intensity intervention by a paraprofessional unless there are significant risk factors dictating otherwise. In matched care a comprehensive mental health assessment will determine which intervention a patient should receive. The full range of effective interventions (both psychological and pharmacological) should be made available in both arms of the trial. The outcomes chosen should reflect both observer and patient-rated assessments of improvement and an assessment of the acceptability of the treatment options. The study needs to be large enough to determine the presence or absence of clinically important effects, and moderators (including the severity of depression) of response should be investigated.

14.11.1.9 The efficacy and cost effectiveness of CBT, IPT and antidepressants in prevention of relapse in people with moderate to severe recurrent depression
In people with moderate to severe recurrent depression, what is the relative efficacy of CBT, IPT and antidepressants in preventing relapse?

Why this is important
Psychological and pharmacological treatments are important therapeutic options for people with depression, but evidence on the prevention of relapse (especially for psychological interventions) is limited. All of these treatments have shown promise in reducing relapse but the relapse rate remains high. New developments in the style

and delivery of CBT and IPT show some promise in reducing relapse but need to be tested in a large-scale trial. The results of this study will have important implications for the provision of psychological treatment in the NHS.

This question should be answered using a randomised controlled trial design which reports short-term and medium-term outcomes (including cost-effectiveness outcomes) of at least 24 months' duration. Particular attention should be paid to the development and evaluation of CBT, IPT and medication interventions tailored specifically to prevent relapse, including the nature and duration of the intervention. The outcomes chosen should reflect both observer and patient-rated assessments of improvement and an assessment of the acceptability of the treatment options. The study needs to be large enough to determine the presence or absence of clinically important effects using a non-inferiority design, and mediators (including the focus of the interventions) and moderators (including the severity of the depression) of response should be investigated.

14.11.1.10 The effectiveness of maintenance ECT for relapse prevention in people with severe and recurring depression that does not respond to pharmacological or psychological interventions

Is maintenance ECT effective for relapse prevention in people with severe and recurring depression that does not respond to pharmacological or psychological interventions?

Why this is important
A small number of people do not benefit in any significant way from pharmacological or psychological interventions but do respond to ECT. However, many of these people relapse and need repeated treatment with ECT. This results in considerable suffering to them and it is also costly, because ECT often necessitates inpatient care. A small number of studies suggest possible benefits from maintenance ECT but it is used little in the NHS. The outcome of the audit and clinical trial should supply information on patient characteristics, outcomes, feasibility and acceptability in relation to the use of maintenance ECT and potentially inform its wider use in the NHS. The results therefore may have important implications for the provision of ECT in the NHS.

This question should be addressed through first establishing a national audit for the collection of data on all people receiving maintenance ECT. The characteristics of the people who are likely to be considered for maintenance ECT make a randomised controlled trial unfeasible, but a clinical trial using alternative methods (for example, mirror image or a carefully characterised non-randomised study) should be undertaken depending on the outcome of the audit.

The number of people receiving maintenance ECT is small, and considerable uncertainty surrounds its use, such as its long-term efficacy and acceptability and possible side effects, which include cognitive impairment. The outcomes chosen for the audit and clinical trial should reflect both observer and patient-rated assessments of improvement, the impact on cognitive function and an assessment of the acceptability of ECT as a maintenance treatment.

15 APPENDICES

Appendix 1: Scope for the development of the clinical guideline   593

Appendix 2: Declarations of interest by Guideline
Development Group members   598

Appendix 3: Special advisers to the Guideline Development Group   610

Appendix 4: Stakeholders and experts who submitted comments
in response to the consultation draft of the guideline   611

Appendix 5: Stakeholders and experts who submitted comments
in response to the pre-publication check   613

Appendix 6: Researchers contacted to request information about
unpublished or soon-to-be published studies   614

Appendix 7: Clinical questions   615

Appendix 8: Search strategies for the identification of clinical studies   619

Appendix 9: Clinical study data extraction form   622

Appendix 10: Quality checklists for clinical studies and reviews   623

Appendix 11: The classification of depression and depression rating
scales/questionnaires   628

Appendix 12: Search strategies for the identification of health
economics evidence   640

Appendix 13: Quality checklist for economic studies   642

Appendix 14: Data extraction form for economic studies   644

Appendix 15: Evidence tables for economic studies   On CD

Appendix 16: Clinical evidence profiles   On CD

Appendices

Appendix 17: Clinical study characteristics tables   On CD

Appendix 18: References to studies from previous guideline   On CD

Appendix 19: Clinical evidence forest plots   On CD

Appendix 20: Case identification included and excluded studies On CD

Appendix 21: Methodology from previous guideline   On CD

APPENDIX 1:
SCOPE FOR THE DEVELOPMENT OF THE CLINICAL GUIDELINE

GUIDELINE TITLE

Depression: the treatment and management of depression in adults (update)

Short title

Depression in adults (update)

BACKGROUND

The National Institute for Health and Clinical Excellence ('NICE' or 'the Institute') has commissioned the National Collaborating Centre for Mental Health to review recent evidence on the treatment and management of depression and to update the existing guideline 'Depression: management of depression in primary and secondary care' (amended) (NICE clinical guideline 23, 2007a). The guideline update will provide recommendations for good practice that are based on the best available evidence of clinical and cost effectiveness.

The Institute's clinical guidelines support the implementation of National Service Frameworks (NSFs) in those aspects of care for which a Framework has been published. The statements in each NSF reflect the evidence that was used at the time the Framework was prepared. The clinical guidelines and technology appraisals published by NICE after an NSF has been issued have the effect of updating the Framework.

NICE clinical guidelines support the role of healthcare professionals in providing care in partnership with service users, taking account of their individual needs and preferences, and ensuring that service users (and their carers and families, if appropriate) can make informed decisions about their care and treatment.

CLINICAL NEED FOR THE GUIDELINE

Depression refers to a range of mental health disorders characterised by the absence of a positive affect (a loss of interest and enjoyment in ordinary things and experiences), low mood and a range of associated emotional, cognitive, physical and behavioural symptoms. It is often accompanied by anxiety, and can be chronic even in milder presentations. People with more severe depression may also develop psychotic symptoms (hallucinations and/or delusions).

The symptoms of depression can be disabling and the effects of the illness pervasive. Depression can have a major detrimental effect on people's personal, social and occupational functioning, placing a heavy burden on individuals and their carers and dependents, as well as placing considerable demands on the healthcare system. Among all diseases, depression is currently the fourth leading cause of burden to society. World Health Organisation projections indicate that it will be the highest ranking cause of disease burden in developed countries by the year 2020.

Each year 6% of adults will experience an episode of depression and over the course of their lifetime more than 15% of the population will experience an episode. The average length of an episode of depression is between 6 and 8 months. For many people the episode will be mild but for more than 30%, the depression with be moderate or severe and have a significant impact on their daily lives. Recurrence rates are high; there is a 50% chance of recurrence after a first episode, rising to 70% and 90% after a second or third episode respectively.

Estimated prevalence rates for men do not vary greatly among ethnic groups but those for women differ remarkably. In the UK significantly higher rates of depression are reported in women of Asian and Oriental family origin or background compared with other groups, with the next highest rates being in white women and the lowest rates in women of West Indian or African family origin or background. However, these estimates are based on relatively small samples.

Depression is the leading cause of suicide, which accounts for less than 1% of all deaths. Nearly two-thirds of deaths by suicide occur in people with depression (that is, about 2,600 suicides per year in England alone).

Data from the Prescription Cost Analysis (PCA; Department of Health, 2008a) system show that in the 12 months to March 2006, antidepressant drugs accounted for 4.1% of all items dispensed in the community in England, at a net ingredient cost of £31 million.

The NICE clinical guideline 'Depression: management of depression in primary and secondary care' (clinical guideline 23) was published in December 2004, and was amended in 2007 to take into account new prescribing advice for venlafaxine. New evidence regarding the care of people with depression involving psychosocial, pharmacological and other physical interventions means that NICE's original guideline on depression needs to be updated.

THE GUIDELINE

The guideline development process is described in detail in two publications that are available from the NICE website (see 'Further information'). 'The guideline development process: an overview for stakeholders, the public and the NHS' (NICE, 2007b) describes how organisations can become involved in the development of a guideline.

'The guidelines manual' (NICE, 2007c) provides advice on the technical aspects of guideline development.

This document is the scope. It defines exactly what this guideline will (and will not) examine, and what the guideline developers will consider. The areas that will be addressed by the guideline are described in the following sections.

POPULATION

Groups that will be covered

- Adults (aged 18 years and older) who have a clinical diagnosis of depression established by a recognised diagnostic system such as DSM–IV or ICD–10. The guideline will be relevant to people with mild, moderate and severe major depressive disorders.
- People in the above group who also have learning difficulties, acquired cognitive impairments, or language difficulties.

Groups that will not be covered

- People with chronic physical disorders. A separate guideline on the treatment of depression in people with chronic physical health problems has been commissioned and will be developed in conjunction with this guideline.
- People with other primary psychiatric disorders, such as schizophrenia or substance misuse.

HEALTHCARE SETTING

Primary, secondary and tertiary care. The guidance will be relevant to all healthcare professionals who provide care for people with depression, irrespective of setting.

CLINICAL MANAGEMENT

- Recognition, assessment and classification of depression, including variations to the assessment to take account of the needs of people with learning difficulties, acquired cognitive impairments or language difficulties.
- Treatment of depressive episodes of differing severity, including the appropriate use of psychosocial interventions (such as guided self-help, formal psychological interventions, support groups and programmes aimed at facilitating employment), pharmacological interventions (including antidepressants and other medication), and physical interventions (such as exercise and electroconvulsive therapy).

- Variations to the systems for accessing and delivering treatment required to take account of the needs of people with learning difficulties, acquired cognitive impairments or language difficulties.
- Interventions to reduce the risk of relapse after an acute depressive episode.
- Assessment and management of the known side effects and other drawbacks of psychotropic medication, physical interventions, and psychosocial interventions, including long-term side effects and risks of suicide.
- Combined psychosocial and pharmacological treatments, the use of combined pharmacological treatments and the sequencing of both pharmacological and psychosocial interventions.
- The safe withdrawal/discontinuation of psychotropic medication.
- Interactions between psychotropic medication and common prescription and over-the-counter drugs.
- The varying approaches of different races and cultures, and issues of internal and external social exclusion.
- The role of the families and carers in the treatment and support of people with depression.
- The ways in which services are delivered, including models of care such as case management and collaborative care, and the structured delivery of care in primary and secondary care services.

Note that guideline recommendations for pharmacological interventions will normally fall within licensed indications; exceptionally, and only if clearly supported by evidence, use outside a licensed indication may be recommended. The guideline will assume that prescribers will use a drug's summary of product characteristics to inform their decisions for individual service users.

The Guideline Development Group will take reasonable steps to identify ineffective interventions and approaches to care. If robust and credible recommendations for re-positioning an intervention for optimal use or changing an approach to care to make more efficient use of resources can be made, they will be clearly stated. If the resources released are substantial, consideration will be given to listing such recommendations in the 'Key priorities for implementation' section of the guideline.

AREAS THAT WILL NOT BE COVERED BY THE GUIDELINE

The guideline will not cover:
- diagnosis of depression
- primary prevention of depression.

STATUS

Scope

This is the final scope.

The guideline will be developed in conjunction with 'Depression: the treatment and management of depression in adults with a chronic physical health problem'; together they will update 'Depression: management of depression in primary and secondary care (amended)' (NICE clinical guideline 23 [2007a]).

They will also update and replace the following NICE guidance:

- Computerised cognitive behaviour therapy for depression and anxiety. NICE technology appraisal guidance 51 (2006a).
- Guidance on the use of electroconvulsive therapy. NICE technology appraisal guidance 59 (2003).

GUIDELINE

The development of the guideline recommendations will begin in November 2007.

FURTHER INFORMATION

Information on the guideline development process is provided in:

- 'The guideline development process: an overview for stakeholders, the public and the NHS' (NICE, 2007b).
- 'The guidelines manual' (NICE, 2007a).

These are available as Portable Document Files (PDFs) from the NICE website (www.nice.org.uk/guidelinesmanual). Information on the progress of the guideline will also be available from the website.

APPENDIX 2:
DECLARATIONS OF INTEREST BY GUIDELINE DEVELOPMENT GROUP MEMBERS

With a range of practical experience relevant to depression in the GDG, members were appointed because of their understanding and expertise in healthcare for people with depression and support for their families and carers, including: scientific issues; health research; the delivery and receipt of healthcare, along with the work of the healthcare industry; and the role of professional organisations and organisations for people with depression and their families and carers.

To minimise and manage any potential conflicts of interest, and to avoid any public concern that commercial or other financial interests have affected the work of the GDG and influenced guidance, members of the GDG must declare as a matter of public record any interests held by themselves or their families which fall under specified categories (see below). These categories include any relationships they have with the healthcare industries, professional organisations and organisations for people with depression and their families and carers.

Individuals invited to join the GDG were asked to declare their interests before being appointed. To allow the management of any potential conflicts of interest that might arise during the development of the guideline, GDG members were also asked to declare their interests at each GDG meeting throughout the guideline development process. The interests of all the members of the GDG are listed below, including interests declared prior to appointment and during the guideline development process.

Categories of interest

- Paid employment
- Personal pecuniary interest: financial payments or other benefits from either the manufacturer or the owner of the product or service under consideration in this guideline, or the industry or sector from which the product or service comes. This includes holding a directorship, or other paid position; carrying out consultancy or fee paid work; having shareholdings or other beneficial interests; receiving expenses and hospitality over and above what would be reasonably expected to attend meetings and conferences.
- Personal family interest: financial payments or other benefits from the healthcare industry that were received by a member of your family.
- Non-personal pecuniary interest: financial payments or other benefits received by the GDG member's organisation or department, but where the GDG member has not personally received payment, including fellowships and other support

provided by the healthcare industry. This includes a grant or fellowship or other payment to sponsor a post, or contribute to the running costs of the department; commissioning of research or other work; contracts with, or grants from, NICE.

- Personal non-pecuniary interest: these include, but are not limited to, clear opinions or public statements you have made about depression, holding office in a professional organisation or advocacy group with a direct interest in depression, other reputational risks relevant to depression.

Declarations of interest – GDG members	
Professor Ian Anderson, Chair, Guideline Development Group	
Employment	Professor of Psychiatry, University of Manchester
Personal pecuniary interest	Consultant for Wyeth Ltd Global Depression and Anxiety Strategy Consultant Board (specific), ended August 2007 Consultant for Bristol-Myers Squibb Pharmaceuticals Ltd/Otsuka Pharmaceuticals UK Ltd Bipolar Disorder Advisory Board (non-specific), ended August 2007 Consultant for Servier Ltd Agomelatine Advisory Board, ended August 2007 Honoraria for speaking at non-promotional meetings from the following companies: AstraZeneca, Wyeth, Janssen Cilag, Lundbeck, 2007–2008
Personal family interest	None
Non-personal pecuniary interest	AstraZeneca investigator – initiated grant (specific) Honorarium paid into university research fund by Wyeth Ltd for speaking at non-promotional meeting Talk on Managing Depression (independent content) at meeting supported by Lilly P1vital commercial study sponsored by Servier

Continued

Declarations of interest – GDG members (*Continued*)	
Personal non-pecuniary interest	Member of MHRA Psychiatry Expert Advisory Group Member of Royal College of Psychiatrists Special Committee on ECT
Ms Alison Barnes	
Employment	Social Worker
Personal pecuniary interest	None
Personal family interest	None
Non-personal pecuniary interest	None
Personal non-pecuniary interest	None
Dr Carolyn Chew-Graham	
Employment	General Practitioner and Senior Lecturer in Primary Care, University of Manchester
Personal pecuniary interest	Mental health clinical adviser for Manchester Joint Commissioning Team (Manchester Primary Care Trust, Central PBC Hub)
Personal family interest	None
Non-personal pecuniary interest	None
Personal non-pecuniary interest	None
Mr Jeremy Clarke	
Employment	Psychological Therapist, Lambeth Primary Care Trust
Personal pecuniary interest	None
Personal family interest	None
Non-personal pecuniary interest	None
Personal non-pecuniary interest	Research and development lead for the Association of Psychoanalytic Psychotherapy in the NHS

Continued

Declarations of interest – GDG members (*Continued*)	
	Member of Expert Reference Group for Improving Access to Psychological Therapies (IAPT)
Ms Catherine Harris	
Employment	Labour Councillor for Haringey
Personal pecuniary interest	Mental Health Act Commissioner from April 2008
Personal family interest	None
Non-personal pecuniary interest	None
Personal non-pecuniary interest	Role as councillor does not entail a portfolio for health issues although the Labour Party campaigns on health issues Member of Mental Health Carers Support Association
Dr Mark Kenwright	
Employment	Consultant Cognitive Behavioural Psychotherapist, Ealing Cognitive Behavioural Therapy Service
Personal pecuniary interest	None
Personal family interest	None
Non-personal pecuniary interest	None
Personal non-pecuniary interest	Coordinator of two pilot studies and an RCT on computerised cognitive behavioural therapy (CCBT), guided self-help for panic disorder and phobias formed focus of doctoral thesis and three publications in *British Journal of Psychiatry* (1999 to 2002) Manager of Stress Self-Help Clinic research project in first CCBT clinic in primary care which offered CCBT for panic/phobia (Fearfighter), obsessive-compulsive disorder (BT Steps) and depression (COPE). Published in *Psychological Medicine* (2001 to 2003)

Continued

Declarations of interest – GDG members (*Continued*)	
	Project lead for Improving Access to Psychological Therapies (IAPT) Pathfinder Site for London and South East (Ealing CBT Service). The service received £200,000 from IAPT for the period October 2007 to 2008
Professor Willem Kuyken	
Employment	Professor of Clinical Psychology and Co-Director Mood Disorders Centre, University of Exeter Psychology
Personal pecuniary interest	None
Personal family interest	None
Non-personal pecuniary interest	None
Personal non-pecuniary interest	Co-director of Mood Disorders Centre, funded by Devon Partnership NHS Trust and Devon Primary Care Trust Co-principal investigator, NHS HTA (£1.2 million, 1.7 million with NHS costs). Cognitive behavioural therapy as an adjunct to pharmacotherapy for treatment resistant depression in primary care: a randomised control trial. 2008 to 2011. (Principal Investigator: Dr Nicola Wiles, University of Bristol) Principal Investigator, Medical Research Council (£233,000). Trial platform: Preventing depression relapse in NHS practice using mindfulness-based cognitive therapy (MBCT) 2005 to 2007
Professor Glyn Lewis	
Employment	Professor of Psychiatric Epidemiology, University of Bristol
Personal pecuniary interest	Occasional payment from pharmaceutical companies for non-promotional talks, for example, to other departments of psychiatry or at conferences
Personal family interest	None

Continued

Declarations of interest – GDG members (*Continued*)	
Non-personal pecuniary interest	Colleagues in department at Bristol University received funds from pharmaceutical industry to carry out research which I am not involved in
Personal non-pecuniary interest	None
Mr Brendan Masterson	
Employment	Clinical Nurse Leader, Affective Disorders Unit, Bethlem Royal Hospital
Personal pecuniary interest	Presented a session on NICE guidelines for bipolar disorder at a study day sponsored by Janssen Cilag (February 2007)
Personal family interest	None
Non-personal pecuniary interest	None
Personal non-pecuniary interest	None
Mr Alan Meudell	
Employment	Healthy Minds at Work
Personal pecuniary interest	None
Personal family interest	None
Non-personal pecuniary interest	None
Personal non-pecuniary interest	Member of Mind Expert Policy Group on Psychiatric Medicine and other Therapies
	Member of Pwyllgor Cymru (Governance body of Mind Cymru, Mind Wales)
	Member of Caerphilly Borough Council Mental Health Strategy Group
	Member of Adult Mental Health NSF Implementation Advisory Group (WAG)
Dr Alex Mitchell	
Employment	Consultant Psychiatrist and Honorary Lecturer in Liaison Psychiatry, University of Leicester

Continued

Declarations of interest – GDG members (*Continued*)	
Personal pecuniary interest	None
Personal family interest	None
Non-personal pecuniary interest	None
Personal non-pecuniary interest	None
Dr Richard Moore	
Employment	Clinical Psychologist, Cambridge and Peterborough NHS Foundation Trust
Personal pecuniary interest	None
Personal family interest	None
Non-personal pecuniary interest	None
Personal non-pecuniary interest	Interest in effectiveness of treatments for depression including taking part in related RCTs and the production of a treatment manual for treatment of chronic depression
Ms Carol Paton	
Employment	Chief Pharmacist, Oxleas NHS Foundation Trust
Personal pecuniary interest	Eli Lilly Advisory Board and consultancy for duloxetine. Involvement has been since phase three trials and is not ongoing (2003–2007)
	Attendance at European Congress of Neuropsychopharmacology (ECNP) 2007, sponsored by Janssen Cilag, without personal financial gain
	Eli Lilly Advisory Board for other products currently subject to clinical trials: depot IM olanzapine and novel drugs in phase two studies. None of these drugs was currently licensed and none was intended to treat depression (February 2008)
Personal family interest	None
Non-personal pecuniary interest	None

Continued

Declarations of interest – GDG members (*Continued*)	
Personal non-pecuniary interest	Co-author of paper describing clinical use of depot antipsychotics in the United Kingdom, to be published in *British Medical Journal* supplement. The supplement is funded by Eli Lilly who have no influence over the content. No personal payment has been or will be received for this (April 2008)
Dr Thomas Shackleton	
Employment	General Practitioner, Suffolk
Personal pecuniary interest	None
Personal family interest	None
Non-personal pecuniary interest	None
Personal non-pecuniary interest	None
Ms Jane Wood	
Employment	Nurse, Strategic Development Manager, Mental Health, Leeds Primary Care Trust
Personal pecuniary interest	None
Personal family interest	None
Non-personal pecuniary interest	None
Personal non-pecuniary interest	None

Declarations of interest – NCCMH staff	
Professor Stephen Pilling – Facilitator, Guideline Development Group	
Employment	Director, NCCMH Director, Centre for Outcomes Research and Effectiveness, University College London
Personal pecuniary interest	In receipt of funding from NICE to develop clinical guidelines
Personal family interest	None

Continued

Declarations of interest – NCCMH staff *(Continued)*	
Non-personal pecuniary interest	RCT to evaluate multi-systemic therapy. Chief Investigator is Professor Peter Fonagy. Department of Health funding of £1,000,000 (2008 to 2012)
Personal non-pecuniary interest	None
Ms Victoria Bird	
Employment	Research Assistant, NCCMH
Personal pecuniary interest	None
Personal family interest	None
Non-personal pecuniary interest	None
Personal non-pecuniary interest	None
Ms Rachel Burbeck	
Employment	Systematic Reviewer, NCCMH
Personal pecuniary interest	None
Personal family interest	None
Non-personal pecuniary interest	None
Personal non-pecuniary interest	None
Mr Matthew Dyer (from 2008)	
Employment	Health Economist, NCCMH
Personal pecuniary interest	None
Personal family interest	None
Non-personal pecuniary interest	None
Personal non-pecuniary interest	None
Ms Sarah Hopkins (2007 to 2008)	
Employment	Project Manager, NCCMH
Personal pecuniary interest	None
Personal family interest	None
Non-personal pecuniary interest	None
Personal non-pecuniary interest	None

Continued

Declarations of interest – NCCMH staff *(Continued)*	
Ms Angela Lewis	
Employment	Research Assistant, NCCMH
Personal pecuniary interest	None
Personal family interest	None
Non-personal pecuniary interest	None
Personal non-pecuniary interest	None
Mr Ryan Li (2008)	
Employment	Project Manager, NCCMH
Personal pecuniary interest	None
Personal family interest	None
Non-personal pecuniary interest	None
Personal non-pecuniary interest	None
Mr Nick Meader	
Employment	Systematic Reviewer, NCCMH
Personal pecuniary interest	None
Personal family interest	None
Non-personal pecuniary interest	None
Personal non-pecuniary interest	None
Dr Suffiya Omarjee (from 2008)	
Employment	Health Economist, NCCMH
Personal pecuniary interest	None
Personal family interest	None
Non-personal pecuniary interest	None
Personal non-pecuniary interest	None
Ms Peny Retsa (until 2008)	
Employment	Health Economist, NCCMH
Personal pecuniary interest	None
Personal family interest	None

Continued

Declarations of interest – NCCMH staff *(Continued)*	
Non-personal pecuniary interest	None
Personal non-pecuniary interest	None
Ms Maria Rizzo	
Employment	Research Assistant, NCCMH
Personal pecuniary interest	None
Personal family interest	None
Non-personal pecuniary interest	None
Personal non-pecuniary interest	None
Ms Jennie Robertson	
Employment	Research Assistant, NCCMH
Personal pecuniary interest	None
Personal family interest	None
Non-personal pecuniary interest	None
Personal non-pecuniary interest	None
Mr Rob Saunders	
Employment	Research Assistant, NCCMH
Personal pecuniary interest	None
Personal family interest	None
Non-personal pecuniary interest	None
Personal non-pecuniary interest	None
Ms Christine Sealey (from 2008)	
Employment	Centre Manager, NCCMH
Personal pecuniary interest	On secondment from NICE
Personal family interest	None
Non-personal pecuniary interest	None
Personal non-pecuniary interest	None
Ms Beth Shackleton (until 2008)	
Employment	Project Manager, NCCMH
Personal pecuniary interest	None

Continued

Declarations of interest – NCCMH staff *(Continued)*	
Personal family interest	None
Non-personal pecuniary interest	None
Personal non-pecuniary interest	None
Ms Sarah Stockton	
Employment	Information Scientist, NCCMH
Personal pecuniary interest	None
Personal family interest	None
Non-personal pecuniary interest	None
Personal non-pecuniary interest	None
Dr Clare Taylor	
Employment	Editor, NCCMH
Personal pecuniary interest	None
Personal family interest	None
Non-personal pecuniary interest	None
Personal non-pecuniary interest	None

APPENDIX 3:
SPECIAL ADVISERS TO THE GUIDELINE DEVELOPMENT GROUP

Dr John Eagles
Professor Steven Hollon

APPENDIX 4:

STAKEHOLDERS AND EXPERTS WHO SUBMITTED COMMENTS IN RESPONSE TO THE CONSULTATION DRAFT OF THE GUIDELINE

STAKEHOLDERS

Association for Family Therapy
Association for Psychoanalytic Psychotherapy in the NHS
Association of Counsellors and Psychotherapists in Primary Care (CPC)
AstraZeneca UK Ltd
British Association for Behavioural and Cognitive Psychotherapies (BABCP)
British Association for Counselling and Psychotherapy
British Association for Psychopharmacology
British Association of Art Therapists
British Psychoanalytic Council
British Psychological Society
Central and North West London NHS Foundation Trust
Centre for Clinical Practice Health Economists, NICE
Centre for Clinical Practice Technical Adviser
Centre for Psychological Services Research
Counselling Haverhill
Critical Psychiatry Network
Department of Health
Depression Alliance
Diabetes UK
Eli Lilly and Company Limited and Boehringer Ingelheim
GlaxoSmithKline UK Limited
Headway – The Brain Injury Association
Institute of Group Analysis
Institute of Psychiatry
Intapsych Ltd
Leeds Partnerships NHS Foundation Trust
Lundbeck Ltd
Medicines and Healthcare products Regulatory Agency
Mental Health Providers Forum
Mind

NHS Direct
Oxfordshire and Buckinghamshire Mental Health NHS Foundation Trust
Royal College of General Practitioners
Royal College of Midwives
Royal College of Nursing
Royal College of Pathologists
Royal College of Psychiatrists
Royal Pharmaceutical Society of Great Britain (RPSGB)
Servier Labatories Ltd
Sheffield Health and Social Care Foundation Trust
South London and Maudsley NHS Foundation Trust
St Mungo's
Tavistock and Portman NHS Foundation Trust
Tees Esk and Wear Valleys NHS Foundation Trust
Tuke Centre
UK Psychiatric Pharmacy Group (UKPPG)
Ultrasis UK Limited
United Kingdom Council for Psychotherapy (UKCP)
Young Minds
Youth Access

EXPERTS

Professor Aaron Beck
Professor John Cape
Professor Mick Cooper
Professor Steven Hollon
Professor Wayne Katon
Professor Tony Kendrick
Dr Roslyn Law
Professor Helen Lester
Dr John Markowitz
Professor Keith Matthews
Professor Declan McLoughlin
Professor Robert Peveler
Professor David Richards
Professor Myrna Weissman

APPENDIX 5:
STAKEHOLDERS AND EXPERTS WHO SUBMITTED COMMENTS IN RESPONSE TO THE PRE-PUBLICATION CHECK

STAKEHOLDERS

Association of British Neurologists
Cambridgeshire and Peterborough NHS Foundation Trust
CPC Association of Counsellors in Primary Care
Department of Health
Eli Lilly and Company Limited and Boehringer Ingelheim Ltd
GlaxoSmithKline UK Limited
Lundbeck Ltd
National Hospital for Neurology and Neurosurgery (NHNN)
Ultrasis UK Limited

EXPERTS

Dr David Healy

APPENDIX 6:
RESEARCHERS CONTACTED TO REQUEST INFORMATION ABOUT UNPUBLISHED OR SOON-TO-BE PUBLISHED STUDIES

Dr Allan Abbass
Professor Anthony Bateman
Professor Paul Crits-Christoph
Dr John Eagles
Dr Robert Golden
Professor Hayes
Dr Mark Hilsenroth
Professor Peter Fonagy
Professor Charles Kellner
Professor Falk Leichsenring
Dr Chris Martell
Professor Glenys Parry
Professor Carolyn Webster-Stratton
Professor Kenneth Wilson

APPENDIX 7:

CLINICAL QUESTIONS

Clinical questions for Depression Update Guideline		Clinical question in previous guideline
A	*Service configuration for people with depression*	
A1	What methods are effective in identifying people with depression in primary care and community settings, including sexual health clinics, emergency departments, and drug and alcohol services? In which populations (excluding those with chronic physical health problems) should identification methods be used?	A1
A2	In the treatment of depression (major depressive disorder, dysthymia, subthreshold depression and subthreshold depressive symptoms), which models of care produce the best outcomes? – collaborative care – stepped care – case management – stratified (matched) care – attached professional model Are different models appropriate to the care of people in different phases of the illness, such as treatment resistant depression and relapse prevention?	A5
B	*Psychology/psychosocial interventions for people with depression*	
B1	In depression, does guided self-help improve outcomes compared with other interventions?	A2
B2	Does computerised CBT (CCBT) improve patient outcomes compared with other treatments?	A3
B3	In the treatment of depression (major depressive disorder, dysthymia, subthreshold depression and subthreshold	A4

	depressive symptoms), do any of the following improve outcomes compared with other interventions? – exercise – support including groups, befriending, and non-statutory provision – programmes to facilitate employment	
B4	Do non-statutory support groups improve outcomes?	A6
B5	In the treatment of depression (major depressive disorder, dysthymia, subthreshold depression and subthreshold depressive symptoms), do any of the following (either alone or in combination with pharmacotherapy) improve outcomes compared with other interventions (including treatment as usual): – CBT – BT/behavioural activation – counselling/person-centred therapy – problem solving – psychodynamic psychotherapy – family interventions/couples therapy – ACT (acceptance and commitment therapy) – systemic interventions – psychoeducation – cognitive analytic therapy (CAT) – solution-focused therapy – self-help, including guided self-help – CCBT Does mode of delivery (group-based or individual) impact on outcomes? Are there specific therapist characteristics that improve outcomes? Are there specific patient characteristics (for example, anxiety, previous episodes) that predict outcomes? Are brief interventions (for example, 6 to 8 weeks) effective? Are psychological interventions harmful?	B1 B2
B6	Following poor response to treatment of depression (major depressive disorder, dysthymia, subthreshold depression and subthreshold depressive symptoms), which psychological or psychosocial interventions are appropriate?	

B7	In people whose depression has responded to treatment, what psychological and psychosocial strategies are effective in preventing relapse (including maintenance treatment)?	
C	***Pharmacological/physical interventions***	
C1	In the treatment of depression (major depressive disorder, dysthymia, subthreshold depression and subthreshold depressive symptoms), which drugs (either not covered by the previous guideline or where significant new evidence exists) improve outcomes compared with other drugs and with placebo? – TCAs – duloxetine – desvenlafaxine – escitalopram – agomelatine – St John's wort – antipsychotics (for example, quetiapine)	C1
C2	In the treatment of depression (major depressive disorder, dysthymia, subthreshold depression and subthreshold depressive symptoms), to what extent do the following factors affect the choice of drug? – adverse events (in particular, cardiotoxicity), including long-term adverse events – discontinuation problems	C2
C3	In the pharmacological treatment of depression, what are the most effective strategies for treating patients experiencing treatment side effects, including sexual dysfunction and weight gain?	C3
C4	In people whose depression has responded to treatment, what strategies are effective in preventing relapse (including maintenance treatment)?	C6
C5	In people whose depression has atypical features, what are the most effective treatment strategies?	C6
C6	In the treatment of depression (major depressive disorder, dysthymia, subthreshold depression and subthreshold depressive symptoms), do any of the following improve outcomes compared with other interventions? – ECT – TMS (integrate NICE Interventional Procedure Guidance)	C7 A9

	– light therapy – VNS – neurosurgery – deep brain stimulation	
C7	For people with depression (major depressive disorder, dysthymia, and so on), who are receiving pharmacological treatment, does therapeutic drug monitoring improve outcomes?	
C8	What are appropriate ways to promote adherence? (Link to NICE guideline on medicines adherence, CG76)	
C9	In the treatment of depression (major depressive disorder, dysthymia, subthreshold depression and subthreshold depressive symptoms), how can equal access to services for all be ensured? [What promotes access to effective care particularly for people with learning difficulties, acquired cognitive impairment and language difficulties?]	A9
D	**General**	
D1	In the treatment of depression, which patient characteristics predict response and relapse? For example, childhood trauma, age of onset, number of previous episodes, gender, and so on.	
D2	In the treatment of depression, are there specific clinician approaches that improve outcomes?	

APPENDIX 8:
SEARCH STRATEGIES FOR THE IDENTIFICATION
OF CLINICAL STUDIES

1. General search strategies

    a. MEDLINE, EMBASE, PsycINFO, CINAHL – Ovid SP interface

1   (depression or depressive disorder or depression, postpartum or depressive disorder, major or dysthymic disorder or mood disorders or seasonal affective disorder).sh,id.

2   (affective disorders or depression or depression, postpartum or depression, reactive or dysthymic disorder or seasonal affective disorder).sh,id.

3   (depression or agitated depression or atypical depression or depressive psychosis or dysphoria or dysthymia or endogenous depression or involutional depression or major depression or masked depression or melancholia or mood disorder or mourning syndrome or organic depression or postoperative depression or premenstrual dysphoric disorder or pseudodementia or puerperal depression or reactive depression or recurrent brief depression or seasonal affective disorder).sh,id. or "mixed anxiety and depression"/ or "mixed depression and dementia"/

4   (affective disorders or anaclitic depression or dysthymic disorder or endogenous depression or major depression or postpartum depression or reactive depression or recurrent depression or treatment resistant depression or atypical depression or pseudodementia or sadness or seasonal affective disorder).sh,id. or "depression (emotion)"/

5   (depress$ or dysphori$ or dysthym$ or melanchol$ or seasonal affective disorder$).tw.

6   or/1-5

    b. Cochrane Database of Systematic Reviews, Database of Abstracts of Reviews of Effects, Cochrane Central Register of Controlled Trials – Wiley Interscience interface[230]

#1 MeSH descriptor Depression, this term only
#2 MeSH descriptor Depressive Disorder explode all trees

---

[230]With respect to 1b, this search was generated for the *Depression in Adults with a Chronic Physical Health Problem* guideline (NCCMH, 2010) and was sifted for relevance to the clinical areas of both that guideline and this guideline update.

#3 MeSH descriptor Mood Disorders, this term only
#4 (depress* or dysphori* or dysthym* or seasonal affective disorder* or melanchol*):ti or (depress* or dysphori* or dysthym* or seasonal affective disorder* or melanchol*):ab
#5 (#1 OR #2 OR #3 OR #4)

2. *Systematic review search filters*

   a. MEDLINE, EMBASE, PsycINFO, CINAHL – Ovid interface

1 (literature searching or (systematic review$ or metaanal$ or meta anal$)).sh,id.
2 ((analy$ or assessment$ or evidence$ or methodol$ or qualitativ$ or quantativ$ or systematic$) adj5 (overview$ or review$)).tw. or ((analy$ or assessment$ or evidence$ or methodol$ or quantativ$ or qualitativ$ or systematic$).ti. and review$.ti,pt.) or (systematic$ adj5 search$).ti,ab.
3 ((electronic database$ or bibliographic database$ or computeri?ed database$ or online database$).tw,sh. or (bids or cochrane or index medicus or isi citation or psyclit or psychlit or scisearch or science citation or (web adj2 science)).tw. or cochrane$.sh.) and (review$.ti,ab,sh,pt. or systematic$.ti,ab.)
4 (metaanal$ or meta anal$ or metasynthes$ or meta synethes$).ti,ab.
5 (research adj (review$ or integration)).ti,ab.
6 reference list$.ab.
7 bibliograph$.ab.
8 published studies.ab.
9 relevant journals.ab.
10 selection criteria.ab.
11 (data adj (extraction or synthesis)).ab.
12 (handsearch$ or ((hand or manual) adj search$)).ti,ab.
13 (mantel haenszel or peto or dersimonian or der simonian).ti,ab.
14 (fixed effect$ or random effect$).ti,ab.
15 (systematic$ or meta$).pt. or (literature review or meta analysis or systematic review).md.
16 ((pool$ or combined or combining) adj2 (data or trials or studies or results)).ti,ab.
17 or/1-16

3. *Randomised controlled trial search filters*

   a. MEDLINE, EMBASE, PsycINFO, CINAHL – Ovid interface

1 exp clinical trial/ or exp clinical trials/ or exp clinical trials as topic/ or exp controlled clinical trials/
2 (placebo$1 or random allocation or random assignment or random sample or random sampling or randomization).sh,id.
3 (double blind$ or single blind$ or triple blind$).sh,id.

4   (crossover procedure or crossover design or cross over studies).sh,id.

5   (clinical adj2 trial$).tw.

6   (crossover or cross over).tw.

7   (((single$ or doubl$ or trebl$ or tripl$) adj5 (blind$ or mask$ or dummy)) or (singleblind$ or doubleblind$ or trebleblind$)).tw.

8   (placebo$ or random$).mp.

9   (clinical trial$ or controlled clinical trial$ or random$).pt. or treatment outcome$.md.

10   animals/ not (animals/ and human$.mp.)

11   animal$/ not (animal$/ and human$/)

12   (animal not (animal and human)).po.

13   (or/1-9) not (or/10-12)

Details of additional searches undertaken to support the development of this guideline are available on request.

APPENDIX 9:

CLINICAL STUDY DATA EXTRACTION FORM

Topic Area:			Report reference ID:		
Comparisons:					Total N
Ref List checked		Rev Man		Study Database	
Data Checked		Reference Manager updated		Excluded (record reason in Notes below)	

Randomised?		Blind?		
Age:		Young/Elderly (mean age over 65) Mean Age % Women		
Setting:		In/Out/Mixed/Primary Care (80% patients)		
Analysis:		Completer/ITT (continuous data)		
Diagnosis			% Comorbid Axis I	
			% Comorbid Axis II	
Mean baseline				

Trial length:
Interventions (Dose): 1   2   3

Notes:

APPENDIX 10:
QUALITY CHECKLISTS FOR CLINICAL STUDIES AND REVIEWS

See pages 624–627.

Completed by:	Report reference ID:

1 TREATMENT GROUP:

Leaving treatment early (any reason)		Leaving treatment early (side effects) reporting		Side Effects (total number		Remission [non-remission]	
n	N	n	N	n	N	n	N

Definition of remission

Definition of response

Post-treatment means

n	Mean	SD	n	Mean	SD	n	Mean	SD

Response [non-response]

n	N

Other data

n	Mean	SD	n	Mean	SD

2 TREATMENT GROUP:

Leaving treatment early (any reason) (side effects)		Leaving treatment early reporting		Side Effects (total number)		Remission [non-remission]	
n	N	n	N	n	N	n	N

Definition of remission

Definition of response

Post-treatment means

n	Mean	SD	n	Mean	SD	n	Mean	SD

Other data

n	N	Mean	SD	n	Mean	SD

Comparisons entered:

3 TREATMENT GROUP:

Leaving treatment early (any reason) (side effects)		Leaving treatment early reporting		Side Effects (total number)		Remission [non-remission]	
n	N	n	N	n	N	n	N

Definition of remission

Definition of response

Post-treatment means

n	Mean	SD	n	Mean	SD	n	Mean	SD

Other data

n	N	n	Mean	SD	n	Mean	SD

4 TREATMENT GROUP:

Leaving treatment early (any reason) (side effects)		Leaving treatment early reporting		Side Effects (total number)		Remission [non-remission]	
n	N	n	N	n	N	n	N

Definition of remission

Definition of response

Post-treatment means

n	Mean	SD	n	Mean	SD	n	Mean	SD	n	Mean	SD

Other data

n	N	Mean	SD	n	N	Mean	SD

APPENDIX 11:

THE CLASSIFICATION OF DEPRESSION AND DEPRESSION RATING SCALES/QUESTIONNAIRES

BACKGROUND

This appendix sets out an approach to the classification of depression that was used in the development of the guideline update (including the analysis of the evidence and the development of recommendations) and will be of value in routine clinical use.

Depression is a heterogeneous disorder in which a number of underlying presentations may share a common phenomenology but have different aetiologies. Despite considerable work on the aetiology of depression including neurobiological, genetic and psychological studies, no reliable classificatory system has emerged that links either to the underlying aetiology or has proven strongly predictive of response to treatment. A number of classification systems/subgroupings have been used, including reactive and endogenous depression, melancholia, atypical depression, depression with a seasonal pattern/seasonal affective disorder and dysthymia. These have been based on varying combinations of the nature, number, severity, pattern and duration of symptoms, and in some cases the assumed aetiology. Over time pragmatic definitions have emerged, enshrined in the current two major classification systems, DSM–IV-TR (APA, 2000c) and ICD–10 (WHO, 1992). These have defined a threshold of severity of clinical significance with further classification in terms of severity (for example, mild, moderate or severe as adopted in DSM–IV with regard to major depressive disorder), duration and course of the disorder (for example, recurrent, presence of residual symptoms) and subtype based on symptom profile (for example, melancholic, atypical). Other aspects of depression such as response to treatment (for example, treatment resistant, refractory) and aetiology (for example, preceding life events) do not feature specifically in the classifications and lack accepted definitions, although are used in clinical practice. The classification has some use in describing likely outcome and course (Khan *et al.*, 1991; Barrett *et al.*, 2001; Sullivan *et al.*, 2003; Blom *et al.*, 2007; Jackson *et al.*, 2007; Conradi *et al.*, 2008; Holma *et al.*, 2008; Van *et al.*, 2008) although social support, social impairment or personality factors also need to be taken into account. Lower severity and duration of a depressive episode predicts, to some extent, a greater likelihood of spontaneous or earlier and eventual improvement whereas greater severity, chronicity and number of previous episodes predict a higher chance of subsequent relapse.

The lack of a highly reliable or valid classificatory system has significant and practical clinical consequences, particularly in primary care where the full range of depression presents. A major concern is whether depression should be classified using dimensions or categories. Categories help distinguish cases from non-cases, while dimensions help distinguish severe disorder from mild (Cole *et al.*, 2008). Clinicians are often required to make a categorical decisions – for example to treat with antidepressants or not, to refer for further interventions or not – and consequently there can be pressure to interpret data on a single dimension in a categorical way, for example, treat or not treat based solely on a symptom severity rating (for example, a PHQ-9 score alone). This conflicts with the recognised need to take multiple factors/dimensions into consideration within a consultation, including the patient's view on the cause of symptoms and acceptable treatment, and in the guideline update a major challenge has been to provide a useful categorisation that adequately captures the complexity.

CLASSIFICATION OF DEPRESSION AND NICE GUIDANCE

The approach adopted in the previous depression guideline (NICE, 2004a; NCCMH, 2004) was based on ICD–10 and rested on a dimensional approach based on a symptom count further elaborated by taking into account the presence of social role impairment and the duration of both symptoms and social impairment. The subsequent categorisation of depression into mild, moderate and severe has led to a number of concerns in practice. First this classification appears to have often been implemented with an emphasis on a symptom count alone with other important factors such as duration and social impairment ignored, although it should be noted that in general there is a relationship between the number of symptoms and severity of functional impairment (Faravelli *et al.*, 1996). Second it implies that the different symptoms experienced are equivalent, although, in fact, symptom patterns may be important. Third, it does not take into account illness duration and course. This tendency may be exacerbated by the use of measures such as the Patient Health Questionnaire (PHQ-9; Kroenke *et al.*, 2001) or Hospital Anxiety and Depression Scale (HADS; Zigmond & Snaith, 1983) under the Quality and Outcomes Framework (Department of Health, 2004).

A drawback inherent in using ICD–10 depression criteria is that most of the treatment research on which the guideline has to be based uses DSM–IV or previous, essentially similar, versions of DSM (DSM–III and DSM–III-R) criteria. As discussed below, the criteria are similar but not identical, and this has particular relevance for the 'threshold' of the diagnosis of a clinically significant depressive episode and therefore what are considered subthreshold depressive symptoms.

DIAGNOSIS OF A DEPRESSIVE/MAJOR DEPRESSIVE EPISODE

The criteria for diagnosing depressive episodes in ICD–10 and DSM–IV overlap considerably but have some differences of emphasis. In ICD–10 the patient must have two of the first three symptoms (depressed mood, loss of interest in everyday activities, reduction in energy) plus at least two of the remaining seven symptoms; while in

DSM–IV the patient must have five or more out of nine symptoms with at least one from the first two (depressed mood and loss of interest). Both diagnostic systems require symptoms to have been present for at least 2 weeks to make a diagnosis (but can be shorter in ICD–10 if symptoms are unusually severe or of rapid onset). In both ICD–10 and DSM–IV the symptoms must result in impairment of functioning that increases with the episode severity. Table 143 compares the symptoms required in ICD–10 and DSM–IV.

DETERMINING SEVERITY OF A DEPRESSIVE/MAJOR DEPRESSIVE EPISODE

Both ICD–10 and DSM–IV classify clinically important depressive episodes as mild, moderate and severe based on the number, type and severity of symptoms present and degree of functional impairment. Table 144 shows the number of symptoms required by each diagnostic system, which are less specific than DSM–IV. The prescriptive

Table 143: Comparison of symptoms of depression in ICD–10 and DSM–IV

ICD–10	DSM–IV major/minor depressive disorder
Depressed mood*	Depressed mood by self-report or observation made by others*
Loss of interest*	Loss of interest or pleasure*
Reduction in energy*	Fatigue/loss of energy
Loss of confidence or self-esteem	Worthlessness/excessive or inappropriate guilt
Unreasonable feelings of self-reproach or inappropriate guilt	
Recurrent thoughts of death or suicide	Recurrent thoughts of death, suicidal thoughts or actual suicide attempts
Diminished ability to think/concentrate or indecisiveness	Diminished ability to think/concentrate or indecisiveness
Change in psychomotor activity with agitation or retardation	Psychomotor agitation or retardation
Sleep disturbance	Insomnia/hypersomnia
Change in appetite with weight change	Significant appetite and/or weight loss

*Core symptoms.

Table 144: Number of symptoms required in ICD–10 and DSM–IV for a diagnosis of depressive episode/major depression (but note they also need assessment of severity and functional impairment to ascertain diagnosis and severity)

	ICD–10 depressive episode	DSM–IV major depression
Mild	4	Minimal above the minimum (5)
Moderate	5–6	Between mild and severe
Severe	7+	Several symptoms in excess of 5

symptom counting approach of ICD–10 tends to lend itself to using symptom counting alone to determine severity.

As ICD–10 requires only four symptoms for a diagnosis of a mild depressive episode, it can identify more people as having a depressive episode compared with a DSM–IV major depressive episode. One study in primary care in Europe identified two to three times more people as depressed using ICD–10 criteria compared with DSM–IV (11.3% versus 4.2%; Wittchen *et al.*, 2001a). However another study in Australia (Andrews *et al.*, 2008) found similar rates using the two criteria (6.8% versus 6.3%) but slightly different populations were identified (83% concordance), which appears to be related to the need for only one of two core symptoms for DSM–IV but two out of three for ICD–10. These studies emphasise that, although similar, the two systems are not identical and that this is particularly apparent at the threshold taken to indicate clinical importance.

DIAGNOSIS OF SUBTHRESHOLD DEPRESSIVE SYMPTOMS

Given how common milder forms of depression are, and the problems inherent in defining a 'threshold' of clinical importance because of the diagnostic system differences and the lack of any natural discontinuity identifying a critical threshold (Andrews *et al.*, 2008), this guideline update has broadened its scope to include consideration of depression that is 'subthreshold', that is, does not meet the full criteria for a depressive/major depressive episode. A further reason is that subthreshold depression has been increasingly recognised as causing considerable morbidity and human and economic costs, is more common in those with a history of major depression and is a risk factor for future major depression (Rowe & Rapaport, 2006).

There is no accepted classification for this in the current diagnostic systems with the closest being minor depression, a research diagnosis in DSM–IV. At least two but less than five symptoms are required, of which one must be depressed mood or diminished interest. This includes ICD–10 depressive episode with four symptoms and, given the practical difficulty and inherent uncertainty in deciding thresholds for significant symptom severity and disability, there is no natural discontinuity between minor depression and mild major depression in routine clinical practice. There is however a danger of 'medicalising' distress by adopting minor depression as a discrete diagnosis, which would inevitably broaden the concept of depression. For this guideline update the GDG therefore use the term 'subthreshold depressive symptoms' to avoid this problem while providing a way of describing this part of the depressive spectrum.

Both DSM–IV and ICD–10 do have the category of dysthymia, which consists of depressive symptoms which are subthreshold for major depression but which persist (by definition for more than 2 years). There appears to be no empirical evidence that dysthymia is distinct from subthreshold depressive symptoms apart from duration of symptoms.

ICD–10 has a category of mixed anxiety and depression, which is less clearly defined than minor depression, and is largely a diagnosis of exclusion in those with anxiety and depressive symptoms subthreshold for specific disorders. Not unexpectedly it appears to be a heterogeneous category with a lack of diagnostic stability over time (Wittchen *et al.*, 2001b; Barkow *et al.*, 2004). For this reason it has not been included in this guideline.

DURATION

The duration of a depressive episode can vary considerably among individuals. The average course of an untreated depressive episode is between 6 and 8 months with much of the improvement occurring in the first 3 months, and 80% recovered by 1 year (Coryell *et al.*, 1994). There is evidence to suggest that patients who do not seek treatment for their depression may recover more quickly than those who seek but do not receive treatment (Posternak *et al.*, 2006). There is also some evidence to suggest that people who do not seek help have a shorter mean duration of depressive episode (Posternak *et al.*, 2006).

Traditionally the minimum duration of persistent symptoms for major depression is 2 weeks and for chronic depression (or dysthymia) 2 years. These conventional definitions have been adopted in the absence of good evidence as there is only a modest empirical base for the minimum duration (for example, Angst & Merikangas, 2001) and none that we could find for the 'cut-off' between acute and chronic depression. As with severity, duration is better thought of as a dimension with a decreased likelihood of remission with increasing chronicity over a given time frame (Van *et al.*, 2008). The conventional criteria are therefore better viewed as guides rather than cut-offs. It is likely that that the minimum duration after which therapy provides more benefit than occurs by spontaneous improvement is somewhat longer than 2 weeks (possibly 2 to 3 months, Posternak *et al.*, 2006), but this has never been tested empirically. By 2 years it does appear that outcome is poorer, supporting consideration of chronicity in describing the disorder; nevertheless the point at which acute becomes chronic is not clear, and indeed may not be a meaningful question. There is some evidence that outcome is poorer after about 1 year (for example, Khan *et al.*, 1991). However there seems little to be gained by redefining duration for the guideline as long as it is recognised that the conventional definitions are merely signposts to include consideration of duration in relation to outcome and need for treatment.

COURSE OF DEPRESSION

An influential model of the course of major depression proposes that the onset of an episode of depression consists of a worsening of symptoms in a continuum going from depressive symptoms through to major depression. Phases of improvement with treatment consist of response (significant improvement) to remission (absence of depressive symptoms) which if stable for 4 to 6 months results in (symptomatic) recovery, meaning that the episode is over (Frank *et al.*, 1991). It is important to distinguish this use of recovery from more recent concepts related to quality and meaning of life in spite of continued symptoms. After recovery a further episode of depression is viewed as a recurrence to distinguish it from a relapse of the same episode. There has been no consensus as to how long a period of remission should be in order to be able to declare recovery; different definitions result in different definitions of episode length and time to full or subthreshold depressive recurrence (Furukawa *et al.*, 2008). Therefore, in practice it can be difficult to distinguish between relapse and recurrence, particularly when people have mild residual symptoms. Follow-up studies of people with depression have shown that, overall, more time is spent with subthreshold depressive symptoms than major depression and there is a variable individual pattern ranging from persisting chronic major depression, through significant but not full improvement (partial remission), to full remission and recovery (Judd *et al.*, 1998). DSM–IV defines full remission when there has been an absence of symptoms for at least 2 months. For partial remission, full criteria for a major depressive episode are no longer met, or there are no substantial symptoms but 2 months have not yet passed. DSM–IV specifies 'with full interepisode recovery' if full remission is attained between the two most recent depressive episodes and 'without full inter-episode recovery' if full remission is not attained. In DSM–IV, therefore, separate episodes are distinguished by at least 2 months of not meeting major depression criteria, which is in contrast to the more stringent ICD–10 requirements of 2 months without any significant symptoms. There is therefore some ambiguity as to whether full remission is required to define separate episodes.

Nevertheless the number of episodes and degree of symptom resolution have important implications for considering the course of an individual patient's depressive disorder. The risk of a further episode of major depression within a given time frame is greater with an increasing number of previous episodes (Solomon *et al.*, 2000; Kessing & Andersen, 2005) and also if there has not been full remission/symptomatic recovery (Paykel *et al.*, 1995; Kanai *et al.*, 2003; Dombrovski *et al.*, 2007). If someone presents with minor depressive symptoms it is therefore crucial to determine whether or not this directly follows an episode of major depression.

DEPRESSION SUBTYPES

Different symptom profiles have been described and are included in the classification systems. In DSM–IV, severe major depression can be without or with psychosis (psychotic depression) and there are specifiers that include melancholia, atypical features, catatonia, depression with a seasonal pattern (seasonal affective disorder) and post-partum onset. ICD–10 also provides specifiers for psychotic and somatic symptoms, the latter similar to DSM–IV melancholia. However, these subtypes do not form distinct categories (for example, Kendell, 1968; Angst *et al.*, 2007) and they add a further complexity to the diagnosis of depression. The GDG judged that these specifiers were best considered where appropriate after the diagnosis of a depressive disorder is made and they are not discussed in detail here. Some specifiers, particularly psychosis and seasonal pattern depression, have potential treatment implications and are considered in the guideline update where evidence is available.

CLASSIFICATION OF DEPRESSION IN THE GUIDELINE UPDATE

The depression classification system adopted for the guideline update had to meet a number of criteria, notably the use of:
- a system that reflects the non-categorical, multidimensional nature of depression
- a system that makes best use of the available evidence on both efficacy and effectiveness
- a system that could be distilled for practical day-to-day use in healthcare settings without potentially harmful over-simplification or distortion
- terms that can be easily understood and are not open to misinterpretation by a wide range of healthcare staff and service users
- a system that would facilitate the generation of clinical recommendations.

These criteria led the GDG to adopt a classificatory system for depression based on DSM–IV criteria. When assessing an individual it is important to assess three dimensions to diagnose a depressive disorder – a) severity (symptomatology and social impairment), b) duration, and c) course – as linked, but separate, factors (see below). In addition there was recognition that a single dimension of severity was insufficient to fully capture its multidimensional nature.

As discussed above the following depressive symptoms require assessment to determine the presence of major depression. **The symptoms need to be experienced to a sufficient degree of severity and persistence to be counted as definitely present.** At least one core symptom is required; both core symptoms would be expected in moderate and severe major depression.

Core symptoms of depression
1) Depressed mood most of the day, nearly every day.
2) Markedly diminished interest or pleasure in all, or almost all, activities most of the day, nearly every day.

Somatic symptoms

3) Significant weight loss when not dieting or weight gain (for example, a change of more than 5% of body weight in a month), or decrease or increase in appetite nearly every day.
4) Insomnia or hypersomnia nearly every day.
5) Psychomotor agitation or retardation nearly every day (observable by others, not merely subjective feelings of restlessness or being slowed down).
6) Fatigue or loss of energy nearly every day.

Other symptoms

7) Feelings of worthlessness or excessive or inappropriate guilt (which may be delusional) nearly every day (not merely self-reproach or guilt about being sick).
8) Diminished ability to think or concentrate, or indecisiveness, nearly every day.
9) Recurrent thoughts of death (not just fear of dying), recurrent suicidal ideation without a specific plan, or a suicide attempt or a specific plan for committing suicide.

The symptoms are not due to the direct physiological effects of a substance (for example, a drug of misuse or a medication) or a general medical condition (for example, hypothyroidism) or better accounted for by bereavement.

There is evidence that doctors have difficulty in remembering the nine DSM–IV depressive symptoms (Rapp & Davis, 1989; Krupinski & Tiller, 2001), which has important implications for the application of these criteria. In addition there is need to be able to consistently diagnose depression in patients where physical symptoms may be due to medical illness. Zimmerman and colleagues (2006) and Andrews and colleagues (2008) have demonstrated that, compared with the diagnosis using the full DSM–IV criteria, there is a high agreement (94 to 97%) and good sensitivity (93%) and specificity (95 to 98%) when a reduced list (excluding the four somatic symptoms) is used with a requirement for three out of the remaining five symptoms.

It is therefore possible to use an abridged list, first asking about the two core symptoms of depression:

● persistent depressed mood
● markedly diminished interest or pleasure.

Then if either or both are present going on to ask about:

● feelings of worthlessness or guilt
● impaired concentration
● recurrent thoughts of death or suicide.

Three or more symptoms indicate a very high probability of major depression. This does not however replace the need to go on to assess somatic symptoms as an aid to determining severity and to help judge subsequent response to treatment. This limits the usefulness of the abridged list in practice and it may be most useful when there are confounding somatic symptoms due to physical illness.

Severity

While recognising that severity is not a unitary dimension, practically it is useful to make a judgement of severity consisting, at least, of number of symptoms, severity of individual symptoms and functional impairment. This leads to a classification of depression into the following severity groupings based on DSM–IV criteria, which should be viewed as exemplars not discrete categories. In the guideline update the term 'depression' refers to major depression:

- subthreshold depressive symptoms: fewer than five symptoms of depression
- mild depression: few, if any, symptoms in excess of the five required to make the diagnosis, and the symptoms result in only minor functional impairment
- moderate depression: symptoms or functional impairment are between 'mild' and 'severe'
- severe depression: most symptoms, and the symptoms markedly interfere with functioning; can occur with or without psychotic symptoms.

Symptom severity and degree of functional impairment correlate highly (for example, Zimmerman *et al.*, 2008), but in individual cases this may not be the case and some mildly symptomatic individuals may have marked functional impairment while some people who are severely symptomatic may, at least for a time, maintain good function, employment and so on.

Duration

By convention the duration of persistent symptoms is required to be at least 2 weeks and once they have persisted for 2 years or more they are called chronic in the case of major depression or dysthymia in the case of subthreshold depressive symptoms. While the specific values may not be particularly helpful there are insufficient empirical data to change these:

1) **Acute** – meeting one of the severity criteria for a minimum of 2 weeks and not longer than 2 years.
2) **Chronic** – meeting one of the severity criteria for longer than 2 years.

Given that the cut-off of 2 years is arbitrary it is best in practice to consider the specific duration and degree of persistence of symptoms for an individual in the context of the severity and course of the disorder.

Course

This was not explicitly considered as a classificatory issue in the previous guideline but it has important treatment implications, particularly for the likelihood of relapse/recurrence:

1) Number of lifetime depressive episodes and the interval between recent episodes: the number varies from a single/first episode to increasingly frequent recurrences. At least 2 months of full or partial remission is required to distinguish episodes.
2) Stage of episode: this refers to where an individual is in the course of their depression. In an episode it is useful to determine if the depression is worsening, static or improving and whether subthreshold depressive symptoms may reflect partial remission from prior major depression.

Conventionally, classification has distinguished between a single episode and two or more episodes (recurrent depression) irrespective of how long there has been between episodes and how many recurrences have occurred. However, someone who has had two episodes separated by decades has a different clinical course from someone with three episodes in a few years, therefore, noting the number of episodes and their recent pattern is important. There is uncertainty about the duration and extent of the recovery that is required to distinguish between different episodes of depression and a fluctuating course of a single episode. In practice this is less important than recognising the risk of persistent symptoms and of major depressive relapse/recurrence.

CLASSIFICATION IN RELATION TO DEPRESSION RATING SCALES AND QUESTIONNAIRES

Depression rating scales and questionnaires give ranges that are proposed to describe different severities of depression. Some of these were described in Appendix 13 of the previous guideline. In reconsidering this for the update it quickly became apparent, not only that there is no consensus for the proposed ranges, but also that the ranges in different rating scales and questionnaires do not correspond with each other. In addition there is a variable degree of correlation between different scales, which indicates that they do not measure precisely the same aspects of depression. When these factors are added to the need to consider more than symptoms in determining severity, and more than severity in considering diagnosis, the GDG was concerned not to perpetuate a spurious precision in relating scores in depression rating scales and questionnaires to the diagnosis or severity of depression, which must in the end be a clinical judgement.

Nevertheless it is necessary to try and translate trial evidence (which may only provide rating scales or questionnaire scores) into a meaningful clinical context as well as relating this guideline update to the previous guideline which used the APA (2000a) cut-offs. The change to DSM–IV-based diagnosis and the inclusion of minor depression (subthreshold depressive symptoms) in the update means that the descriptors of ranges previously given are no longer tenable. Table 145 gives the descriptors and ranges used in this guideline update, with the important caveat that these must not be taken as clear cut-offs or a short-cut to classify people with depression.

IMPLICATIONS OF THE PROPOSED CLASSIFICATION

An important implication is that symptom counts alone (for example, using the PHQ-9) should not be used to determine the presence or absence of a depressive disorder although this is an important part of the assessment. The score on a rating scale or questionnaire can contribute to the assessment of depression and rating scales are also useful to monitor treatment progress.

Another very important point to emphasise is that making a diagnosis of depression does not automatically imply a specific treatment. Making and agreeing a diagnosis of depression is a starting point in considering the most appropriate way of helping that individual in their particular circumstances. The evidence base for treatments considered in this guideline are based primarily on RCTs in which

Table 146: **Levels of depression in relation to the HRSD and BDI in the guideline update compared with those suggested by the APA (2000a)**

17-item Hamilton Rating Scale for Depression (HRSD)

Guideline update	Not depressed	Subthreshold	Mild	Moderate	Severe
APA (2000a)*	Not depressed	Mild	Moderate	Severe	Very severe
Score	0–7	8–13	14–18	19–22	23+

Beck Depression Inventory (BDI)

Guideline update	Not depressed	Subthreshold	Mild to moderate	Moderate to severe
APA (2000a)*	Not depressed	Mild	Moderate	Severe
Score	0–9	10–16	17–29	30+

*Used in the previous guideline.

standardised criteria have been used to determine entry into the trial. Patients seen clinically are rarely assessed using standardised criteria reinforcing the need to be circumspect about an over-rigid extrapolation from RCTs to clinical practice.

Diagnosis using severity, duration and course (see above) necessarily only provides a partial description of the individual experience of depression. People with depression vary in the pattern of symptoms they experience, their family history, personalities, pre-morbid difficulties (for example, sexual abuse), psychological mindedness and current relational and social problems – all of which may significantly affect outcomes. It is also common for people with depression to have a comorbid psychiatric diagnosis, such as anxiety, social phobia, panic and various personality disorders (Brown *et al.*, 2001), and physical comorbidity, or for the depression to occur in the context of bipolar disorder (not considered in this guideline). Gender and socioeconomic factors account for large variations in the population rates of depression, and few studies of pharmacological, psychological and other treatments for depression control for or examine these variations. This emphasises that choice of treatment is a complex process and involves negotiation and discussion with patients. Given the current limited knowledge about which factors are associated with better antidepressant or psychotherapy response, most decisions will rely upon clinical judgement and patient preference until there is further research evidence. Trials of treatment in unclear cases may be warranted but the uncertainty needs to be discussed with the patient and benefits from treatment carefully monitored.

APPENDIX 12:
SEARCH STRATEGIES FOR THE IDENTIFICATION OF HEALTH ECONOMIC EVIDENCE

1. General search strategies

    a.   MEDLINE, EMBASE, PsycINFO, CINAHL – Ovid interface

1   (depression or depressive disorder or depression, postpartum or depressive disorder, major or dysthymic disorder or mood disorders or seasonal affective disorder).sh,id.

2   (affective disorders or depression or depression, postpartum or depression, reactive or dysthymic disorder or seasonal affective disorder).sh,id.

3   (depression or agitated depression or atypical depression or depressive psychosis or dysphoria or dysthymia or endogenous depression or involutional depression or major depression or masked depression or melancholia or mood disorder or mourning syndrome or organic depression or postoperative depression or premenstrual dysphoric disorder or pseudodementia or puerperal depression or reactive depression or recurrent brief depression or seasonal affective disorder).sh,id. or "mixed anxiety and depression"/ or "mixed depression and dementia"/

4   (affective disorders or anaclitic depression or dysthymic disorder or endogenous depression or major depression or postpartum depression or reactive depression or recurrent depression or treatment resistant depression or atypical depression or pseudodementia or sadness or seasonal affective disorder).sh,id. or "depression (emotion)"/

5   (depress$ or dysphori$ or dysthym$ or melanchol$ or seasonal affective disorder$).tw.

6   or/1–5

    b.   NHS Economic Evaluation Database, Health Technology Assessment Database – Wiley interface

#1   MeSH descriptor Depression, this term only
#2   MeSH descriptor Depressive Disorder explode all trees
#3   MeSH descriptor Mood Disorders, this term only

#4 (depress* or dysphori* or dysthym* or seasonal affective disorder* or melan-
chol*):ti or (depress* or dysphori* or dysthym* or seasonal affective disorder*
or melanchol*):ab

#5 (#1 OR #2 OR #3 OR #4)

c. OHE HEED – Wiley interface

1 AX = depress*
2 AX = dysthym*
3 AX = dysphori*
4 AX = seasonal AND affective AND disorder*
5 CS = 1 OR 2 OR 3 OR 4

2. *Health economics and quality-of-life search filters*

a. MEDLINE, EMBASE, PsycINFO, CINAHL – Ovid interface[231]

1 (budget$ or cost$ or economic$ or expenditure$ or fee$1 or fees$ or financ$ or
health resource$ or money or pharmacoeconomic$ or socioeconomic$).hw,id.
2 (health care rationing or health priorities or medical savings accounts or quality
adjusted life years or quality of life or resource allocation or value of life).sh,id.
or "deductibles and coinsurance"/ or "health services needs and demand"/
3 (budget$ or cost$ or econom$ or expenditure$ or financ$ or fiscal$ or funding
or pharmacoeconomic$ or price or prices or pricing).tw.
4 (QALY$ or lifeyear$ or life year$ or ((qualit$3 or value) adj3 (life or
survival))).tw.
5 ((burden adj3 (disease or illness)) or (resource adj3 (allocation$ or utilit$)) or
(value adj5 money)).tw.
6 ec.fs.
7 (or/1–6)

---

[231]With respect to 2a, search request 6 was ANDed with or/1–4 from the general search strategy only.

APPENDIX 13:

QUALITY CHECKLIST FOR ECONOMIC STUDIES

Author: **Date:**

Title:

	Study design	Yes	No	NA
1	The research question is stated	❑	❑	
2	The economic importance of the research question is stated	❑	❑	
3	The viewpoint(s) of the analysis are clearly stated and justified	❑	❑	
4	The rationale for choosing the alternative programmes or interventions compared is stated	❑	❑	
5	The alternatives being compared are clearly described	❑	❑	
6	The form of economic evaluation is stated	❑	❑	
7	The choice of form of economic evaluation used is justified in relation to the questions addressed	❑	❑	
	Data collection			
1	The source of effectiveness estimates used is stated	❑	❑	
2	Details of the design and results of effectiveness study are given (if based on a single study)	❑	❑	❑
3	Details of the method of synthesis or meta-analysis of estimates are given (if based on an overview of a number of effectiveness studies)	❑	❑	❑
4	The primary outcome measure(s) for the economic evaluation are clearly stated	❑	❑	
5	Methods to value health states and other benefits are stated	❑	❑	❑
6	Details of the subjects from whom valuations were obtained are given	❑	❑	❑

7	Indirect costs (if included) are reported separately	❑	❑	❑
8	The relevance of indirect costs to the study question is discussed	❑	❑	❑
9	Quantities of resources are reported separately from their unit costs	❑	❑	
10	Methods for the estimation of quantities and unit costs are described	❑	❑	
11	Currency and price data are recorded	❑	❑	
12	Details of currency, price adjustments for inflation or currency conversion are given	❑	❑	
13	Details of any model used are given	❑	❑	❑
14	The choice of model used and the key parameters on which it is based are justified	❑	❑	❑
	Analysis and interpretation of results			
1	The time horizon of costs and benefits is stated	❑	❑	
2	The discount rate(s) is stated	❑	❑	❑
3	The choice of rate(s) is justified	❑	❑	❑
4	An explanation is given if costs or benefits are not discounted	❑	❑	❑
5	Details of statistical tests and confidence intervals are given for stochastic data	❑	❑	❑
6	The approach to sensitivity analysis is given	❑	❑	❑
7	The choice of variables for sensitivity analysis is given	❑	❑	❑
8	The ranges over which the variables are varied are stated	❑	❑	❑
9	Relevant alternatives are compared	❑	❑	
10	Incremental analysis is reported	❑	❑	❑
11	Major outcomes are presented in a disaggregated as well as aggregated form	❑	❑	
12	The answer to the study question is given	❑	❑	
13	Conclusions follow from the data reported	❑	❑	
14	Conclusions are accompanied by the appropriate caveats	❑	❑	

Validity score: Yes/No/NA:

APPENDIX 14:

DATA EXTRACTION FORM FOR ECONOMIC STUDIES

Reviewer: **Date of review:**

Authors:

Publication Date:

Title:

Country:

Language:

Economic study design:

□ CEA   □ CCA   □ CUA

□ CBA   □ CA   □ CMA

Modelling:

□ No   □ Yes

Source of data for effect size measure(s):

□ Meta-analysis   □ Cohort study

□ RCT   □ Mirror image (before-after) study

□ Quasi experimental study   □ Expert opinion

Comments _____

Primary outcome measure(s) (please list):

_____

Interventions compared (please describe):

Treatment: _____

Comparator: _____

Setting (please describe):

_____

_____

Patient population characteristics (please describe):

_____

_____

_____

Perspective of analysis:

❑ Societal   ❑ Other: _____

❑ Patient and family

❑ Healthcare system

❑ Healthcare provider

❑ Third party payer

Time frame of analysis: _____

Cost data:

❑ Primary   ❑ Secondary

If secondary please specify: _____

Costs included:

Direct medical   Direct non-medical   Lost productivity

❑ direct treatment   ❑ social care   ❑ income forgone due
❑ inpatient   ❑ social benefits   to illness
❑ outpatient   ❑ travel costs   ❑ income forgone due to
❑ day care   ❑ caregiver   death
❑ community healthcare   out-of-pocket   ❑ income forgone by
❑ medication   ❑ criminal justice   caregiver
                           ❑ training of staff

Or

❑ staff

❑ medication

❑ consumables

❑ overhead

❑ capital equipment

❑ real estate   Others: _____

Appendix 14

Currency: _____   **Year of costing:** _____

Was discounting used?

❑ Yes, for benefits and costs   ❑ Yes, but only for costs   ❑ No

    Discount rate used for costs: _____

    Discount rate used for benefits: _____

16   REFERENCES

Please note that due to reasons of space, references to studies reviewed in clinical evidence reviews are in Appendix 17.[232]

Abas, M. (1996) Depression and anxiety among older Caribbean people in the UK: screening, unmet need and the provision of appropriate services. *International Journal of Geriatric Psychiatry, 11*, 377–382.

Abas, M. A., Phillips, C., Carter, J., *et al.* (1998) Culturally sensitive validation of screening questionnaires for depression in older African–Caribbean people living in south London. *British Journal of Psychiatry, 173*, 249–254.

Abbass, A., Sheldon, A., Gyra, J., *et al.* (2008) Intensive short-term dynamic psychotherapy for DSM–IV personality disorders: a randomized controlled trial. *Journal of Nervous and Mental Disease, 196*, 211–216.

Adli, M., Baethge, C., Heinz, A., *et al.* (2005) Is dose escalation of antidepressants a rational strategy after a medium-dose treatment has failed? *European Archives of Psychiatry and Clinical Neuroscience, 255*, 387–400.

AGREE Collaboration (2003) Development and validation of an international appraisal instrument for assessing the quality of clinical practice guidelines: the AGREE project. *Quality and Safety in Health Care, 12*, 18–23.

Ahn, H. & Wampold, B. E. (2001) Where oh where are the specific ingredients? A meta-analysis of component studies in counseling and psychotherapy. *Journal of Counseling Psychology, 48*, 251–257.

Akiskal, H. S. (1986) A developmental perspective on recurrent mood disorders: a review of studies in man. *Psychopharmacology Bulletin, 22*, 579–586.

Almond, S. & Healey, A. (2003) Mental health and absence from work. *Work, Employment and Society, 17*, 731–742.

Altman, D. & Bland, M. (1994a) Statistics notes: Diagnostic tests 2: predictive values. *British Medical Journal, 309*, 102.

Altman, D. & Bland, M. (1994b) Statistics notes: Diagnostic tests 1: sensitivity and specificity. *British Medical Journal, 308*, 1552.

Altshuler, L. L., Bauer, M., Frye, M. A., *et al.* (2001) Does thyroid supplementation accelerate tricyclic antidepressant response? A review and meta-analysis of the literature. *American Journal of Psychiatry, 158*, 1617–1622.

American College of Sports Medicine (1980) *Guidelines for Graded Exercise Testing and Exercise Prescription.* Madison, Wisconsin: American College of Sports Medicine.

---

[232]Where more than one paper has been published from a study, the guideline adopts the convention of the Cochrane Collaboration so that the study is referred to by the author and date of the original study regardless of whether data have been extracted from subsequent papers. The additional papers are listed under the first paper in the appendices.

Anderson, I. M. & Edwards, J. G. (2001) Guidelines for choice of selective serotonin reuptake inhibitor in depressive illness. *Advances in Psychiatric Treatment, 7,* 170–180.

Anderson, I. M., Nutt, D. J. & Deakin, J. F. (2000) Evidence-based guidelines for treating depressive disorders with antidepressants: a revision of the 1993 British Association for Psychopharmacology guidelines. *Journal of Psychopharmacology, 14,* 3–20.

Anderson, I. M., Ferrier, I. N, Baldwin, R. C., *et al.* (2008) Evidence-based guidelines for treating depressive disorders with antidepressants: a revision of the 2000 British Association for Psychopharmacology guidelines. *Journal of Psychopharmacology, 22,* 343–396.

Andrews, G. & Jenkins, R. (eds) (1999) *Management of Mental Disorders* (UK edn, vol. 1). Sydney: WHO Collaborating Centre for Mental Health and Substance Misuse.

Andrews G., Anderson, T. M., Slade, T., *et al.* (2008) Classification of anxiety and depressive disorders: problems and solutions. *Depression and Anxiety, 25,* 274–281.

Anghelescu, I. G., Kohnen, R., Szegedi, A., *et al.* (2006) Comparison of hypericum extract WS 5570 and paroxetine in ongoing treatment after recovery from an episode of moderate to severe depression: results from a randomised multi-centre study. *Pharmacopsychiatry, 39,* 213–219.

Angst, J. (1993) Severity of depression and benzodiazepine co-medication in relationship to efficacy of antidepressants in acute trials: a meta-analysis of moclobemide trials. *Human Psychopharmacology, 8,* 401–407.

Angst, J. & Merikangas, K. R. (2001) Multi-dimensional criteria for the diagnosis of depression. *Journal of Affective Disorders, 62,* 7–15.

Angst, J. & Preisig, M. (1995) Course of a clinical cohort of unipolar, bipolar and schizoaffective patients. Results of a prospective study from 1959 to 1985. *Schweizer Archiv für Neurologie und Psychiatrie, 146,* 5–16.

Angst, J., Gamma, A., Benazzi, F., *et al.* (2007) Melancholia and atypical depression in the Zurich study: epidemiology, clinical characteristics, course, comorbidty and personality. *Acta Psychiatrica Scandinavica, 115* (Suppl. 433), 72–84.

APA (1980) *Diagnostic and Statistical Manual of Mental Disorders* (3rd edn) (DSM–III). Washington, DC: APA.

APA (1994) *Diagnostic and Statistical Manual of Mental Disorders* (4th edn) (DSM–IV). Washington, DC: APA.

APA (2000a) *Handbook of Psychiatric Measures.* Washington, DC: APA.

APA (2000b) Practice guideline for the treatment of patients with major depressive disorder (revision). *American Journal of Psychiatry, 157* (Suppl. 4), 1–45.

APA (2000c) *Diagnostic and Statistical Manual of Mental Disorders* (4th edn Text Revision) (DSM–IV-TR). Washington, DC: APA.

Aragones, E., Pinol, J. L. & Labad, A. (2006) The overdiagnosis of depression in non-depressed patients in primary care. *Family Practice,* 23, 363–368.

Aronson, R., Offman, H. J., Joffe, R. T., *et al.* (1996) Triiodothyronine augmentation in the treatment of refractory depression. A meta-analysis. *Archives of General Psychiatry, 53,* 842–848.

Arroll, B., Goodyear-Smith, F. & Kerse, N. (2005) Effect of the addition of a 'help' question to two screening questions on specificity for diagnosis of depression in general practice: diagnostic validation study. *British Medical Journal, 331,* 884–886.

Association of the British Pharmaceutical Industry (2003) *Edronax (reboxetine) SPC. Compendium of Data Sheets and Summaries of Product Characteristics.* SPC available at: http://www.medicines.org.uk/EMC/medicine/8386/SPC/Edronax + 4mg+Tablets/

Avery, D. & Winokur, G. (1976) Mortality in depressed patients treated with electroconvulsive therapy and antidepressants. *Archives of General Psychiatry, 33,* 1029–1037.

Baca, E., Garcia-Garcia, M. & Porras-Chavarino, A. (2004) Gender differences in treatment response to sertraline versus imipramine in patients with nonmelancholic depressive disorders. *Progressive Neuro-psychopharmacology and Biology Psychiatry, 28,* 57–65.

Badamgarav, E., Weingarten, S. R., Henning, J. M., *et al.* (2003) Effectiveness of disease management programs in depression: a systematic review. *American Journal of Psychiatry, 160,* 2080–2090.

Baer, R. A. (2003) Mindfulness training as a clinical intervention: a conceptual and empirical review. *Clinical Psychology: Science and Practice, 10,* 125–143.

Bailine, S. H., Rifkin, A., Kayne, E., *et al.* (2000) Comparison of bifrontal and bitemporal ECT for major depression. *American Journal of Psychiatry, 157,* 121–123.

Baldomero, E. B., Ubago, J. G., Cercós, C. L., *et al.* (2005) Venlafaxine extended release versus conventional antidepressants in the remission of depressive disorders after previous antidepressant failure: ARGOS study. *Depression and Anxiety, 22,* 68–76.

Baldwin, D. S., Cooper, J. A., Huusom, A. K., *et al.* (2006) A double-blind, randomized, parallel-group, flexible-dose study to evaluate the tolerability, efficacy and effects of treatment discontinuation with escitalopram and paroxetine in patients with major depressive disorder. *International Journal of Clinical Psychopharmacology, 21,* 159–169.

Baldwin, D. S., Stein, D. J., Dolberg, O. T., *et al.* (2009) How long should a trial of escitalopram treatment be in patients with major depressive disorder, generalised anxiety disorder or social anxiety disorder? An exploration of the randomised controlled trial database. *Human Psychopharmacology: Clinical and Experimental, 24,* 269–275.

Ballard, C., Bannister, C., Solis, M., *et al.* (1996) The prevalence, associations and symptoms of depression amongst dementia sufferers. *Journal of Affective Disorders, 36,* 135–144.

Barber, J. P., Crits-Christoph, P. & Luborsky, L. (1996) Effects of therapist adherence and competence on patient outcome in brief dynamic therapy. *Journal of Consulting and Clinical Psychology, 64,* 619–622.

Barber, J. P., Gallop, R., Crits-Christoph, P., *et al.* (2006) The role of therapist adherence, therapist competence, and the alliance in predicting outcome of individual drug counseling: results from the NIDA Collaborative Cocaine Treatment Study. *Psychotherapy Research*, 16, 229–240.

Barbey, J. T. & Roose, S. P. (1998) SSRI safety in overdose. *Journal of Clinical Psychiatry, 59* (Suppl. 15), 42–48.

Barbosa, L., Berk, M. & Vorster, M. (2003) A double-blind, randomised, placebo-controlled trial of augmentation with lamotrigine or placebo in patients concomitantly treated with fluoxetine for resistant major depressive episodes. *Journal of Clinical Psychiatry, 64*, 403–407.

Barbui, C. & Hotopf, M. (2001) Amitriptyline v. the rest: still the leading antidepressant after 40 years of randomised controlled trials. *British Journal of Psychiatry, 178*, 129–144.

Barbui, C., Esposito, E. & Cipriani, A. (2009) Selective serotonin reuptake inhibitors and risk of suicide: a systematic review of observational studies. *Canadian Medical Association Journal, 180*, 291–297.

Barkow, K., Heun, R., Wittchen, H. U., *et al.* (2004) Mixed anxiety-depression in a 1 year follow-up study: shift to other diagnoses or remission? *Journal of Affective Disorders, 79*, 235–239.

Barrett, J. E., Williams, J. W., Oxman, T. E., *et al.* (1999) The treatment effectiveness project. A comparison of the effectiveness of paroxetine, problem-solving therapy, and placebo in the treatment of minor depression and dysthymia in primary care patients: background and research plan. *General Hospital Psychiatry, 21*, 260–273.

Barrett, J. E., Williams, Jr, J. W., Oxman, T. E., *et al.* (2001) Treatment of dysthymia and minor depression in primary care: a randomized trial in patients aged 18 to 59 years. *Journal of Family Practice, 50*, 405–412.

Bauer, M. S. & Dunner, D. L. (1993) Validity of seasonal pattern as a modifier for recurrent mood disorders for DSM–IV. *Comprehensive Psychiatry, 34*, 159–170.

Bauer, M., Whybrow, P. C., Angst, J., *et al.* (2002a) World Federation of Societies of Biological Psychiatry (WFSBP) Guidelines for biological treatment of unipolar depressive disorders, Part 1: Acute and continuation treatment of major depressive disorder. *The World Journal of Biological Psychiatry, 3*, 5–43.

Bauer, M., Whybrow, P. C., Angst, J., *et al.* (2002b) World Federation of Societies of Biological Psychiatry (WFSBP) guidelines for biological treatment of unipolar depressive disorders, Part 2: Maintenance treatment of major depressive disorder and treatment of chronic depressive disorders and subthreshold depressions. *The World Journal of Biological Psychiatry, 3*, 69–86.

Beck, A. T. (1997) The past and future of cognitive therapy. *Journal of Psychotherapy Practice and Research, 6*, 276–284.

Beck, A. T. (2008) The evolution of the cognitive model of depression and its neurobiological correlates. *American Journal of Psychiatry, 165*, 969–977.

Beck, A. T. & Beck, J. S. (1991) *The Personality Belief Questionnaire*. Unpublished manuscript, University of Pennsylvania.

Beck, A. T., Ward, C. H., Mendelson, M., *et al.* (1961) An inventory for measuring depression. *Archives of General Psychiatry, 4*, 561–571.

Beck, A. T., Rush, A. J., Shaw, B. F., *et al.* (1979) *Cognitive Therapy of Depression.* New York: Wiley.

Beck, A. T., Steer, A. & Brown, G. K. (1996) *Beck Depression Inventory Manual* (2nd edn). San Antonio, Texas: The Psychological Corporation.

Beck, A. T., Guth, D., Steer, R. A., *et al.* (1997) Screening for major depression disorders in medical inpatients with the Beck Depression Inventory for primary care. *Behaviour Research and Therapy, 35*, 785–791.

Beck, A. T., Steer, R. A. & Brown, G. K. (2000) *BDI-Fast Screen for Medical Patients: Manual.* San Antonio, Texas: The Psychological Corporation.

Beck, J. S. (1995) *Cognitive Therapy: Basics and Beyond.* New York: Guilford Press.

Beekman, A. F. T., Copeland, J. R. M. & Prince, M. J. (1999) Review of community prevalence of depression in later life. *British Journal of Psychiatry, 174*, 307–311.

Benedicte, Á., Arellano, J., De Cock, E., *et al.* (2010) Economic evaluation of duloxetine versus serotonin selective reuptake inhibitors and venlafaxine XR in treating major depressive disorder in Scotland. *Journal of Affective Disorders, 120*, 94-104.

Benkert, O., Szegedi, A., Wetzel, H., *et al.* (1997)[233] Dose escalation vs. continued doses of paroxetine and maprotiline: a prospective study in depressed out-patients with inadequate treatment response. *Acta Psychiatrica Scandinavica, 95*, 288–296.

Bennett, K. J., Torrance, G. W., Boyle, M. H., *et al.* (2000) Cost-utility analysis in depression: the McSad utility measure for depression health states. *Psychiatric Services, 51*, 1171–1176.

Berlanga, C. & Flores-Ramos, M. (2006) Different gender response to serotonergic and noradrenergic antidepressants. A comparative study of the efficacy of citalopram and reboxetine. *Journal of Affective Disorders, 95*, 119–123.

Berlin, J. A. (1997) Does blinding of readers affect the results of meta-analyses? *Lancet, 350*, 185–186.

Bhugra, D. & Cochrane, R. (2001) Psychiatry in a multi-ethnic context. In *Psychiatry in Multicultural Britain* (eds D. Bhugra & R. Cochrane). London: Gaskell.

Bhui, K., Bhugra, D. & Goldberg, D. (2000) Cross-cultural validity of the Amritsar Depression Inventory and the General Health Questionnaire amongst English and Punjabi primary care attenders. *Social Psychiatry and Psychiatric Epidemiology, 35*, 248–254.

Bhui, K., Bhugra, D., Goldberg, D., *et al.* (2001) Cultural influences on the prevalence of common mental disorders, general practitioners' assessments and help-seeking among Punjabi and English people visiting their general practitioner. *Psychological Medicine, 31*, 815–825.

Bhui, K., Stansfeld, S., Hull, S., *et al.* (2003) Ethnic variations in pathways to and use of specialist mental health services in the UK. *British Journal of Psychiatry, 182*, 105–116.

Biddle, L., Donovan, J. L., Gunnell, D., *et al.* (2006) Young adults' perceptions of GPs as a help source for mental distress: a qualitative study. *British Journal of General Practice*, 56, 924–931.

---

[233]This is also the reference for Benkert *et al.*, 1997 (2nd cf).

References

Biddle, S., Fox, K. & Edmund, L. (1994) *Physical Activity in Primary Care in England.* London: Health Education Authority.

Black, N. (1996) Why we need observational studies to evaluate the effectiveness of health care. *British Medical Journal, 312,* 1215–1218.

Blackburn, I. M., Euson, K. & Bishop, S. (1986) A two-year naturalistic follow-up of depressed patients treated with cognitive therapy, pharmacotherapy and a combination of both. *Journal of Affective Disorders, 10,* 67–75.

Blashki, T. G., Mowbray, R. & Davies, B. (1971) Controlled trial of amitriptyline in general practice. *British Medical Journal, 1,* 133–138.

Blom, M. B., Spinhoven, P., Hoffman, T., *et al.* (2007) Severity and duration of depression, not personality factors, predict short term outcome in the treatment of major depression. *Journal of Affective Disorders, 104,* 119–126.

Boeck, V., Overo, K. F. & Svendsen, O. (1982) Studies on acute toxicity and drug levels of citalopram in the dog. *Acta Pharmacologica et Toxicologica, 50,* 169–174.

Bogetto, F., Bellino, S., Revello, R. B., *et al.* (2002) Discontinuation syndrome in dysthymic patients treated with selective serotonin reuptake inhibitors: a clinical investigation. *CNS Drugs, 16,* 273–283.

Bollini, P., Pampallona, S., Tibaldi, G., *et al.* (1999) Effectiveness of antidepressants. Meta-analysis of dose-effect relationships in randomised clinical trials. *British Journal of Psychiatry, 174,* 297–303.

Bordin, E. S. (1979) The generalizability of the psychoanalytic concept of the working alliance. *Psychotherapy: Theory, Research and Practice, 16,* 252–260.

Borghi, J. & Guest, J. F. (2000) Economic impact of using mirtazapine compared to amitriptyline and fluoxetine in the treatment of moderate and severe depression in the UK. *European Psychiatry, 15,* 378–387.

Bostwick, J. M. & Pankratz, V. S. (2000) Affective disorders and suicide risk: a reexamination. *American Journal of Psychiatry, 157,* 1925–1932.

Bower, P. & Gilbody, S. (2005a) Stepped care in psychological therapies: access, effectiveness and efficiency: narrative literature review. *British Journal of Psychiatry, 186,* 11–17.

Bower, P. & Sibbald, B. (2000) On-site mental health workers in primary care: effects on professional practice. *Cochrane Database of Systematic Reviews.* Available at: http://www.cochrane.org/reviews/en/ab000532.html

Bower, P., Byford, S., Sibbald, B., *et al.* (2000) Randomised controlled trial of non-directive counselling, cognitive-behaviour therapy, and usual general practitioner care for patients with depression. II: Cost-effectiveness. *British Medical Journal, 321,* 1389–1392.

Bower, P., Rowland, N. & Hardy, R. (2003) The clinical effectiveness of counselling in primary care: a systematic review and meta-analysis. *Psychological Medicine, 33,* 203–215.

Bower, P., Gilbody, S., Richards, D., *et al.* (2006) Collaborative care for depression in primary care. Making sense of a complex intervention: systematic review and meta-regression. *British Journal of Psychiatry, 189,* 484–493.

Braun, V. & Clarke, V. (2006) Using thematic analysis in psychology. *Qualitative Research in Psychology, 3,* 77–101.

Bridges, K. W. & Goldberg, D. P. (1987) Somatic presentations of depressive illness in primary care. In *The Presentation of Depression: Current Approaches* (eds P. Freeling, L. J. Downey & J. C. Malkin), pp. 9–11. London: Royal College of General Practitioners.

Briggs, A. H. (2000) Handling uncertainty in cost-effectiveness models. *Pharmacoeconomics, 17*, 479–500.

British Medical Association and the Royal Pharmaceutical Society of Great Britain (2003) *British National Formulary (BNF* 45). London: British Medical Association and the Royal Pharmaceutical Society of Great Britain.

British Medical Association and the Royal Pharmaceutical Society of Great Britain (2008) *British National Formulary (BNF* 56). London: British Medical Association and the Royal Pharmaceutical Society of Great Britain.

British Medical Association and the Royal Pharmaceutical Society of Great Britain (2009) *British National Formulary (BNF 57).* London: British Medical Association and the Royal Pharmaceutical Society of Great Britain.

Brosan, L., Moore, R. & Reynolds, S. (2007) Factors associated with competence in cognitive therapists. *Behavioural and Cognitive Psychotherapy, 35*, 179–190.

Brotman, M. A., Strunk, D. R. & DeRubeis, R. J. (2009) Therapeutic alliance and adherence in cognitive therapy for depression. In preparation.

Brown, G. & Harris, T. (1978) *The Social Origins of Depression: A Study of Psychiatric Disorder in Women.* London: Tavistock Publications.

Brown, T. A., Campbell, L. A., Lehman, C. L., *et al.* (2001) Current and lifetime comorbidity of the DSM–IV anxiety and mood disorders in a large clinical sample. *Journal of Abnormal Psychology, 110*, 585–599.

Bryant, M. J., Simons, A. D. & Thase, M. E. (1999) Therapist skill and patient variables in homework compliance: controlling an uncontrolled variable in cognitive therapy outcome research. *Cognitive Therapy and Research, 23*, 381–399.

Buckley, N. A. & McManus, P. R. (2002) Fatal toxicity of serotoninergic and other antidepressant drugs: analysis of UK mortality data. *British Medical Journal, 325*, 1332–1333.

Buckley, N. A., Dawson, A. H., Whyte, I. M., *et al.* (1994) Greater toxicity in overdose of dothiepin than of other tricyclic antidepressants. *Lancet, 343*, 159–162.

Bucknall, C., Brooks, D., Curry, P. V., *et al.* (1988) Mianserin and trazodone for cardiac patients with depression. *European Journal of Clinical Pharmacology, 33*, 565–569.

Burns, D. D. (1980) *Feeling Good: the New Mood Therapy.* New York: William Morrow.

Burns, D. D. & Nolen-Hoeksema, S. (1992) Therapeutic empathy and homework compliance in cognitive-behavioral therapy. *Journal of Consulting and Clinical Psychology, 60*, 441–449.

Burroughs, H., Morley, M., Lovell, K., *et al.* (2006) 'Justifiable depression': how health professionals and patients view late-life depression; a qualitative study. *Family Practice*, 23, 369–377.

Byford, S., Knapp, M., Greenshields, J., *et al.* (2003) Cost-effectiveness of brief cognitive behaviour therapy versus treatment as usual in recurrent deliberate self-harm: a decision-making approach. *Psychological Medicine, 33*, 977–986.

References

Cahill, J., Barkham, M., Hardy, G., *et al.* (2003) Outcomes of patients completing and not completing cognitive therapy for depression. *British Journal of Clinical Psychology, 42*, 133–143.

Cameron, D. E. (1947) The day hospital. An experimental form of hospitalisation for psychiatric patients. *Modern Hospital, 68*, 60–62.

Campbell, M., Fitzpatrick, R., Haines, A., *et al.* (2000) Framework for design and evaluation of complex interventions to improve health. *British Medical Journal, 321*, 694–696.

Carcone, B., Vial, T., Chaillet, N., *et al.* (1991) Symptomatic bradycardia caused by mianserin at therapeutic doses. *Human Experimental Toxicology, 10*, 383–384.

Carels, R., Darby, L., Cacciapaglia, H., *et al.* (2005) Applying a stepped-care approach to the treatment of obesity. *Journal of Psychosomatic Research, 59*, 375–383.

Carney, R. M., Freedland, K. E., Sheline, Y. I., *et al.* (1997) Depression and coronary heart disease: a review for cardiologists. *Clinical Cardiology, 20*, 196–200.

Caspi, A., Sugden, K., Moffitt, T. E., *et al.* (2003) Influence of life stress on depression: moderation by a polymorphism in the 5-HTT gene. *Science, 301*, 386–389.

Cassano, P. & Fava, M. (2002) Depression and public health: an overview. *Journal of Psychosomatic Research, 53*, 849–857.

Catalano, G., Catalano, M. C., Epstein, M. A., *et al.* (2001) QTc interval prolongation associated with citalopram overdose: a case report and literature review. *Clinical Neuropharmacology, 24*, 158–162.

Chew-Graham, C. A., May, C. R., Cole, H., *et al.* (2000) The burden of depression in primary care: a qualitative investigation of general practitioners' constructs of depressed people in primary care. *Primary Care Psychiatry, 6*, 137–141.

Chew-Graham, C. A., Bashir, C., Chantler, K., *et al.* (2002) South Asian women, psychological distress and self-harm: lessons for primary care trusts. *Health and Social Care in the Community, 10*, 339–347.

Chew-Graham, C. A., Lovell, K., Roberts, C., *et al.* (2007) A randomized controlled trial to test the feasibility of a collaborative care model for the management of depression in older people. *British Journal of General Practice, 57*, 364–369.

Chew-Graham, C. A., Chamberlain, E., Turner, K., *et al.* (2008) General practitioners' and health visitors' views on the diagnosis and management of postnatal depression: a qualitative study. *British Journal of General Practice, 58*, 169–176.

Chong, S. A., Mythily, S. & Mahendran, R. (2001) Cardiac effects of psychotropic drugs. *Annals, Academy of Medicine, Singapore, 30*, 625–631.

Christensen, H., Griffiths, K. M. & Korten, A. (2002) Web-based cognitive behaviour therapy: analysis of site usage and changes in depression and anxiety scores. *Journal of Medical Internet Research, 4*, e3.

Christensen, H., Griffiths, K. M. & Jorm, A. (2004) Delivering interventions for depression by using the internet: randomised controlled trial. *British Medical Journal, 328*, 265–268.

Christian, J. L., O'Leary, K. D. & Vivian, D. (1994) Depressive symptomatology in maritally discordant women and men: the role of individual and relationship variables. *Journal of Family Psychiatry, 8*, 32–42.

Cipriani, A., Furukawa, T. A., Geddes, J. R., *et al.* (2008) Does randomized evidence support sertraline as first-line antidepressant for adults with acute major depression? A systematic review and meta-analysis. *Journal of Clinical Psychiatry, 69*, 1732–1742.

Cipriani, A., Furukawa, T. A., Salanti, G., *et al.* (2009) Comparative efficacy and acceptability of 12 new generation antidepressants: a multiple treatments meta-analysis. *The Lancet, 373*, 746–758.

Clark, D. M., Layard, R. & Smithies, R. (2008) *Improving Access to Psychological Therapy: Initial Evaluation of the Two Demonstration Sites.* CEP Discussion Papers, dp0897. London: Centre for Economic Performance, LSE.

Cochrane Collaboration (2003) *Review Manager (RevMan) Version 4.2.* Copenhagen: The Nordic Cochrane Centre, The Cochrane Collaboration. [Computer programme].

Cochrane Collaboration (2008) *Review Manager (RevMan) Version 5.0.* Copenhagen: The Nordic Cochrane Centre, The Cochrane Collaboration. [Computer programme].

Cohen, H. W., Gibson, G. & Alderman, M. H. (2000) Excess risk of myocardial infarction in patients treated with antidepressant medication: association with use of tricyclic agents. *American Journal of Medicine, 108*, 2–8.

Cole, J., McGuffin, P. & Farmer, A. E. (2008) The classification of depression: are we still confused? *British Journal of Psychiatry, 192*, 83–85.

Commander, M. J., Sashidharan, S. P., Odell, S. M., *et al.* (1997) Access to mental health care in an inner city health district, I: Pathways into and within specialist psychiatric services. *British Journal of Psychiatry, 176*, 407–411.

Committee on Safety of Medicines (2000) Reminder: St John's wort (hypericum perforatum) interactions. *Current Problems in Pharmacovigilance, 26*, 6–7.

Conradi, H. J., de Jonge, P. & Ormel, J. (2008) Prediction of the three-year course of recurrent depression in primary care patients: different risk factors for different outcomes. *Journal of Affective Disorders, 105*, 267–271.

Cooper-Patrick, L., Powe, N. R., Jenckes, M. W., *et al.* (1997) Identification of patient attitudes and preferences regarding treatment of depression. *Journal of General Internal Medicine, 12*, 431–438.

Coryell, W., Akiskal, H., Leon, A. C., *et al.* (1994) The time course of nonchronic major depressive disorder. Uniformity across episodes and samples. National Institute of Mental Health Collaborative Program in the Psychobiology of Depression – Clinical Studies. *Archives of General Psychiatry, 51*, 405–410.

Cowen, P.J. (1998) Pharmacological management of treatment resistant depression. *Advances in Psychiatric Treatment, 4*, 320–327.

Coyne, J. C., Pepper, C. M. & Flynn, H. (1999) Significance of prior episodes of depression in two patient populations. *Journal of Consulting and Clinical Psychology, 67*, 76–81.

Craig, P., Dieppe, P., Macintyre, S., *et al.* (2008) Developing and evaluating complex interventions: the new Medical Research Council guidance. *British Medical Journal, 337*, a1655.

Creed, F., Black, D., Anthony, P., *et al.* (1990) Randomised controlled trial of day patient versus inpatient psychiatric treatment. *British Medical Journal, 300*, 1033–1037.

References

Creed, F. & Marks, B. (1989) Liaison psychiatry in general practice: a comparison of the liaison-attachment scheme and shifted outpatient clinic models. *Journal of the Royal College of General Practice, 39*, 514–517.

Crowther, R. E., Marshall, M., Bond, G. R., *et al.* (2001) Helping people with severe mental illness to obtain work: systematic review. *British Medical Journal, 322*, 204–208.

Cuijpers, P. (1997) Bibliotherapy in unipolar depression: a meta-analysis. *Journal of Behavioural Therapy and Experimental Psychiatry, 28*, 139–147.

Cuijpers, P., Smit, F. & van Straten, A. (2007) Psychological treatments of subthreshold depression: a meta-analytic review. *Acta Psychiatrica Scandinavica, 115*, 434–444.

Cuijpers, P., van Straten, A., van Oppen, P., *et al.* (2008a) Are psychological and pharmacologic interventions equally effective in the treatment of adult depressive disorders? A meta-analysis of comparative studies. *Journal of Clinical Psychiatry, 69*, 1675–1685.

Cuijpers, P., van Straten, A., Warmerdam, L., *et al.* (2008b) Psychological treatmeant of depression: a meta-analytic database of randomized studies. *BMC Psychiatry, 8*, 36–41.

Cullen, J. M., Mitchell, P., Brodaty, H., *et al.* (1991) Carbamazepine for treatment-resistant melancholia. *Journal of Clinical Psychiatry, 52*, 472–476.

Cullen, J. M., Spates, C. R., Pagoto, S., *et al.* (2006) Behavioral activation treatment for major depressive disorder: a pilot investigation. *The Behavior Analyst Today, 7*, 151–166.

Curtis, L. (2009) *Unit Costs of Health and Social Care 2008*. Canterbury: Personal Social Services Research Unit, University of Kent.

Dago, P. L. & Quitkin, F. M. (1995) Role of the placebo response in the treatment of depressive disorders. *CNS Drugs, 4*, 335–340.

Darling, C. & Tyler, P. (1990) Brief encounters in general practice: liaison in general practice psychiatry clinics. *Psychiatric Bulletin, 14*, 592–594.

David, D., Szentagotai, A., Lupu, V., *et al.* (2008) Rational emotive behavior therapy, cognitive therapy, and medication in the treatment of major depressive disorder: a randomized clinical trial, posttreatment outcomes, and six-month follow-up. *Journal of Clinical Psychology, 64*, 728–746.

Davidson, J. & Pelton, S. (1986) Forms of atypical depression and their response to antidepressant drugs. *Psychiatry Research, 17*, 87–95.

Davidson, K., Scott, J., Schmidt, U., *et al.* (2004) Therapist competence and clinical outcome in the prevention of parasuicide by manual assisted cognitive behaviour therapy trial: the POPMACT study. *Psychological Medicine, 34*, 855–863.

Davis, L. L., Kabel, D., Patel, D., *et al.* (1996) Valproate as an antidepressant in major depressive disorder. *Psychopharmacology Bulletin, 32*, 647–652.

Davison, G. C. (2000) Stepped care: doing more with less? *Journal of Consulting and Clinical Psychology, 68*, 580–585.

Delgrado, P. L. (2006) Monoamine depletion studies: implications for antidepressant discontinuation syndrome. *Journal of Clinical Psychiatry, 67* (Suppl. 4), 22–26.

De Los Reyes, A. & Kazdin, A. E. (2008) When the evidence says, 'Yes, no, and maybe so': attending to and interpreting inconsistent findings among evidence-based interventions. *Current Directions in Psychological Science, 17,* 47–51.

Del Piccolo, L., Saltini, A. & Zimmermann, C. (1998) Which patients talk about stressful life events and social problems to the general practitioner? *Psychological Medicine, 28,* 1289–1299.

Department of Health (1999) *National Service Framework for Mental Health.* London: Department of Health.

Department of Health (2000) *The NHS Plan. A Plan for Investment. A Plan for Reform.* London: HMSO.

Department of Health (2001) *Exercise Referral Systems: A National Quality Assurance Framework.* London: Department of Health.

Department of Health (2003) *Fast-forwarding Primary Care Mental Health: Graduate Primary Care Mental Health Workers – Best Practice Guidance.* London: Department of Health.

Department of Health (2004) *Quality and Outcomes Framework: Guidance.* London: Department of Health.

Department of Health (2007) *Improving Access to Psychological Therapies: Specification for the Commissioner-led Pathfinder Programme.* London: Department of Health.

Department of Health (2008a) *Prescription Cost Analysis: England 2007.* London: Department of Health.

Department of Health (2008b) *Report on Self Reported Experience of Patients From Black and Minority Ethnic Groups.* London: Department of Health.

Department of Health & Social Care Institute for Excellence (2009) *SCIE Guide 30: Think Child, Think Parent, Think Family: a Guide to Parental Mental Health and Child Welfare.* London: Department of Health.

Department of Health, Social Care Institute for Excellence & Care Services Improvement Partnership (2008) *Care Programme Approach (CPA) Briefing: Parents with Mental Health Problems and Their Children.* http://www.cpaa.co.uk/cpa-briefing

Derogatis, L. R. (1974) The Hopkins Symptom Checklist (HSCL): a self-report symptom inventory. *Behavioral Science,* 19, 1–15.

DerSimonian, R. & Laird, N. (1986) Meta-analysis in clinical trials. *Controlled Clinical Trials, 7,* 177–188.

DeRubeis, R. J. & Feeley, M. (1990) Determinants of change in cognitive therapy for depression. *Cognitive Therapy and Research, 14,* 469–482.

DeRubeis, R. J., Hollon, S. D., Amsterdam, J. D., *et al.* (2005) Cognitive therapy versus medications in the treatment of moderate to severe depression. *Archives of General Psychiatry, 62,* 409–416.

Dick, P., Cameron, L., Cohen, D., *et al.* (1985) Day and full-time psychiatric treatment: a controlled comparison. *British Journal of Psychiatry, 147,* 246–249.

Dietrich, D. E. & Emrich, H. M. (1998) The use of anticonvulsants to augment antidepressant medication. *Journal of Clinical Psychiatry, 59* (Suppl. 5), 51–58.

References

Dolan, P. & Williams, A. (1995) *A Social Tariff for EuroQol: Results from a UK General Population Survey.* York: Centre for Health Economics, University of York.

Dombrovski, A. Y., Mulsant, B. H., Houck, P. R., *et al.* (2007) Residual symptoms and recurrence during maintenance treatment of late-life depression. *Journal of Affective Disorders, 103,* 77–82.

Donoghue, J. (2000) Antidepressant use patterns in clinical practices: comparisons among tricyclic antidepressants and selective serotonin reuptake inhibitors. *Acta Psychiatrica Scandinavica, 101* (Suppl. 403), 57–61.

Donoghue, J. & Hylan, T. R. (2001) Antidepressant use in clinical practice: efficacy v. effectiveness. *British Journal of Psychiatry, 179* (Suppl. 42), 9–17.

Donoghue, J. & Tylee, A. (1996) The treatment of depression: prescribing patterns of antidepressants in primary care in the UK. *British Journal of Psychiatry, 168,* 164–168.

Donoghue, J., Tylee, A. & Wildgust, H. (1996) Cross-sectional database analysis of antidepressant prescribing in general practice in the UK, 1993–1995. *British Medical Journal, 313,* 861–862.

Dornseif, B. E., Dunlop, S. R., Potvin, J. H., *et al.* (1989) Effect of dose escalation after low-dose fluoxetine therapy. *Psychopharmacology Bulletin, 25,* 71–79.

Dowrick, C. F. (2004) *Beyond Depression.* Oxford: Oxford University Press.

Dowrick, C., Dunn, G., Ayuso-Mateos, J. T., *et al.* (2000) Problem solving treatment and group psychoeducation for depression: multicentre randomised controlled trial. *British Medical Journal, 321,* 1450–1454.

Doyle, J. J., Casciano, J., Arikian, S., *et al.* (2001) A multinational pharmacoeconomic evaluation of acute major depressive disorder (MDD): a comparison of cost-effectiveness between venlafaxine, SSRIs and TCAs. *Value in Health, 4,* 16–31.

Drevets, W. C., Price, J. L. & Furey, M. L. (2008) Brain structural and functional abnormalities in mood disorders: implications for neurocircuitry models of depression. *Brain Structure and Function, 213,* 93–118.

Drummond, M. F. & Jefferson, T. O. (on behalf of the *BMJ* Economic Evaluation Working Party) (1996) Guidelines for authors and peer reviewers of economic submissions to the *BMJ. British Medical Journal, 313,* 275–283.

Dunbar, G. C., Cohn, J. B., Fabre, L. F., *et al.* (1991) A comparison of paroxetine, imipramine and placebo in depressed outpatients. *British Journal of Psychiatry, 159,* 394–398.

Dunn, R. L., Donoghue, J. M., Ozminkowski, R. J., *et al.* (1999) Longitudinal patterns of antidepressant prescribing in primary care in the UK: comparison with treatment guidelines. *Journal of Psychopharmacology, 13,* 136–143.

Dwamena, B. (2007) *MIDAS: Stata Module for Meta-analytical Integration of Diagnostic Test Accuracy Studies.* Statistical Software Components S456880. Boston, Massachusetts: Boston College Department of Economics.

Eagles, J. M., Wileman, S. M., Cameron, I. M., *et al.* (1999) Seasonal affective disorder among primary care attenders and a community sample in Aberdeen. *British Journal of Psychiatry, 175,* 472–475.

Eccles, M., Freemantle, N. & Mason, J. (1998) North of England evidence-based guideline development project: methods of developing guidelines for efficient drug use in primary care. *British Medical Journal, 316*, 1232–1235.

Edwards, J. G. & Goldie, A. (1983) Mianserin, maprotiline and intracardiac conduction. *British Journal of Clinical Pharmacology, 15* (Suppl. 2), 249–254.

Egan, G. (1990) *The Skilled Helper: A Systematic Approach to Effective Helping.* Pacific Grove, California: Brooks/Cole.

Einarson, T. R., Arikian, S. R., Casciano, J., *et al.* (1999) Comparison of extended-release venlafaxine, selective serotonin reuptake inhibitors, and tricyclic antidepressants in the treatment of depression: a meta-analysis of randomised controlled trials. *Clinical Therapeutics, 21*, 296–308.

Ekers, D., Richards, D. & Gilbody, S. (2007) A meta-analysis of randomized trials of behavioural treatment of depression. *Psychological Medicine, 38*, 611–623.

Elgie, R. (2006) A patient and primary care perspective: a patient's perspective on the treatment of depression. *Journal of Clinical Psychiatry, 67* (Suppl. 6), 38–40.

Eli Lilly and Co. Ltd (2009) *Cymbalta. Summary of Product Characteristics.* Basingstoke: Eli Lilly. Available at: http://www.medicines.org.uk/emc/medicine/15694

Elkin, I. (1994) The NIMH treatment of depression collaborative research programme: where we began and where we are. In *Handbook of Psychotherapy and Behaviour Change* (eds A.E. Bergin & S.L. Garfield), 4th edn. New York: Wiley.

Elkin, I., Shea, M. T., Watkins, J., *et al.* (1989) National Institute of Mental Health Treatment of Depression Collaborative Research Programme. General effectiveness of treatments. *Archives of General Psychiatry, 46*, 971–982.

Ellis, A. E. (1962) *Reason and Emotion in Psychotherapy: A Comprehensive Method of Treating Human Disturbances: Revised and Updated.* Secaucus, New Jersey: Carol Publishing Corporation.

Ellis, C. G. (1996) Chronic unhappiness: investigating the phenomenon in family practice. *Canadian Family Physician, 42*, 645–651.

Emery, G. (1981) Cognitive therapy with the elderly. In G. Emery, S. D. Hollon & R. C. Bedrosian (Eds.) *New Directions in Cognitive Therapy* (pp. 84–98). New York: Guilford Press.

Evans, C., Mellor-Clark, J., Margison, F., *et al.* (2000) Clinical Outcomes in Routine Evaluation: The CORE-OM. *Journal of Mental Health, 9*, 247–255.

Faravelli, C., Servi, P., Arends, J. A., *et al.* (1996) Number of symptoms, quantification and qualification of depression. *Comprehensive Psychiatry, 37*, 307–315.

Fava, G. A., Ruini, C., Rafanelli, C., *et al.* (2004) Six-year outcome of cognitive behavior therapy for prevention of recurrent depression. *The American Journal of Psychiatry, 161*, 1872–1876.

Fava, M. & Kendler, K. (2000) Major depressive disorder. *Neuron, 28*, 335–341.

Fava, M., Mulroy, R., Alpert, J., *et al.* (1997) Emergence of adverse events following discontinuation of treatment with extended-release venlafaxine. *American Journal of Psychiatry, 154*, 1760–1762.

Feeley, M., DeRubeis, R. J. & Gelfand, L. A. (1999) The temporal relation of adherence and alliance to symptom change in cognitive therapy for depression. *Journal of Consulting and Clinical Psychology*, 67, 578–582.

Feighner, J. P. (1995) Cardiovascular safety in depressed patients: focus on venlafaxine. *Journal of Clinical Psychiatry*, 56, 574–579.

Feighner, J. P. & Boyer, W. F. (1989) Paroxetine in the treatment of depression: a comparison with imipramine and placebo. *Acta Psychiatrica Scandinavica Supplementum*, 350, 125–129.

Fergusson, D., Doucette, S., Glass, K. C., *et al.* (2005) Association between suicide attempts and selective serotonin reuptake inhibitors: systematic review of randomised controlled trials. *British Medical Journal*, 330, 396–403.

Fernandez, J. L., Montgomery, S. & Francois, C. (2005) Evaluation of the cost effectiveness of escitalopram versus venlafaxine XR in major depressive disorder. *Pharmacoeconomics*, 23, 155–167.

Fischer, J. E., Bachmann, L. M. & Jaeschke, R. (2003) A readers' guide to the interpretation of diagnostic test properties: clinical example of sepsis. *Intensive Care Medicine*, 29, 1043–1051.

Fleishaker, J. C., Francom, S. F., Herman, B. D., *et al.* (2001) Lack of effect of reboxetine on cardiac repolarisation. *Clinical Pharmacological Therapy*, 70, 261–269.

Fonagy, P. (2003) Some complexities in the relationship of psychoanalytic theory to technique. *Psychoanalytic Quarterly*, 72, 13–47.

Ford, D. E., Mead, L. A., Chang, P. P., *et al.* (1998) Depression is a risk factor for coronary artery disease in men: the precursors study. *Archives of Internal Medicine*, 158, 1422–1426.

Frank, E., Prien, R. F., Jarrett, J. B., *et al.* (1991) Conceptualization and rationale for consensus definitions of terms in major depressive disorder. Remission, recovery, relapse, and recurrence. *Archives of General Psychiatry*, 48, 851–855.

Fredman, S. J., Fava, M., Kienke, A. S., *et al.* (2000) Partial response, non-response and relapse with selective serotonin reuptake inhibitors in major depression: a survey of current 'next-step' practices. *Journal of Clinical Psychiatry*, 61, 403–408.

Freud, S. (1917; reprinted 1953–1974) *Mourning and Melancholia*. In *The Standard Edition of the Complete Psychological Works of Sigmund Freud* (trans. & ed. by J. Strachey), vol. 14. London: Hogarth Press.

Friedli, K., King, M. B., Lloyd, M., *et al.* (1997) Randomised controlled assessment of non-directive psychotherapy versus routine general-practitioner care. *Lancet*, 350, 1662–1665.

Friedli, K., King, M. B. & Lloyd, M. (2000) The economics of employing a counsellor in general practice: analysis of data from a randomised controlled trial. *British Journal of General Practice*, 50, 276–283.

Fulton, B. & Benfield, P. (1996) Moclobemide. An update of its pharmacological properties and therapeutic use. *Drugs*, 52, 450–474.

Furukawa, T. A., Kitamura, T. & Takahashi, K. (2000) Time to recovery from an inception cohort with hitherto untreated unipolar major depressive episodes. *British Journal of Psychiatry*, 177, 331–335.

Furukawa, T. A., McGuire, H. & Barbui, C. (2002a) Meta-analysis of effects and side effects of low dosage tricyclic antidepressants in depression: systematic review. *British Medical Journal, 325*, 991–995.

Furukawa, T. A., Streiner, D. L. & Young, L. T. (2002b) Antidepressant and benzodiazepine for major depression (Cochrane Review). In *Cochrane Library*, Issue 4. Oxford: Update Software.

Furukawa, T. A., Fujita, A., Harai, H., *et al.* (2008) Definitions of recovery and outcomes of major depression: results from a 10-year follow up. *Acta Psychiatrica Scandinavica, 117*, 35–40.

Garnier, R., Azoyan, P., Chataigner, D., *et al.* (1993) Acute fluvoxamine poisoning. *Journal of International Medical Research, 21*, 197–208.

Gartlehner, G., Gaynes, B. N., Hansen, R. A., *et al.* (2008) Comparative benefits and harms of second-generation antidepressants: background paper for the American College of Physicians. *Annals of Internal Medicine, 149*, 734–750.

Gask, L., Goldberg, D., Lesser, A. L., *et al.* (1988) Improving the psychiatric skills of the general practice trainee: an evaluation of a group training course. *Medical Education, 22*, 132–138.

Gask, L., Sibbald, B. & Creed, F. (1997) Evaluating models of working at the interface between mental health services and primary care. *British Journal of Psychiatry*, 170, 6–11.

Gask, L., Rogers, A., Oliver, D., *et al.* (2003) Qualitative study of patients' perceptions of the quality of care for depression in general practice. *British Journal of General Practice*, 53, 278–283.

Geddes, J. R. (2009) Clinical trial design: horses for courses. *World Psychiatry, 8*, 28–29.

Geddes, J. R., Freemantle, N., Mason, J., *et al.* (2002) Selective serotonin reuptake inhibitors (SSRIs) for depression (Cochrane Review). In *Cochrane Library*, Issue 1. Oxford: Update Software.

Geddes, J. R., Carney, S. M., Davies, C., *et al.* (2003a) Relapse prevention with antidepressant drug treatment in depressive disorders: a systematic review. *Lancet, 361*, 653–661.

Geddes, J., Carney, S., Cowen, P., *et al.* (2003b) Efficacy and safety of electroconvulsive therapy in depressive disorders: a systematic review and meta-analysis. *Lancet, 361*, 799–808.

Geddes, J. R., Calabrese, J. R. & Goodwin, G. M. (2009) Lamotrigine for treatment of bipolar depression: independent meta-analysis and meta-regression of individual patient data from five randomised trials. *British Journal of Psychiatry, 194*, 4–9.

Gellatly, J., Bower, P., Hennessy, S., *et al.* (2007) What makes self-help interventions effective in the management of depressive symptoms? Meta-analysis and meta-regression. *Psychological Medicine, 37*, 1217–1228.

Gensichen, J., Beyer, M., Muth, C., *et al.* (2006) Case management to improve major depression in primary health care: a systematic review. *Psychological Medicine, 36*, 7–14.

Gerber, P. D., Barrett, J. E., Barrett, J. A., *et al.* (1992) The relationship of presenting physical complaints to depressive symptoms in primary care patients. *Journal of General Internal Medicine, 7*, 170–173.

References

Gibbons, R. D., Hur, K., Bhaumik, D. K., *et al.* (2005) The relationship between antidepressant medication use and rate of suicide. *Archives of General Psychiatry, 62*, 165–172.

Gilbody, S., Bower, P., Fletcher, J., *et al.* (2006) Collaborative care for depression: a cumulative meta-analysis and review of longer-term outcomes. *Archives of Internal Medicine,* 166, 2314–2321.

Gilbody, S., Richards, D. & Barkham, M. (2007) Diagnosing depression in primary care using self completed instruments: UK validation of PHQ-9 and CORE-OM. *British Journal of General Practice, 57,* 650–652.

Giles, D. E., Jarrett, R. B., Biggs, M. M., *et al.* (1989) Clinical predictors of recurrence in depression. *American Journal of Psychiatry, 146,* 764–767.

Gitlin, M. J., Weiner, H., Fairbanks L., *et al.* (1987) Failure of T3 to potentiate tricyclic antidepressant response. *Journal of Affective Disorders, 13,* 267–272.

Glassman, A. H. (1997) Citalopram toxicity. *Lancet, 350,* 818.

Glassman, A. H. & Shapiro, P. A. (1998) Depression and the course of coronary artery disease. *American Journal of Psychiatry, 155,* 4–11.

Glassman, A. H., Roose, S. P. & Bigger, Jr, J. T. (1993) The safety of tricyclic antidepressants in cardiac patients. Risk–benefit reconsidered. *Journal of the American Medical Association, 269,* 2673–2675.

Glassman, A. H., O'Connor, C. M., Califf, R. M., *et al.* (2002) Sertraline treatment of major depression in patients with acute MI or unstable angina. *Journal of the American Medical Association, 288,* 701–709.

Goeringer, K. E., Raymond, L., Christian, G. D., *et al.* (2000) Post mortem forensic toxicology of selective serotonin reuptake inhibitors: a review of pharmacology and report of 168 cases. *Journal of Forensic Sciences, 45,* 633–648.

Goldberg, D. P. & Bridges, K. (1988) Somatic presentations of psychiatric illness in primary care settings. *Journal of Psychosomatic Research, 32,* 137–144.

Goldberg, D. & Huxley, P. (1980) *Mental Illness in the Community: The Pathway to Psychiatric Care.* London: Tavistock.

Goldberg, D. P. & Huxley, P. J. (1992) *Common Mental Disorders: A Bio-Social Model.* London: Tavistock/Routledge.

Goldberg, D. P. & Williams, P. (1991) *A User's Guide to the General Health Questionnaire.* Windsor: NFER-Nelson.

Goldberg, D. P., Jenkins, L., Millar, T., *et al.* (1993) The ability of trainee general practitioners to identify psychological distress among their patients. *Psychological Medicine, 23,* 185–193.

Goldberg, D. P., Privett, M., Ustun, B., *et al.* (1998) The effects of detection and treatment on the outcome of major depression in primary care: a naturalistic study in 15 cities. *British Journal of General Practice, 48,* 1840–1844.

Golden, R. N., Gaynes, B. N., Ekstrom, R. D., *et al.* (2005) The efficacy of light therapy in the treatment of mood disorders: a review and meta-analysis of the evidence. *American Journal of Psychiatry, 162,* 656–662.

Goodwin, G. (2000) Neurobiological aetiology of mood disorders. In *New Oxford Textbook of Psychiatry* (eds M. G. Gelder, J. J. Lopez-Ibor, & N. Andreasen), pp. 711–719. Oxford: Oxford University Press.

GRADE Working Group (2004) Grading quality of evidence and strength of recommendations. *British Medical Journal, 328*, 1490–1497.

Grant, C., Goodenough, T., Harvey, I., *et al.* (2000) A randomised controlled trial and economic evaluation of a referrals facilitator between primary care and the voluntary sector. *British Medical Journal, 320*, 419–423.

Grayer, J. & Rudge, R. (2005) Recruitment: lessons on setting up primary care mental health teams. *Health Service Journal, 115* (Suppl. 13).

Greenberg, J. R. & Mitchell, S. A. (1983) *Object Relations in Psychoanalytic Theory.* Cambridge, Massachusetts: Harvard University Press.

Greene, R., Pugh, R. & Roberts. D. (2008) *Black and Minority Ethnic Parents with Mental Health Problems and Their Children.* Research Briefing No. 29. London: Social Care Institute for Excellence.

Greenhalgh, J., Knight, C., Hind, D., *et al.* (2005) Clinical and cost-effectiveness of electroconvulsive therapy for depressive illness, schizophrenia, catatonia and mania: systematic reviews and economic modeling studies. *Health Technology Assessment, 9,* 9.

Gregor, K. J., Overhage, J. M., Coons, S. J., *et al.* (1994) Selective serotonin reuptake inhibitor dose titration in the naturalistic setting. *Clinical Therapeutics, 16*, 306–315.

Greist, J., Mundt, J. C. & Kobak, K. (2002) Factors contributing to failed trials of new agents: can technology prevent some problems? *Journal of Clinical Psychiatry, 63* (Suppl. 2), 8–13.

Grundemar, L., Wohlfart, B., Lagerstedt, C., *et al.* (1997) Symptoms and signs of severe citalopram overdose. *Lancet, 349*, 1602.

Gunnell, D. & Ashby, D. (2004) Antidepressants and suicide: what is the balance of benefit and harm? *British Medical Journal, 329*, 34–38.

Gunnell, D., Saperia, J. & Ashby, D. (2005) Selective serotonin reuptake inhibitors (SSRIs) and suicide in adults: meta-analysis of drug company data from placebo controlled, randomised controlled trials submitted to the MHRA's safety review. *British Medical Journal, 330*, 385–395.

Guthrie, E., Moorey, J. & Margison, F. (1999) Cost-effectiveness of brief psychodynamic-interpersonal therapy in high utilisers of psychiatric services. *Archives of General Psychiatry, 56*, 519–526.

Guy, W. (1976) *Early Clinical Drug Evaluation Programme Assessment Manual for Psychopharmacology – Revised.* Rockville, MD: US Department of Health, Education, and Welfare, Public Health Service, Alcohol, Drug Abuse, and Mental Health Administration, NIMH.

Haddad, P. M. (2001) Antidepressant discontinuation syndromes. *Drug Safety, 24*, 183–197.

Haefeli, W. E., Schoenenberger, R. A. & Scholer, A. (1991) Recurrent ventricular fibrillation in mianserin intoxication. *British Medical Journal, 302*, 415–416.

Hakkart-van Roijen, L., van Straten, A., Al, M., *et al.* (2006) Cost-utility of brief psychological treatment for depression and anxiety. *British Journal of Psychiatry, 188*, 323–329.

Hall, W. D. & Lucke, J. (2006) How have the selective serotonin reuptake inhibitor antidepressants affected suicide mortality? *Australian and New Zealand Journal of Psychiatry, 40*, 941–950.

Hall, W. D., Mant, A., Mitchell, P. B., *et al.* (2003) Association between antidepressant prescribing and suicide in Australia, 1991–2000: trend analysis. *British Medical Journal, 326*, 1008–1011.

Hamilton, J. A., Grant, M. & Jensvold, M. F. (1996) Sex and treatment of depression. In *Psychopharmacology and Women: Sex, Gender and Hormones* (eds M. F. Jensvold, U. Halbreich & J. A. Hamilton), pp. 241–260. Washington, DC: American Psychiatric Press.

Hamilton, M. (1960) A rating scale for depression. *Journal of Neurology and Neurosurgical Psychiatry, 23*, 56–62.

Hammen, C., Henry, R. & Daley, S. E. (2000) Depression and sensitisation to stressors among young women as a function of childhood adversity. *Journal of Consulting and Clinical Psychology, 68*, 782–787.

Harden, C. L., Pulver, M. C., Ravdin, L. D., *et al.* (2000) A pilot study of mood in epilepsy patients treated with vagus nerve stimulation. *Epilepsy and Behavior, 1*, 93–99.

Haringsma, R., Engels, G. I., Beekman, A. T. F., *et al.* (2004) The criterion validity of the Center for Epidemiological Studies Depression Scale (CES-D) in a sample of self-referred elders with depressive symptomatology. *International Journal of Geriatric Psychiatry, 19*, 558–563.

Harris, E. C. & Barraclough, B. (1997) Suicide as an outcome for mental disorders. A meta-analysis. *British Journal of Psychiatry, 170*, 205–228.

Harris, T. (2000) Introduction to the work of George Brown. In *Where Inner and Outer Worlds Meet: Psychosocial Research in the Tradition of George W. Brown*, (ed T. Harris), pp. 1–52. London & New York: Routledge.

Harris, T., Brown, G. W. & Robinson, R. (1999) Befriending as an intervention for chronic depression among women in an inner city. 1: Randomised controlled trial. *British Journal of Psychiatry, 174*, 219–224.

Hayhurst, H., Cooper, Z., Paykel, E. S., *et al.* (1997) Expressed emotion and depression: a longitudinal study. *British Journal of Psychiatry, 171*, 439–443.

Healey, D. (2003) The emergence of antidepressant induced suicidality. *Primary Care Psychiatry, 6*, 23–28.

Health and Safety Executive (2008) *Self-Reported Work-Related Illness and Workplace Injuries in 2006/07: Results from the Labour Force Survey.* Caerphilly: HSE Information Services.

Hemels, M. E. H., Kasper, S., Walter, E., *et al.* (2004) Cost effectiveness of escitalopram versus citalopram in the treatment of severe depression. *The Annals of Pharmacotherapy, 38*, 954–960.

Henkel, V., Seemüller, F., Obermeier, M., *et al.* (2009) Does early improvement triggered by antidepressants predict response/remission? Analysis of data from a naturalistic study on a large sample of inpatients with major depression. *Journal of Affective Disorders, 115*, 439–449.

Henry, J. A. & Antao, C. A. (1992) Suicide and fatal antidepressant poisoning. *European Journal of Medicine, 1*, 343–348.

Herrmann, L. L. & Ebmeier, K. P. (2006) Factors modifying the efficacy of transcranial magnetic stimulation in the treatment of depression. *Journal of Clinical Psychiatry, 67*, 1870–1876.

Herz, M. I., Endicott, J., Spitzer, R. L., *et al.* (1971) Day versus inpatient hospitalisation: a controlled study. *American Journal of Psychiatry, 127*, 1371–1382.

Hewer, W., Rost, W. & Gattaz, W. F. (1995) Cardiovascular effects of fluvoxamine and maprotiline antidepressant treatment: effects on cognitive function and psychomotor performance. *International Clinical Psychopharmacology, 15*, 305–318.

Higgins, J. P. T. & Green, S. (eds) (2008) *Cochrane Handbook for Systematic Reviews of Interventions*. Version 5.0.1. The Cochrane Collaboration. Available at: www.cochrane-handbook.org

Higgins, J. P. T. & Thompson, S. G. (2002) Quantifying heterogeneity in a meta-analysis. *Statistics in Medicine, 21*, 1539–1558.

Hildebrandt, M. G., Steyerberg, E. W., Stage, K. B., *et al.* (2003) Are gender differences important for the clinical effects of antidepressants? *American Journal of Psychiatry, 160*, 1643–1650.

Hindmarch, I., Kimber, S., & Cockle, S. M. (2000) Abrupt and brief discontinuation of antidepressant treatment: effects on cognitive function and psychomotor performance. *International Clinical Psychopharmacology, 15*, 305–318.

Hippisley-Cox, J., Pringle, M., Hammersley, V., *et al.* (2001) Antidepressants as risk factor for ischaemic heart disease: case-control study in primary care. *British Medical Journal, 323*, 666–669.

Hla, K. K. & Boyd, O. (1987) Mianserin and complete heart block. *Human Toxicology, 6*, 401–402.

Hollon, S. D., Evans, M. D., Auerbarch, A., *et al.* (1988) Development of a system for rating therapies for depression: differentiating cognitive therapy, interpersonal psychotherapy, and clinical management. Unpublished manuscript. Nashville, Tennessee: Vanderbilt University.

Hollon, S. D., Stewart, M. O. & Strunk, D. (2005) Enduring effects for cognitive behavior therapy in the treatment of depression and anxiety. *Annual Review of Psychology, 57*, 285–315.

Holm, K. J. & Spencer, C. M. (1999) Reboxetine: a review of its use in depression. *CNS Drugs, 12*, 65–83.

Holma, K. M., Holma, I. A., Melartin, T. K., *et al.* (2008) Long-term outcome of major depressive disorder in psychiatric patients is variable. *Journal of Clinical Psychology, 69*, 270–276.

Holmes, J. (2001) *The Search for a Secure Base: Attachment Theory and Psychotherapy*. London: Brunner-Routledge.

Hooley, J. M. & Teasdale, J. D. (1989) Predictors of relapse in unipolar depressives: expressed emotion, marital distress and perceived criticism. *Journal of Abnormal Psychology, 98*, 229–235.

Hopko, D. R., Lejuez, C. W., Ruggiero, K. J., *et al.* (2003) Contemporary behavioural activation treatments for depression: procedures, principles, and progress. *Clinical Psychology Review, 23*, 699–717.

References

Howe, D. (1995) *Attachment Theory for Social Work in Practice*. Basingstoke: Palgrave.

Hunkeler, E. M., Meresman, J. F., Hargreaves, W. A., *et al.* (2000) Efficacy of nurse tele-health care and peer support in augmenting treatment of depression in primary care. *Archives of Family Medicine, 9*, 700–708.

Hunkeler, E. M., Katon, W., Tang, L., *et al.* (2006) Long term outcomes from the IMPACT randomised trial for depressed elderly patients in primary care. *British Medical Journal, 332*, 259–263.

Hurley, S. C. (2002) Lamotrigine update and its use in mood disorders. *Annals of Pharmacotherapy, 36*, 860–873.

Husain, N., Creed, F. & Tomenson, B. (2000) Depression and social stress in Pakistan. *Psychological Medicine, 30*, 395–402.

Husain, N., Waheed, W., Tomenson, B., *et al.* (2007) The validation of personal health questionnaire amongst people of Pakistani family origin living in the United Kingdom. *Journal of Affective Disorders, 97*, 261–264.

IAPT (2009) IAPT *Workforce Capacity Tool: Guidance for Use*. Available at: http://www.iapt.nhs.uk/2008/01/17/workforce-capacity-tool/ [accessed May 2009].

Iliffe, S., Haines, A., Gallivan, S., *et al.* (1991) Assessment of elderly people in general practice. 1. Social circumstances and mental state. *British Journal of General Practice, 41*, 9–12.

Ingram, A., Saling, M. M. & Schweitzer, I. (2008) Cognitive side effects of brief pulse electroconvulsive therapy: a review. *Journal of ECT, 24*, 3–9.

Institute of Medicine (US), Board on Global Health & Committee on Nervous System Disorders in Developing Countries (2001) *Neurological, Psychiatric and Developmental Disorders: Meeting the Challenge in the Developing World*. Washington, DC: National Academy Press.

Isacsson, G., Holmgren, P., Druid, H., *et al.* (1997) The utilisation of antidepressants – a key issue in the prevention of suicide: an analysis of 5281 suicides in Sweden during the period 1992–1994. *Acta Psychiatrica Scandinavica, 96*, 94–100.

Isacsson, G., Boethius, G., Henriksson, S., *et al.* (1999) Selective serotonin reuptake inhibitors have broadened the utilisation of antidepressant treatment in accordance with recommendations. Findings from a Swedish prescription database. *Journal of Affective Disorders, 53*, 15–22.

Isbister, G. K., Prior, F. H. & Foy, A. (2001) Citalopram-induced bradycardia and presyncope. *The Annals of Pharmacotherapy, 35*, 1552–1555.

Jackson, J. L., Passamonti, M. & Kroenke, K. (2007) Outcome and impact of mental disorders in primary care at 5 years. *Psychosomatic Medicine, 69*, 270–276.

Jackson, W. K., Roose, S. P. & Glassman, A. H. (1987) Cardiovascular toxicity of antidepressant medications. *Psychopathology, 20* (Suppl. 1), 64–74.

Jacobson, N. S., Fruzzetti, A., Dobson, K. S., *et al.* (1993) Marital therapy as a treatment for depression II: The effects of relationship quality and therapy on depressive relapse. *Journal of Consulting and Clinical Psychology, 61*, 516–519.

Jacobson, N. S., Martell, C. R., & Dimidjian, S. (2001) Behavioral activation therapy for depression: returning to contextual roots. *Clinical Psychology: Science and Practice, 8*, 255–270.

Jadad, A. R., Moore, R. A., Carroll, D., *et al.* (1996) Assessing the quality of reports of randomised clinical trials: is blinding necessary? *Controlled Clinical Trials, 17,* 1–12.

James, I. A., Blackburn, I.-M., Milne, D. L., *et al.* (2001) Moderators of trainee therapists' competence in cognitive therapy. *British Journal of Clinical Psychology, 40,* 131–141.

Janowsky, D., Curtis, G., Zisook, S., *et al.* (1983) Trazodone-aggravated ventricular arrhythmias. *Journal of Clinical Psychopharmacology, 3,* 372–376.

Jick, H., Kaye, J. A. & Jick, S. S. (2004) Antidepressants and the risk or suicidal behaviours. *Journal of the American Medical Association, 292,* 338–343.

Joffe, R. T. & Singer, W. (1990) A comparison of triiodothyronine and thyroxine in the potentiation of tricyclic antidepressants. *Psychiatry Research, 32,* 241–251.

Johnson, J., Howarth, E. & Weissman, M. M. (1991) The validity of major depression with psychotic features based on a community sample. *Archives of General Psychiatry, 48,* 1075–1081.

Johnston, O., Kumar, S., Kendall, K., *et al.* (2007) Qualitative study of depression management in primary care: GP and patient goals, and the value of listening. *British Journal of General Practice, 57,* e1–e14.

Jones, E. & Asen, E. (1999) *Systemic Couple Therapy and Depression.* London: Karnac.

Joy, C. B., Adams, C. E. & Rice, K. (2003) Crisis intervention for people with severe mental illnesses (Cochrane Review). In *Cochrane Library*, Issue 3. Oxford: Update Software.

Joyce, P. R., Mulder, R. T., Luty, S. E., *et al.* (2002) Patterns and predictors of remission, response and recovery in major depression treated with fluoxetine or nortriptyline. *Australian and New Zealand Journal of Psychiatry, 36,* 384–391.

Judd, L. L., Akiskal, H. S., Maser, J. D., *et al.* (1998) A prospective 12-year study of subsyndromal and syndromal depressive symptoms in unipolar major depressive disorders. *Archives of General Psychiatry, 55,* 694–700.

Judge, R., Parry, M. G., Quail, D., *et al.* (2002) Discontinuation symptoms: comparison of brief interruption in fluoxetine and paroxetine treatment. *International Clinical Psychopharmacology, 17,* 217–225.

Kabat-Zinn, J. (1990) *Full Catastrophe Living: Using the Wisdom of Your Body and Mind to Face Stress, Pain, and Illness.* New York: Dell Publishing.

Kahn, E. (1985) Heinz Kohut and Carl Rogers: a timely comparison. *American Psychologist, 40,* 893–904.

Kaltenthaler, E., Shackley, P., Stevens, K., *et al.* (2002) A systematic review and economic evaluation of computerised cognitive behaviour therapy for depression and anxiety. *Health Technology Assessment, 6,* 1–89.

Kaltenthaler, E., Parry, G., Beverley, C., *et al.* (2008) Computerised cognitive-behavioural therapy for depression: systematic review. *British Journal of Psychiatry,* 193, 181–184.

Kanai, T., Takeuchi, H., Furukawa, T. A., *et al.* (2003) Time to recurrence after recovery from major depressive episodes and its predictors. *Psychological Medicine, 33,* 839–845.

Kasper, S., Wehr, T. A., Bartko, J. J., *et al.* (1989) Epidemiological findings of seasonal changes in mood and behavior. A telephone survey of Montgomery County, Maryland. *Archives of General Psychiatry, 46*, 823–833.

Kasper, S., Volz, H. P., Möller, A., *et al.* (2008) Continuation and long-term maintenance treatment with hypericum extract WS 5570 after recovery from an acute episode of moderate depression: a double-blind, randomized, placebo controlled long-term trial. *European Neuropsychopharmacology, 18*, 803–813.

Katon, W., von Korff, M., Lin, E., *et al.* (1992) Adequacy and duration of antidepressant treatment in primary care. *Medical Care, 30*, 67–76.

Katon, W., von Korff, M., Lin, E., *et al.* (1995) Collaborative management to achieve treatment guidelines. Impact on depression in primary care. *Journal of the American Medical Association, 273*, 1026–1031.

Katon, W., Robinson, P., von Korff, M., *et al.* (1996) A multifaceted intervention to improve treatment of depression in primary care. *Archives of General Psychiatry, 53*, 924–932.

Katon, W., von Korff, M., Lin, E., *et al.* (1999) Stepped collaborative care for primary care patients with persistent symptoms of depression: a randomised trial. *Archives of General Psychiatry, 56*, 1109–1115.

Katon, W., von Korff, M., Lin, E., *et al.* (2001) Rethinking practitioner roles in chronic illness: the specialist, primary care physician and the practice nurse. *General Hospital Psychiatry*, 23, 138–144.

Katon, W., Russo, J., von Korff, M., *et al.* (2002) Long-term effects of a collaborative care intervention in persistently depressed primary care patients. *Journal of General Internal Medicine, 17*, 741–748.

Katzelnick, D. J., Simon, G. E., Pearson, S. D., *et al.* (2000) Randomised trial of a depression management programme in high utilisers of medical care. *Archives of Family Medicine, 9*, 345–351.

Kazantzis, N., Deane, F. P. & Ronan, K. R. (2000) Homework assignments in cognitive and behavioral therapy: a meta-analysis. *Clinical Psychology: Science and Practice, 7*, 189–202.

Kazdin, A. E. (2008) Evidence-based treatment and practice: new opportunities to bridge clinical research and practice, enhance the knowledge base, and improve patient care. *American Psychologist, 63*, 146–159.

Keller, M. B., Lavori, P. W., Rice, J., *et al.* (1986) The persistent risk of chronicity in recurrent episodes of non-bipolar major depressive disorder: a prospective follow-up. *American Journal of Psychiatry, 143*, 24–28.

Kellner, C. H., Knapp, R. G., Petrides, G., *et al.* (2007) Continuation electroconvulsive therapy vs pharmacotherapy for relapse prevention in major depression: a multisite study from the consortium for research in electroconvulsive therapy (CORE). *Archives of General Psychiatry, 63*, 1337–1344.

Kendell, R. E. (1968) *The Classification of Depressive Illness.* Maudsley Monographs 18, 1st edn. Oxford: Oxford Unversity Press.

Kendler, L. & Prescott, C. (1999) A population-based twin study of lifetime major depression in men and women. *Archives of General Psychiatry, 56*, 39–44.

Kendler, K. S., Gardner, C. O., Neale, M. C., *et al.* (2001) Genetic risk factors for major depression in men and women: similar or different heritabilities and same or partly distinct genes? *Psychological Medicine, 31*, 605–616.

Kendrick, T., Stevens, L., Bryant, A., *et al.* (2001) Hampshire depression project: changes in the process of care and cost consequences. *British Journal of General Practice, 51*, 911–913.

Kendrick, T., King, F., Albertella, L., *et al.* (2005) GP treatment decisions for patients with depression: an observational study. *British Journal of General Practice, 55*, 280–286.

Kendrick, T., Simons, L., Mynors-Wallis, L., *et al.* (2006a) Cost-effectiveness of referral for generic care or problem-solving treatment from community mental health nurses, compared with usual general practitioner care for common mental disorders: randomised controlled trial. *British Journal of Psychiatry*, 189, 50–59.

Kendrick, T., Peveler, R., Longworth, L., *et al.* (2006b) Cost-effectiveness and cost-utility of tricyclic antidepressants, selective serotonin reuptake inhibitors and lofepramine: randomised controlled trial. *British Journal of Psychiatry, 188*, 337–345.

Kendrick, T., Chatwin, J., Dowrick, C., *et al.* (2009) Randomised controlled trial to determine the clinical effectiveness and cost effectiveness of selective serotonin reuptake inhibitors plus supportive care, versus supportive care alone, for mild to moderate depression with somatic symptoms in primary care: the THREAD (THREshold for AntiDepressant response) study. *Health Technology Assessment, 13*, 22.

Kennedy, N. & Foy, K. (2005) The impact of residual symptoms on outcome of major depression. *Current Psychiatry Reports, 7*, 441–446.

Kessing, L. V. (2007) Epidemiology of subtypes of depression. *Acta Psychiatrica Scandinavica, 115* (Suppl. 433), 85–89.

Kessing, L. V. & Anderson, P. K. (2005) Predictive effects of previous episodes on the risk of recurrence in depressive and bipolar disorders. *Current Psychiatry Reports, 7*, 413–420.

Kessler, D., Bennewith, O., Lewis, G., *et al.* (2002) Detection of depression and anxiety in primary care: follow up study. *British Medical Journal, 325*, 1016–1017.

Kessler, R. C., Greenberg, P. E., Mickelson, K. D., *et al.* (2001) The effects of chronic mental health conditions on work loss and work cut back. *Journal of Occupational and Environmental Medicine*, 43, 218–225.

Kessler, R. C., Berglund, P., Demler, O., *et al.* (2003) The epidemiology of major depressive disorder: results from the National Comorbidity Survey Replication (NCS-R). *Journal of the American Medical Association, 289*, 3095–3105.

Ketter, T. A., Post, R. M., Parekh, P. I., *et al.* (1995) Addition of monoamine oxidase inhibitors to carbamazepine: preliminary evidence of safety and antidepressant efficacy in treatment-resistant depression. *Journal of Clinical Psychiatry, 56*, 471–475.

Khan, A., Dager, S. R., Cohen, S., *et al.* (1991) Chronicity of depressive episode in relation to antidepressant-placebo response. *Neuropsychopharmacology, 4*, 125–130.

Khan, A., Leventhal, R., Khan, S., *et al.* (2002) Severity of depression and response to antidepressants and placebo: an analysis of the Food and Drug Administration database. *Journal of Clinical Psychopharmacology, 22*, 40–45.

Khan, N., Bower, P. & Rogers, A. (2007) Guided self-help in primary care mental health: meta-synthesis of qualitative studies of patient experience. *British Journal of Psychiatry, 191*, 206–211.

King, M., Sibbald, B., Ward, E., *et al.* (2000) Randomised controlled trial of non-directive counselling, cognitive-behaviour therapy and usual general practitioner care in the management of depression as well as mixed anxiety and depression in primary care. *Health Technology Assessment, 4*, 1–83.

Kingdon, D., Tyrer, P., Seivewright, N., *et al.* (1996) The Nottingham study of neurotic disorder: influence of cognitive therapists on outcome. *British Journal of Psychiatry, 169*, 93–97.

Kirsch, I. & Sapirstein, G. (1998) Listening to Prozac but hearing placebo: a meta-analysis of antidepressant medication. http://journals.apa.org/prevention/volume1/pre0010002a.html

Kirsch, I. & Scoboria, A. (2001) Apples, oranges, and placebos: heterogeneity in a meta-analysis of placebo effects. *Advances in Mind-Body Medicine, 17*, 307–309.

Kirsch, I., Moore, T. J., Scoboria, A., *et al.* (2002a) The emperor's new drugs: an analysis of antidepressant medication data submitted to the US Food and Drug Administration. Available at: http://journals.apa.org/prevention/volume5/pre0050023a.html

Kirsch, I., Scoboria, A. & Moore, T. J. (2002b) Antidepressants and placebos: secrets, revelations, and unanswered questions. Available at: http://journals.apa.org/prevention/volume5/pre0050033r.html

Kirsch, I., Deacon, B. J., Huedo-Medina, T. B., *et al.* (2008) Initial severity and antidepressant benefits: a meta-analysis of data submitted to the Food and Drug Administration. *Public Library of Science Medicine, 5*, 260–268.

Kisely, S., Gater, R. & Goldberg, D. P. (1995) Results from the Manchester Centre. In *Mental Illness in General Health Care: An International Study* (eds T. B. Üstün & N. Sartorius), pp. 175–191. Chichester: Wiley.

Klerman, G. L., Weissman, M. M., Rounsaville, B. J., *et al.* (1984) *Interpersonal Psychotherapy of Depression.* New York: Basic Books.

Knapp, M. (2003) Hidden costs of mental illness. *British Journal of Psychiatry, 183*, 477–478.

Knapp, M. & Ilson, S. (2002) Economic aspects of depression and its treatment. *Current Opinion in Psychiatry, 15*, 69–75.

Knekt, P., Lindfors, O., Harkanaen, T., *et al.* (2008) Randomized trial on the effectiveness of long-and short-term psychodynamic psychotherapy and solution-focused therapy on psychiatric symptoms during a 3-year follow-up. *Psychological Medicine, 38*, 689–703.

Kornstein, S. G., Schatzberg, A. F., Thase, M. E., *et al.* (2000) Gender differences in treatment response to sertraline versus imipramine in chronic depression. *American Journal of Psychiatry, 157*, 1445–1452.

Kornstein, S. G., Wohlreich, M. M., Mallinckrodt, C. H., *et al.* (2006) Duloxetine efficacy for major depressive disorder in male vs. female patients: data from 7 randomized, double-blind, placebo-controlled trials. *Journal of Clinical Psychiatry, 67*, 761–770.

Kovacs, M. (1996) Presentation and course of major depressive disorder during childhood and later years of the life span. *Journal of the American Academy of Child Adolescent Psychiatry, 35*, 705–715.

Kovacs, M., Rush, A. T., Beck, A. T., *et al.* (1981) Depressed outpatients treated with cognitive therapy or pharmacotherapy: a one-year follow-up. *Archives of General Psychiatry, 38*, 33–39.

Kris, E. B. (1965) Day hospitals. *Current Therapeutic Research, 7*, 320–323.

Kroenke, K., Spitzer, R. L. & Williams, J. B. (2001) The Patient Health Questionnaire-9: validity of a brief depression severity measure. *Journal of General Internal Medicine, 16*, 606–613.

Kroenke, K., Spitzer, R. L. & Williams, J. B. (2003) The Patient Health Questionnaire-2: validity of a two-item depression screener. *Medical Care, 41*, 1284–1292.

Krupinski, J. & Tiller, J. W. (2001) The identification and treatment of depression by general practitioners. *Australian and New Zealand Journal of Psychiatry, 35*, 827–832.

Kuehner, C. (2005) An evaluation of the 'Coping with Depression Course' for relapse prevention with unipolar depressed patients. *Psychotherapy and Psychosomatics, 74*, 254–259.

Kuhn, R. (1958) The treatment of depressive states with G 22355 (imipramine hydrochloride). *American Journal of Psychiatry, 115*, 459–464.

Kupfer, D. J. (1991) Long-term treatment of depression. *Journal of Clinical Psychiatry, 52* (Suppl. 5), 28–34.

Kuyken, W. & Tsivrikos, D. (2009) Therapist competence, comorbidity and cognitive-behavioral therapy for depression. *Psychotherapy and Psychosomatics, 78*, 42–48.

Kuyken, W., Taylor, R. S., Barrett, B., *et al.* (2008) Mindfulness-based cognitive therapy to prevent relapse in recurrent depression. *Journal of Consulting and Clinical Psychology, 76*, 966–978.

Lam, R. W., Chan, P., Wilkins-Ho, M., *et al.* (2008) Repetitive transcranial magnetic stimulation for treatment-resistant depression: a systematic review and metaanalysis. *Canadian Journal of Psychiatry, 53*, 621–671.

Lambert, M. & Ogles, B. (2004) The efficacy and effectiveness of psychotherapy. In *Bergin and Garfield's Handbook of Psychotherapy and Behavior Change*, 5th edn (ed N. M. J. Lambert). New York: Wiley.

Lancaster, S. G. & Gonzalez, J. P. (1989) Lofepramine. A review of its pharmacodynamic and pharmacokinetic properties, and therapeutic efficacy in depressive illness. *Drugs, 37*, 123–140.

Lau, M. A., Segal, Z. V. & Williams, J. M. G. (2004) Teasdale's differential activation hypothesis: implications for mechanisms of depressive relapse and suicidal behaviour. *Behaviour Research and Therapy, 42*, 1001–1017.

Lauritzen, L., Odgaard, K., Clemmesen, L., *et al.* (1996) Relapse prevention by means of paroxetine in ECT-treated patients with major depression: a comparison with imipramine and placebo in medium-term continuation therapy. *Acta Psychiatrica Scandinavica, 94,* 241–251.

Lave, J. R., Franks, R. G., Schulberg, H. C., *et al.* (1998) Cost-effectiveness of treatments for major depression in primary care practice. *Archives of General Psychiatry, 55,* 645–651.

Lawson, J. S., Inglis, J., Delva, N. J., *et al.* (1990) Electrode placement in ECT: cognitive effects. *Psychological Medicine, 20,* 335–344.

Layard, R. (2006) The case for psychological treatment centres. *British Medical Journal, 332,* 1030–1032.

Lebowitz, B. D., Pearson, J. L., Schneider, L. S., *et al.* (1997) Diagnosis and treatment of depression in later life. Consensus statement update. *Journal of the American Medical Association, 278,* 1186–1190.

Lee, A. S. & Murray, R. M. (1988) The long-term outcome of Maudsley depressives. *British Journal of Psychiatry, 153,* 741–751.

Leff, J., Vearnals, S., Brewin, C. R., *et al.* (2000) The London Depression Intervention Trial. Randomised controlled trial of antidepressants vs. couple therapy in the treatment and maintenance of people with depression living with a partner: clinical outcome and costs. *British Journal of Psychiatry, 177,* 95–100.

Leichsenring, F. (2004) Randomized controlled versus naturalistic studies: a new research agenda. *Bulletin of the Menninger Clinic, 68,* 137–151.

Leichsenring, F. & Rabung, S. (2008) Effectiveness of long-term psychodynamic psychotherapy: a meta-analysis. *Journal of the American Medical Association, 300,* 1551–1565.

Leichsenring, F., Rabung, S. & Leibing, E. (2004) The efficacy of short-term psychodynamic psychotherapy in specific psychiatric disorders. A meta-analysis. *Archives of General Psychiatry, 61,* 1208–1216.

Leith, L. M. (1994) *Foundations of Exercise and Mental Health.* Morgantown, West Virginia: Fitness Information Technology.

Lejoyeux, M. & Ades, J. (1997) Antidepressant discontinuation: a review of the literature. *Journal of Clinical Psychiatry, 58* (Suppl. 7), 11–15.

Lejoyeux, M., Ades, J., Mourad, I., *et al.* (1996) Antidepressant withdrawal syndrome: recognition, prevention and management. *CNS Drugs, 5,* 278–292.

Lenert, L. A. (2000) The reliability and internal consistency of an internet capable program for measuring utilities. *Quality of Life Research, 9,* 811–817.

Lepine, J. P., Gastpar, M., Mendlewicz, J., *et al.* (1997) Depression in the community: the first pan-European study DEPRES (Depression Research in European Society). *International Clinical Psychopharmacology, 12,* 19–29.

Lepore, S. J. (1997) Expressive writing moderates the relation between intrusive thoughts and depressive symptoms. *Journal of Personality and Social Psychology, 73,* 1030–1037.

Letemendia, F. J. J., Delva, N. J., Rodenburg, M., *et al.* (1993) Therapeutic advantage of bifrontal electrode placement in ECT. *Psychological Medicine, 23,* 349–360.

Lewinsohn, P. M. (1975) The behavioural study and treatment of depression. In *Progress in Behavior Modification*, vol. 1 (eds M. Hersen, R. M. Eisler & P. M. Miller), pp. 19–64. New York: Academic Press.

Lewinsohn, P. M., Antonuccio, D. O., Steinmetz-Breckenridge, J. L., *et al.* (1984) *The Coping with Depression Course: A Psychoeducational Intervention for Unipolar Depression*. Eugene, Oregon: Castalia Publishing.

Lewinsohn, P. M., Munoz, R. F., Youngren, M. A., *et al.* (1986) *Control Your Depression* (2nd edn). Englewood Cliffs, New Jersey: Prentice-Hall.

Lewinsohn, P. M., Clarke, G. N. & Hoberman, H. M. (1989) The Coping with Depression course: review and future directions. *Canadian Journal of Behavioral Science, 21*, 470–493.

Lewinsohn, P. M., Solomon, A., Seeley, J. R., *et al.* (2000) Clinical implications of 'sub-threshold' depressive symptoms. *Journal of Abnormal Psychology, 109*, 345–351.

Lexchin, J., Bero, L. A., Djulbegovic, B., *et al.* (2003) Pharmaceutical industry sponsorship and research outcome and quality: systematic review. *British Medical Journal, 326*, 1167–1170.

Licht, R. W. & Qvitzau, S. (2002) Treatment strategies in patients with major depression not responding to first-line sertraline treatment. A randomised study of extended duration of treatment, dose increase or mianserin augmentation. *Psychopharmacology, 161*, 143–151.

Linde, K. & Mulrow, C. D. (2004) St John's wort for depression (Cochrane Review). In *Cochrane Library*, Issue 1. Chichester: Wiley.

Linde, K., Berner, M. M., Kriston, L., *et al.* (2008) St John's Wort for major depression. *Cochrane Database of Systematic Reviews 2008*. CD000448. DOI10.1002/14651858.CD000448.pub3.

Lindert, J., Schouler-Ocak, M., Heinz, A., *et al.* (2008) Mental health, health care utilisation of migrants in Europe. *European Psychiatry, 23* (Suppl. 1), 14–20.

Lingam, R. & Scott, J. (2002) Treatment non-adherence in affective disorders. *Acta Psychiatrica Scandinavica, 105*, 164–172.

Livingstone, M. G. & Livingstone, H. M. (1996) Monoamine oxidase inhibitors: an update on drug interactions. *Drug Safety, 14*, 219–227.

Loosen, P. T. (1987) The TRH stimulation test in psychiatric disorders: a review. In *Handbook of Clinical Psychoneuroendocrinology* (eds P. T. Loosen & C. B. Nemeroff), pp. 336–360. Chichester: Wiley.

Lovell, K. & Richards, D. (2000) Multiple access points and levels of entry (MAPLE): ensuring choice, accessibility and equity for CBT services. *Behavioural and Cognitive Psychotherapy, 28*, 379–392.

Lovell, K. & Richards, D. (2008) *A Recovery Programme for Depression*. London: Rethink.

Luborsky, L., Singer, B. & Luborsky, L. (1975) Comparative studies of psychotherapies: is it true that 'everyone has won and all must have prizes'? *Archives of General Psychiatry, 32*, 995–1008.

Lundbeck Ltd. (2009) *Cipralex. Summary of Product Characteristics*. Milton Keynes: Lundbeck Ltd. Available at: http://www.medicines.org.uk/EMC/medicine/21976/SPC

References

MacDonald, T. M., McMahon, A. D., Reid, I. C., *et al.* (1996) Antidepressant drug use in primary care: a record linkage study in Tayside, Scotland. *British Medical Journal, 313*, 860–861.

MacMillan, H. L., Patterson, C. J. & Wathen, C. N. (2005) Screening for depression in primary care: recommendation statement from the Canadian Task Force on Preventive Health Care. *Canadian Medical Association Journal*, 172, 33–35.

Maes, M., Meltzer, H. Y., Cosyns, P., *et al.* (1993) An evaluation of basal hypothalamic-pituitary-thyroid axis function in depression: results of a large-scaled and controlled study. *Psychoneuroendocrinology, 18*, 607–620.

Magnusson, A. & Partonen, T. (2005) The diagnosis, symptomatology, and epidemiology of seasonal affective disorder. *CNS Spectrums, 10*, 625–634.

The MaGPIe Research Group (2005a) The effectiveness of case-finding for mental health problems in primary care. *British Journal of General Practice, 55*, 665–669.

The MaGPIe Research Group (2005b) Do patients want to disclose psychological problems to GPs? *Family Practice, 22*, 631–637.

Malhi, G. S., Parker, G. B. & Greenwood, J. (2005) Structural and functional models of depression: from sub-types to substrates. *Acta Psychiatrica Scandinavica, 111*, 94–105.

Malitz, S., Sackeim, H. A., Decina, P., *et al.* (1986) The efficacy of electroconvulsive therapy: dose-response interactions with modality. *Annals of the New York Academy of Sciences, 462*, 56–64.

Mallen, C. & Peat, G. (2008) Screening older people with joint pain for depression in primary care. *British Journal of General Practice*, 58, 687–692.

Malt, U. F., Robak, O. H., Madsbu, H.-P., *et al.* (1999) The Norwegian naturalistic treatment study of depression in general practice (NORDEP). I: Randomised double-blind study. *British Medical Journal, 318*, 1180–1184.

Mann, A. H., Blizard, R., Murray, J., *et al.* (1998) An evaluation of practice nurses working with general practitioners to treat people with depression. *British Journal of General Practice, 48*, 875–879.

Mann, T. (1996) *Clinical Guidelines: Using Clinical Guidelines to Improve Patient Care Within the NHS.* London: NHS Executive.

Markowitz, J. S., DeVane, C. L., Liston, H. L., *et al.* (2000) An assessment of selective serotonin reuptake inhibitor discontinuation symptoms with citalopram. *International Clinical Psychopharmacology, 15*, 329–333.

Marks, I. M., Mataix-Cols, D., Kenwright, M., *et al.* (2003) Pragmatic evaluation of computer-aided self-help for anxiety and depression. *British Journal of Psychiatry, 183*, 57–65.

Marmor, J. (1973) The future of psychoanalytic therapy. *American Journal of Psychiatry, 130*, 1197–1202.

Marmor, J. (1975) Academic lecture: the nature of the psychotherapeutic process revisited. *Canadian Psychiatric Association Journal, 20*, 557–565.

Marriott, M. & Kellett, S. (2009) Evaluating a cognitive analytic therapy service: practice-based outcomes and comparisons with person-centred and cognitive-behavioural therapies. *Psychology and Psychotherapy, 82*, 57–72.

Marshall, M., Crowther, R., Almaraz-Serrano, A. M., *et al.* (2001) Systematic reviews of the effectiveness of day care for people with severe mental disorders: (1) acute day hospital versus admission; (2) vocational rehabilitation; (3) day hospital versus outpatient care. *Health Technology Assessment, 5*, 1–75.

Marshall, M., Crowther, R., Almaraz-Serrano, A. M., *et al.* (2003) Day hospital versus outpatient care for psychiatric disorders (Cochrane Review). In *Cochrane Library*, Issue 3. Oxford: Update Software.

Marteau, T. M. (1989) Psychological costs of screening. *British Medical Journal, 299*, 527.

Martenyi, F., Dossenbach, M., Mraz, K., *et al.* (2001) Gender differences in the efficacy of fluoxetine and maprotiline in depressed patients: a double-blind trial of antidepressants with serotonergic or norepinephrinergic reuptake inhibition profile. *European Neuropsychopharmacology, 11*, 227–232.

Martin, D. J., Garske, J. P. & Davis, M. K. (2000) Relation of the therapeutic alliance with outcome and other variables: a meta-analytic review. *Journal of Consulting and Clinical Psychology, 68*, 438–450.

Martinez, C., Rietbrock, S., Wise, L., *et al.* (2005) Antidepressant treatment and the risk of fatal and non-fatal self harm in first episode depression: nested case-control study. *British Medical Journal, 330*, 389–395.

May, C. M., Allison, G., Chapple, A., *et al.* (2004) Framing the doctor-patient relationship in chronic illness: a comparative study of general practitioners' accounts. *Sociology of Health and Illness, 26*, 135–158.

McCrone, P., Chisholm, D., Knapp, M., *et al.* (the INCAT Study Group) (2003) Cost-utility analysis of intravenous immunoglobulin and prednisolone for chronic inflammatory demyelinating polyradiculoneuropathy. *European Journal of Neurology, 10*, 687–694.

McCrone, P., Dhanasiri, S., Patel, A., *et al.* (2008) *Paying the Price: The Cost of Mental Health Care in England to 2026.* London: King's Fund.

McGorry, P. & Jackson, H. (1999) *Recognition and Management of Early Psychosis: A Preventative Approach.* Cambridge: Cambridge University Press.

McGrath, P. J., Blood, D. K., Stewart, J. W., *et al.* (1987a) A comparative study of the electrocardiographic effects of phenelzine, tricyclic antidepressants, mianserin and placebo. *Journal of Clinical Psychopharmacology, 7*, 335–339.

McGrath, P. J., Stewart, J. W., Harrison, W., *et al.* (1987b) Treatment of refractory depression with a monoamine oxidase inhibitor antidepressant. *Psychopharmacology Bulletin, 23*, 169–172.

McGrath, P. J., Stewart, J. W., Nunes, E. V., *et al.* (1993) A double-blind crossover trial of imipramine and phenelzine for outpatients with treatment-refractory depression. *American Journal of Psychiatry, 150*, 118–123.

Mead, G. E., Morley, W., Campbell, P., *et al.* (2008) Exercise for depression. *Cochrane Database of Systematic Reviews, Issue 4.* CD004366.

Meier, C. R., Schlienger, R. G. & Jick, H. (2001) Use of selective serotonin reuptake inhibitors and risk of developing first-time acute myocardial infarction. *British Journal of Clinical Pharmacology, 52*, 179–184.

References

Meijer, W. E. E., Bouvy, M. L., Heerdink, E. R., *et al.* (2001) Spontaneous lapses in dosing during chronic treatment with selective serotonin reuptake inhibitors. *British Journal of Psychiatry, 179*, 519–522.

Melander, H., Ahlqvist-Rastad, J., Meijer, G., *et al.* (2003) Evidence-based medicine – selective reporting from studies sponsored by pharmaceutical industry: review of studies in new drug applications. *British Medical Journal, 326*, 1171–1173.

Meltzer, H., Bebbington, P., Brugha, T., *et al.* (2000) The reluctance to seek treatment for neurotic disorders. *Journal of Mental Health, 9*, 319–327.

Merriman, S. H. (1999) Monoamine oxidase drugs and diet. *Journal of Human Nutrition and Dietetics, 12*, 21–28.

MHRA (2004) *Report of the CSM Expert Working Group on the Safety of Selective Serotonin Reuptake Inhibitor Antidepressants.* Available at: http://www.mhra. gov.uk/home/groups/pl-p/documents/drugsafetymessage/con019472.pdf

MHRA (2006a) Venlafaxine (Efexor) – summary of basis for regulatory position. Available at: http://www.mhra.gov.uk/home/idcplg?IdcService=GET_FILE &dDocName=CON2023840&RevisionSelectionMethod=LatestReleased

MHRA (2006b) Updated prescribing advice for venlafaxine (Efexor/Efexor XL). Available at http://www.mhra.gov.uk/ (accessed May 2009).

Michelson, D., Fava, M., Amsterdam, J., *et al.* (2000) Interruption of selective serotonin reuptake inhibitor treatment. Double-blind, placebo-controlled trial. *British Journal of Psychiatry, 176*, 363–368.

Miller, P., Chilvers, C., Dewey, M., *et al.* (2003) Counselling versus antidepressant therapy for the treatment of mild to moderate depression in primary care: economic analysis. *International Journal of Technology Assessment in Health Care, 19*, 80–90.

Mills, M. & Pound, A. (1996) Mechanisms of change: the Newpin Project. *Mrace Bulletin, 2*, 3–7.

Mind (2007) *Learning Disabilities and Mental Health Problems.* Avaliable from: http://www.mind.org.uk/help/people_groups_and_communities/learning_disabilities_ and_mental_health_problems#incidence

Mindham, R. H. (1982) Tricyclic antidepressants. In *Drugs in Psychiatric Practice* (ed. P. Tyrer). Cambridge: Cambridge University Press.

Mitchell, A. J. & Subramaniam, H. (2005) Prognosis of depression in old age compared to middle age: a systematic review of comparative studies. *American Journal of Psychiatry, 162*, 1588–1601.

Mitchell, A. J., Vaze, A. & Rao, S. (2009) Clinical diagnosis of depression in primary care: a meta-analysis. *Lancet, 374*, 609–619.

Mitchell, P. B. (1997) Drug interactions of clinical significance with selective serotonin reuptake inhibitors. *Drug Safety, 17*, 390–406.

Möller, H. J., Baldwin, D. S., Goodwin, G., *et al.* (2008) Do SSRIs or antidepressants in general increase suicidality? WPA Section on pharmacopsychiatry: consensus statement. *European Archives of Psychiatry and Clinical Neuroscience, 258*, 3–23.

Moncrieff, J., Wessely, S. & Hardy, R. (2001) Active placebos versus antidepressants for depression. In *Cochrane Library*, Issue 4. Oxford: Update Software.

Montgomery, S. A., Kennedy, S. H., Burrows, G. D., *et al. (2004)* Absence of discontinuation symptoms with agomelatine and occurrence of discontinuation symptoms with paroxetine: a randomized, double-blind, placebo-controlled discontinuation study. *International Clinical Psychopharmacology, 19*, 271–280.

Moore, R. & Garland, A. (2003) *Cognitive Therapy for Chronic and Persistent Depression*. Chichester: Wiley.

Morgan, O., Griffiths, C., Baker, A., *et al.* (2004) Fatal toxicity of antidepressants in England and Wales, 1993–2003. *Health Statistics Quarterly, 23*, 18–24.

Mork, A., Kreilgaard, M. & Sanchez, C. (2003) The R-enantiomer of citalopram counteracts escitalopram-induced increase in extracellular 5-HT in the frontal cortex of freely moving rats. *Neuropharmacology, 45*, 167–173.

Moussavi, S., Chatterji, S., Verdes, E., *et al.* (2007) Depression, chronic diseases, and decrements in health: results from the World Health Surveys. *Lancet, 370*, 851–858.

Mucci, M. (1997) Reboxetine: a review of antidepressant tolerability. *Journal of Psychopharmacology, 11* (Suppl. 4), S33–S37.

Murphy, G. E., Simons, A. D.,Wetzel, R. D., *et al.* (1984) Cognitive therapy and pharmacotherapy singly and together in the treatment of depression. *Archives of General Psychiatry, 41*, 33–41.

Murray, C. J. L. & Lopez, A. D. (eds) (1997a) *The Global Burden of Disease. A Comprehensive Assessment of Mortality and Disability from Diseases, Injuries and Risk Factors in 1990 and Projected to 2020*. Cambridge, Massachussetts: Harvard University Press.

Murray, C. J. & Lopez, A. D. (1997b) Global mortality, disability, and the contribution of risk factors: Global Burden of Disease Study. *Lancet, 349*, 1436–1442.

Murray, C. J. L., Lopez, A. D. & Jamison, D. T. (1994) The global burden of disease in 1990: summary results, sensitivity analysis and future directions. *Bulletin of the World Health Organization, 72*, 495–509.

Musselman, D. L., Evans, D. L. & Nemeroff, C. B. (1998) The relationship of depression to cardiovascular disease: epidemiology, biology, and treatment. *Archives of General Psychiatry, 55*, 580–592.

Mynors-Wallis, L. M., Gath, D. H. & Baker, F. (2000) Randomised controlled trial of problem-solving treatment, antidepressant medication, and combined treatment for major depression in primary care. *British Medical Journal, 320*, 26–30.

National Center for Education Statistics (1997) *Adult Literacy in America: A First Look at the Results of the National Adult Literacy Survey*. US Department of Education.

NCCMH (2004) *Depression: Management of Depression in Primary and Secondary Care*. Leicester & London: British Psychological Society and the Royal College of Psychiatrists.

NCCMH (2010) *Depression in Adults with a Chronic Physical Health Problem: Treatment and Management*. Leicester & London: British Psychological Society and the Royal College of Psychiatrists.

Nemeroff, C. B., Entsuah, R., Benattia, I., *et al.* (2008) Comprehensive analysis of remission (COMPARE) with venlafaxine versus SSRIs. *Biological Psychiatry, 63*, 424–434.

References

Neumeyer-Gromen, A., Lampert, T., Stark, K., *et al.* (2004) Disease management programs for depression: a systematic review and meta-analysis of randomized controlled trials. *Medical Care, 42*, 1211–1221.

Nezu, A. M. (1987) A problem-solving formulation of depression: a literature review and proposal of a pluralistic model. *Clinical Psychology Review, 7*, 121–144.

Nezu, A. M., Nezu, C. M. & Perri, M. G. (1989) *Problem-Solving Therapy for Depression: Theory Research and Clinical Guidelines.* New York: Wiley.

NHS, Business Services Authority, Prescription Pricing Division (2009) *Electronic Drug Tariff for England and Wales, May 2009.* Compiled on behalf of the Department of Health. Available at: http://www.ppa.org.uk/edt/May_2009/mindex.htm [accessed 23 May 2009].

NICE (2002) *Guidance on the Use of Computerised Cognitive Behavioural Therapy for Anxiety and Depression.* Technology Appraisal 51. London: NICE.

NICE (2003) *Guidance on the Use of Electroconvulsive Therapy.* Technology Appraisal 59. London: NICE.

NICE (2004a) *Depression: Management of Depression in Primary and Secondary Care.* Clinical Guideline 23. London: NICE.

NICE (2004b) *Anxiety: Management of Anxiety (Panic Disorder, with or without Agoraphobia, and Generalised Anxiety Disorder) in Adults in Primary, Secondary and Community Care.* Clinical Guideline 22. London: NICE.

NICE (2004c) *Vagus Nerve Stimulation for Refractory Depression in Children.* Interventional Procedures Guidance 50. London: NICE.

NICE (2005) *Depression in Children and Young People: Identification and Management in Primary, Community and Secondary Care.* Clinical Guideline 28. London: NICE.

NICE (2006a) *Computerised Cognitive Behaviour Therapy for the Treatment of Depression and Anxiety.* NICE Technology Appraisal 97. Review of Technology Appraisal 51. London: NICE.

NICE (2006b) *Dementia: Supporting People with Dementia and their Carers in Health and Social Care.* Clinical Guideline 42. London: NICE & SCIE.

NICE (2006c) *Bipolar Disorder: The Management of Bipolar Disorder in Adults, Children and Adolescents, in Primary and Secondary care.* NICE Clinical Guideline 38. London: NICE.

NICE (2007a) *Depression: Management of Depression in Primary and Secondary Care.* Clinical Guideline 23 (amended). London: NICE.

NICE (2007b) *The Guideline Development Process – An Overview for Stakeholders, the Public and the NHS.* 3rd edn. London: NICE.

NICE (2007c) *The Guidelines Manual.* London: NICE.

NICE (2007d) *Transcranial Magnetic Stimulation for Severe Depression.* Interventional Procedure Guidance 242. London: NICE

NICE (2007e) *Antenatal and Postnatal Mental Health: Clinical Management and Service Guidance.* Clinical Guideline 45. London: NICE.

NICE (2008a) *Guide to the Methods of Technology Appraisal.* London: NICE.

NICE (2008b) *Social Value Judgements. Principles for the Development of NICE guidance.* 2nd edn. London: NICE.

NICE (2009a) *The Guidelines Manual.* London: NICE.

NICE (2009b) *Medicines Adherence: Involving Patients in Decisions about Prescribed Medicines and Supporting Adherence.* Clinical Guideline 76. London: NICE.

NICE (2009c) *Depression in Adults with a Chronic Physical Health Problem: Treatment and Management.* Clinical Guideline 91. London: NICE.

Nicholson, A., Kuper, H. & Hemingway, H. (2006) Depression as an aetiologic and prognostic factor in coronary heart disease: a meta-analysis of 6362 events among 146,538 participants in 54 observational studies. *European Heart Journal, 27,* 2763–2774.

Nierenberg, A. A. & Amsterdam, J. D. (1990) Treatment-resistant depression: definition and treatment approaches. *Journal of Clinical Psychiatry, 51,* 39–47.

Nierenberg, A. A., McLean, N. E., Alpert, J. E., *et al.* (1995) Early nonresponse to fluoxetine as a predictor of poor 8-week outcome. *American Journal of Psychiatry, 152,* 1500–1503.

Nierenberg, A. A., Farabaugh, A. H., Alpert, J. E., *et al.* (2000) Timing of onsent of antidepressant response with fluoxetine treatment. American Journal of Psychiatry, 157, 1423–1428.

Nolan, P., Murray, E. & Dallender, J. (1999) Practice nurses' perceptions of services for clients with psychological problems in primary care. International Journal of Nursing Studies, 36, 97–104.

Nolen, W. A., van de Putte, J. J., Dijken, W. A., *et al.* (1988) Treatment strategy in depression. II: MAO inhibitors in depression resistant to cyclic antidepressants – two controlled crossover studies with tranylcypromine versus L-5-hydroxytryptophan and nomifensine. *Acta Psychiatrica Scandinavica, 78,* 676–683.

Nolen, W. A., Hoencampe, E. & Halmans, P. M. J. (1994) Classical and selective monoamine oxidase inhibitors in refractory major depression. In *Refractory Depression: Current Strategies and Future Directions* (eds W. A. Nolen, S. P. Zohar, S. P. Roose & J. D. Amsterdam), pp. 59–68. Chichester: Wiley.

Normann, C., Hummel, B., Schärer, L. O., *et al.* (2002) Lamotrigine as adjunct to paroxetine in acute depression: a placebo-controlled, double-blind study. *Journal of Clinical Psychiatry, 63,* 337–344.

Nuechterlein, K. H. & Dawson, M. E. (1984) A heuristic vulnerability/stress model of schizophrenic episodes. *Schizophrenia Bulletin, 10,* 300–312.

Nutt, D. J. (2002) Tolerability and safety aspects of mirtazapine. *Human Psychopharmacology, 17* (Suppl. 1), S37–S41.

Ofman, J. J., Badamgarav, E., Henning, J. M., *et al.* (2004) Does disease management improve clinical and economic outcomes in patients with chronic diseases? A systematic review. *American Journal of Medicine, 117,* 182–192.

Okiishi, J., Lambert, M. J., Nielsen, S. L., *et al.* (2003) Waiting for supershrink: an empirical analysis of therapist effects. *Clinical Psychology and Psychotherapy, 10,* 361–373.

Ormel, J. & Costa e Silva, J. A. (1995) The impact of psychopathology on disability and health perceptions. In *Mental Illness in General Health Care: an*

International Study (eds T. B. Üstün & N. Sartorius), pp. 335–346. Chichester: Wiley.

Ormel, J., van den Brink, W., Koeter, M. W. J., *et al.* (1990) Recognition, management and outcome of psychological disorders in primary care: a naturalistic follow-up study. *Psychological Medicine, 20*, 909–923.

Ormel, J., von Korff, M., Oldehinkel, T., *et al.* (1999) Onset of disability in depressed and non-depressed primary care patients. *Psychological Medicine, 29*, 847–853.

Osgood-Hynes, D. J., Greist, D. H., Marks, I. M., *et al.* (1998) Self-administered psychotherapy for depression using a telephone-accessed computer system plus booklets: an open US–UK study. *Journal of Clinical Psychiatry, 59*, 358–365.

Ostler, K., Thompson, C., Kinmonth, A. L. K., *et al.* (2001) Influence of socio-economic deprivation on the prevalence and outcome of depression in primary care: the Hampshire Depression Project. *British Journal of Psychiatry, 178*, 12–17.

Ostrom, M., Eriksson, A., Thorson, J., *et al.* (1996) Fatal overdose with citalopram. *Lancet, 348*, 339–340.

Palmer, S. C. & Coyne, J. C. (2003) Screening for depression in medical care: pitfalls, alternatives, and revised priorities. *Journal of Psychosomatic Research, 54*, 279–287.

Papakostas, G. I., Montgomery, S. A., Thase, M. E., *et al.* (2007) Comparing the rapidity of response during treatment of major depressive disorder with bupropion and the SSRIs: a pooled survival analysis of 7 double-blind, randomized clinical trials. *Journal of Clinical Psychiatry, 68*, 1907–1912.

Patten, S. B. (1991) Are the Brown and Harris 'vulnerability factors' risk factors for depression? *Journal of Psychiatry and Neuroscience, 16*, 267–271.

Paykel, E. S., Freeling, P. & Hollyman, J. A. (1988) Are tricyclic antidepressants useful for mild depression? A placebo-controlled trial. *Pharmacopsychiatry, 21*, 15–18.

Paykel, E. S., Ramana, R., Cooper, Z., *et al.* (1995) Residual symptoms after partial remission: an important outcome in depression. *Psychological Medicine, 25*, 1171–1180.

Paykel, E. S., Scott, J., Teasdale, J. D., *et al.* (1999) Prevention of relapse in residual depression by cognitive therapy. *Archives of General Psychiatry, 56*, 829–835.

Peckham, C. S. & Dezateux, C. (1998) Issues underlying the evaluation of screening programmes. *British Medical Bulletin, 54*, 767–778.

Peet, M., Tienari, P. & Jaskari, M. O. (1977) A comparison of the cardiac effects of mianserin and amitriptyline in man. *Pharmakopsychiatrie Neuropsychopharmakologie, 10*, 309–312.

Penttinen, J. & Valonen, P. (1996) Use of psychotropic drugs and risk of myocardial infarction: a case-control study in Finnish farmers. *International Journal of Epidemiology, 25*, 760–762.

Personne, M., Sjoberg, G. & Persson, H. (1997a) Citalopram overdose: review of cases treated in Swedish hospitals. *Journal of Toxicology and Clinical Toxicology, 35*, 237–240.

Personne, M., Sjoberg, G. & Persson, H. (1997b) Citalopram toxicity. *Lancet, 350*, 518–519.

Peselow, E. D., Filippi, A. M., Goodnick, P., *et al.* (1989) The short- and long-term efficacy of paroxetine HCl: A. Data from a six-week double-blind parallel design trial vs. imipramine and placebo. *Psychopharmacology Bulletin, 25*, 267–271.

Peveler, R., George, C., Kinmonth, A. L., *et al.* (1999) Effect of antidepressant drug counselling and information leaflets on adherence to drug treatment in primary care: randomised controlled trial. *British Medical Journal, 319*, 612–615.

Peveler, R., Kendrick, T., Buxton, M., *et al.* (2005) A randomised controlled trial to compare the cost-effectiveness of tricyclic antidepressants, selective serotonin reuptake inhibitors and lofepramine. *Health Technology Assessment, 9*, 1–134.

Piaggio, G., Elbourne, D. R., Altman, D. G., *et al.* (2006) Reporting of noninferiority and equivalence randomized trials: an extension of the CONSORT statement. *Journal of the American Medical Association, 295*, 1152–1160.

Pignone, M. P., Gaynes, B. N., Rushton, J. L., *et al.* (2002) Screening for depression in adults: a summary of the evidence for the US Preventive Services Task Force. *Annals of Internal Medicine, 136*, 765–776.

Pilgrim, D. & Bentall, R. (1999) The medicalisation of misery: a critical realist analysis of the concept of depression. *Journal of Mental Health*, 8, 261–274.

Pilgrim, D. & Dowrick, C. (2006) From a diagnostic-therapeutic to a social-existential response to 'depression'. *Journal of Public Mental Health*, 5, 6–12.

Pilling, S. (2008) History, context, process, and rationale for the development of clinical guidelines. *Psychology and Psychotherapy, 81*, 331–350.

Pilling, S. A., Cape, J., Liebowitz, J. A., *et al.* (2010) Enhanced care for depression: a study in primary care (unpublished).

Plummer, S., Ritter, S. A. H., Leach, R. E., *et al.* (1997) A controlled comparison of the ability of practice nurses to detect psychological distress in patients who attend their clinics. *Journal of Psychiatric and Mental Health Nursing, 4*, 221–223.

Pollock, K. & Grime, J. (2002) Patients' perceptions of entitlement to time in general practice consultations for depression: a qualitative study. *British Medical Journal*, 325, 687–690.

Pollock, B. G., Laghrissi-Thode, F. & Wagner, W. R. (2000) Evaluation of platelet activation in depressed patients with ischemic heart disease after paroxetine or nortriptyline treatment. *Journal of Clinical Psychopharmacology, 20*, 137–140.

Popay, J., Kowarzik, U., Mallinson, S., *et al.* (2007) Social problems, primary care and pathways to at the individual level. Part I: the GP perspective help and support: addressing health inequalities. *Journal of Epidemiology and Community Health, 61*, 966–971.

Porter, R. J., Douglas, K. & Knight, R. G. (2008) Monitoring of cognitive effects during a course of electroconvulsive therapy: recommendations for clinical practice. *Journal of ECT, 24*, 25–34.

Posternak, M. A. & Miller, I. (2001) Untreated short-term course of major depression: a meta-analysis of outcomes from studies using wait-list control groups. *Journal of Affective Disorders, 66*, 139–146.

Posternak, M. A. & Zimmerman, M. (2005) Is there a delay in the antidepressant effect? *Journal of Clinical Psychiatry, 66*, 148–158.

References

Posternak, M. A. & Zimmerman, M. (2007) Therapeutic effect of follow-up assessments on antidepressant and placebo response rates in antidepressant efficacy trials. *British Journal of Psychiatry, 190*, 287–292.

Posternak, M. A., Solomon, D. A., Leon, A. C., *et al.* (2006) The naturalistic course of unipolar major depression in the absence of somatic therapy. *Journal of Nervous and Mental Disorders, 194*, 324–329.

Prasher, V. (1999) Presentation and management of depression in people with learning disability. *Advances in Psychiatric Treatment, 5*, 447–454.

Pratt, L. A., Ford, D. F., Crum, R. M., *et al.* (1996) Depression, psychotropic medication, and risk of myocardial infarction. Prospective data from the Baltimore ECA follow-up. *Circulation, 94*, 3123–3129.

Price, L. H., Carpenter, L. L. & Rasmussen, S. A. (2001) Drug combination strategies. In *Treatment Resistant Mood Disorders* (eds J. D. Amsterdam, M. Hornig & A. A. Nierenberg), pp. 194–222. Cambridge: Cambridge University Press.

Priest, R. G., Vize, C., Roberts, A., *et al.* (1996) Lay people's attitudes to treatment of depression: results of opinion poll for Defeat Depression Campaign just before its launch. *British Medical Journal, 313*, 858–859.

Prins, M. A., Verhaak, P. F. M., Bensing, J. M., *et al.* (2008) Health beliefs and perceived need for mental health care of anxiety and depression: the patients' perspective explored. *Clinical Psychology Review, 28*, 1038–1058.

Proudfoot, J., Ryden, C., Everitt, B., *et al.* (2004) Clinical efficacy of computerised cognitive-behavioural therapy for anxiety and depression in primary care: randomised controlled trial. *British Journal of Psychiatry, 185*, 46–54.

Pyne, J., Sieber, W., David, K., *et al.* (2003) Use of the quality of well-being self-administered version (QWB-SA) in assessing health-related quality of life in depressed patients. *Journal of Affective Disorders, 76*, 237–247.

Quitkin, F. M., Rabkin, J. D., Markowitz, J. M., *et al.* (1987) Use of pattern analysis to identify true drug response. A replication. *Archives of General Psychiatry, 44*, 259–264.

Quitkin, F. M., Harrison, W., Stewart, J. W., *et al.* (1991) Response to phenelzine and imipramine in placebo non-responders with atypical depression. A new application of the crossover design. *Archives of General Psychiatry, 48*, 319–323.

Quitkin, F. M., Stewart, J. W. & McGrath, P. J. (2001) Gender differences in treatment response. *American Journal of Psychiatry, 158*, 1531–1533.

Quitkin, F. M., Petkova, E., McGrath, P. J., *et al.* (2003) When should a trial of fluoxetine for major depression be declared failed? *American Journal of Psychiatry, 160*, 734–740.

Rabins, P. (1996) Barriers to diagnosis and treatment of depression in elderly patients. *American Journal of Geriatric Psychiatry, 4*, 79–84.

Rabkin, J. G., Markowitz, J. S., Stewart, J. W., *et al.* (1986) How blind is blind? Assessment of patient and doctor medication guesses in a placebo-controlled trial of imipramine and phenelzine. *Psychiatry Research, 19*, 75–86.

Radloff, L. S. (1977) The CES-D scale: a self-report depression scale for research in the general population. *Applied Psychological Measurement, 1*, 385–401.

Raine, R., Lewis, L., Sensky, T., *et al.* (2000) Patient determinants of mental health interventions in primary care. *British Journal of General Practice, 50*, 620–625.

Rait, G., Burns, A., Baldwin, R., *et al.* (1999) Screening for depression in African-Caribbean elders. *Family Practice, 16*, 591–595.

Ramachandani, P. & Stein, A. (2003) The impact of parental psychiatric disorder on children. *British Medical Journal, 327*, 242–243.

Ramana, R., Paykel, E. S., Surtees, P. G., *et al.* (1999) Medication received by patients with depression following the acute episode: adequacy and relation to outcome. *British Journal of Psychiatry, 174*, 128–134.

Rami, L., Bernardo, M., Boget, T., *et al.* (2004) Cognitive status of psychiatric patients under maintenance electroconvulsive therapy: a one-year longitudinal study. *Journal of Neuropsychiatry and Clinical Neuroscience, 16*, 465–471.

Rami-Gonzalez, L., Salamero, M., Boget, T., *et al.* (2003) Pattern of cognitive dysfunction in depressive patients during maintenance electroconvulsive therapy. *Psychological Medicine, 33*, 345–350.

Rapp, S. R. & Davis, K. M. (1989) Geriatric depression: physicians' knowledge, perceptions, and diagnostic practices. *Gerontologist, 29*, 252–257.

Rasmussen, S. L., Overo, K. F. & Tanghoj, P. (1999) Cardiac safety of citalopram: prospective trials and retrospective analyses. *Journal of Clinical Psychopharmacology, 19*, 407–415.

Rawlins, M. D. (2008) *De Testimonio. On the Evidence for Decisions about the Use of Therapeutic Interventions.* The Harveian Oration of 2008. Delivered before the Fellows of The Royal College of Physicians of London on Thursday 16 October 2008. London: Royal College of Physicians. Available at: http://www.rcplondon.ac.uk/pubs/contents/304df931-2ddc-4a54-894e-e0cdb03e84a5.pdf

Reilly, J. G., Ayis, S. A., Ferrier, I. N., *et al.* (2000) QTc-interval abnormalities and psychotropic drug therapy in psychiatric patients. *Lancet, 355*, 1048–1052.

Revicki, D. A. & Wood, M. (1998) Patient-assigned health state utilities for depression-related outcomes: differences by depression severity and anti-depressant medications. *Journal of Affective Disorders, 48*, 25–36.

Richards, A., Barkham, M., Cahill, J., *et al.* (2003) PHASE: a randomised, controlled trial of supervised self-help cognitive behavioural therapy in primary care. *British Journal of General Practice, 53*, 764–770.

Richards, D. A. & Suckling, R. (2008) Improving access to psychological therapy: the Doncaster demonstration site organisational model. *Clinical Psychology Forum, 181*, 9–16.

Richards, D. & Whyte, M. (2008) Reach out: national programme student materials to support the delivery of training for practitioners delivering low intensity interventions. London: Rethink. Available at: http://www.iapt.nhs.uk/wp-content/uploads/2008/07/0725_student-manual-18july.pdf

Richards, D. A., Lovell, K., Gilbody, S., *et al.* (2008) Collaborative care for depression in UK primary care: a randomized comtrolled trial. *Psychological Medicine, 38*, 279–287.

Richardson, R., Richards, D. A. & Barkham, M. (2008) Self-help books for people with depression: a scoping review. *Journal of Mental Health, 17*, 543–552.

Ridge, D. & Ziebland, S. (2006) 'The old me could never have done that': how people give meaning to recovery following depression. *Qualitative Health Research, 16*, 1038–1053.

Rinaldi, M., Perkins, R., Glynn, E., *et al.* (2008) Individual placement and support: from research to practice. *Advances in Psychiatric Treatment, 14*, 50–60.

Roberts, D., Bernard, M., Misca, G., *et al.* (2008) *Experiences of Children and Young People Caring for a Parent with a Mental Health Problem*. Research Briefing No. 24. London: Social Care Institute for Excellence.

Robinson, L. A., Berman, J. S. & Neimeyer, R. A. (1990) Psychotherapy for the treatment of depression: a comprehensive review of controlled outcome research. *Psychological Bulletin, 108*, 30–49.

Rodin, I. & Thompson, C. (1997) Seasonal affective disorder. *Advances in Psychiatric Treatment, 3*, 352–359.

Rogers, A., Hassell, K. & Nicolaas, G. (1999) *Demanding Patients? Analysing the Use of Primary Care*. Milton Keynes: Open University Press.

Rogers, A., May, C. & Oliver, D. (2001) Experiencing depression, experiencing the depressed: the separate worlds of patients and doctors. *Journal of Mental Health, 10*, 317–333.

Rogers, C. R. (1951) *Client-Centered Therapy: Its Current Practice, Implications, and Theory*. Oxford: Houghton Miffin.

Rogers, C. R. (1957) The necessary and sufficient conditions of therapeutic personality change. *Journal of Consulting Psychology, 21*, 95–103.

Rogers, C. R. (1986) Rogers, Kohut and Erikson. A personal perspective on some similarities and differences. *Person-Centered Review, 1*, 125–140.

Romeo, R., Patel, A., Knapp, M., *et al.* (2004) The cost-effectiveness of mirtazapine versus paroxetine in treating people with depression in primary care. *International Clinical Psychopharmacology, 19*, 125–134.

Roose, S. P. (2001) Depression, anxiety, and the cardiovascular system: the psychiatrist's perspective. *Journal of Clinical Psychiatry, 62* (Suppl. 8), 19–22.

Roose, S. P. (2003) Treatment of depression in patients with heart disease. *Biological Psychiatry, 54*, 262–268.

Roose, S. P. & Glassman, A. H. (1989) Cardiovascular effects of tricyclic antidepressants in depressed patients with and without heart disease. *Journal of Clinical Psychiatry Monograph, 7*, 1–19.

Roose, S. P., Glassman, A. H., Giardina, E. G. V., *et al.* (1987) Tricyclic antidepressants in depressed patients with cardiac conduction disease. *Archives of General Psychiatry, 44*, 273–275.

Roose, S. P., Laghrissi-Thode, F., Kennedy, J. S., *et al.* (1998a) Comparison of paroxetine to nortriptyline in depressed patients with ischemic heart disease. *Journal of the American Medical Association, 279*, 287–291.

Roose, S. P., Glassman, A. H., Attia, E., *et al.* (1998b) Cardiovascular effects of fluoxetine in depressed patients with heart disease. *American Journal of Psychiatry, 155*, 660–665.

Rose, D., Fleischmann, P., Wykes, T., *et al.* (2003) Patients' perspectives on electroconvulsive therapy: systematic review. *British Medical Journal, 326*, 1363.

Rosenbaum, J. F., Fava, M., Hoog, S. L., *et al.* (1998) Selective serotonin reuptake inhibitor discontinuation syndrome: a randomised clinical trial. *Biological Psychiatry, 44*, 77–87.

Rosenthal, N. E., Sack, D. A., Gillin, J. C., *et al.* (1984) Seasonal affective disorder. A description of the syndrome and preliminary findings with light therapy. *Archives of General Psychiatry, 41*, 72–80.

Ross, D. C., Quitkin, F. M. & Klein, D. F. (2002) A typological model for estimation of drug and placebo effects in depression. *Journal of Clinical Psychopharmacology, 22*, 414–418.

Rost, K., Humphrey, J. & Kelleher, K. (1994) Physician management preferences and barriers to care for rural patients with depression. *Archives of Family Medicine, 3*, 409–414.

Rost, K., Williams, C., Wherry, J., *et al.* (1995) The process and outcomes of care for major depression in rural family practice settings. *Journal of Rural Health, 11*, 114–121.

Rost, K., Nutting, P. A., Smith, J., *et al.* (2000) Designing and implementing a primary care intervention trial to improve the quality and outcome of care for major depression. *General Hospital Psychiatry, 22*, 66–77.

Rost, K., Nutting, P., Smith, J., *et al.* (2001) Improving depression outcomes in community primary care practices: a randomized trial of the QuEST intervention. *Journal of General Internal Medicine, 16*, 143–149.

Roter, D. L., Hall, J. A., Kern, D. E., *et al.* (1995) Improving physicians' interviewing skills and reducing patients' emotional distress. A randomised clinical trial. *Archives of Internal Medicine, 155*, 1877–1884.

Roth, A. & Fonagy, P. (1996) *What Works for Whom: A Critical Review of Psychotherapy Research*. New York: Guilford.

Roth, A. D. & Pilling, S. (2009) The impact of adherence and competence on outcome in CBT and psychological therapies. In preparation.

Roth, A. J., Kornblith, A. B., Batel-Copel, L., *et al.* (1998) Rapid screening for psychologic distress in men with prostate carcinoma: a pilot study. *Cancer, 82*, 1904–1908.

Rothschild, A. J. (2003) Challenges in the treatment of depression with psychotic features. *Biological Psychiatry, 53*, 680–690.

Rounsaville, B. J., Carroll, K. M. & Onken, L. S. (2001) NIDA's stage model of behavioral therapies research: getting started and moving on from Stage I. *Clinical Psychology: Science and Practice, 8*, 133–142.

Rowe, D. (1983) *Depression: the Way out of Your Prison*. London: Routledge & Kegan Paul.

Rowe, S. K. & Rapaport, M. H. (2006) Classification and treatment of sub-threshold depression. *Current Opinion in Psychiatry, 19*, 9–13.

References

Royal College of Psychiatrists (1997) *Benzodiazepines: Risks, Benefits or Dependence. A Re-evaluation.* Council Report CR59. London: Royal College of Psychiatrists.

Royal College of Psychiatrists (2005) *The ECT Handbook Second Edition. The Third Report of the Royal College of Psychiatrists' Special Committee on ECT* (ed A. I. F. Scott). Council Report CR128. London: Royal College of Psychiatrists.

Royal College of Psychiatrists (2008) *Mental Health and Work.* London: Royal College of Psychiatrists.

Rush, A. J., Beck, A. T., Kovacs, M., *et al.* (1977) Comparative efficacy of cognitive therapy and pharmacotherapy in the treatment of depressed outpatients. *Cognitive Therapy and Research, 1,* 17–37.

Rush, A. J., Kovacs, M., Beck, A. T., *et al.* (1981) Differential effects of cognitive therapy and pharmacotherapy on depressive symptoms. *Journal of Affective Disorders, 3,* 221–229.

Rush, A. J., Trivedi, M. & Fava, M. (2003) STAR*D treatment trial for depression. *American Journal of Psychiatry, 160,* 237.

Rush, A. J., Trivedi, M. H., Wisniewski, S. R., *et al.* (2006) Acute and longer-term outcomes in depressed outpatients requiring one or several treatment steps: a STAR*D report. *American Journal of Psychiatry, 163,* 1905–1917.

Russell, J. C., Rasmussen, K. G., O'Connor, M. K., *et al.* (2003) Long-term maintenance ECT: a retrospective review of efficacy and cognitive outcome. *Journal of ECT, 19,* 4–9.

Sackeim, H. A., Decina, P., Kanzler, M., *et al.* (1987) Effects of electrode placement on the efficacy of titrated, low-does ECT. *American Journal of Psychiatry, 144,* 1449–1455.

Sainsbury Centre for Mental Health (2007) *Mental Health at Work: Developing the Business Case.* Policy Paper 8. London: Sainsbury Centre for Mental Health.

Salkovskis, P.M. (1995) Demonstrating specific effects in cognitive and behavioural therapy. In *Research Foundations for Psychotherapy Research* (eds M. Aveline & D. A. Shapiro), pp. 191–228. Chichester: Wiley and Sons.

Santos, M. A., Rocha, F. L., Hara, C., *et al.* (2008) Efficacy and safety of antidepressant augmentation with lamotrigine in patients with treatment-resistant depression: a randomized, placebo-controlled, double-blind study. *Journal of Clinical Psychiatry, 10,* 187–190.

Sapin, C., Fantino, B., Nowicki, M. L., *et al.* (2004) Usefulness of EQ-5D in assessing health status in primary care patients with major depressive disorder. *Health and Quality of Life Outcomes, 2,* 20.

Sartorius, N. (2001) The economic and social burden of depression. *Journal of Clinical Psychiatry, 62* (Suppl. 15), 8–11.

Sartorius, N. (2002) Eines der letzen Hindernisse einer verbesserten psychiatrischen Versorgung: das Stigma psychisher Erkrankung [One of the last obstacles to better mental health care: the stigma of mental illness]. *Neuropsychiatrie, 16,* 5–10.

Sauer, W. H., Berlin, J. A. & Kimmel, S. E. (2001) Selective serotonin reuptake inhibitors and myocardial infarction. *Circulation, 104,* 1894–1898.

Saver, B. G., Van-Nguyen, V., Keppel, G., *et al.* (2007) A qualitative study of depression in primary care: missed opportunities for diagnosis and education. *The Journal of the American Board of Family Medicine, 20*, 28–35.

Schaffer, A., Levitt, A. J., Hershkop, S. K., *et al.* (2002) Utility scores of symptom profiles in major depression. *Psychiatry Research, 110*, 189–197.

Schindler, F. & Anghelescu, I. G. (2007) Lithium versus lamotrigine augmentation in treatment resistant unipolar depression: a randomized, open-label study. *International Clinical Psychopharmacology, 22*, 179–182.

Schneider, L. S. & Small, G. W. (2002) The increasing power of placebos in trials of antidepressants. *Journal of the American Medical Association, 288*, 450.

Schweizer, E., Rickels, K., Amsterdam., J. D., *et al.* (1990) What constitutes an adequate antidepressant trial for fluoxetine? *Journal of Clinical Psychiatry, 51*, 8–11.

Schweizer, E., Rynn, M., Mandos, L. A., *et al.* (2001) The antidepressant effect of sertraline is not enhanced by dose titration: results from an outpatient clinical trial. *International Clinical Psychopharmacology, 16*, 137–143.

Scott, C., Tacchi, M. J., Jones, R., *et al.* (1997) Acute and one-year outcome of a randomised controlled trial of brief cognitive therapy for major depressive disorder in primary care. *British Journal of Psychiatry, 171*, 131–134.

Scott, J., Teasdale, J. D., Paykel, E. S., *et al.* (2000) Effects of cognitive therapy on psychological symptoms and social functioning in residual depression. *British Journal of Psychiatry, 177*, 440–446.

Scott, J., Palmer, S., Paykel, E., *et al.* (2003) Use of cognitive therapy for relapse prevention in chronic depression. Cost-effectiveness study. *British Journal of Psychiatry, 182*, 221–227.

Segal, Z., Teasdale, J. & Williams, M. (2002) *Mindfulness-Based Cognitive Therapy for Depression.* New York: Guilford Press.

Selmi, P. M., Klein, M. H., Greist, J. H., *et al.* (1990) Computer-administered cognitive-behavioural therapy for depression. *American Journal of Psychiatry, 147*, 51–56.

Serby, M. & Yu, M. (2003) Overview: depression in the elderly. *Mount Sinai Journal of Medicine, 70*, 38–44.

Shah, R., Uren, Z., Baker, A., *et al.* (2001) Trends in deaths from drug overdose and poisoning in England and Wales 1993–1998. *Journal of Public Health Medicine, 23*, 242–246.

Shaw, C. M., Creed, F., Tomenson, B., *et al.* (1999) Prevalence of anxiety and depressive illness and help seeking behaviour in African Caribbeans and white Europeans: two phase general population survey. *British Medical Journal, 318*, 302–306.

Simon, G. (2006) Collaborative care for depression: is effective in older people, as IMPACT trial shows. *British Medical Journal, 332*, 249–250.

Simon, G. E. & Savarino, J. (2007) Suicide attempts among patients starting depression treatment with medications or psychotherapy. *American Journal of Psychiatry, 164*, 1029–1034.

References

Simon, G. E., von Korff, M., Heiligenstein, J. H., *et al.* (1996) Initial antidepressant choice in primary care. Effectiveness and cost of fluoxetine vs tricyclic antidepressants. *Journal of the American Medical Association, 275*, 1897–1902.

Simon, G. E., Goldberg, D. P., von Korff, M., *et al.* (2002) Understanding cross-national differences in depression prevalence. *Psychological Medicine, 32*, 585–594.

Simon, G. E., Ludman, E. J., Tutty, S., *et al.* (2004) Telephone psychotherapy and telephone care management for primary care patients starting antidepressant treatment: a randomized trial. *Journal of the American Medical Association, 292*, 935–942.

Simon, G. E., Savarino, J., Operskalski, B., *et al.* (2006) Suicide risk during antidepressant treatment. *American Journal of Psychiatry, 163*, 41–47.

Simpson, S., Corney, R., Fitzgerald, P., *et al.* (2003) A randomized controlled trial to evaluate the effectiveness and cost-effectiveness of psychodynamic counselling for general practice patients with chronic depression. *Psychological Medicine, 33*, 229–239.

Singh, G., Verma, H. C., Verma, R. S., *et al.* (1974) A new depressive inventory. *Indian Journal of Psychiatry, 161*, 83–188.

Singleton, N., Bumpstead, R., O'Brien, M., *et al.* (2001) *Psychiatric Morbidity Among Adults Living in Private Households, 2000.* London: The Stationery Office.

Sir, A., D'Souza, R. F., Uguz, S., *et al.* (2005) Randomised trial of sertraline versus venlafaxine XR in major depression: efficacy and discontinuation symptoms. *Journal of Clinical Psychiatry, 66*, 1312–1320.

Skodol, A. E., Oldman, J. M. & Gallaher, P. E. (1999) Axis II comorbidity of substance use disorders among patients referred for treatment of personality disorders. *American Journal of Psychiatry, 156*, 733–738.

Smith, D., Dempster, C., Glanville, J., *et al.* (2002) Efficacy and tolerability of venlafaxine compared with selective serotonin reuptake inhibitors and other antidepressants: a meta-analysis. *British Journal of Psychiatry, 180*, 396–404.

Sneed, J. R., Rutherford, B. R., Rindskopf, D., *et al.* (2008) Design makes a difference: a meta-analysis of antidepressant response rates in placebo-controlled versus comparator trials in late-life depression. *American Journal of Geriatric Psychiatry, 16*, 65–73.

Sobin, C., Sackeim, H. A., Prudic, J., *et al* (1995) Predictors of retrograde amnesia following ECT. *American Journal of Psychiatry, 152*, 995–1001.

Solomon, D. A., Keller, M. B., Leon, A. C., *et al.* (1997) Recovery from major depression. A 10-year prospective follow-up across multiple episodes. *Archives of General Psychiatry, 54*, 1001–1006.

Solomon, D. A., Keller, M. B., Leon, A. C., *et al.* (2000) Multiple recurrences of major depressive disorder. *American Journal of Psychiatry, 157*, 229–233.

Sotsky, S. M., Glass, D. R., Shea, M. T., *et al.* (1991) Patient predictors of response to psychotherapy and pharmacotherapy: findings in the NIMH Treatment of Depression Collaborative Research Programme. *American Journal of Psychiatry, 148*, 997–1008.

Spitzer, R. L., Williams, J. B., Kroenke, K., *et al.* (1994) Utility of a new procedure for diagnosing mental disorders in primary care. The PRIME-MD 1000 study. *Journal of the American Medical Assocaition, 272,* 1749–1756.

Spitzer, R. L., Kroenke, K., Williams, J. B., *et al.* (1999) Validation and utility of a self-report version of the PRIME-MD: the PHQ primary care study. *Journal of the American Medical Association, 282,* 1737–1744.

Stassen, H. H., Delini-Stula, A. & Angst, J. (1993) Time course of improvement under antidepressant treatment: a survival-analytical approach. *European Neuropsychopharmacology, 3,* 127–135.

Steiner, M., Radwan, M., Elizur, A., *et al.* (1978) Failure of L-triiodothyronine (T3) to potentiate tricyclic antidepressant response. *Current Therapeutic Research, Clinical and Experimental, 23,* 655–659.

Stewart, J. W., Quitkin, F. M., Liebowitz, M. R., *et al.* (1983) Efficacy of desipramine in depressed outpatients. Response according to research diagnosis criteria diagnoses and severity of illness. *Archives of General Psychiatry, 40,* 202–207.

Stiles, W. B., Barkham, M., Twigg, E., *et al.* (2006) Effectiveness of cognitive-behavioural, person-centred and psychodynamic therapies as practised in UK National Health Service settings. *Psychological Medicine, 36,* 555–566.

Stiles, W. B., Barkham, M., Mellor-Clark, J., *et al.* (2008) Effectiveness of cognitive-behavioural, person-centred and psychodynamic therapies in UK primary-care routine practice: replication in a larger sample. *Psychological Medicine, 38,* 677–688.

Stirman, S. W., Derubeis, R. J., Crits-Christoph, P., *et al.* (2005) Can the randomized controlled trial literature generalize to nonrandomized patients? *Journal of Consulting and Clinical Psychology, 73,* 127–135.

Strik, J. J., Honig, A., Lousberg, R., *et al.* (2000) Efficacy and safety of fluoxetine in the treatment of patients with major depression after first myocardial infarction: findings from a double-blind, placebo-controlled trial. *Psychosomatic Medicine, 62,* 783–789.

Sullivan, M. D., Katon, W. J., Russo, J. E., *et al.* (2003) Patients' beliefs predict responses to paroxetine among primary care patients with dysthymia and minor depression. *The Journal of the American Board of Family Practice, 16,* 22–31.

Swindle, R. W., Rao, J. K., Helmy, A., *et al.* (2003) Integrating clinical nurse specialists into the treatment of primary care patients with depression. *International Journal of Psychiatry in Medicine, 33,* 17–37.

Szegedi, A., Muller, M. J., Anghelescu, I., *et al.* (2003) Early improvement under mirtazapine and paroxetine predicts later stable response and remission with high sensitivity in patients with major depression. *Journal of Clinical Psychiatry, 64,* 413–420.

Szegedi, A., Jansen, W. T., van Willigenburg, A. P. P., *et al.* (2009) Early improvement in the first 2 weeks as a predictor of treatment outcome in patients with major depressive disorder: a meta-analysis including 6562 patients. *Journal of Clinical Psychiatry, 70,* 344–353.

Tamminga, C. A., Nemeroff, C. B., Blakely, R. D., *et al.* (2002) Developing novel treatments for mood disorders: accelerating discovery. *Biological Psychiatry, 52,* 589–609.

Taylor, D. (1995) Selective serotonin reuptake inhibitors and tricyclic antidepressants in combination. Interactions and therapeutic uses. *British Journal of Psychiatry, 167*, 575–580.

Taylor, D., Stewart, S. & Connolly, A. (2006) Antidepressant withdrawal symptoms: telephone calls to a national medication helpline. *Journal of Affective Disorders, 95*, 129–133.

Taylor, D., Paton, C. & Kerwin, R. (2007) *The Maudsley Prescribing Guidelines* (9th edn). London: Informa Healthcare.

Thase, M. E. (2002) Studying new antidepressants: if there were a light at the end of the tunnel, could we see it? *Journal of Clinical Psychiatry, 63* (Suppl. 2), 24–27.

Thase, M. E. & Rush, A. J. (1997) When at first you don't succeed: sequential strategies for antidepressant non-responders. *Journal of Clinical Psychiatry, 58* (Suppl. 13), 23–29.

Thase, M. E., Kupfer, D. J. & Jarrett, D. B. (1989) Treatment of imipramine-resistant recurrent depression. I: An open clinical trial of adjunctive L-triiodothyronine. *Journal of Clinical Psychiatry, 50*, 385–388.

Thase, M. E., Mallinger, A. G., McKnight, D., *et al.* (1992) Treatment of imipramine-resistant recurrent depression. IV: A double-blind crossover study of tranylcypromine for anergic bipolar depression. *American Journal of Psychiatry, 149*, 195–198.

Thiels, C., Schmidt, U., Treasure, J., *et al.* (1998) Guided self change for bulimia nervosa incorporating use of a self-care manual. *American Journal of Psychiatry, 155*, 947–953.

Thiels, C., Linden, M., Grieger, F., *et al.* (2005) Gender differences in routine treatment of depressed outpatients with the selective serotonin reuptake inhibitor sertraline. *International Clinical Psychopharmacology, 20*, 1–7.

Thomas, C. M. & Morris, S. (2003) Cost of depression among adults in England in 2000. *British Journal of Psychiatry, 183*, 514–519.

Thompson, C. & Thompson, C. M. (1989) The prescribing of antidepressants in general practice. II: A placebo-controlled trial of low-dose dothiepin. *Human Psychopharmacology, 4*, 191–204.

Thompson, C., Kinmonth, A. L., Stevens, L., *et al.* (2000) Effects of good practice guidelines and practice-based education on the detection and treatment of depression in primary care. Hampshire Depression Project randomised controlled trial. *Lancet, 355*, 185–191.

Thompson, C., Ostler, K., Peveler, R. C., *et al.* (2001) Dimensional perspective on the recognition of depressive symptoms in primary care: the Hampshire Depression Project 3. *British Journal of Psychiatry, 179*, 317–323.

Thompson, C., Thompson, S. & Smith, R. (2004) Prevalence of seasonal affective disorder in primary care: a comparison of the seasonal health questionnaire and the seasonal pattern assessment questionnaire. *Journal of Affective Disorders, 78*, 219–226.

Thompson, L. W., Gallagher, D. & Breckenridge, J. S. (1987) Comparative effectiveness of psychotherapies for depressed elders. *Journal of Consulting and Clinical Psychology, 55*, 385–390.

Thoren, P., Floras, J. S., Hoffmann, P., *et al.* (1990) Endorphins and exercise: physiological mechanisms and clinical implications. *Medical Science, Sports and Exercise, 22,* 417–428.

Thorogood, M., Cowen, P., Mann, J., *et al.* (1992) Fatal myocardial infarction and use of psychotropic drugs in young women. *Lancet, 340,* 1067–1068.

Tiemens, B., Ormel, J., Jenner, J. A., *et al.* (1999) Training primary-care physicians to recognise, diagnose and manage depression: does it improve patient outcomes? *Psychological Medicine, 29,* 833–845.

Tint, A., Haddad, P. M. & Anderson, I. M. (2008) The effect of rate of antidepressant tapering on the incidence of discontinuation symptoms: a randomized study. *Journal of Psychopharmacology, 22,* 330–332.

Treasure, J., Schmidt, U., Troop, N., *et al.* (1996) Sequential treatment for bulimia nervosa incorporating a self-care manual. *British Journal of Psychiatry, 168,* 94–98.

Trepka, C., Rees, A., Shapiro, D. A., *et al.* (2004) Therapist competence and outcome of cognitive therapy for depression. *Cognitive Therapy and Research, 28,* 143–157.

Trivedi, M. H., Rush, A. J., Wisniewski, S. R., *et al.* (2006) Evaluation of outcomes with citalopram for depression using measurement-based care in STAR*D: implications for clinical practice. *American Journal of Psychiatry, 163,* 28–40.

Truax, C. B. & Carkhuff, R. R. (1967) *Toward Effective Counseling and Psychotherapy: Training and Practice.* Chicago, Illinois: Aldine.

Unutzer, J., Katon, W., Callahan, C. M., *et al.* (2002) Collaborative care management of late-life depression in the primary care setting: a randomised controlled trial. *Journal of the American Medical Association, 288,* 2836–2845.

Üstün, T. B. & Sartorius, N. (eds) (1995) *Mental Illness in General Health Care: An International Study.* Chichester: Wiley.

Van, H. L., Schoevers, R. A. & Dekker, J. (2008) Predicting the outcome of antidepressants and psychotherapy for depression: a qualitative, systematic review. *Harvard Review of Psychiatry, 16,* 225–234.

Van der Burght, M. (1994) *Citalopram Product Monography.* Copenhagen, Denmark: H Lundbeck A/S.

Van Os, T. W., van den Brink, R. H., Tiemens, B. G., *et al.* (2004) Are effects of depression management training for general practitioners on patient outcomes mediated by improvements in the process of care? *Journal of Affective Disorders, 80,* 173–179.

Van Schaik, D. J. F, Klijn, A. F. J., van Hout, H. P. J., *et al.* (2004) Patients' preferences in the treatment of depressive disorder in primary care. *General Hospital Psychiatry,* 26, 184–189.

Van Straten, A., Tiemens, B., Hakkaart, L., *et al.* (2006) Stepped care vs. matched care for mood and anxiety disorders: a randomized trial in routine practice. *Acta Psychiatrica Scandinavica, 113,* 468–476.

Velazquez, C., Carlson, A., Stokes, K. A., *et al.* (2001) Relative safety of mirtazapine overdose. *Veterinary and Human Toxicology, 43,* 342–344.

Vergouwen, A. C., Bakker, A., Katon, W. J., *et al.* (2003) Improving adherence to antidepressants: a systematic review of interventions. *Journal of Clinical Psychiatry, 64,* 1415–1420.

Vize, C. M. & Priest, R. G. (1993) Defeat Depression Campaign: attitudes to depression. *Psychiatric Bulletin, 17*, 573–574.

Von Korff, M. (1999) Pain management in primary care: an individualized stepped-care approach. In *Psychosocial Factors in Pain* (eds R.J. Gatchel & D.C. Turk), pp. 360–373. New York: Guilford Press.

Von Korff, M. & Goldberg, D. (2001) Improving outcomes in depression: the whole process of care needs to be enhanced. *British Medical Journal, 323*, 948–949.

Von Korff, M., Gruman, J., Schaefer, J., *et al.* (1997) Collaborative management of chronic illness. *Annals of Internal Medicine, 127*, 1097–1102.

Vothknecht, S., Kho, K. H., van Schaick, H. W., *et al.* (2003) Effects of maintenance electroconvulsive therapy on cognitive functions. *Journal of ECT, 19*, 151–157.

Wade, A. G., Toumi, I. & Hemels, M. E. H. (2005a) A pharmacological evaluation of escitalopram versus citalopram in the treatment of severe depression in the United Kingdom. *Clinical Therapeutics, 27*, 486–496.

Wade, A. G., Toumi, I. & Hemels, M. E. H. (2005b) A probabilistic cost-effectiveness analysis of escitalopram, generic citalopram and venlafaxine as a first-line treatment of major depressive disorder in the UK. *Current Medical Research and Opinion, 21*, 631–642.

Wade, A. G., Fernàndez, J. L., François, C., *et al.* (2008) Escitalopram and duloxetine in major depressive disorder: a pharmacoeconomic comparison using UK cost data. *Pharmacoeconomics, 26*, 969–981.

Waddell, G. & Burton A. K. (2006) *Is Work Good for Your Health and Well-being?* London: The Stationery Office.

Wagner, E. H. (1997) Managed care and chronic illness: health services research needs. *Health Services Research, 32*, 702–14.

Wagner, E. H. & Groves, T. (2002) Care for chronic diseases. *British Medical Journal, 325*, 913–914.

Wagner, E., Austin, B. & von Korff, M. (1996) Organizing care for patients with chronic illness. *Milbank Quarterly, 74*, 511–543.

Wagner, H. & Bladt, S. (1994) Pharmaceutical quality of hypericum extracts. *Journal of Geriatric Psychiatry and Neurology, 7* (Suppl. 1), S65–S68.

Walraven, C., van Mamdani, M. M., Wells, P. S., *et al.* (2001) Inhibition of serotonin reuptake by antidepressants and upper gastrointestinal bleeding in elderly patients: retrospective cohort study. *British Medical Journal, 323*, 655–658.

Walsh, B. T., Seidman, S. N., Sysko, R., *et al.* (2002) Placebo response in studies of major depression: variable, substantial, and growing. *Journal of the American Medical Association, 287*, 1840–1847.

Wang, Z.-J., Lin, S.-M. & Hu, M. L. (2004) Contents of hypericin and psuedohypericin in five commercial products of St John's Wort (Hypericum perforatum). *Journal of the Science of Food and Agriculture, 84*, 395–397.

Waraich, P., Goldner, E. M., Somers, J. M., *et al.* (2004) Prevalence and incidence studies of mood disorders: a systematic review of the literature. *Canadian Journal of Psychiatry, 49*, 124–138.

Watkins, E., Scott, J., Wingrove, J., *et al.* (2007) Rumination-focused cognitive behaviour therapy for residual depression: a case series. *Behaviour Research and Therapy, 45*, 2144–2154.

Waugh, J. & Goa, K. L. (2003) Escitalopram: a review of its use in the management of major depressive and anxiety disorders. *CNS Drugs, 17*, 343–362.

Weich, S., Nazroo, J., Sproston, K., *et al.* (2004) Common mental disorders and ethnicity in England: the EMPIRIC study. *Psychological Medicine, 34*, 1543–1551.

Weinmann, S., Becker, T. & Koesters, M. (2008) Re-evaluation of the efficacy and tolerability of venlafaxine V SSRIs: meta-analysis. *Psychopharmacology, 196*, 511–520.

Weissman, M. M. (2007) Cognitive therapy and interpersonal psychotherapy: 30 years later. *American Journal of Psychiatry, 164*, 693–696.

Weissman, M. M., Bland, R., Joyce, P. R., *et al.* (1993) Sex differences in rates of depression: cross-national perspectives. *Journal of Affective Disorders, 29*, 77–84.

Weissman, M. M., Markowitz, J. C. & Klerman, G. L. (2000) *Comprehensive Guide to Interpersonal Psychotherapy.* New York: Basic Books.

Westen, D., Novotny, C. M. & Thompson-Brenner, H. (2004) The empirical status of empirically supported psychotherapies: assumptions, findings, and reporting in controlled clinical trials. *Psychological Bulletin, 130*, 631–663.

Westrin, A. & Lam, R. W. (2007) Seasonal affective disorder: a clinical update. *Annals of Clinical Psychiatry, 19*, 239–246.

Whitfield, G., Williams, C. & Shapiro, D. (2001) Assessing the take up and acceptability of a self-help room used by patients awaiting their initial outpatient appointment. *Behavioral and Cognitive Psychotherapy, 29*, 333–343.

Whittington, C., Cape, J., Buszewicz, M., *et al.* (2009) Comparison of collaborative care for depression and anxiety in primary care with traditional general practice attachments: a meta-analysis and meta-regression. Manuscript in preparation.

WHO (1992) *The ICD–10 Classification of Mental and Behavioural Disorders: Clinical Descriptions and Diagnostic Guidelines.* Geneva, Switzerland: WHO.

WHO (2001) *World Health Report 2001: Mental Health: New Understanding, New Hope.* Geneva, Switzerland: WHO.

WHO (2002) *The World Health Report 2002: Reducing Risks, Promoting Healthy Life.* Geneva, Switzerland: WHO.

Whooley, M. A., Avins, A. L., Miranda, J., *et al.* (1997) Case-finding instruments for depression. Two questions are as good as many. *Journal of General Internal Medicine, 12*, 439–445.

Whyte, I. M., Dawson, A. H. & Buckley, N. A. (2003) Relative toxicity of venlafaxine and selective serotonin reuptake inhibitors in overdose compared to tricyclic antidepressants. *QJM, 96*, 369–374.

Wiersma, D., Kluiter, H., Nienhuis, F., *et al.* (1989) *Day-treatment with Community Care as an Alternative to Standard Hospitalisation: An Experiment in the Netherlands. A Preliminary Communication.* Groningen, the Netherlands: Department of Social Psychiatry, University of Groningen.

References

Wijkstra, J. & Nolen, W. A. (2005) Successful maintenance electroconvulsive therapy for more than seven years. *Journal of ECT, 21,* 171–173.

Wilfley, D. E, MacKenzie, K. R., Welch, R. R., *et al.* (2000) *Interpersonal Psychotherapy for Group.* New York: Basic Books.

Williams, J. B. W., Link, M. J., Rosenthal, N. E., *et al.* (1988) *Structured Interview Guide for the Hamilton Depression Rating Scale: Seasonal Affective Disorders Version (SIGH-SAD).* New York: New York Psychiatric Institute.

Williams, J. M, Russell, I. & Russell, D. (2008) Mindfulness-based cognitive therapy: further issues in current evidence and future research. *Journal of Consulting and Clinical Psychology, 76,* 524–529.

Williams, Jr, J. W., Kerber, C. A., Mulrow, C. D., *et al.* (1995) Depressive disorders in primary care: prevalence, functional disability, and identification. *Journal of General Internal Medicine, 10,* 7–12.

Williams, M. D., Rummans, T., Sampson, S., *et al.* (2008) Outcome of electroconvulsive therapy by race in the Consortium for Research on Electroconvulsive Therapy multisite study. *Journal of ECT, 24,* 117–121.

Williams, R. & Hunt, K. (1997) Psychological distress among British South Asians: the contribution of stressful situations and subcultural differences in the West of Scotland Twenty-07 Study. *Psychological Medicine, 24,* 113–119.

Wilson, K., Mottram, P., Sivanranthan, A., *et al.* (2001) Antidepressant versus placebo for depressed elderly (Cochrane Review). In *Cochrane Library,* Issue 2. Oxford: Update Software.

Wilson, M. & MacCarthy, B. (1994) GP consultation as a factor in the low rate of mental health service use by Asians. *Psychological Medicine, 27,* 1173–1181.

Winokur, G., Coryell, W. & Keller, M. (1993) A prospective study of patients with bipolar and unipolar affective disorder. *Archives of General Psychiatry, 50,* 457–465.

Wisniewski, S. R., Rush, A. J., Nierenberg, A. A., *et al.* (2009) Can phase III trial results of antidepressant medications be generalized to clinical practice? A STAR*D Report. *American Journal of Psychiatry, 166,* 599–607.

Wittchen, H. U., Hofler, M. & Meister, W. (2001a) Prevalence and recognition of depressive syndromes in German primary care settings: poorly recognized and treated? *International Clinical Psychopharmacology, 16,* 121–135.

Wittchen, H. U., Schuster, P. & Lieb, R. (2001b) Comorbidity and mixed anxiety–depressive disorder: clinical curiosity or pathophysiological need? *Human Psychopharmacology, 16* (Suppl. 1), S21–S30.

Wolberg, L. R. (1967) *Short-term Psychotherapy.* New York: Grune & Stratton.

Wolpe, J. (1971) Neurotic depression: experimental analogue, clinical syndromes and treatment. *American Journal of Psychotherapy, 25,* 362–368.

Wolpe, J. (1979) The experimental model and treatment of neurotic depression. *Behaviour Research and Therapy, 17,* 555–565.

World Bank (1993) *World Development Report: Investing in Health Research Development.* Geneva, Switzerland: World Bank.

Wyeth Pharmaceuticals (2008) *Efexor XL. Summary of Product Characteristics.* Maidenhead: Wyeth. Available at: http://www.medicines.org.uk/EMC/history/ 2210/SPC/Efexor+XL

Yesavage, J. A., Brink, T. L., Rose, T. L., *et al.* (1983) Development and validation of a geriatric depression screening scale: a preliminary report. *Journal of Psychiatric Research, 17*, 37–49.

Zajecka, J., Fawcett, J., Amsterdam, J., *et al.* (1998) Safety of abrupt discontinuation of fluoxetine: a randomised, placebo-controlled study. *Journal of Clinical Psychopharmacology, 18*, 193–197.

Zanarini, M. C., Frankenburg, F. R, Dubo, E. D., *et al.* (1998) Axis I comorbidity of borderline personality disorder. *The American Journal of Psychiatry, 155*, 1733–1739.

Zhang, Z. J., Tan, Q. R., Tong, Y., *et al.* (2008) The effectiveness of carbamazepine in unipolar depression: a double blind, randomised, placebo controlled study. *Journal of Affective Disorders, 109*, 91–97.

Zigmond, A. S. & Snaith, R. D. (1983) The Hospital Anxiety and Depression Scale. *Acta Psychiatrica Scandinavica, 67*, 361–370.

Zimmerman, M. & Thongy, T. (2007) How often do SSRIs and other new-generation antidepressants lose their effect during continuation treatment? Evidence suggesting the rate of true tachyphylaxis during continuation treatment is low. *Journal of Clinical Psychiatry*, 68, 1271–1276.

Zimmerman, M., Chelminski, I., McGlinchey, J. B., *et al.* (2006) Diagnosing major depressive disorder X: can the utility of the DSM–IV symptom criteria be improved? *The Journal of Nervous and Mental Disease, 194*, 893–897.

Zimmerman, M., McGlinchey, J. B., Posternak, M. A., *et al.* (2008) Remission in depressed outpatients: more than just symptom resolution? *Journal of Psychiatric Research, 42*, 797–801.

Zisselman, M. H., Rosenquist, P. B. & Curlik, S. M. (2007) Long-term weekly continuation electroconvulsive therapy: a case series. *Journal of ECT, 23*, 274–277.

Zung, W. W. K. (1965) A self-rating depression scale. *Archives of General Psychiatry, 12*, 63–70.

17   ABBREVIATIONS

3MSE	Modified Mini-Mental State Examination
5-HT	5-hydroxytryptymine
AD	antidepressant (in the Appendices only)
AD	antidepressant treatment given for 12 weeks with 6 months' maintenance therapy and 6 months' follow-up (*Strategy A* in this guideline)
ADI	Amritsar Depression Inventory
ADQ	average daily quantities
A&E	Accident and Emergency Department
AfC	Agenda for Change
AGREE	Appraisal of Guidelines for Research and Evaluation Instrument
AMED	Allied and Alternative Medicine Database
AMI	autobiographical memory impairment
AMI/AMT	amitriptyline (in the Appendices only)
AMS	amisulpride
AP	antipsychotic
APA	American Psychiatric Association
APNR	acute phase non-responders
ASEX	Arizona Sexual Experience scale
AUC	area under the curve
BABCP	British Association for Behavioural and Cognitive Psychotherapies
BAC	British Association for Counselling
BACP	British Association for Counselling and Psychotherapy
BAI	Beck Anxiety Inventory
BASDEC	Brief Assessment Schedule depression cards
BD	bipolar disorder
BDI	Beck Depression Inventory
BDT	brief dynamic therapy
BIDS	Brief Inventory for Depressive Symptoms
BLIPS	Brief Limited Intermittent Psychotic Symptons
BLRI	Barrett-Lennard Relationship Inventory
BME	black and minority ethnic
BMJ	*British Medical Journal*
BMQ	Beliefs about Medicines Questionnaire
BMT	behavioural marital therapy

BPD	borderline personality disorder
BPI	Brief Pain Inventory
BPIT	brief psychodynamic-interpersonal therapy
Bpn	bupropion XL
BSP/BS	brief supportive psychotherapy
BT	behaviour therapy
BtB	Beating the Blues
BZD	benzodiazepine
C	completers analysis
CADET	Collaborative Depression Trial
CAGE	A short assessment for alcohol misuse
CARE	Comprehensive Assessment and Referral Evaluation
CAT	cognitive analytic therapy
CAU	care as usual
C-BDI	Chinese Beck Depression Inventory
CBT	cognitive behavioural therapy
CCBT/cCBT	computerised cognitive behavioural therapy
CCSS	Caribbean Culture-Specific Screen for emotional disorders
CCT	client-centered treatment
CDRS-SR	Carroll Depression Rating Scale (Self-Report)
CDS	Chronic Disease Score
CEAC	cost-effectiveness acceptability curve
CEEG	continuous electroencephalography
CES-D	Centre of Epidemiology Studies-Depression
CGI	Clinical Global Impressions
CI	confidence interval
CIDI (-SF)	Composite International Diagnostic Interview (-Short Form)
CIGP-CD	cognitive-interpersonal group psychotherapy for chronic depression
CINAHL	*Cumulative Index to Nursing and Allied Health Literature*
CIS (-R)	Clinical Interview Schedule (-Revised)
Cit/cital	citalopram
clr	cluster randomised (adjusted)
CM	care management/clinical management
CMB	combined
CMBN	combined arms
CMHN	community mental health nurse
CMHT	community mental health team
CNS	central nervous system
CNSLNG	counselling
Cntl	control
CNTRL	control

COMB	Combination of 12 weeks' antidepressant treatment and 16 sessions of CBT with 6 months' maintenance therapy and 6 months' follow-up (*Strategy B* in this guideline)
Combo	combined treatment (used in the Appendices only)
COPE	Calendar of Premenstrual Experiences
CORE	Centre for Outcomes, Research and Effectiveness
CORE (-OM)	Clinical Outcomes in Routine Evaluation (-Outcome Measure)
CPA	Care Programme Approach
CPN	community psychiatric nurse
C-R	clinician-reported
CRHTT	crisis resolution and home treatment team
CSPRS	Collaborative Study Psychotherapy Rating Scale
CSQ (-8)	Client Satisfaction Questionnaire (-8 items)
CT	cognitive therapy
Ctp	citalopram
CTS	Cognitive Therapy Scale
CWD	Coping with Depression
D	dysthymia
DA	dopamine
DAI	Drug Attitude Index
DALY	disability adjusted life years
DBM	demineralised bone matrix
DESS	Discontinuation Emergent Signs and Symptoms
df	degrees of freedom
DIS	Diagnostic Interview Schedule
DP	day patient
DPDS	depression subscale of the Short-CARE
DRP (-PC)	Depression Recurrence Prevention Program (-psychiatric consultation)
DSM (–II, –III, –IV, –TR, –R)	*Diagnostic and Statistical Manual of Mental Disorders* of the American Psychiatric Association (2nd edition, 3rd edition, 4th edition, Text Revision, Revision)
Dsp	desipramine
dul/dulox	duloxetine
ECG	electrocardiogram
ECT	electroconvulsive therapy
EDS	Edinburgh Depression Scale
EED	Economic Evaluation Database
EEG	electroencephalography
EFT	emotion-focused therapy
EMBASE	Excerpta Medica Database

EQ-5D	European Quality of Life-5 Dimensions
ER	extended release
ERIC	Education Resources Information Center
Escit/esc	escitalopram
EuroQOL	European Quality of Life
F	female
FDA	US Food and Drug Administration
Flp	flupenthixol
FLU/fluox/flx/flu	fluoxetine
Flv/Fvx	fluvoxamine
G	group
GAD	generalised anxiety disorder
GAF	Global Assessment of Functioning
GAS	Global Assessment Scale
gCBT	group cognitive behavioural therapy
GDG	Guideline Development Group
GDS	Geriatric Depression Scale
GHC	Group Health Cooperative
GHQ	General Health Questionnaire
GMS-AGECAT	Geriatric Mental State-Automated Geriatric Examination for Computer Assisted Taxonomy
GP	general practitioner
GPc	general practitioner care
GPRD	General Practice Research Database
GPT	group psychotherapy
GRADE	Grades of Recommendation Assessment, Development and Evaluation
GRP	Guideline Review Panel
GSH	guided self-help
GSS	Global Seasonality Score
HADS (-D)	Hospital Anxiety and Depression Scale (-Depression)
HAM-A	Hamilton Anxiety Rating Scale
HAMD/HAM-D	Hamilton Depression Rating Scale
HAP	Human Activities Profile
HAQ	Health Assessment Questionnaire
HCl	hydrochloride
HLM	hierarchical linear modelling
HMIC	Health Management Information Consortium
HMO	health maintenance organisation
HMSO	Her Majesty's Stationery Office
HMU	head-mounted unit
HRQoL	health-related quality of life

Abbreviations

HRSD	Hamilton Rating Scale for Depression
HRT	hormone replacement therapy
HSCL	Hopkins Symptom Checklist
HTA	Health Technology Assessment
IAPT	Improving Access to Psychological Therapies
ICC	intracluster correlation coefficient
ICD (-9, -10)	*International Classification of Diseases* (9th revision; 10th revision)
ICER	incremental cost-effectiveness ratio
ICM	imipramine + clinical management
ICSD-2	International Classification of Sleep Disorders-2
ICT	integrative cognitive therapy
IDS	Inventory for Depressive Symptomatology
IHD	ischaemic heart disease
Imp	imipramine
IMPACT	A collaborative care for depression programme at the University of Washington
Int	intervention
Ip	interpersonal therapy for dysthymic disorder
IP	inpatient
IPD	interpersonal difficulties
IPT (-M, -D)	interpersonal therapy (-maintenance, -for dysthymia)
ITT	intention to treat
JAMA	*Journal of the American Medical Association*
K	number of studies
K10	Kessler-10
KPDS	Kleinian Psychoanalytic Diagnostic Scale
LD3	low dose (three times per week)
LD5	low dose (five times per week)
LED	light-emitting diode
li	lithium
LOCF	last observation carried forward
LOF	lofepramine
LR−	negative likelihood ratio
LR+	positive likelihood ratio
LVCF	last value carried forward
M	male
MADRS	Montgomery–Åsberg Depression Rating Scale
MAJOR	major depression arm of study
MAOI	monoamine oxidase inhibitor

MBCBT	mindfulness-based CBT
MBCT	mindfulness-based cognitive therapy
MBSR	mindfulness-based stress reduction
mcl	moclobemide
MD	mean difference/major depression
MDD	major depressive disorder
MEDLINE	Medical Literature Analysis and Retrieval System Online
MHI (-5)	Mental Health Inventory (-5 items)
MHRA	Medicines and Healthcare products Regulatory Agency
MHT	Mental Health Team
MI	myocardial infarction
MIDAS	Module for Meta-analytical Integration of Diagnostic Test Accuracy Studies
MINI	Mini International Neuropsychiatric Interview
MINOR	minor depression arm of study
MMPI	Minnesota Multiphasic Personality Inventory
MMQ	Maudsley Marital Questionnaire
MMRM	Mixed-Effect Model Repeated Measure
MMSE	Mini-Mental State Examination
Mnp	minaprine
MOS-SF-20	Medical Outcomes Study-Short Form-20 items
MPS	Maier and Philipp (core mood stability) Subscale
Mpt	maprotiline
MRC	Medical Research Council
MSE	Mental State Examination
MSQ	Mental Status Questionnaire
N/A	not applicable
N/n	number of participants
N/R	not reported
NA	noradrenaline
NA	not available
NARI	noradrenaline reuptake inhibitor
NaSSA	noradrenaline and specific serotonin antidepressant
NCC	National Collaborating Centre
NCCMH	National Collaborating Centre for Mental Health
ND	non-directive
NEF	nefazodone
NEO (-FFI)	NEO Personality Inventory (-Five-Factor Inventory)
NHS	National Health Service
NICE	National Institute for Clinical Excellence
NIMH (TDCRP)	National Institute of Mental Health (Treatment of Depression Collaborative Research Program)
nm	nanometers

NNH	number needed to harm
NNT	number needed to treat
Nort	nortriptyline
NOS	not otherwise specified
NPV	negative predictive value
NSAID	non-steroidal anti-inflammatory drug
NSF	National Service Framework
OCD	obsessive-compulsive disorder
OHE HEED	Office of Health Economics Health Economic Evaluations Database
Olz	olanzapine
OpenSIGLE	System for information on Grey Literature in Europe
OR	odds ratio
OT	occupational therapy/therapist
Parox/prx/px	paroxetine
PARQ	Physical Activity Readiness Questionnaire
PASE	Physical Activity Scale for the Elderly
PCA	Prescription Cost Analysis
P-CM	placebo + clinical management
PCMHW	primary care mental health worker
PCP	primary care practitioner
PCT	Primary Care Trust
PD	personality disorder
PE	process experiential treatment
PEP (+PC)	psychoeducational prevention programme (+psychiatric consultation)
PF-SOC	Problem-Focused Style of Coping scale
PGEM	pharmacist guided education and monitoring
PGI	Patient Global Impression scale
PGMS	Philadelphia Geriatric Morale Scale
PHD3	public health dose (180 minutes of moderate-intensity exercise per week, three times per week)
PHD5	public health dose (180 minutes of moderate-intensity exercise per week, five times per week)
PHQ (-9)	Patient Health Questionnaire (-9 items)
Phz	phenelzine
PICO	patient, intervention, comparison and outcome
PLA/Plb/pbo/pb	placebo
POMS	Profile of Mood States
PP	psychodynamic psychotherapy
PRIME-MD	Primary Care Evaluation of Mental Disorders